UNDERSTANDING TRUSTS AND ESTATES

THIRD EDITION

Roger W. Andersen
Professor of Law
University of Toledo
College of Law

ISBN#: 0820557269

Editorial Offices
744 Broad Street, Newark, NJ 07102 (973) 820-2000
201 Mission St., San Francisco, CA 94105-1831 (415) 908-3200
701 East Water Street, Charlottesville, VA 22902-7587 (804) 972-7600
www.lexis.com

(Pub.00728)

HOW TO USE THIS BOOK

This textbook is designed to help law students understand their Trusts and Estates courses. Practicing attorneys may also find it useful if they are new to the subject or have been away from it for some time. The text's structure allows different ways of using the book in different situations.

If you are a law student using the book as a regular supplement to your casebook, try reading the text and ignoring the footnotes until you need more examples or greater depth. You will find that the organization here differs from your casebook in various particulars. Scanning the Table of Contents or using the Index should help you find the relevant sections.

If you are consulting the book with a particular problem in mind, start with the Index or one of the tables (Cases, UPC or UTC). This book uses as examples many of the cases found in popular casebooks. Because details should enrich your understanding, read the footnotes.

If you are studying for finals, start by reading the Table of Contents, to get a sense of the whole. Then concentrate on the text, but be sure to scan the footnotes for those which cross-reference to other sections of the book. These references help identify the interconnections holding the subject together.

PREFACE TO THE THIRD EDITION

This volume takes into account recent developments while retaining the structure of earlier editions. The principal changes involve revisions to the tax chapter in light of Congress's decision to phase out (for now at least) the estate tax and integration of the Uniform Trust Code into discussions of topics it covers. Citations to new cases, articles, and Restatements appear throughout.

I owe thanks to a team of research assistants, especially Jenn Brumby and Jessica Straub. Ken Crislip, Joe Fantozzi, and Ryan Weikart also contributed significantly to the project. All are students at the University of Toledo College of Law.

I gratefully acknowledge financial support from the College through my appointment as Charles W. Fornoff Professor of Law and Values for 2002-2003.

Special thanks to Adriana M. Sciortino, my editor, for her insights and efforts as she shepherded another project through the production process.

Most importantly, I thank my family — Kyanne, Michael, & Jessica — for their continued support of my scholarly efforts.

To

Kyanne

———

For

Michael and Jessica

TABLE OF CONTENTS

CHAPTER 1

LAWYERS, ESTATES, AND TRUSTS

CHAPTER 2

INTESTACY

CHAPTER 3

WILLS

CHAPTER 4

PRIVATE EXPRESS TRUSTS

CHAPTER 5

OTHER NONPROBATE DEVICES

CHAPTER 6

PLANNING FOR INCAPACITY

CHAPTER 7

CHANGING THE SHARE

CHAPTER 8

PROTECTING THE FAMILY

CHAPTER 9

PRESENT AND FUTURE INTERESTS

CHAPTER 10

POWERS OF APPOINTMENT

CHAPTER 12

THE RULE AGAINST PERPETUITIES

CHAPTER 13

PROBLEMS OF ADMINISTRATION

CHAPTER 14

A SKETCH OF FEDERAL WEALTH TRANSFER TAXES

CHAPTER 15

LOOKING AHEAD

TABLE OF AUTHORITIES

The law of wills, trusts, and future interests enjoys a rich variety of source material. The list below gives the short forms for citations in this text.

1. Statutes

IRC — Internal Revenue Code, 26 U.S.C. § 1 et seq. (current).

UPC — Uniform Probate Code (current).

UPC (pre-1990) — Uniform Probate Code (earlier versions).

UTC — Uniform Trust Code (current).

2. Single-Volume Texts

Atkinson — Thomas E. Atkinson, Law of Wills (West 2d ed. 1953).

Bergin & Haskell — Thomas F. Bergin & Paul G. Haskell, Preface to Estates in Land and Future Interests (Foundation Press 2d ed. 1984).

Bogert — George T. Bogert, Trusts (West 6th ed. 1987).

Cribbet & Johnson — John E. Cribbet & Corwin W. Johnson, Principles of the Law of Property (Foundation Press 3d ed. 1989).

Haskell — Paul G. Haskell, Preface to Wills, Trusts and Administration (Foundation Press 2d ed. 1993).

McGovern & Kurtz — William M. McGovern, Jr. & Sheldon F. Kurtz Wills, Trusts and Estates Including Taxation and Future Interests (West 2d ed. 2001).

Moynihan & Kurtz — Cornelius J. Moynihan & Sheldon F. Kurtz, Introduction to the Law of Real Property (West 3d ed. 2002).

Reutlinger — Mark Reutlinger, Wills, Trusts & Estates (Aspen 2d ed. 1998).

Scott — Austin W. Scott, Abridgment of the Law of Trusts (Little Brown 1960).

Shaffer, Mooney & Boettcher — Thomas L. Shaffer, Carol A. Mooney & Amy Jo Boettcher, The Planning and Drafting of Wills and Trusts (Foundation Press 4th ed. 2001).

Simes — Lewis M. Simes, Law of Future Interests (West 2d ed. 1966).

3. Multi-Volume Treatises

ALP — American Law of Property (A. James Casner, ed., Little, Brown 1952).

Bogert & Bogert — George G. Bogert, George T. Bogert & Amy Morris Hess, The Law of Trusts and Trustees (West rev. 2d ed. 1984–1988 & Supp. 2001).

Page — William J. Bowe & Douglas H. Parker or Jeffrey A. Schoenblum, Page on the Law of Wills (Anderson 1960–91 & Supp. 2002).

Powell — Richard R. Powell & Patrick J. Rohan, Powell on Real Property (Matthew Bender 2002).

Scott on Trusts — Austin W. Scott & William F. Fratcher, The Law of Trusts (Little, Brown 4th ed. 1987–1991).

Simes & Smith — Lewis M. Simes & Allan F. Smith, The Law of Future Interests (West 2d ed. 1956 & Supp. 2000).

4. The Restatements

Restatement of Property (1936–44).

Restatement (Second) of Property: Donative Transfers (1983–92).

Restatement (Third) of Property: Wills and Other Donative Transfers (1998-2001).

Restatement of Trusts (1935).

Restatement (Second) of Trusts (1959).

Restatement (Third) of Trusts (1992-1996).

5. Casebooks and Guides

Andersen & Bloom — Roger W. Andersen & Ira M. Bloom, Fundamentals of Trusts and Estates (Matthew Bender 2d ed. 2002).

Clark, Lusky, Murphy, Ascher & McCouch — Elias Clark, Louis Lusky, Arthur W. Murphy, Mark L. Ascher & Grayson M.P. McCouch Gratuitous Transfers: Wills, Intestate Succession, Trusts, Gifts, Future Interests and Estate and Gift Taxation (West 4th ed. 1999).

Dobris & Sterk — Joel C. Dobris & Stewart E. Sterk, Estates and Trusts (Foundation Press 1998).

Dukeminier & Johanson — Jesse Dukeminier & Stanley M. Johanson, Wills, Trusts and Estates (Little, Brown 6th ed. 2000).

Laurence & Minzner — Robert Laurence & Pamela B. Minzner, A Student's Guide to Estates in Land and Future Interests (Matthew Bender 2d ed. 1993).

Marsh — Lucy A. Marsh, [Drafting] Wills, Trusts & Estates (Aspen 1998).

Scoles, Halbach, Link & Roberts — Eugene F. Scoles, Edward C. Halbach, Jr., Ronald C. Link & Patricia Gilchrist Roberts, Decedents' Estates and Trust (Little, Brown 6th ed. 2000).

Waggoner, Alexander, Fellows & Gallanis — Lawrence W. Waggoner, Gregory S. Alexander, Mary L. Fellows & Thomas P. Gallanis, Family Property Law (Foundation Press 3d ed. 2002).

6. Web Sites

www.abanet.org/rppt/home.html (American Bar Association's Section of Real Property, Probate and Trust Law)

www.actec.org (The American College of Trust and Estate Counsel)

www.courttv.com/library/newsmakers/wills/ (wills of notable people)

www.naela.org (National Academy of Elder Law Attorneys, Inc.)

www.seniorlaw.com/seniorla.html (Senior Law Home Page: articles, resources and supplements in the areas of elder law, estate planning and trusts)

www.aarp.org/ (American Association of Retired Persons)

www.rights.org/~deathnet/ (Deathnet: legal aspects of euthanasia and living wills)

www.hg.org/family.html (Sources and links on family, elder law and estate planning)

Chapter 1

LAWYERS, ESTATES, AND TRUSTS

§ 1 Serving the Living

You may be pleasantly surprised to learn that Trusts and Estates is not about dead people. Rather, it is the study of ways to help living people solve real family problems. If your clients have aging parents, if they have just lost a spouse, if they have young children, if they seek to save taxes, if they are anticipating their own retirement and possible disability, you can help. You will have the opportunity to offer them a wide variety of ideas, tools you can use together to craft a solution.

Such a task is both interesting and challenging: interesting because of the interplay between intellectual ideas and individual personalities; challenging because of the required attention to detail and the number of choices faced.

Recognizing that lawyer conduct affects the living, courts have broken down traditional defenses and held lawyers responsible to will beneficiaries who were not their clients. In *Ogle v. Fuiten*,[1] for example, two nephews brought an action for malpractice and breach of contract against the law partner of their aunt and uncle's then-deceased lawyer.[2]

The nephews claimed that the aunt and uncle had wanted the property to go to whichever of them survived the other by 30 days; otherwise the nephews were to get the property. Because of a drafting error, the nephews did not get the property, even though the aunt did not survive the uncle by 30 days.

The lawyer's mistake was easy to make: he left a gap in coverage when he combined two different kinds of clauses in the wills. First, in each spouse's will he made the gift to the other spouse contingent on survival by 30 days. Then, he provided that if both spouses were killed in a "common disaster" the nephews would take.[3]

As luck would have it, neither event occurred. The uncle died of a stroke, and 15 days later the aunt died of cancer. Neither spouse survived long enough to get the other's property, but the nephews did not qualify to take

---

[1] 466 N.E.2d 224 (Ill. 1984).

[2] The estate was also named as a defendant.

[3] The common disaster clause is a particularly bad way to deal with survivorship problems. *See* § 45[B][2][a], *infra*.

In this case, one wonders if the lawyer merely inserted the clause as standard "boilerplate," without discussing it with his clients. If so, the nephews might have had another ground for recovery. *See generally* Roger W. Andersen, *Informed Decision Making in an Office Practice*, 28 B.C. L. Rev. 225 (1987).

it because there was no common disaster.[4] The lawyer had left a gap, and the nephews lost out.

The court allowed the nephews' claim, following a growing, but not uniform, trend toward ignoring defenses based on lack of privity—"they were not my clients"—and statutes of limitation—"the claim is too late because it arose when the will was drafted, not at the later death."[5] Courts have recognized that unless lawyers' duties are extended to will beneficiaries and unless statutes of limitation are applied from the time a mistake is likely to be found, lawyers will escape liability for their mistakes.[6] After all, by the time most will drafting errors are identified, the client is in no position to complain.

Cases like *Ogle* are important because they remind us that we serve people whose lives are affected by how carefully we practice our craft. As you work your way through this text, keep in mind that the doctrine you learn is not important in its own right, but because the use and abuse of this doctrine can affect the lives of real people.

§ 2   An Overview of Intergenerational Wealth Transfer

This section introduces some terminology and basic concepts discussed in later chapters. Its major purpose is to provide a "big picture," so you will know the context in which particular doctrines operate. After a discussion of the probate system for transferring decedents' property, we will examine probate-avoidance devices, lifetime transfers that can serve as substitutes for wills. The section closes with a word about the uniform statutes and Restatements.

---

[4] The estate went to other relatives under what is called an *intestate statute,* a topic covered in the next chapter.

[5] *See* Lucas v. Hamm, 364 P.2d 685 (Cal. 1961) (will beneficiaries have cause of action against drafting attorney in both tort and contract); Auric v. Continental Casualty Co., 331 N.W.2d 325 (Wis. 1983) (will beneficiary allowed to maintain an action against attorney). *But see* Miller v. Mooney, 725 N.E.2d 545 (Mass. 2000) (rejecting tort liability); Barcelo v. Elliott, 923 S.W.2d 575 (Tex. 1996) (lack of privity barred will beneficiary's claim against drafting attorney). *See generally* Martin D. Begleiter, *Attorney Malpractice in Estate Planning—You've Got to Know When to Hold Up, Know When to Fold Up,* 38 U. Kan. L. Rev. 193 (1990); Bradley E.S. Fogel, *Attorney v. Client – Privity Malpractice, and the Lack of Respect for the Privacy of the Attorney-Client Relationship in Estate Planning,* 68 Tenn. L. Rev. 261 (2001). Helen Bishop Jenkins, *Privity—A Texas-Sized Barrier to Third Parties for Negligent Will Drafting—An Assessment and Proposal,* 42 Baylor L. Rev. 687 (1990); Mary Elizabeth Phelan, *Unleashing the Limits on Lawyers' Liability?* Mieras v. DeBona: *Michigan Joins the Mainstream . . .* 72 U. Det. Mercy L. Rev. 327 (1995).

Some courts have abolished the privity defense in contexts not involving wills. *See, e.g.,* Holsapple v. McGrath, 521 N.W.2d 711 (Iowa 1994) (allowing a claim by grantees of a faulty deed).

The increased malpractice exposure serves as a spur to reform outmoded doctrines which haunt this area of law. *See* Jesse Dukeminier, *Cleansing the Stables of Property: A River Found at Last,* 65 Iowa L. Rev. 151 (1979).

[6] Lawyers may also be liable for the mistakes of their employees. *See* John W. Wade, *Tort Liability of Paralegals and Lawyers Who Utilize Their Services,* 24 Vand. L. Rev. 1133 (1971).

[A] Probate

[1] The Process

Probate systems collect the assets of decedents, satisfy creditors, resolve conflicts among beneficiaries, and distribute what is left to the appropriate persons or institutions.[1] Procedural details vary from place to place, but the basic concept of probate carries through differing approaches.

Only some property interests are "subject to probate." Property that the decedent held alone or as a tenant in common is subject to the system. On the other hand, a number of sources of wealth do not pass through probate.[2] Joint tenancy (or tenancy by the entirety) property, life insurance proceeds on the decedent's life, and property in lifetime trusts are all outside of probate.[3]

Notice how little wealth may actually be subject to probate. A typical married couple may hold virtually everything in joint tenancy—house, cars, bank accounts, investments. There may be no probate assets until the surviving spouse dies. If a wealthy family adopts a sophisticated plan, they may have most of their property in trust—again, not subject to probate.

Despite the relatively narrow coverage, the probate system is fundamentally important to the entire intergenerational wealth transfer process. Much of the law governing wealth transfer developed in the context of probate. Moreover, it is the ultimate "fail-safe" system. If no other theory authorizes a shift of property from a decedent to another, the probate system comes into play.

When a person dies and a decision is made to probate his estate, someone—usually a family member—will petition a court[4] in the decedent's state of domicile to appoint a "personal representative" to handle the work.[5] If the decedent owned property in other states, a separate, "ancillary" probate might have to be opened (and a personal representative appointed) in each of those states.[6] Ancillary probate is designed to protect local creditors and is particularly likely if the out-of-state asset is real property.

---

[1] Technically, "probate" refers to the proving of a will and "administration" refers to the process under which assets are collected and dispersed to successors, whether there is a will or not. *See* McGovern & Kurtz at 467-68. In more common usage, however, "probate" has come to mean the entire process, and the term is used in that sense here.

[2] *See generally* § 2[B], *infra.*

[3] Several states allow married couples to hold property as "community property," which is shared equally. At death, the decedent's one-half of the community property may pass through probate or may pass directly to the other spouse. *See generally* Robert L. Mennell and Thomas M. Boykoff, Community Property in a Nutshell (2d ed. 1988). *See also* § 28[A], *infra.*

[4] The court may be called a probate court, a surrogate's court, or even an orphan's court.

[5] The personal representative owes fiduciary duties to the estate's beneficiaries. *See generally* Chapter 14, *infra.*

[6] *See generally* McGovern & Kurtz at 973-77.

The term "personal representative" is a generic term that covers any of the various categories of people[7] named to handle an estate. If there is a will,[8] the first choice for a personal representative would be the person named in the will as "executor."[9] If there is no will, the decedent has died "intestate," and a state statute[10] will direct how the property is to be distributed[11] and provide a hierarchy[12] from which to choose an "administrator."[13]

States differ in the level of judicial supervision they require. Modern probate procedures evolved from two approaches taken in English ecclesiastical courts. "Common form" probate was an ex parte process. After the validity of the will was proved, the court would allow the executor to begin administration without further court involvement. Anyone who objected could petition for probate in "solemn form," which involved notice to interested parties and court supervision. Sensing trouble ahead, an executor might simply elect the solemn form from the start. While some states permit a variant of common form probate,[14] most states' courts supervise the entire process.[15]

In part as a response to complaints that there is too much supervision,[16] at too high a cost,[17] the Uniform Probate Code (UPC) takes a different

---

[7] Trust companies and trust departments of commercial banks often serve in these various capacities as well.

[8] Anyone who wants to transfer probate property at death must make a valid will. People who make wills are called "testators" and are said to die "testate." *See generally* Chapter 3, *infra*.

[9] In the past, the term "executrix" has been used if the personal representative was female. Since gender has no legal consequence in this context, "trix" endings are gradually making their way out of our language. In this text, use of the "or" suffix makes no assumption about the gender of the person involved.

[10] If a decedent owns property in different jurisdictions, different statutes may apply to identify who inherits. Personal property is governed by the law of the decedent's domicile, and real property is governed by the law of its location. *See generally* William M. Richman & William L. Reynolds, Understanding Conflict of Laws §§ 66, 86 & 87 (2d ed. 1993).

[11] *See generally* Chapter 2, *infra*.

[12] Usually the surviving spouse is first on the list, followed by other relatives and, finally, other qualified persons.

[13] Other titles sometimes indicate special circumstances. If the named executor is out of the country for a while, it might be necessary to appoint a "special administrator" to get things started. If the will only names people who cannot serve, a court will appoint someone who could be called an "administrator with will annexed," to indicate that—despite the "administrator" title—there is indeed a will.

[14] *E.g.*, N.C. Gen. Stat. § 31-12.

[15] Many states allow small estates to pass without court administration, or with minimal court involvement. *See, e.g.*, Ind. Code Ann. § 29-1-8-1; Ohio Rev. Code Ann. § 2113.03. *See also* UPC §§ 3-1201 to 3-1204. A few states allow an administration independent of judicial supervision once the will has been proved and there has been an inventory, an appraisal, and a list of claims established. *See* Tex. Prob. Code Ann. § 145.

[16] *See* Richard V. Wellman, *The Uniform Probate Code: A Possible Answer to Probate Avoidance*, 44 Ind. L.J. 191 (1969).

[17] *See, e.g.*, Norman F. Dacey, How to Avoid Probate (Rev. ed. 1990).

approach. Although the traditional approach of full su
able,[18] administration also may be largely unsupervise
called upon as needed. An interested party who feels †
should be reviewed, for example, can obtain court su
controversy without generating supervision of all othe॒

In addition, the UPC offers the choice of universal succession, whिҵ.
administration entirely and gives title to the heirs[20] or residuary devisees,[21] subject to the claims of creditors and any other devisees.[22]

The discussion that follows assumes a court's continuing supervision.

Upon appointment of the personal representative, the court issues
appropriately titled "letters" to evidence the individual's authority. Armed
with official copies of letters and of death certificates, the personal representative can contact banks, stock transfer agents, and the like, to collect the
decedent's assets.[23]

An inventory is then filed.

While the personal representative is collecting assets, she also should be
notifying creditors. The traditional method of giving such notice (and
thereby starting fairly short statutes of limitation running against the as-
sertion of any claims) had been publication in a local newspaper. All that
changed in 1988 when the U.S. Supreme Court ruled, in *Tulsa Professional
Collection Services, Inc. v. Pope*,[24] that more was required.

In *Pope*, the executor (the widow) published appropriate notices in the
local paper, giving creditors two months to file their claims. The hospital
in which the decedent died did not file in time, so the local court denied
the claim. On appeal, the hospital argued that notice-by-publication was
insufficient under the due process clause.[25] The Supreme Court distinguished this situation from mere "self-executing" statutes of limitation not
subject to due process notice requirements,[26] because in the probate context

---

[18] UPC § 3-501.

[19] *See* UPC § 3-107 (comment).

[20] The "heirs" are those who would take under the intestate statute if there were no will.

[21] Historically, the term "devisee" meant someone who took real property by will. The UPC
expands that term to include anyone who takes real or personal property by will. UPC
§ 1-201(10), (11). The "residuary devisees" are those who would take under a will clause which
follows any gifts to individuals or groups and reads: "I give all the rest of my property to . . ."

[22] *See* UPC §§ 3-312 to 3-322. *See also* Eugene Scoles, *Succession Without Administration:
Past and Future*, 48 Mo. L. Rev. 371 (1983).

[23] For an example of a personal representative that failed to meet its obligation to exercise
due care in this context, see *In re First Nat'l Bank of Mansfield*, 307 N.E.2d 23 (Ohio 1974),
discussed in § 56[B], *infra*.

[24] 485 U.S. 478, 99 L. Ed. 2d 565, 108 S. Ct. 1340 (1988). *See generally* Sarajane Love, *Estate
Creditors, The Constitution, and the Uniform Probate Code*, 30 U. Rich. L. Rev. 411 (1996).

[25] *Pope* also illustrates the folly of not being thoughtful (or at least wary) of others involved
in the probate process. Here, the executor and the hospital each knew of the death and pending
bill, yet neither bothered to contact the other in the context of settling the estate. Instead,
they spent substantial funds litigating.

[26] *See* Texaco, Inc. v. Short, 454 U.S. 516, 70 L. Ed. 2d 738, 102 S. Ct. 781 (1982).

re is significant state action throughout the process. Harkening back
o *Mullane v. Central Hanover Bank & Trust Co.*,[27] the Court held that
due process requires actual notice (like mail) to known or reasonably
ascertainable creditors before their claims can be cut off.

Once the assets are assembled and the creditors have been contacted,
estate administration enters a holding period. Appraisals are made; tax
forms are filed; sometimes property is sold to pay creditors or because no
one wants it. If there is a will that an interested party[28] believes should
not be enforced, there may be a will contest.[29] If there is a dispute about
the will's meaning or whether a substantive rule (like the Rule Against
Perpetuities) has been violated, there may be litigation.

Traditionally, the scope of a personal representative's duty to protect the
estate's assets during this period fit the short-term nature of estate
administration: the focus was on supervision and preservation.[30] Because
courts have been moving toward treating personal representatives in much
the same way as trustees, we will discuss the duties of each after we have
examined the law of trusts.[31]

Once assets have been assembled, creditors paid, and problem areas
addressed, the personal representative closes the estate by distributing the
remaining property to those entitled to it. Distributions might be to
individuals, to charities, to trustees of already existing trusts, or to trustees
of trusts created by the decedent's will.

[2] Is Probate Necessary?

We sometimes assume that because the probate system is available, it
must be used. Instead, in each case, we ought to be recalling the functions
of the system and asking whether this particular probate is necessary.

Imagine that Marge Gorski comes into your office to tell you of the death
of her husband, Ed. Ed was recently retired from Monroe Tool Works;
Marge still works for Ace Hardware. They owned a house in joint tenancy,
and had joint checking and savings accounts, and a car titled in both names.

---

[27] 339 U.S. 306, 94 L. Ed. 865, 70 S. Ct. 652 (1950). In *Mullane,* the Court announced due
process standards for adequate notice, which now apply to both *in personam* and *in rem* actions.

[28] In this context, an "interested party" is someone who would benefit from the will being
invalidated. Most commonly, challengers are persons who would take under an earlier will
or under the intestate statute if there were no valid will.

[29] The most common grounds for contest are that the testator (will maker) lacked mental
capacity, was subject to undue influence, or failed to follow technical rules regarding the will's
execution. *See* Jeffrey A. Schoenblum, *Will Contests—An Empirical Study,* 22 Real Prop. Prob.
& Tr. J. 607 (1987). *See generally* Chapter 3, *infra.*

Procedures for contesting wills vary. In some jurisdictions, a contest may be brought in the
probate court. In others, it must be in the court of general jurisdiction. *See generally* Page
ch. 26.

[30] For a good illustration of the problems a personal representative might face, see *Estate
of Baldwin,* 442 A.2d 529 (Me. 1982).

[31] *See* Chapter 13, *infra.*

Ed's retirement plan names Marge as the next beneficiary, and there is some life insurance, again payable to Marge. They have no other assets beyond clothes, jewelry, and furniture. The only debts are pending charge card bills. Ed's will gives everything to Marge; the children are making no claims.

On these facts, there is no good reason to bother probating Ed's estate. The only assets Ed owned alone (the tangible personal property) are already in the house, so there is no problem with assembling estate assets. Marge fully intends to pay off the charge cards, so creditors are not a worry. Since Marge's survivorship interest gives her the house, there is no potential title problem.

The example suggests some situations that could call for probate. If a bank account were in Ed's name alone, letters of authority from a probate court might be the only way to get the bank to release the money. On the other hand, perhaps something else could be worked out informally. If Ed had owned a business, cutting off creditor's claims might be important. Though the *Pope* case, discussed above, would require reasonable efforts to find and notify creditors, going through probate would provide some security against creditors who appeared later. Before deciding, you would want to know how likely their appearance would be. If children from a former marriage are questioning the will's validity, you may need a hearing, but you may be able to reach a settlement. If the house had been in Ed's name alone, probate probably would be necessary to vest a clear title in Marge. Some title insurance companies, however, might be willing to insure a title in Marge's name on the strength of affidavits, instead of requiring a probate court order. For any number of reasons, you may want to advise Marge to use the probate process, but you ought to have reasons.

When someone has died, we need to collect the assets, take care of creditors, resolve any disputes among claimants, and get clear title into the hands of the right survivors. If we need the probate system to accomplish one of those tasks, we should use it. If not, we shouldn't.

[B] Lifetime Transfers

We now turn to devices that effectively transfer wealth at someone's death, but that are not subject to the probate system. For this reason, they are often called "will substitutes." Principal among them is the trust, which we will cover in detail later.[32] This section introduces the trust concept and some terminology, and then describes other nonprobate transfers.[33]

Be sure to distinguish probate avoidance from tax avoidance. Many forms of wealth that do not pass through probate are nonetheless subject to tax.[34]

---

[32] *See* Chapter 4, *infra.*

[33] *See generally* Chapter 5, *infra.*

[34] The federal gift and estate tax system is discussed in Chapter 14, *infra.*

[1] Trusts

Because trusts are so flexible, they are the most useful single estate planning device. Professor Scott, the dominant figure of 20th century trust law, reminds us that "[t]he purposes for which trusts can be created are as unlimited as the imagination of lawyers."[35] Scott challenges us to use trusts creatively to meet the needs of our clients. Trusts are flexible because the essential elements are so few: (1) an intention to create a trust with (2) property (sometimes called the res) (3) held by someone (the trustee) (4) to benefit someone else (the beneficiary). The property serves as the principal (or corpus) of the trust, invested to generate income for the beneficiaries. Of course, there must be someone to create the trust. This person might be called the settlor, donor, trustor, or testator, depending upon the situation and local custom.

One person can assume any number of different roles, just so long as the trustee owes a duty to *someone* else. The settlor could be a trustee, by announcing that property she owned was now being held in trust for the benefit of others. One of those beneficiaries could even be the settlor/trustee herself. The only limit is that one person cannot be both trustee and *sole* beneficiary.[36] Of course, different people might assume each of those roles. It is quite common, for example, for a settlor to give money to a bank as trustee to invest for members of the settlor's family.

A trust may be created by lifetime transfer or by will. If a trust is created during the life of the settlor, it is called a "living" (or "lifetime" or "inter vivos") trust. If a trust is created by will, it is called a "testamentary" trust. Questions involving living trusts can be resolved in courts of general jurisdiction, but there is no ongoing judicial supervision. Testamentary trusts are typically subject to the continuing jurisdiction and supervision of the probate court.

To see when a trust might be appropriate, consider a couple who want to provide for their young children if the parents die while the children are minors. Each of the parent's wills could give everything to the surviving parent. If one died but the other survived, the survivor would continue to care for the children. If there were no surviving parent,[37] however, the will could give everything in trust to the local bank to manage for the children. In addition, life insurance might be made payable to the trustee. While the children were young, the income (and perhaps principal) from the trust would help support them. Once the children reached adulthood, the trustee could distribute the principal. Later we will examine some of the variations

---

[35] 1 Austin W. Scott & William F. Fratcher, The Law of Trusts 4 (Little, Brown 4th ed. 1987-1991).

[36] The basic notion is that without *someone* to enforce a trustee's duties, there are no duties. Technically, we may say there is no separation between legal title (held by the trustee) and equitable title (held by the beneficiaries). For discussion, see §§ 12[B], [C], [D], *infra*.

[37] Suppose a car crash, or deaths from different causes but close in time, as in *Ogle*, discussed in § 1, *supra*.

available to shape the trust to the needs of particular families. For now, concentrate on understanding the trust's basic structure.

[2] Other Lifetime Transfers

While the trust is the most complex probate-avoidance device, others are more common. You will recall from your Property course how the surviving joint tenants own the entire property when one joint tenant dies. This survivorship feature makes joint tenancy holdings extraordinarily popular, especially among persons of modest means. Real estate, bank accounts, stocks, and bonds can all be held in "joint with survivorship" form. Because the survivor no longer shares ownership with the one who has died, the decedent effectively has transferred wealth at death. Because of the legal theory that the survivor has owned the property all along, however, no will is required.

The law of contracts supplies another way around probate. Funds paid by a third party at the death of someone are often treated as contract rights of the beneficiary, rather than property of the one who died.

Life insurance is the most common example of this way of giving money at death. Though the industry has developed a wide array of products in recent years, they commonly fall into one of two basic categories. Term insurance covers the risk of someone dying during the term of the policy. [38] Other products incorporate an investment feature as well. [39]

Death benefits from life insurance bypass the probate system because courts do not consider, for purposes of transferring title, those benefits as property of the decedent. In recent years, the use of "payable-on-death" and "transfer-on-death" accounts has expanded significantly. Statutes have authorized bank accounts and, more recently, mutual funds, other securities [40] and even land, [41] to be held in these forms. The explosion of retirement plans also has produced a new way of accumulating wealth and leaving it to survivors outside of probate. [42]

Professor John Langbein has noted how these developments have profound implications for the law of wealth transfer. [43] On the one hand, the law of wills could learn from the law that has developed around these other devices. On the other, what Langbein calls the subsidiary law of wills— rules about how to interpret documents in various situations—holds many

---

[38] If there is a death, the company pays the face amount to the beneficiary.

[39] If the insured dies while the policy is in force, the beneficiary is paid. Because of the investment feature, however, the owner has the option of drawing out the built-up value of the policy before death.

[40] See Richard V. Wellman, *Transfer-on-Death Securities Registration: A New Title Form*, 21 Ga. L. Rev. 789 (1987).

[41] Ohio Rev. Code § 302.22-.23.

[42] Sometimes retirement benefits are created by contract and sometimes the trust form is used, but the probate avoidance result is the same.

[43] See John H. Langbein, *The Nonprobate Revolution and the Future of the Law of Succession*, 97 Harv. L. Rev. 1108 (1984).

lessons for nonprobate transfers. For example, if someone makes a will in favor of a spouse whom he later divorces, the will provision commonly is treated as revoked.[44] Should we not get the same result if the gift had been in trust? The notion that we should have an integrated wealth-transfer system, which depends more on substance than on form, is gaining increasing attention. As we consider the various doctrines discussed in this text, we will be asking whether good reasons support the different approaches traditionally taken toward these various devices.

[C] The Uniform Codes and the Restatements

Law reform engines have significantly affected the law of trusts and estates. The Uniform Probate Code (UPC) and the Uniform Trust Code (UTC) offer statutory language and commentary to state legislatures considering reform (and indirectly influence court decisions). The Restatements of Property and of Trusts provide guidance to courts (and indirectly influence legislatures). This subsection briefly introduces these vehicles for reform.

In 1969, the Commissioners on Uniform State Laws promulgated the UPC as a comprehensive statute covering a broad range of issues related to family wealth transfers: jurisdiction, intestacy, wills, probate procedure, guardianship, trust administration.[45] Since then, a number of revisions have been made, most notably in 1990.[46]

The UTC was approved in 2000 and is being considered in a number of states.[47] The act codifies an area of law traditionally established by court decisions that necessarily left large gaps in some jurisdictions.[48]

The UPC is a continually evolving document, sheparded by the Joint Editorial Board for the Uniform Probate Code (JEB-UPC). This group of

---

[44] *See, e.g.*, UPC (pre-1990) § 2-508. *See generally* 45[B][1], *infra.*

[45] For brief discussions of the process of creating and marketing uniform laws, see John H. Langbein & Lawrence W. Waggoner, *Reforming the Law of Gratuitous Transfers: The New Uniform Probate Code*, 55 Alb. L. Rev. 871, 875-899 (1992), and Lawrence H. Averill, Jr., *An Eclectic History and Analysis of the 1990 Uniform Probate Code*, 55 Alb. L. Rev. 891, 901-906 (1992).

[46] Many of the changes are analyzed in an extensive symposium. *See Symposium on the Uniform Probate Code: Reflections on Recent Revisions*, 55 Alb. L. Rev. No. 4 (1992). *See also* Mark L. Ascher, *The 1990 Uniform Probate Code: Older and Better, or More Like the Internal Revenue Code*, 77 Minn. L. Rev. 639 (1993); Mary L. Fellows, *Traveling the Road of Probate Reform: Finding the Way to Your Will (A Response to Professor Ascher)*, 77 Minn. L. Rev. 659 (1993); Bruce H. Mann, *Formalities and Formalism in the Uniform Probate Code*, 142 U. Pa. L. Rev. 1033 (1994). The Uniform Laws Annotated lists 16 adopting states of various UPC versions: Alaska, Arizona, Colorado, Florida, Hawaii, Idaho, Maine, Michigan, Minnesota, Montana, Nebraska, New Mexico, North Dakota, South Carolina, South Dakota and Utah. 8 U.L.A. 1 (2002 Pocket Part).

[47] Iowa's new trust code is based on a UTC draft. *See* Martin D. Begleiter, *In the Code We Trust—Some Trust Law for Iowa at Last,* 49 Drake L. Rev. 165 (2001).

[48] *See generally* David M. English, *The Uniform Trust Code (2000): Significant Provisions and Policy Issues*, 67 Mo. L. Rev. 143 (2002).

academic lawyers and practitioners monitors how the UPC is working and recommends both piecemeal and comprehensive (as in 1990) revisions. Facilitated by overlap of interest and personnel, the JEB-UPC has worked cooperatively with groups revising the Restatement of Property and the Restatement of Trusts.

Those Restatements, like others you have learned about, are the product of the American Law Institute, an organization of judges, lawyers and law professors founded in 1923 to clarify, simplify and otherwise reform the law. Two projects are particularly relevant to our topic: The Restatement (Third) of Property (Wills and Other Donative Transfers) and the Restatement (Third) of Trusts. Both are ongoing efforts, but the directions in which they are moving can guide us as to how the law of the future—the law you will be using—will look.

As unlikely as it may seem, the law of wills and trusts is full of life. Its subject matter is people, and its doctrine is in the process of reforming to take advantage of newly developed approaches and to meet new needs.

Chapter 2

INTESTACY

§ 3 Overview

The law governing intestate distributions supports the entire field of family wealth transfers. You might compare these rules to the default provisions of a word-processing computer program. Unless the user (owner) overrides the system with specific instructions, these rules apply to all probate property.[1]

For those who die without a will, and there are many,[2] an intestate statute provides an "estate plan" designed by the state legislature. Even if there is a will, it might not cover all of a decedent's probate property. For example, the will might only say "I give all of my real property to Helen." In the usual case, Helen would have no right to the decedent's personal property.[3] The decedent would then be "partially intestate" as to the personalty, which would pass according to the intestate statute.

What guides legislatures as they decide which survivors[4] should get what shares? The major goal is to reflect the presumed desires of the decedent by asking "Where would most people in this situation want their property

---

[1] Section 2 discusses the distinction between probate and nonprobate assets. In general, intestate shares are fixed without reference to property that passes by other means to the same persons. This approach may change, however, if states react favorably to the revised augmented estate created for purposes of spouses electing to take a statutory share of an estate. *See* § 28[C][3][b], *infra*. The next step could be to view at-death transfers as a whole, and to fix all intestate shares with reference to the larger picture. The "hotchpotch" device (developed to deal with advancements) might be used by analogy. *See* § 24, *infra*.

[2] As you might expect, the wealthier and older the decedent, the more likely he or she will have a will. *See* Mary Louise Fellows, Rita J. Simon & William Rau, *Public Attitudes About Property Distribution at Death and Intestate Succession Laws in the United States*, 1978 Am. B. Found. Res. J. 319. Nonetheless, even very wealthy people sometimes die intestate: neither Howard Hughes nor Pablo Picasso left a valid will.

[3] *See, e.g.*, Estate of Russell, 444 P.2d 353 (Cal. 1968) (Decedent's will made only a specific bequest of jewelry and gift of real estate. When part of the gift of realty failed, that property passed by intestacy.). *Russell* is discussed in § 41[B][1], *infra*.

[4] Deciding *whether* someone is a survivor can be difficult. *See, e.g.*, Janus v. Tarasewicz, 482 N.E.2d 418 (Ill. App. 1985) (Husband and wife each died of tampered Tylenol laced with cyanide.). Moreover, if someone survives, but only for a short time, distributing the property to the short-term survivor only wastes time and effort. For these reasons, the UPC requires someone to survive by 120 hours to qualify to take under the intestate statute. UPC § 2-104. Section 2-702 applies the same limit on wills, life insurance, joint tenancies and other will substitutes. *See generally* Edward C. Halbach, Jr. & Lawrence W. Waggoner, *The UPC's New Survivorship and Antilapse Provisions*, 55 Alb. L. Rev. 1091-1099 (1992).

Careful document drafters will define "survivorship" to include a time requirement. *See* § 45[B][2][a], *infra*.

to go?" Other considerations may include protecting dependent family members, keeping property titles simple, keeping property from breaking into very small shares,[5] promoting the nuclear family, and encouraging individuals to accumulate property.[6] Moreover, conceptions of "family" are changing from a tradition of "wife-husband-children" to a broader view including stepchildren and non-marital cohabitants.[7]

As you will see, states vary in their choices of who, among many survivors, take the property and what their shares should be. Commentators debate about whether various choices further the policies articulated above.[8]

The influence of intestate statutes extends well beyond intestate estates. Often these statutes serve as models for other laws that mandate shares for disinherited spouses or forgotten children.[9] Many of the concepts and definitions developed with reference to intestacy have carried over into will and trust law generally. In addition, intestate schemes provide document drafters with a large variety of choices to present to their clients who want wills or trusts.

This chapter will first discuss intestate shares for surviving spouses. Then it will cover the shares given to other relatives.[10]

---

[5] *See, e.g.*, Hodel v. Irving, 481 U.S. 704, 95 L. Ed. 2d 668, 107 S. Ct. 2076 (1987) (upholding the right of both federal and state governments to modify the rules governing devise and descent in order to prevent further division of small parcels of land, but finding unconstitutional the statute abolishing descent and devise in some situations on Indian reservations); Babbitt v. Youpee, 519 U.S. 234, 136 L. Ed. 2d 696, 117 S. Ct. 727 (1997) (invalidating Congress's response to *Hodel v. Irving*). *See generally* Ronald Chester, *Is the Right to Devise Property Constitutionally Protected—The Strange Case of* Hodel v. Irving, 24 Sw. U. L. Rev. 1195 (1995).

[6] *See* Mary Louise Fellows, Rita J. Simon & William Rau, *Public Attitudes About Property Distribution at Death and Intestate Succession Laws in the United States*, 1978 Am. B. Found. Res. J. at 324. *See also* John H. Beckstrom, *Sociobiology and Intestate Wealth Transfer*, 76 Nw. U. L. Rev. 216 (1981) (discussing the design of intestate statutes in relation to gene theory).

[7] *See generally*, Susan N. Gary, *Adapting Intestacy Laws to Changing Families*, 18 Law & Ineq. J. 1 (2000).

[8] *See, e.g.*, Mary Louise Fellows, Rita J. Simon & William Rau, *Public Attitudes About Property Distribution at Death and Intestate Succession Laws in the United States*, 1978 Am. B. Found. Res. J. at 348-84; Mary Louise Fellows, Rita J. Simon, Teal E. Snapp & William D. Snapp, *An Empirical Study of the Illinois Statutory Estate Plan*, 1976 U. Ill. L.F. 717, 725-736; John R. Price, *The Transmission of Wealth at Death in a Community Property Jurisdiction*, 50 Wash. L. Rev. 277 (1975).

[9] *Compare* Ohio Rev. Code Ann. § 2106.01 (giving a spousal election right) *with* § 2105.06 (the basic intestate statute); *compare* Idaho Code § 15-2-302 (giving omitted children a share equivalent to the share they would have received if the testator had died intestate) *with* § 15-2-103 (the basic intestate statute). Doctrines which protect family members from disinheritance are discussed in Chapter 8, *infra*.

[10] Some states extend inheritance rights to stepchildren. *See, e.g.*, Ohio Rev. Code Ann. § 2105.06(J). If no one listed in the statute survives, the state takes "by escheat." *See, e.g.*, Ohio Rev. Code Ann. § 2105.06(K).

§ 4   Spouses[1]

Like much of the law of spousal relations generally, the law governing spouses' intestate shares is changing. Traditionally, blood relationships were the key to inheritance rights, and spouses suffered by comparison.[2] Now spouses can inherit, and the law has started to respond to the reality that many persons have more than one spouse during a lifetime.[3] The next policy question probably will be the extent the law treats unmarried domestic partners as spouses.[4]

The size of a surviving spouse's share[5] varies, depending upon both state law and who else survives. If the decedent left no children, the spouse might get everything,[6] or might share with the decedent's parents.[7] If the decedent left children, the spouse will often share with them, taking half if there is one child, and one-third if there are more than one child.[8]

Dividing an estate between the spouse and the children might not leave enough to support the spouse. In addition, if the children are minors, they may need separate, costly guardianships. Especially when the amounts are small, splitting the estate may not be wise. As a rough way to avoid these

---

[1] For a discussion of how a spousal relationship is established, see Homer H. Clark, Jr., The Law of Domestic Relations in the United States 68-124 (2d ed. 1988). One might not be a spouse for all purposes. *Compare In re* Estate of Goick, 909 P.2d 1165 (Mont. 1996) (wife was surviving spouse even though divorce was pending when husband died) with N.Y. Est. Powers & Trusts Law § 5-1.2 (separation decree terminates spousal inheritance rights).

[2] In England, at one time spouses had no rights to inherit their dead consorts' land. The doctrines of dower and curtesy, however, protected them against being left with no rights to the land. Wives also got one-third of their husbands' personal property if they left surviving issue, and one-half if they left no surviving issue. Husbands did not need such a right, because they generally became owners of their wives' personalty upon marriage. *See* McGovern, Kurtz & Rein at 3.

Dower and curtesy are discussed in § 28[B], *infra*.

[3] *See generally* Lawrence W. Waggoner, *The Multiple-Marriage Society and Spousal Rights Under the Revised Uniform Probate Code*, 76 Iowa L. Rev. 223 (1991) [hereinafter Waggoner, *Multiple-Marriage*].

[4] *See* 15 Vt. Stat. Ann. § 1204(b) ("spouse" includes parties to a civil union). *See also* Virginia Grainer, *What's Yours is Mine: Reform of the Property Division Regime for Unmarried Couples in New Zealand*, 11 Pac. Rim L. & Pol'y J. 285 (2002); Mary Louise Fellows, Monica Kirkpatrick Johanson, Amy Chiericozzi, Ann Hale, Christopher Lee, Robin Premble & Michael Voran, *Committed Partners and Inheritance: An Empirical Study*, Law & Ineq. J. 1 (1998); Lawrence W. Waggoner, *Marital Property Rights in Transition*, 59 Mo. L. Rev. 21 (1994). Someone who has cohabited under a good faith, but mistaken, belief that he or she was married may be able to claim an intestate share as a *putative spouse*. *See* Restatement (Third) of Property § 2.2 cmt. e.

[5] The shares described here are shares of the probate estate after debts and expenses, which lower the total value of the estate. They do not include exemptions and allowances (as for support), which increase the total of the spouse's share. *See* UPC §§ 2-401 to 2-405.

[6] *See, e.g.,* Ohio Rev. Code Ann. § 2105.06(E).

[7] *See, e.g.,* UPC (pre-1990) § 2-102(2) (Spouse takes $50,000 plus one-half of the balance.); UPC § 2-102(2) (Spouse takes $200,000 plus three-fourths of the balance.). In each case, the parents take the rest. UPC § 2-103(2).

[8] *See, e.g.,* Va. Code Ann. § 64.1-1; Ind. Code Ann. § 29-1-2-1.

problems, some states give the spouse a lump-sum amount, sometimes called "front money," and then divide the balance between the spouse and the children. For example, if Jack dies leaving a wife, Wilma, and their two children, under pre-1990 UPC § 2-102(3), Wilma would take $50,000 plus one-half of the balance. The other half of the balance would go to the children. Of course, if the estate is under $50,000, the children get nothing. They have to rely upon their mother serving as a conduit, leaving them anything that is left over at her death.

The conduit theory may work well in the traditional situation of spouses who marry, raise children, and die without having divorced or remarried. When the surviving spouse is not the parent of some or all of the decedent's children, however, the survivor may be less likely to favor those children and, thus, be less reliable as a conduit.

The revised UPC proposes some significant reforms. In the single-marriage situation, it relies more heavily on the conduit theory. If the surviving children are all children of the decedent and surviving spouse, the surviving spouse gets everything.[9]

The code recognizes, however, two situations common to this day of multiple marriages. First, if the surviving spouse is the parent of the decedent's children, but also has other children, the survivor takes $150,000,[10] plus one-half of the balance. This sharing provides some assurance that the decedent's children will get something in larger estates where the surviving spouse has divided loyalties. On the other hand, if the *decedent* left children who are not children of the surviving spouse, the survivor takes only $100,000, plus one-half of the balance.[11] Here the Code recognizes that the spouse has no natural loyalty to the decedent's children, and protects them in somewhat smaller estates.[12]

The UPC proposals have advanced the debate about how the law of inheritance should respond to a society increasingly characterized by multiple marriages.[13] The solutions offered, however, may favor surviving

---

[9] UPC § 2-102.

[10] UPC § 2-102(3). The larger amount is a reflection of inflation between the time the UPC was originally proposed and 1990. *See* Comment to UPC §§ 2-402, 2-403, 2-404, 2-405. As a practical matter, dollar amounts given for front money understate the actual amounts available to the spouse. Under the current version, exemptions and allowances add at least $43,000. *See* UPC §§ 2-404, 2-405.

[11] UPC § 2-102(4).

[12] Another example of the UPC recognizing the divided loyalty problem arises in connection with pretermitted children. These are children left out of a will. In some situations, they get an intestate share. However, if the decedent left most everything to the *parent* of the omitted child, the child will not get a full intestate share. UPC § 2-302(a)(1). The code relies on the parent (but not just any spouse) to serve as a conduit to the children. Pretermitted shares are discussed in § 29, *infra*.

[13] For discussions by persons who helped develop the UPC proposals, see Waggoner, *Multiple-Marriage*, 76 Iowa L. Rev. 223 (1991); Lawrence W. Waggoner, *Spousal Probate Rights in a Multiple-Marriage Society*, 45 Rec. Ass'n B. City New York 339 (1990) (Mortimer H. Hess Memorial Lecture); John W. Fisher II & Scott A. Curnutte, *Reforming The Law of Intestate Succession and Elective Shares: New Solutions to Age-Old Problems*, 93 W. Va. L. Rev. 61 (1990).

spouses too much, at the expense of surviving descendants. In particular, if a decedent leaves only a spouse and "joint" children, the surviving spouse gets everything.[14] Professor Waggoner notes, "The 1990 UPC is predicated on the notion that decedents . . . see the surviving spouses as occupying somewhat of a dual role, not only as their primary beneficiaries, but also as conduits through which to benefit their children."[15] However, we should ask whether the spousal share should be limited, in light of the number of widowers and widows who remarry. Because surviving spouses' loyalty to their children from a first marriage may wane in the face of a later marriage, spouses may not be reliable conduits.[16]

As we have seen, the revised UPC does recognize divided loyalties when either (or both) the decedent and the surviving spouse had other children. Depending upon who had the other children, the surviving spouse's front money is set at either $100,000 or $150,000. After that, the estate is shared with the decedent's children. The question here is whether, as a practical matter, very many children are given very much protection. Though evidence is spotty, intestate estates over $100,000 are thought to be relatively rare.[17]

Moreover, the intestate estate of a married person is likely to be only a portion, sometimes a very small portion, of his or her total wealth.[18] The rest will be in joint property, retirement accounts, or life insurance, much of which is likely to go to the surviving spouse to the exclusion of the children. Despite a structure that appears to protect children in split families, the revised UPC will likely protect them only in rare cases, and in small amounts relative to the overall size of their deceased parent's wealth. Of course, protecting more children would mean depriving more spouses.[19]

---

[14] UPC § 2-102.

[15] Waggoner, *Multiple-Marriage*, 76 Iowa L. Rev. at 232 (1991).

[16] Traditionally, estates have been divided according to facts known at the decedent's death, and at that time no one knows what the future holds. See Waggoner, *Multiple-Marriage*, 76 Iowa L. Rev. at 233 n.34 (1991). When designing spousal shares, however, perhaps the law should take the possibility of future remarriage into account.

One possibility would be to create a statutory trust for the surviving spouse, giving the spouse lifetime income, coupled with a power to invade the corpus, but giving anything left over to the children. See Waggoner, *Multiple-Marriage*, 76 Iowa L. Rev. at 235 (1991) (criticizing the idea as impractical). Compare the UPC's approach when an incompetent spouse elects against a will. See § 28[C][4], *infra*. Compare also the QTIP trust created to qualify for an estate tax marital deduction. See § 62[B], *infra*.

[17] *Cf.* Mary L. Fellows, Rita J. Simon & William Rau, *Public Attitudes About Property Distribution at Death and Intestate Succession Laws in the United States*, 1978 Am. B. Found. Res. J. at 336-39 (69 percent of persons surveyed with estates over $100,000 had wills); Note, *A Comparison of Iowans' Dispositive Preferences with Selected Provisions of the Iowa and Uniform Probate Codes*, 63 Iowa L. Rev. 1041, 1072 (1978) (24 percent of persons with estates between $100,000 and $249,999 did not have wills).

[18] *See* § 2[B], *supra*.

[19] "The dominant objective is to grant the surviving spouse an adequate share. By this, the revised UPC does not mean to restrict the spouse's share to no more than necessary to provide him or her with the bare necessities of life, but rather to grant a share that is commensurate

As the law governing family relationships continues to evolve, the intestacy shares given to surviving spouses will also change. As we shall see, in designing a system that guarantees a surviving spouse some share of a decedent's estate, the UPC places substantial emphasis on the theory that marriage is a partnership.[20] We may eventually see the partnership theory working its way into intestacy patterns as well.[21]

§ 5   Other Family Members

We now shift our attention from surviving spouses to other members of the decedent's family. First we examine a series of questions revolving around whether a particular survivor is related to the decedent in a way that will allow the survivor to take an intestate share. Then we view the principal schemes that allocate shares among those who qualify to take.

[A]   Qualifying to Take

[1]   Nonmarital Children

For many centuries, children born to unmarried mothers have been called "illegitimate."[1] Such children have been denied a wide range of benefits available to children of married persons.[2]

Originally, nonmarital children could not inherit from anyone.[3] Though the law has moved toward equalizing treatment among marital and non-marital children, differences remain. In the context of inheritance, the controversy now involves when nonmarital children can inherit from their fathers (and vice versa). Legislatures have struggled with how to resolve what have been two conflicting goals. On the one hand, they often want to protect children from discrimination based upon their status. On the other, they also want to protect against fraudulent claims.[4] To do that, a state might preclude a child from claiming a share of her father's estate

---

with the size of the estate and the circumstances of the family make-up." Lawrence W. Waggoner, *Multiple-Marriage*, 76 Iowa L. Rev. at 233 (1991).

[20] For discussion of the partnership theory of marriage, see § 28[C], *infra*.

[21] *See* Martin L. Fried, *The Uniform Probate Code: Intestate Succession and Related Matters*, 55 Alb. L. Rev. 927, 933 (1992).

[1] This label is avoided in the text because it carries the message that such persons are less worthy than persons born to a married couple. Consider further how the more vulgar synonym "bastard" also means an offensive person. Each term places an unfair burden on its subject, since none of us had any control over who our parents are.

[2] *See generally* Jenny Teichman, Illegitimacy: An Examination of Bastardy (1982).

For a fascinating look at how children were caught in the polygamy crossfire between Utah's Mormons and the U.S. Congress, see Barry Cushman, *Intestate Succession in a Polygamous Society*, 23 Conn. L. Rev. 281 (1991).

[3] *See* Thomas E. Atkinson, Law of Wills 40 (West 2d ed. 1953).

[4] Note that the claims can involve *either* children *or* fathers who suddenly arrive to claim a relationship when there is money to be had.

unless the father had acknowledged her as his child.[5] While such a rule might have been justifiable even a few years ago, it is harder to defend in light of new scientific techniques that can establish bloodlines to a virtual certainty.[6] Such requirements now look more like devices for discrimination against the child than like methods for assuring the orderly and accurate administration of estates.

Much of the movement toward more equal treatment for nonmarital children has come from pressure by the U.S. Supreme Court. In 1968, the Court used the Fourteenth Amendment's Equal Protection Clause to protect such children against discrimination under the terms of a wrongful death statute.[7] Since then, the Court has struggled with just how far that protection should go in the context of inheritance between children and their fathers. In 1971, *Labine v. Vincent*[8] upheld a Louisiana statute challenged on equal protection grounds. Although a father had acknowledged his nonmarital daughter, under the statute she could not inherit from him because he had not legitimated her. Deference to states' traditional control over inheritance prevailed over the emerging rights of nonmarital children.

By 1977, a closely divided Court backed away from *Labine*. Giving less deference to a state legislature,[9] the Court in *Trimble v. Gordon*[10] invalidated an Illinois statute that allowed nonmarital children to inherit from their fathers only if their parents eventually married and the fathers acknowledged the children. Justice Powell wrote that "[d]ifficulties of proving paternity in some situations do not justify the total statutory disinheritance of illegitimate children whose fathers die intestate."[11] The burdens those "difficulties" can justify were identified, in part, a year later.

In *Lalli v. Lalli*,[12] an even more-divided Court[13] upheld a New York statute which, it said, bore "an evident and substantial relation to . . .

---

[5] *See, e.g.,* N.Y. Est. Powers & Trusts Law § 4-1.2 (An illegitimate child inherits from her father if the father acknowledges the child, if a filiation order is made during the father's lifetime, or (as provided in a 1987 amendment) if a blood genetic marker test is administered to the father that establishes paternity.).

[6] Traditional HLA blood tests, which can exclude the possibility of paternity with 99.9 percent accuracy, in combination with modern DNA typing, which can establish a probability of paternity greater than 99.9 percent, leave little room for doubt. *See* Sidney B. Schatkin, Disputed Paternity Proceedings Chapters 8-11B (4th ed. 1992).

[7] *See* Levy v. Louisiana, 391 U.S. 68, 20 L. Ed. 2d 436, 88 S. Ct. 1509 (1968) (invalidating a wrongful death statute that denied recovery to nonmarital children).

[8] 401 U.S. 532, 28 L. Ed. 2d 288, 91 S. Ct. 1017 (1971).

[9] *See* Trimble v. Gordon, 430 U.S. 762, 767 n.12, 769. (1977).

[10] 430 U.S. 762, 52 L. Ed. 2d 31, 97 S. Ct. 1459 (1977). The vote was 5-4.

[11] 430 U.S. at 772.

[12] 439 U.S. 259, 58 L. Ed. 2d 503, 99 S. Ct. 518 (1978).

[13] Justice Powell wrote the Opinion of the Court and was joined by Chief Justice Burger and Justice Stewart, who also wrote a separate opinion. Justice Rehnquist concurred in the judgment. Justice Blackmun concurred in the judgment and wrote a separate opinion. Justices Brennan, White, Marshall and Stevens dissented.

particular state interests."[14] The statute allowed a nonmarital child to inherit from her father only if the man had been found to be the father in a paternity action brought both within two years of the child's birth and while the man was alive. Justice Powell again focused on the difficulty of proving paternity. In language reminiscent of *Labine*, he found the requirements justified by the need "to provide for the just and orderly disposition of property at death."[15]

Since *Trimble* and *Lalli*, the Court has made it clear that it will apply an "intermediate" standard of review in illegitimacy cases.[16] As the proof problems get easier, it becomes increasingly harder to justify disproportionate burdens placed on nonmarital children.[17]

A related question, still in the process of being resolved, is how to treat children who are conceived by artificial insemination or other means, after their parent's death.[18]

[2] Adopted Children

Because adoption creates new relationships with new families, it also creates a series of problems regarding inheritance rights.[19] The first step in examining adoption situations is to identify the various parties. The adoptee commands center stage. In the wings on one side we might have the adoptee's genetic parents[20] and their relatives. On the other side, we might find the adoptive parents and their relatives.

Inheritance questions can flow in all directions:[21] If the adoptee dies, can

---

[14] 439 U.S. at 268.

[15] 439 U.S. at 268.

[16] Any classification based on illegitimacy "must be substantially related to an important governmental objective." Clark v. Jeter, 486 U.S. 456, 461, 100 L. Ed. 2d 465, 108 S. Ct. 1910 (1988). *See generally* John E. Nowak & Ronald D. Rotunda, Constitutional Law § 14.19 (6th ed. 2000).

[17] For purposes of inheritance under the UPC, a person is the child of his or her natural parents, "regardless of their marital status." UPC § 2-114.

[18] *Compare* Uniform Status of Children of Assisted Conception Act § 4(b) (decedent is not child's parent) *with In re* Estate of Kolacy, 753 A.2d 1257 (N.J. 2000) (child qualifies as heir where donor was mother's husband who had died of cancer before insemination). *See also* Restatement (Third) of Prop. § 2.5,comment 1 (To inherit, a child must be born within a reasonable time and "in circumstances indicating that the decedent would have approved of the child's right to inherit."). *See generally,* Lori B. Andrews, The Clone Age: Adventures in the New World of Reproductive Technology (1999); Susan Kerr, *Post-Mortem Sperm Procurement: Is It Legal?*, 3 DePaul J. Health Care L. 39 (1999); Christopher A. Scharman, *Not Without My Father: The Legal Status of the Posthumously Conceived Child*, 55. Vand. L. Rev. 1001 (2002).

[19] This section considers the impact of adoption in the context of intestate inheritance. A related problem arises in the context of interpreting documents, as when a will gives property to "children." *See* § 44[E][2], *infra*.

[20] The term "natural parents" is commonly used to designate the biological parents of an adopted person. It is avoided here because it carries the connotation that the adoptive parents are somehow "unnatural." "Genetic," "birth" or "biological" are terms that carry no such baggage.

[21] *See generally* Jan Rein, *Relatives by Blood, Adoptions, and Association: Who Should Get What and Why*, 37 Vand. L. Rev. 711 (1984).

either side inherit? If parents on either side die, can the adoptee inherit? What about more distant relatives? Can the adoptee inherit from them, or vice versa? Should special rules apply when the adoptive parent is married to a genetic parent? At least in situations not involving adoption by stepparents, some states remove the adoptee from the families of the genetic parents and place her in a new family, that of the adoptive parents.[22] Some place the child in both families for all inheritance purposes.[23] Some allow the child to inherit *from* both her genetic and her adopted families, but cut off the genetic parents from inheriting from the child.[24]

In re Estates of Donnelly[25] illustrates some of the issues that arise in the context of adoptee inheritance. Jean's father (John) died while Jean was a baby. Two years later, her mother married Richard, who adopted Jean soon after the wedding. Jean grew up in the new household. When John's father (Jean's grandfather) died leaving only a daughter (Jean's aunt) and Jean, Jean claimed a share of his estate. The Supreme Court of Washington held that Jean's adoption by Richard cut off her claim to share her grandfather's estate.

Neither the Probate nor the Domestic Relations titles of the Washington statutes addressed the precise question of whether an adoptee could inherit *through* a genetic parent.[26] The court reviewed the patchwork of statutes and discerned a legislative policy to provide adopted children a "fresh start"[27] by removing them from the bloodlines of their genetic parents and "plac[ing] them entirely within the adopted family."[28] Jean could not inherit through her biological father.

Several arguments support the "replacement" approach taken in *Donnelly*. It is simple to understand and apply. It treats adopted and non-adopted children similarly, by not giving the adopted child the bonus of a third family from which to inherit. Perhaps most important, a replacement approach also avoids the need to keep track of genetic families, in case inheritance rights should arise. It allows closure of the old relationship.[29]

---

[22] *See, e.g.*, Ohio Rev. Code § 3107.15. *See also* MacCallum v. Seymour, 686 A.2d 935 (Vt. 1996) (holding unconstitutional a statute that allowed adopted children to inherit from their adopting parents, but not from relatives of those adopting parents).

[23] Wyo. Stat. Ann. § 2-4-107.

[24] *See, e.g.*, R.I. Gen. Laws § 15-7-17; Tex. Prob. Code Ann. § 40.

[25] 502 P.2d 1163 (Wash. 1972).

[26] The probate statute kept Jean from being an heir of her birth father, but said nothing about grandparents. Wash. Rev. Code Ann. § 11.04.085. The adoption statute freed her from obligations to her genetic parents and placed her in Richard's family as if she had been born into it but, again, made no specific mention of inheritance from relatives of the genetic parents. 1955 Wash. Laws ch. 291 § 14 (repealed 1984).

[27] *Donnelly*, 502 P.2d at 1166.

[28] *Donnelly*, 502 P.2d at 1167.

[29] *See* Jan Rein, *Relatives by Blood, Adoptions, and Association: Who Should Get What and Why*, 37 Vand. L. Rev. 711, 717 (1984) ("[I]t is apparent that an adoptee's retention of ties with his biological family can undermine the psychological aspect of this assimilation.").

In particular, when a nonmarital child is given up for adoption, there may be substantial benefits in providing the child, to use the court's words, a "clean slate"[30] for the start of a new life.

On the other hand, family law may be moving away from the "fresh start" approach. The concept of "open" adoptions is gaining adherents. In part to encourage people to put their children up for adoption, some states allow genetic parents to help choose the adoptive parents or even maintain contact with the child.[31] In addition, as the four dissenting justices in *Donnelly* noted, the policy of cutting off the genetic family does not fit as well when there has been a stepparent adoption.[32] In that case, as Jean grew up, she presumably learned that her father had died young and that her grandparents were still alive. In many such situations, the grandparents could be expected to play significant roles in the child's life. When there has been a stepparent adoption, whether occasioned by death or divorce, the grandparents may be a major source of continuity and support for the child. Cutting off that relationship may be ill-advised.[33]

Many states have established rules governing inheritance in the special situation of a stepparent adoption.[34] There is no widespread agreement, however, on what those rules should be. The pre-1990 UPC simply said that "adoption of a child by the spouse of a natural parent has no effect on the relationship between the child and either natural parent."[35] Because of the structure of the code, that language meant the child was "not detached from any natural relatives."[36] This option leaves open the possibility that the noncustodial parent or relatives could inherit from the child, even though the child was no longer a part of their lives. Imagine a father with two young children; he divorces his wife and leaves. She remarries to someone who adopts the children with the father's permission. When one of the children is killed in a car crash, the genetic father appears to claim a share of the tort award.

In response to concerns that such results would be unfair, the 1990 revisions to the UPC distinguish between custodial and noncustodial genetic parents. In the context of a stepparent adoption, the full parent-child relationship is maintained with the custodial genetic parent, but the

---

[30] *Donnelly*, 502 P.2d at 1167.

[31] *Cf.* Michaud v. Wawruck, 551 A.2d 738 (Conn. 1988) (Written visitation agreement between genetic mother and adoptive parents does not violate state's public policy.).

[32] *Donnelly*, 502 P.2d at 1168.

[33] *But see* Troxel v. Granville, 530 U.S. 57 (2000) (parent can veto visitation by grandparent).

[34] *See generally* Lisa A. Fuller, *Note, Intestate Succession Rights of Adopted Children: Should the Stepparent Exception be Extended?*, 77 Cornell L. Rev. 1188, 1209-1231 (1992).

A related issue is how to handle a "second-parent adoption," an adoption by a nonmarital cohabiting partner of the child's legal parent. *See* Unif. Adoption Act § 4.102 (treating a second-parent adoption like a stepparent adoption). *See generally* Suzanne Bryant, *Second Parent Adoption: A Model Brief*, 2 Duke J. Gender L. & Pol'y 233 (1995); Deborah Lashman, *Second Parent Adoption: A Personal Perspective*, 2 Duke J. Gender L. & Pol'y 227 (1995).

[35] UPC (pre-1990) § 2-109.

[36] UPC (pre-1990) § 2-109, at comment.

relationship with the noncustodial genetic parent's family runs only to the benefit of the child.[37] The child can inherit from the noncustodial side of the genetic family, but they can not inherit from her. This approach avoids both penalizing the child for the adoption and rewarding the deadbeat parent who effectively abandoned the child.[38] Cutting off the family of the noncustodial genetic parent may be overkill, however, in situations like *Donnelly*, in which one genetic parent has died and the surviving genetic parent has remarried. Because relatives of the predeceased parent may well stay close to the child, perhaps they should be able to inherit from the child.[39]

Adopted persons are now likely to be included as full members of their adoptive families for purposes of inheritance.[40] The extent to which they retain legal ties to their genetic families is an open question, especially when they have been adopted by a stepparent. We should expect the law to keep changing as we adjust to new concepts of "family."

[3] Half-Bloods

A few states discriminate against half-blood, as opposed to whole-blood, relatives. Two people are in a half-blood relationship when they have one common ancestor. Consider the following family:

---

[37] UPC § 2-114(b).

[38] The principle that one who has not treated the child as his or her own should not benefit from the relationship with the child is also covered in a broad provision that cuts off any genetic parent unless the parent has openly treated the child as his or hers and has not refused to support the child. UPC § 2-114.

[39] Pennsylvania takes a flexible approach, which may be the wave of the future. It allows an adopted child to inherit from "natural kin . . . who has maintained a family relationship with the adopted person," 20 Pa. Cons. Stat. Ann. § 2108. *See also* Restatement (Third) of Property § 2.5 cmt. f. *See generally* Lisa A. Fuller, *Note, Intestate Succession Rights of Adopted Children: Should the Stepparent Exception be Extended?*, 77 Cornell L. Rev. 1188 (1992).

[40] Even someone who has not been adopted may still be able to inherit from her custodial parent's spouse. The child may be treated as having been adopted, under the "equitable adoption" (sometimes "virtual adoption") doctrine. *Compare* O'Neal v. Wilkes, 439 S.E.2d 490 (Ga. 1994) (after shuffling among relatives, girl eventually raised by non-relatives, but not entitled to protection as "adopted" because aunt who last took care of her had no authority to enter into adoption contract) *with In re* Heirs of Hodge, 470 So. 2d 740 (Fla. App. 1985) (girl raised by others since age three and given their name). *See generally* Homer C. Clark, Jr., The Law of Domestic Relations in the United States § 20.9 (2d ed. 1988).

In a few states, the child may take as a stepchild. *See* Md. Code Ann., Est. & Trusts § 3-104(e); Ohio Rev. Code Ann. § 2105.06(I). For a proposal to extend the inheritance rights to step-family members when they have become the likely objects of each other's bounty, see Margaret M. Mahoney, *Step-families in the Law of Intestate Succession and Wills*, 22 U.C. Davis L. Rev. 917 (1989). *See also* Thomas M. Hanson, *Intestate Succession For Stepchildren: California Leads the Way, But Has It Gone Far Enough?*, 47 Hast. L.J. 257 (1995).

H1-----┬--------M-------┬-----H2
       │   │
       │   │
       A   B───┴─ C

M and H1 had son A. After a death or divorce, M and H2 had daughters B and C. As to C, A is a half-brother and B is a whole-blooded sister.

The favoritism of the whole-blood, a holdover from England's traditionally narrow conception of family, has largely disappeared. [41] A few states, however, give the whole-blood a larger share [42] or prefer the whole-blood over a half-blood of the same degree of relationship. [43] The ancestral property doctrine also serves to keep property in the bloodline. Under this doctrine, in the family situation above, A would not inherit from C property that C got from H2. Largely abolished, the doctrine is still around in a few places. [44]

[4] Degree of Relationship

If you were to die tomorrow, some of your relatives would be your heirs and others would not. How do we go about identifying the lucky ones? First, we will consider methods of searching a family tree for survivors who inherit. Next, we will ask whether limits should be placed on the size of the tree we search.

While details vary in different places, usually you will be well served by starting with the "look down, look up, look down, look up" principle. [45] Consider the accompanying chart and treat the decedent's spouse as a special case.

When looking for heirs, first look down for descendants. If there are more than one child, follow each child's line down, stopping when you find a survivor. [46] If there are no descendants, look up to the parents. If none, look down again, to sisters and brothers and, if necessary, nieces and nephews. If none, go up to the grandparents (on both sides). Then it's down again,

---

[41] *See, e.g.,* UPC § 2-107.

[42] *See, e.g.,* Fla. Stat. § 732.105.

[43] *See, e.g.,* Conn. Gen. Stat. Ann. § 45a-439.

[44] *See, e.g.,* Wash. Rev. Code § 11.04.035.

[45] This is sometimes called the "parentelic" principle. It is not strictly applied, but serves as a useful starting place when getting a sense of how these schemes are likely to work.

[46] Descendants of living takers do not share; if a decedent leaves a child who also has children, the grandchildren are out.

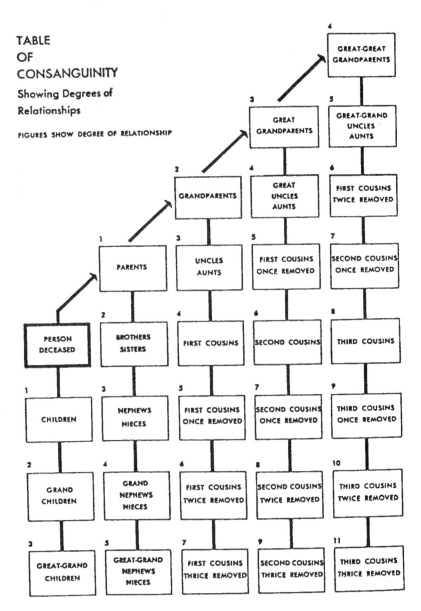

TABLE OF CONSANGUINITY

Showing Degrees of Relationships

FIGURES SHOW DEGREE OF RELATIONSHIP

this time to aunts, uncles, and cousins. A large number of states follow this approach this far (to descendants of grandparents).[47]

When survivors get more remote than grandparents and their descendants, many states designate the "next of kin" to take the estate. The typical way of determining who is "next" is to count people connecting the decedent to the survivor. The numbers in the boxes on the Table of Consanguinity indicate the number of steps ("degrees") from the decedent to various survivors. The closest survivor wins.[48] Ties are sometimes resolved by applying the "first up, then down" principle,[49] and sometimes result in equal sharing among those of equal degree.[50]

Although giving the property to next of kin keeps it in the family, sometimes only very distant relatives survive a decedent. The cost of identifying them may be high, and their ties to the decedent may be minimal.[51] Also, when the estate is large, many persons may be tempted to claim relationships they do not have.[52] To avoid these problems, the UPC cuts off relatives more distant than descendants of grandparents of the decedent.[53] If no one fits that description, the estate "escheats" to the state.[54]

Once we have identified the survivors who qualify as heirs, we need to determine the relative size of their shares. We now turn to that question.

[B] Allocating Shares

[1] The Problem

Two basic notions work both independently and together in various schemes for allocating intestate estates among the heirs. One, called a "per

---

[47] Different share arrangements appear at the grandparent level. The UPC, for example, splits the estate in half between the maternal grandparents (and their issue) and the paternal grandparents (and theirs). UPC § 2-103(4). Note that this division can result in unequal shares for those equally related to the decedent. For example, a decedent might have one cousin on one side of the family and two on the other. Instead of one-third shares for each, the estate would be split 1/2, 1/4, 1/4. *See* Martin L. Fried, *The Uniform Probate Code: Intestate Succession and Related Matters*, 55 Alb. L. Rev. 927, 934-935 (1992).

[48] This method is generally called the "civil law" method. You may find reference to a "Canon Law" method, which now seems to be used only in Arkansas. Under that system, the number of steps to the nearest common relative is determined for both the decedent and for the collateral relative in question. The larger of the two numbers (the larger number of steps to the common ancestor) determines the degree of relationship.

[49] *See, e.g.*, Toomey v. Turner, 186 So. 301 (Miss. 1939).

[50] *See, e.g.*, Dahood v. Frankovich, 746 P.2d 115 (Mont. 1987).

[51] Because they receive a windfall, intestate takers in this situation are sometimes called "laughing heirs" all the way to the bank.

[52] When Ella Wendel died in 1931, leaving about $40,000,000 to charity, 2303 persons claimed next of kin status so they could contest her will. *See* Jesse Dukeminier & Stanley M. Johanson, Wills, Trusts and Estates at 94.

[53] UPC § 2-103.

[54] UPC § 2-105.

capita" approach, counts people. The other goes by either of two names, "per stirpes" or "by right of representation,"[55] and views the family vertically, "by the stocks."

A *per capita* approach is common when all of the takers are in the same generation.[56] When the survivors are in different generations among the descendants of grandparents of the decedent,[57] virtually all states provide for some form of representation. For example, if the decedent left only a sister and two nephews (the sons of a predeceased brother), the sister would likely take one-half of the estate, and the nephews would share the other half as representatives of their father. Especially when the survivors are stretched out among three or more generations, states take different approaches in deciding just how to "represent." Familiarity with these various schemes is important, both because you may encounter any of them, and especially because they serve as alternative models you should present to your clients when they design their own estate plans.

Consider the hypothetical Jones family, long led by Mother Jones. Mother (M) outlived her husband and children, but left a grandchild (B) and great-grandchildren, as follows:

Chart 2-1

Jones Family Tree

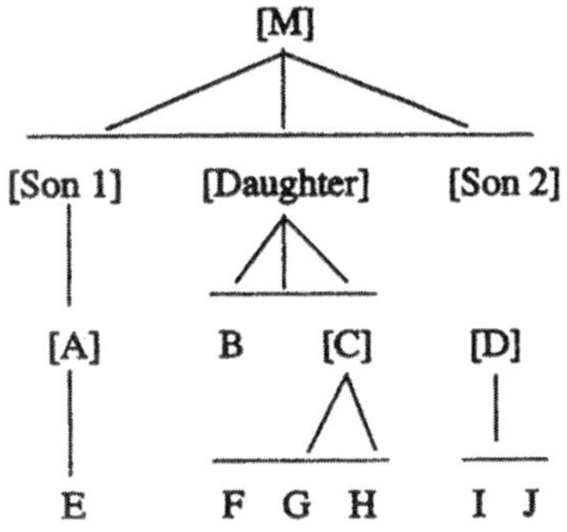

As suggested, M's estate might be divided several ways.

[2] *Per Capita*

One possibility would be for M's estate to be divided among her descendants *per capita*: B, E, F, G, H, I and J would each take 1/7 shares. No intestate statute would adopt such a scheme, but it is introduced here

---

[55] Because it is more easily understood by clients, "by right of representation" is the better term to use in documents.

[56] *See, e.g.*, Ohio Rev. Code Ann. § 2105.12, UPC § 2-103.

[57] Such survivors may be identified as "under the grandparents' umbrella." The metaphor is changed from a tree to an open umbrella with the grandparents at the tip, the direct line of descent as the handle, and the collateral relatives coming down from the spokes.

because the concept of counting heads of survivors appears in other schemes.[58]

[3] Representation: Strict *Per Stirpes*

When people from different generations survive, some form of representation is used. Be careful, however. Do not assume you know what *"per stirpes"* or "by right of representation" means in a particular statute or document. Different states use different definitions. A single state may even define the same language differently, depending upon whether the language appears in the intestate statute or in a will.[59]

Some states, taking an approach often called "strict *per stirpes*," divide at the first generation of descendants.[60] Because Mother Jones had three children who left survivors, the estate would be divided into three shares, one for each stock. E would get 1/3. B would get 1/6 (half of Daughter's 1/3), and F, G, and H would each get 1/18 (sharing the other half of Daughter's 1/3). I and J would each get 1/6.

Those who prefer this system view the family in vertical terms. In our example, they see Son 1's family, Daughter's family, and Son 2's family. Property is shared equally among those families. As a result, however, persons closer to the decedent may get smaller shares than those more distant. Grandchild B got only 1/6, while great-grandchild E got 1/3. Moreover, people in the same generation may get widely differing shares. Different ones of Mother Jones' great-grandchildren got shares of 1/3, 1/6, and 1/18. Their shares depend on how prolific their parents or grandparents were.

---

[58] Poorly drawn wills sometimes use phrases like "issue *per capita*." Such language is particularly troublesome in situations where survivors include both the parent and child in a family. For example, if Mother Jones' grandchild C had survived, the question arises whether F, G, and H would share, or whether C's presence would cut them off. Sometimes the failure to specify between per capita and by right of representation prompts litigation. *See* Petry v. Petry, 175 N.Y.S. 30 (N.Y. App. Div. 1919) ("[I]ssue of my deceased brother" was interpreted to mean that the brother's children and grandchildren all took equally even if the grandchildren's parents were alive.).

[59] *Contrast* Restatement of Prop. § 303 (1940) (defining words in documents according to the way they are defined under the intestate statute in the jurisdiction) and UPC § 2-705 (same) *with* Restatement (Second) of Prop. § 28.2 cmt. a (defining terms irrespective of the intestate statute's definition).

[60] *See, e.g.*, Lombardi v. Blois, 40 Cal. Rptr. 899 (Cal. App. 1964); Godwin v. Marvel, 99 A.2d 354 (Del. Orphans' Ct. 1953).

CHART 2-2
DIFFERENT SCHEMES FOR DIVIDING
MOTHER JONES' ESTATE

	PER CAPITA		STRICT PER STIRPES		PER CAPITA WITH REP.		PER CAPITA AT EACH GEN.	
B	1/7	▪	1/6	▪	1/4	▪	1/4	▪
E	1/7	▪	1/3	▪	1/4	▪	1/8	▪
F	1/7	▪	1/18	▪	1/12	▪	1/8	▪
G	1/7	▪	1/18	▪	1/12	▪	1/8	▪
H	1/7	▪	1/18	▪	1/12	▪	1/8	▪
I	1/7	▪	1/6	▪	1/8	▪	1/8	▪
J	1/7	▪	1/6	▪	1/8	▪	1/8	▪

[4]   Representation: *Per Capita* with Representation

As a partial response to such uneven results, the pre-1990 UPC[61] and some states[62] adopted a compromise interpretation of "representation." The estate is divided into shares at the first generation leaving survivors. Older, "empty" generations are skipped. While sometimes called division by "representation,"[63] this technique often is called "*per capita* with representation." It is "*per capita*" at the first level that has survivors, and "with representation" after that.

If *per capita* with representation were applied to Mother Jones' family, the estate would be divided into four shares: one for B, and one for each of the grandchildren who predeceased Mother leaving surviving descendants. E then takes 1/4; F, G, and H each get 1/12 (1/3 of C's 1/4); I and J each get 1/8. Those closer to the testator get shares at least as large as those more distant, but those in the same generation may still be treated unequally.

[5]   Representation: *Per Capita* at Each Generation

A few states[64] and the revised UPC[65] emphasize equal treatment of each

---

[61] UPC (pre-1990) § 2-106.

[62] *See, e.g.*, Ohio Rev. Code Ann. § 2105.13.

[63] UPC (pre-1990) §§ 2-103 & 2-106.

[64] *See* Me. Rev. Stat. Ann. tit. 18A, §§ 2-103, 2-106; N.C. Gen. Stat. § 29-16.

[65] UPC § 2-106.

generation.[66] Called *"per capita* at each generation," this approach views the family horizontally. To use it, divide the estate in a series of steps. First, find the first generation with survivors and add the number of survivors plus the number of those who died leaving descendants who survive. Give each survivor in the older generation a share based on the total. Next, move down a generation and divide the *remainder* of the estate according to the same principle. How many survivors are there in this generation, and how many in this generation have died leaving descendants? Keep repeating the process until you run out of takers.

Consider again Mother Jones' family. A *per-capita*-at-each-generation approach would ignore the children's generation because none survived. Start at the grandchildren's generation and divide it four ways. B gets 1/4. The remaining 3/4 is put into a pot to be divided by the great-grandchildren. E, F, G, H, I, and J would each take 1/8 of the estate (1/6 each of the 3/4 left after B's share). This scheme has the advantage of treating equally those who are equally distant from the decedent.[67]

In a continuing effort to adjust to shifting family patterns and the presence of nonprobate wealth, the law of intestacy will be changing over the next several years. Intestate statutes will reflect legislative judgments about the distributions most people would want, and about what is fair.[68] The statutes also provide a series of models, which can be used when counseling clients about which alternatives best suit their needs. We now turn to the doctrines that allow us to change the "estate plan" established by intestate statutes.

---

[66] The seeds of law reform sometimes lay dormant for long periods before producing fruit. The 1990 UPC changes were prompted by an article written by Professor Lawrence Waggoner almost 20 years earlier. Lawrence W. Waggoner, *A Proposed Alternative to the Uniform Probate Code's System for Intestate Distribution among Descendants*, 66 Nw. U. L. Rev. 626 (1971). Waggoner, in turn, suggests that a North Carolina statute, which uses the same system, grew out of a 1933 article, Frederick B. McCall & Allen Langston, *A New Intestate Succession Statute for North Carolina*, 11 N.C. L. Rev. 266, 292 (1933). *See* Waggoner, 66 Nw. U. L. Rev. at 633 n.15.

[67] Empirical studies indicate the general public prefers this approach. *See* UPC § 2-106, comment.

[68] One possibility would be to abandon the fixed share approach for one that allows courts more discretion to fit the distribution to each family's circumstances. Questions about close or hostile family relationships and relative needs of the survivors are not now relevant. We might look to our own divorce law and England's law of inheritance for how to add flexibility to our system. *See generally* Mary Ann Glendon, *Fixed Rules and Discretion in Contemporary Family Law and Succession Law*, 60 Tul. L. Rev. 1165 (1986) (rejecting the discretionary approach).

Chapter 3

WILLS

§ 6 Overview

We now shift our attention from default doctrines, which apply when a plan is lacking, to a series of devices for constructing estate plans. The fundamental tool is the will, the subject of this chapter. First, we examine the requirements for creating wills, in terms of both the mental state of a testator and the formal rules for executing a will. Next, we view questions about just what language is considered to be part of a will. Because wills once put together also can be taken apart, doctrines surrounding will revocation come next. The chapter closes with a discussion of contracts to make wills.

Working through this material will require some mental gymnastics. As you consider each topic, view it from different angles. You should master the various rules with an eye to challenging things proffered as "wills." Here you are a litigator in a will contest, looking back upon existing documents and making arguments for your position while anticipating counterarguments. You should also view these topics as raising problems to be avoided. Here you are a planner, looking forward, paying particular attention to the details that make a plan able to withstand future challenges while retaining the flexibility to adapt to unforeseeable change. An important part of planning is staying alert to potential conflicts between family members, so you can head off disputes. Moreover, legal ethics problems lurk in the background of family estate planning, because several family members may want to use the same lawyer. Before you can accept multiple representation, you need to obtain each party's informed consent.[1] Finally, you should step back and ask what is going on here. What policies are being pursued? What, sometimes hidden, assumptions are present? Which rules support and which undermine appropriate policies? Questions like these are not merely academic exercises pursued to please a law professor. They are directly

---

[1] *See* Model Rules of Professional Conduct Rules 1.6-1.8 (2002). Perhaps the best advice is to offer potential clients (like a husband and wife) three choices: (1) They might each get a separate lawyer; (2) You might represent both, but only if they understand that if either wants to change the plan later, your loyalty to the other would prevent you from doing so and your duty of confidentiality would have you keep the request secret; (3) You might represent both if they waive confidentiality, so each understood that anything they tell you would be disclosed to the other. *See generally* Teresa S. Collett, *And the Two Shall Become as One . . . Until the Lawyers Are Done*, 7 Notre Dame J.L. Ethics & Pub. Pol'y 101 (1993); Bruce S. Ross, *I Do, I Don't & I Won't: The Ethics of Engagement Letters*, 31 U. Miami Inst. on Est. Plan. Ch. 8 (1997).

Compare the situations of representing a couple seeking a contract regarding a will (discussed in § 10, *infra*) or one seeking a premarital agreement (discussed in § 26, *infra*).

relevant to your ability to represent clients. To serve them, you should be sensitive to the pressures for change in this area of law. You will need to anticipate, and may have a hand in shaping, the direction the law takes.

§ 7   Creation

[A]   The Mental Element

To be given legal effect, a document ought to reflect the intention of the one signing it. In the context of wills, this concern for intention has two aspects. First, we focus on the act of executing the document. Did the person intend this document to be a will? Did the testator understand what was going on? Was there some delusion that skewed the choices the document reflects? Was there overreaching or fraud? Second, we focus on the meaning of the words themselves. What did the testator mean by the words "my house" or "Mary and her heirs"? This section examines the first set of questions; a later one considers the second.[2]

[1]   Intention

As a threshold matter, for a will to be valid, the testator must have had a "testamentary intention" at the time the will was executed. This requirement is seldom a problem when a lawyer has drafted a document labeled a "will."[3] Testamentary intention is more likely to be an issue, however, when wills are homemade.[4] Moreover, if the law follows the lead of the revised UPC and validates documents despite flaws in their execution when the documents were intended to be wills,[5] then testamentary intention will become a more common subject for dispute.[6]

[2]   Capacity

The law is full of requirements that persons must have "capacity" before their acts have legal effect. The capacity element in wills law stems directly from statutory requirements that testators be "of sound mind."[7] Courts have given substantial content to that simple-sounding element.

---

[2] *See* Chapter 10, *infra*.

[3] Traditionally, courts have not recognized as "wills" documents that only disinherited people, but did not make any gifts. *See generally* J. Andrew Heaton, Note, *The Intestate Claims of Heirs Excluded by Will: Should "Negative Wills" Be Enforced?*, 52 U. Chi. L. Rev. 177 (1985). The revised UPC reverses that position. UPC § 2-101(b).

[4] *See, e.g., In re* Estate of Kuralt, 15 P.3d 931 (Mont. 2000) (Language in letter: "I'll have the lawyer visit the hospital to be sure you inherit the rest of the place in MT. if it comes to that" was intended as an amendment to a will.). *In re* Kauffman's Estate, 76 A.2d 414 (Pa. 1950) ("dear bill i want you to have farm Annie Kauffman" was a will.).

[5] This development is discussed in § 7[B][4][c], *infra*.

[6] *See* James Lindgren, *The Fall of Formalism*, 55 Alb. L. Rev. 1009, 1016-1020 (1992).

[7] *See, e.g.,* UPC § 2-501. Testators may also lack capacity because they are under age. *See, e.g.,* UPC § 2-501 (testator must be 18). For a discussion of the theoretical basis of the capacity requirement, see Alexander M. Meiklejohn, *Contractual and Donative Capacity*, 39 Case W. Res. L. Rev. 307 (1989).

Capacity can be lacking in either of two senses. First, the testator might be suffering from mental deficiency. The question here is general: "Can you figure it out?" Second, the testator might be operating under an "insane delusion."[8] This condition relates to being very confused about something in particular. Unhappy relatives may bring will contests on either ground.[9]

Mental deficiency concerns the general capacity to make a will. Thus, a testator who has a guardian because he cannot handle his own affairs may still be able to make a will.[10] A testator with unorthodox habits can still make a will.[11] The key question is whether the testator understands enough things relating to the will-making process. Though courts use a variety of formulations, they tend to require a testator to:[12]

(1)   Know the nature and extent of his or her property,

(2)   Know which persons would be expected to take the property,[13]

(3)   Understand the basics of the plan for disposing of the property, and

(4)   Understand how the above elements interrelate.

The testator's knowledge and understanding need not be perfect.[14] Rather, they must be sufficient under the circumstances. The larger and more complex the estate, the greater the capacity required.

If a testator suffers from mental deficiency at the time the will was executed,[15] the whole will is invalid.

Insane delusion is different. It is a false belief adhered to against reason. If that false belief affects provisions of the will, those provisions are invalid. If I believe the world is flat, even in the face of those pictures from the moon shots, and I give money to the newly created Foundation for the Flat Earth,

---

[8] Sometimes this condition is called a "mental derangement," but "insane delusion" is both more graphic and easier to remember.

[9] Some jurisdictions place the burden of proof on the capacity issue on the proponent of the will; others, on the contestant. *Compare In re* Estate of Hastings, 347 N.W.2d 347 (S.D. 1984) (proponents) *with* Sessions v. Handley, 470 So. 2d 1164 (Ala. 1985) (contestant).

[10] *See* Gilmer v. Brown, 44 S.E.2d 16 (Va. 1947) (In the morning, a court named committees (guardians) to care for testator's property. In the afternoon, she executed her will. The court upheld the will, but criticized the attorneys who handled both projects.).

[11] *See, e.g.,* Olsen v. Corporation of New Melleray, 60 N.W.2d 832 (Iowa 1953) (Testator was capable of making a will even though he engaged in such habits as wearing dirty clothes, going to the bathroom outside, and wearing a winter coat year-round.).

[12] *See* Atkinson at 232; Dukeminier & Johanson at 163.

[13] Typically, these are the testator's family members. Often they are referred to as "the natural objects of his [or her] bounty."

[14] One will was upheld even though the testator did not know that his wife and daughter had died. *See* Williams v. Vollman, 738 S.W.2d 849 (Ky. Ct. App. 1987). Another was valid even though the testator was unclear about the full amount of her estate. *See In re* Estate of Jenks, 189 N.W.2d 695 (Minn. 1971).

[15] If a testator fades in and out, but executes the will during a lucid interval, the will is valid. Restatement (Third) of Property: Wills and Other DonativeTransfers § 8.1, comment M. *See, e.g.,* Bye v. Mattingly, 975 S.W.2d 451 (Ky. 1998) (Alzheimer's patient).

that gift may be invalid. On the other hand, if I give my entire estate to my wife, my will is valid. Challenges on insane delusion grounds often involve beliefs about family members: a testator may think his wife has been unfaithful or a child is not his.[16]

Mental deficiency relates to the whole package. If competence is lacking, the whole will is bad. Insane delusion is specific. If particular provisions are the result of the delusion, they are void.[17]

[3] Undue Influence

Contests based on lack of capacity often include the additional claim that the will was the product of undue influence. While distinct theories, the two arise from the same sorts of fact patterns: disappointed relatives believe someone else got an unfair share of the estate. If the person who benefited from the will also participated in its preparation, an undue influence claim is likely.

Coercion, usually by psychological domination,[18] is the key concept. If a will reflects what an influencer wants instead of what the testator wants, the law should not validate that document. Courts have struggled to articulate a test for undue influence.[19] A number of factors are relevant: the testator's condition,[20] the opportunity of the influencer to exercise control, some activity on the part of the influencer, the effect on the mind of the testator, the level of secrecy, whether there was a confidential relationship between the influencer and the testator, whether the testator received independent advice, and whether the influencer received an undue benefit. The last factor is crucial; without any undue benefit, there is nothing to correct.

---

[16] *See, e.g., In re* Honigman's Will, 168 N.E.2d 676 (N.Y. 1960) (wife); *In re* Hargrove's Will, 42 N.E.2d 608 (N.Y. 1942) (children). There is a wide gray area between insane delusion, for which relief can be granted, and mistake, for which traditionally there is no remedy. *See, e.g.,* Bowerman v. Burris, 197 S.W. 490 (Tenn. 1917) (mistake); *In re* Honigman's Will, 168 N.E.2d 676 (N.Y. 1960) (insane delusion).

[17] If the offending gift is so central to the plan that the plan fails without it, the whole will is invalidated. *See, e.g.,* Williams v. Crickman, 405 N.E.2d 799 (Ill. 1980) (The contested gift gave one beneficiary an option to purchase for $200,000 land valued at $1,280,000. If the provision failed, the residuary takers would get substantially larger amounts.). Courts have taken the same approach toward specific gifts invalidated on grounds of undue influence.

[18] *See* Haskell at 44.

[19] *See generally* 1 Page §§ 15.1-15.13. Some courts focus more on the testator, others more on the overreaching conduct of the influencer. *Compare* Estate of Hull, 146 P.2d 242 (Cal. App. 1944) (testator) *with* Evans v. Liston, 568 P.2d 1116 (Ariz. App. 1977) (influencer).

[20] A weak testator is more susceptible to undue influence. For this reason, lack of capacity arguments are often used to set up undue influence claims. Even if one loses on the capacity claim, the effect of having made it may be to raise doubts about the ability of the testator to hold out against an influencer. *See, e.g.,* Olsen v. Corporation of New Melleray, 60 N.W.2d 832 (Iowa 1953) (capacity argument failed, but undue influence claim upheld). *See generally,* Lawrence A. Frolik, *The Strange Interplay of Testamentary Capacity and the Doctrine of Undue Influence – Are We Protecting Older Testators or Overriding Individual Preferences?*, 24 Int'l J.L. & Psych. 253 (2001).

Proof[21] of undue influence in any particular case will often rely upon circumstantial evidence. In such situations, presumptions are important. The most common way of creating a presumption of undue influence is proving that a confidential relationship existed between the influencer and the testator. Some relationships are almost automatically "confidential": priest-parishioner, guardian-ward, attorney-client,[22] doctor-patient. Depending upon their nature, other relationships—like family members, business partners, or lovers—may be confidential. Spouses easily overcome presumptions of undue influence, because courts expect spouses to influence each other and expect surviving spouses to get significant benefits under a will.[23]

Although establishing a confidential relationship between the influencer and the testator will often be the key to winning an undue influence contest, be careful not to overemphasize its importance. Contestants can establish undue influence in the absence of a confidential relationship.[24] Moreover, even if a presumption is created, it may be overcome.

Courts disagree on the effect of creating a presumption of undue influence.[25] It may[26] or may not[27] shift the burden of production to the will's proponent. Such a proponent may be able to overcome the presumption by a preponderance of the evidence, or might need clear and convincing evidence.[28] Evidence that the testator received independent advice often can overcome (we might say "cure") the presumption.[29]

---

[21] The burden of proving undue influence may be on the contestant, *see, e.g.,* UPC § 3-407, or the proponent of the will may have to show there was no undue influence, *see, e.g.,* Heinrich v. Silvernail, 500 N.E.2d 835 (Mass. App. 1986).

[22] Lawyers who draft wills naming themselves as beneficiaries not only expose the will to challenge on undue influence grounds, but also may run afoul of the rules of professional ethics. *See, e.g.,* Office of Disciplinary Counsel v. Slavens, 586 N.E.2d 92 (Ohio 1992) (attorney suspended after, among other things, arranging for testator to execute new will giving attorney 35% of estate); Committee on Prof'l Ethics & Conduct v. Randall, 285 N.W.2d 161 (Iowa 1979) (former ABA president disbarred for naming himself as beneficiary of a client's estate). *See generally* Joseph W. de Furia, *Testamentary Gifts from Client to the Attorney-Draftsman: From Probate Presumption to Ethical Prohibition,* 66 Neb. L. Rev. 695 (1987).

[23] *See, e.g.,* Hughes v. Hughes, 634 P.2d 1271 (N.M. 1981) (Wife's testimony that husband wanted to protect family was enough to rebut presumption of undue influence.).

Spouses' close relationships can also work in the other direction, to extend the reach of undue influence when one spouse is the influencer. *See* Estate of Gerard, 911 P.2d 266 (Okla. 1995) (imputing the influencing activity of one spouse to the other, so both are capable of exerting undue influence).

[24] *See, e.g.,* Schmidt v. Schwear, 424 N.E.2d 401 (Ill. App. 1981) (Beneficiary's actions in procuring the execution of the will to her benefit at the expense of others was sufficient to raise the presumption of undue influence without a finding of a confidential relationship.).

[25] *See generally* McGovern & Kurtz at 284-286.

[26] *See* Franciscan Sisters Health Care Corp. v. Dean, 448 N.E.2d 872 (Ill. 1983).

[27] *See* Bryan v. Norton, 265 S.E.2d 282 (Ga. 1980).

[28] *Compare* Williams v. McCarroll, 97 A.2d 14 (Pa. 1953) (preponderance) *with* Koppang v. Hudon, 672 P.2d 1279 (Wash. App. 1983) (clear and convincing).

[29] *See, e.g.,* Heinrich v. Silvernail, 500 N.E.2d 835 (Mass. App. 1986) (Undue influence did not exist because the decedent received independent legal advice.).

Like insane delusion, an undue influence challenge often leaves most of the will alone, invalidating only the tainted provisions. If the influence extends to the whole will, or if the offending gift is so central to the estate plan that the plan collapses without it, the whole will fails.[30]

[4] Fraud

Though it seldom happens, contestants can also challenge wills for having been procured by fraud.[31] Fraud might be either in the inducement, which involves fooling the testator into making or changing will provisions, or in the execution, which involves getting the testator to sign the wrong document.[32] Whatever the circumstances, the elements have been stated as follows: "A will is invalid if the testator has been willfully deceived by the beneficiary as to the character or contents of the instrument, or as to extrinsic facts which are material to the disposition and in fact caused it."[33]

Fraud in the inducement is the more common claim, and the disputes often center on whether the extrinsic facts that induced the will were "material."[34] Consider, for example, the situation of Art who, although already married to Bonnie, went through a marriage ceremony with Carol.[35] Assume that Art lied about his marital status and Carol believed him. Carol died, leaving her residuary estate to Art. The question becomes whether the residuary gift was the fruit of Art's fraud: would Carol have left him the property even if she had known the truth? If Art and Carol and been "married" only a short time, a court might well invalidate the gift. On the other hand, if they had been together for many years, one might attribute the gift to their relationship, as opposed to their marital status, and conclude that the gift should stand because it was not the result of the fraud.

If there has been fraud, the remedy will often be denying probate to the will or part of it. Denying probate will not fix the problem, however, unless the injured party would be made whole. In *Latham v. Father Divine*,[36] for

---

[30] *See, e.g., In re* Estate of Marsh, 342 N.W.2d 373 (Neb. 1984) (Where substantial gift is void because of undue influence and other gifts would increase contrary to testator's expressed wishes, whole will fails.).

[31] *See* Atkinson § 56; Jeffrey A. Schoenblum, *Will Contests—An Empirical Study*, 22 Real Prop. Prob. & Tr. J. 607, 648 (1987) (out of 66 cases surveyed, only six were contested on the grounds of fraud).

[32] Similarly, fraud can accompany revocations or the failure to revoke. Revocation is covered in § 9, *infra*.

[33] Atkinson § 56.

[34] Fraud is different from insane delusion. In fraud situations, someone leads the testator to believe some false information. In insane delusion situations, the testator clings to his own beliefs in the face of proffered evidence.

Fraud also differs from undue influence. In a fraud situation, the testator is still acting under her own free will. If under undue influence, the testator is not. *See, e.g.,* Rood v. Newberg, 218 N.E.2d 886 (Mass. App. 1999) (fraud where person in confidential relationship did not correct donor's mistaken accusations about another beneficiary).

[35] The facts are adapted from *In re* Estate of Carson, 184 Cal. 437 (1920).

[36] 85 N.E.2d 168 (N.Y. 1949).

example, the plaintiffs claimed that the defendants had kept the testator from executing a new will benefitting the plaintiffs. Denying probate to the old will would not help the plaintiffs, but the court held that a constructive trust[37] could be imposed on the takers under the old will, for the benefit of the plaintiffs.[38]

[5] Planning Considerations

One of the secondary themes these doctrines present is their potential for abuse. In part to give themselves flexibility when facing widely varying fact situations, courts have avoided giving distinct shape to concepts like "mental capacity" and "undue influence." One consequence of this lack of definition is that judges[39] and juries[40] can use these doctrines to impose their own views of morality on testators who make "unnatural" dispositions. Lawyers need to be ready with ways to protect their clients' plans against challenge.[41] This section discusses a number of the devices available.[42]

Protection starts with heightened awareness. Which situations are likely to invite challenges? Who is likely to bring one? Some situations are obvious: the client may show signs of lack of capacity or overdependence upon one person. Others may take some digging. The testator may want

---

[37] Constructive trust is a remedy principally used to prevent unjust enrichment. *See* § 12[F], *infra*.

[38] A tort claim, for interference with an inheritance, might also be available on facts like these. *See* Restatement (Second) of Torts § 774B (1979); M. Read Moore, *At the Frontier of Probate Litigation: Intentional Interference With the Right to Inherit*, Prob. & Prop., Nov.–Dec. 1993, at 6-9.

[39] *See, e.g., In re* Strittmater's Estate, 53 A.2d 205 (N.J. 1947) (will leaving testator's estate to the National Women's Party set aside because of testator's "morbid aversion to men" and "feminism to a neurotic extreme"); *In re* Will of Moses, 227 So. 2d 829 (Miss. 1969) (will, which left the bulk of testator's estate to her younger lover, invalidated). We can hope that courts would now be less judgmental about nontraditional lifestyles.

[40] *See, e.g.,* Will of Kaufmann, 205 N.E.2d 864 (N.Y. 1965) (will benefitting presumed homosexual lover overturned for undue influence); Fletcher v. DeLoach, 360 So. 2d 316 (Ala. 1978) (will giving all of estate to only one child invalidated on slender evidence of lack of capacity). *But see* Evans v. May, 923 S.W.2d 712 (Tex. Ct. App. 1996) (relationship of "lifemate" does not constitute undue influence as a matter of law). *See generally* Lawrence A. Frolik, *The Biological Roots of the Undue Influence Doctrine: What's Love Got to Do With It?*, 57. U. Pitt. L. Rev. 842 (1996); Jeffrey A. Schoenblum, *Will Contests—An Empirical Study,* 22 Real Prop. Prob. & Tr. J. 607 (1987).

One way to reduce the potential for abuse is to restrict will contests to bench trials, eliminating juries from the process. *See* Cal. Prob. Code § 8252(b) ("The court shall try and determine any contested issue of fact that affects the validity of the will."). Another suggestion is to abolish the mental capacity requirement. *See* Mary L. Fellows, *The Case Against Living Probate*, 78 Mich. L. Rev. 1066, 1110-1112 (1980).

[41] Some people seem eager to invite challenges, if only to take one last shot. Consider the woman reported to have "left instructions for her executor to take one dollar from her estate, invest it and pay the interest to her husband 'as evidence of my estimate of his worth.' " Henry N. Ferguson, *he who laughs last . . .* , Friends at 13 (Feb. 1982).

[42] *See generally*, Dennis W. Collins, *Avoiding a Will Contest – The Impossible Dream?*, 34 Creighton L. Rev. (2000).

to make a substantial gift outside the biological family.[43] The testator may have children from each of two marriages. Second-marriage situations are particularly tricky, because all may seem well when the common parent is planning the estate, only to degenerate after the common parent's death.[44] Challenges are likely to come from those who would take more, either under an earlier will or by intestacy. Strategies for protecting clients' intentions in these situations fall into two categories: structural elements in the plan, and conduct when carrying out the plan.[45]

[a]   Structural Elements

The estate plan might include any combination of a number of features designed to discourage bringing, or limit the chances of succeeding at, a will contest.

[i]   No-Contest Clauses

One obvious possibility when you anticipate a contest is to include a no-contest clause.[46] The clause can work, however, only if it is accompanied by a gift to the potential contestants. For an example of a useless no-contest clause, consider *Lipper v. Weslow*.[47] The testator had two sons, only one of whom survived her. Because she was favoring her surviving son over the family of her predeceased son and she wanted to discourage a contest by the losers, she provided that any legatee who contested the will would lose his or her share. The will, however, entirely disinherited her predeceased son's family; they had nothing to lose by bringing the contest.[48] She

---

[43] For an example of a will overturned when the lawyer never inquired about why the testator had chosen a particular beneficiary, who turned out to be her lover, see *In re Will of Moses*, 227 So. 2d 829 (Miss. 1969).

Gifts outside the biological family might be prompted by a heterosexual or homosexual relationship. Friendship could explain gifts in situations where people live together to share expenses and mutual support. Ultimately, the law may come to view "family" in broader terms. *See generally* Amy L. Brown, Note, *Broadening Anachronistic Notions of "Family" in Proxy Decisionmaking for Unmarried Adults*, 41 Hastings L.J. 1029 (1990); Jeffrey G. Sherman, *Undue Influence and the Homosexual Testator*, 42 U. Pitt. L. Rev. 225 (1981).

[44] *See, e.g.*, Oursler v. Armstrong, 179 N.E.2d 489 (N.Y. 1961) (Two sides of a "split family" fought over whether there was a contract not to revoke a will.).

[45] *See generally* Leon Jaworski, *The Will Contest*, 10 Baylor L. Rev. 87, 91-93 (1958).

Because lawyers may be unable to prevent a contest, they need to be alert to the problems that arise if litigants call them as witnesses. If needed as a witness, a lawyer will be unable to represent the estate. Planning ahead, lawyers should be sure other witnesses will be available. *See generally* Charles W. Wolfram, Modern Legal Ethics § 7.5 (1986).

[46] Such clauses are sometimes called "in terrorem" clauses, because they serve to intimidate a beneficiary from challenging the will.

[47] 369 S.W.2d 698 (Tex. Civ. App. 1963).

[48] The mistake is ironic, since the will was drafted by her surviving son, a lawyer. In most places, a gift to the lawyer-drafter will give rise to a presumption of undue influence. *See* § 7[A][2], *supra*. Sometimes clear and convincing evidence is required to overcome the presumption in that situation. *See* Franciscan Sisters Health Care Corp. v. Dean, 448 N.E.2d 872 (Ill. 1983).

should have included a gift[49] to the potential contestants large enough to make them think about whether the amount they would gain through a successful contest was enough to justify the risk of losing everything if they lost the contest and the clause were enforced.

Notice that in most capacity and undue influence cases, if the contest is successful, the no-contest clause will have no effect. It will fail with the will or the other challenged clauses. If the contest fails, the question becomes whether to enforce the clause against the contestant. Courts are divided on whether no-contest clauses are a good idea.[50] To the extent they actually discourage litigation, they reduce the incidence of "strike suits."[51] These are suits filed to get the estate beneficiaries to settle with the contestants so the estate can be closed. Discouraging such suits may preserve some measure of family harmony. Since, on their faces, the clauses apply to all contests, however, they may also stifle valid claims. To balance these competing consequences, many jurisdictions refuse to apply no-contest clauses if there was "probable cause" to bring the contest.[52] In other words, even if you lose the contest, if you had probable cause for bringing it, there will be no penalty. In addition, courts often construe such clauses narrowly so that, for example, a petition to interpret the no-contest clause,[53] an objection to the petition for final accounts,[54] and a suit to remove a co-trustee[55] have been found not to be "contests" for the purpose of invoking a no-contest clause.[56] Before Inserting a no-contest clause in a document, lawyers should review local law carefully; subtle differences separate how such clauses are treated in various jurisdictions.[57]

[ii] Explanations

When a testator wants to leave out some family members or reduce their shares, one option is for the testator to explain in the will the reasons for the different treatment. If the testator is equalizing treatment among various takers, as when one child's gift is reduced to take into account a lifetime gift,[58] this technique may work well. What otherwise would have

---

[49] Can we call it a bribe?

[50] *See generally* Martin D. Begleiter, *Anti-Content Clauses: When You Care Enough to Send the Final Threat*, 26 Ariz. St. L.J. 629 (1994).

[51] Professor Langbein notes, in a graphic phrase referring to capacity litigation, ". . . the odor of the strike suit hangs heavily over this field." John H. Langbein, *Living Probate: The Conservatorship Model*, 77 Mich. L. Rev. 63, 66 (1978).

[52] *See* Restatement (Second) of Prop. § 9.1; UPC § 3-905.

[53] *See* Estate of Black, 206 Cal. Rptr. 663 (Cal. App. 1984).

[54] *See In re* Estate of Ikuta, 639 P.2d 400 (Haw. 1981).

[55] *See* Conte v. Conte, 56 S.W.3d 830 (Tex. App. 2001).

[56] On the other hand, when Star Trek creator Gene Roddenberry's daughter brought a will contest, but voluntarily dismissed her claim the day before the case was to go to trial, the no-context clause applied. She forfeited both her substantial cash legacy and her share of a trust. Los Angeles Times, June 28, 1996, at B4.

[57] *See* Restatement (Second) of Prop. § 9.1, reporters note.

[58] Under the doctrine of "satisfaction," this result may follow without language in the will. *See* § 24, *infra*.

looked like unjustified favoritism (and might have prompted a bitter response) becomes understandable.

When favoritism of one side of the family is prompted by ill will toward the other side, displaying the family laundry in public can be risky. In *Lipper v. Weslow*,[59] discussed above, the testator complained in a long paragraph about how she had been ignored by the wife and children of her predeceased son. Airing such complaints is unlikely to discourage a contest from the disinherited relatives. Moreover, such an approach may fuel a contest. Failure to get the facts right could strengthen a challenge based on lack of capacity. Unfounded accusations could produce testamentary libel.[60] Language like that used in the paragraph in *Lipper* may prompt an undue influence claim. Phrases like "my said granddaughter," drafted by the favored son, a lawyer, suggest that the paragraph may not reflect the testator's views.

If explanations of unequal treatment can serve to defuse a family fight, they may belong in the document. Otherwise, you should probably leave them out.[61]

[iii]   Living Probate[62]

A few jurisdictions allow wills to be admitted to probate before the death of the testator.[63] Though the details vary, the basic idea is to allow a testator to give notice to interested parties of an intent to probate the will. If anyone objects, a court holds a hearing. If there are no objections, or if proponents overcome them, the court admits the will to probate. That will, unless it is later revoked, controls distribution of the estate.

Commentators debate the system's merits.[64] Like no-contest clauses, living probate may preclude family disputes, but at the expense of squelching valid claims. If you have questions about Uncle Harry's sanity, are you really likely to risk his and other family members' wrath by saying so to

---

[59] 369 S.W.2d 698 (Tex. Civ. App. 1963).

[60] An estate may be found liable for defamation in the will. *See generally* Paul T. Whitcombe, *Defamation by Will: Theories and Liabilities,* 27 J. Marshall L. Rev. 749 (1994).

[61] In some circumstances, a lawyer may want a testator to explain herself in a writing kept in law office files. *See* § 7[A][5][b], *infra.*

[62] Sometimes this topic is called "ante-mortem," or pre-death, probate. Until we succeed in banning Latin from legal writing, you might want to follow the advice of Professor Richman, "All Latin phrases mean 'let the buyer beware.'" *See* David H. Vernon, Louise Weinberg, William L. Reynolds, William M. Richman, Conflict of Laws: Cases, Materials and Problems 179 (1990).

[63] *See, e.g.,* Ohio Rev. Code Ann. § 2107.081; Ark. Code Ann. § 28-40-202; N.D. Cent. Code § 30.1-08.1-01.

[64] A series of articles in the Michigan Law Review explores the issues in detail. *See* Gregory S. Alexander, *The Conservatorship Model: A Modification,* 77 Mich. L. Rev. 86 (1978); Gregory S. Alexander & Albert M. Pearson, *Alternative Models of Ante-Mortem Probate and Procedural Due Process Limitations on Succession,* 78 Mich. L. Rev. 89 (1979); Mary L. Fellows, *The Case Against Living Probate,* 78 Mich. L. Rev. 1066 (1980); John H. Langbein, *Living Probate: The Conservatorship Model,* 77 Mich. L. Rev. 63 (1978).

his face? From the testator's perspective, one disadvantage is that this system places the will in the public record for the rest of the family to see. Technical questions also arise. Should an order naming current heirs bind those who actually become heirs at the testator's death? Should an order admitting a will to probate through this process in one jurisdiction be honored in jurisdictions that do not allow living probate?

Where it is available, the living probate device may be useful when a testator contemplates a particularly unpopular will provision and is willing to tell the family. Consider, for example, a testator who wants to give everything to a life partner, whether of the same or the opposite sex. Invoking the living probate process could help educate the family and preclude later challenges. The public nature of the whole process, however, may limit its use to relatively rare situations.

[iv] Living Trusts and Other Gifts

Another way to get property to a favored beneficiary without risking a will contest is to make lifetime gifts. Family members could challenge gifts while the client is alive[65] but, as a practical matter, challenges are unlikely. Because the property would not be in the estate,[66] a will contest would be irrelevant. If the client made a gift by creating a lifetime trust[67] with an independent trustee,[68] the continuing nature of the trust during the lifetime of the client/donor may negate challenges of incapacity or undue influence. Other choices would be outright gifts, the creation of joint and survivor or payable-on-death accounts, and life insurance.[69] Of course, the client should have the financial means to make gifts like these and still maintain an appropriate standard of living.

[v] Family Law Options

In some situations, testators may be able to protect their estate plans by using devices from family law. Though detailed examination of these options is beyond the scope of this text, a brief list suggests the sorts of things planners should raise with their clients. Couples who are not married may decide that the protections they gain through marriage outweigh the disadvantages. Adoption may be a good choice if the client has no children and wants to give the estate to a non-family member. By adopting the beneficiary, the client may be able to prevent relatives from challenging the will.[70] Civil union or marriage is not yet an option for most

---

[65] *See generally* Jan Rein-Francovich, *An Ounce of Prevention: Grounds for Upsetting Wills and Will Substitutes*, 20 Gonz. L. Rev. 1 (1984/85).

[66] *See* § 2, *supra*.

[67] Other sections of the book introduce the trust and discuss it in some detail. *See* § 2[B][1], *supra*, and Chapter 4, *infra*.

[68] An independent trustee is someone not closely tied to the client/donor.

[69] *See generally* Chapter 5, *infra*.

[70] Only those who would benefit from a finding of invalidity have standing to contest the

homosexual couples,[71] but adoption may be.[72] Another possibility would be for a couple to agree to a cohabitation contract, setting out their rights and obligations.[73]

Lawyers have an obligation to suggest estate plans that minimize the possibility of a successful challenge. They can also protect estate plans by taking particular precautions as they execute the plans.

[b] Conduct

By acting defensively, lawyers can build a record to discourage contests. Working with one eye viewing the elements of mental capacity and undue influence, they can preserve evidence that their clients were acting competently on their own at the time they executed the wills.[74]

If the testator is disinheriting someone for reasons that he would rather keep private, the lawyer could ask the testator to write out an explanation to keep on file for later use.[75] Having the testator use his own handwriting supports both the authenticity of the document and its weight as actually reflecting the testator's intention. A videotape of the testator explaining the will could be powerful evidence of competency and actual intention.[76] Even

---

will. *See generally* McGovern & Kurtz at 463-465. If a client wanted to benefit his lover instead of his nieces, for example, he could adopt her. As a daughter, her intestate claim would be superior to the nieces, so they would not have standing to contest the will. *See, e.g.*, Greene v. Fitzpatrick, 295 S.W. 896 (Ky. 1927) (Because they had no standing to contest the will, nieces and nephews of the decedent attacked the validity of an adoption. They lost.).

Compare the related tactic of adopting someone to defeat other claimants to a class gift under a will or trust. *See, e.g.*, Evans v. McCoy, 436 A.2d 436 (Md. 1981) (Older woman adopted neighbor and cousin to defeat claims of other cousins.). The question of when adoptees are included in class gifts is discussed in § 44[E][2], *infra*.

[71] *See generally*, Andrew R. Lee, *Estate & Disposition Planning Issues for Same Sex or Other Unmarried Couples*, Tr. & Est. (Jan. 2002) at 51. *But see* 15 Vt. Stat. Ann. § 1204(b) ("spouse" includes parties to a civil union).

[72] *But see In re* Adoption of Robert Paul P., 471 N.E.2d 424 (N.Y. 1984) (A 57-year-old male was not allowed to adopt a 50-year-old male with whom he had shared a homosexual relationship for more than 25 years because it would not establish a parent-child relationship, the primary purpose of adoption.). If adoption or marriage is not an option, the client may be able to designate an heir, a procedure available in a few states. *See, e.g.*, Ohio Rev. Code Ann. § 2105.15.

[73] *See* Marvin v. Marvin, 557 P.2d 106 (Cal. 1976) (Court enforced oral contract between cohabitating couple, thereby giving nonworking partner who provided domestic services legal rights in working partner's property.). *See generally* Symposium, *Unmarried Partners and the Legacy of Marvin v. Marvin*, 76 Notre Dame L. Rev. 1261 (2001).

[74] *See generally* Leon Jaworski, *The Will Contest*, 10 Baylor L. Rev. 87, 91-93 (1958). For guidance on relating to clients who have diminished capacity, see Model Rules of Prof'l Conduct, Rule 1.14 (2002).

[75] Contrast the advice given here with that offered above for situations in which public disclosure might be preferred. *See* § 7[A][5][a][ii], *supra*.

[76] Audio tapes were useful in defending against an undue influence challenge in *Green v. Jones*, 326 S.E.2d 448 (Ga. 1985).

if the tape is not admissible in court,[77] it may well convince the family that the testator really wanted the result shown in the will.

Because witnesses in these situations are more likely to be called to appear in court, clients should choose them with care. Are they young enough to be likely survivors of the testator? Will they come across as strong, independent people? Right after the will execution ceremony, lawyers could ask the witnesses to dictate their recollections of the event. These statements could then be used in later litigation to refresh recollections. Using a psychiatrist as a witness is probably a bad idea, because it would alert challengers to the competency issue. It might be prudent, however, to include a psychiatrist's statement in the file for later use.

In many situations, one child may assume the role of caretaker for a parent. In appreciation of the help, the parent may want to give that child a disproportionately large share of the estate. Disappointed siblings may later claim undue influence, stressing the regular contact between the caretaker and the testator. To overcome this evidence, the testator's lawyer should be sure to exclude the caretaker from discussions about how the testator wants the estate divided. If the caretaker is the one who selected the lawyer—and, especially, if the lawyer and the caretaker have an ongoing relationship—it would be prudent to have the testator consult another lawyer, at least to the extent of discussing the dispository scheme. The second lawyer would be providing the independent advice that can cleanse the taint of undue influence.[78]

[B] Execution

In addition to being mentally competent and free from undue influence, a testator must meet particular formal, statutorily-mandated requirements to create a valid will. Most states recognize a will if it complies with one of the following: the local statute; the law of the place where it was executed, when it was executed; or the law the decedent's domicile.[79] With historical roots extending at least back to the Statute of Wills adopted during the reign of Henry VIII,[80] many modern statutes draw heavily from more recent English statutes: the Statute of Frauds (1677)[81] and the Wills Act (1837).[82] States that have followed the UPC have eliminated many of the technical requirements these older acts established.[83]

As you work through this material, recall the need to view it as a litigator, a planner, and an evaluator. This section first explores various policies that

---

[77] *See generally* McKen V. Carrington, *Estate Planning for the Non-Taxable Estate*, 21 St. Mary's L.J. 367 (1989); Gerry W. Beyer & William R. Buckley, *Videotape and the Probate Process: The Nexus Grows*, 42 Okla. L. Rev. 43 (1989).

[78] *See* § 7[A][3], *supra*.

[79] *See* UPC § 2-506.

[80] 32 Hen. VIII, c. 1 (1540).

[81] 29 Chas. II, c. 3.

[82] 7 Wm. IV & 1 Vict., c. 26.

[83] *See* UPC § 2-502.

might be present in a will-making situation. Then, a typical state statute is dissected to reveal problems hidden in simple-sounding words. The special problems holographs pose are covered next. Differing approaches for what to do when there has been a mistake in the execution of a will are then discussed. The section closes with suggestions for conducting a will execution ceremony.

[1] The Policies

Two themes run through any analysis of various Statute of Wills elements: Why are they included? How strictly should courts interpret them?

Commentators have identified four principal functions of Statutes of Wills.[84] Preservation of evidence is the most obvious one. We want to be confident that we have reliable information about what the testator wanted. Second, there is some value in "channeling" testators to use similar forms, features, and procedures. Such uniformity makes it easier for testators, lawyers, and courts to be confident about how they interpret particular provisions. Third, requiring a level of ceremony serves a cautionary function. It warns the testator, "This is something special." The very formality itself focuses the testator's mind, and gives survivors more confidence that a purported will is not just a set of tentative notes reflecting an unformed intention. Finally, Statute of Wills elements may have a protective purpose, preventing others from overreaching. Once perhaps justifiable, this last element in particular has been roundly criticized as inappropriate to a society in which wills are executed by persons "in the prime of life and in the presence of attorneys."[85]

Traditionally, courts have strictly construed Statute of Wills requirements. The following comments are typical:

It is possible that at times an honest attempt to execute a last will and testament is defeated by the failure to include some one or more of the statutory requirements. However, it is far more important that this should happen under a proper construction of the statute than that the individual case should be permitted to weaken the legislative mandate calculated to protect testators generally from fraud, duress, bad faith, overreaching, or undue influence . . . . [T]he testator's intent to execute a valid will is not by itself sufficient to give validity to an instrument not executed in accordance with the statutory requirements.[86]

In emphasizing the protective function, courts have lost sight of other appropriate policies and have gotten hung up on the details. Concerned that liberal interpretations would weaken the structure, they have thrown out

---

[84] *See generally* Ashbel Gulliver & Catherine Tilson, *Classification of Gratuitous Transfers*, 51 Yale L.J. 1, 5-13 (1941); John H. Langbein, *Substantial Compliance With the Wills Act*, 88 Harv. L. Rev. 489, 492-97 (1975).

[85] Langbein, *Substantial Compliance With the Wills Act*, 88 Harv. L. Rev. at 497. *See* Robert A. Stein & Ian G. Fierstein, *The Demography of Probate Distribution*, 15 U. Balt. L. Rev. 54 (1985) (average testator executes a will five to seven years prior to death).

[86] *In re* Estate of Weber, 387 P.2d 165, 169 (Kan. 1963).

wills that almost certainly reflected the desires of the particular testators.[87] In a word, courts have been picky.

In a direct assault on the traditional approach, the revised UPC provides that, notwithstanding noncompliance with the statutory elements, wills will be effective "if the proponent . . . establishes by clear and convincing evidence that the decedent intended the document" to be a will.[88] Because this provision can be used to undo mistakes, it is discussed later.[89] It is mentioned here, however, to show the contrast between traditional and developing approaches toward the technical requirements of wills statutes. Even jurisdictions that do not adopt the UPC revision may well liberalize their thinking about whether testators complied with the statute in the first place.[90]

[2] A Typical "Statute of Wills"

Dissecting a typical Statute of Wills provides many lessons. It illustrates how carefully these statutes must be read, because individual words often carry potential for mistakes and, thus, for litigation. It relates a variety of doctrines to each other. Our example statute comes from Ohio,[91] but the discussion that follows is drawn from the law of many states.[92] Along the way, notice how the UPC has simplified or eliminated many of the traditional elements of wills statutes.

[a] In Writing

With minor exceptions, wills must be written. They may be handwritten, typed, or printed from a word processor.[93] Under traditional rules, neither tapes[94] nor blips in a computer's memory bank[95] will suffice. That situation

---

[87] Some examples appear in the discussion that follows. For others, see Langbein, *Substantial Compliance With the Wills Act*, 88 Harv. L. Rev. at 498-503.

[88] UPC § 2-503. The section also applies to revocations, changes, and revivals of formerly revoked wills.

[89] *See* § 7[B][4], *infra*.

[90] *See* Restatement (Second) of Prop. § 33.1 cmt. g.

[91] Ohio Rev. Code Ann. § 2107.03 reads as follows:

Except oral wills, every last will and testament shall be in writing, but may be handwritten or typewritten. Such will shall be signed at the end by the party making it, or by some other person in such party's presence and at his express direction, and be attested and subscribed in the presence of such party, by two or more competent witnesses, who saw the testator subscribe, or heard him acknowledge his signature.

[92] For citations to wills statutes around the country, see Restatement (Third) of Prop. § 3.1, Statutory Note.

[93] They need not be on paper. For some interesting examples, see Dukeminier and Johanson at 274-276. *See also* Atkinson § 63.

[94] *See In re* Estate of Reed, 672 P.2d 829 (Wyo. 1983) (audio tape). *See generally* Gerry W. Beyer & William R. Buckley, *Videotape and the Probate Process: The Nexus Grows*, 42 Okla. L. Rev. 43 (1989); Lisa L. McGarry, Note, *Videotaped Wills: An Evidentiary Tool or a Written Will Substitute?*, 77 Iowa L. Rev. 1187 (1992).

[95] Nevada now allows electronic wills. 2001 Nev. Stat. ch. 458. *See generally* Christopher J. Caldwell, *Should "e-wills" Be Wills: Will Advances in Technology Be Recognized for Will Execution?*, 63 U. Pitt. L. Rev. 467 (2002).

may be changing, however. The revised UPC leaves the door open by being silent on the question of whether a videotape is a "writing."[96]

Some states allow oral wills[97] in particular situations. Sometimes called "Soldiers' and Sailors' Wills" because they apply only to last-illness gifts (and sometimes are only available to armed services personnel), they may be limited to giving personal property only,[98] or to giving amounts under a stated value.[99] Although formal, written wills are the superior alternative, in states which allow oral wills, they may be useful in emergency situations.

[b] Signed [At the End?]

The requirement that the testator sign the will has two aspects. First, there must be some sort of mark on the will. While a formal, complete signature is common, a label of relationship,[100] initials,[101] or even an "X"[102] is acceptable. The second element is intention. The signature must have been intended as an operative, validating act.[103] The more casual the signature, the more likely a claim that the mark was made without any intention to validate the document.

In re Estate of McKellar[104] illustrates how the signature requirement can invalidate a purported will. While in the hospital, the testator wrote out her will. The document opened, "To Whom it May Concern I, Greta Meador McKellar, being of sound mind and body, declare this to be my last Will. . . ."[105] Greta's name did not appear elsewhere, and the court invalidated the will because it was not signed. The name, in Greta's handwriting, could have been found to be a signature, had the court accepted other evidence that this was a final document.[106] Instead of asking whether the document was likely to be genuine, the court took a picky approach to the signature requirement.[107]

---

[96] *See* UPC § 2-502 comment; James Lindgren, *The Fall of Formalism*, 55 Alb. L. Rev. 1009, 1022-1023 (1992) (reporting comments by John Langbein and Lawrence Waggoner).

[97] Sometimes these are called "nuncupative wills."

[98] *See, e.g.,* Nev. Rev. Stat. § 133.100, Okla. Stat. Ann. tit. 84, § 46.

[99] *See, e.g.,* Tenn. Code Ann. § 32-1-106.

[100] *See, e.g., In re* Estate of Guinane, 213 N.E.2d 30 (Ill. App. 1965) ("Aunt Margaret").

[101] *See, e.g.,* Quimby v. Greenhawk, 171 A. 59 (Md. 1934).

[102] Some states require additional procedures if a mark is used. *See, e.g.,* Cal. Civil Code § 14.

[103] This requirement is closely related to the one that the testator have the intention to make a will at all. *See* § 7[A][1], *supra.*

[104] 380 So. 2d 1273 (Miss. 1980).

[105] This typical opening is called the "exordium." For a similar case, in which the court invalidates a "will" written on 3" × 5" notecards, see *In re Estate of Erickson*, 806 P.2d 1186 (Utah 1991).

[106] The rule dates from Lemayne v. Stanley, 3 Lev. 1, 83 Eng. Rep. 545 (1681). *See also* Restatement (Second) of Prop. § 32.1 cmt. c.

[107] Courts have also split over whether handwritten names in dispositive clauses ("I give the Helen Jones Estate to Charlie.") count as signatures. *Compare* Estate of MacLeod, 254

The title to this section includes "at the end?" in brackets because that requirement, while in the sample statute from Ohio, is included in the statutes of only about eight states.[108] On its face, such a requirement seems innocent enough. After all, wouldn't we normally expect someone to sign at the end? The problem is that, once faced with the requirement, many courts have applied it strictly, invalidating wills without reference to the broader policy of giving effect to testators' intentions. For example, one will was struck because the signature came before a clause appointing the executors;[109] another failed because the testator signed below the end, in an attestation clause.[110] Jurisdictions without the "at the end" requirement have at least avoided these excesses of formalism.[111]

[c] By the Testator or Another

So that physically disabled persons can make wills, virtually all states allow someone else to sign on behalf of the testator. Usually the proxy must sign in the testator's presence,[112] at his direction.[113] The more clear the testator's direction, the better.[114]

Cal. Rptr. 156 (Cal. App. 1988) (allowing signature in dispositive clause to validate holographic will), *with In re* Estate of Fegley, 589 P.2d 80 (Colo. App. 1978) (holographic will not admitted to probate because no signature on signature space).

[108] *See* Restatement (Second) of Prop. § 33.1, Statutory Note. Had such a provision applied in *McKellar*, it would have precluded any claim that Greta's "signature" was sufficient.

[109] *In re* Winter's Will, 98 N.Y.S.2d 312 (N.Y. App. 1950), *aff'd*, 98 N.E.2d 477 (1951).

[110] Sears v. Sears, 82 N.E. 1067 (Ohio 1907). An attestation clause is a statement by the witnesses, appearing at the end of the will and reciting that the various elements of the local statute were followed.

The UPC's "Self-Proved" affidavit has caused similar confusion, with like results. The affidavit is a notarized statement, which appears at the end of the will and recites the elements of the wills statute that have been followed. UPC § 2-504. When testators have signed there, instead of at the end of the will, courts have invalidated the wills. *See* Bruce M. Mann, *Self-Proving Affidavits and Formalism in Wills Adjudication*, 63 Wash. U. L.Q. 39 (1985). The revised UPC expressly corrects the problem, by considering the signature on the affidavit as also affixed to the will. UPC § 2-504(c).

For more on attestation clauses and self-proved affidavits see § 7[B][2][g], *infra*. For more on how courts resolve mistakes like these, see § 7[B][4], *infra*.

[111] The presence of an "at the end" requirement need not lead to bad results. In one case, the testator folded a sheet of paper in half, making four pages. She wrote on the first and third pages (like a greeting card reads), and then finished and signed on the second page. The court sensibly held that the signature should appear at the logical end of the will, not necessarily the place furthest removed from the start. *In re* Stinson's Estate, 77 A. 807 (Pa. 1910).

[112] "Presence" appears as an element several times in most statutes. It is discussed in § 7[B][2][d], *infra*.

[113] *See* UPC § 2-502.

[114] *See, e.g.*, Waite v. Frisbie, 47 N.W. 1069 (Minn. 1891) (To signify testator's approval, testator placed hand on top of proxy's hand while the proxy made a mark.).

[d] Attested in the Testator's Presence

Unless the state allows so-called "holographic" wills,[115] wills must be witnessed. Virtually all states require two witnesses;[116] some states formerly mandated three, but Vermont seems to be the only one now.[117]

Commonly, the witnesses must themselves sign "in the presence of" the testator. Sometimes they must also sign in the presence of each other. As noted above, if someone is signing the testator's signature on his behalf, the proxy must be in the testator's presence. In all of these contexts, courts have struggled with what "presence" means. They have generally followed either a "line-of-sight" test or, more commonly, a "conscious presence" approach.[118] The cases, as lawyers like to say when conflicts are rampant, tend to be resolved on their own facts.

Two cases illustrate the problems a presence requirement can pose. *In re Demaris' Estate*[119] involved a will executed in a doctor's office. With the doctor and his wife in the room to serve as witnesses, the testator signed the will while he was on the bed in the treatment room. (See diagram.)

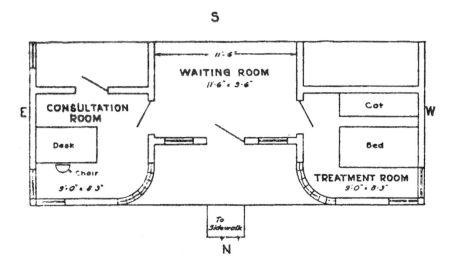

The witnesses then took the will to the desk in the consultation room to sign it themselves. The doors between the rooms remained open. The doctor's wife signed while standing on the south side of the desk, where

---

[115] Unwitnessed wills in the testator's handwriting are allowed in some circumstances. *See* § 7[B][3], *infra*.

[116] UPC § 2-502.

[117] *See* Vt. Stat. Ann. tit. 14, § 5. *See generally* McGovern & Kurtz at 183-185.

[118] *See generally* Page § 19.111 *et seq.*

[119] 110 P.2d 571 (Or. 1941).

she could have been seen by the testator. The doctor then sat at the chair, out of the testator's vision, and signed. Later, the doctor's signature was challenged as not having been made in the presence of the testator.

The court discussed, and rejected, the "line of sight" test. If applied, it would have invalidated the doctor's signature, and maybe his wife's as well.[120] Instead, the court drew upon a standard developed for blind testators and applied the "conscious presence" test: "[I]f [the witnesses] are so near at hand that they are within the range of any of [the testator's] senses, so that he knows what is going on, the requirement has been met."[121] Because the court believed the testator knew what was going on, it upheld the will.

Keeping one eye on the policies involved, the court avoided getting hung up on the rule. Because it believed in the integrity of the will, it stretched the doctrine to save the will. It also foreshadowed recent reforms:

> [I]f Dr. Gillis and his wife failed to comply with the strict letter of the statute when they attested the will, they, nevertheless, substantially complied with its requirements. To hold otherwise would be to observe the letter of the statute as interpreted strictly, and fail to give heed to the statute's obvious purpose. Thus, the statute would be turned against those for whose protection it had been written.[122]

Demaris' Estate illustrates both how mechanistic the "presence" requirement can become, and how a court can be sensible in ignoring that approach when it would defeat a testator's intentions.[123]

In contrast, an English court in *Groffman's Estate*[124] made little effort to save a will, although the court believed the document was genuine. The will was witnessed at a social occasion. With guests seated around a coffee table in a parlor, the testator and one witness crossed a small hall to the dining room, where that witness signed. The other witness moved more slowly and was still in the parlor when the first witness returned. The second witness then joined the testator in the dining room and signed. Because the applicable statute required the testator's acknowledgment before two witnesses in each other's presence, and the court narrowly defined "presence," the will was invalid.[125] A "did everyone know what was going on?" approach could have saved the will.

---

[120] Some authorities require that the testator actually see the witness' hands and the paper, rather than, as here, merely being able to see. *Compare* Graham v. Graham, 32 N.C. 219 (1849) (must see) *with* Burney v. Allen, 125 N.C. 314, 34 S.E. 500 (1899) (must have been able to see, if he had looked).

[121] 110 P.2d 571, 585 (Or. 1941). *See also* UPC § 2-502 comment to subsection (a).

[122] 110 P.2d 571, 586 (Or. 1941).

[123] For a case with similar facts and result, see *Cunningham v. Cunningham*, 83 N.W. 58 (Minn. 1900).

[124] [1969] 1 W.L.R. 733, [1969] 2 All E.R. 108.

[125] A similar celebrated case is *Estate of Weber*, 387 P.2d 165 (Kan. 1963). The testator signed the will in his parked car while witnesses watched from a bank window. Held: no presence. *See also* Stevens v. Casdorph, 508 S.E.2d 610 (W. Va. 1998) (will not valid when bank employee took will to other employees to sign, but testator did not accompany her).

To avoid litigation like these cases illustrate, the UPC eliminated the presence requirement, except for proxy signatures (where conscious presence is required).[126] Be clear about what was dropped. Witnesses must still "witness" something the testator did: the signing itself, an acknowledgment of the signature, or an acknowledgment of the will.[127] Their own signatures, however, need not be affixed in the testator's presence. Under the 1990 version, the signatures need only be placed on the will within a "reasonable time" after the witnessing took place, even if that is after the testator's death.[128] The UPC drafters believed, quite reasonably, that a presence requirement invalidates more good wills than it prevents bad ones.

[e] By Competent Witnesses

Witnesses must not only be competent[129] at the time of the will's execution but also, many states say, part of being competent is being "disinterested," in the sense of not taking any gifts under the will. A holdover from a time when evidentiary rules were much more restrictive, the rule has little modern justification. Strictly applied, the rule would invalidate most wills signed by interested witnesses.[130] Rather than letting the will fail, however, states that follow this rule usually save the will through "purging statutes," which eliminate the gain[131] to the interested witness.[132] If the witness would have had a share under an earlier will or the intestate statute, the new gift is reduced to the size of the earlier share.[133]

---

[126] UPC § 2-502.

[127] Authorities disagree about whether the UPC requires "in-person" contact between the testator and a witness or whether, for example, a testator could sign a will, mail it to the witnesses, and acknowledge the signature by telephone. *See* Julian R. Kossow, *Probate Law and the Uniform Probate Code: One for the Money . . .* , 61 Geo. L.J. 1357, 1380 (1973) (suggesting the example as possibly valid under the UPC, but arguing that the statute should not be so interpreted). *See also In re* Estate of McGurrin, 743 P.2d 994 (Idaho App. 1987) (Idaho's UPC requires in-person contact.). *See generally* C. Douglas Miller, *Will Formality, Judicial Formalism, and Legislative Reform: An Examination of the New Uniform Probate Code "Harmless Error" Rule and the Movement Toward Aphorism—Part One*, 43 Fla. L. Rev. 167, 209-11 (1991).

[128] *See* UPC § 2-502(a)(3) & comment. For more discussion of the timing of witness's signatures, see § 7[B][4][b], *infra*.

[129] "Competency" in this context includes notions of mental deficiency, age, eyesight and influence of drugs or alcohol. *See generally* Page §§ 19.79; 19.83. *See, e.g.,* Norton v. Hinson, 989 S.W.2d 535 (Ark. 1999) (will invalid because witness was under 18). For discussion of competency issues as they relate to testators, see § 7[A][1], *supra*.

[130] In a few cases, there may be extra witnesses. If the required number of witnesses can be met without counting interested witnesses, gifts to extra ("supernumerary") witnesses are irrelevant. *See, e.g.,* King v. Smith, 302 A.2d 144 (N.J. Super. 1973).

[131] Some states eliminate the whole gift, not just the gain. *See* Rosenbloom v. Kokofsky, 369 N.E.2d 1142 (Mass. 1977).

[132] Some states also invalidate gifts to witnesses' spouses. *See, e.g.,* Wis. Stat. Ann. § 853.07. This approach was upheld on constitutional grounds in Dorfman v. Allen, 434 N.E.2d 1012 (Mass. 1982) (construing Mass. Gen. L. ch. 191, § 2).

[133] Because comparisons must often be made between different assets, valuation problems can arise in this context. *See generally* Page §§ 19.76, 19.87, 19.88.

The original rule—invalidating the will—was a crude device to protect against overreaching by witnesses.[134] Because of the way purging statutes operate, however, they substantially undercut the protection rationale. Purging statutes commonly invalidate innocent gifts to friends who happen to have served as witnesses.

Estate of Parsons[135] illustrates why the interested-witness rule and its accompanying purging statutes should be dropped. The will was witnessed by three persons: Evelyn, Marie, and Bob (a notary public). It gave Evelyn $100 and Marie some real estate. The testator's token gift to Evelyn ultimately allowed relatives who were intentionally omitted from the will to take the property anyway. The applicable statute invalidated gifts to witnesses, unless two other disinterested witnesses had signed.[136] Because Evelyn and Marie could not take them, the legacy and the real estate went to the testator's heirs by partial intestacy.

Trying to avoid that result, Evelyn disclaimed[137] her $100 after the testator's death. She hoped the disclaimer would make her the second disinterested witness (with Bob) and allow Marie to take the real estate. The court held that disinterestedness had to be present at the time of the will's execution; the later disclaimer could not save Marie's gift.[138] The court criticized the rule, but felt bound by the statute.

Certainly, if the point of interested-witness rules is protection of the testator, that protection should be judged as of the will's execution. The purging statute, however, already has undercut the protective function. Allowing a disclaimer to cure a bad will after the fact is not different from having a purging statute do the same thing.

In light of the protective function's declining importance and the intention-defeating tendency of purging statutes, many states are adopting the UPC's solution: "The signing of a will by an interested witness does not invalidate the will or any provision of it."[139] Perhaps states eventually will simply abolish the witness requirement.[140]

---

[134] The device was crude, both because it invalidated the whole will, instead of just the part benefiting the witness, and because it invalidated the gift in all cases, whether there was overreaching or not. Compare undue influence, which invalidates only those portions of the will that have been shown to be tainted by the influence. *See* § 7[A][2], *supra*.

[135] 163 Cal. Rptr. 70 (Cal. App. 1980).

[136] California Probate Code § 6112 now allows "any person generally competent" to witness a will, but sets up a presumption that a witness who receives a devise "procured the devise by duress, menace, fraud, or undue influence."

[137] Statutes allow beneficiaries to refuse gifts by filing a disclaimer. The device is usually used to save taxes, as where a wealthy parent will disclaim so that her children would get a gift that would otherwise come to her. The disclaiming parent thereby manages to get property to the children without gift tax consequences. For more discussion, see § 27, *infra*.

[138] The court rejected arguments that the disclaimer related back in time to the execution.

[139] UPC § 2-505(b).

[140] *See generally* James Lindgren, *Abolishing the Attestation Requirement for Wills*, 68 N.C. L. Rev. 541 (1990).

[f] Some Other Rules

A few jurisdictions require elements in addition to those in the sample statute. Some require witnesses to sign in each other's presence.[141] Some require publication, which generally means the testator identifies the document as his will.[142] Some require the testator to request the witnesses to sign.[143] Some require that the testator actually sign before the witnesses do,[144] but most places allow wills if they are executed as part of one continuous transaction.[145]

[g] Attestation Clauses and Self-Proving Affidavits

Neither attestation clauses nor self-proving affidavits are required as part of a valid will, but they are commonly included. They are also commonly confused.

Attestation clauses typically appear after the testator's signature, but above the witnesses' signatures. They are phrased from the witnesses' point of view, attesting that the elements of the local statute have been followed.[146] They are important because in most states, they set up a rebuttable presumption that the facts stated in the clause are correct.[147] This feature can be particularly useful if, between the time of the ceremony and the time for admitting the will to probate, witnesses have died or forgotten the relevant events. In *In re Estate of Collins*,[148] for example, the witnesses were bank employees who had, as a service to their customers, witnessed numerous wills. Though they could not recall the details of the particular will execution in question, the will was upheld on the strength of the attestation clause. If someone challenges a will, the attestation clause can be used to refresh witnesses' recollections or to impeach their testimony.

The Uniform Probate Code has popularized self-proving affidavits. The big differences between self-proving affidavits and traditional attestation clauses are: (1) the testator also signs the self-proving affidavit, and (2) the

---

[141] *See, e.g.*, Groffman's Estate, [1969] 1 W.L.R. 733, [1969] 1 All E.R. 108, discussed in § 7[B][2][d], *supra*.

[142] N.Y. EPTL § 3-2.1(a)(3), (4). *See generally* Atkinson at 327-330.

[143] N.Y. EPTL § 3-2.1(a)(3), (4).

[144] *See, e.g.*, Wheat v. Wheat, 244 A.2d 359 (Conn. 1968).

[145] *See* Haskell at 31.

[146] Here is a typical attestation clause:

> On this 16th day of September, 1994, Mary Smith declared to us, the undersigned witnesses, that the foregoing instrument was her last will, and she asked us to act as witnesses to her signature thereon. She then signed the will in our mutual presence. We now, at her request, in her presence. and in our mutual presence, subscribe our names as witnesses, each declaring that in his or her opinion the testator is of sound mind and not operating under undue influence.

You might look through the clause to identify the statutory elements it is intended to cover.

[147] *See generally* Roger L. Severns, *The True Function of the Attestation Clause in a Will*, 11 Chi.-Kent L. Rev. 11 (1932).

[148] 458 N.E.2d 797 (N.Y. 1983).

affidavit is notarized. Under the UPC, self-proving affidavits raise a conclusive presumption that the statute's signature requirements have been met; they avoid the need for calling witnesses and they limit the grounds of challenge.[149]

One reason for the confusion between attestation clauses and self-proving affidavits is that the UPC provides a form that serves both functions at the same time.[150] This form is designed to be used as part of the execution ceremony. To allow self-proving to come after the execution ceremony, the UPC provides a different, but similar, form.[151] Even in states that have not adopted the UPC provision, parties should execute this alternative form directly[152] after a will execution ceremony. Stapled to the back of the will, the form easily can be ignored by probate judges unfamiliar with it, but it would be available if the testator moved to a UPC state, and it might be useful[153] even in non-UPC states.

Like all parts of the will execution ceremony, lawyers should handle self-proved affidavits with particular care. Some courts have held that signatures that appear in the affidavit, but not earlier, are insufficient to validate the will.[154] The revised UPC allows such signatures.[155]

[3] Holographs

Most of the discussion so far has contemplated a formal will execution ceremony in a law office. Recognizing that in some situations, formality is not possible, and that some testators simply believe it is not necessary, many states allow informal wills, in particular circumstances. Called "holographs," these wills should be viewed as qualifying for recognition under an alternative set of rules.

Most importantly, holographs need not be witnessed. In return for eliminating the need for witnesses, however, states require additional elements, mostly aimed at assuring the genuineness of the document. The revised UPC sets bare-bones requirements: the signature and "material portions" must be in the testator's handwriting.[156] More traditional statutes require the document to be "entirely" in the testator's handwriting.[157]

---

[149] UPC § 2-504 comment.

[150] UPC § 2-504(a).

[151] UPC § 2-504(b).

[152] There need be no delay.

[153] *See generally* Bruce M. Mann, *Self-Proving Affidavits and Formalism in Wills Adjudication*, 63 Wash. U. L.Q. 39 (1985).

[154] *See* Orrell v. Cochran, 695 S.W.2d 552 (Tex. 1985) (testator); Boren v. Boren, 402 S.W.2d 728 (Tex. 1966) (witnesses); *In re* Estate of Ricketts, 773 P.2d 93 (Wash. App. 1989) (witnesses). This problem is discussed further in regard to how the law might react to such mistakes. *See* § 7[B][4][a], *infra*.

[155] UPC § 2-504(c).

[156] UPC § 2-502(b).

[157] *See, e.g.,* Ky. Rev. Stat. Ann. § 394.040.

Some require a date.[158] Some carry over other elements from those applicable to attested wills.[159] Each of these separate elements has spawned its own set of cases.

One frequent question is the extent to which the document must be in the testator's handwriting. Courts typically ignore extraneous material, like the letterhead on motel stationery, even in jurisdictions that follow the "entirely-in-the-handwriting" approach.[160]

More troublesome has been what to do with forms on which testators fill in blanks. Two cases—a liberal one interpreting a narrow statute and a narrow one interpreting a liberal statute—illustrate the problem.

The will contested in *Estate of Black*[161] was written on three copies of the same printed form. The testator started by filling in blanks in the opening clause on each page, identifying herself and her residency and declaring the document to be her will. Then she wrote, "I wish to disburse certain moneys and properties to the following:" and proceeded to write out her wishes. She used the large blank areas on all three forms, crossing out printed material where it did not fit her needs. At the end, she again used some of the form's blanks to identify her executor, the date and place. Then she signed the last page. Faced with a statute requiring the will to be "entirely written" by the testator, the court nonetheless validated the will. To uphold a document it trusted and avoid what would have been an intestate gift to a stranger, the court overlooked what it termed "her superfluous utilization of a small portion of the language of the preprinted form."[162]

In re Estate of Johnson[163] involved a different style statute and different style will form. The statute required the "material provisions"[164] to be in the testator's handwriting.[165] The will form included printed language, which read "I give devise and bequeath to" and left a space. There the testator listed eight people and showed their 1/8 shares. Because the handwriting itself did not express a testamentary intent (that came from the printed words), the court disallowed the will. The court refused to look beyond the handwritten words to the context in which they were written in order to identify the testator's intention.[166]

---

[158] Page § 20.6.

[159] *See, e.g.*, Estate of Blake v. Benza, 587 P.2d 271 (Ariz. App. 1978) (A postscript to a letter was a valid holographic will because the formal signature appeared following the phrase "you can have my entire estate.").

[160] *See, e.g.*, Succession of Burke, 365 So. 2d 858 (La. App. 1978) (Court disregarded the printed portions of the will, but ruled it valid because the handwritten portions contained all the formalities of a holographic will.).

[161] 641 P.2d 754 (Cal. 1982).

[162] *Estate of Black*, 641 P.2d 754, 759 (Cal. 1982).

[163] 630 P.2d 1039 (Ariz. App. 1981).

[164] This is the language in UPC (pre-1990) § 2-503.

[165] If such a statute had been present in *Black,* the will would have been sustained easily.

[166] This position is no longer the law in Arizona. *See In re* Estate of Muder, 765 P.2d 997 (Ariz. 1988). *Compare* Estate of Foxley, 575 N.W.2d 150 (Neb. 1998). There the testator had

In response to cases like *Johnson*, the UPC made two revisions in 1990. "Material portions," rather than "material provisions," must be in the testator's handwriting.[167] The tone is now broader. In particular, even if a printed form includes "give, devise and bequeath" language, the will can be allowed. Second, the revised UPC provides that extrinsic evidence, including portions of a holograph not in the testator's handwriting, can be used to establish testamentary intent.[168]

Because of their minimal requirements, holographic wills can crop up in unlikely places. They may take the form of notes or letters.[169] They may be written on furniture, briefcases, walls, even car bumpers.[170] Short notes on other documents might be valid codicils.[171] Once courts validate these writings, however, they carry the same weight as a beautifully drafted document executed with all the trimmings in a law office. Keep your eyes open for holographs and the arguments they can prompt.

[4] Mistake in Execution[172]

As the prior discussion indicates by example, mistakes happen, especially, but not exclusively, when lawyers are absent from the will execution ceremony. One way the law can lower the chances of mistake is follow the UPC's lead and reduce the number of elements required for a valid will.[173] This approach still leaves in place rules that courts can interpret strictly. Faced with statutory rules, courts have been reluctant to soften this traditionally hard-edged set of doctrine.

But change is on the way. The once-solid wall is finally cracking under onslaughts led by Professor John Langbein. Langbein first suggested that courts allow wills to be probated if there had been "substantial compliance" with the statute.[174] More recently, he has endorsed a "harmless error"

---

marked out words in her printed will, added a note giving a new disposition, her initials and a date. The court held that the handwritten words on their own—without reference to the printed words—did not evidence testamentary intent.

[167] UPC § 2-502(b).

[168] UPC § 2-502(c). This provision is not limited to holographs.

[169] *See* Estate of Wong (Zhao v. Wong), 47 Cal. Rptr. 2d 707 (Cal. App. 1995) (Note reading "All Tai-Kin Wong's Xi Zhao, my best half TKW 12/31/92" was not a will.); Atkinson at 207-210. Letters that might be wills are often challenged on the ground that testators wrote them without any intention that they act as wills. *See In re* Kuralt, 15 P.3d 931 (Mont. 2000) (letter validated as will; discussed in § 7[A][1], *supra*).

[170] For some pictures, see Dukeminier & Johanson at 258-59. For more examples, see Elmer M. Million, *Wills: Witty, Witless, and Wicked*, 7 Wayne L. Rev. 335 (1960).

[171] *See, e.g.*, Johnson v. Johnson, 279 P.2d 928 (Okla. 1954), discussed in § 8[B], *infra*.

[172] Sometimes disappointed relatives challenge a will because there has been a mistake in the inducement to make the will. Unless the will itself shows both the mistake and what the testator would have done differently, courts will deny relief. *See* Atkinson § 59. For related discussions, see § 7[A][4] (fraud), *supra,* and § 41[B] (mistake and extrinsic evidence), *infra*.

[173] For the suggestion that the law only requires a writing and a signature, see James Lindgren, *Abolishing the Attestation Requirement for Wills*, 68 N.C. L. Rev. 541 (1990).

[174] John H. Langbein, *Substantial Compliance With the Wills Act*, 88 Harv. L. Rev. 489 (1975).

theory under which courts can validate a will, despite noncompliance with the statute, if the document reflects the testator's desires.[175] With boosts from prestigious organizations, the reform movement is moving ahead on two fronts. The revised UPC allows courts to ignore harmless errors if the proponent of a document can show by clear and convincing evidence that the document was intended to be effective to create or revoke a will.[176] One important goal of this change is to bring the law of wills more into line with the law regarding the validity of will substitutes.[177]

The following sections examine the traditional doctrine, the substantial compliance doctrine, and the harmless error doctrine. The discussion closes with some examples of how to work with these doctrines.

[a] Traditional Law

Two cases illustrate the law's traditional refusal to remedy a mistake in will execution; a third shows a small step toward reform. Each involved a simple error regarding a will that appeared to be genuine.

Orrell v. Cochran[178] involved a will accompanied by a self-proved affidavit.[179] A witness signed the will where the testator should have, and the testator only signed in the affidavit following the will. Because the testator did not sign the will itself, it was denied probate.

A second example is *In re Estate of Pavlinko.*[180] When Vasil and Hellen Pavlinko visited their lawyer to execute their wills, they mistakenly signed each other's. When Vasil died, the will intended for him did not bear his signature and the one he signed did not make sense, since it was written for his wife. The majority followed the well-established rule:[181] neither could be admitted to probate.

---

[175] John H. Langbein, *Excusing Harmless Errors in the Execution of Wills: A Report on Australia's Tranquil Revolution in Probate Law*, 87 Colum. L. Rev. 1 (1987). Sometimes this approach is known as "excused noncompliance" or granting courts a "dispensing power." The Restatement now uses the "harmless error" term. Restatement (Third) of Property § 3.3.

[176] UPC § 2-503.

[177] Will substitutes are discussed in Chapters 4 and 5, *infra.*

The UPC reform has been criticized as offering only a bridge over, rather than a repair of, the chasm between the rules for lifetime and testamentary transfers. For a comprehensive discussion of the reforms discussed in the text, see C. Douglas Miller, *Will Formality, Judicial Formalism, and Legislative Reform: An Examination of the New Uniform Probate Code "Harmless Error" Rule and the Movement Toward Amorphism—Part One: The Wills Act Formula, the Rite of Testation, and the Question of Intent: A Problem in Search of a Solution,* 43 Fla. L. Rev. 167 (1991) and *Part Two: Uniform Probate Code Section 2-503 and a Counterproposal,* 43 Fla. L. Rev. 599 (1991). To repair the problem, Professor Miller proposes a comprehensive succession act, "a legislative formulation . . . incorporating all ambulatory and revocable dispositions of property—i.e., all essentially testamentary dispositions." 43 Fla. L. Rev. at 711.

[178] 695 S.W.2d 552 (Tex. 1985).

[179] *See* § 7[B][2][g], *supra,* discussing self-proved affidavits.

[180] 148 A.2d 528 (Pa. 1959).

[181] The 1953 edition of Atkinson's wills hornbook—a book dominant long after that date— could say with confidence: "Probate will be denied when the testator through mistake executed the wrong document as his will." Atkinson at 273.

A colorful dissent[182] argued that the will prepared for Hellen, but signed by Vasil, should be probated. Under the guise of interpreting "Vasil's" will, the court could just ignore that the will referred, for example, to Vasil's brother-in-law as "my brother." Although the dissenter did not prevail, the opinion reflects one way courts have responded to a doctrine which precludes reformation of wills. They do not reform; they merely "interpret," sometimes quite liberally.[183]

What the dissent in Pavlinko sought to do indirectly, the Court of Appeals of New York was willing to do directly, about 20 years later. *In re Snide*[184] involved Harvey and Rose, who—like the Pavlinkos—had signed each other's wills. After Harvey died, the mistake was discovered. The Surrogate admitted the will Harvey signed, even though it clearly referred to "Rose" as the testator. To make sense of it, the court reformed it, substituting "Harvey" wherever "Rose" appeared, and vice versa. Presto! We now have a will signed by Harvey that also makes sense. While endorsing this approach, the Court of Appeals also sought to calm any fears that reformation of wills would become commonplace. It stressed the narrow facts: "[W]e are dealing here solely with identical mutual wills both simultaneously executed with statutory formality."[185]

Seeing cases like *Snide* as an opening for (rather than the limits of) reform, commentators pressed for more use of reformation as a remedy for various kinds of mistakes.[186] As applied to mistakes in execution, however, attention has shifted from reforming wills to liberalizing statutory requirements.

[b] Substantial Compliance

One solution for those frustrated with the tradition of strict interpretation of will statutes' requirements is to suggest that a will is valid if there has been "substantial compliance" with the statutory elements.[187] The American Law Institute has endorsed the approach as a "better-than-nothing" solution in places that have not adopted a statute allowing courts to excuse noncompliance.[188]

---

[182] The dissenting opinion ends, "Where there's a will there's a way." 148 A.2d 528, 534 (Pa. 1959).

[183] *See* John H. Langbein & Lawrence W. Waggoner, *Reformation of Wills on the Ground of Mistake: Change of Direction in American Law?*, 130 U. Pa. L. Rev. 521, 555-566 (1982).

[184] 418 N.E.2d 656 (N.Y. 1981).

[185] 418 N.E.2d at 658. Mutual wills are separate documents with reciprocal provisions. *See* Atkinson at 222.

[186] John H. Langbein & Lawrence W. Waggoner, *Reformation of Wills on the Ground of Mistake: Change of Direction in American Law?*, 130 U. Pa. L. Rev. 521 (1982).

[187] *See generally* John H. Langbein, *Substantial Compliance With the Wills Act*, 88 Harv. L. Rev. 489 (1975).

[188] Restatement (Second) of Prop. § 31.1 cmt. g suggests a substantial compliance doctrine under which a will is found validly executed if the document was executed in substantial compliance with the statutory formalities and if the proponent established by clear and convincing evidence that the decedent intended the document to constitute his or her will

. . . .

The doctrine is not without its drawbacks. Most important is that courts have "read into their substantial compliance doctrine a near miss standard, ignoring the central issue of whether the testator's conduct evidenced testamentary intent."[189] Two cases from New Jersey illustrate how the doctrine holds potential for both failure and triumph.

In re Estate of Peters [190] shows a court that was tempted to use substantial compliance but which lost sight of the goal of validating trustworthy documents. The result was particularly harsh. Conrad and Marie were married; Marie had a son, Joseph, from a prior marriage. The couple made reciprocal wills, giving property to each other and, alternatively, to Joseph. Conrad was in the hospital when his will was executed and, in the emotion of the moment, the witnesses failed to sign. The will was notarized, but was still short one witness's signature. After about 15 months, Marie died, followed by Conrad a few days later. When the mistake on Conrad's will was discovered, the trial court allowed the second witness to sign, some 18 months after the testator. Because the witnesses did not sign within "a reasonable time," the New Jersey Supreme Court refused to approve the will. As a result, Conrad and Marie's property escheated to the state.[191]

While leaving open the possibility of applying substantial compliance in future cases, the court limited the doctrine to situations "where, unlike this case, there has been a clear attempt to comply with a statutory formality but compliance is deficient."[192] The court viewed legislative adoption of the UPC's streamlined formalities as an indication that simplifying requirements was the only permissible approach to avoiding the harm mistakes cause. "[S]trict, if not literal, adherence to [the remaining] statutory requirements" was still appropriate.[193] The court did not explain why, in light of the witnesses' ability to testify about the facts surrounding the execution, their timely signatures on the will were so important. The court made the signature requirement itself, rather than the credibility of the will, the central question.

In *In re Will of Ranney*,[194] the New Jersey court lived up to its pledge to consider using the substantial compliance doctrine. Here, witnesses did not sign the will but, instead, signed the self-proving affidavit,[195] which

---

[189] John H. Langbein, *Excusing Harmless Errors in the Execution of Wills: A Report on Australia's Tranquil Revolution in Probate Law*, 87 Colum. L. Rev. 1, 7 (1987). Another problem is the difficulty of deciding just how much compliance is "substantial." *See* Charles I. Nelson and Jeanne M. Starck, *Formalities and Formalism: A Critical Look at the Execution of Wills*, 6 Pepp. L. Rev. 331 (1979).

[190] 526 A.2d 1005 (N.J. 1987).

[191] Marie's will had given everything to Conrad, who survived her. Without the disputed will, Conrad died intestate and without surviving relatives. As a stepson, Joseph had no claim.

[192] 526 A.2d 1005, 1014 n.4 (N.J. 1987).

[193] 526 A.2d at 1014.

[194] 589 A.2d 1339 (N.J. 1991).

[195] Notice the similarity to *Orrell v. Cochran*, discussed above in § 7[B][4][a], where a *testator's* signature only on the self-proving affidavit was insufficient.

appeared on a separate page.[196] The court held that the substantial compliance doctrine could save the will, despite the mistake.[197]

In contrast to its approach in *Peters*, the court saw New Jersey's adoption of the UPC execution rules as reflecting "a more relaxed attitude toward the execution of wills."[198] Focusing on the purposes behind the statutory requirements,[199] the court noted: "It would be ironic to insist on literal compliance with the statutory formalities when that insistence would invalidate a will that is the deliberate and voluntary act of the testator."[200]

The *Ranney* court's support for substantial compliance moved the doctrine forward.[201] The decision may be the source of some confusion, however, because it uses the language of "substantial compliance" while seemingly endorsing an approach of excusing harmless error, which is different. After an explanation of the theory of excusing harmless error, we will return to *Ranney* to sort out the confusion.

[c]   Excusing Harmless Error

In response to decisions like *Peters*, which lost sight of the underlying integrity of the document in its focus on the requirement of a witness's signature, Professor Langbein urged legislatures to give courts the power to validate documents that do not meet traditional statutory elements, but do reflect the testator's intention.[202] In 1990, the UPC reworked Section 2-503 to provide a far-reaching remedy for mistakes:[203]

> Although a document or writing added upon a document was not executed in compliance with Section 2-502 [which gives the basic elements], the document or writing is treated as if it had been executed in compliance

---

[196] Some courts had earlier allowed witnesses' signatures which appeared in self-proving affidavits on the same page as the *testator's* signature. *See, e.g.*, *In re* Estate of Petty, 608 P.2d 987 (Kan. 1980).

[197] UPC § 2-504(c) solves this problem directly by treating the signatures as affixed to the will.

[198] 589 A.2d at 1345.

[199] *See* § 6, *supra*.

[200] 589 A.2d at 1344.

[201] This case illustrates the importance to practicing lawyers of keeping current on directions in legal commentary. Langbein's endorsement of substantial compliance came in 1975. Nelson and Stark added more in 1979. Langbein shifted gears, but kept up the pressure, in 1987. Lawyers who saw the change coming and helped it along, including both the winners here and the losers in *Peters*, served their clients well.

[202] John H. Langbein, *Excusing Harmless Errors in the Execution of Wills: A Report on Australia's Tranquil Revolution in Probate Law*, 87 Colum. L. Rev. 1 (1987). This approach is taken in Israel; Manitoba, Canada; and South Australia, Australia.

In addition to upholding testators' intentions, a harmless error doctrine would benefit lawyers. Professor Begleiter believes "[t]his section would cure most of the execution errors that have generated the bulk of the malpractice actions over the past thirty years." Martin D. Begleiter, *Article II of the Uniform Probate Code and the Malpractice Revolution*, 59 Tenn. L. Rev. 101, 115 (1991).

[203] The section also applies to revocations and other changes in a will.

with that section if the proponent . . . establishes by clear and convincing evidence that the decedent intended the document or writing to constitute (i) the decedent's will . . . .

The reform is variously called a rule of excusing "harmless error,"[204] "excused noncompliance,"[205] and a "dispensing power."[206] Those terms are used interchangeably here.

Note carefully that recognizing that a document is technically deficient, but allowing it anyway, is different from deciding that the document meets statutory elements by being in substantial compliance with them. "Substantial compliance" focuses on being "close." Even if it can justify eschewing the traditional strict-compliance approach, a court using substantial compliance must eventually apply the statutory elements themselves.[207] In contrast, excused noncompliance has been proposed as a statutorily created exception. It ignores the traditional statutory elements and focuses directly on whether the testator intended the document to be effective.

The distinction between these two approaches was blurred by the New Jersey court in *Ranney*. Avoiding the terms "dispensing power" or "harmless error," the court described a doctrine that looks very much like it, but which the court called by another name: "substantial compliance better serves the goals of statutory formalities by permitting probate of formally-defective wills that nevertheless represent the intent of the testator."[208] Perhaps the court, already breaking new ground, was trying to stay within the language (substantial compliance) it had endorsed in *Peters*, even though it was taking a distinctly different approach from that earlier decision. More likely, however, the court did not focus on the distinction between the two theories. Under the facts of the case—the misplaced signatures—the will could be saved under either a substantial compliance or a harmless error approach.[209]

Even if a court or legislature endorses a harmless error approach, some purported "wills" will fail. Consider *Estate of Sky Dancer*.[210] There the decedent left a series of papers that included incomplete portions and blank pages. Signatures appeared on a page separate from any testamentary text.

---

[204] Restatement (Third) of Prop. § 3.3; Restatement (Second) of Prop. § 33.1 cmt. g; UPC § 2-503.

[205] Restatement (Second) of Prop. § 31.1 cmt. g (Tentative Draft No. 12).

[206] UPC § 2-503 (1990), comment.

[207] "Ushers may be given discretion to seat latecomers. But at some point the performance must begin, and to those . . . . who must wait in the wings, the relaxed rule is as harsh as any other formality." James L. Robertson, *Myth and Reality—Or, Is It "Perception and Taste"?—In the Reading of Donative Documents*, 61 Fordham L. Rev. 1045, 2058 (1993).

[208] 589 A.2d at 1344.

[209] Another source of confusion was that the court had before it a Tentative Draft to the Restatement that used "excused noncompliance" language instead of the "substantial compliance" language that appears in the final version. *Compare* Restatement (Second) of Prop. § 33.1 cmt. g (Tentative Draft No. 13), *with* Restatement (Second) of Prop. § 33.1 cmt. g (Final Official Draft).

[210] 13 P.3d 1231 (Colo. App. 2000).

Applying Colorado's version of UPC § 2-503, the court found there was not clear and convincing evidence that the decedent intended the papers to be her will.[211]

Whatever direction the law takes, be clear that there is a practical difference between allowing wills executed in substantial compliance with the statute, on the one hand, and excusing harmless errors, on the other. The next section offers some examples.

[d] Working with the Doctrines

With the advent of these reform doctrines, the legal analysis required in a particular will-execution case is now more complicated. This section first applies the reforms to the cases already discussed. Then it offers a framework for handling will-execution questions in the current changing climate.

Recall the cases discussed above. Two involved switched wills: *Pavlinko* and *Snide*. The absence of a signature on the right will is likely to be fatal under a substantial compliance approach; a will missing a signature is not "close." Two cases involved signatures in the self-proving affidavit, instead of on the will. In *Orrell*, the testator goofed; in *Ranney*, it was the witnesses. Each should be saved by substantial compliance; there were signatures, just in the wrong places. One case, *Peters*, involved a delayed witness's signature. Although the court declined to approve the will under a substantial compliance approach, it could have. All of these should be fairly easy cases, however, for applying a harmless error doctrine. In none was there any doubt about whether the testator had intended the document to be a will. A doctrine excusing noncompliance, coupled with a clear and convincing standard to protect against fraud, is more likely than a substantial compliance standard to validate documents really intended to be wills. That is why the UPC and the Restatement (Third) of Property endorse a harmless error rule.

At a time when the law is changing, keeping track of the various arguments can be a daunting task. A series of questions can help. First, you should ask if the document strictly complies with the statutory elements for an attested will. If that fails, ask if your jurisdiction recognizes holographic wills. If so, would the document work as a holograph? If not (or if holographs are not recognized), do the facts show "substantial compliance" with the statutory elements? Finally, should the will be allowed under a harmless error approach?[212] Consider a hypothetical:

---

[211] *See generally* Emily Sherwin, *Clear and Convincing Evidence of Testamentary Intent: The Search for a Compromise Between Formality and Adjudicative Justice*, 34 Conn. L. Rev. 453 (2002).

[212] This list of questions reflects, in somewhat broader terms, what has been called the "multi-tiered approach to due execution" of the UPC. *See* C. Douglas Miller, *Will Formality, Judicial Formalism, and Legislative Reform: An Examination of the New Uniform Probate Code "Harmless Error" Rule and the Movement Toward Amorphism—Part Two: Uniform Probate Code Section 2-503 and a Counterproposal*, 43 Fla. L. Rev. 599, 686 (1991).

Mi-Ling Wong, a resident of a nursing home, sat in her room with two friends. After a conversation about the need for making a will, she wrote out the following: "I give all of my property at my death to my good friend Robert. Mi-Ling Wong." She then said to her friends, "Now I want both of you to sign this." Before they could do so, however, the fire alarm rang, and everyone fled the room. Mi-Ling died in the fire. Both of the witnesses survived, found the paper, and signed it. Is the paper a valid will?

Now work through the various steps.

(1) This document would fail under a strict construction of the typical statute described early in this section:[213] the witnesses did not sign in the testator's presence. It would be fine under the UPC, because witnesses did sign within a reasonable time.

(2) It would also work as a holograph in most places that recognize holographs, but it would fail in jurisdictions that require a date.

(3) Under a substantial compliance approach, the late signatures of the witnesses might be close enough.

(4) Given the nature of the conversation, Mi-Ling's request for the witnesses to sign, and the interruption, a court should find clear and convincing evidence that this document was intended to be a will, and therefore could allow it under a harmless error rule.

Especially if multiple documents are involved, keeping track of the various arguments and their impact on the ultimate result can be difficult. The key is remembering to ask each of these questions with respect to each document you review.

[5] The Execution Ceremony

Anyone familiar with courts' traditionally picky approach to will execution and the ease with which mistakes can happen should approach a will execution ceremony with great care.[214] If you face special problems, like the likelihood of a contest, take special precautions.[215] Do not be afraid to work from a list.[216] Rather, put a copy of one in each file, so it will be unobtrusively handy when you conduct the ceremony.

Most important, remember that the moment of executing a will is an important time for a client. It involves facing one's own mortality.[217] It may

---

[213] See § 7[B][2], supra.

[214] See generally Gerry W. Beyer, The Will Execution Ceremony—History, Significance, and Strategies, 29 S. Tex. L.J. 413 (1988). Lawyers who cause a will to be badly executed may be liable to the devisees who otherwise would have taken. See § 1, supra.

[215] See § 7[A][5], supra.

[216] Checklists designed to assure compliance with the rules of all states are widely available. See, e.g., Restatement (Second) of Prop. § 33.1 cmt. c.

[217] For a good short discussion, see Shaffer, Mooney & Boettcher at 9-16. See generally John M. Astrachan, Easing the Anxiety of Will-Making, Case & Comment, Jan.–Feb. 1982, at 3.

be one of the few times that person ever visits a law office. Fight the tendency to let the whole exercise become routine.[218]

§ 8 Components

A separate set of issues centers around the question: What items constitute the will? The doctrine of integration addresses the question in the physical sense: Which pieces of paper were meant to be in the will when it was executed?[1] The doctrine of incorporation by reference allows giving testamentary effect to words not physically present at the execution ceremony. We now turn to each of these doctrines.

[A] Integration

Integration is not often a problem. Usually, all of the will's pages are found stapled together, with the signatures at the end. Presumably, that is the way they were when the will was executed. Sometimes there is even more evidence: the attestation clause may specify the number of pages, the words may carry over from one page to the next to show continuity, or the testator and witnesses may have initialed each page.[2]

If the will is executed informally, however, problems can arise. For example, in *In re Beale's Estate*,[3] the testator appears as a classic "absent-minded professor." Preparing for a trip to Russia, the professor dictated a new will. He took the loose pages with him to a going-away party, where he placed them in a pile on a table and asked three colleagues to witness his "will." He signed, they signed, and then he stuffed the papers back into his briefcase. On the same day, either before or after the ceremony, the testator wrote his secretary, requesting some changes and enclosing pages 12 and 13 from the will. She made the corrections on the original pages and sent them to Moscow.[4] Deciding that the original pages 12 and 13 probably had been present at the will execution ceremony, the court allowed the uncorrected will.[5] The key to an integration question is: What papers

---

[218] Consider how much more you appreciate a doctor who expresses sympathy over your sore throat (even if it's the 15th one seen that day) than a doctor who simply dashes off a prescription and hurries on to another patient.

[1] Restatement (Third) of Prop. § 3.5.

[2] As a planning matter, you might want to adopt each of these ideas. The practice of initialing pages is risky, however, because it is so easy to miss a page and thereby raise a suspicion that something is wrong.

[3] 113 N.W.2d 380 (Wis. 1962).

[4] After the testator's death she retyped the pages at the request of the testator's son. Amazingly, these pages also had the testator's initials on them All of the original pages were found after the testator's death: most were loose in one office; page one was stuck in some history notes in another office.

[5] The court rejected two other arguments of interest. One was that because the changes followed so closely on the heels of the will execution ceremony, the testator never really intended the original will as his. Another was that in attempting to make the changes, the testator revoked the will. Intention is discussed in § 7[A][1], *supra*, and revocation, in § 9, *infra*.

were present and intended to be part of the will at the time of the execution ceremony?

Basic to wills law, the integration doctrine may be useful for avoiding the tendency to get distracted by more complicated doctrines. It should have served that function in *Keener v. Archibald.* [6] Four pages were found stapled together. The top two were a printed will form (signed by the testator and three witnesses, but otherwise blank) and a self-proving affidavit (signed by the witnesses and notarized); these were executed the same day. The last two pages were a homemade list showing devisees and amounts they should get; it was signed by the testator and had been notarized about four months earlier. Evidently the testator learned that he needed to do more than sign and notarize a list, so he went out and got a will form. The claimants under the will invited the court to apply the integration doctrine, giving effect to all of the papers present at the time of the will execution. [7] Without adequate discussion, the court declined. [8] Because the papers were found stapled together, the court should have recognized a presumption that they all were present when the will was executed. [9]

[B] Incorporation by Reference

Incorporation by reference is a way to give testamentary effect to a document not present at the execution ceremony. A testator who wants to keep the details of a gift private could, for example, identify the amount and donee in a separate writing and then incorporate that writing into the will by reference. [10]

In most states, the following elements must be met for a document to be incorporated by reference: (1) the document being incorporated must exist at the time of the execution ceremony; (2) the will must indicate an intention to incorporate; (3) the will must refer to the document sufficiently to allow its identification; and (4) the will must say that the document is in existence. [11] Because the last element has proved troublesome in practice, [12] the UPC requires only the first three. [13]

---

[6] 533 N.E.2d 1268 (Ind. App. 1989).

[7] Because the will form did not mention the attached list, the list could not be incorporated into the will by reference. *See* § 8[B], *infra.*

[8] The court said that Indiana had not adopted the integration doctrine by case law or statute. That failure may be because wills law simply *assumes* that when it speaks of a "will," it means the papers present at the time of execution and intended to dispose of the testator's property at death.

[9] Even if the list of devisees was not present, a court following the harmless error doctrine might well allow the list, based on clear and convincing evidence that the testator intended the list to act as a will. *See* § 7[B][4][c], *supra.*

[10] Though the doctrine is widely accepted, it has been rejected in a few states, most notably New York and Connecticut. *See* Booth v. Baptist Church, 28 N.E. 238 (N.Y. 1891); Hatheway v. Smith, 65 A. 1058 (Conn. 1907).

[11] *See generally* Haskell Ch. 6, § 2.

[12] Perhaps the most famous example is Appeal of Bryan, 58 A. 748 (Conn. 1904), in which frequent presidential candidate William Jennings Bryan claimed a gift made by a letter

Simon v. Grayson [14] shows a court liberally using incorporation by reference to save a gift. The opinion also illustrates the relationship between that doctrine and a number of others. First, the facts. The decedent left a will dated March 25, 1932, giving his executors $6,000 to be paid according to directions left in a letter carrying the same date. No such letter was found. With the will, however, was a letter dated July 3, 1933, referring to the gift to the executors and detailing the testator's wishes. In addition, the testator left a codicil dated November 25, 1933.

The most obvious reason for refusing to incorporate the letter is that it fails to meet the first element. It clearly did not exist at the time of execution. To solve that problem, the court used the doctrine of republication by codicil. This theory says that when a codicil is executed it "republishes" the will, as of that date. [15] In this case, the will speaks from November, 1933, after the letter. The letter existed when the will was [re-]executed.

Was the letter sufficiently identified? The court said "yes," although the will spoke of a letter dated March 25, 1932, and the letter found was dated the following July 3. The letter was addressed to the executors and it referred to the gift in the will; pretty clearly, the testator intended the July 3 letter to be operative. [16] A court less willing to save the gift might well have found the reference inadequate. [17]

If incorporation by reference did not work, two other theories might still save the letter's gift. Because the letter was dated and in the testator's handwriting, it would probably qualify as a holographic codicil, if such are allowed in the jurisdiction. [18] Because the letter was clearly intended as a testamentary document, it could also be upheld in jurisdictions recognizing a harmless error doctrine. [19]

---

referred to in a will. Maybe because Bryan had helped prepare the letter, the court was unsympathetic to his claim. The letter could not be incorporated by reference because the will did not refer to it as something existing and known to the testator at the time of the will's execution.

[13] UPC § 2-510. *See also* Restatement (Third) of Prop. § 3.6.

[14] 102 P.2d 1081 (Cal. 1940).

[15] *See* Restatement (Third) of Prop. § 3.4. Republication by codicil can also be relevant in other situations in which timing is important. *See* §§ 9 (will revocation) and 29 (omitted family members), *infra*.

[16] For a similar case and result, see Clark v. Greenhalge, 582 N.E.2d 949 (Mass. 1991). There, the will referred to a "memorandum," but the court allowed incorporation by reference of a later "notebook," when the testator had executed codicils after she had prepared the notebook.

[17] *See, e.g., In re* Estate of Norton, 410 S.E.2d 484 (N.C. 1991) (Though stapled to incomplete "will," codicil made no specific reference to the will and did not incorporate it by reference.); Estate of Sweet, 519 A.2d 1260 (Me. 1987) ("any memorandum or memoranda . . . in existence at the time of my death" was insufficient reference because court could not have determined how many writings testator intended to reference).

[18] Holographs are discussed in § 7[B][3], *supra*.

[19] Recall that a court would require "clear and convincing" evidence under that approach. *See* § 7[B][4][c], *supra*.

Testators often have specific desires about who should get various pieces of personal property: "I want the silver platter from Aunt Martha to go to her son George and the green wing-back chair to go to Marjorie, because she's always liked it." Lists like this can be long. They are also especially subject to change. The testator may get into a fight with George, or Marjorie may buy her own green wing-back. Executing a new codicil each time a change is needed is a cumbersome (and expensive) process. Because incorporation by reference requires the document to exist when the will is executed, that doctrine does not cope with changes.[20] To address these problems, the UPC allows wills to refer to a separate, signed writing that identifies who should get particular items of tangible personal property.[21] The writing can be changed after the will has been executed.

In properly planned situations, the doctrine of integration should never cause a problem, and incorporation by reference should be reserved for rare, special situations. The safest way to be sure that all the parts of the will are recognized is to have them all there at the time of the will's execution.

§ 9   Revocation

A testator can revoke a will by either of two methods established by statute. A later writing meeting the statutory requirements can expressly or impliedly supersede the earlier will. Testators can also revoke wills by specific acts that do physical damage to the document. Either method might cause a total or a partial revocation, but in any case, the testator must have an intention to revoke. Wills can also be revoked by operation of law. This section addresses issues surrounding those revocation methods and then considers how wills, once revoked, can be "revived." With the basics in place, the section discusses the odd-sounding doctrine of dependent relative revocation. It closes with a discussion of ethical problems posed by attorneys safeguarding wills for their clients.[1]

[A]   By a Writing

The most common, and surest, way to revoke a will is by executing a later document that expressly revokes the will. Usually this later document is a new will, which simply replaces the old one. Note carefully that the revoking document itself must meet the requirements for a will.[2]

---

[20] For this reason, creating a separate list and incorporating it by reference is asking for trouble if the client takes home the list. Without appreciating that a new will execution is required, the client faces a strong temptation to change the list and endanger its validity.

[21] UPC § 2-513. Even if the writing is not signed, it might be allowed under the harmless error approach of § 2-503.

[1] Many of the topics covered in this section are discussed in Robert Whitman, *Revocation and Revival: An Analysis of the 1990 Revision of the Uniform Probate Code and Suggestions for the Future*, 55 Alb. L. Rev. 1035 (1992).

[2] The analysis of a multiple-document problem can get messy. Imagine two wills, creatively labeled Will I and Will II. To determine whether Will II revoked Will I, you would need to test Will II's validity against the standards discussed in § 7[B], *supra*. For suggestions on how to keep track of the analysis, see § 7[B][4][d], *supra*.

Courts traditionally have taken the same strict approach toward revocation requirements as they have toward will executions, with the same intention-defeating results. Consider *In re McGill's Will*.[3] Margaret had made a will giving her residuary estate to Thomas Hart, but then she changed her mind. At her request, a friend wrote a note to the executor, who had the will, saying, "Please destroy the will I made in favor of Thomas Hart." Margaret signed the letter and two friends witnessed it. She died without the will having been destroyed. Because the paper *itself* did not declare the will revoked, but merely requested the executor to destroy it, the court held the revocation inadequate.[4] The distinction between executing a document that itself revokes a will and executing a document that directs someone else to do so was important to the court, but seems unlikely to have dawned on the testator.

Writings can also revoke a will in part. Codicils (amendments) are the classic method. Usually they make specific changes and expressly reaffirm the will in all other respects.[5]

If a later will is inconsistent with a prior will, but lacks a clause expressly revoking the prior one, complicated problems can arise. The second will might impliedly revoke the first to the extent of the inconsistency. If the inconsistency is too great, however, the second may totally revoke the first. Courts have struggled with where to draw the line.[6] To avoid litigation in these situations, the revised UPC codified the approach recommended by the Restatement (Second) of Property.[7] The key is whether the later will made a complete disposition of the estate. If so, it is presumed to have revoked the prior will completely. If not, it is presumed to have been intended as a supplement to the prior will. In either case, the presumption can be overcome by clear and convincing evidence.

[B] By Physical Act

Despite the high level of formality statutes (and courts) traditionally have required for someone to create a valid will,[8] testators can revoke wills by physically altering the document with the intent to revoke it. There need not be any writing, nor witnesses; just the appropriate act plus intention. After all the trouble the law requires of people to create valid wills, at first blush it seems surprising that people can undo them so easily. After all,

---

[3] 128 N.E. 194 (N.Y. 1920).

[4] *Compare* Estate of Kuralt, 15 P.3d 931 (Mont. 2000). There a letter said "I'll have the lawyer visit the hospital to be sure you inherit . . . ." The letter writer died before the lawyer visited, but the court found that under the circumstances the letter was intended as a will.

[5] If the changes get numerous, make a whole new will to avoid interpretation problems later.

[6] *See, e.g.*, Gilbert v. Gilbert, 652 S.W.2d 663 (Ky. Ct. App. 1983) (Court read two wills together, harmonizing the conflicting provisions.); *In re* Wolfe's Will, 117 S.E. 804 (N.C. 1923) (The language "all my effects," contained in testator's second will was not so inconsistent with the specific devise of real property in testator's first will as to render the first will invalid.).

[7] *See* UPC § 2-507(b)–(d); Restatement (Second) of Prop. § 34.2 cmt. b.

[8] *See* § 7[B], *supra*.

revoking a will can take property away from one set of beneficiaries and give it to another.[9] The law allows informal revocations because people believe, reasonably enough, that tearing up a will revokes it. To require more formal methods of revocation would defeat intention much more often than it would prevent fraud. Also, through intestate statutes, the law expresses its preferred approach. Ease of will revocation allows people to get back to that scheme.

Statutes list specific acts that revoke a will. Typically, the list includes tearing, burning, canceling, and obliterating.[10] The acts must be done by the testator, or in the testator's presence at his direction.[11] Resolving whether the testator is in the "presence" of those doing the act involves the same issues as whether witnesses are in the testator's "presence" at a will's execution.[12] The revised UPC requires only "conscious presence."[13]

A common source of litigation has been whether particular physical acts were enough to revoke the will in question.[14] Typically, words like "burning" or "tearing" refer to acts done to the paper;[15] words like "canceling" or "obliterating" refer to the language on the page. "Canceling" has caused the most trouble.

Consider, for example, *Thompson v. Royall*.[16] The testator had given her will to her executor and a codicil to her lawyer, for safekeeping. A few weeks before her death, she asked them to destroy both documents. Her lawyer convinced her, however, to keep the papers as memoranda to be used if she changed her mind and wanted a will. On the back of the codicil and on the cover of the will, the lawyer wrote similar statements declaring each document "null and void." The testator, but no witnesses, signed the statements. The testator died without making a new will, and her disappointed relatives challenged the will and codicil in question, claiming they had been revoked by cancellation.[17] Applying a widely held approach, the

---

[9] If there has been one will, intestacy would result. If there has been more than one, an earlier will may become effective again. *See* § 9[D], *infra*, discussing revival.

[10] *See, e.g.,* UPC § 2-507(a)(2).

[11] *See, e.g.,* UPC § 2-507(a)(2).

[12] *See* § 7[B][2][d], *supra*. Not all states require acts in the testator's presence. Ohio allows a physical revocation if it comes after the testator's express written direction. *See* Ohio Rev. Code Ann. § 2107.33. Thus, if the *McGill* case discussed above had arisen in Ohio, and if the executor promptly had destroyed the will as requested, the destruction would have revoked the will.

[13] *See, e.g.,* UPC § 2-507(a)(2).

[14] *See, e.g.,* White v. Casten, 46 N.C. 197 (1853) (slight burning sufficient to revoke will); Tinsley v. Carwile, 10 N.E.2d 597 (Ind. 1937) (writing need not be rendered illegible in order to destroy or mutilate the will).

[15] *See, e.g., In re* Bakhaus' Estate, 102 N.E.2d 818 (Ill. 1951) (will revoked when signature cut off).

[16] 175 S.E. 748 (Va. 1934).

[17] Different advice by the lawyer might have assured the will's revocation. If the lawyer and executor had witnessed the testator's signature, the "null and void" statement would have been effective as a writing meeting the statutory requirements for an attested will. If the testator had both written and signed the statement, it could have qualified as a holograph.

court upheld the will, because the revoking statement did not physically interfere with the written parts of the will.[18] In contrast, the revised UPC allows revocation by burning, tearing or canceling, even if the act does not touch the words on the will.[19]

Sometimes a previously executed will cannot be found after the testator's death. The question then becomes whether the will was revoked by physical act. If the will was last in the testator's hands, it will be presumed revoked. The presumption, however, can be overcome. In *Estate of Markofske v. Cotter*,[20] for example, the testator moved to a nursing home, where she died. Her sister, who was an intestate heir but was not named in the will, cleaned out her house and collected her important papers, some of which had not been stored carefully. No will was found. The sister's interest in not finding the will, coupled with evidence that a few months before her death the testator had mentioned her will, helped overcome the presumption that the testator had revoked the will.[21]

Though it is frequently criticized as a bad idea, some testators execute two copies of a will, one for the testator and one for the lawyer to keep.[22] Since the will is thought of as one entity, destruction of one copy (with intent to revoke) usually revokes the will.[23] As when there is only one copy and the testator's copy cannot be found, a presumption of destruction with intent to revoke will usually arise.

Ambiguities can arise when a testator has altered only part of a will. A clause might be crossed out, or a beneficiary's name obliterated. Because

---

In addition, if the UPC's harmless error doctrine had been available, the revoking statement could have been validated on the clear evidence that the testator intended the document to be effective. Section 7[B][3], *supra*, covers holographs, and § 7[B][4][c], *supra*, harmless error.

[18] Courts sometimes make it similarly difficult to revoke a will by obliterating language. Paragraphs or words "penciled through" may not be enough. *See* Estate of Eglee, 383 A.2d 586 (R.I. 1978).

[19] UPC § 2-507(a)(2).

[20] 178 N.W.2d 9 (Wis. 1970).

[21] For a case reaching the same result on less-suspicious facts, see First Interstate Bank v. Henson-Hammer, 779 P.2d 167 (Or. App. 1989).

If a will has not been revoked, but nonetheless cannot be located, its validity and terms can be proved by other evidence. Most states have "lost wills" statutes directed to the problem; some are quite restrictive. Particularly difficult is the requirement that the will be proved to have been "in existence" at the time of the testator's death or to have been "fraudulently destroyed." *See, e.g.*, Ohio Rev. Code Ann. § 2107.26. Some courts have been creative in avoiding the literal meaning of these terms. *See, e.g.*, *In re* Eder's Estate, 29 P.2d 631 (Colo. 1934) ("existence" means legal, not physical, existence); *In re* Will of Fox, 174 N.E.2d 499 (N.Y. 1961) ("fraudulently destroyed" includes constructive fraud, which means destruction not done by the testator or under the testator's authority).

[22] The better practice is to execute only one copy, and then make photocopies for interested parties.

[23] *See, e.g.*, Succession of Beard, 483 So. 2d 1228 (La. App. 1986); Restatement (Third) of Prop. § 4.1 cmt. f.

Revocation of an *unexecuted* copy might be a sufficient revocation under a harmless error approach. *See* § [7][B][4][c], *supra*.

many states allow partial revocation by physical act, the question becomes whether the physical act was intended to revoke the whole will, or only a particular section.

A different sort of partial revocation problem arises if there are both a will and a codicil, but only one document is touched.

Imagining the will as a base, with the codicil resting on top, helps the general rules make sense. If the intention is to revoke both documents, destroying the will is usually sufficient. If the intention is unclear, however, the codicil may remain valid if it can sensibly stand alone, but it will fail if it needs the will's support. Conversely, tearing up a codicil normally leaves the supporting will in place. This last situation really involves the doctrine of revival, which we cover below.[24]

[C] By Operation of Law

Sometimes people marry or divorce, but do not amend their wills to take into account the change in their lives. Many states have statutes that revoke all or part of a will in one or both of these circumstances.[25] Because the logic of these doctrines should also apply to nonprobate transfers, discussion is postponed to a later section.[26] Closely related to statutes that revoke wills or specific gifts are those that give new spouses or children rights to claim intestate shares if a will omits them. These statutes are discussed in connection with other devices to protect family members from disinheritance.[27]

[D] Revival

Suppose a testator executes Will I, and then sometime later executes Will II, which revokes Will I. Changing his mind again, the testator revokes Will II. Various jurisdictions take different approaches regarding whether Will I is good again. Though strictly speaking only one approach amounts to "revival," that term is generally used to identify the issues surrounding this circumstance.[28]

Some places follow the English common law rule, which said that because wills speak only at the testator's death, Will I was never really revoked by Will II, so Will I still stands as the testator's "last will."

Under this view, Will I is not revived so much as it is uncovered. Other jurisdictions say that because Will I was revoked by Will II, the only way to get back Will I is to re-execute it.

---

[24] See § 9[D], infra.

[25] See Haskell at 67-68; Restatement (Third) of Prop. § 4.1(b) (marriage dissolution presumptively revokes provisions in favor of former spouse). Virtually all states have a statute covering divorce.

[26] See § 45, infra.

[27] See § 29, infra.

[28] Virtually all states have statutes on the question. For a compilation, see Restatement (Third) of Prop. § 4.2, Statutory Note.

Under this approach, Will I is not revived so much as it is reborn. The most common approach really is revival: if the testator intends to revive Will I at the time of revoking Will II, that intention will prevail. Otherwise, Will I stays revoked. Even here, however, there is a split. A more traditional approach would say Will I is revived only if the "terms of the revocation" of Will II indicate an intention to revive.

A more liberal view would consider the "circumstances of the revocation" and the testator's declarations, whether at the time or later, regarding intention to revive. [29]

Identifying a testator's intention can be difficult, as illustrated in *In re Estate of Boysen*. [30] In 1964, Chris Boysen, a widower, executed a will giving his son, Raymond, his real estate on the condition that Raymond pay $7,000 to Raymond's sister, Genevieve. Chris split the personal property equally between the children. Believing the 1964 will was lost, Chris executed a new will in 1975. He seems to have intended the new will to recreate the terms of the old one, but no one could remember what the old will had said. The 1975 will again gave the real estate to Raymond, but this time Raymond had to pay his sister one fourth the value of the land. Since the land was worth about $600,000, Genevieve's share under the second will was much greater.

Thereafter, the 1964 will was located. Chris then tore up the 1975 will, but kept the torn pieces as a precaution against the 1964 will being lost again. Evidently Chris believed the two wills provided the same thing. After Chris died, the question was whether Chris revived the 1964 will when he revoked the 1975 version.

The court, interpreting pre-1990 UPC Section 2-509(a), struggled with whether "the circumstances of the revocation" of the second will evidenced an intent that the first will control. Reluctant to revive a will whose terms were so different, the court imposed a three-part test for examining a testator's intent: [31]

1. Did the testator, at the time he revoked the later will, know whether the earlier will was in existence?

2. If the testator did know that the earlier will was in existence, did he know the nature and extent of his property and the disposition made of his property by the earlier will, particularly with respect to persons with a natural claim on his bounty?

3. Did the testator, by action or nonaction, disclose an intent to make the disposition which the earlier will directs?

---

[29] The pre-1990 UPC took this basic approach, putting the burden on the proponent of Will I to show that the testator intended to revive it. UPC (pre-1990) § 2-509.

[30] 309 N.W.2d 45 (Minn. 1981).

[31] 309 N.W.2d at 47-48.

Asking these questions on remand, the trial court held that the 1964 will was not revived.[32] Chris died intestate.

Because requiring the three specific elements puts a much heavier burden on those seeking to prove revival, commentators have criticized,[33] and the comments to the revised UPC explicitly reject,[34] that approach. A court taking the more flexible view contemplated by the UPC drafters[35] might still have reached the same result under the facts in *Boysen*. The statute requires the party arguing for revocation to establish that the testator's intention was for the previous will to take effect "as executed."[36] Since Chris clearly did not know the terms of his 1964 will, he could not have made an informed intent to revive it, and the will should stay revoked.[37]

The revised UPC adds some details about revival not found in most statutes.[38] It distinguishes between complete and partial revocations, and revocations by physical act and those by written instrument. If Will II totally revoked Will I and is itself later revoked by physical act, the UPC applies a presumption against revival of the first will. Will I is revived only "if it is evident from the circumstances of the revocation of the subsequent will or from the testator's contemporary or subsequent declarations" that the testator intended Will I to be effective.[39] If Will II only partially revoked Will I, the presumption works the other way when Will II is later physically revoked. In that situation, the previously revoked parts of Will I are revived, "unless it is evident . . . that the testator did not intend" the revival.[40] If

---

[32] *See In re* Estate of Boysen, 351 N.W.2d 398 (Minn. App. 1984). The trial court, however, "saved" the 1975 will by applying the doctrine of dependent relative revocation. That holding was reversed on appeal. 351 N.W.2d 398. Dependent relative revocation is discussed in § 9[E], *infra*.

[33] *See* John H. Langbein and Lawrence W. Waggoner, *Reforming the Law of Gratuitous Transfers: The New Uniform Probate Code*, 55 Alb. L. Rev. 871, 885-887 (1992).

[34] Citing *Boysen*, the comments read, "[T]he open-ended statutory language is not to be undermined by translating it into discrete subsidiary elements, all of which must be met . . . ." UPC § 2-509 comment.

[35] Perhaps better communication between the courts and the Joint Editorial Board, which monitors the UPC, could reduce the number of decisions that conflict with the drafters' intention. *See* Robert Whitman, *Revocation and Revival: An Analysis of the 1990 Revision of the Uniform Probate Code and Suggestions for the Future*, 55 Alb. L. Rev. 1035, 1063-1065 (1992).

[36] Both versions use this phrase. *See* UPC (pre-1990) § 2-509(a); UPC § 2-509(b).

[37] *See* John H. Langbein and Lawrence W. Waggoner, *Reforming the Law of Gratuitous Transfers: The New Uniform Probate Code*, 55 Alb. L. Rev. 871, 886-887 (1992). The notion that clients' decisions should be informed ones has implications in a wide range of cases involving wills and trusts. *See generally* Roger W. Andersen, *Informed Decisionmaking in an Office Practice*, 28 B.C. L. Rev. 225 (1987).

[38] *See also* Restatement (Third) of Prop. § 4.2.

[39] UPC § 2-509(a). This is substantially the same rule as the pre-1990 version interpreted in *Boysen. See* UPC (pre-1990) § 2-509(a). The evidentiary rule, allowing the testator's contemporary or later statements, is more liberal than some jurisdictions would allow.

[40] UPC § 2-509(b). Recall the image of a will as a base, with the codicil resting on top, mentioned in § 9[B], *supra*.

a third will is involved (revoking all or part of Will II), Will I is revived "to the extent it appears *from the terms of the later will* that the testator intended" the revival.[41]

[E] Dependent Relative Revocation (Ineffective Revocation)

The most intriguing of the doctrines relating to will revocation is the one carrying the name "dependent relative revocation," known to generations of law students as "DRR."[42] Fundamentally a doctrine for undoing mistakes, it carries an odd title because courts—traditionally reluctant to correct mistakes involving wills—engage in a fiction. When they decide to ignore a mistaken revocation, they traditionally pretend that the revocation itself was really dependent on some condition. When (because of the mistake) the condition is not met, the courts may then presume that the mistaken revocation never really happened in the first place. Because there has been no revocation, the will in question stands.

Consider Hans Schmidt, who wanted to redo his will. At the execution ceremony for the new will, Hans somehow managed not to sign it. Wrongly believing the new will to be effective, he tore up the old one. When the mistake is discovered after Hans' death, a court unable to probate the new will (because there is no signature) might well use DRR to ignore the revocation of the old will. In theory, Hans' revocation of the old will was dependent upon the new will being effective; since the new will fails, the old will was never revoked when Hans tore it up.[43]

The doctrine does not give Hans what he really wanted, and thought he had: the new will. Rather, he gets a consolation prize: the old will he thought he had revoked.[44] Because DRR typically does not have the capacity to validate the will that the testator preferred,[45] one continuing problem in these cases is trying to choose among unfavored alternatives.

---

[41] UPC § 2-509(c) (emphasis added). Note that now the evidence must come from the new will. Written evidence is not generally available in the context of revocation by physical act, covered by the rules of subsections (a) and (b).

[42] *See generally* George E. Palmer, *Dependent Relative Revocation and Its Relation to Relief for Mistake*, 69 Mich. L. Rev. 989 (1971).

The new Restatement adds some clarity by calling this topic "Ineffective Revocation." Restatement (Third) of Prop. § 4.3.

[43] Any revocation clause in the new will has no impact because the new will itself was not properly executed.

[44] The UPC refers to dependent relative revocation as "the law of second best." UPC § 2-507 comment.

[45] It is possible, if very rare, for DRR to realize the testator's first choice. In re Estate of Boysen, 309 N.W.2d 45 (Minn. 1981), is one such situation. The testator, apparently believing both wills provided the same distribution when they in fact did not, revoked Will II. Lack of intention to revive Will I left the decedent intestate. Had DRR been applied to ignore Will II's revocation, the testator's intention would have been honored. *See* John H. Langbein & Lawrence W. Waggoner, *Reforming the Law of Gratuitous Transfers: The New Uniform Probate Code*, 55 Alb. L. Rev. 871, 887 n.34 (1992). The *Boysen* case is discussed in § 9[D], *supra*.

Most courts look at the circumstances, compare the various wills and the intestate statute, and then choose what they believe the testator would have done had the testator known what hindsight has revealed. In Hans' case, they would ask whether—now knowing he cannot have the new will—he would rather get the old will back or have the property pass by intestacy.[46]

Sometimes courts get hung up in the conditional revocation fiction. *In re Estate of Patten*[47] involved two wills Ella Patten had executed. The first was properly executed in 1968; the second was invalidly executed in 1970. Only the second will could be found, and it, of course, was denied probate. Ella's son then sought to admit the 1968 will as a lost will by proving the contents with a copy. The problem with that approach is that lost wills are presumed revoked if last known to be in the testator's possession.[48] The son argued that DRR should overcome the presumption. The court refused to apply DRR because it could not be sure that Ella's revocation of the first will was conditioned upon the validity of the second. By focusing on the so-called conditional revocation, the court missed the central question: What were the choices here? The court should have been asking whether Ella would have preferred the 1968 will or intestacy. Perhaps problems like this can be avoided if courts adopt the Restatement of Property's term for DRR: ineffective revocation.[49]

Dependent relative revocation also ties in with the revival rules.[50] Consider *In re Estate of Alburn*.[51] In 1955, Ottilie Alburn executed a will in Milwaukee, Wisconsin. In 1959, she executed a revised will in Kankakee, Illinois. Returning to Wisconsin in 1960, she tore up the Kankakee will and told a friend she wanted the Milwaukee will to stand. Under Wisconsin law at the time, however, she could only get the Milwaukee will back by re-executing it.[52] Because Ottilie did not re-execute, the court faced two choices. It could declare her intestate, because the Milwaukee will had been revoked by the Kankakee will and the Kankakee will had been revoked by tearing. Or it could apply DRR to save the Kankakee will by using the fiction that Ottilie's revocation was dependent upon the Milwaukee will being revived, which could not happen. Because the court thought Ottilie would rather die having the Kankakee will she tore up than with no will at all, it applied DRR to save the Kankakee will.[53]

---

[46] Reform of will execution rules to include a doctrine of harmless error would avoid the need for the consolation prize approach of DRR. Hans' faulty new will itself could be validated. *See* § 7[B][4][c], *supra.*

[47] 587 P.2d 1307 (Mont. 1978).

[48] *See* § 9[B] n.20, *supra.*

[49] Restatement (Third) of Prop. § 4.3.

[50] *See* § 9[C], *supra.*

[51] 118 N.W.2d 919 (Wis. 1963).

[52] Wisconsin now allows revival if there is clear and convincing evidence of an intent to revive the former will. Wis. Stat. § 853.11(6).

[53] A more liberal revival rule would have given Ottilie the will she wanted, and avoided the need to use DRR to provide the consolation prize. *See* UPC § 2-507 comment.

Dependent relative revocation can also apply when there has been a partial revocation by physical act. Imagine a will that includes a gift of "$5,000 to my friend Michael Andrews." The "$5,000" is crossed out and "$7,500" is written above in the testator's handwriting. In states allowing partial revocation by physical act, courts would probably treat the $5,000 gift as revoked, based on the circumstantial evidence that the testator made the change. The new $7,500 gift fails, however, because the writing does not meet will execution requirements.[54]

Now, things start to get a little weird. Despite the fact that the new disposition fails for lack of formalities, courts tend to consider it as an indication of the testator's intention. Courts (and most of us) look at the $7,500 "gift" and conclude that the testator would surely prefer Michael getting $5,000 to his getting nothing. To reach that result, a court might apply DRR to ignore the crossout. Theoretically, the court would view testator's revocation as having been conditional on the effectiveness of the larger gift. Since the larger gift fails, there was no revocation. In fact, of course, the testator simply assumed the new gift would be valid.

The problem is more difficult if the testator inserted a new gift of only $2,500. We now see a testator less happy with Michael. The question is: Since the $2,500 gift fails, would the testator rather have Michael left with the original $5,000 or left with nothing? Unless there is other evidence indicating a continuing desire to benefit Michael, a court might be quite reluctant on these facts to apply DRR to undo the revocation.[55]

Because physical revocations are ambiguous, courts can use DRR with some comfort when they believe testators would not have revoked the will if the testators had known more. Written revocations, on the other hand, carry more weight. In light of absolute language like "I revoke all my prior wills," a court may have trouble saying the revocation was nonetheless conditional. In some situations, however, courts have applied DRR to correct a mistaken revocation by written instrument. For example, a testator may execute a new will, revoking the old one and creating a new gift that itself is invalid because it is too ambiguous to be enforceable,[56]

---

[54] If the change had included the testator's signature, or even initials, a court might (but probably would not) allow it as a holographic codicil. *See* § 7[B][3], *supra*. Similarly, the change might be allowed in a jurisdiction granting courts the authority to ignore harmless errors. *See* § 7[B][4][c], *supra*.

[55] The case for letting the revocation stand (by not applying DRR) is stronger if the new gift is substantially smaller than the original gift. *See, e.g.*, Schneider v. Harrington, 71 N.E.2d 242 (Mass. 1947) (gift of one-third of estate reduced to zero); *In re* Will of Shuler, 132 A.2d 33 (N.J. 1957) (gift to a mother canceled in favor of a gift to her daughter).

If the testator has made several changes like the example in the text, a court might either treat them independently or as part of a whole, depending upon which approach would best approximate the testator's intention. *See* Restatement (Third) of Prop. § 4.3 cmt. d.

[56] *See, e.g.*, *In re* Estate of Casselman, 364 N.W.2d 27 (Neb. 1985) (A codicil first stated, "I hereby revoke and hold for naught any or all bequests made to and on behalf of my son." Later paragraphs said testator's son "shall be provided a room, a TV and $10.00 a month for funny books or records until he reaches legal age." Because of the codicil's conflicting language, it was denied probate.); Anderson v. Griggs, 402 So. 2d 904 (Ala. 1981) (Court refused to revoke testator's first will when the subsequent will was lost and its contents could not be proved.).

or it violates the Rule Against Perpetuities,[57] or it exceeds limits on gifts to charity.[58] To enforce the revocation clause of the new will, but not allow the new disposition, strikes such courts as being unfair to the testator. They correct the mistake by viewing the new will's revocation clauses as having been conditional on the effectiveness of the new gift. Since the new gift fails, the revocation clause is ignored.[59] Other courts enforce the revocation clause, however, because its language is clearly not conditional.[60]

DRR can apply in many situations: complete revocation by physical act, partial revocation by physical act, total or partial revocations by written instruments.[61] Because it can arise so often, students sometimes see DRR cropping up everywhere. As a device for keeping DRR under control, treat every revocation separately and ask, "Did this happen by mistake?" If not, ignore DRR. If so, proceed to analyze what alternative dispositions would be available if the mistake were undone, asking of each, "Would the testator have preferred this one?"

[F] The Ethics of Safeguarding Wills

As much of the material in this section indicates, wills can be dangerous instruments in the hands of some clients. They can lose them, mangle them, "correct" them, use them for scratch paper. For good reason, lawyers have long wanted to keep wills out of temptation's reach. One solution is for the lawyer to keep the will for the client. That way it will be protected from harm and easily available when needed. Not so coincidentally, later updating and, most lucratively, the ultimate probating, are likely to be handled by the law office where the will has been stored.[62]

Because such safekeeping smacks of overreaching by lawyers, the Wisconsin Supreme Court concluded that "[t]he correct practice is that the

---

[57] *See, e.g., In re* Estate of Jones, 352 So. 2d 1182 (Fla. App. 1977). The Rule is covered in Chapter 12, *infra*.

[58] *See, e.g.*, Linkins v. Protestant Episcopal Cathedral Found., 187 F.2d 357 (D.C. Cir. 1950) (Testator executed new will devising certain parts of his estate to religious organizations. Some of these devises later turned out to be invalid, but the court invoked DRR and held that the testator did not intend the first will to be revoked until the second will became effective.); *In re* Kaufman's Estate, 155 P.2d 831 (Cal. 1945) (Testator executed new will in California with almost identical provisions of his first will executed in New York. However, the provisions regarding charities were invalid under California law. DRR allowed the first will to be probated in New York.).

[59] The Restatement is more direct: "The revocation of the earlier will is presumptively ineffective to the extent necessary to give effect to the dispositive provision in the earlier will that the failed dispositive provision in the later will replaced." Restatement (Third) of Prop. § 4.3 cmt. e.

[60] *See, e.g.*, Crosby v. Alton Ochsner Med. Found., 276 So. 2d 661 (Miss. 1973) (DRR did not allow ignoring express revocation clause in later will, although charitable gifts under that will were invalidated by statute.).

[61] It may even apply to will substitutes. *See* Restatement (Third) of Prop. § 4.3 cmt. k.

[62] One of the major "assets" of many firms is a collection of wills, waiting to be probated. Current lawyers cash in on the investments of their predecessors and, in turn, are obligated to place new wills "in storage" for those lawyers who will join the firm in the future.

original will should be delivered to the testator, and should only be kept by the attorney upon specific unsolicited request of the client."[63] Because of the difficulty of identifying who requested the safekeeping, Professor Johnston would prohibit attorneys from keeping the documents at all.[64] At a minimum, lawyers should be very sensitive to the conflict of interest they face and should fully inform their clients about the pros and cons of various storage options.[65]

§ 10 Contracts Regarding Wills

In addition to being able to create and revoke wills, people can also execute contracts to make, or not make, or revoke, or not revoke, wills.[1] These contracts do not change wills law—wills can still be made or revoked, despite the promises—but they do affect how property is ultimately distributed. The two most common areas of dispute involve contracts to make wills and contracts not to revoke them. This section will address those areas in turn, and then close with a discussion of planning issues.

One person might promise another to make a will in their favor, but then not follow through as expected. If the promise is enforceable under contract law, it will be enforceable against the estate of the breaching promisor. A common remedy will be to create a constructive trust[2] in favor of the promisee and enforce it against estate assets. As a practical matter, the promisee takes the property as a creditor, before will beneficiaries or intestate heirs.

Litigation over contracts to make wills frequently involves someone who worked for a testator in return for a promise to share the testator's estate.[3] Often the promise was oral, and therefore unenforceable under the applicable Statute of Frauds.[4] However, the promisee may bring a quantum meruit

---

[63] State v. Gulbankian, 196 N.W.2d 733, 736 (Wis. 1972).

[64] Gerald P. Johnston, *An Ethical Analysis of Common Estate Planning Practices—Is Good Business Bad Ethics?*, 45 Ohio St. L.J. 57, 133 (1984).

[65] *See* Roger W. Andersen, *Informed Decisionmaking in an Office Practice*, 28 B.C. L. Rev. 225, 234 n.34 (1987); Report, *Developments Regarding the Professional Responsibility of the Estate Planning Lawyer: The Effect of the Model Rules of Professional Conduct*, 22 Real Prop. Prob. & Tr. J. 1, 28 (1987).

[1] *See generally* Bertel M. Sparks, Contracts to Make Wills (1956).

[2] A constructive trust is a remedy to cure unjust enrichment. The "trustee" is ordered to transfer title to the "beneficiary." For further discussion and other examples of the doctrine's use, see §§ 12[f] (oral trusts), 25 (misconduct), and 28[C][1] (spousal election), *infra*. *See generally* Dan B. Dobbs, Remedies § 4.3 (2d ed. 1993).

[3] A charming cartoon shows a dismayed Sidney listening to a lawyer reading from a will, ". . . And to my faithful valet, Sidney, who I promised to remember in my will—Hi there, Sidney." The cartoon, from Playboy Magazine, is reproduced in Dukeminier & Johanson at 321.

[4] The UPC requires contracts concerning succession to be in writing or, at the very least, to be referred to in a will and then proved by extrinsic evidence. The relevant section was moved in 1990, but the substance was not changed. *See* UPC § 2-514; UPC (pre-1990) § 2-701. An important purpose of the section is to discourage litigation about whether there was such a contract. For commentary on the earlier version, see Dennis W. Collins, *Oral Contracts to Make a Will and the Uniform Probate Code: Boon or Boondoggle?*, 20 Creighton L. Rev. 413 (1987).

action for the value of services rendered. *Green v. Richmond* [5] involved such a claim. Max met and proposed to Bernyce, but then backed out because of his "mental hang-up" about marriage. He instead orally promised that if she would stay with him, he would give her his entire estate. Bernyce stayed, providing a variety of social, domestic and business services. When Max died with an estate of over $7,000,000, but evidently gave her nothing, Bernyce sued for the value of her services. [6] The court upheld the contract, despite a claim that it was illegal as a contract for sexual relations. [7] Bernyce came away better than she might have, but one lesson of her experience is familiar: get it in writing.

Individuals can also agree not to revoke their wills. [8] Questions about whether there has been such an agreement generally arise between spouses who execute wills with reciprocal terms. [9] Sometimes these wills are "joint," one will serving two persons. [10] The use of a joint and reciprocal will may create a presumption that the survivor promised not to revoke the will. [11] For this and other reasons, experts caution against using joint wills, [12] but they persist, perhaps because forms tend to have lives of their own.

Wills can also be reciprocal without being joint. Indeed, married couples typically execute wills with reciprocal terms. Although there may have been no intention to restrict the survivor's right to revoke such a will, mirror-image wills may prompt claims of such a promise, especially when the survivor of a second marriage changes the will.

Junot v. Estate of Gilliam [13] is typical of the way courts approach these sad cases. When Emma and Thaddeas married, they each had children by prior marriages. They executed reciprocal wills, giving the property to each other or, if the other spouse had already died, to all of the children equally. Thaddeas died, and Emma took under his will. She then made a new will, giving everything to her children and leaving out Thaddeas'. When Emma died, Thaddeas' children sought to set aside her new will because her earlier will had by contract become irrevocable on the death of their father. [14]

---

[5] 337 N.E.2d 691 (Mass. 1975).

[6] If the contract had been in writing, her claim would have been for the entire estate.

[7] There was enough evidence to submit the question to the jury, which found that sexual relations were only incidental to their relationship. Bernyce maintained her own apartment and job, and Max often traveled with another woman.

The court also allowed evidence of the size of Max's estate, as probative to determining the value of Bernyce's services.

[8] As discussed later in this section, such contracts are usually a bad idea.

[9] Often these are called "mutual wills."

[10] In most situations, a joint will is probated twice, once for each testator. Sometimes the will is not discovered (or not disclosed) until the death of the surviving testator.

[11] *See* Atkinson § 49. The UPC specifically negates any such presumption. UPC § 2-514 (1990); UPC § (pre-1990) 2-701.

[12] *See* Dukeminier & Johanson at 322 ("[J]oint wills are notorious litigation-breeders that should not be used at all.").

[13] 759 S.W.2d 654 (Tenn. 1988).

[14] In most states, probate of the new will is allowed and, if the disappointed parties prevail, they get a claim against the estate.

Applying the general rule, the court said that the wills' reciprocal provisions were not clear and convincing evidence of a contract not to revoke, so Thaddeas' children got nothing.[15]

Perhaps the most important lesson from *Junot* is that lawyers should anticipate the possibility that a surviving spouse may decide to favor different beneficiaries than those identified at the time a set of reciprocal wills is made. This result is more likely when there already is a "combined family" where one or both spouses have children from other marriages, but could also occur if the survivor remarried and had more children. If the couple executed reciprocal wills and the survivor favors one side of the family in a later will, the disappointed relatives may well sue, even if they are unlikely to prove there was an enforceable contract. To avoid the litigation threat, most reciprocal wills should include a clause specifically negating any implication that a contract not to revoke was intended.

On the other hand, seeing a result like the one in *Junot*, you might be tempted to recommend that your clients create an express contract to "lock in" the original plan. Usually this is a bad idea. Especially if the surviving spouse outlives the first to die by a substantial time, a contract could saddle the survivor with an inflexible estate plan that no longer fits the family's needs. The survivor could also face tax problems.[16]

Moreover, these contracts are notorious litigation-breeders.[17] In virtually all situations a trust will better protect the interests of all the survivors.[18]

Counseling clients about these problems can be difficult, especially if you are representing both husband and wife. It requires asking how much each trusts the other not to change the plan. As with any joint representation, it may create particularly difficult ethical questions.[19] Recently, the ethics rules have been restructured to provide better guidance on how to handle conflict of interest and confidentiality problems in a planning context.[20] The first step, however, is to recognize that such problems do arise. That way, you can at least see them coming.[21]

---

[15] For a case with similar facts and results, see Oursler v. Armstrong, 179 N.E.2d 489 (N.Y. 1961).

[16] *See* Amy M. Hess, *The Federal Transfer Tax Consequences of Joint and Mutual Wills,* 24 Real Prop. Prob. & Tr. J. 469 (1990).

[17] *See, e.g.,* Bergheger v. Boyle, 629 N.E.2d 1168 (Ill. App. Ct. 1994) (contract does not apply to life insurance proceeds); *In re* Estate of Jud, 710 P.2d 1241 (Kan. 1985) (contract does apply to wrongful death award); Kretzer v. Brubaker, 660 N.E.2d 446 (Ohio 1996) (contract to keep property on one side of the family met by will provision that excluded nieces on that side).

[18] Trusts are discussed in Chapter 4, *infra.*

[19] One of the most vexing problems is what to do when a client tells you one thing in a joint meeting with their spouse, and then indicates privately that he or she has a different plan in mind. Anticipating this situation before you agree to represent both spouses, you can obtain an agreement from each as to how to handle such conflicts. *See* A v. B. v. Hill Wallack, 726 A. 2d 924 (N.J. 1999) (law firm could disclose to wife existence of husband's non-marital child). For further discussion, see § 6, *supra* (couples seeking wills), and § 28[E], *infra* (waiving marital rights).

[20] *See* Model Rules of Prof'l Conduct, Rules 1.6-1.8.

[21] For other discussions of this problem, see §§ 6 n.1, *supra,* and 28[E], *infra.*

The law of contracts as it applies to wills provides a long list of potential sources of litigation. With little to recommend them as planning devices, contracts regarding wills should be understood, mostly so they can be avoided.

Chapter 4

PRIVATE EXPRESS TRUSTS

Trusts provide lawyers with a continuing series of exciting opportunities. Because trusts are so flexible, they allow us to help clients in an enormous range of circumstances. This chapter opens with an overview designed to supplement the brief introduction to trusts that appears earlier.[1] Then come discussions of what is needed to create a trust, how big a beneficiary's interest might be, and how a trust can be changed or terminated. The chapter closes with a discussion of how to use wills and trusts together, with one "pouring" assets into the other.

§ 11   An Overview

Trusts have been around for a long time,[2] but really caught on in this country after World War II as a way of holding family wealth, usually in the form of personal property. In the context of private express trusts,[3] clients can choose to create either living trusts[4] established during their lifetimes, or testamentary trusts created by will. To establish a living trust, the settlor can either give the property to someone[5] else to hold as trustee or declare herself to be the trustee. To create a testamentary trust, the will simply gives estate assets to someone to be held in trust according to directions in the will.

People create trusts for many different reasons.[6] One is to provide asset management. A trustee has the burden of managing the trust property on behalf of the beneficiaries. Whether the beneficiaries are young children, disabled adults, rich people who do not want to be bothered with the details, or politicians who want to remain disinterested public servants, the trust device can take the burdens of management out of their hands. In addition, these benefits can be stretched into three generations or longer.[7]

---

[1] This might be a good time to reread § 2[B][1], *supra*.

[2] If you wish to explore the long, rich history of trusts, a good place to start is Clark, Lusky, Murphy, Ascher & McCouch, Gratuitous Transfers: Wills, Intestate Succession, Trusts, Gifts, Future Interests and Estate and Gift Taxation 454-467, where a variety of additional sources are cited.

[3] The trust form is also used in some business situations. *See generally* Harry G. Henn and John R. Alexander, Laws of Corporations and Other Business Enterprises §§ 58-67 (West 3d ed. 1983).

[4] These trusts are sometimes called "lifetime" trusts and sometimes go by the Latin term "intervivos" trusts.

[5] Both individuals and companies can be trustees.

[6] *See generally* Scoles, Halbach, Link & Roberts at 347-352.

[7] Although it does not apply directly against trusts' duration, the Rule Against Perpetuities is the principal device for limiting how long trusts can continue. *See* Chapter 12, *infra*.

Living trusts were given a big boost by Norman Dacey's book, *How to Avoid Probate!*, which first appeared in 1965.[8] As the title suggests, one of the principal attractions of a living trust is that its assets are not considered probate assets.[9] As a result, the costs of probate—both in terms of time and of money—are saved. Moreover, the terms of the trust are not part of the public record.[10]

Trusts can also save estate taxes. In particular, they provide a means for splitting family assets among various family members to maximize the use of the unified credit available under federal gift and estate tax law.[11] Because tax savings can be very large, estate planners sometimes overemphasize achieving those savings, at the expense of other client goals. As always, the client should be the one weighing the choices.

Another client choice is whether to use a living trust, a testamentary trust, or both. Of course, if management is needed while the settlor is alive, then he would need to create a living trust. If the trust will not be needed until the settlor's death, either option can be used. A testamentary trust could be created as part of the will, or a living trust could be opened, but left to sit as an empty shell[12] until death.[13]

In general, living trusts are more complicated to set up, but are more flexible once they are in operation. Testamentary trusts are easier to establish, but generally subject to more restrictions when funded. If someone other than the settlor is to serve as trustee of a living trust, that person (or institution) must take part in creating and amending the trust. On the other hand, a testamentary trust can be set up or changed unilaterally. Once the testator has died, however, a testamentary trust becomes subject to the jurisdiction of the probate court. Regular reporting usually will be required; there may be restrictions on investments; the court may retain control even if the family moves out of the jurisdiction. A living trust

---

[8] In 1993, the fifth edition was issued.

[9] Be aware that even if the trust assets do not "pass through" probate, they may be subject to the claims of creditors or surviving spouses. *See* § 12[E], *infra*.

[10] The popularity of revocable living trusts has made them good moneymakers for financial planners and for lawyers. When the two professions work too closely together, trouble can follow. *See, e.g.,* Committee on Prof'l Ethics v. Baker, 492 N.W.2d 695 (Iowa 1992) (lawyer reprimanded for aiding in the unauthorized practice of law and for engaging in conflicts of interest).

The "selling" of living trusts to clients who don't need them continues to draw criticism. *See* Richard Gould, *The Living Trust: Fact v. Fiction*, 15 Quinnipac. Prob. L.J. 133 (2000); David M. Patrick, *Living Trusts: Snake Oil or Better Than Sliced Bread?*, 27 Wm. Mitchell L. Rev. 1083 (2000).

[11] *See* § 62[C], *infra*.

[12] Traditionally, the law has required a trust to have some asset before the trust will be given effect. *See* § 12[B], *infra*. Because a "shell" which is effectively funded at death has many estate planning uses, courts and legislatures have validated "unfunded" trusts. *See* § 16, *infra*.

[13] Sometimes these trusts are funded before death, by someone acting under a durable power of attorney on behalf of a beneficiary who has become disabled and needs the management features a trust provides. For more on durable powers of attorney, see § 22[B], *infra*.

avoids probate and its attendant restrictions. To overgeneralize a bit, testamentary trusts are usually easier unless you have to use them.[14]

§ 12   Creation

An important reason that trusts are so wonderfully flexible is that the law requires so little to create a trust. Generally agreed upon elements are:[1] an intention to create a fiduciary relationship, property that is transferred to (or held by)[2] the trustee, a beneficiary, a valid trust purpose[3] and compliance with formalities (like the Statute of Frauds). Such a list is misleading, however, because courts are so flexible in interpreting the elements that it can hardly be said any particular one is required in any particular case.[4] The key concept is creation of a fiduciary relationship by separating ownership into two parts: "legal title" in a trustee with management duties,[5] and "equitable title" in a beneficiary who can enforce those duties. If a court has confidence that a trust could be useful and would not offend some identifiable policy, it may try very hard to find the necessary elements.[6] In virtually all planning contexts, moreover, the elements are easy to meet.

[A] Intent

Just as a testator must have testamentary intention to create a will,[7]

---

[14] For this reason, many planners recommend that parents of minor children put contingent testamentary trusts into their wills, to protect the children in case both parents die young. They are easy to set up, and the expectation is that they will never have to be used. If tragedy strikes, the children are protected.

[1] *See* Andersen & Bloom at 344; Haskell at 73-80.

[2] If someone other than the settlor is to be the trustee, subsidiary rules regarding whether there has been a sufficient "delivery" apply. Of course, if the settlor declares herself to be the trustee, there is no need for delivery. Courts could save a gift that fails for want of delivery by applying the fiction that a trust was declared with the settlor as trustee. Traditionally, they have not. *See* Farmers' Loan & Trust Co. v. Winthrop, 144 N.E. 686 (N.Y. 1924). For the view that they should, see Sarajane Love, *Imperfect Gifts as Declarations of Trust: An Unapologetic Anomaly*, 67 Ky. L.J. 309 (1979).

[3] "A trust may be created only to the extent its purposes are lawful, not contrary to public policy, and possible to achieve." UTC § 404.

[4] *See* Shaffer, Mooney & Boettcher, at 97-98.

[5] On rare occasions, one person will give property to a "trustee" to hold for someone else, but will attach no duties. The trust is treated as a "passive," or "dry," trust and both the legal and equitable titles vest in the erstwhile beneficiary. The "trustee" has nothing. *See generally* Bogert, Trusts § 46; Restatement (Third) of Trusts § 6.

[6] For example, courts will not let trusts fail for want of a trustee; they will just appoint one. *See* Restatement (Second) of Trusts § 108. Despite their questionable status as "beneficiaries" who could enforce the trust, animals and monuments have been protected by "honorary" trusts. *See, e.g., In re* Searight's Estate, 95 N.E.2d 779 (Ohio App. 1950) (a dog); *In re* Byrne's Estate, 100 A.2d 157 (N.H. 1953) (a monument). Despite the insubstantiality of a beneficial interest in a life insurance policy, such an interest is enough "property" to support a trust virtually anywhere. *See, e.g.,* Brown v. Brown, 604 So. 2d 365 (Ala. 1992); Ala. Code § 35-4-260.

[7] *See* § 7[A][1], *supra.*

so must a settlor[8] have the intention to create a trust.[9] Usually the intention is quite clear: a multi-page document is labeled "Trust Agreement," or a will section is titled "Family Trust." However, trusts can arise easily without such formalities. In *Jimenez v. Lee*,[10] for example, Elizabeth sued her father for breach of a trust she said arose when her grandmother had purchased a U.S. Savings Bond in the names of Elizabeth and her parents. Everyone agreed that the money was to be used for Elizabeth's education. The question was whether the intention to benefit Elizabeth was enough to impose the stringent duties of a trustee on Elizabeth's father. Though the word "trust" had not been used, the court held that a trust had been created. Because he later treated the trust casually,[11] the father was held liable for breach of fiduciary duty.[12] The case illustrates a simple-sounding, but important, principle: once we have a trust, we have a trust. Although a trust may be created easily, even casually, the full range of fiduciary duties burdens the trustee.[13]

Poorly drafted documents may not make clear whether the settlor intended to impose duties on a particular beneficiary, or only expressed a desire that the beneficiary behave in a certain way. Suppose Jose Hernandez left a will giving $5,000 to his wife, Maria, and expressing the "desire" that she use the money to "take care of our children." Is Maria a trustee or is the money hers to spend as she likes? The result will depend upon whether a court finds the language regarding the children to be "mandatory" (a trust) or "precatory" (no obligation).[14] Cases like these tend

---

[8] For simplicity and consistency, this term is used in this text to describe anyone who creates a trust, whether living or testamentary. Depending upon the situation and local law and custom, others might call this person a "trustor," "testator," or "donor."

[9] If the trust is testamentary, standard rules regarding testamentary capacity apply. *See* § 7[A][2], *supra*. Courts disagree about whether persons creating living trusts need a higher level of capacity. *See* Charles F. Gibbs & Cindy D. Hanson, *Degree of Capacity Required to Create An Inter Vivos Trust*, Tr. & Est., Dec. 1993, at 14. The Restatement distinguishes between revocable living trusts (testamentary capacity) and irrevocable living trusts (capacity for making lifetime transfers). Restatement (Third) of Trusts § 11. *See also* UTC § 601.

[10] 547 P.2d 126 (Or. 1976).

[11] For example, he kept no separate records for the fund.

[12] For another example, see *In re Koziell's Trust*, 194 A.2d 230 (Pa. 1963). There the decedent, who had named his sister as beneficiary of his life insurance, had stated that his sister would "take care of his boys" with the proceeds. This testimony was sufficient to create a trust for the benefit of the sons.

[13] If a lawyer could treat trust obligations so casually, consider how easily non-lawyer clients might make the same mistake. Clients are often tempted to try to save money by appointing family members (or agreeing to serve themselves) as trustees, despite their lack of expertise. Becoming a trustee is a serious business, and clients should be fully informed of the risks before deciding how to proceed. For an example of a niece who was surcharged for breach of duty, see *Witmer v. Blair*, 588 S.W.2d 222 (Mo. Ct. App. 1979), discussed in § 56, *infra*.

[14] A different theory applies in the similar situation of one person giving property to another, subject to a requirement that the donee pay someone else some amount of money. For example, Bob's will may give a farm to Mary, subject to Mary paying $50.00 a month to Bob's child. Mary would hold the property free from any trust, but subject to an "equitable charge" in the child's favor. The child would have a security interest in the farm. If Bob gave the farm "on the condition that Mary pay," then Mary may also be personally liable for the payments. *See generally* Scott § 10.

to be resolved very much on their own facts.[15] Some relevant questions would be: Did the will create any other, more elaborate, trusts?[16] Did Maria get any outright gifts under the will? Did the children? Does Maria have other assets? Do the children? In other contexts, were Jose's "desires" interpreted as orders?[17] The stream of litigation about precatory language teaches us to be specific when drafting documents.[18] If a trust is intended, say so. If not, use language like "I hope, but I impose no obligation."

[B] Trust Property

To have a trust, there must be trust property.[19] That seems obvious enough. After all, there must be *something* for a trustee to protect and manage. In many cases, there is really no question about trust property. Assets from an estate fill a testamentary trust; stocks and bonds fill a living trust.[20] In some situations the items claimed to be held in trust can be very insubstantial, like future profits or the beneficial interest in a life insurance policy.[21] Then the question becomes whether the item can be defined as "property" for the purpose of sustaining a trust. In answering that question, courts should ask whether allowing the particular trust in question would

---

[15] *See, e.g., In re* Estate of Martin, 300 N.Y.S.2d 751 (N.Y. App. Div. 1969) ("request" was mandatory); Brannon v. Morgan, 106 S.W.2d 841 (Tex. Civ. App. 1937) ("request" was precatory); *In re* Estate of Hogan, 146 N.W.2d 257 (Iowa 1966) ("recommendation" was not a mandatory direction); Farmer v. Broadhead, 230 So. 2d 779 (Miss. 1970) ("recommended" use of a trust form referred to in testator's will was mandatory). For some hypothetical examples, see Restatement (Second) of Trusts § 25; Restatement (Third) of Trusts § 13 cmt. d. *See generally* L.A. McElwee, *Precatory Language in Wills: Mere Utterances of the Sibyl?*, 11 Prob. L.J. 145 (1992).

[16] If so, this language would look less mandatory by comparison. Having shown how to create a trust clearly, Jose would have been less likely to have used this casual language to create one.

[17] Some authorities suggest that "requests" to family members are likely to be polite directions. *See* Colton v. Colton, 127 U.S. 300, 32 L. Ed. 138, 8 S. Ct. 1164 (1888). However, in *Burton v. Irwin*, 181 S.E.2d 624 (Va. 1971), a statement that "my brother knows my wishes and will carry them out, to the best of his ability" was insufficient to create a trust with the brother as trustee.

[18] For an example of a "request" which doomed the whole will, see *In re* Moody, 154 A.2d 165 (Me. 1959). The will asked the executor to pay each witness $5.00 as a token of appreciation. The court found the request to be mandatory, so the witnesses got legacies, and the will failed for lack of disinterested witnesses. For more on interested witnesses, see § 7[B][2][e], *supra*.

[19] Sometimes the term "res" is used to denote trust property.

[20] An attempted trust may fail because a court cannot tell what property the settlor intended to put in trust. For example, a will might say, "I give one of my bank accounts in trust for Jane." Unless there is other evidence of which account should be for Jane, the attempted trust will fail. *See* Wilkerson v. McClary, 647 S.W.2d 79 (Tex. Ct. App. 1983). The requirement that particular property must be ascertainable has been criticized in Jane B. Baron, *The Trust Res and Donative Intent*, 61 Tul. L. Rev. 45 (1986).

[21] Or the chance of getting football tickets at Nebraska. *See* Kully v. Goldman, 305 N.W.2d 800 (Neb. 1981) (not enough to support a trust). Interestingly, the rights to acquire those tickets are a sufficient property interest to make them subject to court division in a marriage dissolution action. Kullbom v. Kullbom, 306 N.W.2d 844 (Neb. 1981).

offend some identifiable policy. Instead, they may accept uncritically a characterization of something as "property" or "not property," and then use that characterization as if it were a reason for allowing or not allowing the trust.

Brainard v. Commissioner[22] is a well-known case which held that future profits are not "property" for the purpose of creating a trust. In reaching that result, the court did not explain *why* future profits could not be the subject matter of a trust. The case involved a taxpayer who was trying to reduce his income taxes by spreading his gains among a variety of family members.[23] In December 1927, he orally declared to his wife and mother that he was holding the profits he would make from trading stocks in 1928 in trust for various family members. The IRS argued that no trust was created at that time, so that all trading profits earned in 1928 should be attributable to the taxpayer. The court agreed, because there were no 1928 profits in existence at the time of the declaration of trust. Citing the first Restatement of Trusts, the court said "an interest which has not come into existence . . . can not be held in trust."[24]

Brainard can be contrasted with *Speelman v. Pascal*,[25] which involved the written assignment of profits from the stage and film versions of what later became "My Fair Lady." At the time of the assignment, the assignor, producer Gabriel Pascal, had a license from George Bernard Shaw's estate to produce a musical based on the play "Pygmalion." Pascal had not, however, arranged for the production of "My Fair Lady." He was only assigning the profits he hoped to make from a show he hoped to produce. Noting that "[t]here are many instances of courts enforcing assignments of rights to sums which were expected thereafter to be come due to the assignor,"[26] the court saw no particular reason not to honor this assignment.

Clearly, "future profits" are *something*. They can be transferred. They can be valued.[27] Why would *Brainard* say they are not enough of a "thing" so as to be a trust asset? In *Brainard*, the court may have been concerned about other problems and used the insubstantiality of "future profits" as an easy way to avoid recognizing the trust. One concern may have been the possibility of tax fraud. The court may have wondered whether any

---

[22] 91 F.2d 880 (7th Cir. 1937), *cert. dismissed*, 303 U.S. 665, 82 L. Ed. 1122, 58 S. Ct. 748 (1938).

[23] Always be wary of tax cases as authority for statements regarding other areas of the law. Courts handling tax questions may be relatively unfamiliar with the state law upon which the federal tax law depends, and may be tempted to interpret state law with any eye to what they view as the best *tax* result.

[24] *Brainard*, 91 F.2d at 881. *See* Restatement of Trusts § 75.

[25] 178 N.E.2d 723 (N.Y. 1961).

[26] 178 N.E.2d at 725.

[27] *See, e.g.*, Rockey v. Bacon, 470 P.2d 804 (Kan. 1970) (Lessees obtained damages for loss of future profits from wrongful termination of lease.); McPherson v. Schlemmer, 749 P.2d 51 (Mont. 1988) (Rancher who leased grazing pasture and subsequently lost herd of breeding cows in a highway accident could recover lost future profits in a negligence claim against the owner of the property.).

declaration really took place in December 1927, rather than, say, in late 1928, when the taxpayer realized how much money he had made that year. The only evidence of the taxpayer's declaration of trust was statements by interested witnesses. Another explanation could be that the court saw the trust—even if genuine—as an inappropriate attempt to avoid taxes.[28] The court may have refused to recognize the trust in order to keep the taxpayer from separating his income-producing property from the profits on that property.[29] If any of these reasons were behind the court's decision, it should have said so. The sad consequence of *Brainard* is that now we have a case which says future profits are not a sufficient enough property interest to be the subject matter of a trust, although in different circumstances, someone's legitimate goals could be met by creating just such a trust.[30]

Trust law is flexible enough to allow future profits to be a sufficient "interest" to sustain a trust. If future profits seem too insubstantial for that purpose, consider two examples of "interests" that clearly are big enough: contingent remainders[31] and beneficial interests in life insurance. Suppose that Rattan places property in trust, with income to be paid to his wife for life and at her death the principal paid to whomever his wife identifies in her will, and if she fails to name anyone, to his daughter, if she is then living, and if not, to his son. The son's interest is clearly a contingent remainder;[32] one might say a *very* contingent remainder. Because contingent remainders are recognized as "interests in property," that remainder itself could be placed in a different trust.[33] For a second example, imagine yourself as owner of a life insurance policy; you pay the premiums; you can cancel at any time. You name the First National Bank as beneficiary of the policy, with any proceeds to be administered according to an agreement you have with the bank. Although the only asset of the trust is its possible future claim to the insurance money, the trust would be valid in most states.[34] Surely the future profits contemplated in *Brainard* are no less substantial than the contingent remainder or the possible claim against the insurance company in these hypothetical examples.

A trust needs property. The whole idea of a trust is that someone owes a set of duties to someone else with respect to something. As courts decide

---

[28] There is certainly a long history, dating from the Middle Ages, of lawyers designing devices to avoid taxes, and then courts and legislatures closing those "loopholes."

[29] Now it is well established that the fruits of property are taxed to the owner. If Hassan owns income-producing property, but transfers the rights to future income from that property to Nadia, the income will still be taxed to Hassan. *See* Helvering v. Horst, 311 U.S. 112, 85 L. Ed. 75, 61 S. Ct. 144 (1940).

[30] For a different perspective on the case, consider whether a court would have been as reluctant to validate the trust if the trust *beneficiaries* had been suing the settlor for failure to carry out the trust.

[31] Thanks to Professors Dukeminier and Johanson for the suggestion of comparing future profits and contingent remainders.

[32] If your memory of contingent remainders is a bit dim, see § 35[B][2][b], *infra*.

[33] *See* Restatement of Prop. § 162 and Restatement (Second) of Trusts § 78.

[34] *See, e.g.*, Gordon v. Portland Trust Bank, 271 P.2d 653 (Or. 1954); Restatement (Second) of Trusts § 82 cmt. b. Some states have statutes on the question. *See* UPC § 2-511.

whether something is "property" in this context, however, they should interpret the requirement flexibly, so as to validate individuals' estate plans unless allowing a particular trust would offend some identifiable (and identified) policy.

[C] Beneficiary [35]

Just as virtually all trusts clearly have property, so do they have identifiable beneficiaries separate from the trustee. Doctrinally, beneficiaries are required in order to achieve the separation of legal and equitable title which characterizes the trust relationship. [36] A trustee must owe duties to someone *else.* Otherwise, there would be no one to enforce the duties. In marginal cases in which courts are searching for identifiable beneficiaries, they again face the temptation to be rigid and the opportunity to be flexible.

Morsman v. Commissioner [37] is another tax case which grew out of the 1920's stock market boom that gave us *Brainard.*

Again, a trust that would have saved taxes was invalidated by an ungenerous interpretation of trust law. Robert Morsman sought to lower his income taxes by creating a trust whose income would be taxed at a lower rate. He declared himself (in writing) to be the trustee of particular securities he then owned. After five years of adding the trust income to the principal, the trustee was to pay the trust income to Morsman for life. At his death, the principal was to go to his issue, or if he had none, to his widow, or if he left neither, to his heirs at law. The problem was that he had neither a wife nor children at the time he declared the trust. The court held that without identifiable, living beneficiaries other than the trustee, the trust failed. Morsman (as beneficiary) could not be expected to enforce the trust against Morsman (as trustee), [38] and the court could find no one else to do so. The court declined the opportunity to save the trust by viewing Morsman's brother (and expectant heir) as an identifiable beneficiary. As in *Brainard*, we see a court undermining the flexibility of substantive trust law in order to reach a tax result. [39]

------

[35] A beneficiary may be called a *cestui que trust*, a term from Law French.

[36] *See generally* William F. Fratcher, *Trustee as Sole Trustee and Only Ascertainable Beneficiary*, 47 Mich. L. Rev. 907 (1949).

[37] 90 F.2d 18 (8th Cir. 1937).

[38] When the trustee and sole beneficiary are the same, the legal and equitable titles of each are sometimes said to merge. When this situation occurs at the attempted creation of a trust, a more careful explanation is that no trust was created because no separation of title took place. When, after a trust has been created, the trustee becomes the sole beneficiary (for example, if someone dies), the trust may end by merger. In some circumstances courts will intervene for equitable reasons to prevent a merger. *See* Bogert & Bogert, The Law of Trusts and Trustees § 1003.

[39] Professor Haskell characterizes the result in *Morsman* as "not sound and . . . probably anomalous." Haskell at 85 n.24. *See also* Restatement (Third) of Trusts § 2 cmt. h ("None of the intended [trust] beneficiaries need be identified or in existence at the time of the creation of the trust, provided one or more beneficiaries will be ascertainable within the period allowed by the applicable rule against perpetuities.").

Even under the court's approach, the trust would have worked had the facts been slightly different. If Morsman had transferred the property to someone else, rather than having declared himself to be the trustee, he would have been able to enforce the trust as life tenant.[40] If he had had any children, they would have provided the separation of title the court sought. If Morsman had been married, the remainder to his widow would have been enough to give his wife an equitable interest in the trust.[41]

A doctrine flexible enough to find separation of title when the only beneficiaries are contingent remaindermen who may never benefit, also ought to allow trusts even if all the beneficiaries are unborn.[42] Such a trust might be particularly attractive to a grandparent wishing to provide an education fund for anticipated grandchildren. Martin might, for example, declare that he held property in trust for the children of his son, Howard. Interest on the fund could be accumulated until Howard had children, and they could then enforce it. If Howard had no children, the trust would fail. So long as we have good evidence that Martin intended such a trust, there is no good policy reason for prohibiting it.

Even if the separation of title question is not present, beneficiaries of a private trust must be identifiable.[43] The trustee must be able to tell who should get the property, and a court should have a standard by which to judge whether the trustee distributes trust benefits to the right persons. The question in any particular case is whether the description is sufficient to meet those goals. Some are easy: "children," "husband," "wife," "nieces," "nephews."[44] On the other hand, "relatives" has caused some trouble. If construed to mean *any* relation, the description is probably too broad to be enforceable.[45] If construed to mean those relatives who would take under the intestate statute, the term has enough specificity.[46] "Friends" is too broad.[47]

Somewhat different considerations arise when the settlor names someone, usually the trustee or executor, to choose among the members of a particular class. Will an indefinite term like "friends" carry sufficient content if the settlor gives the trustee the duty to select which friends benefit? *Clark v. Campbell*[48] said no. In *Clark*, the testator wanted tangible

---

[40] For more on life estates, see § 34[C], *infra*. Interestingly, Morsman later turned the property over to the United States Trust Company as Successor Trustee. By then it was too late.

[41] She would have had a contingent remainder contingent on her being his widow.

[42] *See* Haskell at 84.

[43] This rule does not apply to charitable trusts, which are characterized by the lack of particular, identified beneficiaries. Rather, charitable trusts distribute their funds to benefit the society in general. *See* § 15, *infra*.

[44] Although courts routinely sustain gifts like these, questions arise regarding which class members qualify to take. *See* §§ 41 & 42, *infra*.

[45] *See, e.g.*, Binns v. Vick, 538 S.W.2d 283 (Ark. 1976).

[46] *See, e.g.*, Reagh v. Kelley, 89 Cal. Rptr. 425 (Cal. App. 1970).

[47] *See, e.g.*, Early v. Arnold, 89 S.E. 900 (Va. 1916).

[48] 133 A. 166 (N.H. 1926).

personal property (books, photos, artwork) to go to his friends as mementoes of the friendship. Rather than listing which individual items should go to which person, he gave them all to his trustees with the direction to distribute them "to such of my friends as they, my trustees, shall select."[49] Because it found no criterion by which to judge the trustees' choices, the court invalidated the attempted trust. In addition, the court refused to sustain the gift as a discretionary power of appointment.[50] Because of the duty, as opposed to the option, to exercise the choice, the court characterized the power as "imperative."[51] It then applied a stricter rule for identification of trust beneficiaries than is generally applied to the identification of beneficiaries of powers of appointment.[52] The result: the testator's friends lost, and a "resulting trust" gave the property to the residuary takers under the will.[53]

The view expressed in *Clark* is the prevailing rule, but has been under attack for a long time.[54] The Restatement (Second) of Property seeks to reform the rule. It says that rather than failing, a provision like that in *Clark* "should be construed to give the [trustees] a power of appointment exercisable within a reasonable period of time . . . ."[55] The Uniform Trust Code is direct: "A power in a trustee to select a beneficiary from an indefinite class is valid."[56]

The beneficiary requirement also causes problems when someone wants to leave money to take care of a pet or an inanimate object, like a grave site. Recognizing that such funds serve a social purpose, courts usually allow them under a theory of "honorary trusts."[57] The "trustee" who is given

---

[49] 133 A. at 168. Recall that UPC § 2-513 allows a list that can be changed after the will's execution. *See* § 8[B], *supra*.

[50] A power of appointment is a power created by the owner of property giving someone else the power to transfer the property. The permissible transferees might, or might not, be limited to a particular group. *See* Chapter 10, *infra*.

[51] "Imperative" powers are also sometimes known as powers "in trust" because they impose a duty. The latter term can be confusing, however, because trusts can also include discretionary powers. For further discussion of imperative powers, see § 39[C], *infra*.

[52] Rather than requiring the entire membership of a class to be ascertainable (the general trust test), powers of appointment are valid if just some members of the group are ascertainable. *See* George E. Palmer, *Private Trusts For Indefinite Beneficiaries*, 71 Mich. L. Rev. 359 (1972).

[53] A "resulting trust" in this context is a theory to explain what happens when an express trust fails (here for lack of identifiable beneficiaries). Under the will, the trustees were given legal title, but because a trust was intended, they cannot hold the property on their own behalf. Instead, they hold title on behalf of the testator's estate and are directed to transfer the property to the alternative takers (here the residuary beneficiaries) under the will. *See generally* Bogert at 281-283; Restatement (Third) of Trusts §§ 7-8. For more on resulting trusts in different contexts, see §§ 12[F] and 35[A].

[54] *See generally* George E. Palmer, *The Effect of Indefiniteness on the Validity of Trusts and Powers of Appointment*, 10 UCLA L. Rev. 241 (1963).

[55] Restatement (Second) of Property § 12.1 cmt. e. *See also* Restatement (Second) of Trusts § 122; Restatement (Third) of Trusts § 46(2).

[56] UTC § 402(c)

[57] *See* Scott at 244-246. Such trusts are likely to be invalidated if they can extend beyond

the money has the choice of honoring the trust or of returning the money (by way of a resulting trust) to the estate. The Uniform Trust Code goes further and allows a settlor (or a court) to appoint someone to enforce the trust.[58]

[D] Trustee

The requirement that a trust have a trustee is the least onerous of the basic elements. If a trust is intended, but no trustee is named, or if a sitting trustee dies or resigns, a court will appoint a trustee rather than let the trust fail. No one can be forced to serve as a trustee, but once someone takes the job, trustee duties attach.[59]

Settlors should choose trustees with great care.[60] Their duties are many and varied.[61] They must handle both the financial and the personal sides of administration. Identifying a trustee who can monitor investments, file tax forms, *and* make sensitive decisions about how much to spend for a beneficiary's "comfortable support" can be difficult. In an effort to combine professional competence and a personal touch, settlors sometimes appoint two co-trustees, one a corporation and the other an individual. The corporate trustee, usually a bank, provides investment expertise,[62] and the individual provides the personal touch. A co-trustee arrangement can be unwieldy, however, because all trustees traditionally must join in acting on the trust's behalf.[63] To avoid that problem, you might want to suggest that a client consider naming a single trustee, and also naming a trusted friend or relative to serve as a "trust advisor." The trust document could require the trustee to consult with (or get the approval of) the advisor before

---

the period established by the Rule Against Perpetuities. Sometimes a court will strain to save such a trust from the Rule. *See In re* Searight's Estate, 95 N.E.2d 779 (Ohio App. 1950) (Court calculated that funds for a dog's care would run out before the end of the Perpetuities period.). *See generally* Chapter 12, *infra*.

[58] UTC §§ 408(b) & 409.

[59] Recall the ease with which the father became a trustee for his daughter in *Jimenez v. Lee*, discussed in § 12[A], *supra*.

[60] *See generally* McGovern & Kurtz at 478-490; Kathryn A. Johnson & Adam J. Wiensch, *Trustee Selection for Successful Trust Administration*, 8 Prob. & Prop., May/June, 1994, at 38. For a discussion of the special problems and risks that arise when a lawyer also serves as a trustee, see Pamela A. Monopoli, *Fiduciary Duty: A New Ethical Paradigm for Lawyer/Fiduciaries*, 67 Mo. L. Rev. 309 (2002).

[61] *See* Chapter 13, *infra*.

[62] A corporate trustee also provides continuity. Because banks seldom go out of business, they are particularly attractive as successor trustees who can take over when the individual trustees die.

[63] *See* Scott § 184. *But see* UTC § 703(a) (majority decision enough).

Funneling every decision, especially investment choices, through two trustees can be costly. A drafter might try to avoid this problem by giving sole power over investments to one trustee. *See* Bogert & Bogert § 555. *See also* Tex. Rev. Civ. Stat. Ann. tit. 9 § 114.003 (If trust document excludes a trustee from investment or other decisions, the excluded trustee is not liable for losses suffered as a result of those decisions.).

deciding whether and how to distribute the trust's funds.[64] To give the advisor even more authority, the client could grant the advisor the power to order the trustee to spend trust funds as the advisor directs.[65]

Meeting each of the minimum elements necessary to create a trust—intent, property, beneficiaries, and a trustee—is seldom a problem in the real world of estate planning. In marginal cases, however, courts have sometimes interpreted those elements strictly, without regard to the goal of effectuating a particular individual's intention. Once a court has assured itself of the trustworthiness of the evidence supporting the trust, it ought to allow the trust unless some strong public policy consideration indicates otherwise.[66] Certainly, that is how many courts have handled the problem of revocability discussed in the next section.

[E] The Problem of Revocability

Living trusts will be recognized even though the settlor reserves a power to revoke.[67] In most states, the power to revoke a living trust must be reserved expressly in the document.[68] A few states cover the point by statute, putting the burden on those who want *irrevocable* trusts to say so.[69] If the document provides for a specific method of revocation (as it should), the settlor must follow that method.[70] The UTC even allows revocation by a later will.[71]

Revocable trusts pose a problem: they can have a *"testamentary* look."[72] Consider a settlor who creates a trust giving a remainder to his wife, but retaining a life estate (to secure present enjoyment of the property) and a power to revoke (in case he changes his mind). The form is different, but

---

[64] For an example of a trust which required the trustee to get approval from a family member before distributing trust assets to one particular beneficiary, see *Shelley v. Shelley*, 354 P.2d 282 (Or. 1960), discussed in § 13, *infra*.

[65] The advisor would have a power of appointment. *See* Chapter 10, *infra*. If the advisor is wealthy, estate tax concerns may influence how broad to make the advisor's power. *See* §§ 37[D] & 62[A][2], *infra*.

[66] Compare the policy of interpreting Statute of Wills provisions in light of that statute's overall goals. *See* § 7[B][1], *supra*.

[67] A testamentary trust, as part of a will, is revocable under wills law. *See* § 9, *supra*.

[68] Scott on Trusts, § 330.

[69] UTC § 602(a) (applies prospectively).

[70] *See* Estate of Kirk, 907 P.2d 794 (Idaho 1995) (settlor amended trust to create a new amendment procedure and then followed the new procedure), *but see* UTC § 602(c)(I) (recognizing revocation if the settlor *substantially complies* with a method provided in the trust.) *See also In re* Estate of Pilafas, 836 P.2d 420 (Ariz. App. 1992) (trust not found after settlor's death; not presumed revoked). Compare the wills doctrine that a will last known to be in the testator's possession but not found at the testator's death will be presumed to have been revoked. *See* § 9[B], *supra*.

[71] UTC § 602(c)(2)(A). The provision could cause problems of interpretation if the trust and the later will refer to the same disposition of property. *See* § 21 *infra*.

[72] The phrase is from Justice Holmes, who used it referring to a deed. Bromley v. Mitchell, 30 N.E. 83, 84 (Mass. 1892).

the substance is close to the situation of a testator who retains ownership and executes a will leaving everything to his wife. The parallel is even closer if the settlor declares himself to be the trustee. Virtually all courts will sustain such a trust against the charge that it is an attempted testamentary transfer which should be invalidated for not complying with the Statute of Wills.[73] They agree that during the life of the settlor, the remainderman got enough of an interest to sustain the trust as a lifetime gift, but they sometimes struggle to get there.

Farkas v. Williams[74] illustrates the difficulties. Albert Farkas bought some mutual fund shares, each time signing a declaration of trust which identified Farkas as the trustee of the shares and as current income beneficiary. His employee, Richard Williams, was named to take the shares at Farkas' death. In his personal capacity, Farkas retained the right to change the beneficiary and to revoke the whole trust. As trustee, he retained the right to sell any shares he liked and then retain the proceeds in his personal capacity. Farkas' heirs challenged the validity of the trust. The court saw two questions: whether Williams acquired an interest during Farkas' lifetime, and whether Farkas retained so much control as to invalidate the documents as attempted testamentary dispositions. The questions really reflect two sides of the same coin. If Farkas kept too much, Williams got too little.

Valid.

The search for some sort of present transfer to Williams reflects the traditional approach to resolving cases like these: if Williams got something, the trust is valid; if not, it fails. Pretty clearly, Williams did not get very much; he got so little that the court had trouble naming it. Even so, the court said it was enough. This court's willingness to find something when little was there contrasts with the *Brainard* court's unwillingness to see future profits as enough property to sustain a trust.[75] In each case, however, the search for a magical property interest distracts the court from the question of whether such arrangements ought to be allowed.

In examining whether Farkas retained too many powers as settlor, the court rightly notes that if someone retains the power to revoke, subsidiary powers like changing beneficiaries and trustees are largely irrelevant. After all, one can always revoke and start over. The court is also troubled by the powers which Farkas retained as trustee. His heirs argued that as a practical matter he owed no fiduciary duties to Williams. Conceding that Williams would never sue Farkas (because then Farkas would simply revoke the trust), the court nonetheless maintains that "Williams has rights

---

[73] Inter vivos trusts will seldom meet the witness requirement, and few are holographs. *See* §§ 7[B][2] and [3], *supra*.

[74] 125 N.E.2d 600 (Ill. 1955). For an insightful commentary putting this case in context, see John H. Langbein, *The Nonprobate Revolution and the Future of the Law of Succession*, 97 Harv. L. Rev. 1108, 1126-1130 (1984). For more on the modern doctrine of revocable living trusts, see Restatement (Third) of Trusts § 25.

[75] *See* § 12[B], *supra*. Indeed, for another perspective on how "big" Williams' interest is, ask yourself whether it is enough of an interest to be the subject matter of a trust *created by Williams* for someone else.

the same as any beneficiary, although it may not be feasible for him to exercise them."[76] It speculates that Williams might have had a claim against Farkas' estate if Farkas had, for example, given away the stock or lost it by having pledged it as security for his personal debts.[77] Just as the size of Williams' interest seems small, so also is Farkas' real-world liability to his beneficiary.[78]

Sustaining this trust because Williams has "something" or because Farkas owes "some duties" tells us little about why, in any particular case, we should allow the plan to stand, or even how to make that judgment. Fortunately, at the end of its opinion, the court moves away from identifying interests and liabilities. Rather, it focuses on the reality of the transaction: it was formal, provided reliable evidence of intention, and lacked any hint of overreaching. Ultimately, the failure to have the witnesses required by the Statute of Wills was not as important as the trustworthiness of the transaction.

Farkas illustrates that, in spite of theoretical hang-ups, courts often will validate trusts when the trust seems genuine and other policies are not offended.[79] While courts might be willing to allow a trust to pass property in the absence of competing claims, when those claims arise, however, courts might well want to ignore the trust form. The law is coming to recognize that a trust might be recognized for one purpose, but not for another. Two examples follow. One involves creditors' claims; the other, claims of a surviving spouse. In each case, the court ignored the trust form and allowed the claim.

State Street Bank & Trust Co. v. Reiser[80] involved creditors' claims in Wilfred Dunnebier's estate. Dunnebier was a home-builder who set up a living trust to hold the capital stock of five closely-held corporations. He retained both the power to revoke and the power to direct the disposition of income and principal during his lifetime. When he died, a bank tried to collect its substantial working-capital loan, only to find that the probate estate was not large enough to cover the debt. The bank then sought trust assets. Under the traditional rule, the trust form would be honored; the trust property would be treated as different from the settlor's property. The

---

[76] 125 N.E.2d at 608.

[77] Professor Langbein suggests that if such a claim were made, a court would treat the case in two steps. The action claimed to be a breach of fiduciary duty would be viewed as an act revoking the trust. Then the transaction could proceed free of trust obligations. John H. Langbein, *The Nonprobate Revolution and the Future of the Law of Succession*, 97 Harv. L. Rev. 1108, 1127-28 (1984). *But see* Breeze v. Breeze, 428 N.E.2d 286 (Ind. Ct. App. 1981) (suggesting that the trustee's breach of duty might be grounds for removal as trustee, but not grounds for finding the trust was revoked).

[78] Section 603(a) of the UTC solves the problem by stating: if the settlor has the capacity to revoke the trust, the trustee only owes duties to the settlor and not other beneficiaries.

[79] Notice the similarity between upholding a trust like Farkas' and allowing a will under a harmless error rule. *See* § 7[B][4][c], *supra*.

[80] 389 N.E.2d 768 (Mass. App. 1979).

fact that the settlor retained the power to revoke the whole trust would not change the result.[81]

This court, however, recognized reality. Reasoning that it would be "excessive obeisance to the form in which property is held to prevent creditors from reaching property placed in trust under such terms,"[82] the court allowed the claim.[83] Though the form of this trust resembles the form of Farkas' trust, the different results are justified because different interests were involved.[84]

A similar recognition of substance over form took place in *Sullivan v. Burkin*.[85] Ernest had created a living trust, with himself as trustee, retaining a power to revoke the trust and directing that income be payable to himself during his life. When he left a will that left out his wife, she exercised her statutory right to claim a share of the estate.[86] She also sought a share of the trust assets. Reaffirming a position like the one taken in *Farkas*, the court rejected her argument that the trust was an invalid testamentary disposition. Recognizing the general validity of trusts in which settlors retain extensive powers, however, did not prevent the court from holding that *for the purpose of spousal elections*, the trust form would be ignored and the trust assets subject to the spouse's claim.[87]

spouse can reach assets in a revocable trust.

Revocable trusts look a lot like wills. Fortunately, courts have been able to look past the similarity and to recognize revocable trusts as useful estate planning tools. They are also beginning to realize that such trusts need not be either valid or invalid for all purposes. When the situation calls for ignoring the trust form, some courts will.

[F] Formalities (and Constructive and Resulting Trusts)

Although most states allow oral living trusts for personal property,[88] oral living trusts for land typically run afoul the Statute of Frauds' writing

personal property - ok

land - SOF

---

[81] Traditionally, creditors cannot force the exercise of a power to revoke as a way of reaching trust assets. *See* Restatement (Second) of Trusts § 330 cmt. o. *See generally* Richard W. Effland, *Rights of Creditors in Nonprobate Assets*, 48 Mo. L. Rev. 431 (1983).

[82] 389 N.E.2d at 771.

According to the Restatement of Property, property placed in trust subject to a reserved general *power of appointment* will be available to satisfy creditors' claims. *See* Restatement of Prop. § 328. Noting the similarity between a power to revoke and a power to appoint, the *Reiser* court says property subject to each should be treated the same way regarding creditors' claims. For more on powers of appointment, see Chapter 10, *infra*.

[83] *See also* Johnson v. Commercial Bank, 588 P.2d 1096 (Or. 1978).

[84] Section 505 of the Uniform Trust Code subjects property in a revocable trust to creditors' claims during the settlor's lifetime. After the settlor's death, the UTC follows the approach of *Reiser*: creditors can reach trusts property after exhausting the probate estate.

[85] 460 N.E.2d 572 (Mass. 1984).

[86] Election rights of surviving spouses are discussed in § 28[C], *infra*.

[87] The court noted the irony that divorced spouses could have greater rights in the property of each other than would spouses who stayed together. *See Sullivan*, 460 N.E.2d at 577.

Because the traditional rule—that spouses could not elect against such trust assets—was well-known and long-standing, the court applied its approach prospectively.

[88] Oral trusts are usually a bad idea, however, because they lack sufficient detail.

SoW

requirement.[89] Oral [testamentary] trusts conflict with the Statute of Wills.[90] Not allowing an oral trust, however, may enrich a grantee unjustly. Suppose Javier delivers a deed of Blackacre, absolute on its face, to Maria, but Maria orally promises to hold the land in trust for Javier for life and then transfer it to Frank. If Maria refuses to turn over the land to Frank, we have a conflict between the policy of limiting oral evidence (and thereby the danger of false claims) and the policy of preventing people from unjustly enriching themselves.[91] To avoid unfair results, courts sometimes will apply a "constructive trust" against a donee like Maria to prevent the donee from holding in her own behalf.

constructive trust

The term "constructive trust" is misleading. The theory does not impose management duties on the "trustee." Rather, constructive trust is a remedy.[92] The constructive trust theory is a device for preventing unjust enrichment by moving legal title from a person who has title but should not, to someone who should. The doctrine can apply in many circumstances.[93]

In the context of oral living trusts, the most common situations calling for a constructive trust remedy are likely to involve either fraud or abuse of a confidential relationship. Recall Javier giving property to Maria, to be held for Frank. If, at the time of the transfer, Maria had no intention of honoring a duty to Frank, her fraud would justify imposing a constructive trust. Similarly, if Javier had relied on a confidential relationship[94] with Maria, trusting her to complete the plan, a constructive trust would likely arise.

A confidential relationship justified a court imposing a constructive trust in *Hieble v. Hieble*.[95] The facts follow an all-too-familiar pattern. A mother, fearing death from cancer (and probably trying to avoid probate), gave her house to her son and daughter. They orally agreed that if she recovered, they would transfer the house back to the mother. Changes in the family situation led the daughter to drop out of the picture, and the mother and son to hold the property jointly. Five years later, with the cancer risk receding, the mother asked the son for his half of the joint property. He refused. Although the Statute of Frauds prevented the oral promise from being enforced, the court got to the same place by imposing a constructive trust on the son's share, ordering him to reconvey to his mother because at the time of the initial transfer they were in a confidential relationship. The court said that not all parent-child relationships are fiduciary, but that

---

[89] *See generally* Bogert & Bogert §§ 66-71; Restatement (Third) of Trusts §§ 22-24.

[90] Many states permit oral wills in particular circumstances, usually limited to transferring personal property via deathbed gifts. Otherwise, wills must be written. *See* § 7[B][2][a], *supra*.

[91] *See* Scott § 44.

[92] *See generally* Dan B. Dobbs, Remedies.

[93] *See, e.g.*, §§ 10, *supra* (contracts regarding wills); 25[A], *infra*; 28[C][1][a], *infra*.

[94] Recall that abuse of a confidential relationship is often claimed in cases challenging wills on undue influence grounds. *See* § 7[A][2], *supra*.

[95] 316 A.2d 777 (Conn. 1972).

under the circumstances of dependence by the mother and assurances of faithfulness by the son, "this relationship becomes a classic example of the confidentiality to which equity will fasten consequences."[96] Notice that the constructive trust remedy can apply either where a grantee promises to hold the property for a third party or where the grantee promises to return the property to the grantor.

Unjust enrichment can also arise when there is a testamentary gift made subject to a promise to give the property to someone else. *Olliffe v. Wells*[97] is a classic old case which involved a residuary gift to the Reverend Eleazer M. P. Wells, who ran St. Stephen's Mission, a shelter for poor people in mid-19th-century Boston.[98] Ellen Donovan's will required Wells to distribute the property in his discretion "to carry out wishes which I have expressed to him or may express to him."[99] Wells said that Donovan had told him to use the money for charity, especially the Mission. Wells made no claim to the money himself. The question was whether to allow him to have the money for the Mission or to give it to Donovan's heirs.

Donovan's heirs claimed the property under a resulting trust theory. They argued that the trust failed because its terms were not shown in the will.[100] Because a trust was intended, however, Wells could not hold the property on his own behalf. Rather, the heirs said he held title on behalf of the testator's estate.[101] Then the heirs would take under partial intestacy[102] because the failed gift was in the residuary clause. The court agreed.

This sort of a trust is sometimes called "semi-secret." The document shows a trust intention on its face, but the details are oral. A court can exclude the oral evidence and still prevent unjust enrichment by imposing a resulting trust to deny the beneficiary the right to keep the property. This approach both supports the Statute of Wills and prevents the unjust enrichment, but it is not commonly followed. More often, a court will allow the oral evidence and impose a *constructive* trust in favor of the intended beneficiaries.[103] Perhaps one reason for the majority rule is to be consistent with the law regarding "secret" trusts.

A trust is "secret" in this context if the gift under the will is absolute on its face, but there is an oral agreement on the side. In order for a court to prevent unjust enrichment in this situation, the court must admit testimony of the oral agreement. Once the court has the details, it is likely to impose a constructive trust in favor of the intended beneficiaries.[104]

---

[96] 316 A.2d at 780.

[97] 130 Mass. 221 (1881).

[98] For more on Reverend Wells, see Dukeminier & Johanson at 614 n.17.

[99] 130 Mass. at 222.

[100] The Statute of Wills' writing requirement precludes giving effect to the oral instructions. *See* § 7[B][2][a], *supra*.

[101] Recall that a failed trust also gave rise to a resulting trust in *Clark v. Campbell*, discussed in § 12[C], *supra*.

[102] *See* § 3, *supra*.

[103] *See* Bogert §§ 84, 85.

[104] *See* Restatement (Second) of Trusts § 55; Restatement (Third) of Trusts § 18.

Different results in the treatment of secret and semi-secret trusts are hard to justify. Following the *Olliffe* approach leads to defeating trusts where a trust intention appears in the will, but (effectively) allowing them when the will is silent. Imposing constructive trusts for the trust beneficiaries in each case at least avoids that incongruous result. Professor Scott argued that the law could be both consistent and give less offense to the Statute of Wills if the property went backwards—to the estate—instead of forwards to the beneficiaries,[105] but he did not carry the day.

§ 13   The Size of a Beneficiary's Interest

This section identifies a set of devices for achieving flexibility through careful structuring of a trust beneficiary's share. Because the rights of a beneficiary's creditors often depend on the size of the beneficiary's own claim on a trust, the section also covers the doctrines surrounding creditors' claims.

[A] Discretionary and Support Trusts

Trusts can last a long time. Circumstances will change as beneficiaries are born or go to college or get sick or die. Families may get richer or poorer; rates of return may fall; inflation may erode purchasing power. Narrow language can hinder a trustee's ability to respond to change. Consider, for example, well-meaning language like "all income from the trust shall be paid to my wife Kyanne, and at her death the trust principal shall be distributed equally to our then-surviving children." If Kyanne gets sick, the income may not be enough; if she wins the lottery, it may be more than she wants. If one of the children is injured in an auto accident or needs tuition money while the mother is alive, the trust fund cannot help.[1]

Fortunately, trusts can allow trustees to adjust to change. Some trusts authorize the trustee to pay the beneficiaries[2] "such amount of income or principal as the trustee in its absolute discretion shall deem advisable."[3]

---

[105] *See* Scott § 55.9.

[1] *See, e.g.*, Estate of Van Deusen, 182 P.2d 565 (Cal. 1947) (In the absence of authority in the document, the court denied income beneficiaries' requests to invade the trust principal to increase payments to them.).

Except in special circumstances, also avoid making gifts in particular dollar amounts; "$2,000 per month" may sound like a generous stipend, but if inflation proceeds at the historically low rate of only 2% annually, the stipend (in constant dollars) would be worth only $1,600 after 10 years. After 20, it would be worth $1,240. If inflation is 6%, the stipend would be worth $820 after 10 years and nothing after 20.

[2] Or others, like health care providers, on a beneficiary's behalf.

[3] Despite the broad language, courts are likely to place some restraints on the trustee's discretion. *See* Restatement (Second) of Trusts § 187 cmt. j (trustee must be honest and impartial); UTC § 814(a) (trustee must exercise discretionary power in good faith, in accord with trust's terms and conditions, and in interest of beneficiaries). *See generally* McGovern & Kurtz § 8.2; Edward C. Halbach, *Problems of Discretion in Discretionary Trusts*, 61 Colum. L. Rev. 1425 (1961).

Sometimes the discretion is limited to distribution of income or of principal, rather than embracing both.

These are commonly called "discretionary trusts." Some trusts will attempt to control the trustee's discretion by limiting distributions to those "necessary for the comfortable support of the beneficiary." These are commonly called "support trusts."[4] Sometimes a settlor will create a hybrid, a "discretionary support trust," by giving the trustee "uncontrolled discretion" to pay funds "for support."[5] To clarify these categories, Restatement (Third) or Trusts § 50 and Uniform Trust Code § 504 treat support trusts as a type of discretionary trust.

In choosing how to structure such a trust, a client must balance between providing flexibility and controlling abuse of discretion. *Old Colony Trust Co. v. Rodd*[6] illustrates the dilemma. George A. Sanderson directed his trustee to pay such amounts of income and principal as the trustee judged necessary for the "comfortable support" of his father-in-law's descendants. Anything left after the beneficiaries' deaths went to charity. In response to a beneficiary's suit,[7] the trial court called the amounts the trustee had distributed "parsimonious."[8] Even George's admonition to provide for comfortable support was not enough to induce the trustee to release reasonable sums to the beneficiaries.

The search for ways to avoid hard-edged directions while also encouraging trustees to provide adequate funds begins with a look at why trustees are often so conservative about spending trust assets. Most important, the law presents trustees with different risks. If they are too generous, they risk a court later ordering the trustee to repay to the trust the money which should not have been distributed.[9] On the other hand, if they are too stingy, they are likely only to suffer a slap on the wrist. In *Old Colony Trust Co.*, for example, the court ordered the trustee to increase the amounts of future support payments, but did not penalize the trustee for the low payments it had been making.[10] Another reason for trustee conservatism is the fear that as beneficiaries reach old age, their health care costs will soar. Keeping funds available for those expenses is prudent, but may in fact doom the income beneficiary to a bleak old age and unintentionally benefit the

---

[4] *See generally* Haskell at 233-238.

[5] *See generally* Evelyn G. Abravanel, *Discretionary Support Trusts*, 68 Iowa L. Rev. 273 (1983).

[6] 254 N.E.2d 886 (Mass. 1970).

[7] Procedurally, the beneficiary complained about the trustee's action by objecting to the trustee's accounting. That is a common way of challenging a trustee's behavior.

[8] On appeal, the Supreme Judicial Court of Massachusetts "emphatically agree[d]." 254 N.E.2d at 889.

[9] *See In re* Murray, 45 A.2d 636 (Me. 1946) (trustee required to reimburse trust for funds distributed to a beneficiary without first determining whether the distribution was necessary).

[10] Commenting that "[c]omfort cannot be retroactively given," the court also declined to order disbursements from the corpus to make up for the small amounts the beneficiaries had been getting. 254 N.E.2d at 890.

A frustrated court in Emmert v. Old Nat'l Bank of Martinsburg, 246 S.E.2d 236 (W. Va. 1978), complained about the "protracted and expensive litigation" and expressed the hopes that in the future, the trustee would voluntarily increase distributions if needed and the beneficiary voluntarily accept a reduced amount if circumstances warranted that change.

remaindermen if the income beneficiary dies without having needed the money. An unjustifiable, but plausible, reason for trustees to hold onto trust property is that their fees are often calculated as a percentage of trust assets. The smaller the trust, the smaller the fee. Also hovering in the background of some cases is a conflict of interest. For example, the trustee may be an income beneficiary or a remainderman.[11]

Achieving the balance between the flexibility and control appropriate for any particular client can be difficult. Probably the most important factor is the selection of the trustee or trust advisor.[12] Words of guidance in a document may help, but are no substitute for familiarity with the settlor's intentions and the family's circumstances. Second, a trustee who regularly meets with the beneficiaries will be more likely to understand their needs.[13] To encourage communication, the trust document can require trustee visits with beneficiaries. Seeing firsthand the beneficiary's situation may loosen the trustee's purse strings. Third, the document can identify the settlor's priorities. While preserving the trustee's discretion, the trust agreement can, for example, identify the primary purpose as caring for the settlor's surviving spouse. Such language should make it easier for the trustee to be generous with the spouse, because it provides something to rely upon if the children complain later. In addition to identifying priorities between beneficiaries, the document can rank needs. A settlor could encourage the trustee to spend the fund for college expenses, even if that use meant the fund were exhausted, or the settlor could encourage the trustee to conserve resources so the beneficiary would have a lifelong income supplement.[14]

If disputes arise despite the best efforts of the trust's drafter, courts will decide the meanings of terms which seek to limit the trustee's discretion. A common subject of litigation is what constitutes "support."[15] Usually the term has been defined flexibly, tied to the manner of living in which the

---

[11] *See, e.g., In re* Flyer's Will, 245 N.E.2d 718 (N.Y. 1969) (Trustee/remainderman's decision not to invade the trust principal for beneficiary's support was deemed appropriate since the beneficiary had independent income.).

[12] *See generally* § 12[D], *supra.*

[13] Some states mandate communication as part of a trustee's duties. *See generally* § 55[B], *infra.*

[14] If the settlor were concerned that the trustee might spend too much for one beneficiary, the document could limit the trustee's invasion power for any beneficiary to a percentage of the total fund.

A settlor concerned that a trustee might be too stingy might also give to a third person a power to order the trustee to pay more to or for a beneficiary. For example, a guardian of minor children might have the power to demand more funds for the children's support. The guardian would have a special power of appointment. For more on special powers, see Chapter 10, *infra.*

[15] *See generally* Restatement (Second) of Trusts §§ 154, 156 cmt. d; Bogert § 811; Page §§ 39.15, 39.16. Another source of confusion is the word "education." *See, e.g.,* Epstein v. Kuvin, 95 A.2d 753; (N.J. Super. Ct. 1953) ("college education" means a four-year degree and does not include medical school); Mitchell v. Whittier College, 272 P. 748 (Cal. 1928) ("college education" includes the education received at a junior college). Many of these problems can be avoided if the client decides how broadly to define the word and the lawyer includes appropriate language in the document.

beneficiary "has become accustomed." This approach both reveals and reinforces class biases.[16] It may in part explain why the trustee in *Old Colony Trust Co.* was less than generous in its support of a single, middle-aged woman who earned a modest income.[17] Accustomed to a modest lifestyle, she got a modest support payment.[18] A related issue is whether, when deciding on the appropriate level of support, the trustee should consider other funds available to the beneficiary. Because the question is frequently litigated,[19] the trust document should cover the point. Otherwise, courts are likely to infer that the beneficiary is entitled to support payments even though other resources are available.[20] The trust should also say whether "support" for a beneficiary includes funds necessary to support the beneficiary's dependents.[21]

In this area, as in so many others, trust doctrine allows estate plans tailored to the needs of individual clients. Settlors can preserve flexibility by giving their beneficiaries trust shares, defined in part by trustees who have a wide range of powers to allocate income and principal as family needs develop. When deciding how to structure those powers, settlors should also consider the topic which follows, the interplay between the nature of a trustee's power and the transferability of the beneficiaries' interests.

[B] Alienability

Two principles underlie much of the law surrounding the transfer of a trust beneficiary's interest.[22] First, unless a statute or the trust document

---

[16] Professor Haskell comments that the costs of a Florida condominium would not be part of a blue collar worker's "support," but might be covered for "a member of the social and economic establishment in the community." Haskell at 234.

[17] 254 N.E.2d at 888.

[18] One suspects from reading the case that George Sanderson wanted the beneficiaries to be able to use his money to enjoy a higher standard of living. The term "comfortable support" was not enough to accomplish that goal. Perhaps his will should have mandated "support at a level which will allow the beneficiaries to live as well as the judges who review this document."

[19] *See* Marsman v. Nasca, 573 N.E.2d 1025 (Mass. App. Ct. 1991), *review denied*, 579 N.E.2d 1361 (1991) (Trust provided "after having considered the various available sources of support for him," the trustees may invade the principal. Trustees had a duty to inquire into the beneficiary's needs.). Edward C. Halbach, Jr., *Problems of Discretion in Discretionary Trusts*, 61 Colum. L. Rev. 1425 (1961). *See also* § 57, *infra* (Drafting: Powers and Duties).

[20] Restatement (Second) of Trusts § 128 cmt. e (1959). The policy choice is between two perceived evils. A trustee who considers other sources of income may undercut the beneficiary's incentive to work, because any income earned would simply reduce the trust distribution. (Note that if only *unearned* income—like interest—is considered, the disincentive to work is eliminated.). On the other hand, ignoring other sources may undermine the trust's support purpose (or the ability of the trust to support others) if the beneficiary does not really need the help. *See* Haskell at 234-235.

[21] *See, e.g.*, Cavett v. Buck, 397 P.2d 901 (Okla. 1964). Construing language only to provide for the named beneficiary's support and maintenance, the court denied a request for additional support for his wife and children.

[22] *See* UTC § 501.

provides otherwise, a trust beneficiary can transfer his or her interest to someone else. Secondly, creditors' rights typically follow alienability: the creditor usually can get what the beneficiary can transfer. Many settlors combine these principles and restrict the alienability of their beneficiaries' interests as a way of protecting the beneficiaries, both from themselves and from creditors. This section first discusses beneficiaries' voluntary transfers, and then, creditors' claims.

[1] Voluntary Transfers

Abstract though they are, equitable interests in trust are much like the tangible property you know. Just as you can give an old armchair to a friend or sell it at a garage sale, so can a trust beneficiary give away or sell a life estate or a remainder interest in trust.[23] Imagine Ingrid as a client who plans a trust to give income to her son, Sven, and at his death pay the principal to his children. Unless Ingrid restricts their interests, the beneficiaries will be able to transfer them. If Sven is (or becomes) well-off, he may someday want to avoid paying taxes on that income, so he might transfer his life estate to his son, Phil. While Sven stayed alive, Phil would get the income. On the other hand, if Sven is short on cash, he might sell his life estate to moneylender Jeanette. Jeanette would consider the size of the trust and Sven's life expectancy, and then pay what she believed was the present value of Sven's share. Sven's children, so long as they were adults, also could transfer their remainder interests.[24] The recipients would have to wait until Sven's death, of course, before they could get the principal.

In deciding whether or how to restrict the interests of her trust beneficiaries, Ingrid would have to balance various risks. Is Sven a responsible person with a steady income who may need the flexibility of giving up the trust later? Or is Sven likely to be tempted by the opportunity to sell his life estate and use the funds for a get-rich-quick scheme (or a wild vacation)? What about Sven's grandchildren, many of whom may not yet be born? The decision is not easy. Ingrid might restrict Sven's interest or the grandchildren's, or both.

If she does decide to restrict a beneficiary's interest, Ingrid has several options.[25] She might create any combination of the discretionary and support trusts described in the prior section. That way the trustee could monitor the beneficiary's behavior. She might also create a classic "spendthrift" trust.[26] Spendthrift clauses typically both prohibit trust

---

[23] Present and future interests are discussed in Chapter 9, *infra*.

[24] If the remainders were contingent, there is a small chance that they would not be alienable. Holdovers from the common law's hostility toward transfer of contingent future interests still cloud the law. *See* Powell ¶ 845.

[25] The law surrounding restraints on the transfer of beneficial interests in trusts has historical roots in the law regarding restraints on alienation of legal interests, especially those in land. *See generally* 4 ALP §§ 26.1-26.132 (1952).

[26] The shorthand label "spendthrift trust" can be misleading. Beneficiaries of such a trust

beneficiaries from transferring their interests and seek to limit the ability of creditors to reach the trust assets.[27] Such clauses do not affect, however, what happens to the money once it reaches the beneficiaries.

Discretionary, support, and spendthrift trusts are often viewed primarily as devices for avoiding creditors. The next section addresses issues surrounding that use. Keep in mind, however, that such devices can also affect the ability of both trustees and beneficiaries to adjust to changing situations. The discretionary power which can shield Sven from his creditors may also leave him with little recourse against a stingy trustee. Or it may allow the trustee to spend funds where they are needed most. The spendthrift clause which might protect Sven from the temptation to sell his share might also prohibit him from giving it away to save taxes. Clients should understand that these various tools affect both voluntary and involuntary transfers.

[2] Involuntary Transfers: Creditors' Claims

Unless a document or statute provides otherwise, creditors can satisfy their claims by reaching a trust beneficiary's interest.[28] The procedure varies among the states, but familiar creditors' devices like attachment, garnishment and execution tend to be available. Creditors usually have a choice between waiting for the beneficiary's payment to come due and then collecting it, or attempting to sell the beneficiary's interest and taking what the market will bring at that time.[29] Most of the controversy in this area surrounds settlors' attempts to shield their beneficiaries from such fates, especially with spendthrift clauses which provide that the beneficiaries' interests shall not be taken to pay their debts. This section will highlight the policies involved, discuss the general approaches taken, and examine some of the exceptions which have arisen.

Spendthrift clauses put creditors at a distinct disadvantage. In contrast to their ability to reach other assets, creditors cannot obtain their debtor's beneficial interest in a spendthrift trust, nor can they force the trustee to pay them directly. Instead, they must wait until the trustee pays the beneficiary and then try to catch the money there.[30] For over 100 years,

---

need not be spendthrifts irresponsibly running up debts. Any trust which provides that the beneficiary's interest is inalienable is likely to be labeled a "spendthrift trust," regardless of the beneficiary's ability to make competent financial decisions.

[27] A spendthrift clause might read as follows: "No interest of my wife or of any lineal descendant of mine in income or principal shall be anticipated, encumbered or assigned. No such interest shall be subject to the claims of such person's creditors, spouse or divorced spouse or others." *See* Domo v. McCarthy, 612 N.E.2d 706, 709 (Ohio 1993). Under UTC § 502(b), calling it a "spendthrift trust" is enough.

[28] *See generally* Bogert § 39.

[29] A beneficiary's interest will pass to his trustee in bankruptcy. 11 U.S.C. § 541. Sale of a beneficial interest in a trust is a theoretical possibility, but because no market exists in this country for the transfer of such interests, as a practical matter, they may not be salable.

[30] Professor Hirsch calls this a game of hide and seek. Adam J. Hirsch, *Spendthrift Trusts and Public Policy: Economic and Cognitive Perspectives*, 73 Wash. U.L.Q. 1, 3 (1995).

commentators have debated the merits of allowing spendthrift trusts.[31] It may not be too much of an oversimplification to say that those who favor the device tend to view the problem from the perspective of the donor, and those who oppose it take the view of the donee.

In an era of "robber barons," the spendthrift trust appealed to a generation of judges who identified with the desire to preserve assets for future generations. Relying on the notion that the property was the settlor's to give, courts viewed trust shares subject to restraints on alienation as one species of less-than-fee-simple interests:[32]

> We are not able to see that it would violate any sound public policy to permit a testator to give to the object of his bounty such a qualified interest in the income . . . and thus provide against the improvidence or misfortune of the beneficiary.

More than 100 years later, a recent case echoes that view: "the law should allow the property owner, within reason, to dispose of her property as she chooses."[33] However, the argument cuts both ways. To the extent the law recognizes the freedom of donors to shape their gifts by attaching strings, the law also undercuts the freedom of donees to dispose of *their* property as *they* choose.[34]

Other arguments also have at least two sides. Allowing spendthrift trusts may encourage people to work hard and accumulate wealth, knowing that they will be able to leave their progeny more secure. On the other hand, the progeny may become lazy and unproductive because they are sheltered from economic realities. Spendthrift trusts probably do mislead creditors who rely on the wealthy trappings of a loan applicant, and inquiry into the sources of the applicant's funds could be costly. On the other hand, lenders could refuse loans unless the applicants provided copies of the relevant provisions from their trusts.[35] Spendthrift trusts may inhibit economic growth by limiting the amount of capital which can be placed at risk. Trust capital protected from the creditors of beneficiaries and constrained by conservative investment standards[36] is not likely to support entrepreneurial enterprises. Whatever the arguments, spendthrift clauses—except if

---

[31] The most famous works are John C. Gray, Restraints on the Alienation of Property (1883) and Erwin N. Griswold, Spendthrift Trusts (1936). Both appeared in later editions. *See also* Anne S. Emanuel, *Spendthrift Trusts: It's Time to Codify the Compromise*, 72 Neb. L. Rev. 179 (1993).

[32] Broadway Nat'l Bank v. Adams, 133 Mass. 170, 173 (1882).

[33] Scott v. Bank One Trust Co., 577 N.E.2d 1077, 1084 (Ohio 1991).

[34] This conflict has been aptly called the "dead hand dilemma." *See* Gregory S. Alexander, *The Dead Hand and the Law of Trusts in the Nineteenth Century*, 37 Stan. L. Rev. 1189, 1190 (1985).

[35] A creditors' perspective can also arise in other contexts. In response to the argument that restricting alienability is an attribute of ownership, one court said "[T]he right to seize property is . . . a right, not of the owner, but of the creditor." Brahmey v. Rollins, 179 A. 186, 1911 (N.H. 1935).

[36] Standards for trustee investments are discussed in § 56[A], *infra*.

applied to the settlor's creditors[37] —have been approved overwhelmingly[38] by courts and legislatures.[39]

Shelley v. Shelley[40] nicely illustrates how various trust devices affect creditors' claims, and that some special kinds of creditors' claims may be treated more favorably than most. Hugh Shelley left a trust to provide for his wife and his son, Grant. All in one document, he established elements of a spendthrift trust, a support trust, and a discretionary trust. After the death of his mother, Grant got the trust income, subject to a standard spendthrift clause prohibiting him from alienating his interest. In an emergency, the trustee could also spend the corpus to support Grant or his children. Finally, once Grant reached age 30, the trustee could also give him so much of the fund as the trustee[41] thought Grant capable of successfully investing.

Grant had two children and one divorce in each of two marriages. Then he disappeared, leaving obligations for alimony and child support. The former wives sought trust funds to satisfy those claims. The court treated separately claims against each of the three interests Grant held in the trust. As to the income, the question was whether the spendthrift clause barred the claims. While recognizing the validity of spendthrift clauses generally, the court endorsed the Restatement's position that such clauses are ineffective against wives' and children's claims for alimony or support.[42]

---

[37] *See* Restatement (Second) of Trusts § 156; Restatement (Third) Trusts §§ 58 & 60; UTC § 505(a)(3). *But see* Alaska Stat. § 34.40.110 (allowing self-settled spendthrift trusts); Robert T. Danforth, *Rethinking the Law of Creditors' Rights in Trusts*, 53 Hastings L.J. 287 (2001-2002).

[38] But not universally. *See, e.g.,* Brahmey v. Rollins, 179 A. 186 (N.H. 1935); Industrial Nat'l Bank v. Budlong, 264 A.2d 18 (R.I. 1970); Meade v. Rowe's Ex'r & Trustee, 182 S.W.2d 30 (Ky. 1944).

[39] Some states followed New York's practice of allowing spendthrift trusts only to the extent of protecting from creditors the amount needed for the beneficiary's education and support. The loophole proved huge, however, because courts adopted a "station in life" rule, which took into account the beneficiary's economic and social status. "If he had . . . lived a life of luxury and ease . . . , then he was entitled to have the trust protect him to the extent necessary to maintain life in the same style." Bogert & Bogert at ch. 13, § 227, p. 517 (footnote omitted). Compare the similar effect of traditional definitions of "support" for purposes of defining trustees' invasion powers. *See supra* note 16 and accompanying text.

There are other statutory refinements in some states. *See, e.g.,* Cal. Civ. Proc. Code § 709.010, Prob. Code § 15306.5 (limiting a creditor to 25% of the beneficiary's income).

[40] 354 P.2d 282 (Or. 1960).

[41] The trustee could act only after gaining approval of one of Grant's uncles. On the use of trust advisors in just this sort of situation, see § 12[D], *supra.*

[42] *See* Restatement of Trusts § 157(a). *See also In re* Marriage of Chapman, 697 N.E.2d 365 (Ill. App. Ct. 1998) (children of someone who had a special power of appointment could reach trust principal when they had a support order). Powers of appointment are discussed in § 37, *infra. See generally* Carolyn L. Dessin, *Feed a Trust and Starve a Child: The Effectiveness of Trust Protective Techniques Against Claims for Support and Alimony,* 10 Ga. St. U. L. Rev. (1994).

Other exceptions given in the Restatement include: necessary services rendered to the beneficiary or necessary supplies furnished to him; services rendered and materials furnished which preserve or benefit the interest of the beneficiary. Restatement (Second) of Trusts

As to the corpus, the court distinguished between the children's and the wives' claims. The children, as beneficiaries, could force the trustee to invade the corpus for support.[43] Language authorizing expenditures "in case of any emergency" limited the trustee's discretion to deny funds, and the court found an emergency here. The former wives failed, however, to reach the corpus for their alimony claims. Because they were Grant's creditors, they could only get the corpus to the extent he could, and his interest was limited to what the trustee decided to give him. The trustee's discretionary power over the corpus not only provided flexibility for dealing with Grant, but also provided protection against the claims of his creditors.

Another approach is to terminate a beneficiary's interest in the face of claims on the trust.[44] For example, in *Scott v. Bank One Trust Co.*,[45] the settlor prohibited the trustee from distributing assets to the settlor's son if he were insolvent, had filed in bankruptcy, or would not personally enjoy the assets. In other words, if creditors came near, the trustee turned off the spigot; when the danger subsided, the money could flow.[46] Because a creditor can get only whatever interest the beneficiary has, and the beneficiary has nothing while a creditor is around, the creditor loses.[47]

The same basic idea has been used to try to take advantage of government welfare programs, while also providing a fund to supply allowable "extras" for disabled or elderly beneficiaries.[48] Some courts have been troubled by the spectre of a trust beneficiary also getting government aid, so that if a trustee's discretion is limited, as by requiring payments to "support" a

---

§ 157(a) added an exception allowing the United States or a state to satisfy a claim against a beneficiary. *See also* Restatement (Third) of Trusts § 59; UTC § 503. *Sligh v. First Nat'l Bank,* 704 So. 2d 1020 (Miss. 1997) (exception for tort creditors whose claims are based on gross negligence or intentional torts).

[43] *Compare* Matthews v. Matthews, 450 N.E.2d 278 (Ohio App. 1981, reconsidered twice in 1982). William Matthews was the beneficiary of his father's trust, which gave the trustee the power to pay for his support. Even though William's daughter, Glenna, was not a trust beneficiary, William's ex-wife was able to recover support payments on behalf of Glenna.

[44] Trusts using this device are sometimes called "protective trusts." *See generally* Haskell at 238-240.

[45] 577 N.E.2d 1077, 1084 (Ohio 1991).

[46] Some versions of these clauses cut off the beneficiary, but allow interim payments to (or for the benefit of) the beneficiary's spouse and children. In spite of fancy footwork like this, forfeiture clauses will not defeat a federal tax lien. *See* Bank One Ohio Trust Co. v. United States, 80 F.3d 173 (6th Cir. 1996) (applying federal law).

[47] While both this approach and the standard spendthrift clause block creditors' claims against the trust, as a theoretical matter they impact both the creditor and the beneficiary differently. In a protective trust, the beneficiary's interest ends (at least temporarily). In a spendthrift trust, payment continues to the beneficiary and the creditor has a chance of catching it there. In practice, a creditor who cannot force money directly out of the trustee is likely not to pursue the claim, so the two approaches get very close to the same place.

[48] *See generally* Shaffer, Mooney & Boettcher at 213-235; Joseph A. Rosenberg, *Supplemental Needs Trust for People With Disabilities: The Development of a Private Trust in the Public Interest,* 10 Boston Univ. Pub. Int. L.J. 91 (2000); Eleanor M. Crosby & Ira M. Leff, *Ethical Considerations in Medicaid Estate Planning: An Analysis of ABA Model Rules of Professional Conduct,* 62 Ford. L. Rev. 1503 (1994).

beneficiary, the state as creditor may be able to get the funds.[49] Others have recognized that if courts allow governments to invade—and quickly exhaust—such funds, rational planners may simply entirely disinherit persons in need.[50] The safest method of providing funds while protecting against creditors may be a purely discretionary trust, in which the trustee has the power, but not the duty, to spend money for the beneficiaries.[51]

Another creditor-avoidance technique has been to open an "asset-protection trust" overseas, out of the reach of creditors. In an effort to attract trust business, which might go offshore, some states have allowed settlors to place assets in trust and yet be protected for the settlor's creditors.[52] Academic response to these approaches has been negative,[53] and courts have used their contempt powers to thwart some efforts.[54]

One of the pleasures and challenges of practicing in this area of law is the ability to shape estate plans to the needs of individual clients. Trusts can give trustees virtually absolute discretion to allocate income and principal among beneficiaries, or they can limit that discretion in various ways. When deciding whether and how to limit trustee discretion, clients need to appreciate both the advantages of flexibility and the dangers of abuse; both the possible needs of the beneficiaries and the possible claims of creditors.

§ 14   Modification and Termination

Sometimes those involved with a trust want to change it, or end it before its time. Often the motivating factor is an unanticipated financial need which arises after the trust is established. Careful use of the kinds of invasion powers discussed in the prior section can reduce greatly the need for seeking trust modifications; the settlor will have built in the flexibility. Even if invasion powers are missing, a settlor who has reserved a power to amend or revoke can change the document as needed.[1] A second source

---

[49] *See* Third Nat'l Bank in Nashville v. Brown, 691 S.W.2d 557 (Tenn. 1985).

[50] *See* Tidrow v. Director, Missouri State Div. of Fam. Serv., 688 S.W.2d 9 (Mo. App. 1985).

[51] *See* Myers v. Dep't of Soc. & Rehab. Servs., 866 P.2d 1052 (Kan. 1994) (Trustee power to pay "so much or all . . . as my trustee deems advisable" did not preclude beneficiary (settlor's son) from qualifying for state support.). The government, however, might "deem" trust property to be available to the beneficiary, and thus disqualify the beneficiary from claiming government benefits. *See* Cohen v. Commissioner, 668 N.E.2d 769 (Mass. 1996) (trust beneficiaries who were also trust settlors ineligible for Medicaid). Rules on these issues change frequently, so be sure to get the latest information before advising a client.

[52] *See* Alaska Stat. § 34.40.110; Del. Code Ann., title 12, § 3571.

[53] *See, e.g.*, Randall J. Gingiss, *Putting A Stop To "Asset Protection" Trusts*, 51 Baylor L. Rev. 987 (1999); Stewart E. Sterk, *Asset Protection Trusts: Trust Law's Race To the Bottom?*, 85 Cornell L. Rev. 1035 (2000); Henry J. Lischer, Jr., *Domestic Asset Protection Trusts: Pallbearers To Liability?*, 35 Real Prop. Prob. & Tr. J. 479 (2000).

[54] *See* FTC v. Affordable Media, L.L.C., 179 F.3d 1228 (9th Cir. 1999) (settlor in civil contempt for failing to follow order to repatriate trust assets).

[1] The power to terminate includes the power to modify. In this context, the law sensibly avoids requiring terminating only to start over. *See* Scott on Trusts § 331.1.

of pleas for early termination is impatient beneficiaries who want their money sooner. In general, they will have to wait.

This section examines the two principles most likely to block early termination of a trust. First, all beneficiaries must consent to the change. Second, a "material purpose" of the trust will not be violated without the settlor's consent. The section concludes by highlighting recent moves to allow perpetual, indestructible trusts.

[A] Beneficiaries' Consent

If the settlor has not reserved a power to revoke, the trust cannot be terminated without all the beneficiaries' consent.[2] Here there are two catches. First, all of the beneficiaries might not consent. Second, and more likely, some of the beneficiaries may be unidentified or unborn,[3] and obtaining consent on their behalf can be difficult. Two different theories have arisen to help solve the problem. Guardians ad litem might be appointed to represent the unborn,[4] or the doctrine of "virtual representation" might allow older relatives to waive claims of ones not yet on the scene.[5]

Hatch v. Riggs National Bank[6] illustrates how a guardian ad litem might be used. Anna Hatch created an irrevocable trust reserving a lifetime income and a testamentary power of appointment[7] to herself. Her next of kin were to take the property if she did not exercise the power. When she had trouble living on the trust income, Anna sought to revoke the trust, but she needed consent from her next of kin, who would not be identified until her death.[8] To solve the problem, the court suggested that a guardian ad litem be appointed to negotiate on their behalf.

Even if the trust is irrevocable, the settlor and all the beneficiaries can agree to end (or change) the trust. The trustee's desire for a fee is not enough of a stake in the trust's continuation to prevent termination. *See, e.g.*, Johnson v. First Nat'l Bank of Jackson, 386 So. 2d 1112 (Miss. 1980) (Settlor, who was the sole beneficiary of an irrevocable trust, was allowed to terminate the trust even though she was financially irresponsible.).

[2] However, trust *modification* not inconsistent with the trust's material purpose may be possible. *See* Restatement (Third) Trusts § 65, comment f.

[3] Suppose Margaret establishes an irrevocable trust to pay income to her grandchildren and distribute shares of the corpus when each reaches age 21. At least until the first grandchild reaches 21 and can demand the corpus, the class of "grandchildren" remains open to include afterborns. *See* § 43[B], *infra*.

[4] *See* UPC § 1–403; UTC § 305. *See generally* Martin D. Beglieter, *The Guardian Ad Litem in Estate Proceedings*, 20 Willamette L. Rev. 643 (1984).

[5] *See* UPC §1–403; UTC § 304. *See generally* Lawrence B. Rodman and Leroy E. Rodman, *Virtual Representation: Some Possible Extensions*, 6 Real Prop. Prob. & Tr. J. 281 (1971). The UPC codifies both doctrines. *See* UPC § 1-403.

[6] 361 F.2d 559 (D.C. Cir. 1966).

[7] The testamentary power gave her the ability to designate in her will who would take the trust after she died. Powers of appointment are covered in Chapter 10, *infra*.

[8] Recall that intestate statutes speak from the date of death. *See generally* Chapter 2, *supra*.

Whether the solution will work depends on the circumstances. In *Hatch*, the next of kin had something to gain by a settlement. Because their interests were subject to Anna's exercise of the power of appointment, they would get nothing if Anna exercised the power. In return for getting more money, Anna might agree to "lock in" a share for the next of kin.

In other situations, guardians may face family pressures to consent to changes which are not in the best financial interests of the unborn beneficiaries they represent. *In re Wolcott*[9] involved another narrowly drafted trust which proved inadequate to meet the needs of the primary beneficiary. Francis Getty named his wife, Ada, as income beneficiary of his testamentary trust. At her death, the corpus would go to Francis' living issue. The trust income was insufficient to support Ada, but the trustee had no power to invade the principal. Joined by Ada's sons and the guardian ad litem for a minor grandson and possible unborn persons, the trustee sought court approval to invade the corpus. Relying on the principle of allowing modifications to meet circumstances unanticipated by the settlor,[10] the court approved the request. Certainly Ada's situation and the family's willingness to help present a sympathetic case. Note, however, the potential liability of a guardian who supported a petition to give money to Ada by taking it away from the persons he was supposedly protecting. Courts usually will deny an income beneficiary's invasion request if all of the beneficiaries do not consent, even in the face of "unforeseen circumstances."[11] By consenting, the guardian might have been allowing what otherwise would have been prohibited. In any event, the guardian can be criticized for having put the widow's interest ahead of the unborn beneficiaries.

In *Wolcott*, the unborn beneficiaries were said to be bound by the decision for another reason: "they are sufficiently represented by those having like interests . . . ."[12] The court applied the doctrine of "virtual representation," allowing the sons who would take the trust principal after their mother's death to represent the interests of their own issue, who would take if the sons did not survive. The theory is that since the unborn beneficiaries would be standing in the shoes now filled by their ancestors, the ancestors, in protecting their own interests, will protect the unborn beneficiaries.[13]

---

[9] 56 A.2d 641 (N.H. 1948).

[10] The court characterized the trustee's petition as one "seek[ing] authority to do what the testator presumably would have authorized had he foreseen the emergency." 56 A.2d at 643. Given the common use of invasion powers to avoid such situations, perhaps the attorney who drafted the document should be liable for the cost of this litigation if the attorney failed to raise with Francis Getty the possibility that the income might not be enough to support Ada. For more on lawyer's obligations, see § 1, *supra*.

[11] *See* Scott on Trusts § 168. Scholars have criticized this result. *See generally* Paul G. Haskell, *Justifying the Principle of Distributive Deviation in the Law of Trusts*, 18 Hastings L.J. 267 (1967). Some statutes allow invasion of principal for support of the income beneficiary. *See, e.g.*, Cal. Prob. Code § 15409; Wis. Stat. Ann. § 701.13(2).

[12] 56 A.2d at 644.

[13] *See* Restatement of Property § 183(a). For a discussion of whether a donee of a power of appointment can "represent" the potential appointees, see Sheldon F. Kurtz, *Powers of Appointment Under the 1990 Uniform Probate Code: What Was Done—What Remains to Be Done*, 55 Alb. L. Rev. 1151, 1153-1162 (1992). This text discusses powers of appointment in Chapter 10, *infra*.

Virtual representation is attractive because it allows currently living persons to make some decisions even though other beneficiaries may appear later. Its use can be questioned, however, if we presume too much of a coincidence between the interests of one generation and those of the next.[14] In *Wolcott*, for example, the sons wanted to take care of their mother. Whether as-yet-unborn grandchildren would be so willing to give up their trust shares for their grandmother is questionable. On the other hand, perhaps liberal use of virtual representation is appropriate because, as a policy matter, we should not inhibit trust modification on the possibility that remote interests may appear later.

[B] Material Purpose

The second major stumbling block to early termination (or modification) of a trust is the notion that a trust cannot be changed without the settlor's consent if to do so would violate a material purpose of the trust. Since in most cases, the settlor[15] is dead, changes are particularly hard to achieve. Courts have struggled to determine what a trust's "material purpose" might be, and whether a particular change would violate it.

The doctrine stems from *Claflin v. Claflin*,[16] which prohibited a settlor's son from getting the trust corpus early. Wilbur Claflin's will had given Adelbert a one-third share of a trust, with distributions of $10,000 at ages 21 and 25, and the balance at 30. Before he reached 25, Adelbert sought his entire share. When the trustee refused, Adelbert sued. Following a pattern consistent with the approval of spendthrift clauses,[17] the court favored the father's protective purposes over the son's desire to decide on his own how to use the money. The decision established a principle, sometimes called the "*Claflin* Doctrine," that beneficiaries cannot end (or modify) a trust if to do so would violate a "material purpose" of the settlor.[18]

Beneficiaries seeking to terminate a trust can, of course, simply ask the trustee. If the trustee complies, there should be no problem.[19] The trustee

---

[14] UTC § 304 recognizes virtual representation "only to the extent there is no conflict of interest between the representative and the person represented."

[15] Recall that the text uses the term "settlor" to include all those persons who create trusts, whether living or testamentary.

[16] 20 N.E. 454 (Mass. 1889).

[17] *See* § 13[B][2], *supra*.

[18] *See* Restatement (Second) of Trusts § 337.

[19] Except perhaps for the trustee. *Compare* Restatement (Second) of Trusts § 342 ("the trust terminates although the purposes . . . have not been fully accomplished") and Haskell at 246 ("If there is a material purpose which is unfulfilled, and all the beneficiaries request termination, the trustee need not comply, but the trustee is not liable if he does comply."), *with* Whitney v. Whitney, 57 N.E.2d 913 (Mass. 1944) (Trustees' and beneficiaries' conveyance of a trust estate was invalid because a trust cannot be terminated when it has not fulfilled its material purpose, regardless of trustees' and beneficiaries' agreement to do so.), *and In re* Wentworth, 129 N.E. 646 (N.Y. 1920) (trustee liable to beneficiary of a spendthrift trust for having transferred trust property to a third person, even though the complaining beneficiary had consented to the transfer).

may object, however, out of a sense of obligation to the settlor, or in order to preserve an image as the sort of trustee that honors settlor's intentions,[20] or simply to keep the account.

If the trustee objects, the beneficiaries seeking change often will face a very difficult hurdle because of the way courts interpret the use of familiar planning devices. As we have seen, trust law's flexibility allows an enormous variety of solutions to particular family problems. In particular, spendthrift, discretionary and support trusts seek both to protect beneficiaries against creditors' claims, and to provide flexibility to handle their various needs over time.[21] Settlors often include restrictions postponing access to the money until certain ages. Following *Claflin*, courts typically have interpreted the inclusion of each of these devices as an indication that a "material purpose" of the trust would be thwarted if the trust were modified or ended.[22] Although beneficiaries can enjoy many protections, they probably cannot avoid them.[23] In some situations, however, the rule may be changing.[24]

About the only trusts which beneficiaries have been able to change without the trustee's concurrence are successive-beneficiary trusts, without spendthrift clauses.[25] These are the ones that provide income for life to Pedro, principal at his death to Tania. They are notoriously inflexible. Ironically, under *Claflin*, the price of providing flexibility in an estate plan

---

[20] *See* Haskell at 245.

[21] *See* § 13, *supra*.

[22] *See* Restatement (Second) of Trusts § 337, comments l, m and n.

[23] Except, of course, if they disclaim a share. *See* § 28, *infra*.

[24] *See* Restatement (Third) of Trusts § 65, comment e (early termination may be possible even if the trustee has discretion regarding payment of income or principal or if the trust includes a spendthrift clause). Spendthrift clauses, in particular, are often included as standard "boilerplate," and thus are suspect indicia of a trust's material purpose. Under UTC § 411(c), a spendthrift clause "is not presumed to constitute a material purpose of the trust." *See generally* Julia C. Walker, *Get Your Dead Hands Off Me: Beneficiaries' Right to Terminate or Modify a Trust Under the Uniform Trust Code*, 67 Mo. L. Rev. 443 (2002); Ronald Chester, *Modification and Termination of Trusts in the 21st Century: The Uniform Trust Code Leads a Quiet Revolution*, 35 Real Prop. Prob. & Tr. J. 697 (2001).

A related issue is the extent to which *Clafflin* precludes beneficiaries from modifying the trust terms by removing the trustee. Again, the law may be moving toward more flexibility. *See generally* Ronald Chester & Sarah Reid Ziomek, *Removal of Corporate Trustees Under the Uniform Trust Code and Other Current Law: Does a Contractual Lense Help Clarify the Rights of Beneficiaries*, 67 Mo. L. Rev. 241 (2002).

[25] *See* Restatement (Second) of Trusts § 337 cmt. f, *followed in* American Nat'l Bank of Cheyenne v. Miller, 899 P.2d 1337 (Wyo. 1995) (allowing termination).

Testamentary trusts may be terminable as part of a compromise settlement between heirs and trust beneficiaries. *Compare* Budin v. Levy, 180 N.E.2d 74 (Mass. 1962) (allowing premature termination as part of a compromise) and UPC § 3-1101 (endorsing such compromises) *with* Adams v. Link, 145 A.2d 753 (Conn. 1958) (applying the *Claflin* doctrine to disapprove a compromise).

is to deny the ultimate flexibility, opting out and taking the money. The doctrine has been under attack,[26] and is collapsing in Missouri.[27]

[C] Indestructible Trusts

As long as there has been wealth, owners have been tempted to lock up that wealth forever to "protect" their families (and, perhaps, to achieve a form of immortality). The Rule Against Perpetuities has served to limit the time landowners and settlors can achieve that end. In recent years, however, the Rule has been under an attack fueled largely by the existence of the Generation Skipping Tax.[28] We will postpone our discussion of those issues until after we have examined the Rule,[29] but note for now that indestructible trusts could become a problem.

Note also that even if the effect of the material purpose doctrine is time-limited by the Rule Against Perpetuities,[30] agreement of all *living* beneficiaries is unlikely to be able to terminate a trust after the perpetuities period. Perpetual trusts necessarily benefit unborn, unidentified persons, and they are not around to consent. Moreover, the *guardian ad litem* and virtual representation approaches[31] cannot help, because terminating the trust would deprive those unknown beneficiaries of benefits they might enjoy if the trust continued.

§ 15 Charitable Trusts

Because of the broad public policy favoring charitable work, charitable trusts operate under some different rules.[1] First, a charitable trust need not have definite beneficiaries. In most situations, the job of enforcing the trust falls to the state's Attorney General.[2] In addition, a charitable trust

---

[26] *See generally* Gail B. Bird, *Trust Termination: Unborn, Living, and Dead Hands—Too Many Fingers in the Trust Pie*, 36 Hastings L.J. 563 (1985); William F. Fratcher, *Trusts and Succession*, 22 Mo. L. Rev. 390 (1957); Julie Anderson, *Comment, A Proposal for a Variation of Trusts Statute in Washington*, 8 U. Puget Sound L. Rev. 625 (1985).

A related question is the extent to which living settlors can enforce trusts they have created. *See* John T. Gaubatz, *Grantor Enforcement of Trusts: Standing in One Private Law Setting*, 62 N.C. L. Rev. 905 (1984).

[27] *See* Hamerstrom v. Commerce Bank of Kansas City, 808 S.W.2d 434 (Mo. App. 1991) (allowing deviation despite potential interests of unborn remaindermen); Peter J. Wiedenbeck, *Missouri's Repeal of the Claflin Doctrine—New View of the Policy Against Perpetuities*, 50 Mo. L. Rev. 805 (1985); Becky Kilpatrick, *Note, Missouri Takes a Stand; The Death of the Dead Hand in the Control of Trusts*, 57 Mo. L. Rev. 1003 (1992).

[28] *See* Ira Mark Bloom, *The GST Tax is Killing the Rule Against Perpetuities*, 87 Tax Notes 569 (2000). We highlight the GST in § 63 and examine the Rule in Chapter 12.

[29] *See* § 53[C].

[30] *See* Restatement (Second) of Prop. § 2.1.

[31] *See* § 14[A].

[1] *See generally* Haskell at ch. 12.

[2] If the trust's funds benefit a particular individual, that person can enforce the trust. *See, e.g.*, Hooker v. Edes Home, 579 A.2d 608 (D.C. App. 1990) (Four women who benefitted from a charitable trust establishing a free home for widows were found to have standing to challenge the relocation of the free home.).

is not subject to the Rule Against Perpetuities.[3] Finally, there is a long tradition allowing courts to modify charitable trusts to further trust purposes in the face of changed circumstances.

This section examines two particularly troublesome topics: what it takes for a trust to have a "charitable purpose" and when courts can modify trusts to keep them serving such a purpose.

[A] Charitable Purposes

Definitions of "charitable" are necessarily open-ended and, perhaps more than most definitions, a function of the time and place in which they are made. The basic concept of a charitable purpose, however, is something that benefits the community in general. According to Restatement (Third) of Trusts § 28, "Charitable purposes include: (a) the relief of poverty; (b) the advancement of education; (c) the advancement of religion; (d) the promotion of health; (e) governmental or municipal purposes; (f) other purposes the accomplishment of which is beneficial to the community."[4]

In some ways, it is easier to identify what is *not* a charitable purpose:

A Trust for Too Narrow a Benefited Class. For example, a trust to provide for the health and education of the grantor's family would not be charitable, even though trusts for health and education are traditional charitable trust categories.[5] Similarly, a trust to pay for medical insurance for employees of a particular company might be too narrow to be deemed charitable, particularly if the company were small.[6]

The mere fact that only a few individuals will benefit from the trust does not prevent the trust from being charitable. Thus, a trust to provide medical care for victims of a particular disease would be valid even though the disease was rare, because the number of persons who could possibly contract the illness is large. Trusts often favor beneficiaries of particular social groups, regions, or political persuasions. Unless a trust offends the state's public policy, courts will allow its particular agenda. On the other

---

[3] *See generally* Chapter 12, *infra.*

[4] Accord UTC § 405(a).

A trust can be "charitable" for the private-law purposes of avoiding the requirement of definite beneficiaries and the Rule Against Perpetuities, even though some of its activities would preclude it from qualifying as a charity for federal tax purposes. *See In re* Estate of Breeden, 256 Cal. Rptr. 813 (Ct. App. 1989) (trust to advance "the principle of socialism and those causes related to socialism," including "supporting radio, television and the newspaper media and candidates for public office").

[5] *See* Hardage v. Hardage, 84 S.E.2d 54 (Ga. 1954) (income to be used for "blood relatives . . . who because of poverty, hardships or old age are unable to properly provide such care out of their own resources" and for "educational loans" to "dependent[s] of any of my blood relatives").

[6] *See* Bogert § 365.

hand, constitutional limits will apply if the trust's administration or enforcement involves "state action."[7]

Benefits Not Tied to the Charitable Purpose. Occasionally, the trust instrument is phrased in terms of a recognized charitable purpose, but the effect of the trust is not charitable. Moreover, generosity is not "charity" in the sense used here. Consider *Shenandoah Valley National Bank v. Taylor.*[8] Charles Henry left his estate to be invested, and the income divided among the local primary school children on the last day of school before Easter and before Christmas, "in furtherance of his or her obtainment of an education." The court saw the plan for what it was: a generous gift to schoolchildren, not a charitable gift to advance the social interests of the community.[9]

Trusts for Political Purposes. On the theory that society benefits from law reform, courts over time have become more sympathetic to trusts pursuing that purpose.[10] Unless a trust offends the state's public policy, courts will allow it.[11]

[B] Modification (Cy Pres)

Sometimes settlors give property for charitable purposes which later become impossible or impractical to pursue. If the settlor also had a general intention to support charitable purposes, a court can apply the trust proceeds to another charitable purpose consistent with the settlor's general intention.[12] Thus, a fund to educate people to repair typewriters might be used to train computer technicians.

---

[7] *See, e.g.,* Podberesky v. Kirwan, 38 F.3d 147 (4th Cir. 1994), *cert. denied,* 514 U.S. 1128, 131 L. Ed. 2d 1002, 115 S. Ct. 2001 (1995) (invalidating University of Maryland scholarships designated for African-American students only). *See generally* David Luria, *Prying Loose the Dead Hand of the Past: How Courts Apply Cy Pres to Race, Gender and Religiously Restricted Trusts,* 21 U.S.F. L. Rev. 41 (1987).

[8] 63 S.E.2d 786 (Va. 1951).

[9] *Compare* Bakos v. Kryder, 543 S.W.2d 216 (Ark. 1976) (A direction to pay $100 or $200 to each child leaving a specified children's home at about age 18, where most of the children in the home were impoverished and all were in the home because of unfortunate circumstances, was charitable.).

[10] *Compare* Jackson v. Phillips, 96 Mass. (14 Allen) 539 (1867) (trust assisting women to obtain equal rights was not charitable), *with* Register of Wills v. Cook, 216 A.2d 542 (Md. 1966) (trust to further passage of equal rights amendment was charitable).

[11] *See* Restatement (Third) of Trusts § 28, comment f.

[12] *See* Restatement (Third) of Trusts § 67; UTC § 413. *See generally* Frances Howell Rudko, *The Cy Pres Doctrine in the United States: From Extreme Reluctance to Affirmative Action,* 46 Clev. St. L. Rev. 471 (1998); Alex M. Johnson, Jr., *Limiting Dead Hand Control of Charitable Trusts: Expanding the Use of the Cy Pres Doctrine,* 21 U. Haw. L. Rev. 353 (1999); Wendy A. Lee, *Charitable Foundations and the Argument for Efficiency: Balancing Donor Intent with Practicable Solutions through Expanded Use of Cy Pres,* 34 Suffolk U. L. Rev. 173 (2000).

Rather than relying upon *cy pres,* a court might simply give trust language a liberal construction. *See, e.g.,* First Nat'l Bank of Southwestern Ohio v. Miami Univ., 121 Ohio App. 3d 170 (1997) ("Soviet Union" means "former Soviet Union.").

The chance to reach a large pot of money can make it tempting to define broadly what is a "changed circumstance." Consider, for example, how the San Francisco Foundation sought to use Beryl Buck's gift. In 1975, she left the residue of her estate (mostly about $9 million worth of Beldridge Oil stock) to the foundation, to be spent in Marin County, a wealthy area north of the city. After a takeover by Shell and changes in the market, the value ballooned to over $300 million by 1984. Based on the changed circumstances of the increase in value, the foundation sought approval to spend some of the money outside of Marin County. Finding charitable needs in the county, the court denied the request.[13]

Sometimes problems arise because settlors attach discriminatory terms to their gifts. *In re Estate of Wilson*[14] combined appeals involving two trusts with similar provisions for paying college expenses for male high school graduates. According to the "Wilson Trust," the local school superintendent was to choose the recipients and forward their names to the private trustee. In response to complaints about the gender discrimination, the superintendent agreed not to supply the names. The appellate court ultimately reformed the trust to allow male students to apply directly to the trustee, thus eliminating the state's role. Similar complaints and responses about the "Johnson Trust" (for which the school board was the trustee) led a different appellate court to take a different approach. It reformed the trust to eliminate the gender restriction.

In both cases, the New York Court of Appeals followed the *Wilson* court's approach of eliminating the state's role by using a private trustee.[15] Because the trusts' discriminatory terms were central to the testators' charitable intentions, those terms would be upheld unless they substantially impaired the gift's general charitable effect. Noting that a *per se* rule invalidating gender restrictions would also strike down female-only charitable gifts, the court declined to strike the male-only terms on public policy grounds. Finally, the court held that allowing the private discrimination was constitutionally appropriate because there was no state action to invoke the Fourteenth Amendment.[16]

A trust will fail if the original purpose becomes impossible or illegal *and* a court cannot apply *cy pres* because it cannot identify a general charitable purpose. For example, in 1931, George Hoffman created a trust for a hospital, but by 1972 the hospital had to close. George's will provided a gift

---

[13] The story appears with commentary in a series of articles starting at 21 U.S.F. L. Rev. 585 (1987). *See also* Note, *Phantom Selves: The Search for a General Charitable Intent in the Application of the Cy Pres Doctrine,* 40 Stan. L. Rev. 973 (1988).

[14] 452 N.E.2d 1228 (N.Y. 1983).

[15] The court relied upon its equitable powers to allow deviation from administrative terms, rather than upon the *cy pres* power to shift to a different charitable use. For a discussion about the differences between the two powers, see Dalonia v. Franciscan Health Sys., 679 N.E.2d 1084 (Ohio 1997).

[16] Compare the discussion in Dean Barclay, *Dead Hands and State Actors: The Racially Discriminatory Charitable Trusts in Hermitage Methodist Homes,* 7 Wash. & Lee. Race & Ethnich Ancestry L.J. 85 (2001).

over to a non-charity, but that gift violated the Rule Against Perpetuities. The gift-over, however, negated the possibility of applying *cy pres* because that gift showed George had a specific, as opposed to general, charitable intent.[17]

§ 16   Trusts and Pour-Over Wills

Now that you have seen the basic elements of wills and of trusts law, it should be useful to consider the principal device for interrelating wills and trusts, the "pour-over" will. "Pour-over" is the name given to wills[1] that designate a trust as one beneficiary. Often pour-over wills include a number of dispository provisions (cash to individuals, real estate or specifically identified items of personal property to particular family members), and then give the rest of the testator's property to a preexisting trust. The effect is to pour probate assets into the trust.

The most common estate plans using the pour-over device include three elements. First, the client creates a living trust, but intends it as a shell to be activated later, rather than as a current management device. Second, the client creates a will naming the trustee of the living trust as a will beneficiary. Third, the client names the trustee as beneficiary of life insurance policies.[2] After the client's death, the will pours probate property, and the life insurance policy pours insurance proceeds, into the trust, which then serves as a management (and, sometimes, tax-savings) device to care for the survivors.[3] (See Figure 4-1.)

---

[17] Nelson v. Kring, 592 P.2d 438 (Kan. 1979). *Compare In re* Estate of Crawshaw, 819 P.2d 613 (Kan. 1991) (trust for nursing scholarships of Marymount College redirected after nursing program closed).

[1] It is also used for other devices, like life insurance policies.

[2] The trust is often called a "life insurance trust." If, as in the example in the text, the only trust asset is its beneficial interest in the insurance policy, the trust may be called "unfunded." A "funded" life insurance trust would have sufficient assets to generate income to pay the premiums on the insurance.

[3] Sometimes "empty" living trusts are established in case they become needed to care for a donor who becomes incompetent. Someone holding a durable power of attorney can then fill the trust in much the same way as a will pours over into a trust. For further discussion, see § 22[B], *infra*.

Figure 4-1

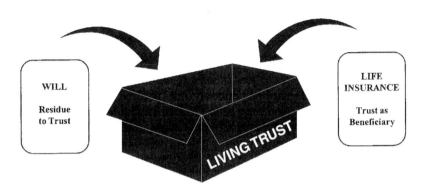

Sometimes clients will use pour-overs with testamentary trusts.[4] For example, Mac and Shirley both may want to create a testamentary trust for their survivor and their children, but they would like the efficiency of one administration. Their individual wills may say, in effect, "If I am the first to die, then give my property to First Bank to be held in trust according to the terms set forth below, but if my spouse has died and established a trust, then add my property to that trust instead." Mac and Shirley could also name the trustee as beneficiary of their life insurance.

The tangled history of the pour-over device can confuse students trying to understand the law. Despite modern statutes which have eliminated the major problems, concepts from the past sometimes haunt the analysis. As living trusts gained popularity, courts struggled with how, and under what circumstances, to allow trust provisions to control the distribution of what had been probate property.[5] Because the terms of a living trust usually would not have met the Statute of Wills' requirements, courts were reluctant to let those terms control the probate property. To the extent that courts allowed such plans, they relied either on incorporation by reference[6] or on the doctrine of independent significance.[7]

Incorporation by reference was a particularly troublesome solution. It failed to cover the situation of a testamentary gift to a living trust that had

---

[4] For a comparison of living trusts and testamentary trusts as planning devices, see § 11, *supra*.

[5] For an excellent short discussion of the development of theories to allow pour-overs, see Restatement (Third) of Trusts § 3.8, Reporter's Note. *See also* Haskell at 101-103.

[6] *See* § 8[B], *supra*.

[7] The theory is that the trust had a non-testamentary significance independent from the will and therefore its terms can be given effect despite the Statute of Wills. *See* § 42, *infra*, for a discussion of this doctrine in the related context of identifying will beneficiaries.

been amended after the will was signed.[8] More fundamentally, testators using the pour-over device had no intention of incorporating the trust into the will; they were trying to avoid probate administration of their trusts by creating living trusts in the first place.[9]

Seeing pour-overs as useful, legislatures acted to allow testamentary gifts to pre-existing trusts. The Uniform Testamentary Additions to Trusts Act appeared in 1960 and was later included in the UPC.[10] The few states which have not adopted the Uniform Act have statutes that reach substantially the same results. The revised UPC's version even allows gifts into living "trusts" that had been left *entirely* empty or that had been executed after the will was signed.[11]

Unless you are considering documents governed by pre-statutory rules or there are gaps in your statute, stay out of the thicket of attempted common law solutions. Only in very rare circumstances should you have any reason to speak about "a pour-over will which incorporates by reference and validates the living trust."[12] Rather, view the gift to the trust as validated by a statute which recognizes the utility and trustworthiness of the device.

The private express trust has gained popularity as a remarkably flexible device for avoiding probate and providing continuing management. It can be shaped to meet the needs of clients in widely varying circumstances. A host of other options, some ancient, some quite modern, are also available to estate planners and their clients. It is to these devices that we now turn.

---

[8] Recall that incorporation by reference requires that the document being incorporated be in existence at the time of the incorporating. *See* § 8[B], *supra*.

[9] Of course, giving a consolation prize of a testamentary trust was probably a better solution than leaving the living trust without assets from the estate. Compare the doctrine of dependent relative revocation discussed in § 9[E].

[10] UPC § 2-511.

[11] UPC § 2-511(a).

[12] One court saved a defectively-executed trust by incorporating it by reference into the will, which had been used to give property to the "trust." Tyson v. Henry, 514 S.E.2d 564 (N.C. App.), *review denied*, 540 S.E.2d 753 (N.C. 1999).

Chapter 5
OTHER NONPROBATE DEVICES

Individuals who want to transfer wealth outside of the probate system can select from a wide variety of options in addition to the trust.[1] While some of these choices may be familiar from your property course, others may not. A brief overview should help both remind you of the basics and place that doctrine in the context of planning wealth transfers. In addition, this chapter introduces some related devices that are part of an estate planning practice: life insurance and retirement plans. The chapter closes with a look at problems that arise when a will attempts to change a will substitute.

In the past, the law treated separately probate and nonprobate transfers, each in its own box with its own set of rules. Now that approach is changing.[2] The presence of relaxed standards for executing nonprobate documents has helped liberalize standards for will execution.[3] In addition, doctrines developed in the context of wills may be usable for will substitutes as well.[4] Over time, the law of probate and of nonprobate transfers will become increasingly integrated. While that change is happening, lawyers must understand both the traditional rules and the likely directions in which the law may move. The sections that follow aim to help meet both needs.

§ 17 Lifetime Gifts

Individuals make gifts for a variety of reasons.[1] Sometimes they are being generous. Sometimes they are trying to save taxes. Sometimes they are trying to avoid probate. Each of these is a legitimate purpose, but to accomplish any, the donor must follow a few basic rules. This section first discusses gifts of personal property, and then turns to real property.[2]

Traditionally, to make an effective gift of personal property, the donor must deliver the property to the donee with the intention to make a gift.[3]

---

[1] *See generally* § 1[B][2], *supra.*

[2] For a wide-ranging discussion of how far the UPC has come and what remains to be done, see Grayson M.P. McCouch, *Will Substitutes Under the Revised Uniform Probate*, 58 Brook. L. Rev. 1123 (1993).

[3] *See* § 7[B], *supra.*

[4] *See, e.g.,* §§ 28[C] (spousal election), 44[E][2] (adoption), 45[B][2][b] (lapse), *infra.*

[1] For a fascinating discussion of the nature of gifts, see the series of articles presented in 44 Fla. L. Rev. at 295-378 (1992).

[2] For an analysis of problems peculiar to gifts to minors, see Thomas E. Allison, *The Uniform Transfers to Minors Act—New and Improved, but Shortcomings Still Exist*, 10 U. Ark. Little Rock L.J. 339 (1987–88).

[3] *See generally* Ray A. Brown, The Law of Personal Property ch. 7-8 (CBC 3d ed. 1975).

There is now developing a rule allowing the donor to use an intervivos donative document instead.[4] Manual delivery is a particularly important element because it is such strong evidence of intention. Some tangible items (like a piano) are too big for easy delivery, so constructive delivery may suffice.[5] Among the more common controversies is whether handing over the key to a locked receptacle is sufficient symbolic delivery to allow the recipient to take the contents. The cases usually turn on whether it was practical for the donor to transfer the stored items manually, instead of merely giving the key. Donors can transfer intangible property (like stocks or bank accounts) by manually delivering the stock certificate or bank book evidencing the property.[6]

Almost over the line between valid lifetime gifts and invalid testamentary gifts are those gifts of personal property made in fear of death then imminent.[7] Like other gifts, they require delivery and an intention to make a present gift, but unlike most other gifts, they are both revocable and conditional (on the donor dying). If the donor changes her mind, she can get the property back. Moreover, if the donor survives, the gift is automatically revoked.

Just over the line are those gifts which in form appear to be lifetime gifts, but are really intended to take effect only at death. They might involve either personal or real property, and are commonly made by persons seeking to avoid probate and acting without a lawyer's advice. The problem is that lay people usually are unaware of the law's distinction between lifetime and testamentary gifts. From the law's perspective, the donor seems to want it both ways. The transfer is intended to look like a lifetime gift, thereby avoiding probate, but is also intended not to be effective until death. If the transfer can be branded an intended "testamentary" transfer, it will usually fail for not having met the Statute of Wills.[8] Many disputes involve whether the donor intended a lifetime or an at-death transfer.

Ferrell v. Stinson[9] illustrates some of the problems in these ambiguous situations. Mary Kamberling owned a farm in Iowa, but moved to Arizona

---

[4] Restatement (Third) of Prop. § 6.2, comment c.

[5] *See* Ray A. Brown, The Law of Personal Property §§ 7.5, 7.6 (CBC 3d ed. 1975). Sometimes "constructive" delivery and "symbolic" delivery are used interchangeably. The classic work on personal property draws a distinction between the two concepts. Constructive delivery involves giving "the means of obtaining possession and control," while symbolic delivery involves handing over some other object in place of the thing itself. Ray A. Brown, The Law of Personal Property at 92. Making symbolic delivery alone, without giving up power and dominion is said to be insufficient to make a gift.

[6] *See* Ray A. Brown, The Law of Personal Property at § 8.3 (CBC 3d ed. 1975).

[7] Such gifts are often called "gifts *causa mortis.*" *See* Restatement (Third) of Prop. § 6.2. *See generally* Ray A. Brown, The Law of Personal Property at §§ 7.15–7.20 (CBC 3d ed. 1975); Adrian J. Bradbrook, *Reassessment of the Scope of the Gift Causa Mortis*, 17 McGill L.J. 567 (1971).

[8] This result may change as jurisdictions adopt the UPC's harmless error rule. *See* § 7[B][4][c], *supra.*

[9] 11 N.W.2d 701 (Iowa 1943).

for health reasons. Bedridden about 10 months before she died, she executed a quitclaim deed to the farm, naming three women as grantees. She then asked her housekeeper to put the deed in a box in her bedroom closet. The next day, Mary executed a will giving property to others. At the time, she told her lawyer that she had executed deeds for the Iowa farm, so that it need not be covered in the will. She also asked her executor to mail the deed after her death to one of the grantees. Mary seems to have treated the deed and the will as equally valid ways of arranging her affairs. By using the deed, she could keep the farm out of probate.

The problem was that in order to sustain the deed, the court had to find delivery to the grantees during Mary's lifetime. This result was possible because manual delivery of a deed is not necessary to transfer title to real estate.[10] Here the court treated the instructions to the executor as a delivery in escrow, with title passing to the grantees at that time. The fact that Mary kept receiving rents from the property until her death could be justified by saying that she impliedly reserved a life estate, giving the grantees only remainder interests.[11] *Ferrell* illustrates that courts will sometimes stretch quite far in their search for something they can say a donee received during the life of the donor, for some way of avoiding the label "testamentary gift."[12] As a planning matter, of course, you would be taking foolhardy risks to use Mary Kamberling's approach. Putting the land in trust would avoid both probate and the litigation challenging delivery.

Henkle v. Henkle[13] shows another risk of using deeds as will substitutes: a court might actually treat the deed as a deed. In this case, Clarriette Henkle gave a deed of the family farm to her grandson, John, and reserved a life estate for herself. John therefore got a remainder. John was operating the farm, and Clarriette no doubt expected him to continue to do so after her death. Her lifetime gift would avoid the need for probate. When John died before his grandmother and left his wife and son as intestate heirs, they got John's remainder interest. Clarriette, faced with the prospect of the farm going out of the bloodline, challenged her earlier deed, but failed. The court saw the deed as an irrevocable gift to John and saw no reason to disturb it. Wills are revocable; deeds (traditionally) are not.

You might be tempted to make a deed revocable, either by reserving the power to revoke in the deed, or by reserving a power to reclaim a deed placed in escrow. As a planning matter, resist the temptation. Courts often invalidate such attempted transfers.[14] On the other hand, if you face a

---

[10] John E. Cribbet & Corwin W. Johnson, Principles of the Law of Property 156-158. In most situations, of course, the Statute of Frauds will require a writing. *See* Cribbet & Johnson at 160-166.

[11] For more on life estates and remainders, *see* §§ 34[C] & 35[B][2], *infra*.

[12] Compare the search for a present transfer in Farkas v. Williams, 125 N.E.2d 600 (Ill. 1955), the case involving a revocable trust of mutual fund shares. It is discussed in § 12[E], *supra*.

[13] 600 N.E.2d 791 (Ohio App. 1991).

[14] *See generally* Powell at ¶ 898[a].

situation where someone has tried such an approach, consider making anal-
ogies to trust law, which has allowed revocable transfers into trust for some
time. Maybe you could convince a court that it is time the law surrounding
deeds caught up with trust law.

People often attempt to use lifetime gifts as will substitutes. As long as
the law applies different rules for effectuating present gifts and testamentary gifts, such efforts are likely to backfire.

§ 18   Joint Interests

Creating joint interests in real or personal property is perhaps the most
common probate-avoidance device. The right of the survivor to own the
whole is the distinguishing feature of these interests.[1] When one owner
dies, her interest simply disappears, leaving the survivor(s) owning the
whole. An important planning point about joint interests is that while they
do avoid probate, they may not save federal estate taxes.[2] A couple whose
assets total more than $600,000 and who want to avoid federal estate tax
will usually need a more complex estate plan than merely holding their
property jointly. Clients often equate "probate avoidance" with "tax avoidance," and lawyers perform a vital service when they explain the difference.

As a doctrinal matter, most estate planning problems involving joint
interests center around whether and when grantors intended a completed
gift. Courts usually, but not always, take people at their word when they
say they are creating joint interests. This section will first discuss real
property joint tenancy, and then turn to personal property.

[A]   Real Property

Following the Great Depression of the 1930s, increasing numbers of
people started holding their land in joint tenancy.[3] Though a variety of
factors contributed to the popularity of joint tenancy, the increasing
attention given to probate avoidance no doubt contributed substantially to
the trend.

Joint tenancy can be an effective probate avoidance device. Clients need
to understand, however, that a deed creating a joint tenancy, unlike a will
identifying a beneficiary, is not revocable.

---

[1] *See* Cribbet & Johnson at 101-117. About half the states allow married couples to own
property as "tenants by the entirety," who also benefit from the survivorship feature. Unlike
interests held in joint tenancy, however, these cannot be transferred by either owner alone,
and they generally are not subject to creditors' claims. *See* Cribbet & Johnson at 102-106.

Tenancy in common, the other principal way for individuals to share ownership, creates
interests which are subject to probate as each co-tenant dies. *See* Cribbet & Johnson at 111-114.

[2] *See* § 62[A], *infra*.

[3] *See generally* N. William Hines, *Real Property Joint Tenancies: Law, Fact, and Fancy*, 51
Iowa L. Rev. 582 (1966). Joint tenancies can be created with a large number of co-tenants,
but typically are used by a husband and wife.

Gross v. Gross[4] illustrates how grantors who change their minds will nonetheless be bound by their prior actions. Peter Gross, in his 80s, wanted to avoid probate, so he executed and recorded deeds creating joint tenancies between himself and his son, Richard. Peter kept the deeds and occupied and maintained the property. Later Peter remarried and then sought to have the deeds declared void, because he had had no intention to give Richard a present interest.[5] The Supreme Court of Montana held that Peter's uncorroborated self-serving testimony was not clear and convincing evidence to overcome the presumption of delivery raised by executing and recording the deeds. Peter wanted both the freedom of absolute ownership and the probate avoidance feature of ownership shared in joint tenancy. He could not have both,[6] and once he elected to make the gift, he bound himself to that choice.[7]

Using joint tenancy for estate planning requires particular care. Clients who at one moment may view probate avoidance as their dominant goal may later change their minds.

[B] Personal Property [Especially Bank Accounts]

Jointly held stocks, bonds, mutual funds and bank accounts are common. Perhaps the principal reason courts have struggled with these forms of ownership is that they do not fit into traditional boxes. A joint account is "neither a common law joint tenancy, an ordinary inter vivos gift, a trust nor a will, yet it partakes of the features of all of these."[8] Bank accounts, perhaps because they are so widespread, have caused the most trouble. Slowly, the law is coming to recognize that people may use the joint form for a variety of reasons. Rather than burdening these devices with the baggage of other doctrines, legislation has emerged to validate various approaches in their own right.[9]

Questions arise regularly about whether a particular jointly held account was opened only for the "convenience" of one depositor.[10] In *Franklin v.*

---

[4] 781 P.2d 284 (Mont. 1989).

[5] Compare the change of heart experienced in *Henkle v. Henkle*, 600 N.E.2d 791 (Ohio App. 1991), when a grandmother tried to undo a gift of remainder to her grandson. The case is discussed in § 17, *supra*.

[6] In Ohio, someone pursuing both goals could use a "transfer-on-death deed" that allows persons to retain a fee simple title, but automatically transfers their interest upon their death to named beneficiaries. Until then, the beneficiaries have no interest. Ohio Rev. Code §§ 5302.22-.23.

[7] For a similar case, see *Estate of Levine*, 178 Cal. Rptr. 275 (Cal. App. 1981) (Husband tried to create joint tenancy for probate avoidance purposes, but to maintain property as community property for purposes of disposition under his will. Absent an agreement with his wife to hold the property as community, she took as surviving joint tenant.).

[8] N. William Hines, *Personal Property Joint Tenancies: More Law, Fact and Fancy*, 54 Minn. L. Rev. 509, 531 (1970).

[9] *See, e.g.*, UPC Article VI.

[10] To avoid litigation like this, courts have begun to interpret joint accounts as conclusively establishing a right of survivorship, at least in the absence of fraud or undue influence. *See, e.g.*, Wright v. Bloom, 635 N.E.2d 31 (Ohio 1994); Robinson v. Delfino, 710 A.2d 154 (R.I. 1998)

Anna National Bank of Anna,[11] Frank was a widower with failing eyesight, whose sister-in-law, Cora, moved in to care for him. To make it easier for Cora to get funds, Frank had Cora's name placed on the savings account he had had with his wife. Cora signed the bank's card, which designated the account as a "joint tenancy with right of survivorship." After Frank's death, Cora (as surviving joint tenant) and Frank's executor (as successor to Frank) both claimed the money. The court found clear and convincing evidence that Frank had not intended to make a gift to Cora but, rather, had added her as a signatory for his own convenience. This evidence was enough to overcome the usual presumption of joint ownership established by the bank's signature card.[12]

Though the most common reason depositors establish "convenience accounts" is to allow a caregiver easy access to funds, such accounts may also be opened for short-term uses, like allowing a friend to pay your bills when you go on vacation. If banks were to offer accounts clearly designated as convenience accounts, much litigation could be avoided.[13]

A form of ownership peculiar to savings accounts is the so-called "Totten Trust," sometimes also known simply as a "savings account trust." The former term comes from the name of a New York case validating the device.[14] In form, the depositor opens an account in his own name, "as trustee" for someone else. In fact, there is really no trust relationship established. Rather, the account functions like a "Payable-on-Death" (POD) account, in which the depositor can withdraw the funds at any time for his own use and the "beneficiary" gets what is left when the depositor/trustee dies. While courts have been hostile to straightforward POD accounts (as too blatantly testamentary), savings accounts trusts have proliferated, often because of specific legislative authorization.[15]

---

[11] 488 N.E.2d 1117 (Ill. App. 1986).

[12] For an unusual case in which a joint account holder argued that the account was *only* a convenience account, see *Estate of Taggart*, 619 P.2d 562 (N.M. 1980). There a widow claimed a share as a pretermitted spouse, but faced the argument that joint accounts with her husband were intended to be in lieu of any testamentary provisions for her. To preserve her pretermitted claim, she argued that the accounts were for convenience only, rather than in lieu of testamentary gifts. The court affirmed lower court findings that the account was not for her convenience.

For discussion of pretermitted spouses, see § 29, *infra*.

[13] *See generally* David M. English, *The UPC and the New Durable Powers*, 27 Real Prop. Prob. & Tr. J. 333, 354-361 (1992). The UPC provides a "check off what you want" form, which includes a "multiple-party account *without* right of survivorship." *See* UPC § 6-204 (emphasis added). Much of the UPC's approach was foreshadowed in N. William Hines, *Personal Property Joint Tenancies: More Law, Fact and Fancy*, 54 Minn. L. Rev. 509, 552-559 (1970).

Another solution is to use a durable power of attorney. *See* § 22[B], *infra*.

[14] *In re* Totten, 71 N.E. 748 (N.Y. 1904).

[15] *See generally* Note, *Totten Trust as a Testamentary Substitute*, 41 Alb. L. Rev. 605 (1977). More recently, legislatures have also allowed POD bank accounts, without the trust fiction. *See* Richard V. Wellman, *Transfer-on-Death Securities Registration: A New Title Form*, 21 Ga. L. Rev. 789, 806 n.50 (1987).

The law regarding the ownership of bank accounts is not very satisfactory. Because statutes may cover one topic, or allow one form but not another, you must read them very carefully. Many states, for example, absolve banks from liability if they pay funds to someone whose name is on the account, but who turns out not to have a right to the money.[16] Often these statutes give no guidance, however, on who has title to the account. The UPC's Article VI offers a wide-ranging attempt to validate many arrangements which prior law might have invalidated as "testamentary."[17] In addition, it clarifies the rights of multi-party[18] bank account owners, both during their lifetimes and at death.[19]

Joint interests will no doubt remain popular probate-avoidance devices. Lawyers who keep their clients well-informed about the tax and non-tax consequences of this method provide valuable service in facilitating efficient wealth transfers. Too often, however, people act without adequate information, and then the laws' technicalities become intention-defeating.

§ 19   Life Insurance and Other Contracts

In terms of estate planning, life insurance may be the most important asset of middle-class Americans.[1] As noted earlier,[2] insurance is often made payable to preexisting living trusts, which then serve to manage the funds for the survivors. In other cases, it is paid directly to the beneficiaries, or is held by the company in some form, usually as an annuity to be paid out over time. Despite its functional similarity to wills,[3] life insurance has

---

[16] Ohio Rev. Code Ann. § 1109.07; Cal. Fin. Code § 852.

[17] See generally William M. McGovern, Jr., Nonprobate Transfers Under the Revised Uniform Probate Code, 55 Alb. L. Rev. 1329 (1992).

[18] These accounts are called "joint accounts" in common parlance. The UPC's term is intended to avoid confusion with common law joint tenancy interests in real property.

[19] See UPC §§ 6-211 & 6-212.

Recent amendments extend the statute's reach to include security transfers on death (TOD). See UPC §§ 6-301 to 6-311. The rules regarding securities, however, differ from those covering bank accounts. See generally William M. McGovern, Jr., Nonprobate Transfers Under the Revised Uniform Probate Code, 55 Alb. L. Rev. 1329 (1992); Richard V. Wellman, Transfer-on-Death Securities Registration: A New Title Form, 21 Ga. L. Rev. 789 (1987).

A TOD statute could have saved the fight in Blanchette v. Blanchette, 287 N.E.2d 459 (Mass. 1972). Robert worked for AT&T and purchased stock by payroll deduction. To avoid probate, he had the stock issued to himself and his wife, Marie, as joint tenants. When they later divorced, Marie claimed an interest in the stock. The court gave the stock to Robert after it found he had had no intention to make a gift.

[1] Indeed, some say they are worth more dead than alive, which is true if you ignore the value of their earning potential over time. A brief description of types of insurance appears in § 2[B][2], supra. For more detailed coverage, see Joel C. Dobris & Stewart E. Sterk, Estates and Trusts ch. 12 (Foundation Press 1998). See also Jon J. Gallo, The Use of Life Insurance in Estate Planning: A Guide to Planning and Drafting — Part I, 33 Real Prop. Prob. & Tr. J. 685 (1999) and Part II, 34 Real Prop. Prob. & Tr. J. 70 (2000).

[2] See § 16, supra.

[3] Life insurance is revocable and benefits are paid at death.

escaped the "testamentary transfer" label. The enforceability of life insurance policies is governed by contract law, not the law of wills.[4] On policy grounds, it makes good sense to validate these transfers; we trust them.[5] On the other hand, it seems odd that courts continue to strike down as "testamentary" arrangements which, while technically different, are very similar to life insurance.

The judicial tendency to put things in various doctrinal boxes and then apply the law for that "box," irrespective of the law regarding functionally equivalent devices, is well illustrated by *Wilhoit v. Peoples Life Insurance Co.*[6] Sarah was beneficiary of a life insurance policy purchased by her husband. After he died, she received the proceeds and then sent them back to the company, to be held at interest and paid to her brother, Robert Owens, at Sarah's death. Robert Owens died about two years later. Sarah died about 20 years later, leaving a will which attempted to give the funds to Robert Wilhoit, her step-grandson. Both Robert Wilhoit and Thomas Owens (as successor to Robert Owens, through his will) claimed the money. The court treated the second contract (under which Sarah returned the funds) as an attempted testamentary gift, which failed because it lacked Statute of Wills formalities. The gift therefore fell into the estate and went to Wilhoit. If, instead of returning the funds to be held by the company, Sarah had used the money to buy a new policy with her brother as beneficiary, that policy certainly would have been honored. Because she chose another form, more like a bank deposit, her gift failed.[7]

Several issues lurking in Wilhoit are covered in other sections of this text. They deal with the extent to which the "subsidiary law of wills" should apply to will substitutes.[8] If the second contract were valid, would Sarah's will provision have been effective to change the beneficiary to Robert Wilhoit?[9] If the contract were valid, but Sarah's will could not change it, who would take the property intended for her predeceased brother?[10] If Sarah and her husband had divorced, would Sarah still have had a claim

---

[4] *See* Atkinson § 39.

[5] For more extended discussion of this point, see § 7[B][4][c] (dispensing power for wills) and § 12[E] (validity of revocable trusts), *supra*.

[6] 218 F.2d 887 (7th Cir. 1955).

[7] By invalidating the gift to Robert Owens, the court managed to honor Sarah's ultimate intention to get the property to Robert Wilhoit. It could have done that, however, without invalidating the gift as a testamentary transfer, by requiring Owens to survive Sarah in order to take. Since he did not, the gift under the policy would fail and pass to Wilhoit under the will.

Compare the result under the UPC. Section 6-201(a) would validate the POD provision, and § 2-706(b) would give the money to Thomas Owens, if he was a descendant of the named beneficiary, Robert Owens. For more discussion of survivorship, see § 45[B][2], *infra*.

[8] *See* John H. Langbein, *The Nonprobate Revolution and the Future of the Law of Succession*, 97 Harv. L. Rev. 1108, 1134-1140 (1984).

[9] Probably not. *See* § 21, *infra*.

[10] Probably her estate, under the terms of the contract. The UPC establishes substitute beneficiaries under a broad anti-lapse statute discussed in § 45[B][2][b][ii], *infra*.

as beneficiary of the policy on his life?[11] Pushed by the UPC, the law is likely to move toward treating like things alike. In the meantime, beware of the law's habit of maintaining separate boxes for each.

§ 20 Retirement Funds

With the support of favorable tax treatment from Congress, private funds designed to support Americans' retirement years have mushroomed in recent years. These funds provide income in addition to that available from the federal government's Social Security system.[1] The rules surrounding such pension plans[2] are extraordinarily complex, and detailed descriptions are beyond the scope of this text. A brief introduction, however, should help you put into a larger context the planning devices emphasized in most wills and trusts courses.[3] This section identifies some basic terminology, and then discusses the problem of federal preemption of state law and the scope of spousal rights to pensions, two issues particularly relevant to lawyers developing estate plans.

As a practical matter, most pension plans are governed by the Employee Retirement Income Security Act (ERISA)[4] and the Internal Revenue Code (IRC). The two statutes work together toward the goals of encouraging investment in such funds, and assuring that the money employers have promised is really available at retirement and that employees are treated fairly. From the individual's perspective, pension plans offer two principal tax benefits. First, contributions to the plan are in "pre-tax" dollars excluded from the employee's income. Secondly, employees can defer taxation until distribution at retirement age. This feature means reinvested income is also pre-tax, and that when taxation does come, the taxpayer may well be in a lower (retirement-level) tax bracket.

Employer plans fall into two broad categories. "Defined benefit" plans establish each employee's benefit according to a formula. For example, someone's retirement pay might be 60% of the average of their highest three years

---

[11] Probably. *See, e.g.*, Cook v. Equitable Life Assurance Soc., 428 N.E.2d 110 (Ind. Ct. App. 1981) (applying the traditional rule that a divorce does not revoke a beneficiary designation in a life insurance policy).

The law may be changing, however. *See* Vasconi v. Guardian Life Ins. Co., 590 A.2d 1161 (N.J. 1991) (divorce presumably revokes life insurance beneficiary designation); UPC § 2-804. Both the *Vasconi* case and UPC statute are discussed in § 45[B][1], *infra*.

[1] The vast majority of workers are covered by Social Security. There is a parallel system for railroad workers. Various public employees, including teachers and persons in the military, have their own state or federal programs.

[2] The term "pension plans" is used in the broad sense to include the range of devices available to employers and employees to set aside funds for the employee's retirement. A narrower definition, describing a plan with "definitely determinable benefits . . . not dependent upon profits," appears in the Treasury Regulations. Treas. Reg. § 1.401-1(b)(1)(ii).

[3] If you desire somewhat more information and citations, but do not want to be overwhelmed with detail, see Andersen & Bloom at 196-199. For greater depth, see Everett T. Allen et al., Pension Planning: Pensions, Profit-sharing, and Other Deferred Compensation Plans (7th ed. 1992).

[4] 29 U.S.C. § 1001 *et seq.*

of salary. Years of service might also be part of the formula. Those with 20 years service might get 40%, while those with 40 years get 60%. The employer then funds the plan according to actuarial calculations regarding age, life expectancy, current salary and the like. Except for the risk that the employer may become insolvent, the employee has no risk of a low return on the investments made during the employee's working years.[5] The benefit is already defined. On the other hand, the employee does not benefit from any return which turns out to be higher than that anticipated.

The second principal category of employer-funded plans is "defined contribution" plans. These come in a variety of forms. Rather than starting at the benefit end and working backwards to determine an employer's obligation, these plans either require or allow employer contributions at various levels. Accounts are kept for each employee, and whatever has been accumulated before retirement becomes available to that person. The employee bears the risk of poor returns and benefits from high returns. Among the most popular of these plans are "profit sharing" arrangements under which the employer has the option of contributing to employees' retirement funds in good years. In contrast, "money purchase" plans require employer contributions. Some kinds of plans allow employee contributions (in pre-tax dollars) to the fund.[6]

As part of the effort to provide basic, nationwide protections to employees, ERISA preempts "any and all State laws insofar as they many now or hereafter relate to any employee benefit plan"[7] covered by the act. ERISA may apply to a number of problems traditionally viewed as part of wills and trusts law. For example, in *Egelhoff v. Egelhoff*,[8] the Supreme Court held that ERISA preempted a Washington State statute that would have revoked the designation of a divorced spouse as a beneficiary of an employer-sponsored group life insurance policy.[9] Lawyers who do private estate planning need to be aware that ERISA may be lurking around the edges.

One federal action deserving further mention is the expansion of spousal rights to pension funds. The Retirement Equity Act mandates that if a plan beneficiary dies before the benefits start, his or her spouse must get some or all of the employee's benefit.[10] Perhaps more importantly, when an

---

[5] The Pension Benefit Guarantee Corp., created on the model of the government corporations which insure bank accounts, protects against underfunded pension funds. *See* 29 U.S.C. § 1322(a).

[6] Self-employed individuals can establish Keogh plans. *See* IRC § 404(e). These are sometimes called "H.R. 10" plans, after the number of the bill establishing the program. Another option is to open an Individual Retirement Account (IRA). Employees can open IRAs, but their tax benefits may be limited if they also are covered by their employer's plan. *See* IRC §§ 219(b) & 408(a).

[7] 29 U.S.C. § 1144(a).

[8] 121 S. Ct. 1322 (2001). *See* Cheyanna L. Jaffke, *Death, Taxes, and Now Divorce — The Dyad Expands to a Triad: ERISA's Social Policy Harms Women's Rights*, 35 U.S.F.L. Rev. 255 (2001).

[9] For more on how state law handles gifts to ex-spouses, see § 45[B][1].

[10] *See generally* Camilla E. Watson, *Broken Promises Revisited: The Window of Vulnerability for Surviving Spouses Under ERISA*, 76 Iowa L. Rev. 431 (1991).

employee retires, the plan usually must pay out in the form of a joint and survivor annuity.[11] The employee's spouse can consent to another arrangement. This statute is consistent with a general trend toward empowering non-employee, non-income-earning spouses.[12]

§ 21   Using a Will to Change a Will Substitute[1]

We have seen that nonlawyers may not appreciate the differences among the legal doctrines which accompany the various devices used to transfer wealth at death. One consequence of this inaccurate merging of doctrine is that sometimes testators will attempt to use their wills to transfer property not subject to probate court jurisdiction. Often those attempts seek to change who benefits from various will substitutes. Generally the efforts fail, but the law is not consistent.[2]

In re Schaech's Will[3] captures the confusion testators sometimes experience. It involved a homemade will by Thomas Schaech, giving all of his personal property to his wife, except as otherwise stipulated. The will then designated who should get a variety of assets, some probate and some not: life insurance policies, bank accounts, jewelry, cash, and even his half (joint tenancy) interest in his home. Sometimes the testator tried to give property to a person different from the one who would have taken it outside of probate. For example, he "gave" his sisters-in-law life insurance in which his wife was named beneficiary, and he "gave" his joint tenancy interest in his home (held with his wife) to his daughter. The court applied standard doctrine and said that the will could not change title to the nonprobate assets.[4] The court, however, did force his widow to choose between taking under the will, but giving up the life insurance and share of the house, or taking the insurance and house, but giving up property she got through the will. The court kept probate and nonprobate doctrines separate, but made some effort to effectuate Thomas's overall intention.

Cases like *Schaech* have prompted discussions about whether a so-called "blockbuster" or "super" will should be allowed for the express purpose of overriding beneficiary designations made in nonprobate documents.[5] Certainly such an option would be convenient in those rare circumstances of

---

[11] A joint and survivor annuity is one which pays out to both spouses while they are both alive, and then pays to the survivor.

[12] Section 28, *infra*, discusses the complex questions regarding claims each spouse has to assets acquired by the other.

[1] The related question of contracts to make or not revoke wills is covered in § 10, *supra*.

[2] For example, UPC § 6-213(b) prohibits changing by will rights of survivorship or POD designations in bank accounts. The UPC takes no position regarding other will substitutes. The UTC allows a will to revoke a lifetime trust. UTC § 602(c)(2)(A).

[3] 31 N.W.2d 614 (Wis. 1948).

[4] *But see* Burkett v. Mott, 733 P.2d 673 (Ariz. Ct. App. 1986) (allowing a will to change a life insurance beneficiary designation).

[5] *See generally* Roberta R. Kwall, *The Superwill Debate: Opening the Pandora's Box?*, 62 Temp. L.Q. 277 (1989).

people making deathbed wills. On the other hand, such wills could raise difficult questions about the scope of their coverage or the consequences of their execution and revocation. Any legislation authorizing blockbuster wills ought to be designed with careful reference both to the rules surrounding nonprobate devices and to traditional wills rules.

Perhaps a better solution to the proliferation of nonprobate devices would be to make trusts more easily available by endorsing standardized forms for their creation.[6] If individuals, without much trouble, could place a wide variety of assets in trust, perhaps the cumbersome use of many devices would decline.

This chapter has brought together a series of doctrines related by the fact that they all involve at-death events which are not part of the probate process. Despite their commonalties, they tend to be governed by different sets of rules. As they continue to gain importance in practice, however, we can expect that these doctrines increasingly will merge into a unified set of concepts, drawing lessons from both the testamentary and the lifetime-transfers sides of their heritage.

---

[6] *See* Gerry W. Beyer, *Simplification of Inter Vivos Trust Instruments—From Incorporation by Reference to the Uniform Custodial Trust Act and Beyond*, 32 S. Tex. L. Rev. 203 (1991).

Chapter 6

PLANNING FOR INCAPACITY

Because people live longer than ever before, and because medical technology often can keep even severely incapacitated people alive, clients often want to plan for their own possible incapacity.[1] Consequently, lawyers who in the past drafted "simple" wills for clients of modest means are now also developing plans for both property management and control of health care decisions during incapacity. On the property side, the trust is still the device of choice because of its great flexibility and well-established legal doctrine. The advent of durable powers of attorney, however, has made available at lower cost some of the advantages of trusts.

On the health care side, the law has been changing rapidly. First came "living wills," which attempt to offer advance directives for how to handle various medical questions in case the patient cannot make the decision at the time. Then came durable powers of attorney, which name someone to make decisions. Now the law is moving to combine these concepts in one document.

This chapter first addresses the property issues, and then turns to the health care questions.

§ 22 Property Management

When lawyers work with clients to develop strategies for how to manage the property of an incapacitated person, many factors come into play: the nature and extent of any incapacity, the amount and kind of property involved, the needs of family members and friends, and the state of the law in the relevant jurisdictions. As noted above, trusts are often the best solution. Less elaborate approaches, however, will fit many situations. This section introduces the principal non-trust options for facing disability.

[A] Guardianship

Much like the way the law of intestacy serves as a foundation for the law of wills, guardianship law undergirds other approaches to property management for incapacitated people. When someone is a minor or is unable to make various kinds of decisions, the law provides for a guardian

---

[1] For guidance on relating to clients who have diminished capacity, see Model Rules of Professional Conduct, Rule 1.14 (2002).

to make decisions on that person's behalf.[1] The disabled person is called a "ward."

In general, in order for a court to appoint a guardian, the ward must be "incompetent."[2] Not so long ago, guardianship was an all-or-nothing proposition almost everywhere: a ward lost virtually all decisionmaking authority. Increasingly, states have recognized that someone might be incompetent to make some decisions, but able to make others. Many states have reformed their laws to allow "limited" or "partial" guardianships, so that a guardian's authority is tailored to the needs of the particular ward.[3] Typically, the basic standard is whether the ward can understand the question at hand, what the options are, and what the likely consequences of a particular decision will be.[4] If the ward cannot understand that much, a guardian can be appointed to handle a particular decision (or category of decisions). Thus, someone might be incompetent for one purpose, but competent for another.

In the planning context, the law distinguishes between two different types of guardianships. A *guardian of the person* has the responsibility to care for the personal needs of the ward. Guardians of the person handle topics like setting bedtimes and monitoring TV viewing for a minor, or supervising travel plans or personal hygiene for an adult. A court may also appoint the same person or another (including an institution) as *guardian of the property* of the ward. This person would handle some or all of the ward's financial affairs.[5]

Guardianship over property offers the advantage of court-supervised administration, which can help avoid arbitrary or fraudulent activity, but the actual level of court supervision varies widely. Moreover, guardianship presents significant disadvantages. By labeling the ward as at least partially "incompetent," guardianship carries a stigma which may hurt the ward's self-esteem. Because it is court-supervised, guardianship is also costly, in terms of both time and money. Evaluations, hearings, reports and the like all take time and drive up costs. In addition, the list of permissible investments may limit flexibility.[6]

---

[1] Your state may not use the term "guardian." In the text, "guardian" includes "conservator," "curator," "committee," and similar terms identifying the person or people making decisions for others. The UPC calls the property manager a "conservator" and the person in charge of personal questions the "guardian." UPC §§ 1-201, 5-306. *See generally* Thomas P. Gallanis, A. Kimberly Dayton & Molly M. Wood, Elder Law 259-320 (2000); Lawrence A. Frolik & Alison Barnes, Elderlaw 449-514 (2d ed. 1999).

[2] It can often be difficult to decide whether someone meets the relevant statutory definition. *See, e.g., In re* Maher, 621 N.Y.S.2d 617 (App. Div. 1994) (stroke victim not "incapacitated").

[3] *See, e.g.,* N.Y. Mental Hygiene Law, Art. 81. A revised Uniform Guardianship and Protective Proceedings Act appeared in 1997. *See* 8A Unif. Laws. Ann., 2002 Pocket Part. *See generally* Lawrence A. Frolik, *Plenary Guardianship: An Analysis, a Critique and a Proposal for Reform,* 23 Ariz. L. Rev. 599 (1981).

[4] Compare the elements for determining the capacity to make a will. *See* § 7[A][2], *supra.*

[5] Choosing guardians can be difficult. Clients need to identify people who are both competent and compassionate. Compare the challenges of choosing a trustee. *See* § 12[D], *supra.*

[6] *See generally* William M. McGovern, *Trusts, Custodianships, and Durable Powers of Attorney,* 27 Real. Prop. Prob. & Tr. J. 1 (1992).

For a variety of reasons, many people decide to leave guardianship as a last resort. At least where adults are concerned, creative use of caretakers, on the personal side, and of trusts or powers of attorney, on the property management side, often can avoid the need for guardianship.

[B] Durable Powers of Attorney

A power of attorney is an arrangement under which one person (the principal) gives another person (the agent) the power to act on behalf of the person executing the power. Powers of attorney might be executed for a specific purpose, like allowing someone else to participate in the closing of a house sale when either the buyer or the seller cannot be present. Powers of attorney can also be quite broad, authorizing the agent to act in all sorts of ways for the principal. They can be particularly useful in allowing a helper to handle the affairs of someone who is homebound.[7] Under traditional agency law, however, the power of the agent ends if the principal becomes incompetent.[8]

To overcome the restrictions of agency law, all states have authorized some form of a "durable" power of attorney, under which the agent retains authority despite the principal's incapacity.[9] The term "durable" can be misleading in this context. The power survives the principal's incapacity, but not the principal's death.[10] Moreover, like all powers of attorney, durable powers are revocable by the principal.

The power's revocability creates problems, both for third parties and for the principal. A bank, for example, may be reluctant to allow the agent to withdraw funds, for fear that the document they see has been revoked. The bank may be more willing to cooperate if the power of attorney form itself

---

[7] "Convenience" bank accounts are often meant to serve this purpose, but can cause numerous problems when the relationship of the parties is not clearly recorded. *See* § 18[B], *supra.*

[8] *See* Restatement (Second) of Agency §§ 120 & 122 (1958). Sometimes relatives disappointed by an agent's decisions will challenge a power of attorney on the ground that the principal lacked capacity at the time the power was signed. *See, e.g.*, Estate of Taggart, 95 N.M. 117, 619 P.2d 562 (1980) (affirming a jury verdict which, on the basis of conflicting evidence, found James Taggart lacked the capacity to grant a power of attorney to his second wife). Compare the problems surrounding testamentary capacity, discussed in § 7[A][2], *supra.*

[9] *See generally* Karen E. Boxx, *The Durable Power of Attorney's Place in the Family of Fiduciary Relationships*, 36 Ga. L. Rev. 1 (2001); Patrick E. Longan, *Middle Class Lawyering in the Age of Alzheimer's: The Lawyer's Duties in Representing a Fiduciary*, 70 Fordham L. Rev. 901 (2001).

The statutes are usually based on proposals that have changed slightly over time and now appear in §§ 5-501 to 5-505 of the UPC. Statutes vary in particulars, but the basic concept has been accepted everywhere. The differences in detail, however, reduce the utility of durable powers for use in an increasingly multi-jurisdictional economy.

[10] Many statutes protect the agent who acts in good faith without actual knowledge of the death. They also bind successors of the principal to such acts. These provisions avoid the problem of having to undo arrangements made after the death, but before people knew of it. *See* UPC § 5-504(a).

absolves from liability third parties who rely on the form without notice of its termination.[11]

A principal who decides to revoke the power should both notify the agent and notify third parties with whom the agent had been working.[12]

Powers of attorney can either be immediately effective, or can be written to "spring" into action upon the happening of a future event, usually the disability of the principal. A springing power has the advantage of keeping complete control in the hands of the principal until the power is needed. One disadvantage, however, is trying to tell when the event activating the power has taken place. Powers invite litigation if they provide simply that they are effective upon the principal's "incapacity," without more elaboration. The power should define "incapacity," and probably should designate a committee (with flexible membership) to certify that incapacity exists. Such a power, accompanied by the committee's certification, should be enough to allow the agent to act, without litigating about the existence of her authority.

Durable powers of attorney have several advantages over other devices. They are easier and less expensive to establish than most trusts. They are more flexible than lifetime gifts and joint tenancies. They avoid the need for invoking the judicial process the way guardianships do.[13] On the other hand, they may raise substantial questions about the scope of the agent's power to do particular acts.[14] Can the agent make a gift of the principal's property? Under what circumstances?[15] Can the agent exercise the

---

[11] Some statutes require banks and other institutions to honor powers in identified circumstances. *See, e.g.*, N.J. Stat. Ann. 46: 2B-8; N.Y. Gen. Oblig. Law § 5-1504.

[12] Powers of attorney can also be set to expire on a fixed date. This device protects the principal against the possibility of abuse by the agent in the future. One might structure the power to expire unless it is renewed by the principal or other designated persons who could keep the power alive if the principal became incapacitated.

[13] The lack of supervision, however, increases the opportunities for abuse.

[14] *See* William M. McGovern, *Trusts, Custodianships, and Durable Powers of Attorney*, 27 Real Prop. Prob. & Tr. J. 1, 32 (1992).

[15] Such a power may be useful to allow tax planning, but presents a serious conflict of interest if the agent can give herself a gift.

All gifts, especially those to an agent, should be expressly authorized in the document. In *Estate of Huston*, 60 Cal. Rptr. 2d 217 (Ct. App. 1997), the court invalidated a gift an agent made to himself at the principal's oral instructions. The written power of attorney prohibited such gifts. *But see* LeCraw v. LeCraw, 401 S.E.2d 697 (Ga. 1991) (Despite lack of specific authorization, gifts were allowed to agents and agents' family members where a gift-giving program was a continuing part of principal's tax planning and where principal was aware of some of the gifts.). *See generally* Robert McLead, *What Are the Limitations to an Attorney-in-Fact's Power to Gift and to Change a Dispositive (Estate) Plan?*, 27 Wm. Mitchell L. Rev. 1143 (2000).

Gifts can produce unintended consequences. While in a nursing home, George gave his grandson Danny a power of attorney. Ostensibly to make it easier to keep Danny's alcoholic father out of George's house, Danny used the power to transfer the house to himself and his wife, Tania. When they later divorced, Tania claimed half of the house. To keep the house in George's family, the court in Miller v. Miller, 872 S.W.2d 654 (Mo. Ct. App. 1994), invalidated the transfer as a breach of Danny's fiduciary duty to George. Compare Henkle v. Henkle, 600 N.E.2d 791 (Ohio Ct. App. 1991), discussed in § 17, *supra*, and Gross v. Gross, 781 P.2d 284 (Mont. 1989), discussed in § 18[A], *supra*.

principal's power to revoke a trust?[16] Can the agent shift assets into a form exempt from Medicaid's "maximum assets" rules?[17] Or elect against a will?[18] Or borrow money? For what purposes? The more a power of attorney form attempts to answer these questions, the more cumbersome (and expensive) it becomes. If the power of attorney arrangement starts to resemble a trust, perhaps the trust device should be used after all, with the added advantage that the trust can continue after the death of the principal.

Some clients do not want to trouble themselves with a living trust while they are competent, but do want its protection should they become incompetent. One solution is to establish a nominally funded trust and create a springing durable power of attorney that authorizes the agent to add funds to the trust.[19] The power of attorney functions much like a pour-over will, but the assets can be transferred to the trust while the principal is still alive.[20] Such a standby trust will be available if it is needed, but need not be used at all if the principal does not become incompetent or if the power of attorney proves sufficient.

Another possible use of a durable power of attorney is to appoint someone to make health care decisions on behalf of an incompetent person. Sometimes clients will give one person power over both property and health care decisions; sometimes those functions will be split. A client might prefer financial decisions to be in one set of hands, and life-and-death decisions in another.[21] Because durable powers for health care decisions raise different issues, they are discussed in the next section.[22]

§ 23   Health Care Decisionmaking

Prompted by changes in medical technology, courts and legislatures have grappled with the question of when and how to allow people to die, even though they might be kept alive. Clients seeking wills now regularly ask their lawyers to prepare appropriate documents to allow the client some control over end-of-life decisions. These variously named documents go under the general title, "advance directives." This section sketches the basic options.

---

[16] *See* Fanzen v. Norwest Bank Colorado, 955 P.2d 1018 (1998) (yes).

[17] For a discussion of Medicaid and trusts, see § 13[B][2], *supra.*

[18] The answer is yes, sometimes. For discussion, see § 28[C][4], *infra.*

[19] *See generally* John J. Lombard, *Planning for Disability: Durable Powers, Standby Trusts and Preserving Eligibility for Government Benefits*, 20 U. Miami Inst. on Est. Plan. ch. 17 (1986).

[20] For a discussion of pour-over wills, see § 16, *supra.*

[21] Similar issues arise when choosing a trustee. *See* § 12[D], *supra.*

[22] Another related topic which lawyers may face is evaluating the terms of their clients' long-term care insurance policies. *See generally* Robert D. Hayes, Nancy G. Boyd & Kenneth W. Hollman, *What Attorney's Should Know About Long-Term Care Insurance*, 7 Elder L.J. 1 (1999); Jan Ellen Rein, *Misinformation and Self-Deception in Recent Long-Term Care Policy Trends,* 12 J.L. & Pol. 195 (1996).

First, a warning: approach any work you do in this area very carefully. Both case law and statutes are changing rapidly, and the details vary widely.[1] More important, your clients may not be ready to execute the documents they believe they want. These documents involve difficult decisions that most of us would rather not face, that many of us have not considered carefully, and that we may not be able to anticipate.[2] They should not be executed casually, but only after the client has had time to think through the choices after being fully informed of what they mean.[3]

The law is now in its third stage of development. The first, running roughly in the 1970s, involved the advent of living wills.[4] Created by analogy to wills disposing of property, living wills speak directly for the patient. They try to anticipate various medical situations which could arise, and say what care the patient would want. Many states impose various execution requirements similar to those which apply to wills of property.[5] For example, most living wills require a writing signed before witnesses.[6]

The second stage, beginning in the 1980s, brought a surge of interest in durable powers for health care decisions.[7] Like their counterparts for dealing with property,[8] these documents name someone else to act on behalf of the patient. The grant of authority may be broad, or may be limited to

[1] A good source for keeping tabs on the changes is Alan Meisel, The Right to Die (2d ed. 1995, with annual supplements).

[2] For an insightful personal account and drafting suggestions, see Stephan R. Leimberg & Albert E. Gibbons, *Drafting an Advance Directive for Health Care: Personal Reflections*, Estate Planning, Aug. 2002, at 422. *See also* Lorraine M. Bellard, *Restraining the Paternalism of Attorneys and Families in End of Life Decision Making While Recognizing that Patients Want More Than Just Autonomy*, 14 Geo. J. Legal Ethics 803 (2001).

[3] Advance directives may also impact more traditional areas of practice. *See* James C. Benson & Russell Austin, *The Impact of Medical Directives on Distribution of Estate Assets Under the Uniform Simultaneous Death Act,* 5 Elder L.J. 1 (1997). *See also* § 45[B][2][a], *infra.*

[4] Living wills got a boost from the publicity surrounding Karen Ann Quinlan, whose father ultimately received court permission to disconnect her respirator. *See In re* Quinlan, 70 N.J. 10, 355 A.2d 647 (1976).

[5] *See* § 7[B], *supra.*

[6] Writing in this area tends to get out of date very quickly. *See generally* Norman L. Cantor, *Twenty-Five Years After* Quinlan: *A Review of the Jurisprudence of Death and Dying,* 29 J. Law, Med. & Ethics 182 (2001); Dretton J. Horttor, *A Survey of Living Wills and Advanced Health Care Directives,* 740 N.D.L. Rev. 233 (1999).

[7] The publicity surrounding the efforts of Nancy Cruzan's parents to remove tubes providing Nancy with nutrition and hydration kept the issue in the public eye. *See* Cruzan v. Director, Mo. Dep't of Health, 497 U.S. 261, 111 L. Ed. 2d 224, 110 S. Ct. 2841 (1990) (upholding a statute which required clear and convincing evidence of a patient's desires as a condition for allowing a surrogate to refuse medical treatment on behalf of the patient); Susan R. Martyn & Henry J. Bourguignon, *Coming to Terms with Death: The Cruzan Case,* 42 Hastings L.J. 817 (1991).

The Patient Self-Determination Act, 42 U.S.C. § 1395, came next, requiring hospitals receiving federal funds to advise patients of their right to sign advance directives. *See* Edward J. Larson & Thomas A. Eaton, *The Limits of Advance Directives: A History and Assessment of the Patient Self-Determination Act,* 32 Wake Forest L. Rev. 249 (1997).

[8] *See* § 22[B], *supra.*

particular situations. Basically, the agent directs the patient's care as the agent believes the patient would have wanted it.

The 1990s brought two significant changes. First, more states adopted "family consent" statutes, which establish procedures for naming surrogate decisionmakers if the patient has not done so. Rather like the way intestate statutes provide default provisions for wills of property, family consent statutes serve variously as backstops for advance directives. The second movement is toward merging living wills and durable powers into a single, simplified document.

A uniform act pushes both of these developments forward, while eliminating many of the restrictive rules many states have established for advance directives. In 1993, the National Conference of Commissioners on Uniform State Laws approved the Uniform Health-Care Decisions Act (UHCDA).[9]

As a model, some of the most important features of the act are the ones that are missing. To avoid picky fights over the wrong issues, the act eliminates most execution requirements.[10] The act recognizes oral instructions from the patient, and allows appointment of a surrogate in a signed writing that need not be witnessed or acknowledged.[11] To avoid problems about whether a patient is in a "terminal condition" or a "permanent vegetative state," the act does not limit its scope to end-of-life decisions.[12] Instead, it authorizes any adult or emancipated minor to "execute a power of attorney for health care, which may authorize the agent to make any health care decision the principal could have made while having capacity."[13]

The act also clarifies some points that have caused problems in various states. For example, if the patient has not left specific instructions and the decisionmaker does not know the patient's wishes, the agent or surrogate decides according to the their view of the patient's best interest.[14] Also, a guardian must comply with the ward's individual health care instructions, and may not revoke the advance directive without court approval.[15] Perhaps most important in our mobile society, the act validates any health care directive which complies with the act's minimal requirements. The

---

[9] 9 (Part IB) U.L.A. 143 (Supp. 1999) (hereinafter cited as UHCDA). The act replaces a series of earlier attempts: the Model Health-Care Consent Law (1982), and two versions of the Uniform Rights of the Terminally Ill Act (1985 and 1989). For a description of the most recent act, see David English & Alan Meisel, *Uniform Health Care Decisions Act Gives New Guidance,* Est. Plan., Nov./Dec. 1994, at 355.

Section 4 of the act provides an optional form which combines features of durable powers and living wills, and allows people to donate organs and tissue and to designate their primary care physician.

[10] Compare the UPC's efforts to liberalize execution requirements for wills. *See* § 7[B], *supra.*

[11] *See* UHCDA § 2(a), (b).

[12] The power will be effective upon the principal's incapacity, unless the document identifies a different time, which could be earlier or later. UHCDA §§ 1(3), 2(c).

[13] UHCDA § 2(b).

[14] UHCDA §§ 2(e), 5(f).

[15] UHCDA § 6.

UHCDA's provisions for naming surrogate decisionmakers includes non-relatives, but gives relatives priority.[16]

It is impossible to predict how advance-directives law will develop.[17] Unquestionably, it will not go away. One can hope that it will achieve a level of uniformity allowing people to live or travel anywhere in the country, confident that their wishes will be honored.

Many of the topics raised in this chapter are part of the developing specialty of "Elder Law." These questions are not, however, only about old people. As you contemplate your personal and your professional plans, consider that Nancy Cruzan was 25 when her auto accident set in motion the events which so profoundly shaped our law of advance directives. Virtually all of your clients should be anticipating the possibility of their own incapacity.

---

[16] *See* UHCDA § 5(b) & (c). Anyone in a nontraditional relationship must execute an advance directive if they want their partner to be able to make the decisions, instead of a family member.

[17] Certainly, pressure from the related move toward physician-assisted suicide will help shape the future. *See* Washington v. Glucksberg, 521 U.S. 702, 138 L. Ed. 2d 772, 117 S. Ct. 2258 (1997) *and* Vacco v. Quill, 521 U.S. 793, 138 L. Ed. 2d 834, 117 S. Ct. 2293 (1997) (companion cases upholding prohibitions of physician-assisted suicide in the face of due process and equal protection challenges); Or. Rev. Stat. § 127.800 (allowing physician-assisted suicide). *See generally* Cass Sunstein, *The Right to Die,* 106 Yale L.J. 1123 (1997).

Chapter 7

CHANGING THE SHARE

This chapter discusses several doctrines which have the effect of changing the shares beneficiaries otherwise would have received by intestate succession, will, or will substitute. Recalling themes from Chapter 5, you will see that the law is coming to treat various wealth transfer devices in similar ways, but that the doctrine is not fully integrated. The first section covers gifts, usually from parents to their children, made with the intention of prepaying some of the beneficiary's ultimate share. Later sections note various ways the conduct of the beneficiaries themselves can affect the shares they get.

§ 24 Advancements and Gifts in Satisfaction

Suppose that Eva (a widow and the mother of Peter, Marta, and Krystyna) gives Marta $10,000 and Krystyna $5,000. When Eva dies, should a court adjust the children's shares of Eva's estate so that the combination of lifetime and at-death transfers treats each child equally? That is the basic question addressed by the related doctrines of "advancements" and "satisfaction." Lifetime gifts intended to come out of an intestate share are called *advancements*.[1] Lifetime gifts intended to take the place of gifts made by will are gifts *in satisfaction*[2] of the bequest. Though the details of the doctrines differ in some respects, this section treats them together because the structures of each are so similar.

[A] Advancements

Two questions predominate. First, how do we tell if a gift is an advancement? Secondly, what is the impact on other shares? The most common candidate for an advancement is a gift from a parent to a child.[3] To decide whether to characterize a gift as an advancement, we look to the donor's intention regarding the impact of the gift on the donee's share of the estate. Was the "gift" really a loan instead? If it was a gift, was it intended to be independent from, or part of, the donee's inheritance? Proof can be difficult.

---

[1] The doctrine is treated in detail in a series of articles by Professor Harold I. Elbert, appearing at 51 Mich. L. Rev. 665 (1953), and 52 Mich. L. Rev. 231 (1953) and 535 (1954).

[2] Sometimes the doctrine is called "ademption by satisfaction," on the theory that the gift under the will is adeemed (lost) because it had been satisfied during the testator's lifetime. *See generally* Barney Barstow, *Ademption by Satisfaction*, 6 Wis. L. Rev. 217 (1931). Other aspects of the ademption doctrine are discussed in § 46[C], *infra*.

[3] Some jurisdictions broaden the traditional rule by recognizing that gifts to heirs (including spouses), rather than only gifts to descendants, can be advancements. *See* UPC § 2-109.

Often testimony will come many years after the gift.[4] Often the evidence will be largely circumstantial.[5] Traditionally, the law presumed that gifts of land or a substantial amount of personalty from parents to children were advancements.[6] This approach invites people to make long lists of whatever gifts were made throughout a lifetime and to fight about which of those gifts qualify as advancements. To avoid litigation, several states have reversed the presumption and required better proof. They treat gifts as advancements only if the donee acknowledges them as such, or if the donor indicates in a contemporaneous writing that the gift is meant as an advancement.[7]

If a particular gift is considered an advancement, the second question becomes how to calculate everyone's shares. Courts conduct what is called a "hotchpotch" calculation. Each advancement is added to the total amount available for distribution from the estate. Each heir's respective share is then calculated with reference to this "hotchpotch," the donee is credited with the gifts already received, and the rest of the property is distributed.[8] Note especially that the lifetime gift itself is not returned to the estate but, rather, its value is added in only for the purpose of calculating shares.[9]

Chart 7-1

Eva's net probate estate	. . . .		$ 60,000
Plus advancements	Marta	. . . .	$ 10,000
	Krystyna	. . . . .	$ 5,000
Total hotchpot	. . . .		$ 75,000

Divided by number of takers (3)	$ 25,000 each

---

[4] *See, e.g.*, *In re* Martinez, 633 P.2d 727 (N.M. App. 1981) (testimony offered in 1980 regarding a 1953 conversation about the intention surrounding a gift made in 1941).

[5] *See, e.g.*, Miller v. Richardson, 85 S.W.2d 41 (Mo. 1935) (A series of gifts by a father to the neediest of his children were found to be advancements.).

[6] *See* Atkinson at 716-725.

[7] *See* McGovern & Kurtz at 63-64. The UPC provision requires such a writing. *See* UPC § 2-109. *Accord* Restatement (Third) of Prop. § 2.6. One observer comments that the UPC's approach "virtually removes the doctrine of advancements from the law of intestate succession." Martin L. Fried, *The Uniform Probate Code: Intestate Succession and Related Matters*, 55 Alb. L. Rev. 927, 937 (1992).

Another solution could be to treat most gifts as advancements, and simply not inquire into the donor's intention. *See* Mary L. Fellows, *Concealing Legislative Reform in the Common-Law Tradition: The Advancements Doctrine and the Uniform Probate Code*, 37 Vand. L. Rev. 671 (1984).

[8] Because the presence or absence of advancements affects the sizes of the intestate shares, the personal representative may be under a duty to inquire about whether there were advancements. Duties of personal representatives are discussed in Chapter 13, *infra*.

[9] A similar technique is sometimes used to calculate the share of a spouse claiming an elective share. *See* § 28[C], *infra*.

Disputes sometimes arise regarding valuation. The UPC values an advancement "as of the time the heir came into possession or enjoyment of the property or as of the time of the decedent's death, whichever first occurs." UPC § 2-109(b). A parallel provision covers gifts made in partial satisfaction. UPC § 2-609(b).

Distribution of estate —

Marta - share of hotchpotch	. . . .	$ 25,000
less amount advanced	. . . .	$ 10,000
share of estate	. . . .	$ 15,000

Krystyna - share of hotchpotch	. . . .	$ 25,000
less amount advanced	. . . .	$ 5,000
share of estate	. . . .	$ 20,000

Peter - share of hotchpotch	. . . .	$ 25,000
less amount advanced	. . . .	-0-
share of estate	. . . .	$ 25,000

Chart 7-1 illustrates how the hotchpotch calculation would work for the hypothetical family introduced at the beginning of this section. It assumes Eva left a net probate estate of $60,000. When the advancements are added, the hotchpotch totals $75,000. The three shares of $25,000 are then adjusted to yield the shares each child gets from the probate estate.[10] If anyone's advancement was greater than her share of the hotchpotch, that person would simply not participate in the distribution of the estate.[11] Again, the doctrine does not require giving property back.

Sometimes the donee of the advancement will die before the donor. The question then arises whether the advancement counts against the share of the donee's children. Traditional rules say it does count,[12] but the UPC says it does not, because there is no guarantee that the children benefited from the advancement.[13]

[B] Satisfaction

Much of the law surrounding lifetime gifts made in satisfaction of testamentary gifts parallels the law of advancements. Some of the details differ, but the idea is the same. For example, courts have presumed that monetary gifts from parents to children after a will's execution were in satisfaction of any legacies under the will.[14] Some courts did not apply satisfaction to real estate, nor to specific gifts of personalty.[15] A more

---

[10] To be prudent, check that the total of those shares equals the net *probate* estate. It is easy to calculate and divide the hotchpotch, and then forget to subtract the amounts already received. Here Marta's $15,000, Krystyna's $20,000, and Peter's $25,000 add up to the $60,000 available in Eva's estate.

[11] For example, if Krystyna had received $50,000, she would simply keep that. Marta and Peter would share a hotchpotch of $70,000 (Eva's estate, plus the advancement to Marta). Marta would get $25,000 from the estate, and Peter would get $35,000.

[12] *See* Atkinson at 722.

[13] *See* UPC § 2-109(c) and comment.

[14] *See* Atkinson at 737-741. For an interesting case in which the court rejected a son's claim that lifetime gifts his father made to the father's "friend" were gifts in satisfaction of the friend's legacy, see *In re* Estate of Lutz, 107 N.Y.S.2d 388 (N.Y. Surr. Ct. 1951).

[15] *See* Haskell at 115. Courts viewed these items as unique, and had trouble saying a testator could replace them with a different gift.

modern view would allow lifetime gifts to replace testamentary gifts of different character, where that is the intention.[16]

Because will beneficiaries need not be heirs, satisfaction potentially covers a wider range of lifetime gifts than does the advancements doctrine. For example, depending upon the donor's intention, a will provision giving "$15,000 to Knox College" might have been satisfied by a lifetime gift of that amount to the college.[17] Also, the UPC allows a lifetime gift to one person to satisfy a testamentary gift made to another.[18] Because the doctrine centers on intention, the same sorts of proof problems surrounding advancements arise here as well. The requirement of a writing, so popular as a solution to advancements, is less commonly applied to gifts in satisfaction.[19] Certainly, the policy of limiting disputes about these questions should apply to both situations.

Once a lifetime gift is identified as one which changes the testamentary gift, the shares under the will must be adjusted accordingly. Sometimes the change will be straightforward; the will beneficiary will get nothing. Sometimes a hotchpotch calculation will be necessary. A hotchpotch would be needed, for example, if a testator gave "$30,000 to my children" and then made lifetime gifts to some of those children, in satisfaction of their testamentary gifts.

Both the doctrines of advancements and of satisfaction allow donors to change — by the act of making lifetime gifts — the way their estates will be divided. The doctrines to which we now turn depend not on the action of donors, but of their beneficiaries.

§ 25 Misconduct

Another way an expected share can change is for a beneficiary to lose the share by the beneficiary's own misconduct. Most commonly, slayers are denied the benefits of their crimes.[1] Sometimes courts have imposed a

---

[16] *See* Atkinson at 740-741. If, after executing the will, the testator gave away property which was also a specific gift identified in the will, the property would simply be unavailable for distribution at death. In that situation, the doctrine of ademption says the testamentary gift fails. For more on the various classes of gifts and on ademption, see § 46, *infra*.

[17] Partial satisfaction is also possible. A $5,000 lifetime gift could have the effect of reducing the testamentary gift to $10,000.

[18] One reason this provision might be desirable is to facilitate tax planning. For example, a wealthy grandparent might find it advantageous to give a lifetime gift to a grandchild, rather than leaving the sum as part of a testamentary legacy to the child's parent. *See* UPC § 2-609 comment.

[19] *See* Roger W. Andersen, *The Influence of the Uniform Probate Code in Nonadopting States*, 8 U. Puget Sound L. Rev. 599, 602 (1985). The UPC requires a writing in both instances. *See* UPC §§ 2-109 & 2-609.

[1] *See generally* McGovern & Kurtz at 68-74; Mary L. Fellows, *The Slayer Rule: Not Solely a Matter of Equity*, 71 Iowa L. Rev. 489 (1986); Linda J. Maki & Alan M. Kaplan, *Elmer's Case Revisited: The Problem of the Murdering Heir*, 41 Ohio St. L.J. 906 (1980).

Some states also cut out adulterers, those who abandon their children, or other undeserving "constructive trust" on the slayer's share and ordered it transferred, instead, to someone else. Because a constructive trust approach is necessarily ad hoc, most jurisdictions now have statutes dealing with some aspects of the problem. Many of these statutes, however, are incomplete, so the common law may fill gaps. This section first addresses constructive trusts, and then highlights the issues raised by statutes.

[A] Constructive Trusts

The constructive trust is a flexible device for remedying bad conduct in a broad range of situations.[2] In particular, it serves to remove title from the slayer who would otherwise get it, and pass that ownership to someone else. Despite the label, a constructive trust is not really a trust, but a remedy. It is a way of shifting title, from someone who has it but does not deserve it, to someone who *should* have it.

In re Estate of Mahoney[3] endorsed imposing a constructive trust when Charlotte Mahoney shot her husband, Howard, and then stood to inherit his estate. The slaying does not seem to have been motivated by money; less than $4,000 was involved. Nonetheless, Howard's parents must have been outraged that Charlotte, then serving time after a conviction for manslaughter, should benefit from killing their son. They sought, and got, an order from the probate court giving the property to them.

Though sympathetic to the parents' claim, the Vermont Supreme Court held that the probate court could not order a distribution to the parents in the face of an intestate statute that clearly gave the estate to Charlotte as surviving spouse.[4] The supreme court would not intrude upon the legislative prerogative by creating an exception to the statute. On the other hand, the court suggested that a constructive trust might be imposed upon Charlotte's share, so that a court could order Charlotte (as "trustee") to pay the funds to Howard's parents (the trust "beneficiaries").[5] Because the result is exactly the same under either approach, use of the constructive trust in this context has been called a "subterfuge"[6] and "fictitious."[7]

---

takers. *See, e.g.*, Cal. Prob. Code § 259(a) (physical abuse, neglect, or fiduciary abuse of elder or dependent adult); Va. Code Ann. § 64.1-16.3 (takers who willfully desert or abandon a child or spouse and such situation continues until the death of the child or spouse); N.Y. E.P.T.L. § 4-1.4 (takers who refuse to provide for, or who abandon, a child under 21 years of age). *See generally* Kymberleigh N. Korpus, *Extinguishing Inheritance Rights: California Breaks New Ground in the Fight Against Elder Abuse but Fails to Build an Effective Foundation*, 52 Hastings L.J. 537 (2001).

[2] For other contexts covered in this text, see §§ 10 (contracts regarding wills), 12[F], *supra* (oral trusts), and 28[C][1], *infra* (spousal election). *See generally* Dan B. Dobbs, Remedies § 4.3.

[3] 220 A.2d 475 (Vt. 1966).

[4] Spousal shares in intestacy are discussed in § 4, *supra*.

[5] Because in Vermont the probate court did not have jurisdiction to impose the constructive trust, the probate action was stayed, so the parents had time to file a petition in a chancery court. For a more direct approach, see Maine Sav. Bank v. Bridges, 431 A.2d 633 (Me. 1981) (awarding the property directly to the other heirs).

[6] Mary L. Fellows, *The Slayer Rule: Not Solely a Matter of Equity*, 71 Iowa L. Rev. 489, 550 (1986).

[7] *In re* Duncan's Estate, 246 P.2d 445, 446-447 (Wash. 1952).

Aside from the deception involved in using the constructive trust to avoid directly contravening the intestate statute, the device also suffers from a lack of precision. The general principle that one should not benefit from his wrongdoing does not offer much guidance on exactly when the doctrine should be applied and what happens once it is.[8] Statutes, to which we now turn, can solve some of these problems.

[B] Statutes

A large number of states have statutes denying slayers property in certain circumstances. Because many statutes cover some topics but not others, it can be helpful to have a series of questions you can ask about whatever statute you face.

First, what bad actions disqualify the slayer? Must the killing have been premeditated? Must the killing have been in the state with jurisdiction over the property? Must the slayer have been convicted?[9] If not, can culpability be established by a mere preponderance of the evidence, or is some higher standard required? Should it matter if the slaying was a mercy killing?[10] What if the slaying came in response to years of spouse abuse?

Second, what property interests are affected? Intestate shares only? Gifts under wills? Trust shares? Retirement benefits?[11] Life insurance? Joint tenancy interests? Remainders following victims' life estates? The narrow coverage of many slayer statutes highlights the point that the law has not yet achieved integration of the rules surrounding probate and nonprobate transfers at death.[12]

Third, what is the effect of applying the statute? Most of the time, the property will pass as if the slayer had predeceased the victim. Sometimes, however, that approach poses problems. In some circumstances, a slayer might actually increase the share available to the slayer's family as a result of the killing.[13] Unlike many statutes, the UPC attempts to

---

[8] *See, e.g.,* Ford v. Ford, 512 A.2d 389 (Md. App. 1986) (killer's insanity meant prohibition on inheritance would not apply); *In re* Estate of Safran, 306 N.W.2d 27 (Wis. 1981) (Killing must be intentional, proved by clear and convincing evidence. Killer treated as predeceased, but killer's unborn issue have no claim. No payment to killer for subsistence. Joint property divided between killer and victim's estate.).

[9] Consider the problem of a slayer who then commits suicide. Do the *slayer's* survivors get the property because there was no chance to deny it to the slayer? What about a juvenile who kills his parents but is too young to commit a felony? *See In re* Estates of Josephson, 297 N.W.2d 444 (N.D. 1980) (denying the child a share).

[10] For the argument that it should, and a model statute, see Kent S. Berk, *Mercy Killing and the Slayer Rule: Should the Legislatures Change Something?*, 67 Tul. L. Rev. 485 (1992). *See also* Jeffrey G. Sherman, *Mercy Killing and the Right to Inherit*, 61 U. Cin. L. Rev. 803 (1993).

[11] Federal law may preempt state statutes which attempt to control what happens to retirement benefits. Preemption is discussed in § 20, *supra.*

[12] For other examples and discussion, see Chapters 4 and 5, *supra.*

[13] Consider a slayer who kills her father. He has four grandchildren, three by his daughter

prohibit this result.[14] Different problems surround property in which the slayer already has an interest. Should the law allow a remainderman to take possession immediately after killing the life tenant? What about one joint tenant who kills the other? What if the slayer paid for life insurance on the victim? One appealing way to deny the slayer any benefit in these situations would be to treat the victim as alive until (according to actuarial tables) the victim would have died. In the meantime, the survivors other than the slayer could use the property.

Fourth, is a bona fide purchaser who takes from the slayer protected? Suppose Rhoda kills Roger and inherits a lake cabin, which she then sells to Phil, who suspects nothing. Surely Phil ought not to lose the property when the murder is later discovered. The UPC so provides,[15] but many statutes fail to clarify the point.

This series of questions should highlight the problems lurking throughout so-called "slayer statutes." The main point, however, is that only a few of the statutes address these questions at all. States with incomplete statutes would do well to consider the UPC's approach.

§ 26   Assignments of Expectancies

Suppose Jill expects to come into some money when her mother dies, but Jill wants someone else to get those funds when the time comes. Perhaps she wants to let her favorite charity know there could be money in its future. Maybe family relationships could be helped if she gives her share to her brother, Gregory. Perhaps she is short of cash, and Gregory is willing to pay something now for the chance he will get more later. In any of these situations, a transferee might end up with nothing. If the mother makes a will disinheriting Jill, her "expectancy" becomes worthless. The tenuous nature of Jill's expectancy has led courts to restrict severely the situations in which any transfer would be effective.

According to orthodox doctrine, outright transfers of expectancies are not allowed.[1] Why this approach should be followed is not at all clear. One "reason" for invalidating such attempted assignments is that the thing being assigned is a "mere expectancy" that does not rise to the level of an "interest," which would be transferable. This, of course, is not a reason, but

---

and one by his predeceased son. If the father had died intestate before his daughter, his estate would have been divided in half between his daughter and his son's child. If, because she killed her father, the slayer/daughter is treated as having predeceased him, her childrens' collective share might increase to 3/4 of their grandfather's estate, while the other grandchild's share would shrink to 1/4. Typical intestate distribution schemes are discussed in § 5[B], *supra*.

[14] Under § 2-803(b), the estate passes as if the slayer had disclaimed. The disclaimer section (2-801(d)) treats the disclaimant as predeceased to allow others to take, but not for the purpose of changing the shares. Disclaimers are covered in § 27, *infra*.

[15] UPC § 2-803(i).

[1] *See* Restatement of Prop. § 313 cmt. a. Despite the rule, transfers are sometimes tried. *See* Harper v. Harper, 243 S.E.2d 74 (Ga. 1978) (a deed transferring grantor's interest from his future inheritance void).

simply a conclusion, like the one that future profits are not a sufficient interest to constitute trust property.[2] One justification for the traditional rule could be that the administration of estates would be complicated if the apparent heirs or will beneficiaries no longer held their interests. This problem could be solved, however, by requiring a writing or clear and convincing evidence of the transfer. There is little justification for banning *all* donative transfers of expectancies.

One way in which courts have softened the doctrine is to enforce in equity contracts to transfer expectancies, if the agreement is supported by fair consideration.[3]

In *Scott v. First National Bank*,[4] for example, as part of a separation agreement, Wilmer Scott assigned to Grace half of his expected inheritance from his father. Grace agreed to support the children beyond the small amounts Wilmer supplied. After the father died, the court enforced the agreement. The court believed that Grace may have "tempered her demands [for support funds] because of the assignment in order to insure that [their] child would receive a share of the expectancy which might otherwise be frittered away."[5] Grace's carrying the support burden supplied the necessary consideration to make the agreement enforceable. The fact that Wilmer's father did not know of the assignment was irrelevant.[6]

A parallel doctrine recognizes transfers of a child's expectancy back to the parent, again if supported by fair consideration. These transfers are called "releases" and are treated like advancements.[7] The parent's payment for the release is really just an early transfer of an expected share.

Releases and assignments of expectancies are made *before* the death of the person supplying the funds. Once the person dies, the heir or beneficiary has the property unless she disclaims, the topic to which we now turn.

§ 27 Disclaimers

Beneficiaries use disclaimers[1] to change the distribution of an estate by refusing to accept its benefits. The most common reason for disclaiming is

---

[2] Indeed, one writer uses the example of an "expectancy that one will inherit by intestacy or under a will" as an example of something which is not "property" and therefore cannot be trust property. *See* Haskell at 86. The same scholar notes that the civil law system of inheritance recognizes a "birthright" of an expectant heir as a property interest. *See* Paul G. Haskell, *The Power of Disinheritance: Proposal for Reform*, 52 Geo. L.J. 499, 517-518 (1964).

The question of what is sufficient "property" to be the subject matter of a trust is discussed in § 12[D], *supra*.

[3] *See* Atkinson at 729.

[4] 168 A.2d 349 (Md. 1961).

[5] 168 A.2d at 353.

[6] This is the prevailing view, although there is some authority to the contrary. *See* 3 American Law of Property § 14.12.

[7] *See* Atkinson at 725. Advancements are discussed in § 24[A], *supra*.

[1] "Disclaimer" is the term used in the Internal Revenue Code. IRC § 2518. In the past,

to save taxes. Consider Laurie, a person of independent means. Her father's will names her as beneficiary, and provides that if she predeceases him, her share goes to her children. After her father's death, if Laurie disclaims her share, the disclaimer "relates back" in time to her father's death. Laurie never acquires ownership. Under most statutes, the property would pass as if she had predeceased her father; in this case it would go to her children.

Laurie effectively would be making a gift to her children, but if she followed the IRS's disclaimer rules,[2] she would not be taxed on the gift.[3] Also, any income the property earned would be taxed at the children's rates. Moreover, the property would not be Laurie's at her death, so would not be subject to estate tax at that time.[4] All of these effects would take place after the death of Laurie's father. Because of their ability to rearrange a testator's plan, disclaimers are one of the most powerful tools for what is known as "postmortem" estate planning.[5]

Both state and federal law apply to disclaimers.[6] State law determines ownership; federal law determines tax consequences. It would therefore be possible for Laurie to disclaim property effectively under state law so that it went directly from her father's estate to her children, but at the same time, fail to follow the federal rules, so that for tax purposes the property came to her first. She would then have made a taxable gift to her children. Unless tax considerations are not a factor, you must pay attention to both sets of rules.

The property doctrine is based on the notion that a gift cannot be forced upon someone. The disclaimer is simply a refusal of a gift that would come at the death of someone else.[7] At common law, disclaimers were not

---

statutes and case opinions tended to use the term "renunciation." *See, e.g.*, UPC § 2-801 (pre-1990). The terms are interchangeable, but "disclaimer" is now probably more common. The UPC now uses "disclaimer." UPC § 2-801.

[2] IRC § 2518.

[3] At the other end of the spectrum, if Laurie were in financial trouble, her disclaimer might well keep the property out of the hands of her creditors. *See generally* Adam J. Hirsch, *The Problem of the Insolvent Heir*, 74 Cornell L. Rev. 587 (1989); Adam J. Hirsch, *Inheritance and Bankruptcy: The Meaning of the "Fresh Start,"* 45 Hastings L.J. 175 (1994); Stephen E. Parker, *Can Debtors Disclaim Inheritances to the Detriment of Their Creditors?*, 25 Loy. U. Chi. L.J. 31 (1993).

Federal tax liens, however, are likely to prevail over a debtor's disclaimer. *See* Drye v. United States, 528 U.S. 49 (1999) (son disclaimed intestate inheritance from mother).

Sometimes disclaimers are used for other purposes. In Estate of Parsons, 163 Cal. Rptr. 70 (Cal. App. 1980), for example, a beneficiary who witnessed a will disclaimed her interest in an unsuccessful attempt to save the will by becoming a disinterested witness. *Parsons* is discussed in § 7[B][2][e], *supra*. For other examples, see S. Alan Medlin, *An Examination of Disclaimers under UPC Section 2-801*, 55 Alb. L. Rev. 1233, 1266-1268 (1992); Patricia J. Roberts, *The Acceleration of Remainders: Manipulating the Identity of the Remaindermen*, 42 S.C. L. Rev. 295 (1991).

[4] Gift and estate taxes are discussed in Chapter 14, *infra*.

[5] *See generally* John R. Price, Contemporary Estate Planning ch. 12 (1983).

[6] For helpful discussions of both topics, see McGovern & Kurtz at 75-82 and S. Alan Medlin, *An Examination of Disclaimers under UPC Section 2-801*, 55 Alb. L. Rev. 1233 (1992).

[7] *See* Estate of Baird, 933 P.2d 1031 (Wash. 1997) (rejecting son's attempt to avoid tort creditor by disclaiming interest from his mother *before* she died).

available to intestate heirs, because they took as a matter of law, not by gift. To eliminate the unequal treatment, modern statutes apply to both testate and intestate transfers. The extent to which disclaimers are effective for nonprobate transfers is unclear in many jurisdictions.[8]

Another problem is whether someone other than a beneficiary can disclaim. In particular, when can a guardian disclaim the interest of his ward? Suppose James and Martha are well-off octogenarians with three children. James is incompetent and his son, Mercer, is his guardian.[9] If Martha dies leaving everything to James, it might make sense for James to disclaim some or all of his share so it could go directly to the children. Should Mercer, as guardian, be able to disclaim on behalf of his father, especially when Mercer would stand to gain? The UPC allows disclaimers by personal representatives,[10] and a comment suggests that such disclaimers are proper "when it is in the ward's best interests."[11] A sensible reading of James' best interests may include achieving tax savings for his family, but a court is likely to scrutinize such action closely, especially in light of Mercer's conflict of interest.[12]

An additional question is how a disclaimer affects the interests of others.[13] Usually a donor's property is distributed as if the disclaimant had predeceased the donor.[14] This approach often works well enough, but it can be subject to abuse. Consider Bill, who died intestate leaving a daughter, Emily, and her three children, and a fourth grandchild, Jacob, the son of Emily's predeceased brother. Most intestate schemes would divide the estate in half between Emily and Jacob.[15] If Emily were to disclaim, however, her being treated as predeceased would leave Bill with four grandchildren, who might well share equally. By disclaiming, Emily could

---

[8] Both the UPC and the tax law recognize disclaimers of nonprobate transfers. *See* UPC § 2-801; Treas. Reg. § 25.2518-2(c)(4).

[9] Other aspects of planning for incapacity are discussed in Chapter 6, *supra.*

[10] UPC § 2-801(a). This section, revised in 1990, also extends the right to disclaim to the personal representative of a decedent. This power allows tax savings when a survivor dies too soon to have had time to disclaim.

For a list of other changes between the two UPC versions, see S. Alan Medlin, *An Examination of Disclaimers under UPC Section 2-801*, 55 Alb. L. Rev. 1233, 1238 n.26 (1992). *See generally* Adam J. Hirsh, *Revisions in Need of Revising: The Uniform Disclaimer of Property Interest Act*, 29 Fla. St. L. Rev. 109 (2001).

[11] UPC (pre-1990) § 2-801(a) comment.

[12] For example, a court denied a mother the power to disclaim on behalf of her children when the disclaimer would have saved estate taxes in her husband's estate by increasing the mother's share. *See In re* Estate of De Domenico, 418 N.Y.S.2d 1012 (N.Y. Surr. 1979).

[13] You would not want to advise a client to disclaim, only to find that the disclaimer did not have the desired result. *See In re* Estate of Fleenor, 17 P.3d 520 (Ore. Ct. App. 2000) (One brother disclaimed his share of the house so his disabled brother could benefit. Instead, the property went to the disclaimant's children.); Webb v. Webb, 301 S.E.2d 570 (W. Va. 1983) (Son disclaimed so that his mother would take more; instead, his share went to his own daughter.).

[14] *See, e.g.*, UPC §§ 2-801(d)(1) & (2).

[15] Descriptions of various intestate schemes appear in § 5[B], *supra.*

grab one-fourth of Bill's estate for her family. The revised UPC attempts to remove the opportunity for this sort of abuse by providing that in this situation, "the disclaimed interest passes by representation to the descendants of the disclaimant who survive the decedent."[16]

It is beyond the scope of this text to address the variety of ways disclaimers can be used to achieve tax savings.[17] A few basics, however, should alert you to the sorts of problems which can arise when seeking tax benefits. The key concept is a "qualified disclaimer."[18] Unless the disclaimer meets the rules to become "qualified," the tax benefits do not follow. In general, a qualified disclaimer must be in writing and filed within nine months of the time of the transfer (often the death of the donor).[19] The disclaimant cannot have accepted the disclaimed interest, nor benefited from it. Upon disclaim, the property must go to someone other than the disclaimant, unless the disclaimant is the donor's spouse.[20] Thus, the ability of a disclaimer to qualify for favorable tax treatment depends in part on its effect under state law.

The availability of disclaimers injects a good deal of flexibility into postmortem planning. Their use, however, requires special care, because both state and federal rules apply.

---

[16] UPC § 2-801(d)(1). Professor Medlin argues that the desired result may not follow from the UPC's language in all situations. *See* S. Alan Medlin, *An Examination of Disclaimers under UPC Section 2-801*, 55 Alb. L. Rev. 1233, 1261 n.162 (1992).

[17] *See generally* Theodore M. David, *Correct Estate Planning Mistakes with the Qualified Disclaimer (with Forms)*, 36 Prac. Law., Mar. 1990, at 27; Malcolm A. Moore, *The Ever-Expanding Use of Disclaimers in Estate Planning: An Update*, 17 ACTEC Notes 255 (1991).

[18] *See* IRC § 2518.

[19] If the disclaimant is under 21, the filing can come later, so long as it is within nine months of her reaching 21. IRC § 2518(b)(2)(B).

[20] The exception is to allow a surviving spouse to maximize the marital deduction by shifting assets among various gifts, some of which benefit the spouse. The marital deduction is discussed in § 62[B], *infra*.

Chapter 8

PROTECTING THE FAMILY

Despite creating a framework to allow people to transfer their property as they wish, the law also imposes some limits on testamentary freedom. One set of restrictions relates mostly to the size of gifts and directions about their use. Protections for family members, the topic of this chapter, fall into this category.[1] Another kind of limit concerns how long a donor's restrictions can last.[2]

In resolving the competing interests of donors, donees, and those who are cut out, legislatures and courts necessarily reflect various views about how families should function. This topic is particularly interesting because our views about families are changing. Decisionmakers face such questions as: What claims should spouses have on property acquired during a marriage? Should those claims be different after one spouse dies? Should children or others have rights parallel to those of surviving spouses? Should the law restrict in other ways the potential caprice of donors?

In providing a framework for analyzing these issues, this chapter first, and primarily, discusses rights of surviving spouses. Next it covers the rights of those relatives (usually children) omitted from a will. The chapter closes with two short sections on other restrictions on testamentary freedom: those relating to charitable gifts and general public policy limits imposed on testamentary gifts.

§ 28 Disinherited Spouses

For a very long time, the law has protected surviving spouses against their predeceasing spouses' attempts to disinherit them. We are now in the midst of a reform movement that is changing the way we view spousal inheritance rights. This movement is itself part of a larger restructuring of family law.[1]

As a vehicle to focus the major issues, consider a prototypical, "traditional" American family. Sam and Nina have been married for 17 years. Sam works outside the home to provide financial security for his family. All of the family's assets are titled in his name. Nina stays home to clean, to cook, and to supervise their two children, Peter and Susan. Suppose that Sam,

---

[1] The related rules surrounding limitations on trust beneficiaries' rights to transfer property they receive are covered in § 13, *supra*.

[2] The Rule Against Perpetuities, the primary rule regarding time limits, is discussed in Chapter 12, *infra*.

[1] *See generally* Mary A. Glendon, The Transformation of Family Law (1989).

unappreciative of Nina's efforts, consults a lawyer and constructs a plan to disinherit Nina. Sam puts his modest stock portfolio into a lifetime trust, reserving a power to revoke and naming himself as trustee.[2] At his death, the trust assets are payable to the children. Sam names the children as beneficiaries of his life insurance, and he executes a new will giving everything to them. He also creates a joint tenancy in the house among himself and his children.[3] Unless Nina has some wealth of her own or is otherwise guaranteed a share of the property held in Sam's name, she will face significant financial hardships if (as is likely) she survives him.

This section addresses the different legal theories which serve to protect disinherited spouses. It reflects how the law is responding to the changing roles of women, as the traditional prototype becomes increasingly less representative of the modern family.[4] If you are not familiar with community property, pay particular attention to the next subsection for some useful background information necessary to understand the reforms proposed for states that have not adopted a community property regime. Following that, dower, the holdover from the common law, is briefly described. Then the discussion turns to this section's principal topic, the evolving right of a surviving spouse to claim a share of property titled in the decedent spouse's name. The section next views the problems posed for couples who migrate between common law and community property jurisdictions. It closes with a look at contracts which spouses can use to adjust (or waive) their rights.

[A] Community Property

Community property states[5] have created a form of property ownership which recognizes the mutuality of marital relationships. Rather than treat

---

[2] For a quick overview of trust terminology and doctrine, see § 2[B][1], *supra*. For more details, see Chapter 4, *supra*.

[3] If, like many couples, Sam and Nina had held their house as joint tenants, Sam might sever the joint tenancy and create instead a tenancy in common. Nina would own her one-half as tenant in common and Sam's half would pass by will to the children. For more on joint interests, see § 18, *supra*.

Courts have allowed and commentators have criticized "secret severances" of the type envisioned here. *See, e.g.*, Riddle v. Harmon, 162 Cal. Rptr. 530 (Cal. App. 1980) (affirming the "indisputable right" of each joint tenant to sever the tenancy without the knowledge or consent of the other). *See generally* Samuel M. Fetters, *An Invitation to Commit Fraud: Secret Destruction of Joint Tenant Survivorship Rights*, 55 Fordham L. Rev. 173 (1986).

[4] For related discussions in the context of intestacy, see §§ 4, 5[A], *supra*.

[5] The states are: Alaska, Arizona, California, Idaho, Louisiana, Nevada, New Mexico, Texas, and Washington. Wisconsin has adopted the Uniform Marital Property Act (which uses different terminology, but basically adopts the same system) and should also be counted as a community property state. *See generally* Howard S. Erlanger & June M. Weisberger, *From Common Law Property to Community Property: Wisconsin's Marital Property Act Four Years Later*, 1990 Wis. L. Rev. 769 (1990).

Instead of using community property as the default system which couples can agree to avoid, Alaska merely allows couples to "opt in" by choosing to hold property as a community. *See generally* Jonathan G. Blattmachr, Howard M. Zaritsky & Mark L. Ascher, *Tax Planning with*

spouses' earnings as the separate property of each, as is the case in most of the country,[6] this doctrine lumps together "the fruits of the marriage" and calls them "community property." Property that each spouse brings into the marriage (or acquires by gift or inheritance intended for themselves individually) is called "separate property." As you can imagine, longer marriages tend to generate more community property.[7] For inheritance purposes, both spouses have the power to dispose of their own separate property and half of the community property.

Recall Sam and Nina, our traditional couple. In a common law state, Sam's paycheck is his, as are assets he acquires with those funds.[8] In a community property state, the paycheck is community property, with each spouse owning half. Under a community property regime, the radio Nina owned before they were married is hers, but the TV they bought later is community. Assets acquired over time pose special problems. For example, Sam may have purchased a house before the marriage, but continued after the marriage to make mortgage payments out of his earnings. Community property states recognize both the separate and the community claims to the property.[9]

The policy basis for community property is broader than simply protecting each spouse against disinheritance. In recognizing that both spouses contribute to a marriage, the doctrine empowers spouses (traditionally women) who provide services rather than dollars.[10] One major consequence

---

Consensual Community Property: Alaska's New Community Property Law, 33 Real Prop., Prob. & Tr. J. 615 (1999).

For brief descriptions of the doctrine, see Haskell at 147-157; McGovern & Kurtz at 146-157. *See also* Robert L. Mennell & Thomas M. Boykoff, Community Property in a Nutshell (2d ed. 1993); Symposium, *American Community Property Regimes*, 56 Law & Contemp. Probs., Spring 1993. For detailed coverage, see W. S. McClanahan, Community Property Law in the United States.

[6] States which follow this view are sometimes called "common law" states because their ideas came from England. In contrast, community property states borrowed their approach from the civil law systems in Europe, mostly by way of Spain.

[7] Newly acquired property can take on "separate" character if the source of acquisition funds can be traced to other separate property. *See, e.g.,* Estate of Hanau v. Hanau, 730 S.W.2d 663 (Tex. 1987) (Husband owned Texaco stock at the time of his marriage, sold Texaco and bought City Investing, and sold that to buy TWA. Although the dollar amounts were not equivalent, the court found the TWA stock to be the husband's separate property.).

[8] He may choose to deposit his check in a joint bank account with Nina, but even then, the money may still be his. Joint accounts are discussed in § 18[B], *supra*.

[9] Some states take an inception-of-title approach, which would leave title in Sam's name, but would give the community a right to reimbursement for community funds expended in paying the mortgage. Other states divide the ownership pro rata between separate and community property. Note that the pro-rata approach allows the community to benefit from any gain in the house's value. *See* William A. Reppy, Jr., *Acquisitions with a Mix of Community and Separate Funds: Displacing California's Presumption of Gift by Recognizing Shared Ownership or a Right of Reimbursement*, 31 Idaho L. Rev. 965 (1995).

Another way property can take on a "mixed" character is if one spouse improves the other spouse's separate property. *See, e.g., In re* Kobylski, 503 N.W.2d 369 (Wis. App. 1993) (husband worked on house his wife owned before marriage.)

[10] In general, each spouse can manage (i.e., spend) the community property. Transfers of real estate or substantial gifts to third parties usually will require consent of both spouses.

of the doctrine, however, is that surviving spouses already own half of the community assets. In a community property state, Sam could give his half to the children at his death, but he could not deny Nina her half.[11] Because surviving spouses are already protected by their ownership interests, they usually do not have the right, available in common law states, to elect against a will that disinherits them.[12]

[B] Dower

In creating protections for surviving spouses, the common law distinguished between widowers and widows.[13] A widower got a life estate in all of the lands his wife owned during the marriage, if issue who could inherit the land were born of that marriage. The widower's right, granted "by the curtesy of England," came to be called "curtesy." A widow, on the other hand, got a life estate in one-third of the lands her husband owned during the marriage; children were not required, but the estate to which the right attached had to be one that issue could inherit if they were born.[14] The widow's right was called "dower." Most states have abolished both doctrines, but some retain various versions of dower and apply them to both men and women.

Dower and curtesy had some utility in a society in which most of the wealth was held as land, but do not work very well to protect surviving spouses today. In particular, most of our wealth is now personal property, to which the doctrines do not apply.[15] There is also a downside to the doctrines: they tend to clog land titles.[16] As a practical matter, the right of modern spouses to elect against a will disinheriting them has replaced dower and curtesy as a protection device.

[C] The Right to Elect

Except in community property states[17] and Georgia,[18] surviving

---

[11] Sam's will could attempt to transfer Nina's interest, for example, to a trust for her and the children. Nina would then face what has been called a "widow's election" as to whether to claim her share of the community property or to give it up for the benefits of the trust. *See* McGovern & Kurtz at 154-155.

[12] In part because of this difference, couples that move between community property and common law jurisdictions face special problems. *See* § 28[D], *infra*. The right to elect is discussed in § 28[C], *infra*.

[13] *See* Atkinson at 104-106; McGovern & Kurtz at 137.

[14] Because the estate must have been capable of being inherited, dower did not attach to a life estate or an interest held in joint tenancy.

[15] They can help some, however. Note that our hypothetical husband, Sam, put his house in a joint tenancy with his children. In a state which recognized dower, Nina would have a life estate in one-third of the property, because Sam owned it while they were married and before it was placed in joint tenancy.

[16] *See* Opinion of the Justices, 151 N.E.2d 475 (Mass. 1958) (upholding legislation limiting dower and noting the problems dower caused to title searchers).

[17] Community property is discussed in § 28[A], *supra*.

spouses[19] have the right to claim a share of their predeceased consort's estate.[20] The size of the share varies among different jurisdictions, as does the size of the "estate" to which the right attaches. We will first discuss the traditional approach to structuring an elective share, and then turn our attention to the two waves of reform the UPC generated. The discussion closes with a look at the election rights of incompetent spouses.

[1] Traditional Approaches

Elective share statutes developed as an alternative to dower. In states where dower was not abolished, spouses were often given the choice of whether to claim dower or an elective share. Now the elective share is the dominant approach.[21] Regardless of a will's provisions, under traditional statutes a surviving spouse can claim a share of the decedent's probate estate.[22] Often the share parallels the spouse's share under the local intestate succession statute.[23] If the survivor is electing in the face of a will, the burden of satisfying the claim might either fall on the residuary taker or be prorated among all the beneficiaries.[24]

Recall Sam and Nina, our traditional couple. Suppose Sam has died leaving his plan intact. Because she was left nothing under Sam's will, Nina might choose to take her elective share.[25] She would get a fraction of Sam's probate estate, which consists of whatever personal property Sam left in his name.[26] Because Nina's election right only extends to Sam's probate

---

[18] Georgia offers only a "year's support." *See* Verner F. Chaffin, *A Reappraisal of the Wealth Transmission Process: The Surviving Spouse, Year's Support and Intestate Succession*, 10 Ga. L. Rev. 447 (1976).

[19] New York has denied such a right to the survivor of a homosexual relationship. *In re* Estate of Cooper, 592 N.Y.S.2d 797 (App. Div. 1993).

[20] Spousal election can also serve as a valuable estate planning device for wealthy taxpayers who need to "balance" their estates to maximize their use of the federal unified credit. *See* § 62[C], *infra*.

[21] *See generally* Sheldon F. Kurtz, *The Augmented Estate Concept Under the Uniform Probate Code: In Search of an Equitable Elective Share*, 62 Iowa L. Rev. 981, 982-1011 (1977).

[22] In some states a spouse can elect in an intestate estate. *See* UPC § 2-202(a). The election would make sense if it provided a larger share than the intestate statute would. The most probable situation in which an election would be better is if the jurisdiction allowed election against nonprobate assets. *See* §§ 28[C][1] (capturing nonprobate assets under traditional elective share statutes) & 28[C][3] (UPC approaches to expanding the range property against which spouses can elect), *infra*.

[23] Thus, any smaller share under the will could prompt an election. For a discussion of intestacy, see Chapter 2, *supra*.

[24] *Compare* Crocker v. Crocker, 120 N.E. 110 (Mass. 1918) (residuary), *with In re* Wilkinson v. Brune, 682 S.W.2d 107 (Mo. Ct. App. 1984) (pro rata). If the electing spouse were giving up a life estate, a court might "sequester" the life estate and use the income to reimburse beneficiaries particularly disadvantaged by the election. *See, e.g.*, Sellick v. Sellick, 173 N.W. 609 (Mich. 1919).

[25] If her intestate share would be greater than her elective share, Nina might also challenge the will's validity. For a discussion of planning techniques Sam might have used to thwart Nina's efforts, see § 7[A][5], *supra*.

[26] The distinction between probate and nonprobate assets is covered in § 2, *supra*.

estate, she has no claim to the house in joint tenancy, the stock portfolio now held in trust, or the life insurance.

[a] Capturing Nonprobate Assets

Some courts have found troubling the specter of someone "emptying" the probate estate to defeat a surviving spouse's claim. In response, these courts have fashioned various theories to protect a disinherited spouse by extending the right of election to nonprobate assets.[27] It may be helpful to group most of the cases along two general lines.[28] One approach focuses on intent (sometimes "fraudulent" intent), and the other asks whether there has been an illusory transfer. A word of caution, however: courts have tended to apply these theories narrowly. They may not be as protective as they first appear. In response to the weaknesses of those approaches, an objective test has appeared. The rest of this section discusses these various methods of protecting spouses.

The intent/fraud cases tend to consider a variety of factors, giving different weight to each in particular instances. In some cases, like our hypothetical, the motive may be clear and determinative. In others, one might look to how soon before death a gift was made,[29] or the amount of support otherwise available to the spouse,[30] or the relationship of the spouses.[31] This loose approach makes prediction difficult in any particular case.[32]

Courts use the illusory transfer test more often, but not to much better effect. The most influential case espousing this view is *Newman v. Dore.*[33] Three days before he died, 80-year-old Ferdinand Straus created a revocable trust containing all of his personal and real property. Though he named

---

[27] The classic text on this topic is William D. Macdonald, Fraud on the Widow's Share (1960).

[28] *See generally* McGovern & Kurtz at 132-144. Any grouping is somewhat arbitrary. One court has observed that the cases show "no single standard which can be applied . . . . Rather, the majority of courts . . . appear to decide the issue on a case by case basis, in light of the particular facts and circumstances." Davis v. KB & T Co., 309 S.E.2d 45, 50 (W. Va. 1983).

[29] *See* McClure v. Stegall, 729 S.W.2d 263 (Tenn. Ct. App. 1987) (Surviving spouse challenged decedent's conveyance to his mother as one made in anticipation of his death. The court upheld the gift because decedent died in an automobile accident.).

[30] *See* Warren v. Compton, 626 S.W.2d 12 (Tenn. App. 1981) (Decedent's $40,000 gift was not fraudulent because decedent's will provided her the exact amount from his estate to which she was entitled by law.).

[31] *See In re* Estate of Fisher, 440 N.Y.S.2d 519 (N.Y. Sur. Ct. 1981) (Poor marital relationship did not establish fraudulent intent on the part of the husband when both parties had signed a separation agreement and divorce proceeding was pending at the time of husband's death.). *See generally* Margaret V. Turano, *Love and Death: Marital Problems, Wills, and the Right of Election*, 49 Brook. L. Rev. 405 (1983).

[32] When Ohio decided to retain its traditional approach, a dissenting justice noted that while under the majority's approach theoretically there could be fraud, "the surviving spouse will rarely be able to reach the trust assets unless perhaps the explicit statement 'this trust is created to defraud my spouse' appears somewhere in the trust instrument . . . ." Dumas v. Estate of Dumas, 627 N.E.2d 978, 985 (1994) (Resnick, dissenting).

[33] 9 N.E.2d 966 (N.Y. 1937).

others as trustees, he reserved income to himself for life and powers to control the trust administration. His thirty-something widow was not pleased with an empty probate estate, so she challenged the trust's validity.[34] Rejecting the approach of examining motive or intent, the Court of Appeals of New York asked instead whether Ferdinand "in good faith divested himself of ownership of his property or has made an illusory transfer."[35] The required good faith referred not to the purpose of disinheriting his wife but, rather, whether he intended to give up his ownership in the property. On these facts, the court found the trust "illusory" and, for the purpose of allowing the widow's election,[36] the trust property was part of Ferdinand's estate.

Despite its potential,[37] the illusory transfer test has been an illusory protection for disinherited spouses. In particular, courts applying the test have upheld revocable trusts with retained life estates[38] in the face of challenges by disinherited surviving spouses.[39] Even Totten Trusts[40] have been found not to be illusory.[41]

In response to the inadequacies of the intent/fraud and illusory transfer approaches, the Massachusetts Supreme Judicial Court, in *Sullivan v. Burkin*,[42] adopted an objective test. If, during the marriage, the deceased spouse created an inter vivos trust over which he or she alone retained a general power of appointment,[43] the assets in the trust would be subject

---

[34] As the age difference suggests, this was not a typical marriage. For some interesting details, see Clark, Lusky, Murphy, Ascher & McCouch at 129 n.2.

[35] Newman, 9 N.E.2d at 969. New York has since changed its approach. *See* N.Y. Est. Powers & Trusts Law § 5-1.1(b). For a discussion focusing on many of the issues which arise in New York, see Sidney Kwestel & Rena C. Seplowitz, *Testamentary Substitutes: Retained Interests, Custodial Accounts and Contractual Transactions—A New Approach*, 38 Am. U. L. Rev. 1 (1988).

[36] For discussion about whether trusts should be recognized for some purposes, but not others, see § 12[E], *supra*.

[37] For a decision citing *Newman v. Dore* and holding a trust illusory, see Seifert v. Southern Nat'l Bank of South Carolina, 409 S.E.2d 337 (S.C. 1991). There the husband retained extensive control over the trustee's investment powers and the court *invalidated* the trust, rather than merely allowing the wife's election against trust assets. The legislature later remedied the problem so such a trust would survive, subject to the claim. S.C. Code Ann. § 62-7-112. *See* S. Alan Medlin, *Result-Oriented Interpretations of the South Carolina Probate Code Create Estate of Confusion*, 44 S.C. L. Rev. 287 (1993).

[38] *See* §§12[E] (revocable trusts) & 16 (trusts and pour-over wills), *supra*.

[39] *See, e.g.*, Leazenby v. Clinton County Bank & Trust Co., 355 N.E.2d 861 (Ind. App. 1976) (husband could not take share of wife's assets held in trust over which wife retained power to revoke). *See also* Restatement (Second) of Trusts § 57 cmt. c.

[40] These are savings accounts held nominally in trust form. *See* § 18[B], *supra*.

[41] *See In re* Halpern's Estate, 100 N.E.2d 120 (N.Y. 1951). *But see* Montgomery v. Michaels, 301 N.E.2d 465 (Ill. 1973) (savings account trust included in the probate estate for purposes of calculating the elective share).

[42] 460 N.E.2d 572 (Mass. 1984).

[43] Under federal tax law, to which the court referred, a general power is one exercisable in favor of the person holding the power (the donee), his estate, his creditors, or creditors of his estate. *See* I.R.C. § 2041(b)(1). This text discusses powers of appointment in Chapter 10, *infra*, and their tax implications in Chapter 14, *infra*.

to spousal election.[44]

The case involved Mary Sullivan's claim against an inter vivos trust her husband, Ernest, created sometime after the couple separated. The facts are incomplete, but it is clear that they had been separated for many years before Ernest died. Ernest named himself as trustee, reserved the income for his life, and kept a power to revoke. The court's approach will allow others[45] in Mary's position to include the trust assets as part of the estate against which they could elect.

Sullivan v. Burkin is noteworthy because of the court's straightforward approach. First, the court resisted the temptation to declare the trust invalid as a "testamentary" transfer not meeting statutory requirements. Revocable inter vivos trusts are simply too valuable as estate planning tools for this court to undermine their general viability to meet the needs of a particular situation.[46] Second, the court avoided the morass of traditional approaches toward recapturing (for purposes of spousal election) assets held as will substitutes. There is no inquiry into intention, motive, fraud, colorability or the illusory nature of the transfer; the objective test is clean. Moreover, the court grounded its decision firmly on the public policy that prompted changes in the law regarding spousal rights at divorce.[47] Finally, the court acknowledged that it was not answering a whole series of related questions,[48] and it called upon the legislature to address the problem. As of this writing, the legislature has not obliged.

Another court to respond creatively in the face of a seemingly rigid law was the New Jersey Supreme Court in *Carr v. Carr*.[49] After 17 years of marriage, Thomas Carr left his wife, Joyce. About a year later, she brought a divorce action against Thomas, but he died before the case got to trial. When Thomas' death ended the divorce action, Joyce lost her chance to claim equitable distribution of the marital assets. New Jersey law also precluded her from taking an elective share of Thomas' estate, because at

---

[44] *See generally* Margaret M. Mahoney, *Elective Share Statutes: The Right to Elect Against Property Subject to a General Power of Appointment in the Decedent*, 55 Notre Dame L. Rev. 99 (1979). *See also* Restatement (Second) of Property § 34.1(3). The Restatement would not require the trust to have been established during the marriage. *See* Restatement (Second) of Property § 34.1(3) at 13.7 cmt. a.

[45] Because it was changing Massachusetts law on the point, the court issued a prospective ruling, applicable to all documents drafted or amended after the opinion's date.

[46] Notice the similarity of the terms of the trust here to the one upheld in *Farkas v. Williams*, 125 N.E.2d 600 (Ill. 1955), discussed in § 12[E], *supra*.

[47] Fairness, rather than how title is held, is the central theme. Courts typically make an "equitable distribution" of the couple's assets. *See generally* John D. Gregory, The Law of Equitable Distribution (1989).

The *Sullivan v. Burkin* court noted that "[i]t is neither equitable nor logical to extend to a divorced spouse greater rights . . . than are extended to a spouse who remains married until the death of his or her spouse." 460 N.E.2d at 577.

[48] Among the acknowledged, unaddressed problems were how to handle assets given to the trust by a third person, what happens if the power of appointment were held in conjunction with someone else, and which assets should be used to satisfy the claim.

[49] 576 A.2d 872 (N.J. 1990).

the time of his death, they were living apart. Joyce was in danger of falling between the gaps in protections offered to spouses.[50]

The court examined both the divorce and the spousal election statutes and identified a principle that "animates both statutes[:] . . . a spouse may acquire an interest in marital property by virtue of the mutuality of efforts during marriage that contribute to the creation, acquisition, and preservation of such property."[51] Notions of "fairness, common decency, and good faith" underlie the principle. To protect that interest, Joyce could assert a constructive trust[52] against the marital property in Thomas' estate.

Cases like *Sullivan v. Burkin* and *Carr v. Carr* illustrate a willingness of some courts to apply to spousal election situations the equitable distribution concepts developed in the context of divorce.[53] These approaches can help to modernize the doctrine, but they are necessarily piecemeal changes. They leave essentially undisturbed fundamental structural problems within the traditional system.

[2] Weaknesses in the Traditional System

Much of the weakness of the traditional elective share system grows out of its title-based approach. If the decedent spouse held property in her or his own name, so that it becomes an asset of the probate estate, the survivor has a shot at it. If property is held in trust (or some other will substitute), survivors normally cannot reach it. Form prevails over substance. The title-based approach is arbitrary in another sense as well. Whether the marriage lasted a day or a half century, the elective share is the same. These results are out of sync with the idea that a marriage is a cooperative venture, to which both parties contribute over time.

The label, "The Partnership Theory of Marriage," is often used as a shorthand way to refer to the notion that both spouses contribute to, and benefit from, a marriage.[54] Use of the word "partnership" does not imply that the technical rules relating to business enterprises should be imported wholesale into the law of family relations. Rather, the term connotes a concept,

---

[50] A separation agreement giving Joyce some rights in Thomas' property might have avoided this problem. Of course, agreement might have been impossible. Contracts regarding marital rights are discussed in § 28[E], *infra*.

[51] *Carr*, 576 A.2d at 879. Compare the rationale for community property discussed in § 28[A], *supra*.

[52] *See generally* Dan B. Dobbs, Law of Remedies § 4.3. For other uses of constructive trusts, see §§ 10 (contracts regarding wills), 25[A] (misconduct), and 12[F] (oral trusts), *supra*.

The *Carr* court also suggested that principles of quasi-contract were relevant, because of Joyce's contributions to the creation and acquisition of the marital assets. 576 A.2d at 880.

[53] The trend is not universal. *See* Dalia v. Lawrence, 627 A.2d 392 (Conn. 1993) (declining the invitation to allow a surviving spouse to reach a savings account trust, even though such trusts are subject to division on a marriage's dissolution); Pezza v. Pezza, 690 A.2d 345 (R.I. 1997) (applying the illusory transfer test to defeat a wife's claim although divorce was pending when husband died).

[54] *See, e.g.*, UPC, Article 2, Part 2 general comment. For an excellent and accessible discussion, with particular attention to topics directly relevant to this text, see Lawrence W. Waggoner, *Marital Property Rights in Transition*, 59 Mo. L. Rev. 21 (1994).

a way of thinking about marriage. This notion may come from a presumption that parties to the marriage agreed to share the fruits of the marriage, or the idea that the parties are each entitled to a return for the contributions they have made, or the hope that this approach itself will shape views of how marriages ought to work.[55] Perhaps the best-known applications of this concept are the community property system[56] and the laws surrounding property division upon divorce.[57]

When viewed from the perspective of a marriage as a partnership, traditional elective share statutes produce two kinds of unfair results. Sometimes they give the survivor too little, sometimes too much.

Under protection of a surviving spouse's interests can be a function of the way title is held or of the length of the marriage. For an illustration of the ways a spouse can end up with too little, recall Sam and Nina, the hypothetical couple introduced at the beginning of this section.[58] You will remember that Sam essentially emptied his probate estate, leaving only a few incidentals against which Nina could elect. Because few assets were titled in Sam's name, Nina was left with an unfairly small share. Even if, instead of using will substitutes, Sam had left a "full" probate estate, Nina's share still would have been inadequate when viewed from the perspective of a partnership theory of marriage. After 17 years of contributions, Nina's elective share under a traditional statute would likely be one-third, not an equal sharing of the fruits of the marriage.

The traditional system can also give the electing spouse too large a share. Suppose that instead of wanting to disinherit Nina, Sam tried to provide for her. He named her as income beneficiary of the trust (worth $11,000) and gave her the power to invade the trust principal for her benefit. He named her joint tenant in the house ($90,000) and beneficiary of his life insurance policies ($10,000). Wanting to leave something to his children, Sam named them as will beneficiaries (net probate estate: $10,000). Out of $121,000, Nina would take $111,000 under Sam's plan. Under a traditional scheme, Nina could also elect to take $3,333 from the probate estate intended for the children.[59]

The traditional system also ignores the relationship between the length of the marriage and the fairness of a spouse's share. Short-term marriages present difficult situations. Suppose Miriam, a wealthy, young heiress, marries Pete, a starving, young artist. Upon returning from their honeymoon, Miriam writes a will giving Pete a modest stipend, but then she dies

---

[55] *See* Waggoner, Alexander, Fellows & Gallanis at 582-584 (citing others).

[56] Community property is discussed in § 28[A], *supra*.

[57] *See generally* Mary A. Glendon, The Transformation of Family Law (1989); Stephen D. Sugarman and Herma H. Kay, Divorce Reform at the Crossroads (1990).

[58] Other easily accessible examples appear in the general comment to Article 2, Part 2, of the UPC.

[59] For a real-world example, see Bravo v. Sauter, 727 So. 2d 1103 (Fla. App. 1999) (spouse electing against will also retains trust interest).

in an unfortunate accident.[60] Despite having made minimal contributions to the marriage, Pete would get the same elective share as someone who had been married 50 years. Later-in-life marriages raise the same problem, with the added complication that children are often involved. Suppose Rae, with two sons, marries Ollie, with two of his own. Each spouse has significant assets, which they keep separate, and each makes a will giving everything to their respective children. When Rae dies two years later, Ollie's exercise of his one-third elective share effectively takes money away from Rae's sons and makes it available to his. By treating all marriages the same, regardless of their length, the traditional system gives some spouses a greater share of the marital assets than would a system based on a partnership theory.

[3] The Uniform Probate Code

The drafters of the Uniform Probate Code have sought, within the confines of a title-based marital property system, to address the basic weaknesses in the traditional approach to spousal election. The UPC's reforms have come in two stages. The original code introduced the concept of an expanded, "augmented" estate against which surviving spouses could elect.[61] The basic idea was to negate the efforts of spouses who emptied their probate estates to defeat their survivor's claims. At the same time, the code sought to prevent surviving spouses, who benefited amply from nonprobate transfers, from adding to their shares by also electing against their spouses' probate estates. The second stage came in 1990. These amendments use two devices to implement the partnership theory of marriage. First, rather than being uniform for all couples, the survivor's share increases over the length of the marriage.[62] Second, the augmented estate has been reformulated; now spouses share the total assets of the marital unit.[63] The 1990 amendments also introduced an element which goes more to providing support than to recognizing a partnership; they mandate a minimum $50,000 share.[64] The following subsections discuss each of these stages in the UPC's development.

[a] The First Augmented Estate

The original version of the augmented estate sought to prevent people from taking advantage of the system.[65] In some ways, it is a system made

---

[60] *See* Janus v. Tarasewicz, 482 N.E.2d 418 (Ill. App. 1985) (newlywed victims of random poisoning by taking tainted Tylenol). Sometimes accidents are not so accidental. If caught a killer is likely to lose the benefit of the crime. *See* § 25, *supra*.

[61] UPC (pre-1990) § 2-202.

[62] UPC § 2-202(a).

[63] UPC § 2-202(b).

[64] UPC § 2-201(b).

[65] For a comprehensive discussion, see Sheldon F. Kurtz, *The Augmented Estate Concept Under the Uniform Probate Code: In Search of an Equitable Elective Share*, 62 Iowa L. Rev. 981, 1011-1063 (1977).

not to be used. The drafters hoped that by making it virtually impossible for one spouse to defeat the other's share, or for a survivor who was well cared for to "double dip" by electing and taking more, people would not bother on either score.[66] To accomplish those goals, they invented the "augmented estate." It includes both will substitutes that do not benefit the surviving spouse, and those that do. The survivor can claim a one-third share of that larger pot,[67] but is credited with the value of property already received.[68]

This version of the augmented estate has three basic parts.[69] The first can be called the "net probate estate." This is the property in the decedent spouse's probate estate, less debts, expenses and allowances. Though the details differ among jurisdictions, this is the estate against which spouses elect under traditional statutes.

To the net probate estate is added the value of will substitutes that benefit persons other than the surviving spouse. In concept, but not detail, this part of the augmented estate draws upon the definition of the gross estate for purposes of the Federal Estate Tax.[70] It reaches property which continued to benefit the decedent, but which was held in a form that avoided probate. In particular, it includes a revocable inter vivos trust with a non-spouse as beneficiary.[71] In an exception to the general thrust of this approach, however, life insurance benefitting a non-spouse is not included.[72] Also, because the goal is to avoid "fraud" on the elective share, only transfers during the marriage are subject to this sort of recapture.[73]

The third part of the augmented estate is property which the decedent gave the surviving spouse before death. This device is meant to preclude elections by spouses who have already gotten a fair share of the decedent's wealth. For this reason, life insurance that benefits the surviving spouse is included. This part of the augmented estate covers not only gifts which the survivor still owns, but also property which the survivor in turn gave away to others, but which would be included in the survivor's augmented estate. The second element prevents a survivor from manipulating the statute by setting up his or her own avoidance devices.

---

[66] *See* UPC (pre-1990) § 2-202 comment.

[67] UPC (pre-1990) § 2-201.

[68] UPC (pre-1990) § 2-207.

[69] *See* UPC (pre-1990) § 2-202. For a helpful checklist, see Sheldon F. Kurtz, *The Augmented Estate Concept Under the Uniform Probate Code: In Search of an Equitable Elective Share*, 62 Iowa L. Rev. 981, 1015-1016 (1977).

[70] *See generally* § 62[A], *infra*.

[71] Recall that *Sullivan v. Burkin*, 460 N.E.2d 572 (Mass. 1984), reached the same result by judicial decision. *Sullivan* is discussed in § 28[C][1], *supra*.

[72] Perhaps influenced by a life insurance industry that wanted to avoid the complications of the statute, the drafters concluded that people do not normally purchase life insurance as a way of emptying a probate estate to defeat an election claim. *See* UPC (pre-1990) § 2-202 comment. The revised version closes this loophole. *See* UPC § 2-205(1)(iv).

[73] In our earlier example, if Rae had created a trust for her children before she married Ollie, he would not be able to include the trust in Rae's augmented estate. Note the importance of premarital planning. *See generally* § 28[E], *infra*.

To see how the pre-1990 augmented estate is put together, again consider Sam and Nina. You will recall that in one version, Sam tried to defeat Nina's claims.[74] His probate estate was worth $10,000. He created with his children a joint tenancy in his house ($90,000). He put his stock in a revocable living trust ($11,000). His life insurance totaled $10,000. He named his children, Peter and Susan, as will, trust, and life insurance beneficiaries. Under the pre-1990 version, Sam's augmented estate would be the total of his probate estate, the joint property, and the revocable trust ($111,000). Nina's share would be $37,000.

In a different version, Sam was relatively more generous to Nina, and she was double dipping. He named her as income beneficiary of the trust and gave her the power to invade the trust principal for her benefit. He left the house in joint tenancy with Nina and named her as beneficiary of his life insurance policies. His children were the beneficiaries of his will. The augmented estate would include all of these assets ($121,000),[75] and Nina's share would be $40,333. Because Nina had already received from Sam property valued more than that, she would receive nothing from the probate estate.[76]

The original augmented estate was a creative approach to the problems of spouses who were left too little, or who could manipulate the system to claim too much. It viewed marital claims, however, through the lens of a who-holds-title system. From the perspective of marriage as a partnership, it falls short. It does not treat assets acquired during the marriage as if both spouses had claims on them. Nor does it provide a floor securing a minimum level of support for the survivor.

[b]   A New Approach

Prompted by Professors Langbein and Waggoner,[77] the UPC's drafters reshaped the spousal election machinery to recognize the partnership theory of marriage in 1990. In 1993, they reorganized the relevant sections and made some minor substantive adjustments. Two changes predominate: the survivor's share now increases over the length of the marriage, and spouses now share the total assets of the marital unit.[78] The revised version

---

[74] See § 28[C][2], supra.

[75] This amount is $10,000 higher than the prior example because life insurance payable to the spouse is included in this version of the augmented estate, whereas life insurance payable to others is not.

[76] See UPC (pre-1990) § 2-207. This approach is similar to the way advancements are treated in a hotchpot. They are added in to determine the total pot; shares are calculated; donees are credited with the amounts they have received already; and then distributions are made. For more discussion, see § 24, supra.

[77] See John H. Langbein & Lawrence W. Waggoner, Redesigning the Spouse's Forced Share, 22 Real Prop. Prob. & Tr. J. 303 (1987).

[78] The drafters chose this accrual method over both divorce law's equitable distribution (too case-specific) and a deferred community property model (too hard to trace and classify marital property). See Lawrence W. Waggoner, The Multiple-Marriage Society and Spousal Rights Under the Revised Uniform Probate Code, 76 Iowa L. Rev. 223, 223-247 (1991); UPC §§ 2-202(a),

also mandates a minimum $50,000 share.[79] Commentary on these proposals has been generally positive.[80]

Working through a problem under the new system requires four basic steps:

(1) Identify the "elective share percentage" to which the surviving spouse is entitled.

This step is easy. Section 2-202(a) includes a chart showing increasing percentages over the length of a marriage. The idea is to approximate the effects of a community property system. As couples stay married longer, more and more of their assets are likely to have come from their joint efforts.[81] The UPC assumes different joint contributions over time. For example, after 7 years of marriage, the survivor can claim a 21% share of the augmented estate.[82] After 15 years, all of the couple's assets are presumed to be marital assets, to which each spouse has a right to half.

(2) Calculate the augmented estate.

Calculating the new augmented estate is similar to, but less complicated than, the same effort under the original UPC.[83] The basic idea is to include all assets of both spouses, regardless of how title is held.[84] The process includes four steps:

    (a)   Start with the decedent's net probate estate.[85]

    (b)   Add the value of nonprobate transfers the decedent made to others than the surviving spouse. Included transfers might have taken many forms: property the decedent effectively owned immediately before death;[86] property the decedent

---

2-203. For a different view, see Alan Newman, *Incorporating the Partnership Theory of Marriage into Elective-Share Law: The Approximation System of the Uniform Probate Code and the Deferred-Community-Property Alternative*, 49 Emory L.J. 487 (2000).

[79] UPC 2-202(b).

[80] *See generally* Ira M. Bloom, *The Treatment of Trust and Other Partial Interests of the Surviving Spouse Under the Redesigned Elective-Share System: Some Concerns and Suggestions*, 55 Alb. L. Rev. 941 (1992); Lawrence W. Waggoner, *Spousal Rights in our Multiple-Marriage Society: The Revised Uniform Probate Code*, 26 Real Prop. Prob. & Tr. J. 683 (1992); Margaret V. Turano, *UPC Section 2-201: Equal Treatment of Spouses?*, 55 Alb. L. Rev. 983 (1992); John W. Fisher, II & Scott A. Curnutte, *Reforming the Law of Intestate Succession and Elective Shares: New Solutions to Age-Old Problems*, 93 W. Va. L. Rev. 61 (1990). For more a critical view, see Charles H. Whitebread, *The Uniform Probate Code's Nod to the Partnership Theory of Marriage: The 1990 Elective Share Revisions*, 11 Prob. L.J. 125 (1992).

[81] The scale is not evenly distributed. In the first 10 years of marriage, each year adds 3%. After 10 years, each year adds 4%.

[82] Because each spouse has a right to half of the marital assets, this percentage assumes that after 7 years 42% of the couple's assets are the result of their joint effort.

[83] *See* § 28[C][3][a], *supra.*

[84] *See* UPC § 2-203.

[85] As before, this amount comes after debts, expenses and allowances (including those for family support). UPC § 2-205(1).

[86] This category includes property subject to a general, presently exercisable power of

transferred during the marriage,[87] but retained the benefits of;[88] and gifts made during the marriage and within two years of death.[89]

(c)   Add the value of nonprobate property going to the surviving spouse.[90]

(d)   Add the value of the spouse's property (including what would have been included among the surviving spouse's nonprobate transfers to others if the spouse had been the decedent).[91] Because the section seeks to implement the partnership theory, the source of assets owned by the surviving spouse is not relevant. We now avoid the complicated task of tracing assets to see if they came from the decedent spouse.

The total of these elements is intended to reflect the value of both spouses' property.

(3)   Determine the elective share by multiplying (1) and (2).

The third step in figuring the elective share just requires multiplying the percentage identified in Step 1 and the value of the augmented estate determined in Step 2. The result is the amount of the augmented estate that the surviving spouse can claim. If the amount is less than $50,000, however, a "supplemental elective-share amount"[92] is available to bring the total up to $50,000. This minimum figure is based on a marital duty to support, so it is not prorated according to the length of the marriage.[93]

---

appointment, joint tenancy property, other survivorship-type property, and insurance proceeds. UPC § 2-202(b)(2)(i). The insurance provision fills a loophole from the original UPC. The UPC comments provide numerous examples. For more on powers of appointment, see Chapter 10, *infra*. Other will substitutes are covered in Chapter 5, *supra*.

[87] For the argument that premarital transfers should be subject to election, see Rena C. Seplowitz, *Transfers Prior to Marriage and the Uniform Probate Code's Redesigned Elective Share: Why the Partnership is Not Yet Complete,* 26 Ind. L. Rev. 1 (1991).

[88] One example would be an irrevocable trust over which the decedent retained a right to income for life. UPC § 2-205(2). The comments provide others.

[89] UPC § 2-205(3). Such gifts are often will substitutes. Outright gifts, which would not otherwise be in the augmented estate, are included to the extent that the same donee has received more than $10,000 in either year. The $10,000 figure comes from the gift tax law, now indexed for inflation. I.R.C. § 2503(b). Like the tax law, the UPC chooses to ignore smaller gifts. The annual exclusion is covered in § 61[B], *infra*.

[90] UPC § 2-206.

[91] Property which would be in the spouse's estate is not valued as if the surviving spouse were deceased. Thus, for example, life insurance on the surviving spouse would not be valued at its face amount, because the insured is still alive. *See* UPC § 2-207. The UPC comments suggest that the insurance could be valued under the method used for federal estate tax purposes under Treas. Reg. § 20.2031-8. *See* UPC § 2-202 comment; UPC § 2-207 comment.

[92] UPC § 2-202(b).

[93] Like other amounts in the UPC, the $50,000 is included in brackets to indicate that states may set their own amounts. Professor Waggoner has commented that "[a] somewhat higher figure might be quite appropriate." Lawrence W. Waggoner, *Marital Rights in Transition*, 18 Prob. Law. 1, 41 (1992).

The supplemental elective share is similar in concept to the "front money" available to surviving spouses under the law of intestacy. *See* UPC § 2-102 (setting minimum amounts of between $100,000 and $200,000). For discussion, see § 4, *supra*.

(4) Identify the property used to satisfy the elective share.

Once we have determined the amount to which the surviving spouse is entitled, the final step is to identify which property can be used to satisfy the claim.[94] Recall that the goal of this whole process is to create an entitlement to half of the assets the marriage produced. If the surviving spouse already has that much, we need look no further. If not, the spouse can get property from the decedent's other beneficiaries.

The starting place for satisfying the survivor's claim, then, is to credit the spouse for property he or she already owns or has received from the decedent. That property can come from several sources:[95]

(a) Property the survivor received by will or intestate succession.[96]

(b) Will substitutes benefiting the surviving spouse.

(c) Property owned by the surviving spouse (including the survivor's nonprobate transfers to others), up to what the Code calls an "applicable percentage."[97] This percentage is twice the spousal election percentage identified in Step 1, based on the length of the marriage. By doubling the elective share percentage, we identify the shares of spouses' assets which ought to be treated as part of the marital pool.[98] Because the percentage is 50% for marriages longer than 15 years, in those cases all of the survivor's property can be credited to satisfy the claim.[99] If the total of this property

---

[94] *See* UPC § 2-209.

[95] Though the rationale for this approach is to create a sharing consistent with the partnership theory, the effect eliminates the problem of "double dipping." *See* § 28[C][3][a], *supra*.

[96] UPC § 2-209(a)(1). Because the elective share rights are additional to other benefits, the spouse is not charged with homestead, family allowance and exempt property benefits. *See* UPC § 2-402 to 2-404. *See also* UPC § 2-209 comment.

[97] UPC § 2-209(a)(2).

[98] A credit for the full amount of property owned would not be fair in a short-term marriage. The UPC assumes that these shorter marriages hold both marital and individual assets. Recall that the elective share percentage identifies the share of the whole to which the survivor was entitled. That percentage also applies to the assets held by each spouse. For example, a seven-year marriage yields an elective share percentage of 21%, on the assumption that after seven years, 42% of a couple's pool of assets is the result of their joint effort and 58% is the result of individual efforts. The code also assumes that 42% of property in the wife's name is marital, and 58%, individual. The same is true for the property titled in the husband.

If 58% of a spouse's assets are not attributable to the marriage, at the time of an election that 58% should not be subject to sharing. Conversely, 42% of the survivor's assets are deemed marital, so those should be credited towards satisfying the elective share.

[99] In 1975, the UPC started crediting the spouse with property the spouse would have received, but disclaimed. Some commentators have criticized this approach because such crediting discourages a spouse from disclaiming a life interest in a trust in order to get an absolute interest under the elective share. *See* Ira M. Bloom, *The Treatment of Trust and Other Partial Interests of the Surviving Spouse Under the Redesigned Elective-Share System: Some Concerns and Suggestions*, 55 Alb. L. Rev. 941, 970-975 (1992). On the other hand, taking disclaimed property into account helps preserve the decedent's testamentary scheme as much

is not enough to satisfy a spouse's share, then the spouse may claim against the decedent's estate and others who received nonprobate transfers from the decedent.

For purposes of satisfying the elective share from property not benefiting the survivor, the UPC distinguishes between two classes of beneficiaries. First in line to share with the spouse are will and will-substitute beneficiaries who effectively receive their benefits as of the decedent's death.[100] They contribute to the spouse's claim in shares proportional to their benefits. Only if these people are unable to satisfy the survivor's claim do we retrieve property from people who had already received irrevocable gifts from the decedent within two years of the death.[101] Gifts shortly before death are included in the augmented estate because they work as will substitutes, but the reliance interests involved and the difficulty of trying to retrieve this property make these gifts the last place for satisfying the spousal claim.

To see how the revised augmented estate works, again consider Sam and Nina.[102] They had been married for 17 years, and Nina had no property titled in her name. You will recall that in one version, Sam tried to defeat Nina's claims.[103] His probate estate was worth $10,000. He created with his children a joint tenancy in his house ($90,000). He put his stock in a revocable living trust ($11,000). His life insurance totaled $10,000. He named his children, Peter and Susan, as will, trust, and life insurance beneficiaries. Because they had been married for more than 15 years, Nina's share of Sam's augmented estate would be $60,500, half the total value of $121,000.[104] Peter and Susan would each contribute $30,250 to satisfy their mother's claim.

If we change the facts to suppose that Nina had assets in her name worth $100,000, the augmented estate would now be $221,000, and Nina's half would be $110,500. Because Nina already had $100,000, Peter and Susan would only lose $5,250 each to their mother.

---

as possible and avoids manipulative moves by the survivor. *See* Patricia J. Roberts, *The 1990 Uniform Probate Code's Elective-Share Provisions — West Virginia's Enactment Paves the Way*, 95 W. Va. L. Rev. 55, 71-73 (1992).

The 1993 "technical" amendments eliminated the rule crediting the spouse with disclaimed property. UPC § 2-209. The comment to amended § 2-209 indicates that this rule was deleted due to the creation of QTIP provisions under the tax code, I.R.C. § 2056A, making computation of the value of the disclaimed interest too difficult. UPC § 2-209 comment. Disclaimers are discussed in § 27, *supra*, and QTIP provisions in § 62[B], *infra*.

[100] UPC § 2-209(b), (c).

[101] UPC §§ 2-209(c); 2-205(3)(i) & (iii).

[102] For other examples, see UPC, Article 2, Part 2, general comment; Patricia J. Roberts, *The 1990 Uniform Probate Code's Elective-Share Provisions — West Virginia's Enactment Paves the Way*, 95 W. Va. L. Rev. 55, 124-128 (1992); Lawrence W. Waggoner, *Spousal Rights in Our Multiple-Marriage Society: The Revised Uniform Probate Code*, 26 Real Prop. Prob. & Tr. J. 683, 734-742 (1992).

[103] *See* § 28[C][2], *supra*.

[104] Contrast the result under the pre-1990 version. The augmented estate is $10,000 larger because it now includes life insurance. The new share is half, instead of one-third.

In a different version of the hypothetical, Nina still held no assets, but Sam was relatively more generous, and Nina was double dipping. He named her as income beneficiary of the trust and gave her the power to invade the trust principal for her benefit. He left the house in joint tenancy with Nina and named her as beneficiary of his life insurance policies. His children were the beneficiaries of his will. The augmented estate would still be $121,000, and Nina's share would be $60,500.[105] Because Nina had already received from Sam property valued at more than that, she would receive nothing from the probate estate.

The UPC's new augmented estate goes a long way toward applying the partnership theory of marriage to spousal claims at death. In some ways it is a political compromise, based on the belief that many common law states are unlikely to adopt community property,[106] and that in most cases, this new system can produce results similar to what community property would yield.[107] The UPC's system works well for most long-term marriages and for short-term, later-in-life marriages.[108] It may, however, disadvantage spouses in long-term marriages who give up job opportunities to stay home and raise a family.[109] In addition, the UPC system may not work well for longer-term, late-in-life marriages in which each spouse acquired wealth before the marriage.[110] The UPC proposals are likely to influence legislators and courts which grapple with elective share questions. Whether the system will gain widespread adherence remains to be seen.

[105] In this example. the only change in result from the pre-1990 version is that Nina's share has increased from one-third to one-half of the augmented estate.

[106] For the suggestion not to give up on the Uniform Marital Property Act as a way of bringing community property to the rest of the country, see Charles H. Whitebread, *The Uniform Probate Code's Nod to the Partnership Theory of Marriage: The 1990 Elective Share Revisions*, 11 Prob. L.J. 125, 141-144 (1992).

[107] It is not, however, a community property system. In particular, community property sets up rebuttable presumptions about whether assets are "separate" or "community." The UPC's sliding scale of percentages is absolute. Also, community property gives each spouse testamentary power over half of the community's assets. The UPC does not give the spouse who "owns" less than half of the property the power to dispose of the marital property of the "richer" spouse. *See* Mary M. Wenig, *The Marital Property Law of Connecticut: Past, Present and Future*, 1990 Wis. L. Rev. 807, 874-78; Charles H. Whitebread, *The Uniform Probate Code's Nod to the Partnership Theory of Marriage: The 1990 Elective Share Revisions*, 11 Prob. L.J. 125, 134-137 (1992). *But see* Lawrence W. Waggoner, *The Multiple-Marriage Society and Spousal Rights Under the Revised Uniform Probate Code*, 76 Iowa L. Rev. 223, 249 n.78 (1991). For an introduction to community property, see § 28[A], *supra*.

[108] For examples, see UPC Article 2, Part 2, general comment.

[109] *See* Margaret V. Turano, *UPC Section 2-201: Equal Treatment of Spouses?*, 55 Alb. L. Rev. 983, 1003-1006 (1992) (suggesting that in this situation, the surviving spouse be given a larger elective share percentage or higher supplemental (support) share).

[110] Imagine Dominic and Rose, widower and widow, each with children, who meet in a retirement community and marry at age 67. If they live into their mid-80s, the UPC will presume all of their assets to be marital, subject to sharing, even though they were not accumulated during this marriage. As a result, each spouse's ability to leave property to their own children is restricted. *See* Charles H. Whitebread, *The Uniform Probate Code's Nod to the Partnership Theory of Marriage: The 1990 Elective Share Revisions*, 11 Prob. L.J. 125, 137-139 (1992).

[4] Incompetent Spouses

One problem which will become increasingly common as our population ages is how to handle the right of election of an incompetent surviving spouse. *In re Estate of Clarkson*[111] involved Joseph and Evelyn, who married later in life, each having children from prior marriages. After Evelyn became incompetent, Joseph executed a will creating a trust for her care. He funded the trust with one-fourth of his net estate, giving Evelyn income from the trust for her life and giving the trustee the power to invade the principal for her benefit.[112] After her death, the trust would go to those persons she named in her will. If (as was certain, given her incompetence) she never named anyone,[113] the trust was to be divided between her children and Sam's. The split was not equal, however. Evelyn's two children each got $25,000; the rest of the roughly $340,000[114] was divided between Sam's two children.

Although the legal question was whether the court should elect against the will on Evelyn's behalf, the fight was really between the children on each side. If the election were allowed, Evelyn would take the money outright, and what was left after her death would go to her children.[115] If not, Evelyn's children would only get their $25,000 each under the trust.

In deciding whether to act in Evelyn's behalf, the court asked if the election would be in her best interests.[116] It took what it called the minority position, evaluating her "best interests" objectively based on what produced the most value. The other view is that courts should interpret "best interests" in light of all the facts and circumstances of the particular case. Under the broader approach, it might be appropriate to consider the needs of the surviving spouse or the interest of preserving the estate plan.[117] Applying the pecuniary-value approach, the Nebraska court affirmed an order giving Evelyn an election for one-fourth of the estate outright, rather than limiting her to the trust. On these facts, Evelyn might actually have come out worse, even though given a fee interest unencumbered by the

---

[111] 226 N.W.2d 334 (Neb. 1975).

[112] For a discussion about trusts of this sort, see § 13[A], *supra*.

[113] Tax reasons no doubt explain why Evelyn was given authority she could not exercise. Because she had a general testamentary power of appointment, Joseph's estate could claim an estate tax marital deduction for the gift in trust. Powers of appointment are discussed in Chapter 10 and the marital deduction is covered in § 62[B], *infra*.

[114] In the early 1970s, Joseph's whole estate was worth around one and a quarter million dollars, but the residence was only worth $22,000. There is a lesson here for lawyers building a practice: many rich people live simply.

[115] In addition, with Evelyn giving up her life estate, the remainder to her children would probably accelerate, giving them an additional $25,000 each from what would have been in the trust.

[116] The "best interests" language—common to many statutes—was drawn from the Nebraska statute. *See* Neb. Rev. Stat. § 30-2315. Some states allow the election only if it is necessary to provide support for the survivor. *See* UPC (pre-1990) § 2-203.

[117] *See* Kinnett v. Hood, 185 N.E.2d 888 (Ill. 1962); Van Steenwyck v. Washburn, 59 Wis. 17 N.W. 289 (Wis. 1883).

trust. Because she was incompetent, she would need a guardian appointed to handle her estate, and guardianship expenses often eat up more funds than would trust administration.[118]

The revised UPC takes a different approach to this question. To the extent that the elective share includes the decedent's property and nonprobate property the spouse transferred to others,[119] that property is placed in trust for an incompetent survivor.[120] The trustee uses the money to support the survivor (and others dependent upon the survivor). Anything left after the survivor's death passes under the predeceased spouse's will or goes to that spouse's intestate heirs.[121] The UPC result is very similar to the estate plan which Joseph Clarkson intended for Evelyn.

The way one views spousal election generally can influence how to handle elections on behalf of incompetents. In this regard, the UPC seems to be pulling against itself. As we have seen, the 1990 revisions generally reflect the partnership theory of marriage, with support considerations playing only a minor, minimum share role. When it comes to election by incompetent spouses, however, support becomes the dominant consideration. A partnership theory would suggest that the assets in any custodial trust be paid according to the *survivor's* wishes.[122] If the survivor has earned an entitlement, it should not be lost by the survivor's incompetence.[123]

Unquestionably, the traditional rules surrounding spousal election are under attack. Courts and statutory reformers are taking a broader view of the legitimate claims each spouse has on what used to be viewed as the property of the other. The details of the change will be emerging for some time to come.

[D] Migrating Couples

Because of the different systems of marital property in common law and in community property jurisdictions, couples who move between the two face a variety of problems. Under traditional conflict of laws rules, different

---

[118] *See* § 22[B], *supra.*

[119] For a discussion of the items in the resdesigned augmented estate, see § 28[C][3][b], *supra.*

[120] *See* UPC § 2-212(b). The UPC also now expressly allows conservators, guardians, and agents acting under a power of attorney to make the election. A recent Florida decision prevented a lawyer from electing on behalf of his incompetent client, when the lawyer was not acting under a durable power of attorney. *See* Harmon v. Williams, 615 So. 2d 681 (Fla. 1993). Durable powers of attorney are discussed in § 22[B], *supra.*

[121] *See* UPC § 2-212(c)

[122] The custodial trust for an incompetent survivor is consistent with either the partnership or the support rationale. The question is what happens to the money left after the survivor dies.

[123] Similarly, the partnership theory undercuts another common rule, that a surviving spouse who dies before an election is made loses the right to elect. *See* UPC § 2-212(a).

Of course, requiring survivorship at all is one feature that distinguishes elective share law from community property, which grants rights at the time assets are acquired. For further discussion, see §§ 28[A] (community property), 28[C][3][b] (evaluating the 1990 UPC), *supra.*

laws can apply to different aspects of marital property. The law of the situs of real property controls that property; the law of the marital domicile at the time personal property is acquired determines its character (community or separate); and the law of the marital domicile at death determines the surviving spouse's rights.[124] Applying the law under these rules can produce some unfair results.

Recall Sam and Nina, our traditional couple. Suppose that during Sam's working years, they live in a common law state and hold everything in Sam's name. After retirement, they move to a community property state, which would characterize the property as Sam's separate property. Because community property states rely on their basic system to allocate wealth between spouses, these states generally do not provide survivors a right of election against their predeceased spouse's property. The survivor merely keeps his or her half of the community property. This arrangement works well where a couple has acquired community property, but the system does not protect propertyless migrant spouses like Nina.[125] Lawyers advising couples planning to move to community property states should make them aware of the different systems for protecting survivors.[126]

Couples moving in the other direction—from a community property state to a common law state—also run into problems. Their community property should continue to retain that characterization,[127] but lawyers, judges, and transfer agents unaccustomed to community property may try to force the couple to change the ownership to something more familiar, like a joint tenancy.[128] If the couple does manage to preserve the community status

---

[124] *See* William M. Richman & William L. Reynolds, Understanding Conflict of Laws, 2d ed. 256-259 (1993). *See generally* Jeffrey A. Schoenblum, Multistate and Multinational Estate Planning (1982 & Supp. 1994).

These rules are not absolute. For example, in the context of divorce, Texas has refused to recognize other jurisdictions' characterization of property subject to equitable distribution, but at the same time has followed the traditional rule in probate situations. *See* Estate of Hanau v. Hanau, 730 S.W.2d 663 (Tex. 1987).

[125] Idaho and California remedy this situation. They recognize something called "quasi-community property," which is personal property acquired elsewhere that would have been community property if acquired in the new home state. If the acquiring spouse dies first, the survivor gets half of the quasi-community property. *See* Cal. Prob. Code §§ 66, 101; Idaho Code § 15-2-202.

[126] One solution is a contract between the spouses, giving each rights in the other's property. These agreements are a subset of the contracts discussed in § 28[E], *infra*. That section also discusses ethical issues raised by multiple-party representation.

[127] *See In re* Estate of Kessler, 203 N.E.2d 221 (Ohio 1964) (Stock shares acquired in California, a community property state, retained their characterization as community property when husband and wife moved to Ohio, a common law state.).

[128] *See generally* John C. Nodggard & Harold T. Pickler, Note, *Community Property in a Common Law Jurisdiction: A Seriously Neglected Area of the Law*, 16 Washburn L.J. 77, 86-90 (1976). Joint tenancy is discussed in § 18, *supra*.

Couples wanting to preserve the community property status of their property should consider taking title in both names and executing a separate document reciting their intention to keep the property "community." *See* Stanley M. Johanson, *The Migrating Client: Estate Planning for the Couple from a Community Property State*, 9 U. Miami Inst. Est. Plan. ¶ 800, ¶ 830.2 (Philip E. Heckerling, ed., 1975).

of its property, they may also be creating a situation in which a surviving spouse can double dip. Unless courts or legislatures adapt elective share laws to reflect the presence of community property, the survivor could retain his or her half of the community and still elect to take part of the decedent's half. The Uniform Disposition of Community Property Rights at Death Act, adopted in several common law states,[129] gives each spouse the right to dispose of half of the community property at death, and removes the right of election as to that property.

[E] Agreements Waiving Marital Rights

Sometimes potential (or current) spouses are not comfortable with their counterparts having available a right to elect or some other claim[130] that comes with the marriage. In particular, people with children from an earlier marriage may want to prevent a new spouse from electing against a will benefiting those children.[131] One solution is for one or both parties to waive their spousal rights.[132] People usually make these agreements before marriage.[133] In a few cases, contracts come after the marriage, but while it is still happy; and sometimes they arise with separation or divorce on the horizon.[134] A lawyer preparing these agreements must be sensitive, both to whether the contract will be enforceable and to whether she is breaching her legal ethics.

In deciding when to enforce such agreements, courts face conflicts between wanting to allow freedom of contract generally, wanting to encourage marriages which might not happen without these agreements, and

---

[129] The states are: Alaska, Arkansas, Colorado, Connecticut, Florida, Hawaii, Kentucky, Michigan, Montana, New York, North Carolina, Oregon, Virginia, and Wyoming. 8A Unif. L. Ann. (2002 Pocket Part).

[130] For example, alimony, support, dower, or community property claims.

[131] Compare the similar situation of spouses who agree not to revoke a will. *See* § 10, *supra*. *See also* Carolyn L. Dessin, *The Troubled Relationship of Will Contracts and Spousal Protection: Time for an Amicable Separation*, 45 Cath. U. L. Rev. 435 (1996); Joanna Lynn Grama, *The "New" Newlyweds: Marriage Among the Elderly, Suggestions to the Elder Law Practitioner*, 7 Elder L.J. 379 (1999).

[132] *See generally* Homer H. Clark, The Law of Domestic Relations in the United States 11-12 (2d ed. 1988); Symposium, *Nuptial Agreements*, 8 J. Am. Acad. Matrim. Law. (Spring 1992); Barbara A. Atwood, *Ten Years Later: Lingering Concerns About the Uniform Premarital Agreement Act*, 19 J. Legis. 127 (1993).

Principles from these agreements may also apply to agreements between nontraditional couples. *See* Brooke Oliver, *Contracting for Cohabitation: Adapting the California Statutory Marital Contract to Life Partnership Agreements Between Lesbian, Gay or Unmarried Heterosexual Couples*, 23 Golden Gate U. L. Rev. 899 (1993).

[133] Sometimes these are called "antenuptial agreements."

[134] Older authority invalidated (as against public policy) agreements setting property rights upon divorce. Most jurisdictions now follow Posner v. Posner, 233 So. 2d 381 (Fla. 1970), and enforce fair and reasonable agreements. They offer the advantage of protecting against the death of one of the parties before the marriage formally ends. For an example of someone who might have benefited from such an agreement, see Carr v. Carr, 576 A.2d 872 (N. J. 1990), discussed in § 28[C][1], *supra*.

wanting to protect against abuse. To resolve these issues, courts tend to use either one or both of two different approaches. One view focuses on process, as courts ask whether the parties have made fair disclosures to each other about how much property they own and what the other is giving up.[135] Another tack is to judge the substantive fairness of the agreement itself.[136] As with many questions surrounding spousal election, society's changing views on the roles of women influence how these approaches are applied to particular facts. Two cases illustrate some of the issues.

In *Rosenberg v. Lipnick*[137] a widow sought to invalidate an antenuptial agreement she had signed with her husband. Charlotte was nearly 60, and Perry, nearly 70, when they met. Each had children from prior marriages. After a courtship lasting 18 months, Perry proposed, and asked Charlotte to sign an agreement stating that she would accept $5,000 from his estate in lieu of whatever rights she would have if she survived him. Charlotte consulted her brother, a lawyer, who encouraged her to learn the extent of Perry's wealth. She ignored the advice and signed the agreement anyway. When Perry died 15 years later, his estate was worth $119,000. Charlotte gave two reasons a court should not enforce the agreement: (1) in light of the size of Perry's estate, limiting her to $5,000 was unfair, and (2) she had signed without full knowledge of Perry's wealth. On the basis of old

[135] In judging whether parties have made fair disclosure, courts may consider a number of factors. *See, e.g.*, *In re* Marriage of Norris, 624 P.2d 636 (Or. App. 1981) (no fair disclosure when agreement was presented on morning of wedding); *In re* Marriage of Matson, 705 P.2d 817 (Wash. App. 1985) (no fair disclosure when one party was much less sophisticated than the other); Hawkins v. Hawkins, 185 N.E.2d 89 (Ohio Prob. Ct. 1962) (fair disclosure when both parties were competent professionals); *In re* Marriage of Foran, 834 P.2d 1081 (Wash. App. 1992) (no fair disclosure when one spouse's net worth was $8200 compared to the other spouse's net worth of $198,500); Geddings v. Geddings, 460 S.E.2d 376 (S.C. 1995) (no fair disclosure, despite language in the agreement that there had been disclosure, when wife had no knowledge of the value of husband's estate).

Courts disagree about whether both parties must have legal representation. *Compare In re* Marriage of Bonds, 5 P.3d 815 (Cal. 2000) (baseball star Barry Bonds' premarital agreement enforceable when wife unrepresented by counsel), *with In re* Estate of Crawford, 730 P.2d 675 (Wash. 1986) (independent counsel required when prenuptial agreement unreasonable).

[136] The relevant factors here overlap some with those used to determine fair disclosure. *See, e.g.*, Greenwald v. Greenwald, 454 N.W.2d 34 (Wis. 1990) (prenuptial agreement, which divided property unequally, was substantively fair when husband's assets totaled over $600,000 compared to wife's minimal assets); Hill v. Hill, 356 N.W.2d 49 (Minn. App. 1984) (because wife was in extremely poor health and unable to provide for herself, prenuptial agreement that denied either party a right to spousal maintenance was unconscionable and substantively unfair at the time of their divorce). *See also* Brandt v. Brandt, 427 N.W.2d 126 (Wis. 1988) (agreement substantively unfair at the time of the divorce because the parties had ignored the agreement up to the time of their divorce by failing to keep their assets separate).

Another question is whether the agreement should be judged as of the time it was made or at the time it becomes enforceable. For the view that a surviving spouse's waiver should not be enforced if the survivor needs support at the time of divorce or death, see Paul G. Haskell, *The Premarital Estate Contract and Social Policy*, 57 N.C. L. Rev. 415 (1979).

[137] 389 N.E.2d 385 (Mass. 1979).

authority, the court upheld the contract, but the court articulated a new approach to be applied in future cases.[138]

The old approach had been to uphold premarital agreements made in the absence of fraud.[139] Despite the confidential relationship of the parties, they were treated as if they had been negotiating at arms' length. So long as neither party lied or prevented the other from learning facts about the extent of his or her wealth, a court would enforce the contract. The *Rosenberg* court overruled that approach and endorsed both of the contemporary views described above, fairness and full disclosure.[140] The court noted, however, that even if it had applied its new rule, it might have reached the same result, especially because Charlotte had rejected her brother's advice to get more information and because there was no evidence of coercion by Perry. This opinion reveals a court willing, but not eager, to invalidate unfair agreements or ones made without adequate information.

Simeone v. Simeone[141] sets a somewhat different tone, which in some ways harkens back to earlier cases that applied general contract principles, despite the special relationship of the parties.[142] Simeone arose in the context of a divorce, but its principles could well apply to waiver of spousal rights at death.[143] When they were married in 1975, Catherine was an unemployed nurse, age 23, and Frederick was a neurosurgeon, age 39, with assets worth about $300,000. The day before their wedding, Frederick presented Catherine with the final version of a prenuptial agreement limiting her to support payments of $200 per week, subject to a maximum of $25,000, if they divorced or separated. The couple later disagreed about whether Catherine knew about the agreement ahead of time, but in any case, she signed. After they separated seven years later, Frederick made payments up to $25,000 and then stopped. Catherine ultimately challenged the agreement, which the court upheld.

The court retained the requirement that the parties make full and fair disclosure of their financial positions,[144] but explicitly rejected those cases

---

[138] For another example of the Massachusetts court's tendency to issue prospective rulings, also applied in the context of spousal election, see Sullivan v. Burkin, 460 N.E.2d 572 (Mass. 1984), discussed in § 28[C][1], *supra.*

[139] Wellington v. Rugg, 136 N.E. 831 (Mass. 1922).

[140] Whether there was a written waiver is also particularly important to this court. Other relevant factors include "the parties' respective worth, . . . ages, . . . intelligence, literacy, and business acumen, and prior family ties or commitments." *Rosenberg*, 389 N.E.2d at 389.

[141] 581 A.2d 162 (Pa. 1990). *See also* Recent Development, *Family Law — Prenuptial Agreements — Pennsylvania Supreme Court Rejects Substantive Review of Prenuptial Agreements*, 104 Harv. L. Rev. 1399 (1991).

[142] *See, e.g., Wellington,* 136 N.E. at 831, effectively overruled by *Rosenberg,* 389 N.E.2d at 385.

[143] For example, Massachusetts went the other way and applied *Rosenberg* in a divorce context. *See* Osborne v. Osborne, 428 N.E.2d 810 (Mass. 1981).

[144] This requirement may not in practice undo many agreements. A recitation in the contract that there has been full disclosure sets up a presumption of disclosure, which

which allow substantive review on fairness grounds. Characterizing such review as the paternalistic approach of a bygone era when women were regarded as weak and in need of protection, the court said premarital agreements should be judged by the same criteria as other contracts. Parties to other contracts sometimes cut bad deals, or circumstances sometimes change so that what seemed a good bargain turns out not to have been one. According to this court, parties to a premarital contract should bear those same risks.

One judge concurred in the result because, applying substantive review, he would not have invalidated this agreement. Despite gains on behalf of women's equality, this judge believed inequality still existed and feared that his colleague who wrote for the court "does not live in the real world."[145] He would have treated these contracts as "in the nature of contracts of adhesion with one party generally having greater authority than the other . . . ."[146]

A dissenting judge would have gone further and allowed substantive review, based either on the circumstances at the time of the agreement or on intervening events. Raising themes which parallel the partnership theory of marriage, he would have allowed courts to invalidate premarital agreements when there is clear and convincing evidence that "the amount of time and energy necessary for [a] spouse to shelter and care for the children of the marriage has rendered the terms of a pre-nuptial agreement inequitable, and unjust and thus, avoidable."[147]

There is little question that courts will continue to debate the extent to which contracts governing marital rights ought to be treated as a special category, subject to more careful judicial oversight. Full disclosure seems here to stay. Even if courts back away from substantive, "reasonableness" review, lawyers ought to be reluctant to draft agreements that appear to be unfair. Such agreements are likely to attract litigation, with all its financial and, perhaps more important in a family context, emotional costs.

Among the most difficult issues lawyers face regarding waiver of marital rights are questions surrounding legal ethics.[148] Suppose that Michael and Rose are each getting married for the second time. Presumably because they want to save money, they both say they trust you to be fair and they each want you to draft a premarital agreement for them. Before you take on such

---

presumption can only be overcome by clear and convincing evidence of fraud or misrepresentation. *Simeone*, 581 A.2d at 167. *See also* Geddings v. Geddings, 460 S.E. 376 (S.C. 1995) (no fair disclosure despite language in the agreement).

[145] 581 A.2d at 168 (Papadakos, J., concurring).

[146] 581 A.2d at 168 (Papadakos, J., concurring). For a more nuanced approach, see *In re* Estate of Greiff, 703 N.E.2d 752 (N.Y. 1998) (avoiding presumptions and mandating "particularized and exceptional scrutiny" of these agreement).

[147] 581 A.2d at 171 (McDermott, J., dissenting).

[148] *See* Jeffrey N. Pennell, *Professional Responsibility: Reforms Are Needed to Accommodate Estate Planning and Family Counselling*, in 25 U. Miami Inst. Est. Plan. ch. 18 (John T. Gaubatz ed., 1991).

a dual representation, carefully explain that their interests necessarily conflict. They should understand that the safest course may be for each to get a separate lawyer.[149] Not only would you avoid potential conflicts, but obtaining the independent review would strengthen the agreement against later challenge.[150] You can represent both only if you first obtain their informed consent.[151] A waiver of confidentiality, so you could tell each client what the other tells you, might also be advisable.[152]

§ 29   Omitted Family Members

Another way in which the law protects families is to guarantee a minimum share to family members omitted from a will.[1] The typical scenario is of someone who makes a will and sometime later marries or has a child (or additional children), but neglects to amend the will. A person not covered is often called "pretermitted," or overlooked. Virtually all states have statutes protecting such family members, especially children.[2] Of course, one way to avoid any problems with these statutes is to give any protected person a share of the estate.[3]

Testators, however, need not make such gifts.[4] Unlike spousal election statutes,[5] these statutes do not guarantee the surviving relative a share.[6]

---

[149] This is a particularly appropriate solution if you have represented one of them in the past and, therefore, have closer bonds to that client.

[150] Compare how independent review can protect against claims of undue influence. See § 7[A][3], supra.

[151] Model Rules of Professional Conduct Rule 1.7 (2002); Model Code of Professional Responsibility DR5-105 (1983).

[152] Compare the situations of representing a couple seeking a will (discussed in § 6, supra) or a contract regarding a will (discussed in § 10, supra), or structuring the estate tax marital deduction (discussed in § 62[B], infra).

[1] The argument that a revocable lifetime trust should be treated like a will for this purpose was rejected in Robbins v. Johnson, 780 A.2d 1282 (N.H. 2001).

[2] Wyoming seems to be the only exception. See Lawrence H. Averill, Jr., The Wyoming Probate Code of 1980: An Analysis and Critique, 16 Land & Water L. Rev. 103, 117 (1981). For a compilation of statutes, see Restatement (Second) of Property § 34.2 statutory note.

[3] For example, alternative gifts to children are sufficient, even if the children do not actually take the property. See Mason v. Stanimer, 403 S.E.2d 605 (N.C. 1991) (testator's will giving his personal effects and the residue of his estate to his wife, if she survived him; if not, passing in trust to his surviving children was sufficient to prevent nonmarital child from taking as a pretermitted heir). A nominal gift may not be enough, especially if it is to a general class. See Estate of Torregano v. Torregano, 352 P.2d 505 (Cal. 1960) (gift of $1 to anyone asserting any claim insufficient to preclude omitted child from claiming a pretermitted share).

[4] Disinheriting relatives is a risky strategy. In addition to creating problems under pretermitted heir statutes, not making such gifts virtually invites a will contest. Moreover, not mentioning spouses and children at all may support a claim of lack of mental capacity. See § 7[A], supra.

[5] See § 28[C], supra.

[6] The one exception is Louisiana, which recognizes the legitime, a device of the civil law that guarantees a share to protected relatives. See La. Civ. Code Ann. art. 1493-1500; Max Nathan, Jr., Forced Heirship: The Unheralded "New" Disinherison Rules, 74 Tul. L. Rev. 1027 (2000).

The survivors' moral (and economic) claims bow to the testator's freedom of choice,[7] but these statutes do force testators to negate the statutes' protections. Because the statutes vary in detail but pose similar issues, it can be helpful to have a series of four questions you can ask about whatever statute you face.[8]

First, which categories of relatives are protected? Many jurisdictions view the problem as one of following a testator's presumed intention in light of changed circumstances; they effectively partially revoke the will to include "after-acquired"[9] relatives.[10] Several protect spouses in this situation,[11] most protect children,[12] and some protect descendants of

---

[7] Especially as we become a society with more noncustodial children, we may need to curb this freedom of testation. *See* Brown v. Drake, 270 S.E.2d 130 (S.C. 1980) (upholding a will provision, drafted in the face of an impending divorce, giving $1 to each child in the custody of the testator's wife). *See generally* Ralph C. Brashier, *Disinheritance and the Modern Family*, 45 Case W. Res. L. Rev. 83 (1994); Brian C. Brennan, *Disinheritance of Dependent Children: Why Isn't America Fulfilling Its Moral Obligation?*, 14 Quinnipiac Prob. L.J. 125 (1999); Ronald Chester, *Should American Children Be Protected Against Disinheritance?*, 32 Real Prop. Prob. & Tr. J. 405 (1997).

[8] *See generally* McGovern & Kurtz at 130-134.

[9] Timing can be important. Azcunce v. Estate of Azcunce, 586 So. 2d 1216 (Fla. App. 1991), involved the claim of a daughter born after her father's will was executed but before the date of a codicil. The court held that the codicil republished the will, so the daughter was not an afterborn child. The Restatement of Property expressly disapproves of the result in this case because the testator's intention was defeated. "The mere fact that the codicil expressly republished the prior will should not require that the doctrine of republication by codicil always be applied." Restatement (Third) of Prop. § 3.4, Reporter's Note. For more on the republication doctrine, see the discussion of *Simon v. Grayson* in § 8[B], *supra*. After the daughter lost this claim, she sued the lawyer who drafted the will. She lost on the ground that the lawyer owed no duty to her. *See* Espinosa v. Sparber, Shevin, Shapo, Rosen & Heilbronner, 612 So. 2d 1378 (Fla. 1993). For more on liability of document drafters, see § 1, *supra*.

[10] Indeed, marriage revokes the whole will in some places. *See, e.g.*, Ga. Code Ann. § 53-2-76. Some require marriage and birth of a child. *See, e.g.*, Kan. Stat. Ann. § 59-610. Some treat the will as revoked only if the new spouse survives the testator. *See, e.g.*, Or. Rev. Stat. § 112.305. In other places, marriage has no effect on a preexisting will. *See, e.g.*, Ohio Rev. Code Ann. § 2107.37. For related discussions, see § 9 (will revocation), *supra*, and § 45[B][1] (interpreting documents in light of a divorce), *infra*.

[11] *See, e.g.*, UPC § 2-301. A spouse's right to claim a pretermitted share differs from the right to elect. First, each may mandate different percentage shares. Second, the pretermitted share is unlikely to extend beyond probate property, but the elective share might. Third, the pretermitted share can be overcome by negating the claim in a will, but the elective share cannot. *See generally* § 28[C], *supra* (spouse's elective share).

One problem that has haunted courts is how to handle a gift to someone who becomes a spouse after the will is executed. *See, e.g.*, Herbach v. Herbach, 583 N.W.2d 541 (Mich App. 1998) (gift in will to woman testator later married precluded her from claiming as a pretermitted spouse.)

[12] *See, e.g.*, UPC § 2-302. One question is whether a statute protects adopted children. The clear trend is to treat adopted children the same as children born into the family. *See* §§ 5[A][2] (adopted children in intestacy), *supra*, and § 44[E][2] (document interpretation to include adopted persons), *infra*. If timing is important, the date of the adoption, not the date of the person's birth, is the relevant time. *See In re* Estate of Markowitz, 312 A.2d 901 (N. J. Super. 1973) (testator's two adopted daughters qualified as pretermitted heirs because they were adopted after the execution of testator's will).

The rights of nonmarital children are covered in §§ 5[A][1] (intestacy), *supra*, and 44[E][2] (document interpretation), *infra*.

omitted children.[13] Some states take a different approach and protect all children, whether born before or after the will's execution.[14] Rather than relying upon a "changed circumstances" rationale, these jurisdictions are simply forcing testators to disinherit expressly, if that is their desire.

Second, does other evidence preclude application of the statute? Even if the omitted person is in a class protected by the statute, he might not get a share. Two types of evidence might prevent that person from taking: evidence of the testator's intention, or statutorily identified family circumstances.

Numerous questions surround evidence of testators' intentions to disinherit. First, states differ on what sort of evidence is admissible. Some places allow extrinsic evidence, but others restrict the evidence to language in the will.[15] Second, the effect of particular statements has been the subject of much litigation.[16] States which allow claims by descendants of omitted children face special problems.[17] Finally, even where the intention is clear, traditionally courts have not allowed so-called "negative wills" to disinherit children if the will does not otherwise dispose of the property.[18] Because there is no strong policy justification for such an intention-defeating rule, the revised UPC allows negative wills.[19]

---

[13] *See, e.g.*, Ark. Code Ann. § 28-39-407. New York reached this result by judicial decision. *See In re* Horst, 190 N.E. 475 (N.Y. 1934) (A child was born after the will was executed, but he predeceased the testator, leaving children. The testator's grandchildren took a pretermitted share under a statute only giving such a right to a "child.").

[14] *See, e.g.*, Mass. Gen. Laws Ann. ch. 191, § 20; Vt. Stat. Ann. tit. 14, § 556.

[15] Those which do allow extrinsic evidence are sometimes called "Massachusetts-type" statutes, and those which do not, "Missouri-type" statutes, although the labels do nothing to reveal the nature of the approaches. *See* Atkinson at 141-143. Simply reading the statute may not be enough to allow placing it in the proper category. *See* Crump's Estate v. Freeman, 614 P.2d 1096 (Okla. 1980) (extrinsic evidence not allowed, despite statutory language like the Massachusetts statute).

[16] In general, the more specific the language, the more likely it will defeat a relative's claim. *See* Russell G. Donaldson, Annotation, *Pretermitted Heir Statutes: What Constitutes Sufficient Testamentary Reference to, or Evidence of Contemplation of, Heir to Render Statute Inapplicable*, 83 A.L.R.4th 779 (1991).

[17] In particular, if a disinherited child predeceases a testator, should the language disinheriting the child also disinherit that person's child? The answer is probably "no," because the grandchild was left with nothing and not specifically mentioned. *See, e.g.*, Estate of Gardner v. Lane, 580 P.2d 684 (Cal. 1978). If, on the other hand, the testator "disinherited" the child by making a nominal gift, and that gift passed to the grandchild under an anti-lapse statute, then the grandchild would have taken something under the will, so presumably would not qualify for a pretermitted share. *See, e.g.*, Reed v. Reed, 332 P.2d 1049 (Or. 1958). For a discussion of anti-lapse statutes, see § 45[B][2][b], *infra*.

[18] *See* Coffman v. Coffman, 8 S.E. 672 (Va. 1888) ("will," which only disinherited son but nothing more, not really a will, and therefore not entitled to probate).

[19] UPC § 2-101(b). The comment to that section offers drafting suggestions. *See also* Restatement (Third) of Prop. § 2.7 (endorsing negative wills).

Under the UPC, the property which would otherwise go to the excluded person passes as if that person had disclaimed. For a discussion of disclaimers, see § 27, *supra*. *In re Estate of Jetter*, 570 N.W.2d 26 (S.D. 1997), refused to recognize a negative will under UPC § 2-101 where the result would have been an escheat.

Under traditional statutes, omitted relatives take pretermitted shares unless there is affirmative evidence that the testator meant to exclude them. This approach can skew estate plans in ways testators probably would not want, if they had thought about the question. Consider David and Edith. After the birth of a daughter, Zena, David executes a will giving everything to Edith, if she survives him, and if not, everything to Zena. Later a second daughter, Rhoda, is born, but David neglects to amend his will to account for the new child.[20] Now suppose David dies, leaving Edith, Zena, and Rhoda. Zena would get nothing.[21] Under many statutes, Rhoda would get her intestate share, despite David's clear intention to give everything to his wife, even though he had a child when he made the will. The statutory assumption that David would want Rhoda to have a share, rather than that he would rely upon Edith to take care of Rhoda, does not fit the facts. Moreover, the two sisters would take drastically different shares.

To avoid cases like this, a statute might assume that in particular circumstances, most testators would not want the afterborn child to take a full intestate share. The UPC applies this approach in several situations.[22] To take Rhoda's case, the UPC assumes that testators would want to treat their afterborn children as nearly as possible the same way they treated the children alive when the will was drafted. Absent other facts, if a testator has one or more children at the time the will is executed, the UPC gives afterborn children the same share as they would have received if the testator had given all children equal shares of the total given to the existing children.[23] Because Zena got nothing, Rhoda would get nothing.

Even if the testator had no children when the will was executed, the UPC denies an afterborn child a pretermitted share if the will gives "all or substantially all" to the other parent and that parent survives to take under the will.[24] This is a change from the pre-1990 version, which cut out afterborns only if the testator had had children when the will was executed and had given most everything to the other parent.[25] The revision is based on research indicating that testators with children give their estates to their spouses, and rely on the spouse to be a conduit to the children.[26] The UPC drafters believe testators also trust their spouses, even if there are no

---

[20] Rhoda would have been covered and the pretermitted problem avoided if the alternative gift had read something like, "to my descendants, by right of representation." "Representation" should have been defined. For a discussion of different methods of dividing an estate among descendants, see § 5[B], *supra*.

[21] In many states she would have no claim because she was born before the will was executed. In those states which protect any child, her pretermitted claim would fail because the will clearly recognizes her and gives her an alternative gift.

[22] *See* UPC §§ 2-301, 2-302.

[23] UPC § 2-302(a)(2).

[24] UPC § 2-302(a)(1). The "substantially all" language leaves room for incidental gifts, but also invites litigation.

[25] *See* UPC (pre-1990) § 2-302(a)(2).

[26] A series of studies are cited in the comment to UPC § 2-102. For discussion of spouses as conduits, see § 4, *supra*.

children when the will is executed.[27] Notice that only the surviving *parent*, not *any* surviving spouse, qualifies as a conduit.

Another situation in which a testator would probably not want a child to take a pretermitted share is when that child already benefits from transfers outside the will. Suppose that David, instead of giving everything to his wife, Edith, had created an unfunded living trust, giving Edith income for life and a remainder to their surviving children. His pour-over will included some incidental gifts and named the trustee as the will's prime beneficiary.[28] Under traditional statutes, because Rhoda, the afterborn daughter, was not mentioned in the will, she could get a pretermitted share. The fact that she benefits under the trust is irrelevant.[29] The UPC changes this rule and denies a pretermitted share to someone "provided for" by nonprobate transfers if "the intent that the transfer be in lieu of a testamentary provision is shown by the testator's statements or is reasonably inferred from the amount of the transfer or other evidence."[30]

Third, what share does the relative take? As noted above, an omitted relative normally takes an intestate share. Some statutes, however, adjust the share in different situations. Under the UPC, if a testator gives something to children living when the will was executed, afterborns get only a share of what was given their older siblings.[31] Ohio gets to about the same place by a different route. There, pretermitted children get the share they would have received if the testator had died with no surviving spouse, and owning only the property not given to the surviving spouse.[32] Wisconsin gives a court the discretion to give the share "it deems would best accord with the probable intent of the testator . . . ."[33] Each of the these approaches limits the damage a pretermitted share can do to an estate plan.

---

[27] *See* UPC § 2-302 comment.

[28] The relationship between trusts and pour-over wills is discussed in § 16, *supra*.

[29] Lawyers drafting pour-over wills should be particularly careful to include in the will language noting that current and future children are not will beneficiaries because they will take from the trust.

[30] UPC § 2-302(b)(2). A parallel provision applies to pretermitted spouses. UPC § 2-301(a)(3). *See also* Estate of Bartell, 776 P.2d 885 (Utah 1989) (wife not mentioned in husband's will could not take as an "omitted spouse" because the court found the husband's lifetime transfer of $230,000 to his wife showed "an intent to provide for his wife in lieu of a testamentary provision").

While the UPC considers nonprobate transfers for the purpose of defeating a pretermitted share, the Code does not extend pretermitted protection to nonprobate assets. This omission is inconsistent with the Code's overall theme of integrating the law surrounding transfers at death. *See generally* Chapter 5, *supra*.

[31] *See* UPC § 2-302(a)(2). For example, if the testator had made gifts to two older children, an afterborn would take one-third of the total of the two gifts.

[32] Ohio Rev. Code Ann. § 2107.34. Despite the similarity, this approach differs with the UPC in two important respects. First, pretermitted children in Ohio are not limited to sharing what their siblings received. Second, the statute seems not to consider second marriages; it relies on the surviving *spouse* to take care of the children. The UPC trusts only a surviving *parent* as a conduit. *See* UPC § 2-302(a)(1).

[33] Wis. Stat. § 853.25(5).

Fourth, where does the money come from? In many states, the taker under the residuary clause will bear the primary burden of satisfying a pretermitted claim.[34] This approach is consistent with the way most claims are handled.[35] In particular circumstances, however, others may pay for the claim. In Ohio, for example, the pretermitted child takes property from all will beneficiaries *except* the surviving spouse.[36] Under the UPC, if the testator made gifts to older children but left out an afterborn, the afterborn's share would come from the gifts to the older children.[37] A pretermitted spouse under the UPC cannot take property from the testator's children born before the marriage (unless they are also the spouse's children).[38]

Pretermitted statutes take a variety of approaches in their attempts to protect family members. Armed with the foregoing series of questions, however, you should be able to attack any statute and identify its danger points.

§ 30 Charitable Gifts[1]

At one time, a number of states had so-called "mortmain statutes,"[2] which limit gifts to charity. Such states had two overlapping aims: to protect family members against disinheritance, and to protect the testator (and the family) from the temptation of buying one's way into heaven by making a deathbed transfer. Mortmain statutes thus took either or both of two approaches. They might limit the percentage of property which testators can give to charity, or they might prohibit (or limit) charitable gifts made in a set period before death.

Virtually no states retain these limitations,[3] but, the move away from mortmain statutes has been a relatively recent development.[4] Untangling some not-so-old cases may require understanding what these statutes were trying to accomplish.[5]

---

[34] Absent specific circumstances, the UPC follows this approach. *See* UPC §§ 2-301(b) (spouses), 2-302(d) (children), 3-902 (order of abatement).

[35] *See* § 46[D], *infra.*

[36] Ohio Rev. Code Ann. § 2107.34. This approach is consistent with limiting the size of the claim to property not given to the surviving spouse. The gifts abate "proportionately, or in such other manner as is necessary to give effect to the intention of the testator as shown by the will . . . ."

[37] UPC § 2-302(a)(2)(iv). If the older children were given different shares, they would contribute pro rata to their younger sibling.

[38] Substitute gifts (under the anti-lapse provisions) to the descendants of such a child are also protected from the spouse's claim. UPC § 2-301(b). For a discussion of anti-lapse statutes, see § 45[B][2][b], *infra.*

[1] For a discussion of charitable trusts, see § 15, *supra.*

[2] The name comes from the English Statute of Mortmain. 7 Edw. 1, stat. 2, ch. 13 (1279).

[3] Georgia does. *See* Ga. Code Ann. § 53-2-10.

[4] A 1970 report listed 11 jurisdictions with mortmain statutes. *See* ABA Committee on Succession, *Restrictions on Charitable Testamentary Gifts*, 5 Real Prop. Prob. & Tr. J. 290, 291-292 (1970).

[5] For an example, see In re Estate of Rothko, 372 N.E.2d 291 (N.Y. 1977), discussed in § 55[A][1][a], *infra.*

§ 31 Public Policy Limits

In this final section of a chapter about protecting the family, we ask how much courts should act on their own to invalidate various will provisions as violative of public policy. Family members are not necessarily the beneficiaries of a court decision striking a particular will directive, but as a practical matter, they often will be. Further, the public policy doctrine nicely illustrates a question central to this chapter and to much of wills and trusts law: How much freedom should we give people to control the use of property after their deaths?[1]

By its very nature, a doctrine labeled "public policy" defies precise definition. This mushiness appropriately restrains many courts when applying the doctrine, for they understand that they might easily use it to justify judicial second-guessing of all sorts of testators' decisions.[2]

Shapira v. Union National Bank[3] reveals a court reluctant to override the plans of a father who had deeply held views about his sons' behavior. David Shapira had three children, a married daughter and two unmarried sons. David gave each child an equal share of the residue of his estate, but he conditioned each son's gift on the son being married "to a Jewish girl whose both parents were Jewish." A son unmarried at the father's death would have seven years to marry such a person, or the son's share would instead go to the State of Israel. Son Daniel, 21 and unmarried, challenged the restriction, which the court upheld.

Daniel claimed that the restriction was invalid as a partial restraint upon marriage.[4] As a general rule, restraints encouraging (or discouraging) marriage to someone of a particular faith are valid if "the restraint does not unreasonably limit the transferee's opportunity to marry."[5] Clearly, Daniel's choices were more limited than had his father imposed no restriction, but the court found that in an era of easy travel and communication, Daniel would have an opportunity to meet plenty of Jewish women.[6] Of course, potential donees do not have to comply; they can give up their gifts. Clearly, however, the restraints are coercive.[7] They extend, beyond death, disagreements which probably took place between parents and children.[8]

---

[1] For a thoughtful look at a related topic – how to handle directions for disposing of the body, see Tanya K. Hernandez, *The Property of Death*, 60 U. Pitt. L. Rev. 971 (1999).

[2] Compare courts' relatively greater willingness to apply the somewhat (barely?) harder-edged doctrines surrounding testamentary capacity. *See* § 7[A], *supra*.

[3] 315 N.E.2d 825 (Ohio Common Pleas 1974).

[4] He also claimed enforcing the provision would violate the Fourteenth Amendment. Finding no state action on these facts, the court rejected the argument.

[5] *See* Restatement (Second) of Prop. § 6.2.

[6] *Contrast* Maddox v. Maddox, 52 Va. (11 Gratt.) 804 (1854), which struck down a provision effectively restricting a woman to marrying a member of the Society of Friends. At that time and place, the number of qualifying men was too small.

[7] The depth of the father's commitment to preserving Jewish blood and traditions also influenced the court.

[8] David Shapira almost certainly had reason to doubt whether his sons would marry Jewish women. One can easily imagine family arguments over whom his boys wanted to date.

One problem with such restrictions is that after the death of the parent, the requirements become etched in stone. No longer does the child have a chance to convince the parent that in a particular situation, the restraint is unreasonable.[9]

Intergenerational restrictions on behavior pose particularly difficult choices for courts. On the one hand, invoking an ill-defined doctrine like "public policy" opens the door to a judge substituting his or her judgment for that of the testator. On the other hand, allowing restrictions to stand locks people in, despite changes in circumstances which the decedent could not have foreseen.[10]

Modern reproductive technology promises to challenge courts in new ways.[11] In *Hecht v. Superior Court*,[12] the question was what to do with frozen sperm. William Kane deposited 15 vials of his sperm at a sperm bank, and his will gave his sperm to his live-in friend of five years, Deborah Hecht. After his death, Kane's children from a prior marriage wanted the sperm destroyed. The court determined that the sperm was part of Kane's estate, and rejected the children's argument that post-mortem artificial insemination by an unmarried woman is against public policy.[13]

Courts regularly invalidate one kind of direction on public policy grounds: instructions to destroy property.[14] In *Eyerman v. Mercantile Trust Co.*,[15] neighbors and certain trustees who had powers similar to those of a homeowner's association sought to enjoin Louise Johnston's executor from razing her house according to directions in her will. Noting that both the neighbors

---

For discussion of the appropriate reach of the dead hand to "protect" the living, see § 13, *supra* (spendthrift trusts).

[9] David Shapira might have relented in the face of a charming, sincere Gentile who promised to convert and to raise David's grandchildren in the Jewish tradition. For similar cases, see United States Nat'l Bank v. Snodgrass, 275 P.2d 860 (Or. 1954) (no Catholic spouse); In re Estate of Keffalas, 233 A.2d 248 (Pa. 1967) (must marry someone "of Greek blood and descent and of Orthodox religion").

[10] For a compelling argument against allowing testators to control personal conduct of the living, see Jeffrey G. Sherman, *Posthumous Meddling: An Instrumentalist Theory of Testamentary Restraints on Conjugal and Religious Choices*, 1999 U. Ill. L. Rev. 1273.

The law is restrictive, but not entirely inflexible in the face of changed circumstances. For example, the doctrine of equitable reformation, or *cy pres*, offers some relief when new conditions make charitable purposes impossible to meet. *See* § 15, *supra*. Also, some courts allow trustees to deviate from investment instructions which, if followed, would harm the trust. *See, e.g., In re* Trusteeship Agreement with Mayo, 105 N.W.2d 900 (Minn. 1960) (court allowed trustees to deviate from the original trust instruction and invest in corporate stock and real estate), discussed in § 57[B], *infra*. In an extreme case, a court might, by analogy to these situations, invalidate a restriction on personal behavior.

[11] *See generally* Lori B. Andrews, The Clone Age: Adventures in the New World of Reproductive Technology (1999).

[12] 20 Cal. Rptr. 2d 275 (Ct. App. 1993).

[13] After a settlement and another appeal, Hecht ultimately got three vials. Kane v. Superior Ct., 44 Cal. Rptr. 2d 578 (Ct. App. 1995). Hecht was unable to get pregnant. She has since married and adopted a child. *See* The Easy Reader, Hermosa Beach, CA, March 29, 2001.

[14] *See* Page § 44.3.

[15] 524 S.W.2d 210 (Mo. Ct. App. 1975).

and the estate beneficiaries would be harmed by the loss of the house, and characterizing the direction as "stemming from apparent whim and caprice,"[16] the court concluded that the destruction would violate public policy. The waste that would be caused in a case such as *Eyerman* makes the result seem obvious.[17] Other directions to destroy may not present such clear cases. How about an artist's direction to destroy works he created for himself, but did not want others to see? Or a movie star's order to burn love letters which have value in the tabloid marketplace, but whose exposure would offend notions of privacy? Sometimes, even destruction may be the proper choice.[18]

The law surrounding family members' claims upon family assets is changing as our society rethinks the meaning of "family." That review opens special opportunities for lawyers because we have such a broad influence, through both lobbying legislatures and presenting creative arguments to courts. Whether you agree with the revised UPC's solutions or not, note their potential, both for getting the attention of legislators and judges and for identifying relevant issues. The UPC can be a valuable tool in an area where traditional assumptions and traditional arguments no longer seem to fit.

---

[16] 524 S.W.2d at 214.

[17] While the law does allow individuals to destroy their own property, usually self-interest keeps them from doing so arbitrarily. By the time a will provision would be followed, however, the testator no longer suffers harm.

[18] For a critique of the traditional rule, see Abagail J. Sykas, *Waste Not Want Not: Can the Public Policy Doctrine Prohibit the Destruction of Property by Testamentary Direction?*, 25 Vt. L. Rev. 911 (2001).

Chapter 9

PRESENT AND FUTURE INTERESTS

This chapter presents an overview of the system of present and future interests. It assumes both that you have seen most of these terms and concepts before, and that a new look may be helpful. Because this is difficult material, sometimes one presentation helps one person, but a slightly different approach makes more sense to another.[1] Part of what this chapter offers is a new set of diagrams to represent graphically how various interests act. It opens with a question many students ask, and then proceeds to the core concepts in the law of present and future interests.

§ 32 Why Bother?

Many students, confronted with a seemingly impenetrable mass of concepts developed in the Middle Ages, reasonably ask why they should bother to learn this stuff. From the narrow view of a course in trusts and estates, the strongest reason for studying present and future interests is that these concepts are the basic building blocks for estate plans. Even if the names fade from your memory, the ideas they represent will be crucial to your ability both to present estate planning choices to your clients and to draft documents which fulfill clients' wishes. The power you have over their plans carries a special responsibility to do the job well. Moreover, even the odd-sounding names themselves are important, for they provide the vehicle for communication among lawyers, courts and legislatures about these topics. As with many trusts and estates topics, law reform is in the air. Reform is not possible, however, unless we all understand what we are talking about.

A broader reason for studying this material stems from law schools' mission of training people to analyze legal problems, irrespective of the particular subject matter. The law is full of densely tangled topics. Learning how to handle them takes practice. The law of present and future interests provides an excellent opportunity for getting that practice: this law is complicated; it presents unfamiliar terminology; and it requires attention to detail. At the same time, however, a basic understanding of the topic's core concepts is manageable within the confines of a law school course.

---

[1] If you need more details and have a favorite text, return to it. If not, consider the following specialized sources: Bergin & Haskel; Laurence & Minzner; Moynihan & Kurtz; Simes; and Lawrence W. Waggoner, Estates in Land and Future Interests in a Nutshell (2d ed. 1993).

As you study the endless examples available, beware of the danger of only learning to recognize various interests while not really understanding what those interests are. One way to test your understanding is to draft your own language, and then figure out what you have created.

185

Consider this topic as affording a chance to develop skills useful for your professional lifetime. As they say of New York, if you can make it here, you can make it anywhere.

§ 33   Present v. Future Interests: Dividing Time

This area of law developed to meet the needs of landowners. Although these concepts now apply most often to personal property held in trust, viewing the question in terms of land can help with the fundamentals. First, the law separates the notion of ownership from the thing owned. We own "interests" in land, rather than the dirt itself. Second, we can divide our interests among different people, according to when they have the right to use the land.[1] Third, we start treating these individual interests as if they were things in themselves. We give them unique characteristics and speak as if they behave in various ways.

The biggest, most complete interest is the *fee simple absolute*. If Howard owns a fee simple absolute interest in a house, he owns an interest which extends forward in time for infinity. Suppose Howard died owning the property. His fee simple absolute would not end just because he died. Rather, it would go to someone else, by intestacy or by will. If the fee simple went intact, the recipient would get exactly what Howard had, an interest extending ahead in time for infinity.

Suppose, however, Howard left a will dividing the ownership: he gave Ethel the right to use the house during her lifetime and said that after her death, Andrew can use it. Howard's will created both a present interest and a future interest. Because Ethel can use the house now, she has what we call a present interest.[2] Her interest is not as large as Howard's was, however, for Ethel's interest ends at her death. Because we know now that Andrew's interest will entitle him (or someone else[3]) to the right to use the house after Ethel's death, we say Andrew now has a future interest. Future interests are not things people get in the future. Rather, they are things people own in the present, but which carry a right of possession in the future, rather like a ticket to next week's concert.

---

[1] Another way of dividing ownership is to let a number of people share property at the same time. This is the law of co-tenancy, and it frequently intersects with the law of future interests. For more on co-tenancy in estate planning, see § 18, *supra*.

[2] Perhaps it helps to imagine a house with a front porch and a rocking chair. The holder of the present interest at any given time has the right to sit in that chair.

[3] We might refer to these others as Andrew's "successors." "Successors" is not a term of art; it simply means those people who take what Andrew had. If Andrew died owning the interest, it would pass under his will or by intestacy. He might also have transferred it to someone else before he died.

Most future interests are fully transferable, but in some places, some kinds of future interests are not transferable in some ways. *See, e.g.*, Goodwine State Bank v. Mullins, 625 N.E.2d 1056 (Ill. App. 1993) (contingent remainder not transferable by quitclaim deed); Powell § 275[2] & [3] (in some states, rights of entry and possibilities of reverter transferable only by release). Creditors' rights in future interests closely track the transferability rules. *See* Simes at 67-87. For discussion of creditors' claims against interests held in trust, see § 13[B][2], *supra*.

Future interests are really just present interests pushed out ahead of us. When Ethel dies, whoever holds Andrew's interest will be able to use the land, so that person then will have a present interest. In this example, what is now Andrew's future interest will become a fee simple absolute. In other situations, what was once a future interest will become a present interest followed by still more future interests.[4] When considering a future interest, look for two labels: on the outside is the term identifying the type of future interest; hidden inside, however, is a present interest waiting to appear.[5]

The notion of dividing ownership according to time has allowed the development of modern trust law. In place of Ethel's right to use the house, we give her the right to receive income from a trust. In place of Andrew's right to use the house next, we give him a right to distribution of the trust principal after Ethel's death. Because the trustee holds legal title, Ethel and Andrew have equitable interests, but these behave in much the same way as the legal interests invented centuries ago.[6]

§ 34 Present Interests

To recognize that individuals were trying to do different things when they divided their property according to time, the common law invented a series of different present interests and gave them different characteristics. This section introduces these various interests and offers a graphic depiction of each, to capture their principal attributes in visual form.

[A] Fee Simple Absolute

In terms of dividing ownership according to time, the fee simple absolute is everything. (See Figure 9-1.) At common law, deed drafters seeking to create this interest had to use words like, "To Suzanne *and her heirs*."[1] The "and her heirs" (or "and his heirs") language was critical. Courts interpreted those words not as words of purchase indicating who got the property—Suzanne's heirs got nothing from such a grant; rather, courts treated the magic words as words of limitation describing the estate granted. The words "and her heirs" came to indicate a grantor's intention to give an estate that would extend beyond the grantee's lifetime and go on forever.[2]

---

[4] For example, Howard might have given the property to Ethel for her life, and then to Andrew for his life. Because Andrew's interest did not account for the rest of time, his interest would be followed by another future interest (a reversion).

[5] It may help to think of sets of hollow dolls or jars or nutshells, one placed inside another. You open one to find another one, and so on.

[6] For more on how the law divides trust ownership between legal and equitable interests, see §§ 11 & 12, *supra*.

[1] For two reasons, the text avoids the abstract "A" and "B" in favor of real names. First, using names underscores that real families create and own these interests. Second, students sometimes have trouble making the jump from abstract formulae to documents which use names. Using names here should ease that transition.

[2] Interestingly, the words were not required to pass a fee simple by will. The presumption that a testator intended to give as much as possible avoided the problem.

FIGURE 9-1
Fee Simple Absolute

The requirement of including "and her heirs" language is almost dead, and this text will not include it in future examples.[3] However, the distinction between words of purchase, which indicate takers, and words of limitation, which identify those takers' interests, remains an important part of document interpretation.[4]

[B]   Defeasible Fees

Sometimes grantors want to give property so that the interest could, but need not, go on forever. Defeasible fee simple estates have that feature. They are still fee simple estates because they could go on forever, but they are "defeasible" because they can be lost. Defeasible fees generally are not used in estate planning, but the concepts surrounding them are.[5] Particularly important is the distinction between the two ways in which a defeasible fee simple ends: expiration and divestment.

One way a defeasible fee can end is by expiring. This can happen if the grantor has placed a limit on the grant. For example, Shannon might give

---

[3] At common law, a grant "to Suzanne," without more, would give her only a life estate. Because following the common law rule would defeat most persons' intentions, most modern courts would give Suzanne a fee simple absolute.

Sometimes the old rules can affect modern cases. Burk v. State, 607 N.E.2d 911 (Ohio App. 1992), involved an 1852 grant of land to the state to be used for two "Lunatic Asylums." The deed also provided that when the land ceased to be used for that purpose, "the same shall revert to the grantors." In 1988, the state closed the facilities and sought to sell the land. Relatives of the grantors appeared, claiming under the reverter language. Applying the law of 1852, the court held that because the deed had not reserved an interest to the grantors *and their heirs*, the possibility of reverter was in effect only during the grantors' lives.

[4] For some examples, see §§ 44 (special cautions) & 45[B][2][b][i] (antilapse statutes), *infra*.

[5] Defeasible fees sometimes appear as land use devices. *See* Gerald Korngold, *For Unifying Servitudes and Defeasible Fees: Property Law's Functional Equivalents*, 66 Tex. L. Rev. 533 (1988).

property "to the School Board so long as the land is used as a school." The school board might keep the property forever, but if they stopped using it as a school, their ownership would end. Language like "so long as," "while," and "until" is called "limitational" language because of the notion that it limits the estate from the start. When used in conjunction with a fee simple's potential for infinite duration, limitational language creates a *fee simple determinable*. To indicate the limitational nature of a fee simple determinable, Figure 9-2 shows it as an empty circle.

FIGURE 9-2
Fee Simple Determinable and Possibility of Reverter

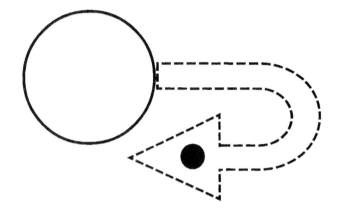

Although future interests are discussed below,[6] for the sake of completeness and clarity, this section matches future interests with their corresponding present interests. To account for the fact that Shannon did not say what would happen to the property if it ceased being used as a school, we would say she retained a future interest called a *possibility of reverter*, indicated by the arrow in Figure 9-2. If the school board's fee simple determinable expired, Shannon would have a fee simple absolute, represented by the solid circle inside the arrow.

A fee simple determinable can also be followed by an interest in someone other than the grantor. For example, Shannon might have said, "To the School Board so long as used as a school, and if the property ceases to be used as a school, to Beneth if she is then living." The board still has a fee simple determinable, but we call Beneth's interest an *executory interest*. The dashed arrow in Figure 9-3 indicates that an executory interest is contingent, and the solid circle shows that if Beneth takes, she will have a fee simple absolute.

---

[6] *See* § 35, *infra.*

FIGURE 9-3
Fee Simple Determinable
followed by an Executory Interest

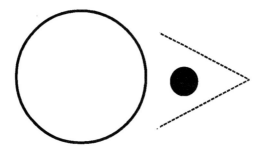

The other way for a defeasible fee simple to end is by being divested, or cut short. This result is possible if the grantor has used "conditional" language like "but if," "provided, however," or "on the condition that." The law recognizes two types of defeasible fees subject to being divested. Which label we use depends upon who holds the future interest that follows.

If the grantor retains the future interest, we call the *present* interest a *fee simple subject to a condition subsequent.* The grantor's accompanying future interest is a *right of entry.*[7] Thus, if Shannon gives property "to the School Board, but if the property is not used as a school, then I reserve the right to reenter and take possession of the property," the school board has a fee simple subject to a condition subsequent, illustrated by the cross-hatched circle in Figure 9-4. Shannon has retained a right of entry, indicated by the arrow. If the board stops using the property for a school and Shannon decides to exercise her right, she will have a fee simple absolute.

---

[7] Sometimes the term "power of termination" is used.

FIGURE 9-4
Fee Simple Subject to a Condition Subsequent and Right of Entry

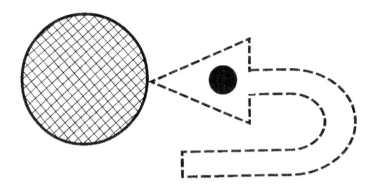

If someone other than the grantor has the future interest following a defeasible fee created by conditional language, we call the *present* interest a *fee simple subject to an executory limitation*. The accompanying future interest is an *executory interest*. Thus, if Shannon gives property "to the School Board, but if the property is not used as a school, then to Beneth if she is then living," the school board has a fee simple subject to an executory limitation, illustrated by the cross-hatched circle in Figure 9-5.

FIGURE 9-5
Fee Simple Subject to an Executory Limitation
and Executory Interest

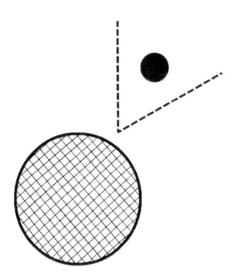

Beneth still has an executory interest. In this case, if the board stops using the property for a school, Beneth's executory interest will automatically divest the board's interest, giving her a fee simple absolute. This time the executory interest arrow points in toward the present interest, to indicate that Beneth's interest might divest the board's interest.

To identify which defeasible fee simple estate has been created, apply a two-part test, as of the time of the grant. First, ask: Is the language limitational (so long as, etc.) or conditional (but if, etc.)? If the language is limitational, the present estate is a fee simple determinable. If the language is conditional, ask the second question: Who holds the future interest? If the future interest is retained by the grantor, then the *present* interest is a fee simple subject to a condition subsequent. If the future interest is given to a third party, then the *present* interest is a fee simple subject to an executory limitation.

The distinction between an estate which expires and one which is subject to divestment can be important. Consider two of the above examples. In Figure 9-3, the school board has a fee simple determinable, followed by Beneth's executory interest. In Figure 9-5, the board has a fee simple subject to an executory limitation, subject to Beneth's executory interest. In each case, Beneth had to survive to take. Suppose Beneth dies and then the board stops using the property for a school. If the board had a fee simple determinable, it still expires. It was only good "so long as" there was a school. Because Beneth had not met the condition of surviving, Shannon would take as grantor.[8] On the other hand, if the board initially had a fee simple subject to an executory limitation, when Beneth died, there was no one around to divest their interest. The board got a fee simple absolute. Their later violation of the condition was irrelevant.

[C] Life Estate

The life estate is probably the favorite estate of law students. It is both easy to recognize[9] and easy to understand. If Cletus gives property "to Helen for life," Helen has a life estate. If the property is realty, Helen has the right to possession during her lifetime.[10] If the gift is in trust, Helen usually will have a right to trust income during her life. Chart 9-6 illustrates the life estate as an empty square. The square

---

[8] Most authorities discuss this question in the context of an executory interest which fails under the Rule Against Perpetuities. For a classic case, see First Universalist Soc'y v. Boland, 29 N.E. 524 (Mass. 1892). There a grantor created deed in 1854, which conveyed real estate to a religious society so long as the land was used for religious purposes. The deed also stated that if the land stopped being used for religious purposes, then it was to go to designated persons. The court held that the 1854 deed conveyed a fee simple determinable and that the executory interest that followed was void for remoteness. Therefore, the grantor retained a possibility of a reverter, and the religious society did not have a fee simple absolute. *See generally* Simes & Smith § 1241.

In the context of a perpetuities violation, the Second Restatement suggests that an invalid executory interest should leave a fee simple absolute, even when the present interest was a fee simple determinable. Restatement (Second) of Prop. § 1.5 cmt. b, c.

The text followed the convention of most authorities and did not account for the grantor's possibility of reverter when first identifying the interests created by this grant. Perhaps we should identify both the executory interest and the possibility of reverter, by analogy to contingent remainders and reversions. For more on the relationship between those latter interests, see § 35[B][2][b], *infra*.

[9] Well, usually. In Edwards v. Bradley, 315 S.E.2d 196 (Va. 1984), Viva's will gave her farm to her daughter, Margaret, subject to the condition that the farm not be encumbered. Because the will used the term "fee simple" in other places but not here, and because Viva's conditions could not be imposed on a fee simple, the court found that Margaret had a life estate.

[10] A legal life estate, like the one envisioned in the text, is useful only in rare circumstances. In almost all situations, creating a trust and giving the beneficiary an equitable life estate will meet client needs while avoiding the problems created by dividing the legal estate.

FIGURE 9-6
Life Estate and Reversion

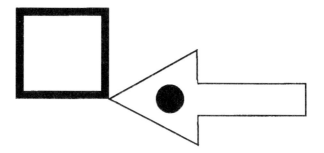

is empty because the life estate, like the fee simple determinable represented by an empty circle, expires. Because Cletus has not identified who should take the property after Helen, we say he has retained a "reversionary interest," in this case a *reversion*, illustrated by the arrow. The solid circle inside the arrow indicates that when Cletus's reversion becomes possessory on Helen's death, it will become a fee simple absolute. If Cletus had identified third parties to take after Helen's death, they would have had *remainders*, which are detailed below.[11]

Not all life estates are as uncluttered as the standard example. Grantors can also create life estates that may end before the death of the life tenant. Like defeasible fees, these life estates can either expire or be divested.[12] If Cletus says "to Helen for life or until she remarries," he would create a life estate determinable, sometimes called a life estate subject to a special limitation.[13] Helen's interest can now expire either of two ways, her remarriage or her death. Figure 9-7 adds a diamond inside the life estate square to indicate the double limitations on Helen's interest. Cletus retains

---

[11] *See* § 35[B][2], *infra.*

[12] If you find the examples in this paragraph difficult, review the discussions of the parallel defeasible fee estates in § 34[B], *supra.*

[13] The general limitation is being alive. The special limitation is the requirement to stay single.

a reversion.[14] Life estates can also be subject to divestment, either by a right of entry[15] or by an executory interest.[16]

FIGURE 9-7
Life Estate Determinable and Reversion

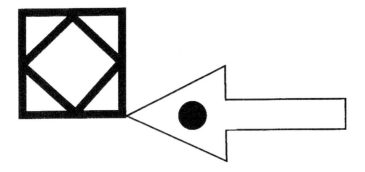

Another, more complicated life estate is one a grantor creates for one person, good for the life of another. Cletus might give property "to Helen for the life of Menelaus." Helen has a life estate for the life of another, illustrated in Figure 9-8 by the letter "M" in the square.[17] When Menelaus dies, Helen's estate ends.[18]

---

[14] There is some disagreement about whether the grantor also retains a possibility of reverter, to account for the possibility of a shortened life estate. The standard view is that Cletus retains a reversion, defined as the interest retained by a grantor who transfers a lesser quantum than he already had. *See* ALP § 4.18; Bergin & Haskell at 56-59; Powell ¶ 271. Since Cletus had a (potentially infinite) fee simple and only gave away a life estate, he kept a reversion, albeit one that could take in two circumstances.

[15] Cletus could give property "to Helen for life, but if Helen remarries, the grantor may re-enter." Helen would have a life estate subject to a condition subsequent. Cletus would have a right of entry (during Helen's life) and a reversion.

[16] Cletus could give property "to Helen for life, but if Helen remarries, then to Joanna at that time, and in any case, to Joanna after Helen's death." Helen would have a life estate subject to an executory limitation. Joanna would have an executory interest (during Helen's life) and a remainder.

[17] Traditional terminology would call Helen's interest a "life estate *pur autre vie*."

[18] Another way Helen could have obtained such an interest is if Menelaus had a life estate for his own life, and he then gave it to Helen. She would get what he had, a life estate for Menelaus' life.

FIGURE 9-8
Life Estate for the Life of Another and Reversion

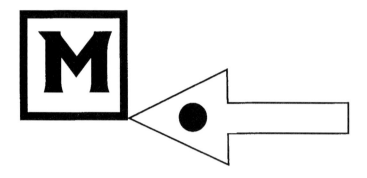

[D] Fee Tail

At common law, if a grantor gave land "to Kelly and the heirs of her body," Kelly would have a fee tail.[19] That interest would then pass to her children, their children, and so on, until the death of Kelly's last descendant. At that point, ownership would either come back to the grantor (who retained a reversion), or move on to someone else identified in the original document (who would have a remainder). Because the fee tail promoted family dynasties and interfered with the marketability of land, virtually all states have abolished it.

Recognizing a fee tail and understanding the basic notion of an estate moving with the generations are important to modern lawyers for two reasons. Sometimes old wills or lay-drafted wills use the "heirs of the body" language. You need to know to check the applicable local statute to see what interests those words create.[20] Also, documents sometimes include language like "and if Kelly dies without issue, to Mark." Interpreting the "dies without issue" language is easier if you understand the fee tail.[21]

§ 35 Future Interests

As we have seen, the system of estates allows grantors to divide ownership in terms of time. When creating a future interest, grantors can either retain rights in the property or give pieces of the future to various

---

[19] For a brief history, see Bergin & Haskell at 28-34.

[20] A good starting place is Powell ¶ 98. Some states create life estates, and others, fee simple estates of varying kinds. *See, e.g.*, Pickens v. Black, 885 S.W.2d 872 (Ark. 1994) (life estate in grantee, remainder in fee simple in grantee's issue).

[21] For discussion of this question, see § 44[B], *infra*.

beneficiaries. This section first reminds you of the interests grantors can retain, and then discusses the future interests grantees own.

[A] In the Grantor

Interests which a grantor retains are called "reversionary" interests. There are three. A possibility of reverter follows a fee simple determinable. A right of entry (sometimes also called a power of termination) follows a fee simple subject to condition subsequent. Because defeasible fees seldom have any part in estate plans, their accompanying reversionary interests seldom appear. The third interest, a reversion, is important to estate planners. It is the interest a grantor retains if he only creates a life estate, or a life estate and contingent remainders. Because modern estate plans regularly create life estates and contingent remainders in trust, reversions are often present.[1]

[B] In Grantees

Grantees can hold two kinds of future interests: executory interests and remainders. The practical differences between them may be minimal,[2] but our common language maintains both labels. One way to help distinguish between the two categories is by assigning each a personality characteristic. Executory interests are aggressive; they go around cutting short other interests; they have hatchets. In contrast, remainders are patient; they snuggle up against a present interest and wait for its natural expiration; they have pillows.

[1] Executory Interests

Executory interests are future interests held by third party grantees.[3] Executory interests usually take over by divesting prior interests. Developed after the Statute of Uses in 1536,[4] executory interests made possible the fee simple subject to an executory limitation.[5] They also allowed a third

---

[1] Recall that a trustee holds legal title so that, like other interests, the settlor's reversion is "equitable." If the reversion were to become possessory, we would say that the trustee held the legal title on a "resulting trust" for the settlor. In this context, the resulting trust theory just means that the trustee cannot claim legal title on its own behalf, so has a duty to turn the property over to the settlor or the settlor's successors. A resulting trust will also arise if an express trust fails, say, for lack of a beneficiary. *See* § 12[C], *supra*. *See generally* Haskell at 297-299.

[2] *See* Jesse J. Dukeminier, Jr., *Contingent Remainders and Executory Interests: A Requiem for the Distinction*, 43 Minn. L. Rev. 13 (1958).

[3] The first party is the grantor, and the second party is the holder of the present interest.

[4] For a brief history of these developments, see Bergin & Haskell at 80-115.

[5] In this situation, traditional descriptions would say the present interest is subject to a *shifting executory interest*, because someday the legal title may shift from one grantee (who holds the present interest) to a second one (who holds the future interest). Executory interests can also be of the *springing* variety, jumping out of the grantor to start in the future. For example, Jessica would have a springing executory interest if a grant read "to Jessica when she graduates from college." Because the distinction has little, if any, modern importance, it is falling into disuse.

party to take following a fee simple determinable. This latter situation is the one exception to the rule that executory interests take possession by divesting. Because a fee simple determinable expires on its own, the executory interest has nothing to divest.[6] In all other cases, however, executory interests take by divesting.

[2] Remainders

Remainders are also interests in third party grantees. Rather than divesting,[7] however, they usually wait around for the expiration of a life estate.[8] Remainders come in two types, vested and contingent, to which we now turn.

[a] Vested Remainders

A remainder is "vested" if it satisfies three tests. First, the holder of the remainder must be someone who has been born. Second, that person must be identified. Third, there can be no express or implied condition precedent to that person taking.[9] Once a remainder jumps through those hoops, the question remains: What type of vested remainder is it? There are three: indefeasibly vested, subject to complete defeasance, and subject to open.

[i] Indefeasibly Vested

Just as a fee simple is the biggest interest, an indefeasibly vested remainder is the biggest remainder. It is just a fee simple absolute, pushed out into the future. Suppose Joseph's will gives property "to Rose for life, remainder to Barbara." Rose has a life estate, shown as a square in Figure 9-9, and Barbara has an indefeasibly vested remainder, shown by the

---

[6] Here the executory interest acts just like a remainder, waiting for the natural termination of the prior estate. Common law judges could not call it a remainder, however, because by the time it came along, the definitions of remainders were carved in stone.

For a discussion of the distinction between present interests subject to divestment and present interests subject to expiration, see § 34[B], *supra*.

[7] The one exception is that when contingent remainders vest in interest, they divest the reversion.

[8] Remainders can also follow a fee tail. For a brief review of the fee tail, see § 34[D], *supra*.

[9] Reforms proposed by the revised UPC would reduce drastically the number of vested remainders created. The UPC would impose a condition of survivorship on future interests under the terms of a trust. UPC § 2-707(b). Because the remainders are subject to a condition precedent, they would be contingent. Grantors could overcome the presumption of required survivorship, but only with specific language. For discussion of this reform proposal, see § 45[B][2][c][iii], *infra*.

FIGURE 9-9
Life Estate and Indefeasibly Vested Remainder

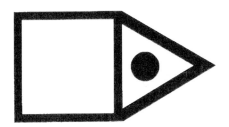

triangle. The solid lines indicate that the remainder is vested, and the solid circle inside indicates that someday it will become a fee simple absolute.[10]

[ii]   Subject to Complete Defeasance

Just as a fee simple can be defeasible, so can a vested remainder. Many vested remainders subject to complete defeasance are just defeasible fees, pushed out into the future. Others are life estates in future garb. Like their present interest counterparts, these remainders can end either by expiration or by divestment. By convention, we do not usually distinguish between the various subcategories of vested remainders subject to complete defeasance. If it helps you, however, you certainly may refer to them by more detailed descriptions.[11]

Suppose Jenn leaves the farm "to Pat for life, then to the School Board so long as they use the land for school purposes." As Figure 9-10 illustrates, Pat has a life estate, the Board has a vested remainder subject to

---

[10] Under traditional rules, if Barbara survived Joseph, but died before Rose, Barbara's remainder would pass to Barbara's successors, who would then take at Rose's death. *See* First Nat'l Bank v. Anthony, 557 A.2d 957 (Me. 1989) (remainder "in equal shares to [settlor's] children" was vested). These rules may change; see the previous footnote.

[11] You might refer to: "a vested remainder in a fee simple determinable," or "a vested remainder in a fee simple subject to a condition subsequent," or "a vested remainder in a fee simple subject to an executory limitation."

FIGURE 9-10
Life Estate and Vested Remainder
Subject to Complete Defeasance (Expiration)

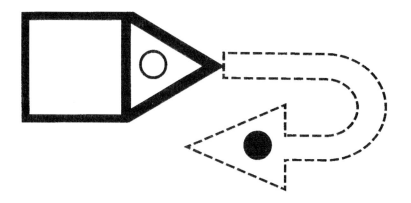

complete defeasance, and Jenn has a possibility of reverter.[12] If Jenn had said, "to Pat for life, then to the School Board, but if the land is not used as a school, then to Beneth if she is then living," the Board still would have a vested remainder subject to complete defeasance.[13] Beneth would have an executory interest. (See Figure 9-11.)

---

[12] Compare Figure 10-2, in § 34[B], *supra*.

[13] In this instance, it would be a vested remainder subject to complete *divestment*. For more on the distinction between the broader term, defeasance, and the narrower one, divestment, see § 34[B], *supra*.

Often remainders anticipate possible divestment during the pending life estate. For example, "to Marjorie for life, remainder to John, but if he predeceases Marjorie, to Planned Parenthood."

FIGURE 9-11
Life Estate and Vested Remainder
Subject to Complete Defeasance (Divestment)

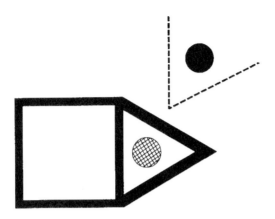

A vested remainder subject to complete defeasance can also come in the form of a life estate. Indeed, these remainders commonly go by the name "vested remainders for life." Suppose Cletus gave property in trust, with the income "to Helen for her life, and then to Carol for her life, and after her death distribute the principal to Ryan." Helen has a life estate; Carol has a vested remainder for life;[14] and Ryan has an indefeasibly vested remainder. (See Figure 9-12.)

---

[14] Although Carol must survive Helen in order to enjoy the trust income, that reality is a function of the limited nature of the interest Carol has (a life estate). Because survival is not an added condition precedent, we classify Carol's remainder as vested, rather than contingent.

FIGURE 9-12
Life Estate, Vested Remainder for Life,
and Indefeasibly Vested Remainder

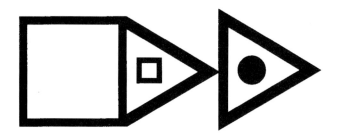

[iii] Subject to Open

Sometimes settlors will give property to a group of people whose membership is not fixed at the time of drafting. The usual idea of using such a class
gift is to allow people born after the drafting, but before the time for
distribution, to share in the gift. For example, Sheppe may give property
"to my wife Mindel for life, and then to our children." We call the remainder
to the children a class gift.[15] Because children born[16] later could qualify
as class members, we say the class is "open" during Mindel's life.[17] Suppose
Sheppe and Mindel have one child, Frieda. Frieda's remainder is vested;
we know who is getting it and there is no condition precedent. There is,
however, the chance that Frieda will have to share her remainder with a
later-born sibling. To account for that possibility, we say her remainder is
vested, subject to partial divestment. Because this situation arises only
when we have an open class, many lawyers use the shorter term "vested,
subject to open." Figure 9-13 illustrates Frieda's remainder as a shaded
triangle to indicate the possibility of its being shared.

---

[15] Other common class gifts are to grandchildren, descendants, nieces and nephews. For
discussion of how to determine whether a gift is a class gift, see § 43[A], *infra*.

[16] Adopted children might also qualify for class membership. *See* § 44[E][2], *infra*.

[17] For discussion of when classes close, so that later potential members do not qualify to
take, see § 43[B], *infra*.

FIGURE 9-13
Life Estate, Vested Remainder Subject to Open and Executory Interest

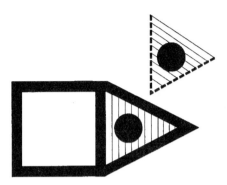

To complete the picture, we often say that the couple's as-yet-unborn children have executory interests.[18] Of course, this habit is silly, because there are no children to own anything. The convention is useful nonetheless, because it reminds us of what would happen if more children appeared. Their executory interest symbols are shaded to indicate that if children do join the class, their interests will also be subject to open.

Vested remainders can be subject to complete defeasance and subject to open at the same time. This situation is common in estate plans which stretch across three generations. Suppose Sheppe gives property "to Mindel for life, then to my children for their joint lives, and then to my grandchildren." Suppose further that Sheppe and Mindel have a daughter, Frieda, and a grandson, Scott. Mindel has a life estate. Frieda has a vested remainder for life, subject to open. Frieda's unborn siblings have executory interests for life (subject to open). Scott has a vested remainder, subject to open. Scott's unborn siblings have executory interests (subject to open). (See Figure 9-14.)

---

[18] They have executory interests because they take by partially divesting their older siblings. See § 35[B][1], *supra*.

FIGURE 9-14
Life Estate, Vested Remainder for Life Subject to Open, Vested Remainder Subject to Open, and Executory Interests

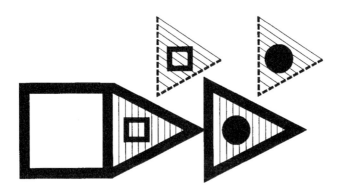

[b] Contingent Remainders[19]

If remainders are not vested, they are contingent. The way to identify contingent remainders, therefore, is to work through the definition of vested remainders to see if the interest in question fails one of those tests. Ask: (1) Is the holder of the remainder someone who has not yet been born? (2) Is the holder of the remainder unidentified? (3) Is there any express or implied condition precedent to that person taking? If the answer to any question is "yes," the remainder is contingent. When you identify a remainder as contingent, be sure you also identify *why* it is contingent.[20]

It may seem silly to ask whether someone who holds a remainder has been born. The question is useful, however, because it helps us identify which people will take what interests if someone is born later.[21] Consider a gift from Joanne "to Scott for life, then to his children." If Scott has no children, he has a life estate and Joanne has a reversion. To indicate that things may change, however, we commonly say that Scott's as-yet-unborn children have contingent remainders, contingent upon being born. To indicate the potential nature of their interest, Figure 9-15 shows the children's remainder as a dashed triangle. If Scott later has a child, the

---

[19] This is the traditional label. The Second Restatement calls these remainders "nonvested." *See* Restatement (Second) of Prop. § 1.4 cmt. b.

[20] That way you will know whether the remainder vests if facts change. Also, knowing why a remainder is contingent is critical to determining its validity under the Rule Against Perpetuities. The Rule is covered in Chapter 12, *infra*.

[21] Recall how we say unborn class members can have executory interests which might partially divest vested remainders, subject to open. *See* § 35[B][2][a][iii], *supra*.

child would take a vested remainder subject to open,[22] and Joanne would lose her reversion.

FIGURE 9-15
Life Estate, Contingent Remainder, and Reversion

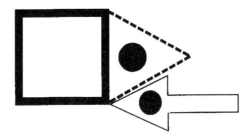

The second way a remainder may be contingent is if the person holding the remainder is unidentified. Assume Joanne grants property "to Scott for life, then to Scott's first child to graduate from college," and that Scott has a child, Taylor, who is in elementary school. Taylor has a remainder contingent upon being identified as the first of Scott's children to graduate from college. If Scott has other children before one of them graduates, they too will have contingent remainders, because each can join the race to qualify. Because it is possible that none of Scott's children will graduate from college and no one will qualify, Joanne has a reversion.[23]

At this point, you might ask what happens if Scott dies while Taylor is in college, but Taylor goes on later graduates. If the grant were of realty, at common law Scott's death while Taylor's remainder was still contingent would have destroyed the remainder.[24] Joanne would have kept the property. Rooted in the doctrine of seisin,[25] the destructibility rule does

---

[22] *See* Figure 9-14, *supra.*

[23] A graph of this grant would look the same as Figure 9-15, *supra.*

[24] At Scott's death, Joanne would get the property via her reversion, because Taylor had not yet qualified to take it. Joanne would keep the property because Taylor's contingent remainder was not powerful enough to divest someone in possession.

Taylor's remainder might also be destroyed by merger. If Joanne gave her reversion to Scott, then Taylor's contingent remainder would be caught in the squeeze between Scott's life estate and his reversion. Not powerful enough to prevent the merger, the remainder would be destroyed.

For short discussions of the Doctrine of Destructibility of Contingent Remainders, see Bergin & Haskell at 77-78, 85-88; Moynihan & Kurtz at 169-177.

[25] "Seisin" is the common law concept that means possession of a freehold. As a force in our law, it is increasingly irrelevant. For a brief discussion, see Moynihan at 98-102.

not apply to trusts and has been abolished virtually everywhere.[26] Today, Joanne almost certainly would keep the property until Taylor graduated, at which point he would take.[27] If there were a trust, Joanne would probably get the income until Taylor graduated and got the principal.[28]

The third way a remainder can be contingent is for it to be subject to a condition precedent. Assume Taylor is still in elementary school. Suppose, however, Joanne uses the language "to Scott for life, then to his first child if that child graduates from college." This time there is no identification problem. Only Taylor can be Scott's "first child." Taylor still has a contingent remainder, this time subject to the condition precedent of graduating. Because Taylor's remainder is contingent, Joanne has a reversion. If Taylor graduates from college before Scott dies, Taylor's remainder vests, and Joanne loses her reversion.

A single remainder may be contingent for more than one reason. Suppose Joanne used the language, "to Scott for life, then to his first child to graduate from college if that child then attends law school." Scott's children would have contingent remainders, contingent upon identification (first to graduate) and a condition precedent (attending law school). Both conditions would have to be met before the remainder would vest.

Settlors should, and often do, create alternative gifts, in case the favored person does not qualify to take. Often these gifts take the form of alternative contingent remainders. Imagine that our hypothetical family now has two children, Taylor and Todd. Suppose Joanne grants property "to Scott for life, then to Taylor if he survives Scott, and if he does not, to Todd." Scott has a life estate. Taylor has a contingent remainder,[29] contingent on survival. Todd has a contingent remainder, contingent upon Taylor's non-survival of their father. To illustrate the alternative nature of the remainders, Figure 9-16 shows them both snuggled next to the life estate. One or the other will take at the expiration of the life estate. Joanne has a reversion.

---

[26] *See* Powell ¶ 272[6] & n.75.

[27] At this point, Taylor's interest would be acting like an executory interest.

[28] Bogert & Bogert §§ 163, 182.

[29] Some would say, an "alternative contingent remainder."

FIGURE 9-16
Life Estate, Alternative Contingent Remainders and Reversion

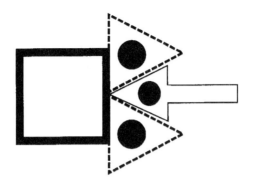

Why does Joanne have a reversion? Surely Taylor will either survive Scott and take the remainder, or not survive, so Todd will take.[30] The answer, like much of the law of future interests, lies in history. One way to remember the rule is to move the grant back to the time of the Wars of the Roses, in which first one family and then another would capture the English Crown. In such an environment, one could commit treason by backing a loser. One consequence of treason might be forfeiting one's life estates, but not one's life. Imagine Scott in the Tower of London, having forfeited his life estate. Neither Taylor nor Todd could take the land, for they had not yet survived Scott. To account for the fact that possession had to go someplace, the law recognized Joanne's reversion. If all that history is too much, simply remember the rule: if there is a contingent remainder, there is a reversion.[31]

Because settlors can give contingent remainders to classes, contingent remainders can be subject to open. Most classification schemes ignore that fact until it becomes relevant, but it is important to know if the remainder is subject to open, whether you say so or not.[32] That way, you can solve problems as facts change.

Suppose Joanne transfers land "to Scott for life, then to his children who graduate from college." While Scott is alive and his children have not yet graduated, the children have contingent remainders, subject to open. (See

---

[30] Because there is no requirement for Todd to survive, under traditional rules his death before getting possession would only mean his successors took. For gifts in trust, the UPC would change this rule and require Todd's survival. UPC § 2-707(b). For discussion of the reform, see § 45[B][2][c][iii], *infra*.

[31] If a jurisdiction followed the destructibility-by-merger rule, the reversion would be important. See the discussion in note 24, *supra*.

[32] Compare the convention of not distinguishing initially between the various ways in which vested remainders may be subject to complete defeasance. *See* § 35[B][2][a][ii], *supra*.

Figure 9-17.) Their unborn younger siblings have executory interests, subject to open. If one of the children graduates while Scott is alive, the

FIGURE 9-17
Life Estate, Contingent Remainders Subject to Open, Executory Interests, and Reversion

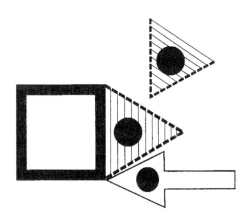

child's remainder will become vested, subject to open.[33] If Scott then dies and some children have not graduated, the ones who have graduated will hold fee simple estates, subject to executory interests held by their siblings who have not graduated.[34]

[c] Vested or Contingent?

When drafters create alternative future interests following a life estate, it may be particularly difficult to classify those interests. Usually two possible constructions appear. There may be a vested remainder and an executory interest,[35] or two alternative contingent remainders and a reversion.[36] This section discusses courts' varying approaches to the problem.

The key to classification in this context usually is the first remainder. If it is contingent, then an alternative contingent remainder construction likely will follow. If the first remainder is vested, then the second interest probably will be an executory interest. Compare two examples:

---

[33] *See* Figure 9-13, *supra.*

[34] You could graph this situation by shading the executory interests represented in Figure 9-5, *supra.* The shading would show that even if these people take, they may still be partially divested later.

[35] *See* Figure 9-11, *supra.*

[36] *See* Figure 9-16, *supra.*

Example 9-1. Wendy grants property "To Arlyn for life, then to Glenn if he graduates from college by age 25, and if not, to Darla."

Example 9-2. "To Arlyn for life, then to Glenn, but if he does not graduate from college by age 25, to Darla."

In Example 9-1, Glenn and Darla get alternative contingent remainders. On the other hand, Example 9-2 yields Glenn a vested remainder, subject to complete defeasance, and Darla an executory interest. In the first example, Glenn's remainder was subject to a condition precedent. In the second, it was subject to a condition subsequent. How can we tell? Look carefully at the words.[37] In Example 9-1, the "if he graduates" language directly followed Glenn's identification. In Example 9-2, a comma followed Glenn's name, and then, a "but."[38]

However picky such an approach may seem, take it seriously, for important consequences flow from the distinction between vested and contingent remainders. Sometimes looking ahead to those consequences can help with the basic classification. In particular, try killing off the life tenant before the contingency has been resolved. If Arlyn dies while Glenn is a 20-year-old undergraduate, who takes? Start reading after the "to Arlyn for life" language. In Example 9-1, we read, "to Glenn if." Neither Glenn nor Darla qualifies as of Arlyn's death, so Wendy takes. In Example 9-2, we read "to Glenn, but . . . ." Glenn has qualified, but may not be able to keep it.

To help decide difficult cases and to further other policies, construction rules may favor one conclusion over another. Classic doctrine, often repeated as if by rote, says that the law favors vested interests.[39] Commentators debate why and whether that principle makes sense today.[40] Of the various rationales they offer for the rule, two are worth noting here.

---

[37] *See* Bergin & Haskell at 72.

[38] In actual documents, the language is often more cumbersome, even when it follows these basic forms. *See, e.g., In re* Krooss, 99 N.E.2d 222 (N.Y. 1951) (finding a vested remainder to the children when the language read, "Upon the death of my beloved wife . . . to my beloved children . . . In the event that either of my children aforesaid should die prior to the death of my beloved wife [to such children's descendants] . . . ").

Also, some courts will ignore the rigid classification formulas. For example, Webb v. Underhill, 882 P.2d 127 (Or. App. 1994) involved an attempt to partition land left to a widow for life, and then to some of the testator's children. In Oregon, only beneficiaries with a vested remainder could maintain a partition action. Despite language giving the remainder to named children, "But if one or more of these shall be dead, their share shall go to their lineal descendants, if any," the court found the children had contingent remainders.

[39] *See generally* Simes & Smith § 573.

[40] Although the principle can apply to questions other than survivorship, as a practical matter survivorship conditions are quite common, and their use dominates the debate. *See generally* Powell ¶ 295; McGovern & Kurtz at 377-383; Susan F. French, *Imposing a General Survival Requirement on Beneficiaries of Future Interests: Solving the Problems Caused by the Death of a Beneficiary Before the Time Set for Distribution*, 27 Ariz. L. Rev. 801 (1985); Edward C. Halbach, Jr., *Future Interests: Express and Implied Conditions of Survival*, 49 Cal. L. Rev. 297 (Part I) and 431 (Part II) (1961); Edward H. Rabin, *The Law Favors the Vesting of Estates. Why?*, 65 Colum. L. Rev. 467 (1965).

First, because a vested construction will tend to limit the number of future interest holders, it may make property more alienable.[41] The rule will achieve that result, however, only in a very small number of cases.[42] In particular, the alienability rationale has no application to trusts. The trustee has legal title to the assets and can transfer them freely, despite the variety of equitable interests held by the beneficiaries.

Second, a vested construction will tend to avoid cutting off one line of a family. This may be the best argument for the rule. Suppose Eva's will creates a trust for Hope for life, with ambiguous remainders to her children, Carleton and Channey. Suppose also that Channey survives Eva, but dies before Hope. If a court construed Channey's gift as contingent upon his surviving Hope, Channey's family may lose out.[43] If, as under the traditional rule, Channey need not survive, his family could be expected to take the remainder by his will or intestacy.[44] There are other ways to protect Channey's family, however, without running the property through Channey's estate.[45]

Although the preference for vesting is under attack, it serves as a warning to drafters who believe they are creating contingent interests. One scary old rule comes from *Edwards v. Hammond*.[46] *Edwards* says, in effect, that if you repeat an age contingency, a court will ignore your first reference as surplusage, leaving a vested, subject construction. Thus, if you grant "to Michael for life, then if Polly reaches 21 to Polly, but if Polly does not reach 21, to Chris," a court following *Edwards* will read it like this: "to Michael for life, then ~~if Polly reaches 21~~ to Polly, but if Polly does not reach 21, to Chris." Polly gets a vested remainder, subject to complete defeasance. Fortunately, the rule does not apply to age contingencies tied to class gifts.[47]

Most of the time, reading the words in order will tell you whether particular language creates a vested or a contingent remainder. In marginal cases, courts are likely to repeat, and often follow, the traditional preference

---

[41] Limiting the possibility of unidentified future interest holders also makes for easier trust modification and termination. For discussion of those issues, see § 14, *supra*.

[42] "[T]he rule facilitates alienation only in cases involving legal estates in land where the interest is an indefeasibly vested estate not subject to open and where ameliorative legislation has not been enacted." Rabin, *The Law Favors the Vesting of Estates. Why?*, 65 Colum. L. Rev. at 482 (1965).

[43] If the gift were a class gift, as the surviving class member, Carleton would take Channey's share. For more on class gifts, see § 43, *infra*.

If this were not a class gift, Channey's share would pass under a residuary clause or by intestacy. Of course, some of Channey's share could come back to his family by either route.

[44] Channey might also give the property to someone else.

[45] We might imply that Channey has a power to appoint the remainder or we could create alternative gifts by statute. For discussion of these options, see § 45[B][2][c][iii], *infra*.

[46] 83 Eng. Rep. 614 (K.B. 1683). The case involved a gift of a copyhold, one of the old forms of ownership in England. For some background on the case, see Waggoner, Alexander, Fellows & Gallanis at 1042 n.1.

[47] *See* Festing v. Allen, 152 Eng. Rep. 1204 (Ex. 1843). There a remainder was, simplified, "to Martha's children who reach 21." Because the age contingency was wrapped up in identifying the class members, the court found the remainder contingent.

for a vested construction. The stone in which that preference has been carved is slowly crumbling, however, so beware of putting too much reliance upon the old rule.[48]

§ 36 Putting It Together

Examining different bits of language with an eye to classifying present and future interests is rather like looking through a kaleidoscope. Every time you turn it a different way, a new pattern appears. Because the patterns are endless, generalizations are dangerous. Rare cases, by definition, will not fit common patterns. Nonetheless, the following chart may help if you treat it as a guide, rather than a mandate, and if you take classification one step at a time.

---

[48] One recent blow comes from the UPC, which presumes that future interests in trust are contingent on the beneficiary surviving until the time for distribution. UPC § 2-707(b). For discussion of the UPC proposal, see § 45[B][2][c][iii], *infra*.

Present and Future Interests

Present Interest	Future Interest*	
	In Grantor	In Third Persons
1) Fee simple absolute ("to B & her heirs") (modern–"to B")	none	none
2) Fee tail ("to B & the heirs of his body")	reversion	vested remainder** contingent remainder executory interest
3) Defeasible fee estates		
(a) fee simple determinable ("to B, so long as . . . .")	possibility of reverter	executory interest
(b) fee simple subject to condition subsequent ("to B, but if . . . .")	right of entry (power of termination)	none
(c) fee simple subject to an executory limitation ("to B, but if . . . .")	none	executory interest
4) Life estate ("to B for life")	reversion	vested remainder** contingent remainder executory interest

---

*In many cases it will not be possible for *both* the grantor *and* a third person to hold future interests following the same present interest. This chart indicates some *possible* future interests following various present interests.

** Vested remainders can be indefeasibly vested, vested subject to complete defeasance, or subject to open.

Chapter 10

POWERS OF APPOINTMENT

Trusts are remarkably flexible devices.[1] That flexibility has two aspects. Part stems from the relatively few basic elements trust doctrine requires, so lawyers can shape trusts to fit the needs of individual clients. Part comes from each individual trust's ability to adapt over time. Powers of appointment are the lifeblood of that adaptability.[2]

A power of appointment is a power one person has to designate who will take property subject to the power or what shares the takers will receive.[3] We have seen such powers already, in the context of defining the size of a trust beneficiary's interest.[4] A trustee's powers to allocate income among various beneficiaries or to invade the trust principal on someone's behalf are powers of appointment. This chapter concerns powers individuals have to allocate the shares of a trust long after it was created.[5] The first section introduces some new terminology and discusses issues which cut across the entire area. The second considers questions surrounding the creation of powers.[6] Issues regarding the exercise of powers of appointment are then covered. The chapter closes with some suggestions regarding drafting powers. This coverage should help you to understand how powers fit into estate plans and to follow later discussions regarding the Rule Against Perpetuities[7] and the federal estate tax.[8]

---

[1] *See generally* Chapter 4, *supra*.

[2] One of the mistakes students sometimes make when reading cases about powers is to cut straight to the narrow issue being decided. Instead, take advantage of the opportunity to review other lawyers' overall estate plans along the way.

[3] *See* Restatement (Second) of Prop. § 11.1. For overviews of this topic, see Bergin & Haskell, ch. 7; McGovern & Kurtz ch. 10; Simes, chs. 12-15; William A. Peithman, *A Look At The Principles And Uses Of Powers Of Appointment*, Tr. & Est., Aug. 1993 38-47. For more in-depth treatment, see American Law of Property §§ 23.1-23.12; Powell ch. 33; Simes & Smith, chs. 28-29.

[4] *See* § 13, *supra*.

[5] Real estate can be, but thankfully seldom is, held subject to a power of appointment. A rule which continues to haunt us from the past is "Chancellor Kent's Rule." If this rule were applied when a grantor gives Blackacre "to Matthew absolutely with full power to consume, and if anything is left over to Robin," the gift to Robin would be void as "repugnant" to the grant to Matthew. For a modern case following this approach, see Sterner v. Nelson, 314 N.W.2d 263 (Neb.1982). For criticism of the rule, see Jesse Dukeminier, *Cleansing the Stables of Property: A River Found at Last*, 65 Iowa L. Rev. 151, 169-170 (1979).

[6] In this chapter, "powers" means "powers of appointment."

[7] *See* Chapter 12, *infra*.

[8] *See* Chapter 13, *infra*.

§ 37   The Basics

[A]   Postponed Decisionmaking

Powers of appointment are useful because they can buy time. For example, they allow members of one generation to give property to their grandchildren's generation, but postpone decisions about exactly how that property will be divided. Consider Edna, a widow with one son, James, a young adult without children. Suppose Edna wants to set up a trust for James. She might give James the trust income for his life, with the principal distributed equally among his (yet unborn) children at James' death. The problem is that Edna cannot know if James will have children, or how many, or what their needs will be by the time James dies. Rather than arbitrarily fixing the shares ahead of time, Edna instead could give James (or someone else) a power of appointment to identify who should take the trust principal, and in what shares. By creating a power of appointment, Edna can keep her trust adaptable to changed circumstances. For a generation, she can postpone decisions about how that money will be spent.[1]

[B]   The Players

The law of powers has its own terminology. It may help to imagine a power of appointment as the authority to operate a large crane which can move property from one person to another. The **donor** is the person who creates the power (authorizes the use of the crane). The person who gets the power is called the **donee**.[2] A word of caution: the donee can operate the crane, but may not necessarily use it to take the property for himself. The donee can give the property only to people the donor identifies as **objects** of the power, which may or may not include the donee. If the donee exercises the power (uses the crane to move the property), the recipient is called an **appointee**. An appointee, then, must come from the class of objects. If the donee does not exercise the power, the property goes to a **taker in default**, if the donor so provided. Depending upon the estate plan, the same person may assume several roles.[3]

[C]   Classification of Powers

Two different ways of classifying powers are critically important.[4] One

---

[1] In addition to providing flexibility, powers of appointment can produce estate tax savings even when the powers are intended to remain unexercised. For an example, see *In re* Estate of Clarkson, 226 N.W.2d 334 (Neb. 1975), discussed in § 28[C][4], *supra*. Powers and estate tax are discussed in §§ 37[D] and 62[A][2], *infra*.

[2] In the example above, Edna is the donor, and James, the donee, of the power.

[3] Someone reserving a power to appoint to himself, and then exercising that power to do, so would be donor, donee, object, and appointee.

[4] You may see references to more detailed branches of these two main divisions. The detailed classifications are largely outmoded, but could matter in a rare case. *See* Bergin & Haskell at 152 n.9; Simes at § 56.

is based on who can get the property subject to the power; the other, on the mechanics of how the power can be exercised.

[1] Permissible Donees

The breadth of the class of objects is one criteria for dividing powers. In this context, lawyers traditionally have referred to powers as either "general" or "special."[5] A **general** power is one in which a donee can give the property to himself, his creditors, his estate, or creditors of his estate. A **special** power is one in which a donee is limited to a particular class of objects. These definitions leave a gap: a power that can be exercised to benefit anyone except the donee, his creditor, his estate, or its creditors. Earlier, the gap caused little trouble because people saw little utility in creating such "**hybrid**" powers.[6] The increased importance of tax planning has prompted drafters to create such powers because they avoid the tax consequences of a general power, yet they also give the donee enormous discretion.

In response to this change, the Second Restatement of Property identifies two categories of powers, similar to those used in the Internal Revenue Code: **general**[7] and **non-general**.[8] The "non-general" category includes both special and hybrid powers. This grouping has the advantage of bringing tax and property terminology closer together, but it can be awkward because not all non-general powers raise the same questions. Some property rules apply to what we traditionally call special powers, but not to all non-general powers.[9]

Lawyers and courts still refer to "general" and "special" powers, and readers will understand the terms according to their context. In most situations, "general" probably means a power exercisable in favor of the donee, his estate, his creditors, or the creditors of his estate. If the question involves tax, "special" probably means "not general." If the question does not involve tax, "special" means "for a limited class of objects" (excluding the donee, the donee's creditors, the donee's estate or creditors of the donee's estate as class members). This text will follow that approach.

---

[5] *See* Restatement of Prop. § 320.

[6] *See* Restatement of Prop. § 320 cmt. a; Simes at 124.

[7] According to the Restatement, a general power is one "exercisable in favor of any one or more of the following: the donee of the power, the donee's creditors, the donee's estate, or the creditors of the donee's estate." Restatement (Second) of Prop. § 11.4(1). *Cf.* I.R.C. § 2041.

[8] Not surprisingly, this term means any power which does not meet the definition of "general." *See* Restatement (Second) of Prop. § 11.4(2).

[9] For example, sometimes people will try to appoint to their grandchildren, even though a power limits them to appointing to their children. Traditional rules regarding special powers would prohibit the appointment, but the problem simply does not arise regarding hybrid powers. In this situation, the Second Restatement distinguishes between "objects of a non-general power not a positively defined limited class" and "objects of a non-general power a positively defined limited class" [formerly called objects of a special power]. Restatement (Second) of Prop. §§ 20.1, 20.2.

[2] Method of Exercise

The other way of classifying powers centers upon how and when powers can be exercised. Donors can create powers exercisable by a deed during the donee's lifetime [10] (**inter vivos powers**), exercisable by a will at death (**testamentary powers**), or exercisable either way at the donee's option. Donors can give specific instructions, which donees must follow in order to exercise the power. [11]

These two basic lines of division—permissible donees and method of exercise—overlap. We can have general inter vivos powers and special inter vivos powers. We can also have general testamentary powers and special testamentary powers. From a planning perspective, these options mean flexibility. From the perspective of interpreting a document someone else has prepared, the first step in analysis is to identify the type of power involved.

[D] Estate Tax Treatment

Although discussion of the federal estate tax appears in Chapter 13, a brief explanation here should aid your understanding of powers of appointment. Settlors often create powers with tax reasons in mind. Therefore, even if cases involve non-tax issues, untangling the estate plan requires some basic knowledge of tax.

The details can get very complex, but the general principles are straightforward. If a donee dies holding a general power of appointment, the property subject to that power will be included in the donee's gross estate for tax purposes. [12] Property subject to a special power, however, will not suffer the same fate. [13] Because of this distinction, donors may create

---

[10] Such powers are often "presently exercisable," able to be used immediately. Sometimes a donor may delay the time for the exercise until a future date, but still during the donee's lifetime.

The time of a power's exercise and the time the appointee actually gets the property subject to the power may be widely separated. For example, Mary may have a life estate in a trust and a presently exercisable power to appoint the principal. Mary could execute a document exercising the power, naming Kendra to get the remainder, but Kendra would have to wait until Mary's death to get the trust principal.

[11] For discussion, see § 38, *infra*.

[12] I.R.C. § 2041(a). For tax purposes, a power is not general if it is properly limited by an ascertainable standard. I.R.C. § 2041(b)(1)(A). For example, a donee may not have a general power, even though she can invade trust principal on her own behalf, if she can only invade to pay the "reasonable expenses of her higher education." Taxpayers who stray from the language of the code and regulations may find that they have not limited their standard narrowly enough and have created a general power. *See, e.g.*, Miller v. United States, 387 F.2d 866 (3d Cir. 1968) (power to invade for "other expenses incidental to her comfort and well-being" was too broad and created a general power).

[13] There is one exception. To fill a gap first opened by Delaware, the code *will* include in the estate of the donee of a special power, property subject to that power, *if* the donee exercises the special power by will to create a general power. IRC § 2041(a)(3). This provision is sometimes called the "Delaware Tax Trap."

different sorts of powers in different situations. For example, planners often recommend that clients create special powers in order to give a donee considerable authority, but still not incur taxes on the property subject to the power.[14] On the other hand, a client may decide to give a surviving spouse a general power as a way of equalizing the estate tax burden between each spouse.[15]

[E] Who Owns the Property?

Like much of the law of property, the law surrounding powers of appointment is moving from strict reliance upon the logic of traditional doctrine to a more flexible examination of the realities involved.[16] One illustration of this development is the conflict surrounding how much interest a donee of a power has in the property subject to the power. The question is important, largely because other persons who have claims on the donee often want to treat the property subject to the power as the donee's property, to which the claimants have access.

Traditionally, the law viewed a donee of a power almost as an agent of the donor, who retained ownership of the property until the donee exercised the power. Under this view, the exercise of the power then relates back to the power's creation, so the exercise fills in blanks which had been left in the document creating the power. The appointee thus gets the property from the donor, not the donee. Because the property subject to the power was not the donee's, claimants against the donee came away empty-handed.[17]

The relation-back theory makes sense in the context of a special power. Because the donee cannot appoint the property to herself, she is rather like a trustee holding other persons' property. The property is not in any practical sense hers,[18] and generally should not be subject to claims against

---

[14] By carefully using the details of the tax laws, a settlor can give a trust beneficiary very extensive authority over property and still avoid taxation at the beneficiary's death. For a list of powers which meet these goals, see Dukeminier & Johanson at 673-674.

[15] Property subject to that power would both qualify for the marital deduction in the donor's estate and put the property in the donee-spouse's gross estate. *See* § 62[B], *infra*.

[16] One example comes from the UTC, which treats the holder of a power of appointment created under a trust as a trust beneficiary (unless the power is held in a trust capacity). UTC § 103(2)(B).

[17] *See, e.g., In re* Estate of Wylie, 342 So. 2d 996 (Fla. Dist. Ct. App. 1977) (property subject to general testamentary power not part of the probate estate for the purpose of determining executors' fees); Quinn v. Tuttle, 177 A.2d 391 (N.H. 1962) (creditors cannot reach property subject to general testamentary power when the beneficiary has yet to exercise that power); Harlan Nat'l Bank v. Brown, 317 S.W.2d 903 (Ky. 1958) (assets of wife's trust over which she had the power to appoint could not be included in her estate for determining husband's dower rights). Under an earlier version of the tax law, property subject to an unexercised general power of appointment was not taxed in the donee's estate. *See* Charles L. B. Lowndes et al., Federal Estate and Gift Taxes §§ 12.2-12.4 (3d ed. 1974)

[18] Merely having the power, however, may increase the donee's chances of getting appropriate attention from potential appointees. For example, grandchildren may visit more often if their grandparent holds the power to change their trust shares.

her.[19]

On the other hand, the donee of a general power is only a paper-thin line away from absolute ownership. All the donee of a presently exercisable general power need do to get the property is sign some forms. In this context, treating the property as the donor's, and thus not subject to claims against the donee, is hard to justify.[20]

The law is split about how to treat property subject to general powers. For example, such property is part of the donee's gross estate under the federal estate tax.[21] In many states, however, creditors of the donee of a general, presently exercisable power cannot force the donee to exercise the power in their behalf.[22] Commentators have criticized this rule.[23] Several state statutes and the UTC have reversed it to allow creditors to get the appointive property after they have exhausted the donee's property.[24] Similarly, surviving spouses traditionally have been unable to elect against property subject to a general power their decedent spouse held, but that rule may be changing.[25] Increasingly, but unevenly, the law is taking the view that if a donee can get the property, so should those who have claims on that donee.

Another example of the continuing influence of the relation-back doctrine is the set of rules regarding which state's law applies to resolve particular powers questions. Because donors and donees often live in different places,

---

[19] *But see, In re* Marriage of Chapman, 697 N.E.2d 365 (Ill. App. Ct. 1998) (children of a donee who had a special power to appoint trust principal to them may reach the principal when they have a support order).

[20] *See* Melanie Leslie, Note, *The Case Against Applying the Relation-Back Doctrine to the Exercise of General Powers of Appointment*, 14 Cardozo L. Rev. 219 (1992).

[21] I.R.C. § 2041(a), discussed in §§ 37[D], *supra*, and 62[A][2], *infra*.

[22] *See, e.g.*, Irwin Union Bank & Trust Co. v. Long, 312 N.E.2d 908 (Ind. App. 1974) (former wife unable to enforce judgment against trust over which former husband held a general power); Restatement (Second) of Prop. § 13.2.

If the donee is also the donor of the power, the creditors can reach the property. *See* 2d Rest. Prop. § 13.3. This rule is similar to the one that a person cannot create a spendthrift trust for himself. *See* Bogert at 155. Spendthrift provisions are discussed in § 13[B], *supra*.

After the donee of a general power exercises the power, in most states the donee's creditors can grab the property before it gets to the appointee. *See* 2d Rest. Prop. § 13.4.

[23] *See, e.g.*, Bergin & Haskell at 173-174.

[24] *See, e.g.*, Mich. Comp. Laws Ann. § 556.123; Wis. Stat. Ann. § 702.17; UTC § 505(b).

Similarly, a general, presently exercisable power is included in the estate of a bankrupt donee. *See* 11 U.S.C. § 541(b).

[25] *See* § 28[C][1], *supra*, for a discussion of Sullivan v. Burkin, 460 N.E.2d 572 (Mass. 1984), which does allow such an election. *See also* Restatement (Second) of Prop. § 34.1(3).

The revised UPC includes in the augmented estate property subject to which "the decedent alone, immediately before death, held a presently exercisable general power of appointment." UPC § 2-205(l)(i). Under the UPC, property subject to a general *testamentary* power, however, is not included. For discussion of the revised augmented estate, see § 28[C][3][b], *supra*.

See generally Margaret M. Mahoney, *Elective Share Statutes: The Right to Elect Against Property Subject to a General Power of Appointment in the Decedent*, 55 Notre Dame L. Rev. 99 (1979).

conflict of laws issues are often critical to powers of appointment cases.[26] For example, disputes may arise about whether the donee of a general power properly exercised the power. The relation-back doctrine, which views the donee as merely filling in blanks in the donor's document, leads to the traditional view that the law of the donor's domicile controls.[27] A less doctrinaire approach recognizes, however, that the donee's will is likely to be drafted with the law of the donee's domicile in mind, so the donee's law should control questions surrounding the adequacy of the exercise.[28]

Overall, the relation-back doctrine has continuing influence, but, especially with respect to general powers, it has fallen to a "look at the realities" approach in a variety of contexts.

§ 38   Creating Powers

The process of creating a power of appointment is one key to its successful use. You may use a first draft as a vehicle for discussing the choices the client must make regarding who should have the power and what the scope of the power should be. Once a client has decided what she wants, a careful final draft can avoid many of the problems which can arise when a donee executes the power.[1]

Sadly, not all powers are well drafted. Indeed, sometimes it is hard to tell if a donor intended to create a power at all. Language like "to my daughter, Kyanne, to be used for the education of her children" could be an outright gift to the daughter, a trust with the daughter as trustee,[2] or a power of appointment.[3] Testators sometimes say something like "to my son, Keoka, for life, and at his death to his executors." From the context it is clear that the executors are not meant to take a remainder in their personal capacities, but guessing at what the testator really intended can be difficult.[4] Powers are wonderful tools, but like most tools, you should treat them with respect.[5]

---

[26] For some proposals on how the UPC might be improved by clarifying several conflict of laws issues, see Sheldon F. Kurtz, *Powers of Appointment Under the 1990 Uniform Probate Code: What Was Done—What Remains to Be Done*, 55 Alb. L. Rev. 1151, 1172-1182 (1992).

[27] *See* Beals v. State St. Bank & Trust Co., 326 N.E.2d 896 (Mass. 1975), discussed in § 39[A], *infra*. *See generally* Harrison F. Durand & Charles L. Herterich, *Conflict of Laws and the Exercise of Powers of Appointment*, 42 Cornell L.Q. 185 (1957).

[28] *See* White v. United States, 680 F.2d 1156, 1160 (7th Cir. 1982) (discussing the exercise of a general testamentary power); Toledo Trust Co. v. Santa Barbara Found., 512 N.E.2d 664 (Ohio 1987) (discussing the exercise of a special testamentary power).

[1] We will return to the question of drafting after discussing problems regarding the exercise of powers. *See* § 40, *infra*.

[2] *See* § 12[A], *supra*.

[3] For more on this question, see § 12[C], *supra*, especially the discussion of *Clark v. Campbell*.

[4] *Compare In re* Thompson's Estate, 80 N.Y.S.2d 1 (N.Y. App. 1948) (finding a power of appointment in the beneficiary), *with* Bredin v. Wilmington Trust Co., 216 A.2d 685 (Del. Ch. 1965) (finding a remainder, by implication, to the issue of the beneficiary).

[5] The question of the validity of a power of appointment under the Rule Against Perpetuities is reserved for § 51, *infra*.

§ 39 Exercising Powers

As noted in the prior section, many problems involving powers can be avoided by careful drafting. As you read through this section, file away ideas for how you might draft around various trouble spots.[1] This section first addresses what it takes to exercise a power. Next, we examine various problems surrounding the scope of special powers. The section closes with a look at what happens when a power has not been exercised.

[A] Getting It Done

The first step for someone about to exercise a power of appointment is to check carefully the document creating the power. It can (and should) specify not only who has the power, but the steps the donee must take to exercise it. For example, Marcia might have a power to allocate the remainder of a trust "according to the terms of a writing delivered to the trustee." Failure to follow the instructions probably means failure of the attempted exercise.[2]

Among the most common problems involving powers of appointment is whether a residuary clause in a donee's will exercises a power.[3] The will may use general, "all of my property" language, or a "blending" clause like "including all property over which I have a power of appointment."[4] If the donor has required specific reference to the power as a condition of its exercise, the question may arise as to whether particular language in the donee's will is enough to qualify as a specific reference.

Sometimes a donee's residuary clause refers to "the rest of my property," but does not mention the power of appointment in question. In this situation, most states presume non-exercise, whether the power is general or special.[5] *Beals v. State Street Bank & Trust Company*[6] took a different

---

[1] *See generally* Alexander A. Bove, Jr. *Exercising Powers of Appointment – A Simple Task or Tricky Business?*, 28 Est. Planning 277 (2001).

[2] *See* Catch v. Phillips, 86 Cal. Rptr. 2d 584 (Cal. App. Ct. 1999) (power not exercised by lifetime document when instrument creating power required a will or codicil); National Shawmut Bank v. Joy, 53 N.E.2d 113 (Mass. 1944) (A will witnessed by a notary did not satisfy the donor's requirements that the power of appointment be exercised by an instrument under seal, acknowledged, and deposited with the trustees.); Restatement (Second) of Prop. § 18.3. Some states' statutes allow donees to ignore formalities imposed by the donor, beyond those the law requires for the instrument in question. *See* Restatement (Second) of Prop. § 18.3, reporter's note. *See also* Restatement (Second) of Prop. § 17.1 cmt. b.

Sometimes a court will recognize an appointment when the donee tried, but failed, to follow the donor's instructions. *See, e.g., In re* Estate of Wood, 32 Cal. App. 3d 862, 108 Cal. Rptr. 522 (Cal. App. 1973) (appointment recognized when donor required delivery of the appointing instrument to the trustee during the donee's lifetime and donee signed it and gave it to her lawyer, but the lawyer failed to forward it until after donee's death). Question: Is the donee's lawyer liable in malpractice for the cost of the litigation in the *Wood's Estate* case? *See generally* § 1, *supra*.

[3] *See generally* Susan F. French, *Exercise of Powers of Appointment: Should Intent to Exercise Be Inferred From a General Disposition of Property?*, 1979 Duke L.J. 747.

[4] Sometimes such language is called a "blanket-exercise" clause.

[5] *See* Simes at 147; Restatement (Second) of Prop. § 17.3. Claimants can overcome the pre

approach. It involved the wills of Arthur Hunnewell and his daughter, Isabella. In 1904, Arthur's will created a trust giving Isabella income for her life and a general testamentary power to appoint the remainder. Arthur's will also provided a gift in default of the exercise. In 1944, Isabella released her power to the extent that she could appoint to anyone other than her father's descendants who survived her.[7] Isabella died in 1968,[8] leaving a will with a residuary clause disposing of all of her property and specifically mentioning her power of appointment under her *husband's* will. Isabella's will made no specific mention of the power she held over her *father's* trust, nor did it use a blending clause.

Taking minority positions along the way, the court held that Isabella's will did exercise the power from her father's trust. The Massachusetts court applied its own law, the law of the donor's domicile, rather than the donee's.[9] In contrast to most states, Massachusetts presumed that a residuary clause exercised a general testamentary power.[10] The court applied this presumption even though Isabella's release had left her with a special power. Moreover, the court found no evidence that Isabella did not intend to exercise the power from her father. (The court might, instead, have noted that she specifically mentioned the power from her husband.

---

sumption by evidence of the donee's contrary intention. Jurisdictions differ, both on the required standard of proof (a preponderance, or clear and convincing), and whether the donee's oral declarations are admissible. *See* Susan F. French, *Exercise of Powers of Appointment: Should Intent to Exercise Be Inferred From a General Disposition of Property?*, 1979 Duke L.J. 747, 786-790.

[6] 326 N.E.2d 896 (Mass. 1975).

[7] She thereby created a special power, no doubt to save estate taxes. Under earlier tax law, property subject to unexercised general powers was not taxed in the donee's estate. In 1942 the law was changed so that now any general power, exercised or not, brings the property into the donee's gross estate. Property subject to special powers is not taxed in the estate of the donee, even when the power is exercised. Because of the change, taxpayers were given until 1951 to amend their estate plans (by turning general into special powers) without adverse tax consequences. *See* Charles L. B. Lowndes et al., Federal Estate and Gift Taxes § 12.3 (3d ed. 1974).

In part because releases had tax benefits in the 1940s, courts and legislatures have allowed releases of general testamentary powers, even though the effect of a release may be to defeat the donor's intention to delay decisionmaking until the donee's death. Because the power was released, the property would go to the takers in default, and that result would be known at the time of the release. *See* Restatement (Second) of Prop. § 14.1 & statutory note.

On the other hand, contracts to exercise testamentary powers cannot be specifically enforced, nor can damages be granted for their breach. See Restatement (Second) of Prop. § 16.2. Allowing such contracts would fly too much in the face of the donor's intention to delay decisions. For a dispute about whether a document was a release or a contract, see *Seidel v. Werner*, 364 N.Y.S.2d 963 (N.Y. Sup. Ct. 1975) (finding a contract), discussed in Samuel M. Fetters, *Future Interests: 1975 Survey of N.Y. Law*, 27 Syracuse L. Rev. 365, 366-377 (1976).

[8] Note that 64 years passed before someone had to decide how the remainder of the trust would be distributed.

[9] While recognizing the trend toward applying the law of the donee's domicile, this court followed the traditional approach. For discussion of the conflict of laws point, see § 37[E], *supra*.

[10] Massachusetts has since changed positions and now presumes non-exercise. *See* Mass. Gen. L. ch. 191, § 1A(4).

Perhaps the contrast of her not naming her power from her father should raise a presumption of non-exercise of that power.) After applying the presumption of exercise and finding no evidence to rebut it, the court held that her general residuary clause was enough to exercise the power from her father.

Under the revised UPC, a general residuary clause, without more, will not exercise a power.[11] A general residuary clause will be presumed to exercise a power, however, if the donor has not required specific reference to the power, and if either of two circumstances occurs: (1) the power is general and there is no gift in default,[12] or (2) the donee's will "manifests an intention to include the property subject to the power."[13]

As noted by the UPC, a donor's will may use language like "this power shall be exercisable only by specific reference to this power of appointment." The donor may be trying to avoid inadvertent exercise of a power,[14] or may be trying to make the exercise more difficult, in hopes that it will fail and the takers in default will get the property.[15] In any case, these requirements raise the question: what is a specific reference? Of course, careful drafting can, and should, identify precisely any power being exercised.[16] Imprecise references breed litigation, like *First National Bank v. Walker*.[17] *Walker* involved Allie's attempted exercise of a power created by her husband, Charles. Charles' will required specific reference; Allie's used a blending clause.[18] The court held that Allie's reference was not specific enough and, despite testimony that Allie intended to exercise the power, gave the property to the takers in default.[19]

Sometimes courts will save an attempted exercise that does not follow the donor's instructions. *In re Strobel*[20] involved Willie Mae Strobel's

[11] *See* UPC § 2-608. *See generally*, Sheldon F. Kurtz, *Powers of Appointment Under the 1990 Uniform Probate Code: What Was Done—What Remains to Be Done*, 55 Alb. L. Rev. 1151, 1162-1168 (1992).

[12] Without a gift in default, the property would go back to the donor. Giving the property to the donee's residuary takers is better than having to reopen the donor's estate.

[13] UPC § 2-608.

[14] The UPC establishes such a presumption. UPC § 2-704. *See generally*, Sheldon F. Kurtz, *Powers of Appointment Under the 1990 Uniform Probate Code: What Was Done—What Remains to Be Done*, 55 Alb. L. Rev. 1151, 1168-1172 (1992).

[15] This might be the case if the donor created the power for tax reasons, but really did not want the donee to change the estate plan. For a short discussion of tax implications, see § 37[D], *supra*.

[16] *See generally* Addison E. Dewey, *Is There a Simple Will? Or Drafting of a Testamentary Power of Appointment Without Specific Reference to Source of the Power: Opportunity for Malpractice?*, 1983 Det. C.L. Rev. 1533.

[17] 607 S.W.2d 469 (Tenn. 1980).

[18] She gave all her property, "including all property over which I shall have any power of appointment at my death . . . ." 607 S.W.2d at 470.

[19] To the same effect as *Walker*, see Clinton County Nat'l & Trust Co. v. First Nat'l Bank, 403 N.E.2d 968 (Ohio1980). *But see* Cross v. Cross, 559 S.W.2d 196 (Mo. Ct. App. 1977), where a blending clause was specific enough.

[20] 717 P.2d 892 (Ariz. 1986).

attempt to exercise a power created by her husband, Oscar. Here the problem was mistake: Willie Mae's will specifically referred to a trust which never came into existence. Because Willie Mae was trying to appoint to a natural object of her bounty, and because the appointment would not undermine Oscar's purpose in preventing unintended exercise, the court found that Willie Mae's bad reference approximated Oscar's instructions and should have been recognized in equity. [21] Effectively, the court reformed the will to exercise the power. [22]

[B] Problems of Scope

Because a donor of a power is creating a new thing, the donor can shape it to his own desires, subject only to the broad limits the law imposes. [23] When drafting leaves gaps, the law fills them with default rules. This section addresses questions about the scope of a donee's authority to create various interests and to choose among the objects of a power.

Fortunately, the donee of a general, presently exercisable power can use the power to create new property interests just as if she owned in fee simple the property subject to the power. In a refreshingly straightforward approach, the law does not force the donee first to exercise the power in her own behalf and then to create new interests. It allows directly what could be done indirectly. [24] The same rule applies, although perhaps somewhat less universally, to general testamentary powers. [25]

Special powers have caused problems in some places. The most common approach is that a donee has the power to create whatever interests she desires, except as the donor has restricted that use. [26] Because special powers limit donees' choices of appointees, however, some courts have viewed special powers as somehow smaller than general powers in other respects as well. For example, in *Loring v. Karri-Davies,* [27] the holder of two special powers was not allowed to exercise them to create trusts for the appointees. Using similar language in a living trust and in his will, William Gaston gave his daughter, Ruth, separate powers to appoint to her issue. She, in turn, left a will attempting to exercise those powers to create new trusts for her children and their issue. The court presumed that Ruth got only the authority William gave her, rather than total authority except as William limited her. Because William's documents showed no intention to

---

[21] *See* Restatement (Second) of Prop. § 18.3. Allowing the exercise in this situation is rather like allowing a will to be probated, despite the lack of formalities. *See* § 7[B][4], *supra.*

[22] *Cf.* § 41[B], *infra.*

[23] *See, e.g.,* Chapter 12, *infra,* and § 31, *supra.*

[24] *See generally* Simes & Smith at § 976; Restatement (Second) of Prop. § 19.1.

[25] *See generally* Simes & Smith at § 976; Restatement (Second) of Prop. § 19.1. Some cases have enforced donor restrictions in general testamentary powers that limit their donees to appointing legal fee simple interests. *See, e.g.,* Dant v. Fidelity & Columbia Trust Co., 193 S.W.2d 399 (Ky. 1946) (invalidating donee's attempt to create a new trust with limitations).

[26] *See* Scott at 62-63; Simes at 153-157; Bergin & Haskell at 155-161.

[27] 357 N.E.2d 11 (Mass. 1976).

allow Ruth to create new trusts, her appointment failed.[28] As William's designated takers-in-default, Ruth's children took the property free from trust. Similar cases have denied donees of special powers the ability to create new powers of appointment.[29] This limited view of the authority granted by special powers is losing favor,[30] but, because of the risk that a court may take a narrow view, good drafting requires donors of special powers to be particularly careful to identify the sorts of interests they want their donees to be able to create.

Special powers do, of course, limit the persons the donee can benefit. Even if a donee of a special power has broad authority to create all sorts of interests, the donee may not, for example, create a trust for someone not an object of the power. The offending part of the exercise, however, would not be the trust, but the fact that it benefited a non-object.[31]

Sometimes disputes arise about whether someone qualifies as an object of a power. Anne Killian gave her son, John, the power to appoint "to his wife" up to one-third of the property in a trust. At the time, John was married to Donna. After they divorced, John married Jan and attempted to exercise the power by appointing the property to her. The Iowa Supreme Court held that "his wife" meant John's wife at the time of the power's exercise, so Jan could take.[32]

Special powers also present the question of how much power the donee has to choose among the class of objects. A special power can be either **exclusive** or **nonexclusive**.[33] In this context, "exclusive" means having the power to exclude some of the objects of the power in favor of others. *Harlan v. Citizens National Bank of Danville*[34] illustrates the majority approach. Annie Harlan died leaving three children, Jay, George, and Sue. Annie gave George a life estate in trust and the power to appoint the remainder "to his widow, his descendants or my descendants." George's will gave everything to Jay, and a disappointed Sue claimed that George did not have the authority to cut her out. The court disagreed. It assumed that a donee has the power to exclude objects of the power unless the donor forbids that practice.[35]

---

[28] The court announced that it would follow a more liberal rule in the future and allow such appointments, absent contrary intention by the donor. *See* 357 N.E.2d at 16.

[29] *See* Thayer v. Rivers, 60 N.E. 796 (Mass. 1901) (denying donee's creation of powers of appointment in her nieces and nephews).

[30] *See* Restatement (Second) of Prop. §§ 19.3, 19.4.

[31] Sometimes donees will try to get around this restriction by giving property to an object, who has in turn agreed to give some of it to a non-object. Such an appointment is invalid as a "fraud on the power." *See* Restatement (Second) of Prop. § 20.2.

[32] *In re* Trust of Killian, 459 N.W.2d 497 (Iowa 1990). Similar questions arise in the context of the Rule Against Perpetuities. *See* § 51, *infra*.

[33] *See generally* Bergin & Haskell at 154-155; Simes & Smith at § 981.

[34] 251 S.W.2d 284 (Ky. 1952).

[35] The minority approach presumes a nonexclusive power. *See, e.g.*, Hopkins v. Dimock, 48 A.2d 204 (N.J. Eq. 1946).

If a special power is nonexclusive, the donee must give each object something. The question is, how much? Some jurisdictions require each object to get a substantial part of the assets subject to the power.[36] Others say that nominal gifts to some objects still satisfy the restriction that a donee cannot exclude anyone.[37] The rule allowing nominal gifts seems odd. If a court interprets a document as requiring all objects to benefit from the power's exercise, why should it then allow its own rule to be so easily circumvented?[38]

Before drafting a document executing a special power in a way that excludes an object, check the donor's document carefully to be sure the donee has that authority. If the power is nonexclusive and the donee nonetheless excludes someone, the entire appointment is void.[39]

[C] Failure to Appoint

Not all powers will be exercised effectively.[40] As a consequence, well-drafted powers of appointment include takers in default. This group will act much like the residuary takers of a will. To the extent that the power is unexercised, they usually will take the appointive property. Sometimes, however, a donor will not name takers in default, or the takers in default will be unable take the property, or the donee will indicate a desire to claim the property for herself if the appointment fails. This section discusses the different rules which apply to general and to special powers in these circumstances.[41]

An unexercised general power simply leaves the property where it was, in the hands of the donor. An ineffective exercise[42] of a general power, however, raises the question of whether the donee intended to assume control over the property for more than the limited purpose of exercising the power. If so, the donee may have "captured" the property for his own estate.[43] Commentators have identified four factors which may convince

---

[36] *See, e.g.*, Barret's Ex'r v. Barret, 179 S.W. 396 (Ky. 1915) (appointment of $1000 out of a $150,000 trust was illusory).

[37] *See, e.g.*, Hodges v. Stegall, 83 S.W.2d 901 (Tenn. 1935) (appointments of nominal amounts to some appointees were sufficient, although the power was nonexclusive).

[38] The problem may be that courts are using the nominal gift rule to avoid enforcing nonexclusive powers, which make little sense. After all, a donor who wants particular (or all) objects protected can require minimum shares. If the donor does not set minimums, perhaps the power should be deemed exclusive. The Restatement takes this approach. *See* Restatement (Second) of Prop. § 21.2.

[39] *See* Simes at 159.

[40] Indeed, powers may be created for tax reasons with no intention that they be exercised. This appears to have been the case in *In re* Estate of Clarkson, 226 N.W.2d 334 (Neb. 1975), discussed in § 28[C][4], *supra*.

[41] *See generally* McGovern & Kurtz at 407; Simes at 149-151, 155-157.

[42] Two common reasons for an appointment to fail are that it violates the Rule Against Perpetuities or that the appointee dies before the appointment becomes effective, so the gift lapses. The question of the validity of a power of appointment under the Rule Against Perpetuities is covered in § 51, *infra*, and the doctrine of lapse in § 45[B][2][b], *infra*.

[43] *See generally* Thomas L. Jones, *Consequences of an Ineffective Appointment—Capture*, 18 Ala. L. Rev. 229 (1966).

a court that a donee intended to capture the property:[44] a blending clause,[45] a residuary clause that is presumed to exercise a power[46] a residuary clause revealing an intent to exercise the power because the donee's estate would otherwise be insufficient to satisfy the donee's gifts, and an appointment in trust.

Talbot v. Riggs[47] illustrates the capture doctrine. Emma Keller's will created a trust with various life estates for her relatives and gave her brother, Thomas, a general testamentary power to appoint the remainder. Thomas' will, in turn, attempted to exercise the power by naming three alternative takers as trustees for various beneficiaries. The first appointment failed because the beneficiaries did not survive the life tenants;[48] the second and third failed for violating the Rule Against Perpetuities.[49] The court held that Thomas' attempts to create trusts showed an intention to remove the property from Emma's trust.[50] The captured property became part of Thomas' estate.[51]

The capture doctrine does not apply to unexercised general powers, because the donee has shown no intention to claim the property. On the other hand, capture may apply even though the donor created a gift in default, because the doctrine focuses on the *donee's* intention.[52] The doctrine does not apply to special powers because these donees do not have the authority to appoint to themselves.

When special powers remain unexercised, or an attempted exercise fails, the property normally passes to the takers in default. If there are no takers in default, the property usually will go equally to the objects of the power, rather than return to the donor. Courts may use either of two theories to reach this result. Some courts imply a gift in default to the objects.[53] The

---

[44] Waggoner, Alexander, Fellows & Gallanis at 1020-21.

[45] A blending clause is one which mixes the donee's own property and the property subject to the power. Such a clause was used in First Nat'l Bank v. Walker, 607 S.W.2d 469 (Tenn. 1980), discussed in § 39[A], *supra*.

[46] Section 39[A], *supra*, discusses whether a residuary clause exercises a power.

[47] 191 N.E. 360 (Mass. 1934).

[48] For a discussion of when gifts lapse because beneficiaries do not survive, see § 45[B][2][b], *infra*.

[49] The question of the validity of a power of appointment under the Rule Against Perpetuities is reserved for § 51, *infra*.

[50] *But see* Northern Trust Co. v. Porter, 13 N.E.2d 487 (Ill. 1938) (an attempted appointment in trust did not capture the property for the donee's estate).

[51] The court treated Thomas as the creator of a trust which failed for want of beneficiaries, so Thomas' trustee held the property in a resulting trust for Thomas' estate, which got the property. Resulting trusts, which resemble reversions, are discussed in § 34[C], *supra*.

[52] Opening a gift-in-default clause with the following language may protect against the capture doctrine: "To the extent the donee does not expressly exercise this power of appointment effectively, ..." Waggoner, Alexander, Fellows & Gallanis at 1021.

[53] *See, e.g.,* Loring v. Marshall, 484 N.E.2d 1315 (Mass. 1985). In this case, the donor had named takers in default, but in a prior decision, the court had held they had not met the condition precedent to their taking. Massachusetts Inst. of Technology v. Loring, 99 N.E.2d 854 (Mass. 1951).

notion is that the donor intended the objects to take, unless the donee decided otherwise. Other courts say the donee has a "power in trust," sometimes called "an imperative power," with a duty to exercise the power.[54] Because the donee has violated that obligation, a court will impose a constructive trust[55] on those who would otherwise take, in favor of the objects of the power. In most cases, either theory gets the property to the objects, equally.[56]

§ 40 Drafting Powers of Appointment

Careful drafting can avoid most of the problems discussed in this chapter.[1] The drafter for a donor has a special opportunity: the draft can both provide choices for donees and protect against a donee's faulty exercise. Examining a draft is one way to see how the doctrine affects individual estate plans.

Consider the following draft as a vehicle for understanding powers of appointment, rather than as a model to be copied. Assume the clause appears in a revocable living trust agreement establishing a life estate for the settlor's son, Michael. This language is intended to give Michael a special power of appointment over the trust principal remaining after his death.

The Restatement takes an implied gift approach. Because the theory is not appropriate for all "non-general" powers, its application is restricted to those powers in which the objects are in a positively defined limited class. *See* Restatement (Second) of Prop. § 24.2 cmt. a. The Restatement's terminology is discussed in § 37[C][1], *supra*. Courts also imply gifts of future interests in some situations. *See* § 44[B], *infra*.

[54] *See, e.g.*, Daniel v. Brown, 159 S.E. 209 (Va. 1931).

[55] A constructive trust is a remedy to avoid unjust enrichment. For other applications and discussion, see §§ 10, 12[F], and 28[C][1], *supra*.

[56] The theory has mattered when a donor has required the donee to choose *one* member of the class of objects. *Compare* Bridgewater v. Turner, 29 S.W.2d 659 (Tenn. 1930) (using an implied gift theory to give the property to all of the objects), *with* Waterman v. New York Life Ins. & Trust Co., 142 N.E. 668 (N.Y. 1923) (applying an imperative power theory, but leaving the power unexercised, because the document creating the power specifically restricted its exercise to benefit *only* one member of the class, and dividing the corpus among the entire class would defeat the donor's intent).

Courts should ask who the donor probably would prefer to benefit: all of the objects sharing equally or the alternative takers if the appointment fails. This approach is similar to the one used in dependent relative revocation cases, discussed in § 9[D], *supra*, where courts must choose a "second best" solution.

[1] For a short list of ideas, see Ronald C. Link, *Revised Provisions of Restatement of Property Provide Important Lessons for Estate Planners*, 13 Est. Plan. 20, 25-26 (1986).

Michael's[2] Special Power of Appointment

Upon Michael's death, the trustee shall pay all remaining principal and undistributed income, or hold it, according to the directions Michael makes under the special power of appointment created by this section. Michael may make such appointment by a written instrument he has signed and delivered to the trustee during Michael's lifetime but after my death or by a provision in a will executed after my death and specifically referring to the power created by this trust agreement.[3] Michael may appoint to, or for the benefit of, any one or more of his lineal descendants,[4] in whatever shares he deems appropriate.[5] He may not appoint to himself, his estate, his creditors or the creditors of his estate.[6]

He may appoint the property outright or in trust according to whatever terms he chooses as if the property were his own, subject to the limitations imposed by this section with regard to the persons who may benefit from this trust. In particular, but not by way of further limiting his discretion, he may: create new powers of appointment and new present or future interests in any appointee; create new powers of appointment in any other person living at my death (including a trustee), except that such new power may not be exercised in favor of persons other than the objects of this power; and impose spendthrift or other lawful restrictions.[7]

---

[2] This form is both personalized to the individual client and relatively easy to understand. Word processing programs allow drafters to offer documents that are much more personalized than was practical in the past. Using the name "Michael" builds rapport with the client, whose son is not a faceless "child of the settlor." Personalizing the draft, using shorter sentences with active verbs, and avoiding legalisms like "hereinbefore" all help keep the client engaged through the difficult task of reviewing the document.

[3] This power is both presently exercisable and testamentary. Requiring the donee to wait until after the donor's death before exercising the power takes advantage of the postponed decisionmaking feature of powers. The restrictions on how to exercise the power are intended to make accidental exercise unlikely.

[4] The term "lineal descendants" should be defined elsewhere in the document. For discussion of whether, without such a definition, non-marital or adopted children are covered by such a term, see § 44[E][2], *infra*.

[5] Limited to his lineal descendants, Michael has a special power. That class of objects, however, might be narrower than necessary to fulfill the settlor's objectives. Michael cannot give the property to his wife, or to the spouses of his children, or to charity. Because any of those might be acceptable to the client, you should ask. If the client wants the tax benefits of a special power, but otherwise had no limits for where the money went, he could create a non-general power authorizing Michael to appoint to anyone except himself, his estate, his creditors or the creditors of his estate.

The "one or more" and "whatever shares" language makes this an exclusive power. The "for the benefit of" language ties into the donee's ability to create trusts.

The power would have been general if it had read "my [meaning the settlor's] lineal descendants." Limiting the class of objects to a defined group does not necessarily create a special power. You must also be sure that the donee does not fall within the group.

[6] Although the donee can only appoint to his lineal descendants, this sentence reassures the IRS that this is not a general power of appointment for tax purposes.

[7] This paragraph is intended to overcome those cases which have read special powers narrowly. Notice also the "for the benefit of" language in the first paragraph. The authority

To the extent that Michael does not expressly exercise this power of appointment effectively, the trustee shall distribute the property subject to this power according to the terms of section III, B, 2, of this trust agreement. [8]

When it later becomes time to exercise a power of appointment, donees face some drafting problems as well. They must be particularly careful to follow the rules the donor established. Those rules might relate to how the power is exercised, who the permissible appointees are, or what kinds of interests the donee can create. Drafting a document to exercise a power, without referring to the document which created the power, is very risky. In addition, donees of general testamentary powers or special powers must be particularly careful to avoid violating the Rule Against Perpetuities. [9] Because some donors do not create obstacles to the unintended exercise of powers, donees may want to try to pick up property subject to powers they do not even know about. General blending clauses, while inadvisable as a way of exercising known powers, can achieve a "blind" exercise. [10]

When used creatively and precisely, powers of appointment are particularly valuable devices. They allow clients to develop adaptable estate plans, able to change to meet new circumstances. Commonly used in tax planning, they also can serve the needs of a wide variety of clients of modest means.

---

to create new powers in other people allows the donee to establish discretionary trusts and give invasion powers to trust advisors and guardians. For discussion of these issues, see § 13[A], *supra*. The requirement that the donee of any new power be someone living at the settlor's death avoids conflict with the Rule Against Perpetuities. For discussion, see § 51[B][1], *infra*.

[8] Often, describing the gift in default is a complicated affair. When powers are part of more general dispository clauses, the powers may get lost in the detail. Donees (and their lawyers) may be unaware the powers exist. Documents should be drafted to make it as easy as possible for future readers to find and understand the various parts.

Cross-referencing to another section is one way to avoid overwhelming a power of appointment clause with other information. If possible, the details of the gift in default should follow directly after this clause. As with all drafting, you cannot assume that the primary beneficiaries will survive until the time of distribution. Alternative gifts are advisable. For more on survivorship, see § 45[B][2], *infra*.

[9] *See* § 51[B][2], *infra*.

[10] *See, e.g.*, John H. Martin, *The Draftsman Views Wills for a Young Family*, 54 N.C. L. Rev. 277, 294 (1976); Edward H. Rabin, *Blind Exercises of Powers of Appointment*, 51 Cornell L.Q. 1, 9 (1965) (recommending using a separate clause, rather than relying upon the residuary clause). Some observers caution against blind exercises because of the nasty surprises they can generate. *See* Edward C. Halbach, Jr. et al., *Use and Drafting of Powers of Appointment*, 1 Real Prop. Prob. & Tr. J. 307, 318 (1966).

Chapter 11

PROBLEMS OF INTERPRETATION

§ 41 Introduction

This chapter discusses a number of doctrines governing what documents mean. Some of these doctrines developed as part of wills law, some as part of future interests law, and others as statutory responses to perceived inadequacies in each. They appear together here to illustrate further how the law regarding probate and nonprobate transfers is collapsing (unevenly) toward one integrated whole.[1] Because this is a long chapter, you might benefit from reviewing the Table of Contents to see the relationships between the various sections.

This section identifies two issues which pervade the entire chapter. First, we ask what it is courts think (or say) they are doing when they attribute meaning to documents. Second, we examine the question of how courts handle mistakes, with particular attention to what evidence is admissible to help courts with their task. Later sections address difficulties in identifying beneficiaries, and what happens when circumstances change between the time a document is drafted and the time the language applies.

[A] The Donor's Intention [?]

Deeply imbedded within our law is the notion that a court seeking the meaning of a donative document should attempt to identify the donor's intention. One court's image captures the central point: "We first place ourselves in the armchair of the testator and remember that the intention of the testator is the polestar in the construction of every will."[2] The canonization of "intention" causes confusion, however, as courts struggle to attribute to donors subjective intentions they almost certainly never had.

The problem is that identifying intention in a particular case can be very difficult. A document's language often will be the best evidence courts have,[3] so that is where they will begin. The document, however, might apply in a situation unanticipated at the time it was drafted.[4] Even if the

---

[1] *See generally* John H. Langbein, *The Nonprobate Revolution and the Future of the Law of Succession*, 97 Harv. L. Rev. 1108 (1984).

[2] *In re* Estate of Houston, 201 A.2d 592, 595 (Pa. 1964).

[3] This statement applies with special force if we are examining a will. We cannot ask a dead testator, "Now, what did you mean here?" In some cases, we might have other persons' memories of what the testator said, but those memories may be clouded by time and self-interest.

[4] *See, e.g.*, Engle v. Siegel, 377 A.2d 892 (N.J. 1977), discussed in § 41[B][2], *infra*.

language is clear, the donor may not have understood it.[5] Finally, of course, the language may not be clear, either because it is tangled, or because when applied to the real world, it does not fit.

When documents fail, courts often look elsewhere. Sometimes extrinsic evidence can help identify what the donor wanted, sometimes it cannot. Lawyers have a special responsibility to push clients to decide among foreseeable options, to help clients understand their plans, and to draft documents which accomplish the clients' goals.[6]

The difficulty (or impossibility) of finding a donor's subjective intent has led some observers to suggest that any such search is misguided and produces uneven results. When sufficient objective evidence is not available, Professor Fellows would apply an "imputed intent" doctrine, showing a preference for families while attributing to donors an intention to do what a competent estate planner would in the circumstances.[7] Professor Robertson would abandon the search for, and language of, intent, and replace it with "circumstanced external standards for reading and interpreting donative documents."[8] At least in some situations, Professor Ascher would impose rules for the sake of having a clear answer, and not worry about testator's intentions.[9]

Despite such criticisms, the goal of finding and following a donor's intention probably will guide courts for some time to come. In the future, however, they may become less inclined to speak about intent when it is clear to everyone that we cannot know whether the donor even had considered the point in question. More courts may come to articulate the policy bases for their decisions, rather than hiding in the mist of "the donor's intention." As you consider decisions seeking to find meaning in language, ask yourself how honest each court has been, with itself and with its readers, about what it has done.

[B] Mistake and Extrinsic Evidence

One way or another, mistakes prompt the search for intent. Perhaps a will's language is confused; perhaps a beneficiary in a trust is misnamed; perhaps a codicil is incomplete. In these situations, courts face two important questions: Is extrinsic evidence admissible? If so, what types of

---

[5] Consider how well informed the testator supposedly was in Proctor v. Lacy, 160 N.E. 441, 443 (Mass. 1928): "The will was drafted by a member of the bar of many years' standing and experience, and it is fair to suppose that the *testator . . .* had in mind the interpretation of similar words and clauses in cases decided in this commonwealth." (emphasis added).

[6] *See generally* Roger W. Andersen, *Informed Decisionmaking in an Office Practice*, 28 B.C. L. Rev. 225 (1987).

[7] Mary L. Fellows, *In Search of Donative Intent*, 73 Iowa L. Rev. 611, 612-614, 657-658 (1988).

[8] James L. Robertson, *Myth and Reality—Or, Is It "Perception and Taste"?—In the Reading of Donative Documents*, 61 Fordham L. Rev. 1045, 1054 (1993).

[9] Mark L. Ascher, *The 1990 Uniform Probate Code: Older and Better, or More Like the Internal Revenue Code?*, 77 Minn. L. Rev. 639 (1993).

evidence? On both counts, there has been a push toward liberalization, but the movement is uneven.[10]

Courts traditionally have been reluctant to look beyond the language of a document when they try to determine its meaning. They may give effect to the "plain meaning"[11] of particular technical words, or stretch a bit further and consider the whole document. In either case, however, they would not consider extrinsic evidence. The problem is that what is plain to a particular judge may not be so plain to other people. Understanding the bigger picture, however, requires a court to admit the extrinsic evidence, and courts traditionally have been unwilling to do so unless that evidence is needed to resolve ambiguity.

This section first distinguishes between two types of ambiguity, and then addresses whether courts are ought to be reforming mistaken donative transfers.

[1] Patent and Latent Ambiguities

A patent ambiguity is one apparent from the face of a document, while a latent ambiguity is one only discoverable by considering evidence extrinsic to the document. For example, "I give Arnie one of my two houses in Toledo" creates a patent ambiguity. The document itself reveals that we cannot tell which house to give Arnie. Following the view that one ought not look beyond the document, some courts faced with a patent ambiguity have excluded extrinsic evidence and relied solely on rules of construction to resolve the problem.[12] In contrast, "I give $5,000 to my cousin in Urbana" looks fine until we learn that the donor had one cousin in Urbana, Ohio, and one in Urbana, Illinois. Then we have a latent ambiguity. The direction of the law, but perhaps not yet the majority position, is to allow extrinsic evidence to resolve ambiguity, whether patent or latent.[13]

It can get a bit circular trying to decide whether one is admitting evidence to identify ambiguity or to resolve it. One authority concludes, "[a]lthough

---

[10] *See generally* Haskell at 105-107; McGovern & Kurtz at 241-251. For detailed discussion, see John H. Langbein & Lawrence W. Waggoner, *Reformation of Wills on the Ground of Mistake: Change of Direction in American Law?*, 130 U. Pa. L. Rev. 521 (1982) [cited below as Langbein & Waggoner].

[11] Mahoney v. Grainger, 186 N.E. 86 (Mass. 1933) ("heirs" given technical meaning). Massachusetts reaffirmed its adherence to the plain meaning rule in Flannery v. McNamara, 738 N.E.2d 739 (Mass. 2000), discussed in § 41[B][2], *infra*.

Professors Langbein and Waggoner refer to this rule by its effect; they call it the "no-extrinsic-evidence rule." *See* Langbein & Waggoner, 130 U. Pa. L. Rev. at 521. *See generally* Andrew W. Cornelison, *Dead Man Talking: Are Courts Ready to Listen? The Erosion of the Plain Meaning Rule*, 35 Real Prop. Prob. & Tr. J. 811 (2001).

[12] The identity of beneficiaries may also be subject to patent ambiguity. If rules of construction do not help, a gift may fail because it cannot be understood. *See, e.g.*, Johnson v. Johnson, 229 S.W.2d 743 (Ky. 1950) (will devising all of testator's property to her "children who have no homes" or "means of living" failed because the court could not determine which children would qualify as a beneficiary). *See* James A. Henderson, Jr., *Mistake and Fraud in Wills—Part I: A Comparative Analysis of Existing Law*, 47 B.U. L. Rev. 303, 358-380 (1967).

[13] *See* Haskell at 107; Restatement (Third) of Prop. § 11.1 cmt. a.

the question posed is usually whether extrinsic evidence is 'admissible,' the trial court usually hears it, and the strength of the evidence may determine the weight it receives."[14] Once a court knows the story, persuasive evidence may overcome technical rules.[15] Such was the situation in *In re Estate of Gibbs*,[16] a case which nicely illustrates latent ambiguities.

George and Lena Gibbs died within about a month of each other, each leaving a will giving a bequest to "Robert J. Krause, now of 4708 North 46th Street, Milwaukee, Wisconsin." The trial court allowed evidence which showed that George and Lena did not know Robert J. Krause. They did, however, know a Robert W. Krause, who had been a longtime employee of George. Evidently, someone picked out the wrong Robert Krause from a telephone book. The problem was that under traditional rules, this evidence should not have been admitted. There was no ambiguity here: the wills clearly gave property to Robert J. Krause and that person lived where the wills said he did. Many courts would be unwilling to second-guess the testators' clearly expressed desires.[17]

Despite the absence of a latent ambiguity, this court could not ignore the clear evidence of mistake. It concluded that details of identification, like middle initials and addresses, "should not be accorded such sanctity as to frustrate an otherwise clearly demonstrable intent."[18] It allowed the evidence and disregarded the mistaken details.

The case would have been easier had the wills created a latent ambiguity. If they had read "to Robert Krause," the language, when applied to the real world, would have yielded more than one person as a possible taker. If they had read "to my longtime employee Robert J. Krause," the language would have described no one in the real world.[19] In either case, courts would allow

---

[14] McGovern & Kurtz at 245 (footnote omitted).

[15] For a thoughtful article encouraging courts to consider facts at the time a document is being interpreted (rather than only the circumstances of its execution), see William M. McGovern, *Facts and Rules in the Construction of Wills*, 26 UCLA L. Rev. 285 (1978).

[16] 111 N.W.2d 413 (Wis. 1961).

[17] Courts sometimes have used the "personal usage" exception to justify ignoring clear identifications. The exception applies when a testator has called someone by a name other than their own and then uses the "personal usage" name in a will. *See* Moseley v. Goodman, 195 S.W. 590 (Tenn. 1917) (Testator had called a Mrs. Trimble by the name "Mrs. Moseley" and left money to "Mrs. Moseley." Mrs. Trimble took the money).

[18] *Gibbs*, 111 N.W.2d at 418.

[19] In cases where a description is partially correct, courts often allow striking the incorrect part, leaving a clear identification. Under this approach, a court would strike initial "J." and leave "my longtime employee, Robert Krause." *Compare* Breckheimer v. Kraft, 273 N.E.2d 468 (Ill. App. 1971) (Will gave property to "Raymond Schneikert and Mable Schneikert his wife," but Raymond had divorced Mable and married Evelyn. In response to evidence that the testator intended a gift to Evelyn, the court struck the reference to Mable and left only "Raymond . . . and his wife."). The doctrine allowing a court to strike an incorrect part is sometimes called *falsa demonstratio non nocet*.

While most courts would never dream of adding language to a will, *Breckheimer* manipulated the doctrine, allowing the striking of language to give Evelyn a gift as effectively as if the court had inserted her name into the will.

some extrinsic evidence to resolve the ambiguity. They disagree, however, about when to allow evidence of a testator's declarations. Some courts will admit evidence of the testator's declarations only when two or more things meet the will's description, but not when there is a partial description.[20]

One modern decision went a long way toward scrapping narrow rules, but then got tangled up in the notion that extrinsic evidence should not be allowed to contradict the clear language of a will. *Estate of Russell v. Quinn*[21] involved a holographic will written on both sides of a small card.[22] Thelma Russell left a coin and diamonds to her niece, Georgia, and everything else "to Chester H. Quinn and Roxy Russell." Roxy was a dog, and dogs cannot own property. Georgia, the intestate heir, argued that because Roxy's gift failed, Georgia should get half of the residue.[23] Chester argued that Thelma must have intended him to get her assets, with an obligation to care for Roxy.[24] Georgia won.

The opinion in *Russell* starts well, with the court rejecting both the plain meaning rule and the notion that patent and latent ambiguities should be treated differently. The court said extrinsic evidence is admissible under a two-stage process, which first considers evidence of the circumstances in which the will was made.[25] If, in light of that evidence, two or more plausible readings appear, evidence regarding the testator's intention is then admissible to resolve the problem. On the other hand, if, knowing the circumstances, a court finds the will's language not susceptible to multiple meanings, the extrinsic evidence showing an intention different from the written words will be inadmissible. That overall approach is typical of modern opinions.

The weakness in the opinion is its insistence that, even though Roxy was a dog, the gift to Chester and Roxy is not reasonably susceptible to meaning Thelma intended a trust for Roxy's care. According to the court, Chester's interpretation would contradict "a disposition which by its language leaves the residuum in equal shares to [Chester] and the dog."[26] Therefore, other evidence, which tended to show Thelma wanted to limit the size of Georgia's gift and wanted to avoid intestacy, was inadmissible. "Interpreting the provisions relating to [Thelma's] residuary estate in accordance with the only meaning to which they are reasonably susceptible," the court concluded

---

[20] *See* McGovern & Kurtz at 242-243.

[21] 444 P.2d 353 (Cal. 1968).

[22] Holographic wills are notorious litigation-breeders. *See* Lord Neaves, *The Jolly Testator Who Makes His Own Will*, in William Prosser, The Judicial Humorist 246 (1952). Execution rules for holographs are discussed in § 7[B][3], *supra*.

[23] Chester might have argued that because he was the surviving residuary taker, he should get Roxy's share. See the discussion in § 45[B][2][b][i], *infra* regarding lapsed gifts in residuary clauses.

[24] "Honorary" trusts of this sort are discussed in § 12[C], *supra*.

[25] *Russell*, 444 P.2d at 358-359.

[26] *Russell*, 444 P. 2d at 363.

that Thelma "intended to make a disposition of all of the residue . . . to [Chester] and the dog in equal shares; therefore, as tenants in common."[27]

The court's reading of Thelma's will seems odd. First, the will says nothing about equal shares. Second, Thelma was a competent person, who owned rental property. Why would a court believe that she actually intended Roxy to get a half share as a tenant in common? Treating a will's language as the starting point for interpreting the document makes sense. Insisting upon an implausible reading does not.

Whatever its weaknesses, *Russell* moved the law in the right direction. Courts are allowing more extrinsic evidence, more often.[28] There is some danger that this approach may encourage litigation because it necessarily opens up more written language to challenge. Given the law's history of overreliance on words, however, the change should be worth the cost.

[2] Interpretation or Reformation?

Courts faced with mistakes in drafting often purport to "interpret" or "construe" a document in order to correct the mistake.[29] One reason they resort to this approach is that traditional rules preclude reforming wills.[30] To do so would give testamentary effect to language not put through the Statute of Wills wringer. In a comprehensive and influential article, Professors Langbein and Waggoner propose that courts recognize a reformation doctrine for wills.[31] The Restatement has endorsed their approach.[32] Not only would such a development allow courts to be more honest about what they are doing,[33] but it would also bring wills law more into

---

[27] *Russell*, 444 P. 2d at 363.

[28] *See also* Erickson v. Erickson, 716 A.2d 92 (Conn. 1998) (allowing extrinsic evidence to show a testator's intent that the will he executed two days before his wedding was not intended to be revoked by marriage).

[29] Traditional analysis distinguishes interpretation, which seeks to identify parties' intentions, from construction, which offers legal rules to fill gaps when we cannot identify a particular intention. *See* Scoles, Halbach, Link & Roberts at 198. Increasingly, the concepts have merged. *See* Restatement of Prop. § 241 cmt. e.

For an example of a court which stretched "interpretation" into *de facto* reformation, see Engle v. Siegel, 377 A.2d 892 (N.J. 1977) (Applying New Jersey's "probable intent" doctrine, the court interpreted a residuary gift to the testator's mother to mean a gift to her as "representative" of her family.).

[30] *See* Atkinson at 808.

[31] Langbein & Waggoner, 130 U. Pa. L. Rev. at 577-590.

For additional commentary, see Joseph W. deFuria, Jr., *Mistakes in Wills Resulting from Scriveners' Errors: The Argument for Reformation*, 40 Cath. U. L. Rev. 1 (1990); Mary L. Fellows, *In Search of Donative Intent*, 73 Iowa L. Rev. 611 (1988); Clark Shores, *Reforming the Doctrine of No Reformation*, 26 Gonz. L. Rev. 475 (1990-91); James L. Robertson, *Myth and Reality—Or, Is It "Perception and Taste"?—In the Reading of Donative Documents*, 61 Fordham L. Rev. 1045 (1993); Pamela R. Champine, *My Will Be Done: Accommodating the Erring and the Atypical Testator,* 80 Neb. L. Rev. 387 (2002).

[32] Restatement (Third) of Prop. § 12.1.

[33] Langbein and Waggoner note that "a reformation doctrine would often constitute less an innovation in principle than in candor." Langbein & Waggoner, 130 U. Pa. L. Rev. at 524.

line with the law of will substitutes. To indicate the tensions the law is facing, this section discusses two illustrative cases (one about a trust, the other, a will). Each involves perhaps the most frequent source of litigation about documents' meanings—documents which fail to anticipate what actually happens.

Despite their functional similarity to wills, trusts have developed under their own set of rules, largely unencumbered by the law of wills.[34] One example of that different treatment is that courts can reform trusts to correct mistakes. Consider *Brinker v. Wobaco Trust Ltd.*[35] Norman and Maureen Brinker established an unfunded living trust and a pour-over will.[36] The trust named Norman as settlor and named "the issue of the settlor" as beneficiaries of the principal. At the time, the Brinkers had two children, Cynthia and Brenda. Maureen died, and money was held in her estate for a while, awaiting payment to the living trust. Later, Norman married Magrit, and they had two children, Christina and Mark. In the context of Norman's divorce from Magrit and its accompanying revelations, the two children from the first marriage sought reformation of the trust to exclude the two children from the second marriage.

Cynthia and Brenda offered testimony from their father and from the lawyer who drafted both the trust and their mother's will. Both supported the view that Norman and Maureen intended the remainder to go to the issue of their marriage. Norman said he and Maureen knew she could not have more children and they intended the trust to be for Cynthia and Brenda. More than likely, no one thought about the fact that Norman might have more children. Norman also said he did not then know what the word "settlor" meant and the lawyer had not told them. The lawyer testified that if the trust were drafted so as to include other children, he had made a mistake.[37] The trial court refused to admit this evidence.

An appeal won a new trial on the ground that trusts can be reformed. The appellate court used broad language: "The fact that the written instrument is couched in unambiguous language, or that the parties knew what words were used and were aware of their ordinary meaning, or that they were negligent in failing to discover the mistake before signing the

---

The authors give examples of several types of cases in which courts effectively reform wills: resolving ambiguity, following the "personal usage" doctrine, implying future interests to fill gaps, invalidating "sham" wills, applying dependent relative revocation, and reforming to cure violations of the Rule Against Perpetuities or to gain a tax benefit. Langbein & Waggoner, 130 U. Pa. L. Rev. at 528-566. They might have added cases allowing beneficiaries to modify the terms of a testamentary trust.

[34] Compare the relative liberality of the rules discussed in Chapter 4 (Trusts) with the narrowness of the traditional approaches covered in Chapter 3 (Wills).

[35] 610 S.W.2d 160 (Tex. Civ. App. 1980).

[36] For discussion of this device, see § 16, *supra*.

[37] The lawyer may be liable in malpractice, either for having failed to explain the document or for having used the wrong language. Presumably, damages would include the cost of bringing the reformation action. *See* Roger W. Andersen, *Informed Decisionmaking in an Office Practice*, 28 B.C. L. Rev. 225 (1987).

instrument, will not preclude relief by reformation."[38] The court also rejected the argument that because the living trust would get assets from Maureen's estate, the trust had become "testamentary" and not subject to reformation.[39] The trust's form saved it from the no-reformation rule.[40]

Focus on form had the opposite result in *Flannery v. McNamara*.[41] William White died leaving a will giving all his property to his wife, Katherine, who had died almost two years before he did. There were no alternative takers identified. William had no children, so the property went by intestacy to cousins identified by a genealogical search. His wife's sisters sought to introduce extrinsic evidence that William intended to give the property to them if Katherine did not survive him. Because the case involved a will (instead of a trust), the Massachusetts court refused to depart from the plain meaning rule barring extrinsic evidence to construe unambiguous wills. Relying primarily on a "floodgates" argument, the court also declined an invitation to adopt the Restatement of Property's proposal to allow reformation of wills for mistake.[42] For this purpose at least, the court said wills are different from intervivos trusts.

In contrast, Massachusetts does allow reformation of will s to achieve a testator's objective of minimizing taxes.[43] On the other hand, because tax benefits often come at the cost of other planning objectives, perhaps courts should be more reluctant to assume that testators will come down on the side of saving taxes.[44] Clearly, these are questions that will continue to attract attention of courts and legislatures.

The current UPC, while not providing for reformation, allows that option. Section 2-601 notes that the Code's rules of construction apply "[i]n the absence of a finding of contrary intention." The earlier version had referred to "contrary intention indicated by the will." The comments explain that "[t]he striking of this sentence removes [a] possible impediment to the

---

[38] *Brinker*, 610 S.W.2d at 164.

[39] *Brinker*, 610 S.W.2d at 165. Maureen's will did not incorporate the trust terms. This is one example of the importance of avoiding the incorporation by reference doctrine when analyzing pour-over wills and their accompanying living trusts. For more discussion, see §§ 8[B] (incorporation by reference) & 16 (trusts and pour-over wills), *supra*.

[40] The fact that Norman was alive and could testify as to what he had meant made reformation easier. However, the suit also claimed that Maureen was a co-settlor, and she was dead. Moreover, courts allow reformation of living trusts even when the settlor had died. *See, e.g.*, Roos v. Roos, 203 A.2d 140 (Del. Ch. 1964) (the court, in 1964, reformed a trust established in 1936, although the settlor had died in 1939); Pond v. Pond, 678 N.E.2d 1321 (Mass. 1997) (trust reformed to provide for settlor's wife when she survived him).

[41] 738 N.E.2d 739 (Mass. 2000).

[42] *See* Restatement (Third) Prop. §12.2. Perhaps the court would have been more willing to consider reformation if the mistake claim had been based on more than "he wanted to give it to us." A concurring opinion argued the court should keep the door open for reformation in an appropriate case. 738 N.E.2d 748 (Greaney, J., concurring in the result).

[43] *See* Putman v. Putman, 628 N.E.2d 1351 (1997). Not surprisingly, the Restatement endorses this view. Restatement (Third) Prop. § 12.2.

[44] *See* Roger W. Andersen, *Informed Decisionmaking in an Office Practice*, 28 B.C. L. Rev. 225, 237-239 (1987).

judicial adoption of a general reformation doctrine for wills . . . ."[45] Courts taking that step would be moving with the tide of continuing integration of the law surrounding probate and nonprobate transfers.

§ 42 Independent Significance

Courts must also rely upon extrinsic evidence in many situations not involving mistake. Hardly thinking about it, they identify people ("my children") and property ("my house on Maple Street") by looking at evidence outside of the will. Other situations require more obvious references to additional information. Suppose Akiko's will reads "all the books in my library to Mitsuo Matsushita" or "$500 to each of the members of the Galesburg Sewing Circle." In order to interpret these gifts, a court might rely upon a library catalog or an after-death inventory, a sewing circle mailing list or a dues record. Courts routinely consider such evidence under the doctrine of independent significance.[1]

The key to the doctrine is the notion of significance independent of the will. Presumably, Akiko would not move books in or out of a library in order to change the gift to Mitsuo. Akiko would not invite people to join a sewing circle in order to qualify under the will. These facts have a separate, non-testamentary significance. Reference to them does no violence to the policies behind the Statute of Wills.[2] On the other hand, some references clearly have no significance other than effecting a disposition. Suppose a will reads "to those persons listed on a paper I will leave in my desk." The list has no significance apart from the will, and would not be admissible under the doctrine of independent significance.[3]

Some situations straddle the line. Suppose Naomi leaves a will which gives "everything in my right-hand desk drawer to Beth and everything in my left-hand desk drawer to Andrea." The designation might be innocent. Perhaps Naomi kept stamps on the right and coins on the left, and Beth collected stamps, while Andrea collected coins. In that case, a court ought to allow the gifts by analogy to ones of "my coin collection."[4] If the evidence showed, however, that Naomi moved things from one side to the other as she changed her mind about who should get what, the gifts should fail. In

---

[45] UPC 2-601 comment.

[1] *See* Atkinson at 394-400.

[2] For discussion of those policies, see § 7[B][1], *supra*.

[3] Depending upon the facts, the list might be incorporated into the will by reference. *See* § 8[B], *supra*. A court applying the harmless error rule might uphold the list as a testamentary document. *See* § 7[B][4][c], *supra*.

For an interesting case, see First Nat'l Bank v. Klein, 234 So. 2d 42 (Ala. 1970) (upholding, on grounds of independent significance, a gift to people named in the testator's son's will).

[4] *See, e.g., In re* Estate of Smith, 580 P.2d 754, 755 (Ariz. 1978) (allowing a gift which read, "I devise my money and coin collection . . . .").

that case, Naomi would have used the drawers to change testamentary gifts without complying with the Statute of Wills.[5]

§ 43 Class Gifts

Class gifts are a familiar part of the estate planning landscape as donors give property to groups whose membership can change after the time of drafting.[1] This section concerns two fundamental questions which apply to all class gifts. First, what is a "class"? The question is important because rules often apply differently to class gifts, as opposed to gifts to individuals. Second, when does a class "close," so that its maximum membership is fixed? This question matters because class closing rules often determine which potential beneficiaries take the property and whether the gift survives the Rule Against Perpetuities.

[A] What Is a Class?

Most class gifts are easily recognizable, like gifts to "children" or "issue." Some are not. On the margin, courts seeking to identify class gifts ask two related questions: Was the testator "group minded"? Did the testator intend for the size of the group to fluctuate?[2] As in many areas of the law where label tends to dictate result, however, courts often seem to work backward, from the specific facts at hand to the language. Whether they say so or not, they often look first to the consequences of applying the "class gift" label.

For example, at common law the share of an individual beneficiary who died between the time of a will's execution and the testator's death would "lapse," or fail.[3] The gift would pass, either under a residuary clause or the intestate statute. In contrast, if a predeceased beneficiary would have taken as a consequence of being a class member, surviving class members would divide the share of the predeceased class member.[4] Because of these different rules, if someone died in the interim, the residuary beneficiary and the surviving "class" members might fight about whether there was a class at all. When courts ask the familiar question, "What did the donor intend?", they are not really asking whether the donor intended a class gift in the abstract, but who, given the facts, the donor intended to benefit.

---

[5] Sometimes testators leave lists of personal property designated for various beneficiaries. Usually neither independent significance nor incorporation by reference can save such lists. UPC § 2-513 recognizes them in some circumstances. Section 8, *supra*, discusses the UPC provision.

[1] *See generally* Bergin & Haskell at 136-148; Simes at 204-213. For comprehensive coverage, see Simes & Smith at chs. 20-23.

[2] *See* Bergin & Haskell at 136-137; Simes at 204.

[3] Today, an "antilapse" statute might save the deceased person's share for relatives of that person. If a statute does not apply, however, the common law rule still applies. *See* § 45[B][2][b], *infra*.

[4] In practice this characteristic works like the survivorship feature of joint tenancy. *See* § 18, *supra*. For discussion of whether antilapse statutes change this result, see § 45[B][2][b][i], *infra*.

Consider *Sullivan v. Sullivan*,[5] in which Kathleen left a gift, simplified, "to my nephews Marshall and David, and to my niece Martha, in equal shares, that is one-third each." Marshall predeceased Kathleen, and the question was what happened to his gift. In the abstract, both naming the individuals and identifying fractional shares indicate that the testator intended individual gifts, rather than a class gift.[6] On the other hand, Kathleen had drafted the will herself and this clause effectively functioned as a residuary clause. If Marshall's gift failed, it would pass by intestacy.[7] In this situation, the court found ambiguity and allowed extrinsic evidence.[8] That evidence showed that Marshall, David, and Martha were the children of one of Kathleen's brothers. Kathleen was particularly close to that whole family, but did not get along with her other brother and his family, who would share any intestate gift. Rather than allowing Marshall's death to create a partial intestacy, the court found Kathleen had created a class gift, so the surviving class members took.[9]

[B] When Does a Class Close?

Virtually everyone who has attended college has had the experience of being shut out of an academic class which closed. Either the size of the classroom or limits set by the instructor fixed a maximum for how many students could enroll. The same idea applies to class gifts. Class closing rules set the maximum size of a class. Just as students can drop out of academic classes, so can members drop out of donative classes, making them smaller. The class closing rules, then, do not establish the exact size of a class, but only its ceiling. Donative classes can close two ways, physiologically or according to the "rule of convenience."

Classes close physiologically when all the persons who can feed the class are dead.[10] For example, if a trust provides income "to Jessica's children,"

---

[5] 529 N.E.2d 890 (Mass. App. 1988).

[6] *See* Restatement of Prop. § 280.

[7] Because he left no children, the antilapse statute did not apply. Antilapse statutes are covered in § 45[B][2][b], *infra*, and intestacy in Chapter 2, *supra*.

[8] For discussion of when extrinsic evidence is admitted to resolve ambiguities, see § 41[B], *supra*.

[9] *Compare In re* Moss, [1899] 2 Ch. 314 (Eng. C.A.) There Walter left a trust share of stock in a newspaper to "E.J. Fowler and the child or children of my sister Emily . . . who shall attain the age of twenty-one years equally to be divided between them as tenants in common." E.J. died before Walter, and the question was whether Emily's children took the stock, or part of it went to residuary takers. Perhaps influenced by the notion that Walter wanted to keep the newspaper stock in the hands of one branch of the family, the court found a class gift, despite the "tenants in common" language.

[10] In general, the law conclusively presumes that living people can procreate. Some courts have allowed proof that particular individuals could not. *See, e.g.,* Brinker v. Wobaco Trust Ltd., 610 S.W.2d 160 (Tex. Civ. App. 1980). *See generally* Scott on Trusts § 340.1.

Whether or not people can have children, they can also increase the size of a class by adopting someone. For discussion of whether such an adoptee would qualify to take as a class member, see § 43[E][2], *infra*.

the class cannot grow after Jessica's death. Often, one class will have many feeders, which can only be identified by extrinsic evidence. A gift "to my nieces and nephews" would close physiologically only after the deaths of all of the donor's siblings. A gift to "Michael's grandchildren" would close physiologically only after the deaths of all of Michael's children.

Classes will close according to the rule of convenience when any class member has a right to demand possession.[11] This rule is not imposed by nature, but was created by courts as a rule of construction, seeking to anticipate a donor's probable intention.[12] The rule strikes a balance between a donor's desire to include all possible members of the class and the desire to allow distribution to those who have qualified to take. It also avoids the administrative problems that would develop if living beneficiaries took property, subject to giving some back as new class members appeared. Because income can be reallocated as new class members arrive, the rule only applies to gifts of principal. Like the students who are not first in line at registration, class members who are born[13] too late are closed out.[14]

Some examples should help your understanding of the rule of convenience. They are simply applications of the basic principle: once one class member has a right to his or her share, afterborn class members are cut out. In all cases, assume that the class feeders are alive. If they were dead, the class would be closed physiologically.

Immediate Gifts. Suppose Howard's will gave $10,000 "to Ethel's children." If Ethel has a child, the class closes at Howard's death. If Ethel has no children, the class remains open until Ethel's death, even if she later has a child who could take. This exception to the general principle is based on the theory that Howard knew Ethel had no children, so he must have intended to benefit all of her children, whenever born.[15]

Suppose Helen's will gave $3,000 "to each of my grandchildren." She has three children and three grandchildren. Because the total amount of the gift varies with the number of grandchildren, the class closes at Helen's death to allow closing of Helen's estate. This result would follow even if Helen had no grandchildren. We can neither keep the estate open until the

---

[11] A more graphic, if less formal, way of expressing this principle is to say a class closes when any member can shout, "Gimmie!"

[12] Because the rule is one of construction, evidence of a donor's contrary intention may prevent the rule's application. The evidence must be very persuasive, however, because the rule "is adhered to more closely than any other rule of construction . . . ." Dukeminier & Johanson at 778.

[13] More accurately, conceived. *See* Bergin & Haskell at 136. When it speaks about qualifying for class membership, the law typically means "conceived" when it says "born," and this text follows that convention.

[14] This result sounds harsh, but as a practical matter the rule seldom excludes people, because afterborns seldom appear. Edward C. Halbach, Jr., *Issues About Issue: Some Recurrent Class Gift Problems*, 48 Mo. L. Rev. 333, 359 & n.106 (1983).

[15] *See* Restatement (Second) of Prop. § 26.1.

class closes physiologically, nor know how many $3,000 shares to set aside for possible future grandchildren.[16]

Postponed Gifts. Suppose Rivke established a trust to pay income to "Noyich for life, remainder to Sylvia's children." At Rivke's death, Sylvia has one child, David. Before Noyich dies, Sylvia has Ricky. The class does not close until Noyich's death, when David[17] can demand distribution. Ricky shares the fund. Any of Sylvia's children born after Noyich's death are cut out.

Suppose Matilda's will gave $10,000 "to Robert's children who reach 21." Robert has one child, Maggie (3). A year later he has Peter. The class closes when Maggie reaches 21, with Maggie and Peter as class members.[18] If Maggie dies before then, the class remains open until Peter reaches 21. If, before the class closes, Robert has another child, that child would share the gift.

Suppose Samuel's will created a trust to pay income to "Ida for life, remainder to Frank's children who reach 21." At Samuel's death, Frank has one child, Ethan. At Ida's death, Ethan is 10. A year later, Casey is born. When Ethan reaches 21, the class closes to allow distribution of half of the fund to him. If Casey reaches 21, she will get the other half. If not, it will go to Ethan.

Questions about when a class closes under the rule of convenience can get complicated because they depend in part on other rules of construction. In order to know whether a particular remainderman, for example, has a right to demand distribution, one must interpret the remainder to determine whether there are any unmet conditions precedent.[19] If there are, then the remainderman cannot close the class. When analyzing a class closing problem, first interpret the grant, then see when the beneficiaries can demand distribution.

---

[16] If, instead of coming from an estate, the funds would come from a trust, this rationale would not apply. Consider *In re Earle's Estate*, 85 A.2d 90 (Pa. 1951). George's will established separate trust funds for each of his grandsons. The residuary clause established yet another trust. The court allowed a grandson born 21 years after George's death to have a separate trust set aside for him out of the ongoing residuary trust. *See also* Central Tr. Co. v. Smith, 139, 553 N.E.2d 265, 272 (Ohio 1990) (Although the trustee had made discretionary distributions to class members, the class stayed open to admit a grandchild adopted before the first mandatory distribution.).

[17] Under traditional rules of construction, David's remainder is vested. If he does not survive the life tenant Noyich, David's successors will get the remainder and can still demand distribution at the end of the life estate. For discussion of survivorship requirements, see § 45[B][2][c], *infra*.

[18] Though Peter is in the class, he can still drop out by dying before 21.

[19] On the question of how to tell whether remainders are vested or contingent, see § 35[B][2][c], *supra*. Other aspects of the problem are discussed in §§ 44 (special cautions) and 45[B][2][c] (survivorship), *infra*.

§ 44 Special Cautions

Phrases which sound lawyerlike may not be. Careless language can destroy an estate plan. This section's main priority is to help you develop a list of "phrases to avoid." When you draft or review documents, those phrases should jump off the page as ones that you should either not use, or use only with great care. Along the way, you should pick up arguments which can be helpful if you face litigation over such language.

[A] "To Delison and His Children"

Suppose Evelyn owned a farm she wanted to give to her son and grandchildren, so her will identified the farm and said it should pass "to Delison and his children."[1] Delison and his two daughters, Susan and Angela, survived Evelyn. A year later, Delison's third child, Sarah, was born. Consider some possible interpretations. Maybe Delison, Susan and Angela own the farm as joint tenants or tenants in common.[2] Maybe Delison has a fee simple.[3] Maybe Delison has a life estate, and the daughters have vested remainders, subject to open. The probable modern interpretation would give Delison, Susan and Angela tenancies in common.[4] If Delison had no children when Evelyn died,[5] most courts would give him a life estate, with a remainder in his yet unborn children.[6] The bottom line: avoid this formulation.

[B] "If Dorthea Dies Without Issue"

Just as first-year law students often cram their initial memos with legalisms in an attempt to sound like lawyers, so do novice drafters use the deadly little phrase, "dies without issue."[7] The phrase haunts in many ways.

---

[1] This language derives from *Wild's Case*, 77 Eng. Rep. 277 (K.B. 1599). *See generally* A. James Casner, *Construction of Gifts, "To A and His Children" (Herein the Rule in Wild's Case)*, 7 U. Chi. L. Rev. 438 (1940); Ronald C. Link, *The Rule in Wild's Case in North Carolina*, 55 N.C. L. Rev. 751 (1977).

[2] If this language creates a co-tenancy, modern doctrine would favor a tenancy in common. *See generally* § 18[A], *supra*.

[3] The argument would be that "and" really means "or," and that Evelyn really intended a substitutional gift. Since Delison survived, he should get everything. Had he predeceased, his children would have taken. *See In re* Parant's Will, 240 N.Y.S.2d 558 (N.Y. Surr. 1963) (rejecting this argument and finding a tenancy in common).

[4] *See* Simes at 225.

[5] Older cases asked who was alive when the will was drafted. That interpretation has changed, so that now the will reads as of the date of death.

[6] A similar bit of language to avoid is "to Blanche and the children of Delison." *See* Restatement (Second) of Prop. § 28.3.

[7] *See generally* Bergin & Haskell at 236-238; Simes at ch. 18. For comprehensive coverage, see Powell ¶¶ 340-343; Simes & Smith §§ 521-551.

First, a bit of history. When the fee tail was still in use, English courts read "if Dorthea dies without issue" to mean "if her line runs out."[8] This indefinite failure of issue construction meant that people did not "die without issue" until their last descendant died.[9] Most states now adopt a definite failure of issue construction, which means we ask if Dorthea has died leaving issue surviving her death.[10]

Another source of trouble is a dispute about whether gifts should be treated as "substitutional" or "successive."[11] Suppose George's will leaves property "to Dorthea, but if she dies without issue, to William." Some authorities say if Dorthea survives George, she gets a fee simple absolute and William gets nothing. The theory here is that "dies without issue" means "dies without issue before George dies." This is a substitutional construction; William is an alternative beneficiary of George's will. Other authorities give Dorthea a fee simple subject to an executory limitation, and William, an executory interest.[12] Under this view, the language means "dies without issue whenever Dorthea dies." This is a successive construction; William can divest Dorthea if she later dies without issue. When the gift involves a present interest, the successive construction is preferred, but not universal.[13]

The same substitutional/successive dispute applies to future interests. Suppose George inserted a life estate before the gift to Dorthea: "to Marilyn for life, remainder to Dorthea, but if she dies without issue, to William." The question again is one of timing. Some courts adopt a substitutional construction, which says the key time is Marilyn's death. If Dorthea survives Marilyn, Dorthea gets a fee simple absolute. William was an alternative taker, in case Dorthea died without issue before Marilyn.[14] Others say the critical moment is Dorthea's death and the gift is successive. If Dorthea survives Marilyn, Dorthea gets a fee simple subject to an executory limitation, and William has an executory interest. In this context,

---

[8] In England, a gift of real estate "to Dorthea, but if she dies without issue, to William" would have created a fee tail in Dorthea and a remainder in William. How the English got that construction from that language is unclear. *See* Simes at 197-198.

[9] Sometimes old rules can influence decisions long after they are abolished. *See* Hayes v. Hammond, 143 N.E.2d 693 (Mass. 1957) (interpreting an 1855 will as contemplating an indefinite failure of issue, because the rule favoring that construction had not been abolished by statute until 1888). For the view that courts should interpret documents according to modern rules, see Edward C. Halbach, Jr., *Stare Decisis and Rules of Construction in Wills and Trusts*, 52 Cal. L. Rev. 921 (1964).

[10] Another conflict surrounds what to do if Dorthea had a child, but the child died before Dorthea. The standard rule is that "dies without issue" means "dies without issue surviving her (or him)." *See* Bergin & Haskell at 237.

[11] *See generally* Simes & Smith at § 533.

[12] For discussion of these interests, see § 34[B], *supra*.

[13] *See* Restatement of Prop. § 263.

[14] If Dorthea dies with issue before Marilyn, the will provides no alternate taker. In this situation, most courts will fill the gap by implying a gift to the issue, on the theory that the donor must have intended such a result. *See* Simes at 202-203. Courts also use the implied gift theory when a donee fails to exercise a special power of appointment. *See* § 39[C], *supra*.

the preferred view is that the language creates a substitutional gift, with the failure of issue question resolved no later than the death of the life tenant. [15]

Similar construction problems arise if someone uses a phrase like "dies with issue." The question remains: When? *Pyne v. Pyne* [16] faces that problem and illustrates how the rules discussed in this section can affect dispositions. Elizabeth Pyne's will gave real estate to various family members in succession. First, her sister got a life estate. Elizabeth's daughter, Caroline, followed with another life estate. The remainder after Caroline's life estate was divided four ways among Caroline's issue (one collective share) and three brothers, John, Henry, and Charles. The brothers' remainders, however, were subject to the following condition: "if any one . . . should die leaving a descendant or descendants, said descendant or descendants to take the share his, her or their parent would have taken had he lived." [17]

Elizabeth died in 1905, leaving her children and sister. The sister died in 1914, and that same year John assigned his interest to Henry. John died in 1935, and his son, John Jr., died in 1943, leaving a daughter, Jennifer. (See Chart 11-1.) After Caroline's death without issue in 1944, Henry (as John's assignee) and Jennifer (as John's descendant) each claimed John's share.

Chart 11-1 — *Pyne v. Pyne* — Family Tree

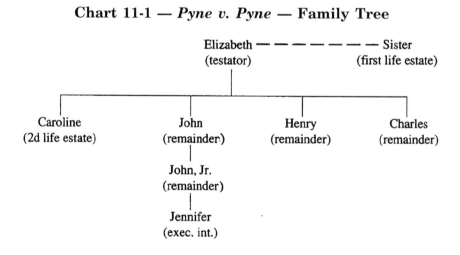

The question was when the clause divesting the brothers applied. Henry said the clause applied only if a brother died before Elizabeth (the testator). That way, the interest John assigned to Henry back in 1914 was a remainder in fee simple absolute; John had already survived Elizabeth and the divesting condition could not be met. Jennifer said the key time was

---

[15] *See* Simes at 201.

[16] 154 F.2d 297 (D.C. Cir. 1946).

[17] *Pyne*, 154 F.2d at 298.

a brother's death before Caroline. That way all John (and then Henry) got was a remainder subject to divestment, which John, Jr. and (ultimately) Jennifer took when John died before Caroline. After examining the document and the various authorities, the court held that the critical time was the death of the life tenant, Caroline.[18]

Using the phrase "dies without issue" is asking for trouble. If you do use it, elaborate its meaning with the greatest care.[19]

[C] "To Vernon's Youngest Grandchild"

Sometimes drafters will insert a descriptive phrase which might apply to different persons at different times. Such was the case in *Lux v. Lux*.[20] Philomena Lux's will said that her real estate "shall be maintained for the benefit of [her] grandchildren and shall not be sold until the youngest of said grandchildren has reached twenty-one years of age." She died leaving a son, Anthony, and five grandchildren.

The court interpreted the quoted language to create a trust,[21] but then had to decide how to identify "the youngest grandchild." According to the court, someone might qualify at any of four times: (1) when the will was executed, (2) when the will was effective (Philomena's death), (3) when the youngest alive at any time reached 21, and (4) when no more grandchildren could join the class (Anthony's death). Deciding that the first two alternatives were too restrictive and the last would not likely have been Philomena's intention, the court settled on the third reading. Of course, the drafter should have clarified the point in the first place.

[D] "To Joyce's Heirs" or "To My Heirs"

Gifts to heirs present some of the most notorious construction problems in the law.[22] This discussion uses "heirs" to mean those people who would

---

[18] Similar "When does it apply?" problems arise when interpreting gifts to "surviving" beneficiaries. *See* § 45[B][2][c][i], *infra*.

[19] For a helpful discussion and drafting suggestions, see John L. Garvey, *Drafting Wills and Trusts: Anticipating the Birth and Death of Possible Beneficiaries*, 71 Or. L. Rev. 47, 66-72 (1992).

[20] 288 A.2d 701 (R.I. 1972). The opinion opens with language which should send chills through anyone who drafts documents: "The artless efforts of a draftsman have precipitated this suit . . . ."

[21] The guardian for the grandchildren argued that there was no trust. An immediate gift would have closed the class, preserving for then-living grandchildren a share free from dilution by afterborn siblings. Class closing rules are discussed in § 43[B], *supra*.

[22] *See generally* Restatement (Second) of Prop. §§ 25.1-25.10, 29.1, 29.7, 30.1-30.2. Other similar terms, like "relatives" and "family," present a myriad of problems beyond the scope of this text. For a good short discussion, see William F. Fratcher, *Class Gifts to "Heirs," "Issue," and Like Groups*, 55 Alb. L. Rev. 1205, 1214-1218 (1992). The UPC treats many of these terms the same. When a document or statute creates a future interest in a designated person's "heirs," "heirs at law," "next of kin," "relatives," or "family," the property passes as it would if that person had died intestate. UPC § 2-711.

take a gift[23] and are identified by reference to an intestate statute.[24] This subsection first examines how heirs are identified, and then turns to two old favorites, the Rule in Shelley's Case and the Doctrine of Worthier Title.

[1] Identifying Heirs

A court deciding who fits the description of "Joyce's heirs" starts by looking at an intestate statute. Two principal problems emerge.[25] First, what statute should apply? Second, when?

Suppose Edwin died an Illinois resident in 1970, leaving personal property in trust "to Lois for life, remainder to Joyce's heirs." Joyce, who lived in Indiana, died in 1980. Should the law of Illinois (the testator's domicile) or Indiana (the designated person's domicile) identify Joyce's heirs? There is authority for each position.[26] If the gift were of a vacation cabin in Wisconsin, that law would probably apply.[27] Suppose Illinois law applies, but the statute was revised in 1975. Should the new or the old version control? Again, the authorities split.[28]

Timing can also be a problem in another sense. As a starting place, we expect to determine someone's heirs at the time of her death.[29] On the other

---

[23] The term is thus used as a word of purchase. Often "and his heirs" or "and her heirs" are used as words of limitation, identifying the estate granted as a fee simple. *See* § 34[A], *supra*.

[24] Traditionally, "heirs" meant those people who would take realty, and "next of kin" or "distributees," those who would take personalty. Some jurisdictions have retained different intestate schemes for realty and personalty. *See, e.g.*, Va. Code Ann. §§ 64.1-1, 64.1-11. Now, almost all states have dropped the distinction.

Sometimes a court, reading "heirs" in light of a particular grant, will find that the donor did not intend a technical meaning but something else, like "children." *See, e.g.*, Faulkner's Guardian v. Faulkner, 35 S.W.2d 6 (Ky. 1931) ("Bodily heirs" meant children because they were the persons who would take under statute of descent and distribution, and because that reading would effectuate the testator's intent.); Jones v. Lewis, 44 N.E.2d 735, 741 (Ohio App. 1941) ("my children's heirs" meant my "grandchildren"). Some statutes provide that when used in a document "heirs" presumably means "children." *See, e.g.*, N.C. Gen. Stat. § 41-6. For discussion of problems regarding who qualify as "children," see § 44[E][2], *infra*.

[25] *See* John L. Garvey, *Drafting Wills and Trusts: Anticipating the Birth and Death of Possible Beneficiaries*, 71 Or. L. Rev. 47, 79-84 (1992). For shorter descriptions, see Bergin & Haskell at 230-232; McGovern & Kurtz at 388-392; Simes at 220-223. For greater detail, see Simes & Smith §§ 728-737.

[26] *See* Tootle v. Tootle, 490 N.E.2d 878 (Ohio 1986) (testator's domicile); *In re* Dodge Testamentary Trust v. Detroit Bank & Trust Co., 330 N.W.2d 72 (Mich. App. 1982) (designated person's domicile).

[27] *See In re* Good's Will, 106 N.E.2d 36 (N.Y. 1952) (law of situs of realty controls). *See generally* William M. Richman & William L. Reynolds, Understanding Conflict of Laws, 257-259 (2d ed. 1993). The UPC appears to apply the law of the designated person's domicile, even if real property is involved. *See* UPC § 2-711.

[28] *Compare In re* Dodge Testamentary Trust v. Detroit Bank & Trust Co., 330 N.W.2d 72 (Mich. App. 1982) (applying revised law in force at time of beneficiary's death), *with* National City Bank v. Ford, 299 N.E.2d 310 (Ohio Common Pleas 1973) (applying law in force at time trust established). One court even applied the law at the time the will was executed. *See In re* Estate of Hughlett, 446 N.E.2d 887 (Ill. App. 1983).

[29] *See* Stanley M. Johanson, *Reversions, Remainders, and the Doctrine of Worthier Title*, 45 Tex. L. Rev. 1, 39 (1966).

hand, in many situations such a reading would not match a donor's likely intention. Interpretation problems can arise with regard to both immediate gifts and gifts of future interests.

Suppose Lois and Joyce were sisters and Lois had predeceased Edwin, making the gift to "Joyce's heirs" an immediate gift. (See Chart 11-2.) Suppose also that Joyce died before Edwin, leaving only her children, Diane and Andy (Situation A). We normally would say they took the gift as Joyce's heirs. Suppose, however, Andy had died after Joyce, but before Edwin (Situation B). Rather than letting "Joyce's heirs" refer to someone

Chart 11-2 — Immediate Gifts

Facts at Irwin's Death

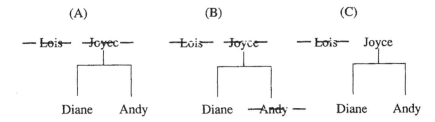

already dead (Andy), most courts would postpone the time for identifying heirs.[30] Interpreting "Joyce's heirs" to mean those who would have inherited from Joyce if she had died when Edwin did, courts would give the property to Diane.[31] In other situations, courts might accelerate determining heirship. If Lois had predeceased Edwin, but Joyce were still alive (Situation C), a court would probably determine "Joyce's heirs" as of Edwin's death and give the property to Dianne and Andy.[32]

Similar problems appear when the gift to heirs is a future interest. Recall our devise from Edwin "to Lois for life, remainder to Joyce's heirs." This time, suppose that before Edwin's death, Joyce had died leaving only her sister, Lois, and Lois's son, Peter. (See Chart 11-3.) Normally, we would expect a court to determine Joyce's heirs at her death, naming Lois.[33] In

---

[30] *See, e.g., In re* Austin's Estate, 20 N.W.2d 445 (Iowa 1945) (Testator's will left a life estate to his daughter with a remainder to her heirs. Testator's daughter predeceased him, leaving him as her sole heir at that time. Rather than giving the remainder back to the now deceased father, the court determined the daughter's heirs as of the testator's death.). *See generally* 5 ALP § 22.60.

[31] Under this approach, Andy's gift would not lapse. Rather, because courts would construe the word "heirs" so as to exclude him, he never had a gift in the first place. *See* Bergin & Haskell at 321-232. Section 45[B][2][b], *infra*, discusses lapse.

[32] *See* Restatement (Second) of Prop. § 29.4 cmt. c. In this situation, some courts interpret "heirs" of the living person to mean "children." *See* A. James Casner, *Construction of Gifts to "Heirs" and the Like*, 53 Harv. L. Rev. 207, 230 (1939).

[33] *See* Simes at 222.

this situation, that interpretation would give Lois both the life estate and the remainder, which would merge into a fee simple.

Chart 11-3 — Future Interests

Facts at Edwin's Death

Courts favoring early vesting as a way of promoting alienability of land might prefer this result.[34] On the other hand, to preserve Edwin's intention to restrict Lois to a life estate, a court might postpone determination of Joyce's heirs until Lois's death.[35] On these facts, that approach would exclude Lois, but keep the property in the family.[36]

[2] "To Joyce for Life, Remainder to Her Heirs": The Rule in Shelley's Case

Perhaps the most infamous of the old rules which continue to haunt estate planners is the Rule in Shelley's Case. Because the purpose of this discussion is to alert you to language with hidden dangers, we can omit many details of the rule's operation. If you face a *Shelley* problem, you will have no shortage of sources for more information.[37] The danger, of course, is not recognizing the problem at all.

Where it is followed, the rule applies to gifts of land to a life tenant, with an attempted remainder to the heirs of the life tenant.[38] It should not,

---

[34] *Cf.* Estate of Woodworth, 22 Cal. Rptr. 2d 676 (Cal. App. 1993) (absent evidence of contrary intent, heirs determined at death of named ancestor who predeceased life tenant). For more on early vesting, see § 35[B][2][c], *supra*.

[35] When a donor creates a future gift to heirs (or other like designations), the UPC identifies heirs as of the time the disposition takes effect "in possession or enjoyment." UPC § 2-711.

[36] *Cf. In re* Latimer's Will, 63 N.W.2d 65 (Wis. 1954). There the testator created a trust for Mary for life, with a series of contingent remainders ending in a wrap-up gift to the heirs of James. As of the testator's death, James' sole heir was Mary. The court delayed determination of James' heirs until the end of Mary's life estate.

For discussions of how careful drafting can avoid problems like these, see John L. Garvey, *Drafting Wills and Trusts: Anticipating the Birth and Death of Possible Beneficiaries*, 71 Or. L. Rev. 47, 83 (1992); Stanley M. Johanson, *Reversions, Remainders, and the Doctrine of Worthier Title*, 45 Tex. L. Rev. 1, 39 (1966).

[37] For short versions, see Cribbet & Johnson at 59-62; Laurence & Minzner at 153-157; McGovern & Kurtz at 393-395; Moynihan & Kurtz at 181-191. For comprehensive coverage of the rule's modern status, see Simes & Smith §§ 1563-1569.

[38] The rule also applies to a fee tail, with a remainder to the heirs of the tenant in tail.

therefore, affect personal property, but it can affect trusts if they include land. The greatest modern danger may be for farmers or developers who pour their landholdings into trusts, and for those who use trusts to hold recreational property for their families.

Regardless of the intention of the donor, the rule invalidates the attempted remainder to the heirs, and substitutes in its place a remainder owned by the life tenant. Thus, if Edwin gave realty "to Joyce for life, remainder to her heirs," the rule would change that grant to read "to Joyce for life, remainder to Joyce." At that point, the doctrine of merger would apply to create a fee simple absolute in Joyce. [39]

Be careful not to collapse the analysis and jump straight to the fee simple. Follow a two-step process. All *Shelley* does is convert the remainder. Whether to apply merger is a separate question. Consider a grant "to Joyce for life, then to Lois for life, then to Joyce's heirs." If *Shelley* applied, the grant would read: "to Joyce for life, then to Lois for life, then to Joyce." There would be no merger, however, because Lois's vested remainder for life would prevent it.

The Rule in Shelley's Case is dying, but not dead. It lingers on in a few states and has only recently been abolished in others. [40] It remains a malpractice trap for lawyers who create remainders to heirs.

[3] "To Joyce for Life, Remainder to My Heirs": The Doctrine of Worthier Title

Like its cousin *Shelley*, the Doctrine of Worthier Title is not in good health. [41] Unlike *Shelley,* in modern form, the doctrine applies to both real and personal property and, rather than an unmodifiable rule of property, it is a rule of construction. [42] The doctrine establishes a presumption that a grantor's [43] gift of a remainder to the grantor's own heirs was not intended

---

[39] The doctrine of merger recognizes that parts may add up to a whole. In this context, merger applies when one estate and the next vested estate come into the same hands. *See generally* Moynihan & Kurtz at 173 & 184.

[40] For citations to statutes changing *Shelley*, see the statutory notes in Restatement (Second) of Property § 30.1. *See generally* John V. Orth, *Requiem for the Rule in Shelley's Case*, 67 N.C. L. Rev. 681 (1989).

[41] The continued health of the Doctrine of Worthier Title remains unclear. For citations to statutes changing Worthier Title, see the statutory notes in Restatement (Second) of Property § 30.2. The UPC abolishes Worthier Title in § 2-710.

[42] For short versions, see Cribbet & Johnson at 63-64; Laurence & Minzner at 157-158; McGovern & Kurtz at 395-396; Moynihan & Kurtz at 191-203. For comprehensive coverage of the rule's modern status, see Simes & Smith §§ 1603, 1605, 1612.

[43] There used to be a "testamentary branch" to the doctrine, which said that gifts to heirs of the testator passed by descent instead of by will. Because in modern law it very seldom makes any difference whether someone takes by will or by descent, this branch of the doctrine is believed dead. *See* Restatement (Second) of Prop. § 30.2(2). It may not be, however. *See In re* Estate of Kern, 274 N.W.2d 325 (Iowa 1979) (prospectively abolishing the testamentary branch of the Doctrine of Worthier Title); Suzanne M. Patterson, *Comment, The Iowa Doctrine of Worthier Title—Why Perpetuate the Testamentary Branch?*, 66 Iowa L. Rev. 439 (1981).

as a remainder at all but, rather, as a way of retaining a reversion. Oddly, saying "remainder to my heirs" is not enough to overcome the presumption; something more is required.[44]

An easy way to remember the doctrine's impact is to say it simply invalidates remainders to heirs of the grantor. Thus, if Edwin created a trust giving "income to Joyce for life, remainder to my heirs," the doctrine would have us strike the remainder, leaving only "income to Joyce for life." Without more granted, Edwin has a reversion.

Despite their dangers, sometimes old doctrines can be tempting to use. *Hatch v. Riggs National Bank*[45] involved Anna Hatch's attempt to revoke an irrevocable trust she had created. She had retained lifetime income, with a remainder in her next of kin. When she wanted more money, she argued that the Doctrine of Worthier Title had prevented her from creating the remainder and left her with a reversion. Therefore, as settlor and sole beneficiary, she could revoke. Fortunately for the sake of the law's development, the court declined to follow the doctrine. The court did suggest, however, that a guardian ad litem be appointed to negotiate on behalf of her next of kin.[46]

Often a gift to heirs will present several problems at once. Such was the case in *Warren-Boynton State Bank v. Wallbaum*,[47] which involved William Wallbaum's deed of 1903. William (then 65) reserved a life estate to himself, and gave his daughter, Emma Mae (then 5), a remainder for her life. After her death, the property went to her surviving children, and if she had none, "to the heirs of said William Wallbaum share and share alike." At the time of the deed, William had two adult sons from a prior marriage; he had another son before he died. All of the sons predeceased Emma Mae, who died in 1984 without having had children.

One question was when to determine William's heirs. The court chose Emma Mae's death. If "heirs" were interpreted in the technical sense of determining heirship at William's death, Emma Mae would be an heir and get both a life estate and a remainder following that life estate. The court thought that William would not have intended that result. Moreover, because of the age differences between William and his older sons, on the one hand, and his daughter, on the other, William probably assumed Emma would outlive them all. Presumably, he would not have wanted to open the estates of people long dead in order to dispose of the remainder. Rather,

---

[44] New York became a particularly notorious breeding ground for litigation on the question of what it takes to overcome the presumption. In response, its legislature abolished the doctrine. *See* Powell ¶ 381.

Language like the following ought to be enough: "By this grant I fully intend to overcome the Doctrine of Worthier Title and to create a remainder in my heirs, and not to retain a reversion for myself." Of course, other language in the document should specify under what statute and when those heirs are to be identified. *See* § 44[D][1], *infra*.

[45] 361 F.2d 559 (D.C. Cir. 1966).

[46] Section 14[A], *supra*, discusses this aspect of the case.

[47] 528 N.E.2d 640 (Ill. 1988).

the gift was intended as a catch-all to keep the property in the family in case Emma died without children. The court interpreted the document sensibly and identified William's heirs as if he had died right after Emma Mae.[48]

Another advantage of the court's approach was to avoid the Doctrine of Worthier Title. Normally, the doctrine would have invalidated the gift of remainder to the grantor's heirs. Because the court determined William's heirs at Emma Mae's death, instead of under the technical definition of identifying them at William's death, the worthier title doctrine did not apply.

The litigants also raised a *Shelley's Case* issue, which the court avoided because William had not *created* a life estate before the gift in remainder to his (a life tenant's) heirs. Rather, he had *reserved* a life estate, so under this court's reading of the rule, *Shelley* did not apply.

Wallbaum illustrates four questions to ask if you see a remainder to the "heirs" of some person:

Is the person alive? If so, the remainder is probably contingent.

Is the person a life tenant? If so, *Shelley* may apply.

Is the person the grantor? If so, Worthier Title may apply.

When should "heirs" be determined? Traditionally, they are identified as of the death of the person, but they may be determined at other times.

Gifts to heirs can often be useful. They serve as the ultimate catch-all if known beneficiaries do not survive until the date for distribution. On the other hand, creating those gifts requires careful drafting to identify which statute applies (and when), and to avoid the ghosts of *Shelley* and Worthier Title.

[E] "To Linda's Issue" or "To Linda's Children"

Gifts to issue and to children present a number of constructional problems. This subsection considers issues already introduced in the context of intestate succession, but with the difference that they now involve interpretation of documents. Two questions predominate here: how to divide a gift to issue, and whether to include adopted or nonmarital children in a class.[49] Issues surrounding survivorship are postponed for discussion later.[50]

---

[48] There was also an argument about whether William said "heirs," but meant "children." Because the document used "children" elsewhere, the court believed William must have intended something different by "heirs."

[49] *See generally* Bergin & Haskell at 232-235; McGovern & Kurtz at 45-52; William F. Fratcher, *Class Gifts to "Heirs," "Issue," and Like Groups*, 55 Alb. L. Rev. 1205, 1218-1230 (1992); Edward C. Halbach, Jr., *Issues About Issue: Some Recurrent Class Gift Problems*, 48 Mo. L. Rev. 333, 334-355 (1983). For more details, see Simes & Smith §§ 723-731; 739-747.

[50] *See* § 45[B][2], *infra*.

[1] Allocating Shares

Suppose Hope executed a will giving her property "to my descendants." Hope dies leaving one son, Gordon, and his three children, Gord, Chuck and Kathy. Hope's other son (Phil) has predeceased, leaving two children, Kendra and James. (See Chart 11-4(A).) Do the descendants take per capita, so each gets 1/6? Or do they take by representation, so Gordon gets half and James and Kendra share the other half? If Gordon has also predeceased (see Chart 11-4 (B)), do the grandchildren take equally, or do Gord, Chuck and Cathy share one half while James and Kendra share the other?

Chart 11-4 — Dividing Gifts to Descendants

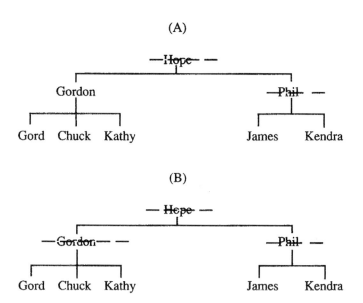

Of course, better drafting could have avoided these questions.[51] When they need clarification, courts often interpret documents according to the way the local intestate statute would handle the problem. The First Restatement endorsed that approach.[52] The Second Restatement established its own rule.[53] The UPC follows the First Restatement, and looks to the intestate

---

[51] For ideas on various options to review with a client, see the discussion of intestate statutes in § 5[B], *supra*. You can adapt these statutory solutions to fit wills and trusts. *See, e.g.*, Edward C. Halbach, Jr., *Issues About Issue: Some Recurrent Class Gift Problems*, 48 Mo. L. Rev. 333, 355 n.92 (1983). For more suggestions, see the statutory note to Restatement (Second) of Property § 28.2; John L. Garvey, *Drafting Wills and Trusts: Anticipating the Birth and Death of Possible Beneficiaries*, 71 Or. L. Rev. 47, 77-78 (1992).

[52] *See* Restatement of Property § 303.

[53] Regardless of the intestacy rules, the Second Restatement would divide the gift at the first generation with a living member, and then give it to those survivors who do not have an ancestor who is a living member of the class. Restatement (Second) of Prop. § 28.2.

provisions.[54]

[2] Identifying Takers

Additional problems arise if individuals claim membership in a class by way of adoption, or if they are nonmarital children. Earlier sections have discussed the increasing tendency to include such persons in the class of intestate takers.[55] While the fairness issues that were considered there are also relevant in this context, an additional factor present when interpreting documents is what the donor intended.

In the absence of an identifiable intent to include nonmarital children in class gifts, traditional rules excluded them. Adopted children fared a bit better. They were presumed included in an appropriate class gift created by their adopting parents, but they were excluded from class gifts created by others who did not know of the adoption. The idea was that "strangers to the adoption" should not have adopted family members foisted upon them.[56]

Presently, both adopted and nonmarital children are more likely than they were in the past to be included in class gifts. Some of the change has come through case law,[57] some through legislation.[58] The UPC distinguishes between class gifts from parents (biological or adoptive) and class gifts from "strangers" to the conception or adoption. Membership in class gifts from parents is determined by the intestacy rules; if the claimant can qualify as an intestate heir, he or she can also qualify to take a class gift.[59] On the other hand, claimants of class gifts from persons not their birth parents do not qualify as children of their birth parents unless the claimant "lived while a minor as a regular member of the household" of the relevant birth parent or other specified relatives.[60] Similarly, claimants for class gifts from persons not their adoptive parents do not qualify as children of those

---

[54] UPC § 2-708.

[55] See §§ 5[A][1], [2], supra.

[56] See generally Atkinson at § 23.

[57] See, e.g., In re Estate of Coe, 201 A.2d 571 (N.J. 1964) (adoptees qualified under gift to "lawful children" of their adoptive mother); Will of Hoffman, 385 N.Y.S.2d 49 (N.Y. App. 1976) (nonmarital grandchildren included in class under the gift to "issue" in grandmother's will).

[58] See 755 Ill. Comp. Stat. 5/2-4(f) (establishing a presumption that an adopted child is deemed a child born to the adopting parent unless (1) the intent to exclude the child is demonstrated by the instrument by clear and convincing evidence or (2) the adopting parent otherwise acted to benefit the child to even things out with other siblings). First Nat'l Bank of Chicago v. King, 651 N.E.2d 127 (Ill. 1995), upheld the statute while applying it to a 1937 trust dividing some of the Swift meat fortune. Compare Newman v. Wells Fargo Bank, N.A., 926 P.2d 969 (Cal. 1996) (excluding adopted person, because that was the law at the time the document was drafted); Matter of Doris Duke, 702 A.2d 1008 (N.J. Super. Ct. 1995) (Doris Duke's adoption, at age 75, of 35-year-old Chandi Heffner did not qualify Heffner to take share of trust established in 1924 by Doris' father).

[59] UPC § 2-705(a).

[60] UPC § 2-705(b).

adoptive parents unless they lived while a minor in the adoptive parent's household.[61]

By limiting class gifts from persons other than parents of the recipient, the UPC avoids some of the problems which broader statutes present.[62] Consider *Minary v. Citizens Fidelity Bank & Trust Co.*[63] Amelia Minary created a trust giving income to her husband for life and then to her sons for their lives. After the death of the last surviving life tenant, the trust would terminate, with the assets distributed to Amelia's then-surviving heirs. Her son Alfred had no children, but after almost 30 years of marriage, adopted his wife, Myra.

The question was whether Myra could qualify as Alfred's daughter (Amelia's granddaughter) and take the remainder under Amelia's trust. Although Kentucky had a very broad statute which treated an adoptee as the child of the adoptive parent for all purposes, the court refused to recognize Myra as an "heir" of Amelia. The court viewed such an adult adoption as a "subterfuge which in effect thwarts the intent of the ancestor . . . and cheats the rightful heirs."[64] Other courts allow adult adoptions as a way of qualifying someone for a class gift.[65]

Good lawyering can solve many of the problems identified in this section. Most importantly, before creating a class gift, talk with your clients about who they want included and why.[66]

§ 45 Changes After Drafting: People

Life goes on between the time someone executes a will or will substitute and the time survivors apply the document to the real world. Changes during that time gap may mean the document does not fit very well to the

---

[61] UPC § 2-705(c).

[62] *See generally* Victoria M. Mather, *The Magic Circle: Inclusion of Adopted Children in Testamentary Class Gifts*, 31 S. Tex. L. Rev. 223 (1990); Jan E. Rein, *Relatives by Blood, Adoption, and Association: Who Should Get What and Why*, 37 Vand. L. Rev. 711, 731-765 (1984).

[63] 419 S.W.2d 340 (Ky. Ct. App. 1967).

[64] 419 S.W.2d at 343. More than likely, neither Amelia nor her lawyers thought about what would happen if one of the children did not have children. They might have anticipated the natural impulse to provide for a spouse and given each son a special power of appointment in favor of his wife. For a discussion of powers uses, see § 37[A], *supra*.

[65] *See, e.g., In re* Estate of Stanford, 315 P.2d 681 (Cal. 1957) (Niece-beneficiary of testator adopted an adult and her two children who later qualified under the will as the niece's children because of public policy considerations and the testator's attitude toward adoption.). *See generally* Donald G. Cohen, *Adult Adoption May Qualify One as a Beneficiary*, 19 Est. Plan. 88 (1992).

[66] *See* Edward C. Halbach, Jr., *Issues About Issue: Some Recurrent Class Gift Problems*, 48 Mo. L. Rev. 333, 348 (1983). Be particularly careful with the tendency to define "children" (or "descendants," etc.) as only including "lawful," as opposed to nonmarital, children. A client may well want to define the terms separately for different situations, depending upon whether he is referring to his own children or those of others. A blanket "lawful" could disinherit grandchildren the client would really want to include. 48 Mo. L. Rev. at 346-347.

new situation. Careful drafters will anticipate change, but not all documents are well drafted and not all changes are foreseeable. The law—especially the law of wills—has developed a number of doctrines to handle common problems. Increasingly but unevenly, courts and legislatures are applying those solutions to will substitutes as well. This section considers changes regarding people: new people appear, familiar ones leave. The following section addresses similar changes to property.

[A] Arrivals

We have already discussed, in different places, various doctrines which affect documents in light of new arrivals. If someone gets married, his whole will may be revoked.[1] The new spouse may have a "pretermitted spouse" claim.[2] In addition, of course, any spouse will have available other protections, like community property or the right to elect against a will.[3] If a testator has a child, the child may be able to take a share of the estate.[4] If a will or trust creates a class gift, a newborn or newly adopted[5] class member may be able to qualify for it, if the class is still open.[6] Some of these doctrines apply only to wills; others have broader impact. Some protect against inadvertence; others protect against disinheritance. In various ways, however, all address the problem of how to handle those who arrive on the scene after a document has been drafted.

[B] Departures

The law recognizes two ways in which beneficiaries depart the scene before a document takes effect. A beneficiary may divorce the donor, or may die before receiving any benefit.

[1] Divorce of the Donor

Suppose Glenn and Tracy marry and have two children. Glenn executes a will giving everything to Tracy or, if she does not survive him, to the children. He makes an identical beneficiary designation for his life insurance. Later the marriage collapses and the parties divorce, but the decree does not mention either the will or the insurance policy. When Glenn dies without having revised either document, Tracy claims the proceeds of each. In most states Tracy would lose under the will, but still take the life insurance. The reason for the different treatment is that virtually every state

---

[1] *See* § 9[C], *supra.*

[2] *See* § 29, *supra.*

[3] *See* § 28, *supra.*

[4] *See* § 29, *supra.*

[5] For discussion of problems involving interpretation of documents in light of adoptions, see § 44[E][2], *supra.*

[6] *See* § 43[B], *supra.*

has a statute denying will benefits to a former spouse,[7] but the statutes seldom apply to will substitutes.[8]

Section 2-508 of the pre-1990 UPC is fairly typical of statutes on the question. It provides that a divorce or annulment after a will execution "revokes any disposition or appointment of property made by the will to the former spouse," and that the property "passes as if the former spouse failed to survive the decedent."[9] Many statutes cover fewer details, but are of the same general effect.[10]

Some courts have stretched doctrine or statutes to cover will substitutes. *Miller v. First National Bank & Trust Co.*[11] involved William Miller's life insurance trust and pour-over will.[12] His wife, Frances, was a principal beneficiary of the trust. Later, William and Frances divorced. In the eight months before he died, William did not revise the trust to eliminate Frances as a beneficiary. Faced with a divorce-revokes-gift statute which applied only to wills, the court stretched the incorporation by reference doctrine, brought the trust into the will, and then applied the statute.[13] Although reaching a sensible result, the court's reasoning confused both the incorporation by reference doctrine and the independent status of living trusts.[14] In order to take advantage of the subsidiary law of wills, the court made the trust into a will.

On similar facts, *Clymer v. Mayo*[15] rejected Miller's approach, but got to the same place. *Clymer* simply stretched the "gifts to divorced spouses

---

[7] These statutes partially revoke the will by operation of law. For other examples of this doctrine, see § 9[C], *supra*.

Unless modified by statute, the doctrine affects only gifts from a donor to a spouse. The doctrine typically does not apply to beneficiaries who themselves divorce. *See, e.g., In re* Estate of Breder; 432 N.Y.S.2d 441 (N.Y. Surr. 1980) (A gift to the testator's nephew and his wife went to both, even though they divorced before testator's death.). *But see* Grady v. Grady, 395 So. 2d 643 (Fla. Dist. Ct. App. 1981) (A gift of trust income to the testator's daughter and her husband for their support went solely to the daughter after the parties dissolved their marriage.).

[8] *See* Lawrence W. Waggoner, *The Multiple-Marriage Society and Spousal Rights Under the Revised Uniform Probate Code*, 76 Iowa L. Rev. 223, 226-227 (1991). *But see* Restatement (Third) of Prop. § 4.1 cmt. p (apply to will substitutes the presumption that a marriage dissolution revokes any provision in favor of the former spouse).

[9] UPC (pre-1990) § 2-508. If the parties remarry, the statute does not affect the will.

[10] Consider the problems a narrow statute caused in Porter v. Porter, 286 N.W.2d 649 (Iowa 1979). Corwin gave everything to his wife, Sena, and if she predeceased Corwin, to her son Wayne. After the marriage dissolved, Corwin died. The statute invalidated Sena's gift, but did not specify what to do next. Under the will's language, Wayne could not take because Sena was still alive. Convinced that Corwin wanted Wayne to take, the court implied a gift to Wayne as an alternate taker, to benefit if for any reason Sena could not take.

[11] 637 P.2d 75 (Okla. 1981).

[12] For more on this sort of an estate plan, see § 16, *supra*.

[13] For discussion of incorporation by reference, see § 8[B], *supra*.

[14] Incorporation by reference requires an intention to incorporate, which was almost certainly lacking in this case. One important feature of this estate plan is to avoid probate, not invoke it. Moreover, if pour-over wills really do incorporate their trusts, a whole series of questions arise about the extent to which trust assets are subject to probate court jurisdiction.

[15] 473 N.E.2d 1084 (Mass. 1985).

are revoked" rule of the wills statute and applied it to the unfunded life insurance trust Clara Mayo had created for her husband before they divorced. The court recognized both the independent legal significance of the trust and its similarity to a will, especially when the proceeds do not arrive until the death of the settlor. It concluded that the legislature intended[16] the statute to cover this situation.[17]

One striking feature of these cases is how the pour-over will and life insurance trust combination served as a hook to bring in wills rules to solve the problem. *Vasconi v. Guardian Life Insurance Co.*[18] lacked the hook, but applied the wills rule anyway. *Vasconi* involved only a life insurance policy from Robert's employer and a beneficiary designation in favor of his former wife, Leah. Recognizing it was rejecting substantial authority to the contrary,[19] the court held that a divorce decree which purported to settle all questions about marital assets presumably revoked Leah's beneficiary designation, even though the settlement agreement did not specifically mention the policy.[20] In the court's view, life insurance was simply too much like a will to treat them differently in the context of divorce.

Cases like these indicate the kind of piecemeal reform that courts can effect. More comprehensive reform requires legislation.[21] Section 2-804 of the UPC provides a model which cuts across a range of will substitutes.[22] It revokes appointments and beneficiary designations of, and severs joint tenancies with, the former spouse.[23] Property which would otherwise go

---

[16] This is an example of a court's willingness to impute to the legislature an intention it probably never had, to fill a gap in a way the court thought made sense. Compare § 41[A], *supra*, discussing interpretation of donative documents.

[17] Another question in the case was whether the divorce revoked a gift to Clara's "nieces and nephews." Standard definitions limit "nieces and nephews" to blood relations. *See* Restatement (Second) of Prop. § 25.8 cmt. e; UPC § 2-705(a). Because Clara had no siblings, the gift must have been intended for James' nieces and nephews. The court saw no legislative intent to bar the relatives of divorced spouse.

A court acting under the UPC would have reached the opposite result. Absent express language to the contrary, the UPC revokes gifts both to the former spouse and to the former spouse's relatives. UPC § 2-804(b)(1).

[18] 590 A.2d 1161 (N.J. 1991).

[19] *See generally* Alan S. Wilmit, Note, *Applying the Doctrine of Revocation by Divorce to Life Insurance Policies*, 73 Cornell L. Rev. 653 (1988); Mark Davis, Note, *Life Insurance Beneficiaries and Divorce*, 65 Tex. L. Rev. 635 (1987).

[20] Again, creative "interpretation" proved a helpful vehicle. Just as *Clymer* had liberally interpreted a statute, this court liberally interpreted a property settlement agreement.

[21] Legislatures can, of course, also engage in piecemeal reform. *See, e.g.*, Ohio Rev. Code Ann. §§ 5302.20(C)(5) (divorce changes joint tenancy property to tenancy in common); 1339.62 (divorce revokes beneficiary designation in revocable living trust); 1339.63 (divorce revokes beneficiary designations in life insurance and retirement plans).

[22] For a good, short description, see Lawrence W. Waggoner, *The Multiple-Marriage Society and Spousal Rights Under the Revised Uniform Probate Code*, 76 Iowa L. Rev. 223, 227-229 (1991).

ERISA, the primary federal statute regulating employee retirement benefits, preempts state statutes that would impact the federal scheme. *See* Egelhoff v. Egelhoff, 532 U.S. 141 (2001) (employer-provided group life insurance).

[23] UPC § 2-804(b).

to the former spouse passes as if the spouse, and the spouse's relatives, had disclaimed.[24] Section 2-804 represents one more step in the UPC's effort to integrate the law of probate and nonprobate transfers.[25]

Extending the doctrine from wills to nonprobate transfers may well effectuate the intentions of a donor. On the other hand, that approach may be unfair to the former spouse. Denying a former spouse the benefits of a will makes sense because the will presumably covers property either allocated to the testator under principles of equitable apportionment or acquired after the divorce.[26] On the other hand, disputes arise about nonprobate assets because they were not considered at the time of the divorce. Although some marital assets were subject to bargaining, these were not, even though the former spouse may well have contributed to the marriage during the time the asset was acquired. To deny a former spouse all benefit when the divorce proceeding missed something is harsh.[27] Perhaps a percentage allocation,[28] or an individualized inquiry into spousal contributions,[29] would produce a fairer result.

---

[24] The UPC keeps the property away from the former spouse's relatives on the theory that ties between the decedent and those relatives are likely to have broken down after the divorce. *See* UPC § 2-804 comment.

[25] UPC provisions apply to all decedents dying after a legislature adopts the code, no matter when the will or will substitute was executed. UPC § 8-101(b)(1). Some courts have invalidated this approach in the context of § 2-804's application to existing life insurance policies because the statute would be violating the contracts clause of the U.S. Constitution. The notion is that reforms cannot retroactively impair contracts. *See, e.g.*, Whirlpool Corp. v. Ritter, 929 F.2d 1318 (8th Cir. 1991). *But see* Means v. Scharbach, 12 P.3d 1048 (Wash. Ct. App. 2000) (upholding Washington's statute).

The Joint Editorial Board for the UPC has defended its approach. *See* Joint Editorial Board Statement Regarding the Constitutionality of Changes in Default Rules as Applied to Pre-existing Documents, 17 ACTEC Notes 161 (1991). *See also* Edward C. Halbach, Jr. & Lawrence W. Waggoner, *The UPC's New Survivorship and Antilapse Provisions*, 55 Alb. L. Rev. 1091, 1128-1130 (1992).

[26] For more on equitable apportionment, see John D. Gregory, The Law of Equitable Distribution (1989).

[27] *See* Robert J. Lynn, *Will Substitutes, Divorce, and Statutory Assistance for the Unthinking Donor*, 71 Marq. L. Rev. 1, 28 (1987).

[28] The UPC formula for figuring spousal election shares might be adapted to this situation. It is discussed in § 28[C][3][b], *supra*.

[29] If a death occurs while a divorce and property distribution are pending, a court may still subject assets to equitable division. *See* White v. White, 319 S.E.2d 447 (Ga. 1984) (When husband died after divorce decree, but pending trial on property division, proceeds of his life insurance, payable to his former wife, were subject to equitable division.). If the property settlement misses assets, perhaps courts should take the same approach, even when the death comes later.

In a community property state, courts would inquire as to how much of the asset was acquired by community funds. *See* Yeats v. Estate of Yeats, 580 P.2d 617 (Wash. 1978) (When policies on husband's life were not covered by the divorce decree and the husband later died, the former wife received half the proceeds, as tenant in common.). For more on community property, see § 28[A], *supra*.

[2] Death: The Need for Survivorship

The most common way for beneficiaries to drop out of a donative document is by dying. In this context, timing is everything. Traditionally, survival of the donor, even by a moment, is enough for someone to qualify. Moreover, unless the document provides otherwise, once someone acquires a future interest, it usually remains valid even if the holder dies before the time for possession. This section first addresses the question of how to determine whether someone has survived, and then covers, in turn, problems surrounding those who fail to survive donors, and those future interest holders who fail to survive until their time for possession.

[a] Survival: Simultaneous Death

Questions about whether one person survives another have two aspects: one medical, the other legal. Sometimes it has been difficult to determine who died first, especially in a "common disaster." Suppose Carol and Greg had wills giving everything to each other, but then died in a plane crash. Who should inherit from whom? In response to this problem, an early version of the Uniform Simultaneous Death Act provided that where "there is no sufficient evidence that the persons have died otherwise than simultaneously, the property of each person shall be disposed of as if he had survived."[30] The idea was to solve the dilemma of insufficient evidence and to distribute property to living people as much as possible. The statute was drafted too narrowly, however. Claimants were able to produce evidence of bare survival and thereby overcome the statute, defeating its second purpose of not giving property to dead people.[31]

In response, the UPC created a legal definition of survival, requiring one person to have survived another by 120 hours before being deemed to have survived for the purpose of interpreting documents.[32] The UPC assumes that in a common accident situation, someone who survives by 120 hours will recover enough to be able to enjoy the property. A time requirement is better than a "simultaneous death" approach, because a time requirement covers deaths that are close together, even if not at the same moment. It is also better than a "common disaster"[33] clause, because the key is not whether people die of the same cause, but whether they die too close to each other in terms of time. For these reasons, careful lawyers recommend that clients include a survival time requirement in their documents, usually

---

[30] Unif. Simultaneous Death Act § 1, 8A U.L.A. 561 (1953).

[31] *See, e.g.*, Estate of Rowley v. Bunnell, 65 Cal. Rptr. 139 (Cal. App. 1967) (car passenger died 1/150,000th of a second before driver); *In re* Bucci's Will, 293 N.Y.S.2d 994 (N.Y. Surr. 1968) (carbon monoxide in blood of wife indicated she had survived husband whose blood had no carbon monoxide after plane crash).

[32] The 1990 amendments extended the 120-hour rule from wills to will substitutes. UPC § 2-702. Section 2-104 applies the rule to intestate succession. In 1991, the Uniform Simultaneous Death Act was also amended to reflect the 120-hour rule. Unif. Simultaneous Death Act § 4 (1991).

[33] "If we should die in a common disaster, then . . . ."

by providing a definition of "survive."[34] Otherwise, trying to repeat the time condition with each gift can get complicated and lead to mistakes.[35]

[b] Surviving the Donor: Lapse

Suppose James leaves a will giving his piano to Jessamal, but that she predeceases him. At common law, Jessamal's gift would "lapse," or fail.[36] The piano would be distributed under the residuary clause, or, if the will lacked one, by intestacy. Because legislators thought that in some cases such a result would be contrary to a common testator's intention, they passed "antilapse" statutes.[37] Rather than letting gifts fail, these statutes give the property to specified alternative takers. The statutes vary in detail, in terms of whose gifts they save and what alternative takers they designate. Questions also arise about the extent to which antilapse statutes, originally applied only to wills, cover will substitutes. This subsection first addresses traditional antilapse statutes, and then turns to the changes proposed by the UPC.

[i] Traditional Antilapse Statutes

Because antilapse statutes vary in detail, it can be helpful to have a series of questions you can ask about whatever statute you face: (1) Is the predeceased beneficiary in a class protected by the statute? (2) Did the beneficiary die before the document was executed? (3) Did the beneficiary leave survivors who qualify under the statute to take the gift? (4) How does the document's language affect the statute? (5) Does the statute apply to documents other than wills?

Is the predeceased beneficiary in a class protected by the statute? The answer depends upon the relationship between the testator and the beneficiary. Some jurisdictions protect gifts to all beneficiaries; some apply

---

[34] A typical clause might read: "If any gift is given subject to a requirement that a beneficiary survive someone, survival for thirty days shall be required in order for the beneficiary to qualify for the gift." Thirty days is a common period, but different planners favor periods of different lengths. The time should be long enough to avoid giving property to someone who has died before they can enjoy it anyway, and short enough to facilitate easy administration. Tax considerations may vary this approach in large estates. See I.R.C. § 2056(b)(3) (you may lose the benefits of the estate tax marital deduction if the survivorship requirement exceeds six months).

[35] The malpractice in Ogle v. Fuiten, 466 N.E.2d 224 (Ill. 1984), occurred because the lawyer mixed a time survival requirement and a common disaster clause. He made each spouse's gift contingent on survival by 30 days, but then said that if they were to die in a common disaster, their nephews would take. The husband died of a stroke 15 days before his wife died of cancer. Because they did not die in a common disaster, the will left a gap. For more discussion, see § 1, *supra*.

[36] Gifts can lapse for reasons other than death of the beneficiary. *See, e.g.,* §§ 7[B][2][e] (will needs competent witnesses), 25 (misconduct), 30 (charitable gifts), *supra*.

On lapse and modern statutes addressing the problem, see generally Atkinson at 777-786; Haskell at 107-111; McGovern & Kurtz at 305-313. For more detailed coverage, see Page § 50.

[37] Restatement (Third) of Property § 5.5, statutory note.

only to gifts to relatives;[38] some only cover gifts to descendants. In our example, if Jessamal had been James' daughter, her gift would qualify for protection anywhere.

Did the beneficiary die before the will was executed? Under the common law, a gift to someone dead when the will was executed did not lapse; rather, it was "void." Most statutes expressly cover both lapsed and void gifts, but some do not, at least in some circumstances.

Did the beneficiary leave survivors who qualify under the statute to take the gift? This time the key is the relationship between the predeceased beneficiary and that person's survivors. If appropriate survivors exist, they will take the gift. By far, the most common substitute takers are issue[39] of the beneficiary. In our example, if Jessamal were of the proper relationship *and* if she had left surviving issue, those issue would take her gift, unless James' will precluded that result.

How does the document's language affect the statute? Because they are remedial statutes designed to effectuate presumed intention, antilapse statutes will yield to contrary expressions of intent.[40] While the combinations of different language and situations are endless, some common topics emerge.

Survivorship. Much confusion surrounds the impact of adding survivorship language to a gift. Recall our example in which James gave a piano to Jessamal and she died first. Suppose James had added, "if she survives me." Is that language enough to indicate that James would prefer the gift to fail, rather than go to Jessamal's issue under an antilapse statute? Authorities sometimes say a mere survivorship requirement is enough to override the statute.[41] The law is not clear, however,[42] so relying upon that approach is risky.[43] In particular, courts may require a "gift over" to

---

[38] For this purpose, spouses usually do not qualify as "relatives," because applying the statute could shift property to the spouse's family. This rule sometimes leads courts to manipulate language to create an alternative gift to children of a predeceased spouse. *See, e.g.,* Jackson v. Schultz, 151 A.2d 284 (Del. Ch. 1959) (in gift to wife "and her heirs and assigns forever," "and" meant "or," creating a substitutional gift to the testator's stepchildren); Estate of Mangel v. Strong, 186 N.W.2d 276 (Wis. 1971) (same). *See also* Estate of Griffen v. Haugland, 543 P.2d 245 (Wash. 1975) (using the same technique to find an alternate for a gift to a predeceased stepdaughter).

[39] This is another situation in which adopted children may not qualify. For discussions, see §§ 5[A][2] and 44[E][2], *supra.*

[40] Extrinsic evidence of the testator's intent is usually inadmissible. *See* McGovern & Kurtz at 242. That approach may change as part of the general movement away from excluding extrinsic evidence that could aid interpretation. *See* § 41, *supra.*

[41] *See, e.g.,* Estate of Rehwinkel, 862 P.2d 639 (Wash. App. 1993) (Gift "to those of the following who are living at the time of my death" precluded antilapse statute.); Atkinson at 780.

[42] *See* McGovern & Kurtz at 309; Edward C. Halbach, Jr., & Lawrence W. Waggoner, *The UPC's New Survivorship and Antilapse Provisions,* 55 Alb. L. Rev. 1091, 1104-1115 (1992).

[43] *See, e.g.,* UPC § 2-603 comment ("Lawyers who believe that the attachment of words of survivorship to a devise is a foolproof method of defeating an antilapse statute are mistaken.").

someone else.[44] Under this view, the statute would apply in our example unless James said "to Jessamal if she survives me, and if not, to Richard."

Whether it is required or not, a gift over following survivorship language is likely, but not certain, to defeat the statute if the alternate taker survives.[45] Courts also disagree about what happens if both the primary and secondary beneficiaries predecease the testator, with one or more of them leaving issue.[46] For this reason, drafters often provide a series of alternative beneficiaries.[47] The disarray surrounding the effect of survivorship language challenges document drafters to be especially careful. They cannot safely assume that its casual use will be enough to override a statute.[48]

Class gifts.[49] Questions also arise about whether antilapse statutes apply to class gifts. Suppose Klavidia left a will giving property "to my children." She left three surviving children, but her daughter Marilyn predeceased her, leaving a son, Boris. Would Boris get his mother's share? Many statutes expressly apply to class gifts. When the statute is not clear, courts are divided.[50] The dispute centers on how courts view antilapse statutes. Recall that class gifts have a built-in survivorship feature, in which remaining members of the class take if another class member's gift fails. If the purpose of an antilapse statute is to prevent the gift from falling into the residuary or passing by intestacy, the statute is not needed. On the other hand, if the purpose is to protect the issue of a predeceased class member, the

---

[44] *See* Detzel v. Nieberding, 219 N.E.2d 327, 336 (Ohio Prob. Ct. 1966) (to avoid the statute, "it is necessary that the testator, in apt language, make an alternative provision in his will providing . . . another specifically named or identifiable" beneficiary).

[45] *Compare In re* Estate of Evans, 227 N.W.2d 603, 604 (Neb. 1975) (statute not applied when testator's daughter predeceased her, because testator specifically excluded her grandchildren by writing "should any of my said children die before my decease I hereby give, will, devise and bequeath the share of said deceased child to the survivor or survivors of my said children, share and share alike"), *with* Estate of Kehler, 411 A.2d 748, 749 (Pa. 1980) (statute applied to save gift for testator's deceased brother's daughter, despite language giving property to testator's siblings "and to the survivor or survivors of them, equally, share and share alike, to have and to hold unto themselves, their heirs and assigns forever"). For more discussion, see Susan F. French, *Antilapse Statutes Are Blunt Instruments: A Blueprint for Reform*, 37 Hastings L.J. 335, 347-349 (1985).

[46] *Compare* Estate of Ulrikson v. Erickson, 290 N.W.2d 757 (Minn. 1980) (statute applied where both beneficiaries were dead, but the alternative beneficiary left issue) *with* Estate of Kerr v. Hall, 433 F.2d 479 (D.C. Cir. 1970) (statute not applied where both beneficiaries were dead, but the alternative beneficiary left issue). *See generally* Page § 50.8.

[47] *See* John L. Garvey, *Drafting Wills and Trusts: Anticipating the Birth and Death of Possible Beneficiaries*, 71 Or. L. Rev. 47, 54-56 (1992).

[48] The confusion prompted the revised UPC's detailed statute. *See* UPC § 2-603, discussed in § 45[B][2][c][iii], *infra*.

[49] For a description of class gifts, see § 43[A], *supra*.

[50] *See generally* Page §§ 35.15, 50.9. The Restatement's position is that antilapse statutes do apply to single-generation class gifts (e.g., children), but not to multiple-generation gifts (e.g., descendants). *See* Restatement (Third) of Prop. § 5.5 cmt. j.

statute should apply, even if doing so gives the property to someone not a member of the class. Most courts apply antilapse statutes to class gifts.[51]

Powers of Appointment.[52] Suppose Stephen is the donee of a power of appointment and he exercises that power by a will provision which reads, "to my daughter, Sammantha." Suppose also there is no identified taker in default and that Sammantha dies before Stephen, leaving two children. Whether Sammantha's children take her gift under an antilapse statute may depend upon what kind of power Stephen had.[53]

When the testator is exercising a general power, courts usually will apply an antilapse statute, if its other terms are met. On the other hand, if the power is special, courts may refuse to apply the statute. Suppose Stephen had a power to appoint among his "children." In this situation, most courts would not apply the statute because to do so would allow appointment to someone outside the class (here, a grandchild).[54] Even if Stephen's power were to appoint among his "descendants," so that the substituted taker would still be an object, some courts would refuse to apply the statute.

Does the statute apply to documents other than wills? By their terms, virtually all antilapse statutes apply only to wills. As with other aspects of the subsidiary law of wills, however, the question arises whether antilapse statutes should cover will substitutes.[55] The only cases so far involve trusts. Suppose Louise established a revocable, inter vivos trust, reserving a life estate to herself and disposing of the corpus to a variety of people, including Selden.[56] For practical purposes, the trust is acting like a will. Should that mean that if Selden dies before Louise, his gift lapses? The conventional view is no, because Selden acquired a vested remainder at the time Louise established the trust. Unless the remainder were contingent on Selden's surviving Louise, it would be Selden's asset and pass

---

[51] Be careful not to assume too much by that statement. Saying that an antilapse statute applies to class gifts will not necessarily save a particular gift. The other elements of the analysis still apply. If, for example, the predeceased class member was not related closely enough to the testator, the gift would fail and go to the other class members.

[52] Powers of appointment are discussed in Chapter 10, *supra.*

[53] *See* Bergin & Haskell at 165-167; McGovern, Kurtz & Rein at 490-491. For more details, see 5 ALP § 23.47; Simes & Smith § 984.

[54] Recall that courts usually do apply antilapse statutes to class gifts, even if the effect is to benefit someone not a member of the class. This difference in treatment is hard to justify. *See* Susan F. French, *Application of Antilapse Statutes to Appointments Made by Will*, 53 Wash. L. Rev. 405, 431 (1978).

   If the issue of objects of a special power can take via an antilapse statute, perhaps they should be considered permissible objects for the purpose of whether the donee can appoint directly to them. *See* Restatement (Second) of Prop. § 18.6(2).

[55] Compare, for example, the discussions in §§ 25 (misconduct), 28[C] (spousal election) and 45[B][1] (divorce), *supra.*

[56] This example is drawn from the facts of Detroit Bank & Trust Co. v. Grout, 289 N.W.2d 898 (Mich. App. 1980).

to his successors at his death.[57] Without a lapse-like rule requiring survivorship, antilapse statutes have no role.[58]

A few cases, however, have applied antilapse statutes to revocable, inter vivos trusts.[59] The Restatement advocates this approach.[60] As in other areas, pressure from courts may prompt more comprehensive legislative reform,[61] because judicial reform is necessarily piecemeal and leaves many unanswered questions. In an attempt to anticipate most questions, the UPC proposes detailed rules extending antilapse statutes to a wide variety of interests.[62]

The list of questions this section provides should help you analyze both a lapse problem and any antilapse statute that could apply. An antilapse statute may not apply for any number of reasons. If that happens, the failed gift may go to alternative beneficiaries named in the will, to surviving class members, to surviving residuary takers,[63] or to intestate heirs.

[ii] The UPC

In a series of related sections, the revised UPC expands and clarifies the scope and operation of antilapse statutes. The result is a comprehensive, complicated system which will dominate the debate on these questions for some time. This section introduces the provisions which apply to wills and various will substitutes.[64] Discussion of the proposal to extend coverage to future interests appears later.[65]

---

[57] For basics on vested and contingent remainders, see § 35[B][2], *supra*.

[58] Saying a beneficiary's gift will lapse unless the beneficiary survives the grantor will not, of course, automatically create an alternative gift under conventional antilapse statutes. The beneficiary still must have the right relationship to the grantor, and must leave the right surviving relatives. In Detroit Bank & Trust, 289 N.W.2d at 898, for example, the beneficiary, Selden, was only a friend of the grantor, so the statute would not have saved his gift.

[59] *See* Dollar Savings & Trust Co. v. Turner, 529 N.E.2d 1261 (Ohio 1988) (later reversed by Ohio Rev. Code Ann. § 2107.52); Estate of Button v. Old Nat'l Bank, 490 P.2d 731 (Wash. 1971).

[60] *See* Restatement (Third) of Property § 5.5 cmt. p.

[61] Recall the comments regarding spousal election law in Sullivan v. Burkin, 460 N.E.2d 572 (Mass. 1984), discussed in § 28[c][1][a], *supra*.

[62] *See* §§ 45[B][2][b][ii] & [c][iii], *infra*.

[63] If the lapsed gift was to a residuary beneficiary and not saved by an antilapse statute, traditional rules give the property to intestate heirs, rather than to the surviving residuary takers. The theory is that there can be no "residue of a residue"; there is nothing to catch the failed gift. *See* Atkinson at 784-785.

Some jurisdictions allow some surviving residuary beneficiaries to take. *See* Ohio Rev. Code Ann. § 2107.52(B); UPC § 2-604(b); Restatement (Third) of Prop. § 5.5 cmt. o. If California had followed this view, the invalid gift to Roxy the dog in Estate of Russell v. Quinn, 444 P.2d 353 (Cal. 1968), would have gone to Chester, the surviving residuary taker. *Russell* is discussed in § 41[B][1], *supra*.

If the residuary gift is *also* a class gift, then surviving beneficiaries will take the lapsed gift as surviving *class* members.

[64] *See generally* Edward C. Halbach, Jr. & Lawrence W. Waggoner, *The UPC's New Survivorship and Antilapse Provisions*, 55 Alb. L. Rev. 1091, 1100-1130 (1992) [cited below as Halbach & Waggoner].

[65] *See* § 45[B][2][c][iii], *infra*.

Consistent with the ongoing theme of integrating the law of wealth transfers, the UPC extends antilapse protection to a variety of will substitutes: life insurance, retirement plans, POD accounts and other nonprobate transfers.[66] In most states, predeceased beneficiaries of these devices lose their claims, just like will beneficiaries. There seems to be no good reason not to apply an antilapse approach, if it protects payors (like insurance companies), which the UPC does.[67]

Another way the UPC extends the antilapse statute's reach is by expanding the class of protected predeceased[68] beneficiaries. The UPC preserves any gift to a grandparent, to a descendant of a grandparent, or to a stepchild of the decedent, for that person's descendants.[69] This step limits the need for courts to manipulate language to save gifts for persons not protected by the statute,[70] but its broad reach may also protect gifts the average testator would rather see fail.[71]

The UPC also clarifies a series of familiar trouble spots. The statute applies to class gifts,[72] to testamentary exercises of powers of appointment,[73] and to void gifts.[74] Its most ambitious and controversial step is to clarify the rules surrounding what language will preclude the application of the statute and who the alternate takers ought to be in various circumstances.

In particular, under the revised UPC, the language "if she survives me," without more, is not enough to prevent the statute from substituting alternative takers if the named beneficiary does not survive.[75] As a general

---

[66] UPC §§ 2-706, 1-201. Coverage of life insurance may run afoul of the contracts clause of the Constitution. See § 45[B][1], supra. The federal ERISA statute may preempt UPC provisions covering retirement plans. See § 20, supra.

The nonprobate devices themselves are covered in Chapter 5, supra.

[67] UPC § 2-706(d).

[68] Recall that the UPC treats someone as predeceased if they do not survive by at least 120 hours. UPC § 2-702. For discussion, see § 45[B][2][a], supra.

[69] UPC § 2-603(b). Notice the similarity to the scope of the UPC's intestacy provisions, discussed in the text in Chapter 2, with the addition here of stepchildren. See UPC § 2-103. A gift to a stepchild may be revoked, under § 2-804, in divorce situations. If the stepchild then predeceased the testator, the antilapse statute would not apply. See § 2-603 comment. For discussion of gifts revoked by divorce, see § 45[B][1], supra.

[70] See Estate of Griffen v. Haugland, 543 P.2d 245 (Wash. 1975) (reading a gift to "herself and her heirs forever" as creating an alternative gift to the heirs of a predeceased stepdaughter whose gift would otherwise have lapsed).

[71] Suppose Kyanne leaves $5,000 to Aunt Dorothy, who was kind to her as a child. If Dorothy dies first, the statute would give the money to her children or grandchildren, rather than have it fall into the residuary and pass to Kyanne's own children. The more distant the protected relative, the less likely that the statute effectuates most testators' intentions.

[72] UPC § 2-603(b)(2).

[73] UPC §§ 2-603(a)(3), (4), (5), (7) & (b)(5). For commentary, see Sheldon F. Kurtz, *Powers of Appointment Under the 1990 Uniform Probate Code: What Was Done—What Remains to be Done*, 55 Alb. L. Rev. 1151, 1182-1201 (1992).

[74] UPC § 2-603(a)(4).

[75] UPC § 2-603(b)(3). For criticism, see Mark L. Ascher, *The 1990 Uniform Probate Code:*

rule, such a phrase has prevented an antilapse statute from applying, but the law is uneven.[76] The UPC drafters were unwilling to believe, without evidence of lawyer-client consultation on the question,[77] that even if testators' wills used words of survivorship, most of those testators had formed an intention to override the antilapse statute. The drafters believe that in most cases, the UPC's alternative gifts are more likely to effectuate testators' intentions than whatever would be the effect of not applying the statute. Only if testators clearly express another intention can they avoid the statute's solutions.

The best way to avoid the statute is to provide an alternative gift, or a series. Here the UPC also adds certainty. Alternative gifts will override the statute only if they are given to someone entitled to take.[78] For example, suppose Sara left her fishing pole "to my son Ben, if he survives me, and if he does not, to my daughter Nancy." Assume Ben predeceased Sara, but left descendants. If Nancy survives, she overrides the statute and takes the pole. If Nancy does not survive, however, the statute still applies. The idea is that Sara had a specific, as opposed to generalized, intention. Her gift to Nancy does not reveal an intention to override the statute's alternative gift in all cases, but only if she could give the property to Nancy.[79]

Suppose Nancy does not survive and that she, too, leaves descendants. Who takes, Ben's or Nancy's descendants? At first, the statute would seem to apply to both, because it applies unless overridden, and nothing overrides either gift.[80] To solve the problem, the Code sets priorities to identify which alternative takers it will substitute. It applies the common-sense concept

---

Older and Better, or More like the Internal Revenue Code?, 77 Minn. L. Rev. 639, 649-657 (1993); Lawrence W. Averill, Jr., *An Eclectic History and Analysis of the 1990 Uniform Probate Code*, 55 Alb. L. Rev. 891, 919-925 (1992); Martin D. Begleiter, *Article II of the Uniform Probate Code and the Malpractice Revolution*, 59 Tenn. L. Rev. 101, 123-124 (1991). For defense of the UPC approach, see Mary L. Fellows, *Traveling the Road of Probate Reform: Finding the Way to Your Will (A Response to Professor Ascher)*, 77 Minn. L. Rev. 659, 674-680 (1993); Halbach & Waggoner, 55 Alb. L. Rev. at 1099-1125 (especially p. 1108 n.62); John H. Langbein & Lawrence W. Waggoner, *Reforming the Law of Gratuitous Transfers: The New Uniform Probate Code*, 55 Alb. L. Rev. 871, 888 n.38 (1992). For the suggestion that such a change may be significant enough to warrant being adopted prospectively only, see Sheldon F. Kurtz, *Powers of Appointment Under the 1990 Uniform Probate Code: What Was Done—What Remains to be Done*, 55 Alb. L. Rev. 1151, 1189 (1992).

For further debate on how to treat survivorship language with respect to antilapse statutes, *compare* Susan F. French, *Antilapse Statutes are Blunt Instruments: A Blueprint for Reform*, 37 Hastings L.J. 335, 348-50, 369-70 (1985), *with* Patricia J. Roberts, *Lapse Statutes: Recurring Construction Problems*, 37 Emory L.J. 323, 349-54 (1988).

[76] See the discussion in § 45[B][2][b], *supra*.

[77] For ideas on how to preserve such evidence, see Roger W. Andersen, *Informed Decision-making in an Office Practice*, 28 B.C. L. Rev. 225, 245-246 (1987).

[78] UPC § 2-603(b)(5).

[79] A gift in the residuary is not an alternate gift, for purposes of defeating the statute, unless the will specifically says lapsed gifts go under the residuary clause. UPC § 2-603(a)(1).

[80] Nancy does not override the statute as to Ben, because she did not survive. No one overrides the statute as to Nancy. (Recall that even if Nancy's gift had read "if she survives me," that language alone would not be enough to override the statute).

of a "primary devise," and then prefers the substitute gift the statute creates for that primary devise.[81] To identify the primary devisee, ask who would take if everybody survived. Because Ben would, his is the primary devise and his descendants take the fishing pole.[82]

The UPC provision is detailed. Reading through the language in the abstract can be intimidating. Anticipating the objection that the statute is too hard to follow, Professors Halbach and Waggoner argue: "The test of a statute is not whether the statute is understandable upon a single reading of its text. The test of a statute is whether it produces a clear and appropriate result when applied to an actual case."[83] The examples presented here are designed to give you a sense of how the statute works,[84] so that you can both evaluate its innovations and use it to solve particular cases.[85]

Overall, the UPC antilapse statute assumes that if someone leaves property to a family member and the beneficiary dies first, the donor would want the beneficiary's descendants to take the property. To that end, it extends protections to a broad range of people and documents, and it requires solid evidence of a different intention before it withdraws that protection.

[c] Future Interests: Surviving Until Possession?

If Peggy left a will giving property to her son, Todd, but he predeceased her, we have seen how an antilapse statute probably would save the gift for Todd's children. Suppose, however, that Peggy left property "to Ricky for life, remainder to Todd," and that Todd survived Peggy, but not Ricky. When Todd survived his mother, he got a vested remainder.[86] Under traditional rules, unless a future interest is subject to a condition requiring survivorship until a particular time, a beneficiary's interest is not lost when the beneficiary dies prior to the time for possession.[87] Thus, when Todd

---

[81] UPC § 2-603(c). Recall that the UPC uses the term "devise" to include both real and personal property. UPC § 1-201(10).

[82] If the substitute gift is to a *descendant* of the primary devisee, however, different rules may apply to give the property to the substitute takers of the younger generation devisee. *See* UPC § 2-603(c)(2) & comment, example 7.

[83] Halbach & Waggoner, 55 Alb. L. Rev. at 1124.

[84] For more examples, consult the detailed comments to UPC § 2-603. *See also* Restatement (Third) of Property § 5.5 cmts.

[85] Solutions will not always come quickly, but in a huge percentage of cases, solutions should come. Professors Halbach and Waggoner state: "If, by working with the statutory language and the official comments for an hour or two in his or her law office, a lawyer can resolve the case, the public is much better served by the statute than it would be by a simpler statute that leaves a number of issues unresolved and requires legal research and perhaps litigation and appeal in order to resolve the case." Halbach & Waggoner, 55 Alb. L. Rev. at 1224. For the view that the UPC has tried to solve too many problems, see Mark L. Ascher, *The 1990 Uniform Probate Code: Older and Better, or More Like the Internal Revenue Code?*, 77 Minn. L. Rev. 639 (1993).

[86] For reminders about remainders, see § 35[B][2], *supra.*

[87] *See, e.g.*, Swanson v. Swanson, 514 S.E.2d 822 (Ga. 1999) (Trust beneficiary had a vested

died later, there would be no lapsed gift for an antilapse statute to save. Rather, the remainder would pass to Todd's successors.

This subsection discusses rules which change that result and require a future interest holder to survive until the time of possession. First, it examines survival requirements created by express language in a grant. Then we see when courts imply survivorship conditions. With that background, we view the UPC's new rules requiring survival. The subsection closes with an example comparing various approaches.

[i] Express Survival Requirements: When?

Donors can, of course, expressly require a beneficiary to survive until a particular time. Problems arise, however, when the document is not clear.[88] In general, the law presumes that words of survivorship refer to the time the beneficiary would come into possession of the property.[89]

In re Gustafson[90] illustrates the problem. Carl Gustafson's will created a trust giving his wife, Elsie, a life estate, and dividing the corpus between his brothers, Leonard and Roy. If either brother predeceased Elsie, his share was be paid "to his surviving child or children."[91] Leonard predeceased Elsie, leaving two children, Jacqueline and Daniel. Then Daniel died, leaving a wife and children. Then Elsie died. (See Chart 11-5.)

Chart 11-5

The Gustafsons

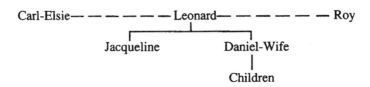

The question was whether the gift to Leonard's "surviving child" meant "surviving Leonard" or "surviving Elsie." If Daniel only had to survive Leonard, his wife and children would take. If Daniel had to survive Elsie, Jacqueline would take all of Leonard's share. Following the typical approach, the court ruled that Daniel had to survive until the time for

remainder subject to divestment by his issue if he died before the life tenant. He died first, but left no issue. The remainder was vested and went to his wife.); *In re* Trust of Holt, 491 N.W.2d 25 (Minn. App. 1992) (remaindermen who survived testator but died before life tenant got vested remainders).

[88] *See generally* Edward C. Halbach, Jr., *Future Interests: Express and Implied Conditions of Survival, Part II*, 49 Cal. L. Rev. 431, 440-451 (1961).

[89] *See* Simes at 190-191.

[90] 547 N.E.2d 1152 (N.Y. 1989).

[91] The trust also provided that if one of the brothers predeceased Elsie "without issue surviving," the surviving brother would take.

distribution, in this case Elsie's death.[92] Because he did not, Jacqueline won.

Although the tendency is to require survivorship until the time of distribution, courts often depart from that rule in particular cases. Sometimes they say "survive" means "survive the testator."[93] Sometimes "survive" means "survive your immediate ancestor."[94] Under either of those rules, Daniel would have survived long enough for his remainder to have vested and ultimately passed to his wife and children. Most of all, these cases teach that document drafters should not rely on presumptions,[95] but rather "should be crystal-clear as to the requirement of survivorship."[96]

[ii] Implied Survival Requirements

In general, courts do not imply survivorship requirements in gifts of future interests.[97] This reluctance reflects the doctrine that the law favors vested interests.[98] There are exceptions, however.

Multi-generational classes. Perhaps the most common situations in which courts will imply conditions of survivorship are when donors give to multi-generational classes, like "issue,"[99] "heirs,"[100] and "descendants."[101] Courts generally define these terms as having a built-in survivorship requirement and alternative gift to those who survive.[102]

"To Thomas for life, remainder to George or Martha." If a gift is phrased in alternative terms, courts usually will read it to mean that the gift to the first person is contingent upon survival.[103] If both of them

---

[92] *See* Restatement of Property § 251 (use of "survive," without saying when, "tends to establish the time of termination of all preceding interests as the time to which survival is required").

A dissenting judge argued that because the document used "children" and "issue" interchangeably, the gift should go to Leonard's "issue," namely, half to Daniel's children and half to Jacqueline. *Gustafson*, 547 N.E.2d at 1155 (Hancock, J., dissenting).

[93] *See, e.g., In re* Nass's Estate, 182 A. 401 (Pa. 1936).

[94] *See, e.g., In re* Colman's Will, 33 N.W.2d 237 (Wis. 1948).

[95] For further discussion, see Halbach & Waggoner, 55 Alb. L. Rev. at 1141-1145.

[96] Bergin & Haskell at 132. For suggestions, see Edward C. Halbach, Jr., *Future Interests: Express and Implied Conditions of Survival, Part II*, 49 Cal. L. Rev. 431, 465-468 (1961).

[97] For a good, short discussion, see Susan F. French, *Imposing a General Survival Requirement on Beneficiaries of Future Interests: Solving the Problems Caused by the Death of a Beneficiary Before the Time Set for Distribution*, 27 Ariz. L. Rev. 801, 807-810 (1985); Edward C. Halbach, Jr., *Issues About Issue: Some Recurrent Class Gift Problems*, 48 Mo. L. Rev. 333, 361-367 (1983). *See also* McGovern & Kurtz at 376-390.

The classic study is Edward C. Halbach, Jr., *Future Interests: Express and Implied Conditions of Survival*, 49 Cal. L. Rev. 297 (Part I), 431 (Part II) (1961).

The UPC proposal to change this approach is discussed in § 45[B][2][c][iii], *infra*.

[98] *See* § 35[B][2][c], *supra*.

[99] For discussion of how gifts to "issue" are divided, see § 44[E][1], *supra*.

[100] For discussion of when "heirs" are determined, see § 44[D][1], *supra*.

[101] *See* Bergin & Haskell at 131; 5 ALP § 21.13; Restatement (Second) of Prop. § 28.2.

[102] *See* UPC § 2-707 comment.

[103] *See, e.g.,* Robertson v. Robertson, 48 N.E.2d 29 (Mass. 1943) (a remainder to Ernest "or

predecease Thomas, the general rule would not imply a survivorship condition with respect to Martha's gift, so Martha's successors will take.[104] Following the general rule, there is no condition of survivorship implied with respect to Martha's gift.

"To Anton for life, remainder to Stanley at 21." If a gift is to someone "at" a particular age, many courts will read "at" as "if he reaches" and require the donee to survive until that age.[105] On the other hand, courts would probably read "to Stanley, payable at 21" to give Stanley a vested interest, with no survival requirement.[106] These different interpretations got their start in *Clobberie's Case*,[107] but whether the addition of "payable" should yield a different meaning is doubtful.[108]

With these exceptions, and an odd decision or two interpreting other language,[109] courts are unlikely to imply conditions of survivorship to future interests. Of course, reliance upon clear language, rather than upon these rules, is the prudent choice.

---

his issue" read as requiring Ernest to survive the life tenant); Landmark Communications, Inc. v. Sovran Bank, N.A., 387 S.E.2d 484 (Va. 1990) (remainder to family members "or their heirs" is contingent). Simes at 191.

This rule sometimes prompts courts to find that "to James and his heirs" means "to James or his heirs." The later construction creates both a survivorship requirement for James and an alternative gift for his heirs. For examples of this use, see § 45[B][2][b][i], *supra*.

[104] *See* 5 ALP § 21.18. The UPC would change this result by also implying a condition of survivorship upon Martha's gift. *See* § 45[B][2][c][iii], *infra*, discussing § UPC 2-707.

[105] *See* Simes at 191-193; 5 ALP § 21.17.

[106] Under this reading, if Stanley dies, his successors can demand payment when Stanley *would have reached* 21 (or at Anton's death later).

[107] 86 Eng. Rep. 476 (K.B. 1677).

[108] Professor Halbach suggests that courts should treat both sets of language the same way, preferably not requiring survival. *See* Edward C. Halbach, Jr., *Future Interests: Express and Implied Conditions of Survival, Part I*, 49 Cal. L. Rev. 297, 302 (1961).

[109] Two minority positions are worth noting. Some courts imply a condition of survival from another condition making a remainder contingent. *See, e.g.*, Lawson v. Lawson, 148 S.E.2d 546 (N.C. 1966). Following a life estate to Opal, there was a gift to her brothers and sisters, expressly contingent upon either Opal having no children or on her leaving no children surviving (the document was not clear). In any case, Opal never had children, so the brothers and sisters took. The court, however, required them also to have survived Opal. From the express contingency regarding Opal's children, the court implied a condition of survivorship. This is a distinctly minority view. *See* Restatement of Prop. § 261. For a discussion of how this approach has haunted Iowa, see N. William Hines, *Implied Conditions of Personal Survivorship in Iowa Future Interests Law*, 75 Iowa L. Rev. 941 (1990).

Some courts have held that if language requires property to be "divided and paid over" to a group of beneficiaries, they must survive until the time for distribution. Largely repudiated or ignored, this old rule was applied in Harris Trust & Savings Bank v. Beach, 513 N.E.2d 833 (Ill. 1987) (The surviving grandchildren and great-grandchildren received the trust principal because the court interpreted the language "divide and/or distribute trust principal among my heirs" to be a contingent class gift requiring the beneficiaries to be alive at the time of distribution.). The Restatement rejects the rule. *See* Restatement of Prop. § 260. For a short description, see Simes at 194.

[iii] The UPC

In light of the confusion surrounding survivorship requirements for future interests, the 1990 UPC proposes significant reform. Taking an approach which parallels the new antilapse statutes discussed above,[110] Section 2-707 applies to future interests under the terms of trusts.[111] Because the sections have similar structures, understanding one will help with the others.[112] The future interests reform takes two basic steps. It requires beneficiaries to survive[113] until the time of distribution, and it provides an alternate distribution of a predeceased beneficiary's interest.

The UPC radically alters traditional learning about future interests by making any future interest in trust contingent upon survival.[114] For centuries, lawyers have learned that a gift in trust to Richard for life, remainder to Stephanie gives her an indefeasibly vested remainder. If she died before Richard, the remainder would not be lost. As a practical matter, it would be likely to go through Stephanie's estate. Often no one discovers such an interest until the life tenant's death and by that time, the remainderman's estate must be reopened. To avoid distributions to and through estates of predeceased beneficiaries,[115] the UPC reverses the common law rule. Under the UPC, Stephanie would have a remainder contingent on surviving Richard.[116]

---

[110] *See* UPC §§ 2-603(b) (wills), 2-706(b) (life insurance and other will substitutes), discussed in § 45[B][2][b][ii], *supra.*

[111] The UPC does not distinguish between revocable, living trusts and other trusts. Some courts have applied traditional antilapse statutes to living trusts because they act so much like wills. *See* § 45[B][2][b][i], *supra.* It might be possible to create a special category for revocable living trusts in which the settlor retains a life estate. Survivorship of the settlor could be treated under rules for wills and life insurance, but survivorship beyond the settlor would be subject to the general rules for future interests. *But see* Halbach & Waggoner, 55 Alb. L. Rev. at 1139 (suggesting that all trusts should be treated alike).

Future interests outside of trusts are not covered. They are also not common. One reason the UPC exempts them may be because the survivorship requirement the statute imposes could impair alienability of land not held in trust. *See* § 35[B][2][c], *supra.*

[112] To avoid confusion, this text will use the term "antilapse" statute to mean the one applied as of the donor's death, and "substitute gift" statute to mean the one applied to future interests.

[113] UPC § 2-707. Recall that under the UPC, "survival" means survival by 120 hours. UPC § 2-702. The 120-hour rule is discussed in § 45[B][2][a], *supra.*

[114] Because the change is so great, Professor Kurtz suggests that perhaps it should, unlike other construction rules of the UPC, be adopted prospectively only. *See* Sheldon F. Kurtz, *Powers of Appointment Under the 1990 Uniform Probate Code: What Was Done — What Remains to be Done,* 55 Alb. L. Rev. 1151, 1189 (1992).

For different views on the wisdom of the UPC proposal, see Laura E. Cunningham, *The Hazards of Tinkering With the Common Law of Future Interests: The California Experience,* 48 Hastings L.J. 667 (1997); Jesse Dukeminier, *The Uniform Probate Code Upends the Law of Remainders,* 94 Mich. L. Rev. 148 (1995); Lawrence W. Waggoner, *The Uniform Probate Code Extends Antilapse Type Protection to Poorly Drafted Trusts,* 94 Mich. L. Rev. 2309 (1996).

[115] *See* UPC § 2-707 comment.

[116] For clarity's sake, the example in the text is a bit oversimplified. Few trusts are drafted without requiring the holder of the first remainder to survive the life tenant. More frequently, however, drafters will fail to supply survivorship language for an alternative gift, and the same analysis will apply to the alternative taker.

Creating a new set of rules also allows the UPC to eliminate trouble spots in the traditional doctrine. For example, the statute sets a specific time for survival—the distribution date.[117] Also, the fights about whether to imply survivorship requirements are irrelevant.[118] On the other hand, because a donor can always override these rules of construction, disputes may arise about whether a particular donor intended to create a gift not contingent upon survival. The statute attempts to limit narrowly the basis for such arguments by requiring express language to overcome the statute.[119]

Creating remainders contingent upon survival until the date of distribution may be a very sensible reform, which would save money and effectuate many donors' intentions. Lawyers should understand that if the UPC is followed, however, they will have to develop new instincts when it comes to interpreting documents. The examples are endless, of course, but one more should illustrate the point. Consider a living trust from Zena "to Richard for life, remainder to Stephanie, but if Stephanie dies before me, to Lisa." Common law rules would give Stephanie a vested remainder, subject to divestment by dying before Zena, and Lisa an executory interest, contingent on Stephanie's dying before Zena. The UPC would give Stephanie a *contingent* remainder, contingent on surviving *Richard*, and Lisa a contingent remainder, contingent upon both Stephanie's non-survival *and* her own survival of Richard.

In some cases, creating all these contingent remainders could cause problems with the Rule Against Perpetuities, which operates against contingent interests.[120] Three factors mitigate the concern. First, a great many trusts do not extend long enough to raise a perpetuities problem. Second, perpetuities reform continues to gain adherents. Third, any jurisdiction adopting the UPC changes regarding survivorship rules would be likely to consider seriously the UPC's companion perpetuity reforms.[121]

Another possible criticism of the reform is that by requiring survivorship of *any* future interest in trust, the substitute gift statute applies to a much broader class than most antilapse statutes. Recall that the UPC limits its antilapse protection to relatives and stepchildren.[122] The testator's loyalty to non-relative beneficiaries is not likely to extend to their descendants, so the statute does not save such gifts. Broader coverage for gifts of future

---

[117] The "distribution date" is the UPC's term for the time the future interest holder would get either income or principal from the trust. *See* UPC § 2-707(a)(4).

[118] For discussion of the problem under traditional doctrine, see § 45[B][2][c][ii], *supra*.

[119] Section 2-707(b)(3) says "words of survivorship . . . are not, in the absence of additional evidence, a sufficient indication of an intent" to override the statute. Moreover, even words of survivorship which relate to a different distribution date or which use condition-subsequent form do not change the result.

The comment suggests two ways to override the statute's survival rule: "remainder to Stephanie whether or not she survives Richard," or "remainder to Stephanie or her estate."

[120] The Rule is addressed in Chapter 12, *infra*.

[121] *See* UPC §§ 2-901 to 2-906.

[122] The antilapse statute applies to gifts to grandparents, their descendants, and stepchildren of the donor. UPC §§ 2-603(b) (wills), 2-706 (life insurance and other will substitutes).

interests may be justifiable in a trust context. First, token gifts to non-relatives are less likely to appear in a trust than in a will, so the narrower coverage is less necessary.[123] Second, the advantage of cleaning up the mess of survivorship law, rather than only part of it, may outweigh the disadvantage of benefiting an occasional person a donor would not have.[124] Third, a donor can always (and careful drafters will) override the statute.

Having imposed a survivorship requirement, the UPC's second step is to establish a set of alternative takers. This part of the future interests statute draws heavily upon the UPC antilapse statute. Unless the gift is to a class with its own alternative gift structure,[125] descendants of the deceased beneficiary take the gift.[126] As in the antilapse statute, if the statute would otherwise identify more than one substitute beneficiary, the statute provides a priority system.[127] Finally, to avoid giving property to dead people, the statute creates ultimate substitute gifts to the donor's residuary takers or heirs.[128]

By requiring survivorship, and then substituting a predeceased beneficiary's descendants or the donor's residuary takers or heirs, the UPC's substitute gift statute shifts power away from beneficiaries and back to donors. Recall that Zena's gift to Richard for life, remainder to Stephanie normally gives Stephanie an indefeasibly vested remainder, which would likely go through her estate if she predeceases Richard. At the cost of higher taxes and administration expenses, Stephanie has control of that remainder. Under the UPC, she loses that power.

Instead of analogizing to antilapse statutes to identify substitute takers, Professor French would look to powers of appointment.[129] Like the UPC, she would impose a survivorship requirement. Rather than giving beneficiaries ownership of their future interests, however, she would limit beneficiaries to a power to dispose of those interests.[130] Some legislatures might

---

[123] See Susan F. French, *Imposing a General Survival Requirement on Beneficiaries of Future Interests: Solving the Problems Caused by the Death of a Beneficiary Before the Time Set for Distribution*, 27 Ariz. L. Rev. 801, 815 (1985).

[124] See Halbach & Waggoner, 55 Alb. L. Rev. at 1139. *Compare* Restatement (Second) of Prop. § 34.6 cmt. b, illustration 3 (extending antilapse protection to trusts, but limiting the application to gifts protected by the local statute).

[125] Gifts to "heirs" and "issue" and the like are defined so as to create substitute takers. Although the alternative gift provisions do not apply to these gifts if there are survivors in the class, class members still hold future interests, so the requirement of surviving until distribution still applies. *See* UPC § 2-707(b).

[126] UPC § 2-707(b)(1), (2).

[127] See UPC § 2-707(c). For discussion of the parallel provisions under the antilapse statute, see § 45[B][2][b][ii], *supra*.

[128] The first choice is takers under the donor's residuary clause (who are treated as having future interests affected by this section), and the second is the donor's intestate heirs, determined at the time of distribution. UPC §§ 2-707(d), 2-711.

[129] On powers of appointment generally, see Chapter 10, *supra*.

[130] See Susan F. French, *Imposing a General Survival Requirement on Beneficiaries of Future Interests: Solving the Problems Caused by the Death of a Beneficiary Before the Time Set for Distribution*, 27 Ariz. L. Rev. 801 (1985). *See also* John L. Garvey, *Drafting Wills and Trusts: Anticipating the Birth and Death of Possible Beneficiaries*, 71 Or. L. Rev. 47, 56 n.42 (1992) (supporting this view).

simulate traditional antilapse statutes by limiting appointment to the beneficiary's surviving issue; others might create a broad hybrid power.[131] So long as the power was not a general power, the property would not be subject to federal estate tax in the estate of the beneficiary.[132] This technique would avoid the tax and administration problems of the traditional vested interest approach, but would preserve beneficiaries' power to make different dispositions. This freedom would allow people to react to circumstances which change after the death of the donor, but while the remainder is still contingent. Leaving control with beneficiaries may, for example, let one benefit a spouse unknown to the donor or adjust shares to help a needy sibling.[133] French's reform statute would still have default rules, in case a beneficiary did not act, but those rules could favor the *beneficiary's* residuary takers or heirs, instead of the donor's.

Both reform proposals establish default rules, which donors can override. The question legislators will face as they debate these proposals is which default rules make the most sense in terms of the dual policies of running an efficient system and effectuating donors' likely intentions.

[iv] Applying the Rules

As a vehicle for understanding how the survival rules apply in the context of future interests, consider *Security Trust Co. v. Irvine.*[134] James Wilson died in 1918, leaving a will whose residuary clause created a trust to care for two of his sisters, Martha and Mary. At the death of their survivor, James declared the fund was to be "equally divided among my brothers and sisters, share and share alike, their heirs and assigns forever, the issue of any deceased brother or sister to take his or her parent's share." The question was who qualified to take the trust principal after the death of the surviving life tenant.

When James died, he left all five of his siblings surviving. By the time Mary died in 1951, all of that generation was gone. However, two of the brothers (Samuel and Henry) left issue. (See Chart 11-6.) Samuel had had four children. Two (Frazier and Jeannette) survived their Aunt Mary, but two others (Sam Jr. and Francis) did not. Sam Jr. had already died without children, and Francis had died leaving a daughter (Grace). In addition, Henry's two daughters (Margaret and Mary) survived.

---

[131] *See* French, 27 Ariz. L. Rev. at 820-821.

[132] *See* IRC § 2041, discussed in § 37[D], *supra*, and § 62[A][2], *infra*.

[133] Professor Waggoner has expressed similar concerns. *See* Lawrence W. Waggoner, *Future Interests Legislation: Implied Conditions of Survivorship and Substitutionary Gifts Under the New Illinois "Anti-lapse" Provision*, 1969 U. Ill. L. Forum 423, 437-438.

[134] 93 A.2d 528 (Del. Ch. 1953).

Chart 11-6

The Wilsons

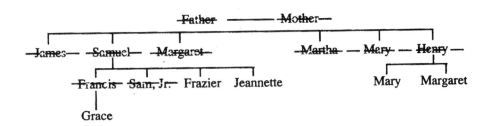

Following the traditional rule, the court declined to imply conditions of survivorship to the single-generational class of brothers and sisters. It also declined to exclude the life tenants from the class holding the remainders. Each of the brothers and sisters thus had vested remainders, subject to divestment by their issue. Because sisters Margaret, Martha, and Mary all died without leaving issue, their remainders went to their estates.[135] Samuel's and Henry's remainders went to their respective issue.

The court did not address who took Samuel's remainder.[136] Recall that the document created executory interests as follows: "the issue of any deceased brother or sister to take his or her parent's share." "Issue" is a multi-generational class to which survivorship conditions are normally implied. One would expect, therefore, that Francis and Sam Jr. would lose out, and Grace, Frazier and Jeannette would divide Samuel's share. On the other hand, the document speaks of issue taking his or her *parent's* share. Perhaps "issue" was really intended to mean "children." If that reading is correct, then the executory interest is in a single-generational class and survivorship is not implied. Under this view, Francis and Sam Jr. would take along with Frazier and Jeannette. Grace would be out as a direct beneficiary, though she might ultimately take a share as successor to her father.

The revised UPC would produce a very different result if applied to these facts. First, of course, all of the future interests would be contingent on surviving until the distribution date (Mary's death). Under the Code, the property which all class members would have shared passes to those who survived and to the surviving descendants of those class members who left surviving descendants. Because James' sisters Margaret, Martha, and

---

[135] All three had wills. Margaret's share went to her husband; Martha's went to Henry's two daughters; Mary's went mostly to one of Henry's daughters. Rather than reopening the estates of Martha and Mary, the court took the sensible, but relatively rare, approach of ordering distribution directly to the beneficiaries of those estates. Margaret's husband was a party to the action, so he probably took directly as well.

[136] *Security Trust*, 93 A.2d at 532.

Mary did not leave descendants surviving Mary, the sisters simply fall out of the class, effectively giving the remaining takers larger shares.[137]

In this case, Samuel's and Henry's issue take. If "issue" really means "issue," Samuel's and Henry's gifts would pass to their then-surviving issue as substitute takers under the trust.[138] If "issue" means "children," the same people take, but as substitute takers identified by the statute.[139] In either case, the survivors take under the "per capita, with representation" approach.[140]

The principal losers under the new rule would be Margaret's husband (who would have taken her remainder under her will and now gets nothing) and Henry's daughter Margaret (who would have taken her Aunt Mary's share under Mary's will). The principal winners would be Samuel's issue, whose shares would jump from 1/15 each (one third of Samuel's 1/5) to 1/5 each.

§ 46 Changes After Drafting: Property

Just as people can come and go between the time a grantor executes a document and the time it becomes effective, so can property. Imagine that Javier drafts a will leaving Antonio 50 shares of Computerwiz stock. Any number of things might happen to affect that gift before Javier dies. The stock might split, with additional shares issued for each share owned. Computerwiz might merge with, or be purchased by, another company. Javier might sell, or give away, the stock. Miriam, acting as Javier's guardian or under a power of attorney, might sell it on his behalf. Javier might develop financial problems and die owning the stock, but fewer total assets than he had anticipated.

This section addresses the doctrines which determine what Antonio would get in these various circumstances. First, it identifies the various classifications the law has created for gifts. Often the way a court classifies a gift will determine how well the donee fares. Next, we will view accessions, those "add-ons" that come after the document was drafted. Third comes the doctrine of ademption, which asks what to do when the subject of the gift is no longer there. The section closes with the abatement doctrine, which sets priorities among will beneficiaries if there are not enough assets to go around.

---

[137] Because the code defines "deceased beneficiary" in this context to mean only those who predeceased *and* left descendants, deceased beneficiaries who left no descendants, like James' sisters in our example, simply drop out. *See* UPC § 2-707(b)(2).

[138] *See* UPC § 2-707(b)(4).

[139] *See* UPC § 2-707(b)(2).

[140] *See* UPC §§ 2-707(b)(2) (beneficiaries substituted by the statute take by representation), 2-708 (documentary gifts to issue divided as they would be in intestate succession), 2-106 (representation defined for purposes of intestate succession). The various systems for dividing gifts among descendants are discussed in § 5[B], *supra*.

[A] Classification of Gifts

For purposes of handling the changes discussed in this section, courts and legislatures have identified four classes of gifts:[1] specific, general, demonstrative, and residuary.[2] Although courts often get formalistic when assigning such labels, the idea of the different categories is to recognize that testators may have different ideas about various gifts. The familiar goal is to identify the testator's intention.

Often classification is easy. Specific gifts are just that: gifts specifically identified as going to someone in particular. "My oak desk," "my 100 shares of General Motors Preferred Stock," and "my house and lot in Pullman" are all specific gifts. General gifts are often legacies, but they need not be. "$3,000 to Marsha" and "my land to Calvin" are both general gifts.[3] Demonstrative gifts are rare. They are a cross between specific and general gifts. Demonstrative gifts are ones which a testator intends to come from a specific source, but which can also come out of general estate assets. "$6,000 to come first from my credit union account, but if the account is too small, from my other funds" is a demonstrative gift. Finally, residuary gifts are the catch-alls giving "everything else I own."[4]

The biggest problem is trying to distinguish—on the margin—between specific and general gifts.[5] One reason for the trouble is that the characterization has different consequences in different circumstances. As we shall see, from the perspective of a will beneficiary, a "specific" label is a good thing if there is not enough money to go around and some gifts cannot be made. Specific gifts usually are the last to go. On the other hand, a "specific" label is bad if the question involves a gift of property that is not an estate asset at the testator's death. In this situation, specific gifts fail, but general gifts do not. Predictably, courts sometimes read similar language in different ways as they strain to push a gift into a particular category to produce the result they believe makes the most sense in the case before them.[6]

---

[1] The term "gifts" includes the traditional categories of bequests (personalty), legacies (money), and devises (realty). Slowly, these distinctions, which serve more to confuse than enlighten, are giving way to more general terms. The UPC uses "devise" to cover all testamentary gifts. UPC § 1-201(10).

[2] See generally Atkinson at 731-737. See also Restatement (Third) of Prop. § 5.1.

[3] Gifts of land used to be specific gifts. Because the will did not cover land acquired after the will's execution, it was possible to determine specifically what land the testator owned at that time and limit the gift to that land. Now, after-acquired property is included, so some gifts of land are general.

[4] Residuary clauses can be particularly verbose, going on and on about "the rest, residue and remainder of my real, personal, and/or mixed property, wheresoever situated" and the like. When you get the chance, save a tree by editing a residuary clause.

[5] For helpful discussion of an area which continues to challenge lawyers, see John C. Paulus, *Special and General Legacies of Securities—Whither Testator's Intent*, 43 Iowa L. Rev. 467 (1958).

[6] *See, e.g.*, Haslam v. De Alvarez, 38 A.2d 158 (R.I. 1944) (For abatement purposes, the language, "I give and devise all real estate owned by me or in which I may have an interest

A more direct approach, however, would be to ignore the label and get directly to the underlying question, whether the testator would have intended the gift to succeed or fail in the particular circumstance. Sometimes it can help to ask whether the testator was primarily thinking of the gift or of the beneficiary. Recall Javier, whose will left Antonio 50 shares of Computerwiz stock. If Antonio is an old friend, perhaps the stock is just a convenient way of saying "I enjoyed our friendship." Applying the law so as to give Antonio *something* becomes paramount. On the other hand, perhaps Antonio has a particular love for computers, or perhaps the 50 shares would give him controlling interest in the company. In those cases, the particular gift of stock becomes more important. Perhaps a court should not favor Antonio so much as a beneficiary, but as a beneficiary *of Computerwiz stock*. Because motives have a way of mixing,[7] trying to identify what a testator might have wanted may yield incomplete information, but at least it seems to be asking the right question in this context.[8]

[B] Increases

People often acquire assets derived from property they already own. Bondholders may receive interest. Stockholders may receive dividends in the form of cash or additional stock. Stocks may split, with the company offering two new shares for each old one. When these changes occur between the time of a will's execution and the testator's death or during the estate administration, questions can arise about which beneficiaries get the "add-ons," the residuary takers or the beneficiaries receiving the underlying property.[9]

---

to my . . . daughter" was a specific bequest.); *In re* Estate of DeVoss, 474 N.W.2d 542 (Iowa 1991) (For abatement purposes, the language, "I give, devise and bequeath . . . all of the real property of which . . . I may be entitled wherever situated" was a general bequest.). Sometimes a court will perform impressive contortions, as in *In re* Fitch's Will, 118 N.Y.S.2d 234 (N.Y. App. 1952), where the court preserved a gift of stock from the ademption doctrine by finding a general gift, but also gave the beneficiary the benefit of a later stock split, which traditionally accompanies only specific gifts.

Such conflicts may be a good thing. A stream of cases consistently construing the same language the same way indicates a court which does not look past the label to its consequence, but only applies the rules in a knee-jerk fashion. *See* John C. Paulus, *Special and General Legacies of Securities—Whither Testator's Intent*, 43 Iowa L. Rev. 467, 518 (1958).

[7] For some examples in this context, see Gregory S. Alexander, *Ademption and The Domain of Formality in Wills Law*, 55 Alb. L. Rev. 1067, 1080-1081 (1992).

[8] Of course, often the circumstance will be one the testator has not anticipated. Then our goal becomes a mix of trying to determine what most testators probably would want and what rules make sense from fairness and efficiency perspectives. For a debate about whether clear, if arbitrary, rules are better in this context, see Mark L. Ascher, *The 1990 Uniform Probate Code: Older and Better, or More Like the Internal Revenue Code?*, 77 Minn. L. Rev. 639 (1993); Mary L. Fellows, *Traveling the Road of Probate Reform: Finding the Way to Your Will (A Response to Professor Ascher)*, 77 Minn. L. Rev. 659 (1993); Mark L. Ascher, *A Response to Professor Fellows*, 77 Minn. L. Rev. 683 (1993).

[9] *See* Atkinson at 749-753. Commentators often refer to these additions as "accessions and accretions," without distinguishing between them, and seldom using either word alone. Dictionary definitions largely overlap, and the dual phrase seems to be with us out of habit, like "null and void."

Absent contrary intention of the testator, specific gifts usually include accrued, but unpaid, income.[10] Gifts of corporate securities, however, have vexed courts for years. Recall Javier's gift to Antonio and consider what to do with dividends. Suppose that after the will's execution, Computerwiz sends Javier a cash dividend. All authorities would agree that Antonio would have no claim to that dividend after Javier's death. There would be no tracing; the cash would be an estate asset, just like any other money Javier earned before he died. If the dividend were paid in Computerwiz stock, however, Antonio might argue that he should get the additional shares as part of his Computerwiz gift. The authorities are split.[11] Most courts say stock dividends do not go along with the underlying gift, because stock dividends, like their cash counterparts, are paid out of corporate earnings.[12] Other courts note that after a stock dividend, the total shares the stockholder owns still reflect the same percentage ownership of the company. To deny the beneficiary the stock dividend dilutes the gift. Therefore, these courts give stock dividends to the beneficiaries of the underlying stock.[13]

Stock splits have also been troublesome. Suppose that before Javier's death, Computerwiz splits its stock, two for one, so that Javier dies owning 100 shares of their stock. The traditional approach of deciding whether Antonio gets 50 or 100 shares was to ask whether his gift was specific or general. If specific, the new shares would go along as part of the basic gift. If general, they would not. A newer view gives the donee the additional shares after a stock split, regardless of the form of the gift, absent a showing of the testator's different intention.

Bostwick v. Hurstel[14] illustrates the modern approach to stock splits. In 1957, Cecile Bostwick gave James 25 shares of AT&T stock. By the time she died in 1965, the stock had split twice. James argued that he should get 150 shares. The court agreed, and took the opportunity to reject the traditional rule, on several grounds. First, relying upon the general/specific distinction in the abstract ignores a testator's intention regarding the specific question at hand; namely, where additional stock from a stock split

---

Similar questions arise during a trust administration, when a trustee must decide whether to allocate receipts to income or principal. *See* § 55[A][2][c], *infra*.

[10] Similarly, gifts of land with growing crops typically include the crops. *See* Cheshire v. Keaton, 190 S.E. 579 (Ga. 1937) (gift of farm included all the crops in the fields).

Because general legacies come out of estate assets, they do not have any increases to carry along. Often, however, they bear interest starting a year after the date of death.

[11] Authorities also question the standard treatment of stock dividends for purposes of corporate accounting. *See* Bayless Manning & James J. Hanks, Jr., Legal Capital 127-130 (3d 1990).

[12] *See* Hicks v. Kerr, 104 A. 426 (Md. 1918). Ella Hicks' will gave 42 shares of stock to her husband. Before she died, she received a stock dividend of 16 more. Her husband took only the original 42 shares.

[13] *See, e.g.*, Butler v. Dobbins, 53 A.2d 270 (Me. 1947) (stock and cash dividends in First National Bank went to specific devisees). This is the approach of the UPC. *See* § 2-605.

[14] 304 N.E.2d 186 (Mass. 1973). *See also* Watson v. Santalucia, 427 S.E. 2d 466 (W. Va. 1993) (following *Bostwick*).

should go. Second, the traditional approach ignores the reality that a stock split dilutes the value of each share. Third, basing different results on the general/specific distinction asks for litigation on what kind of a gift is involved. A rule giving stock splits to the donee of the underlying stock follows the likely intention of testators, recognizes the reality of corporate accounting, and avoids litigation.[15]

[C] Ademption

Recall that Javier's will gave Antonio 50 shares of Computerwiz, but that by the time Javier died, he no longer owned the stock. We might say that because the stock is not there, the gift fails, or we might order Javier's executor to buy Computerwiz for Antonio. The result will depend upon the particular jurisdiction's approach to "ademption by extinction," often shortened to "ademption."[16]

The dominant approach relies upon classifying the gift as general or specific. If the gift is general, Javier's executor uses general estate assets to buy the stock for Antonio. If the gift is specific, Antonio loses out under the "identity" theory, which says that a specific gift fails if the subject matter is not an estate asset at death.[17] The identity theory is easy to understand and, superficially at least, easy to apply.[18] In many situations, however, it defeats testators' probable intentions, so courts have developed various devices for avoiding the strict doctrine. This subsection first gives examples of intention-defeating circumstances, and then examines some avoidance devices. It closes with a look at the changes proposed by the UPC to scrap the identity theory.

---

[15] The UPC adopted the modern approach in 1990. *Compare* UPC (pre-1990) § 2-607 *with* UPC § 2-605. *See also* Restatement (Third) of Prop. § 5.3 (devise carries additional securities "to the extent that the post-execution acquisitions resulted from the testator's ownership of the described securities").

[16] Some authorities speak of another form of ademption, this one "by satisfaction." Ademption by satisfaction occurs if a testator gives someone a lifetime gift to "satisfy" a gift under the will. Because the doctrine is very similar to the theory of making "advancements" of intestate shares, this text discusses advancements and gifts in satisfaction together in § 24, *supra*.

To avoid confusion between ademption by extinction and ademption by satisfaction, this text calls the former doctrine "ademption" and the latter "satisfaction."

[17] The identity theory seems to have gotten its start in decisions penned by Lord Thurlow in the 1780s. For this reason, the doctrine is sometimes called "Lord Thurlow's rule." *See* John C. Paulus, *Ademption by Extinction: Smiting Lord Thurlow's Ghost*, 2 Tex. Tech. L. Rev. 195 (1971). The rule was a response to dissatisfaction with attempted searches for testators' intentions. Interestingly, the law is now moving back to considering intention. For an enlightening, readable discussion of the law's tendency to cycle between clarity and fuzziness, see Carol M. Rose, *Crystals and Mud in Property Law*, 40 Stan. L. Rev. 577 (1988).

For short descriptions of ademption generally, see Atkinson at 741-748; Haskell at 111-115; McGovern & Kurtz at 292-300. For detailed treatment, see Page §§ 54.3-54.5. *See also* Restatement (Third) of Prop. § 5.2.

[18] Because the result depends so directly upon the classification, arguments often arise about which classification fits. *See* § 46[A], *supra*.

Strict adherence to the identity theory can defeat a typical testator's intention in several circumstances.[19] Recall Javier's gift to Antonio and suppose that the will gave "my 50 shares of Computerwiz."[20] One can imagine Javier selling his Computerwiz and buying Solar Energy without ever giving a thought to his will provision.[21] The identity theory would preclude substituting of the Solar Energy stock for the Computerwiz.

Sometimes assets are missing even though testators have taken no action to remove the assets from the estate. In *In re Hilpert's Estate*,[22] John Hilpert left his library to the Bishop of Brooklyn and his two half-brothers. Before Hilpert died, however, the library burned. The Bishop sought the insurance proceeds, but the court applied the identity theory and rejected the claim. In *In re Estate of Nakoneczny*,[23] Michael Nakoneczny left real estate to his son, Paul. The Urban Redevelopment Authority later acquired the land, and Michael put most of the proceeds into bonds. When Paul claimed the bonds after his father's death, the court applied the identity theory and declined to trace the gift.[24]

A particularly poignant case is *McGee v. McGee*.[25] Claire McGee's will gave $20,000 to her friend Fedelma, and her Texaco stock plus "any and all monies standing in my name on deposit in any banking institution" to her grandchildren. Anticipating Claire's death, her son Richard, acting under a power of attorney, withdrew funds from the savings accounts and, among other things, bought U.S. Treasury Bonds which could be used to save money on federal estate taxes.[26] The question was whether the gift to the grandchildren was adeemed, or whether the money from the savings accounts could be traced to the bonds. The court labeled the grandchildren's gift as "specific"[27] and, applying the identity theory, said the trial court should have excluded evidence of Claire's intent and barred the grandchildren's claim to the bonds. The fact that Richard, rather than Claire, made

---

[19] Whether we believe that a particular result thwarts a particular testator's intention depends largely on what we believe that intention would have been. For more discussion of this point in the context of changes in property, see § 46[A], *supra. See also* § 41[A], *supra* (discussing the search for donor intention generally).

[20] Under traditional rules, use of the "my" would make this a specific gift.

[21] A somewhat less likely, but still possible, scenario is that Javier got mad at Antonio and sold the stock to revoke the gift. In either case, the identity theory would not allow an inquiry beyond whether Javier owned Computerwiz at his death.

[22] 300 N.Y.S. 886 (N.Y. Surr. 1937).

[23] 319 A.2d 893 (Pa. 1974).

[24] *See also* Estate of Hume, 984 S.W.2d 602 (Tenn. 1999) (House sold at foreclosure before testator's death; specific gift of house adeemed.).

[25] 413 A.2d 72 (R.I. 1980).

[26] The rule applies to certain bonds issued before 1971. The bonds are purchased at a discounted value and normally not redeemable until maturity. They can be used to pay estate taxes, however, credited at par value plus accrued interest. For this reason, they are often called "flower bonds," which "blossom" at death. *See* John R. Price, Price on Contemporary Estate Planning § 12.48 (1982). Ironically, there was no estate tax liability to Claire's estate.

[27] This characterization can be questioned. For one thing, if the grandchildren got the money in the savings accounts, where was the executor to get Fedelma's $20,000? It seems almost as if the grandchildren's gift was the Texaco stock plus a "residuary" of Claire's cash.

the purchase did not matter, because Claire had expressed her approval of his plan.[28]

Because of the identity rule's harshness, courts have developed several avoidance devices. If the testator is incompetent, courts often trace assets when someone acting on behalf of the incompetent has transferred property subject to a specific devise.[29] Another technique is to manipulate the general/specific distinction so they can avoid the ademption issue altogether.[30] If the gift is clearly "specific," the "change-in-form" exception may come into play. For example, in our continuing hypothetical, if Computerwiz sold out to Apple, which issued Apple stock to Computerwiz stockholders, Antonio would get Javier's (new) Apple stock.[31] Also, courts can sometimes save a gift by construing the will as speaking at the time of the testator's death. Property matching the will's description would be covered, even if acquired later. Thus, a gift of "my car" would almost certainly apply to the car owned at death.

In response to frustrations about the intention-defeating effects of the identity rule and the confusion caused by courts' various attempts to avoid it, the 1990 UPC created an intention-driven rule.[32] Section 2-606 details

---

[28] She approved, however, because she thought the bond purchase would make more money available to the children and grandchildren. Some courts apply the identity theory even if the testator had no opportunity to revise the will. *See In re* Barry's Estate, 252 P.2d 437 (Okla. 1952) (A testator was killed in an accident while driving a car her will gave to her friend. The friend took only the scrap value, not the insured value.).

[29] The leading case is Morse v. Converse, 113 A. 214 (N.H. 1921). There a guardian took money from a savings account to buy a Liberty Bond and for other purposes. The beneficiary of the savings account got the bond, but not the other funds.

[30] Thus a gift of "100 shares of Glowcorp stock" would normally be general, but if Glowcorp were a family corporation, courts would likely find the gift specific. In an ademption setting, they would look ahead to the consequence and avoid sending the executor out to buy stock in a very limited market. *See In re* Buck's Estate, 196 P.2d 769 (Cal. 1948) (In a proceeding to determine partial ademption, the court held that the testator's gifts of 5000 shares of Belridge Oil Company to each of his children were specific devises because the testator's family, along with two other families, controlled 61% of the voting stock, and the stock had never been traded on any stock exchange.).

[31] *See In re* Estate of Watkins, 284 So. 2d 679 (Fla. 1973) (no ademption where testator's gift of 400 shares of Amerada Petroleum Corporation was converted into shares issued by the Amerada Hess corporation after the two corporations merged).

In general, courts have been hostile to applying the change-in-form principle to gifts other than corporate securities. In *McGee*, for example, the court did not consider the bonds merely a change in form from the savings accounts. *But see* Johnston v. Estate of Wheeler, 745 A.2d 345 (D.C. 2000) (no ademption where will referred to testator's "pension" and testator rolled her benefits into an IRA).

[32] For criticism of the earlier version and recommendations of changes which were later adopted, see Richard W. Effland, *Will Construction Under the Uniform Probate Code*, 63 Or. L. Rev. 337, 358 (1984). For discussions of the new version, see Gregory S. Alexander, *Ademption and the Domain of Formality in Wills Law*, 55 Alb. L. Rev. 1067 (1992); Mark L. Ascher, *The 1990 Uniform Probate Code: Older and Better, or More Like the Internal Revenue Code?*, 77 Minn. L. Rev. 639, 643-649 (1993); Mary L. Fellows, *Traveling the Road of Probate Reform: Finding the Way to Your Will (A Response to Professor Ascher)*, 77 Minn. L. Rev. 659, 663-674 (1993).

specific situations in which tracing is appropriate,[33] expands the change-in-form principle,[34] and sets up a presumption *against* ademption by extinction.[35] The adoption of an intent-based approach to ademption is one more step in the UPC's attempt to open up will construction to include extrinsic evidence[36] and, thereby, further integrate the law of wills and will substitutes. Interestingly, however, the UPC does not extend the rules of Section 2-606 to will substitutes.[37]

One recent case contrasts with the UPC's approach. *Wasserman v. Cohen*[38] involved a revocable inter vivos trust which Frieda Drapkin had created, naming herself as trustee. The trust document directed the trustee to convey a specific apartment building to the plaintiff on Frieda's death. Before her death, however, Frieda sold the building without ever having put the building in trust. The court followed its continuing trend of extending wills doctrines to will substitutes,[39] and held (in contrast to the UPC) that the ademption doctrine applied. On the other hand, the court stuck to its traditional identity rule, declaring that its "so-called harsh results" can be avoided by careful drafting.

[D] Abatement and Exoneration

Two other doctrines relate not so much to changes in property as to creditors' claims, but they traditionally depend so heavily upon the classification of gifts that it makes sense to consider them here. Abatement addresses what to do when there is not enough money to go around. Exoneration considers the impact of liens on specifically devised property.

Suppose Ralph's will creates the following gifts: "(1) my woodworking tools to my daughter Victoria, (2) $8,000 to my son Michael, (3) $4,000 to

---

For a decision applying a intention approach, see Estate of Austin v. Shrine Hosp. for Crippled Children, 169 Cal. Rptr. 648 (Cal. App. 1980) (Testator's will gave a promissory note to his friend. The note was paid off after the execution of the will, but was not adeemed. The friend received the face value of the note as cash payment from the estate.). *See also* Restatement (Third) of Prop. § 5.2 (adopting intention theory) and cmt. d (endorsing a liberal change-in-form approach).

[33] *See, e.g.,* UPC §§ 2-606(a)(2) (condemnation awards), (a)(3) (insurance proceeds), (b) (proceeds of property transferred by someone acting for an incapacitated person).

[34] UPC § 2-606(a)(5) (property acquired to replace specifically devised property). Under this section, even a gift of "my 1998 Jeep" would include replacement vehicles.

[35] UPC § 2-606(a)(6). The comment to the section calls the presumption "mild." For discussion of how the presumption should work, see Gregory S. Alexander, *Ademption and the Domain of Formality in Wills Law*, 55 Alb. L. Rev. 1067, 1079-1080 (1992).

[36] *See* UPC § 2-601 (declaring that the construction rules apply "[i]n the absence of a finding of a contrary intention," and not limiting the search to the will's language). For discussion of this point in general, see § 41[B], *supra.*

[37] By presuming against ademption, the UPC may prompt more lawyers to talk about this question with their clients. *See* Gregory S. Alexander, *Ademption and The Domain of Formality in Wills Law*, 55 Alb. L. Rev. 1067, 1086-1087 (1992).

[38] 606 N.E.2d 901 (Mass. 1993).

[39] *See, e.g.,* Clymer v. Mayo, 473 N.E.2d 1084 (Mass. 1985), discussed in § 45[B][1], *supra.*

my daughter Marie, and (4) the rest of my estate to my wife Margaret."
Suppose further that the tools are worth $6,000 and other estate assets total
$24,000, for a total of $30,000. Debts total $15,000. Which beneficiaries'
shares go to pay the creditors? Typically, gifts to will beneficiaries "abate,"
or fail in the face of inadequate funds, in the following order: (1) residuary,
(2) general, and (3) demonstrative and specific as a single class.[40] Multiple
gifts in the same class abate proportionately. This hierarchy would mean
that Margaret would get nothing; Michael would get $6,000; Marie, $3,000;
and Victoria, the tools. A rule making the residuary bear the creditors'
claims presents a warning to drafters. If the residuary beneficiary is primary, the will should not be too generous with specific and general gifts.[41]

Exoneration is the common law doctrine that a specific gift transfers free
from any outstanding mortgage or lien, which has to be paid by the
residuary estate.[42] For example, suppose you owned a house (subject to a
mortgage) and a car (subject to a lien), and suppose your will gave the house
to your sister, the car to your brother and all the rest of your property to
your mother. If your jurisdiction followed the exoneration doctrine, your
mother's gift would be reduced by the amounts necessary to pay off the
mortgage and the car loan. Some jurisdictions recognize the doctrine, while
others do not.[43] The important point for document drafters is that if you
include a specific gift, say whether it passes free from creditors' encum-
brances, or subject to them.[44]

---

[40] Any intestate property would abate first. *See generally* Atkinson at 754; McGovern &
Kurtz at 303-303. If the claimant is not a creditor, but rather a surviving spouse or pretermitted
heir, a different hierarchy may apply. For discussion of those situations, see §§ 28[B] (spousal
election) and 29 (forgotten spouses and children), *supra*.

[41] One way to avoid having general legacies take up too much of the estate is to state them
in percentage terms, instead of dollar amounts.

[42] *See* John C. Paulus, *Exoneration of Specific Devises: Legislation vs. The Common Law*,
6 Willamette L. Rev. 53 (1970).

[43] *Compare* Ashkenazy v. Estate of Ashkenazy, 140 So. 2d 331 (Fla. Dist. Ct. App. 1962)
(residuary taker had to pay off mortgage on real estate given to former wife), *with* UPC § 2-607
(no right of exoneration).

[44] One of the dangers of a clause at the beginning of a will calling for payment of debts
out of the residuary is that a court might read the clause as evidence of intent to apply the
exoneration doctrine. *See* O'Meara v. Shreve, 26 F.2d 998 (D.C. Ct. App. 1928). The UPC
provides that "a general directive in the will to pay debts" is not enough to bring the doctrine
into play. UPC § 2-607.

Chapter 12

THE RULE AGAINST PERPETUITIES

No interest is good unless it must vest, if at all, not later than twenty-one years after some life in being at the creation of the interest.[1]

§ 47 Introduction

Perhaps the most feared doctrine facing law students, the Rule Against Perpetuities has a bad, and somewhat inaccurate, image. Unquestionably, it is complex, both in its own right, and especially because it builds so much on other technical material.[1] With some work, however, the basics of the Rule[2] are understandable. You can learn to spot suspect situations. You can learn a framework for testing different interests for compliance with the Rule. Indeed, it is even possible to become overconfident about your understanding of the Rule. The goals of this chapter are to provide tools you can use to identify and solve perpetuities problems, and to leave you with a healthy respect for the Rule's intricacies.[3]

The Rule is among those rules of law which limit the power of one generation to restrict the uses future generations put to property. Unlike the other "dead hand" doctrines discussed earlier,[4] the Rule does not focus on the substance of various restrictions. Rather, the Rule is concerned with time. It asks: *How long* will a cloud remain? The Rule cuts a balance between the interests of the older and younger generations.[5] Roughly

---

[1] John C. Gray, The Rule Against Perpetuities § 201 (Roland Gray ed., 4th ed. 1942).

[1] Even the legendary John Chipman Gray said it engendered modesty. John C. Gray, The Rule Against Perpetuities at xi (Roland Gray ed., 4th ed. 1942). For a discussion of Gray's influence, see Stephen A. Siegel, *John Chipman Gray, Legal Formalism, and the Transformation of Perpetuities Law*, 36 U. Miami L. Rev. 439 (1982). For a start on the history, see George L. Haskins, *Extending the Grasp of the Dead Hand: Reflections on the Origins of the Rule Against Perpetuities*, 126 U. Pa. L. Rev. 19 (1977).

[2] In this chapter, a capitalized "Rule" means the common law Rule Against Perpetuities.

[3] For an excellent, accessible article which integrates "how-to" explanations with substantive rules, including modern reforms, see Jesse Dukeminier, *A Modern Guide to Perpetuities*, 74 Cal. L. Rev. 1867 (1986). The classic short treatment of the Rule is Professor Leach's article. *See* W. Barton Leach, *Perpetuities in a Nutshell*, 51 Harv. L. Rev. 638 (1938).

For other discussions or sample problems, see the sources cited in § 32, *supra*, and Frederic S. Schwartz, A Student's Guide to the Rule Against Perpetuities (1988). For a modern, comprehensive discussion with particular attention to how the Rule affects planning, see David M. Becker, Perpetuities and Estate Planning (1993).

[4] *See* §§ 13 (restrictions on beneficial interests in trust) and 31 (public policy limits on gifts), *supra*.

[5] *See* Dobris & Sterk at 745-748; Lewis M. Simes, *The Policy Against Perpetuities*, 103 U.

speaking, the old folks get to tie up property for about 100 years; after that, the cycle restarts.

Discussion of the Rule raises a familiar theme: reform. In this area, reform has been moving along for some time, but in fits and starts. Encouraged by Professor W. Barton Leach's colorful writing,[6] legislatures have been making changes since the late 1940s.[7] More recent reform boosts came in 1983 with the Restatement (Second) of Property[8] and, especially, in 1986 with the Uniform Statutory Rule Against Perpetuities.[9] More recently, a movement is growing to abolish the Rule as applied to interests in trust.[10]

In light of widespread movement to change the Rule, why should law students study it? Apart from the reasons for studying present and future interests generally,[11] understanding the Rule is important because even in states which have reformed it, those reforms build upon the basic structure of the Rule.[12] Of course, if you practice in one of the states still following the Rule, you will want to avoid embarrassment[13] or, worse, malpractice.[14]

This chapter first offers a framework for approaching perpetuities questions. Next, it highlights basic principles of the Rule. Finally, the chapter discusses the reforms, which increasingly have grabbed legislative attention.

Pa. L. Rev. 707, 723 (1955). For the view that the Rule may not cut the right balance, see Adam J. Hirsch & William K. S. Wang, *A Qualitative Theory of the Dead Hand*, 68 Ind. L.J. 1, 18-19 (1992). *See also* Jeffrey E. Stake, *Darwin, Donations, and the Illusion of Dead Hand Control*, 64 Tul. L. Rev. 705 (1990).

[6] *See, e.g.*, W. Barton Leach, *Perpetuities in Perspective: Ending the Rule's Reign of Terror*, 65 Harv. L. Rev. 721 (1952); W. Barton Leach, *Perpetuities: Staying the Slaughter of the Innocents*, 68 L.Q. Rev. 35 (1952).

[7] Pennsylvania led the way in 1947. The current version of its statute is found at 20 Pa. Cons. Stat. Ann. § 6104(B). For an endorsement, see W. Barton Leach, *Perpetuities Legislation: Hail Pennsylvania*, 108 U. Pa. L. Rev. 1124 (1960).

[8] Restatement (Second) of Prop. §§ 1.1-1.6.

[9] The statute is now part of the Uniform Probate Code. UPC §§ 2-901 to 2-906.

[10] *See* § 53[C], *infra*.

[11] *See* § 32, *supra*.

[12] *See* David M. Becker, *Estate Planning and the Reality of Perpetuities Problems Today: Reliance upon Statutory Reform and Saving Clauses Is Not Enough*, 64 Wash. U. L.Q. 287 (1986); Robert J. Lynn, *Perpetuities Literacy for the 21st Century*, 50 Ohio St. L.J. 219 (1989).

[13] Do not let it be said of your drafting, as it was of one lawyer's work, "This petition . . . seeks answers to questions arising from an artlessly drafted will that, among its many inadequacies, includes a blatant violation of the rule against perpetuities." Dewire v. Haveles, 534 N.E.2d 782, 783 (Mass. 1989).

[14] Lawyers and law students have sought some comfort in *Lucas v. Hamm*, 364 P.2d 685 (Cal. 1962), which said that the Rule is so confusing that, on the facts of that case, it was not negligence for a lawyer to draft a document so as to violate the Rule. *Lucas'* continued viability as a malpractice shield is in some doubt, however. *See* Wright v. Williams, 121 Cal. Rptr. 194, 199 n.2 (Cal. App. 1975) ("There is reason to doubt that the ultimate conclusion of *Lucas v. Hamm* is valid in today's state of the art."). For a brief discussion of malpractice in estate planning, see § 1, *supra*.

§ 48 A Framework for Analysis

The purpose of this section is to help you identify a perpetuities problem and give you a method to use when you find one. Three ideas permeate the analysis. First, the Rule is concerned about questions which stay unresolved for too long. Second, the Rule judges each interest based on facts we know at the time the interest becomes indestructible in a grantee.[1] Third, the Rule applies a *possibilities* test, so that if anything could go wrong, you must assume it will. These ideas prompt a series of questions to ask about each interest you test.[2]

First, is this interest contingent?[3] In general, the Rule applies to all contingent remainders and executory interests, and it does not apply to vested interests.[4] There are some refinements to that principle, however. A contingent gift to a second charity, following a gift to a first charity, is not subject to the Rule.[5] More importantly, vested remainders subject to open, despite their "vested" label, *are* subject to the Rule.[6] Otherwise, you are safe to limit your inquiry to contingent interests.[7]

---

[1] If a deed creates the interest, the relevant time is that of the deed's delivery. If a will creates the interest, the time is the testator's date of death. If a revocable trust creates the interest, the time is the expiration of the power to revoke (usually the settlor's death). For property subject to a general, presently exercisable power of appointment, the perpetuities period should not start to run until the expiration of the power. *See* Restatement (Second) of Prop. § 1.2.

[2] For different formulations, see David M. Becker, Perpetuities and Estate Planning 233-239 (1993); Frederic S. Schwartz, A Student's Guide to the Rule Against Perpetuities 32-37 (1988).

[3] Here you must consider rules of construction. *See* §§ 35[B][2][c] (vested or contingent remainders) and 45[B][2][c] (survivorship requirements), *supra*.

Authorities disagree about the effect of the Rule on the construction process. At one end of the spectrum is Gray, who separated the analysis into two parts. First, construe the document, then "remorselessly" apply the Rule. *See* John C. Gray, The Rule Against Perpetuities § 629 (Roland Gray ed., 4th ed. 1942). At the other end are authorities that state a preference for construing language in a way that preserves interests. *See, e.g.*, 765 Ill. Comp. Stat. 305/4(c)(1)(A). *See also* White v. Fleet Bank, 739 A.2d 373 Me. 1999) (trust); Coulter & Smith, Ltd. v. Russell, 966 P.2d 852 (Utah 1998) (option under contract).

[4] The Rule also applies to some commercial transactions, like options. *See* McGovern & Kurtz at 444-447. The UPC exempts most non-donative transfers from the Rule. *See* UPC § 2-904(1).

[5] A contingent gift to a charity following a gift to a non-charity *is* subject to the Rule. *See* Bergin & Haskell at 223-224; Simes at 296-297.

[6] The openness of the class is a contingency which must be resolved within the perpetuities period. This aspect of the rule is covered as part of the discussion of how the Rule applies to class gifts. *See* § 50, *infra*.

[7] Despite their ability to cloud titles, possibilities of reverter and rights of entry are not subject to the Rule because they are retained interests. *See* Brown v. Independent Baptist Church of Woburn, 91 N.E.2d 922 (Mass. 1950) (possibility of reverter not subject to the Rule). For criticism, see W. Barton Leach, *Perpetuities in Perspective: Ending the Rule's Reign of Terror*, 65 Harv. L. Rev. 721, 741-745 (1952). For a review of these reversionary interests, see § 35[A], *supra*.

Also, in the rare case when an executory interest is certain to vest in the future ("to Alphonse in 20 years"), the Rule treats it as vested. *See* ALP § 24.20; Jesse Dukeminier, *Contingent Remainders and Executory Interests: A Requiem for the Distinction*, 43 Minn. L. Rev. 13, 23-28 (1958); John Makdisi, *The Vesting of Executory Interests*, 59 Tul. L. Rev. 366, 388 (1984).

Second, what will it take to resolve the contingency? The point here is to be precise. Identify exactly what we will need to know in order to say the interest has vested.

Third, is there someone (or some group) you can identify and say, "Within your lifetime(s) or 21 years thereafter, this contingency will be resolved, one way or the other"?[8]

Identifying this "validating life"[9] poses the biggest initial problem for most students. Take it in two steps.[10] First, narrow your search to "relevant lives," those persons who have something to do with the contingency. In this connection, recall those problems which make interests contingent: identification and conditions precedent.[11] Relevant lives might be: (1) the beneficiaries themselves,[12] (2) people who can affect the identity of the beneficiaries,[13] and (3) people who can affect any condition precedent.[14] In order to help, of course, these people must be alive at the beginning of the perpetuities period.[15] Once you have identified the people who might make a difference, try them out. As to each person, ask "Can we be sure we will have resolved the problem by the time of your death (plus 21 years)?" If so, that life can be a "validating life," establishing that the interest satisfies the Rule. If the answer is no, try another life. When you run out of relevant lives, and none works, the interest is void under the Rule.

Consider some examples, to see the process.

Example 12-1: Suppose a grant from Virgil "to Denise for life, remainder to Nicole if she survives Denise." Denise's life estate is presently vested, not subject to the Rule. Nicole's remainder is contingent upon surviving Denise. Here we have two relevant lives, Denise and Nicole. We also have

---

[8] The question is adapted from one formulated by Professors Clark, Lusky and Murphy. *See* Clark, Lusky & Murphy at 761.

[9] Earlier formulations called it a "measuring life." The term "validating life" better captures the idea. The newer term may have originated in Note, *Understanding the Measuring Life in the Rule Against Perpetuities*, 1974 Wash. U. L.Q. 265. For a tracing of the term's use, see Robert L. Fletcher, *Perpetuities: Basic Clarity, Muddled Reform*, 63 Wash. L. Rev. 791, 804 n.20 (1988). Professor Fletcher's article also offers a different approach to analyzing perpetuities problems. *See also* David M. Becker, *A Methodology for Solving Perpetuities Problems Under the Common Law Rule: A Step-by-Step Process That Carefully Identifies All Testing Lives in Being*, 67 Wash. U. L.Q. 949 (1989); Mark Reutlinger, Wills, Trusts & Estates 187-212.

[10] *See* Jesse Dukeminier, *A Modern Guide to Perpetuities*, 74 Cal. L. Rev. 1867, 1873-1874 (1986).

[11] *See* § 35[B][2][b], *supra*.

[12] Ezra, in a gift of remainder "to Ezra if he reaches 21."

[13] Isadora, in a gift of remainder "to Isadora's children."

[14] Kayla, in a gift of remainder "to Lindsey if Kayla attends college."

[15] Persons who are relevant lives because they fit a *description* (rather than because they are named) will not be validating lives if someone currently unborn could also meet that description. We must be certain that the validating life is someone who was alive at the start of the period. This rule causes the problem of the unborn spouse (see § 49[B], *infra*) and plays havoc with class gifts (see § 50, *infra*).

two validating lives, because we now know that at the death of either one we will be able to tell whether Nicole survives Denise. The remainder is valid. Virgil's reversion is presently vested and not subject to the Rule.

Example 12-2: Suppose Kenneth grants property "to Penny for life, remainder to her first child to get married." At the time, Penny has one child, Allison. Penny's life estate is presently vested and not subject to the Rule. The remainder is contingent upon identification as Penny's first child to get married. Penny is a relevant life, because she supplies the children. She is not a validating life, however, because we cannot be sure that within 21 years after her death one of her children will get married. Allison is also a relevant life. She, too, fails as a validating life. While it is possible that she will get married and thus meet the condition within her lifetime, she might not.[16] Allison might die tomorrow, and Penny might have another child who would get married more than 21 years after Penny's death.[17] Having run out of relevant lives to test, we have established that the remainder is void under the Rule. Kenneth's reversion is presently vested, not subject to the Rule.

Example 12-3: Suppose the same facts as the example above, except that the remainder is "to Penny's first child if he or she gets married." Because we know that Allison is Penny's first child, the remainder is not contingent upon identification but, rather, upon the condition precedent of getting married. Because Allison will either get married or not within her own lifetime, she can serve as the validating life for her remainder. Notice three things about this example. First, a slight change in wording made a big difference, because it changed the nature of the question to be resolved. Second, in order to be valid under the Rule, Allison's remainder need not ever vest. The Rule's concern is not whether the remainder vests, but how long we must wait to find out. We only need to know that the uncertainty definitely will be resolved within the lifetime (plus 21 years) of someone now around. Third, the holder of the interest in question (here, Allison) can be her own validating life.

Example 12-4: For a more complex example, suppose a grant from Helen "to David for life, remainder to Fred if he marries Jennifer before David dies, but if Fred does not marry Jennifer before David dies, to David's firstborn child." David has no children. David's life estate is vested, not subject to the Rule. Fred's remainder is contingent upon the condition precedent of marrying Jennifer before David's death. David, Fred, and Jennifer can all serve as validating lives for that remainder. Because we will know by the death of any of them whether Fred acted in time, Fred's remainder

---

[16] One of the doctrines reforming the Rule would allow us to "wait and see" if Allison gets married. If she does, the interest would be valid, because the contingency would be resolved in time. The common law Rule, however, does not allow waiting to see how things turn out. It demands knowing now that the question will be resolved in time. For discussion of wait and see, see § 53[A], *infra*.

[17] The later child would not be able to serve as a validating life, because that child was not living at the time of the grant.

is valid under the Rule.[18] David's child's remainder is contingent upon Fred's not marrying Jennifer in time and upon the child being identified as first born. You must measure each contingency under the Rule. As before, David, Fred, and Jennifer can also serve as validating lives on the marriage question. David can be the validating life on the identification question. We will know by his death who his first born child is.[19] Because both contingencies will be resolved in time, the second remainder is also valid. Helen's reversion is vested, not subject to the Rule.

Rather than dual contingencies, like the ones attached to David's child's remainder, we might have alternative contingencies. The Rule judges each contingency separately. If one contingency would cause a void gift, but the other, a valid gift, the void contingency fails, but the gift is good, subject to the valid contingency.[20]

Example 12-5: Suppose Vincent's will gives property "to Donald for life, then to the first of Donald's children to reach age 21, or if none reach 21, to the first to attend the University of Michigan." Donald and his daughter, Lee (age 20) survive Vincent. Lee has not yet attended Michigan. Donald's life estate is presently vested, not subject to the Rule. Lee's remainder is contingent upon being identified as the first to reach 21 or attend Michigan. Donald can be the validating life for the age contingency, but the contingency to attend Michigan fails because it is not tied into a validating life.

Example 12-6: Finally, consider a grant which uses successive remainders for life. Suppose Beth gives property "to Ira for life, then for life to Ira's oldest child who survives him, then for life to the first child of that child, then to Samuel." At the time of the grant, Ira has two children, Maia and Alexander. Ira's life estate is presently vested, not subject to the rule. The first remainder for life is contingent upon identification as Ira's oldest child who survives him. Ira is the validating life. Because we will resolve the identity crisis at Ira's death, that remainder is good. The next remainder for life is contingent upon identification as the first child of the one who held the prior remainder for life. Ira cannot serve as the validating life, because his grandchild (who would take the remainder in question) might not be born for more than 21 years after Ira's death. Maia and Alexander cannot be validating lives, because they might have died, leaving an as yet

---

[18] The remainder may be invalid on public policy grounds, because it affords Fred such a narrow choice of spouses. *See* § 31, *supra.*

[19] More accurately, we will know within nine months or so. As with other areas of the law, people are considered "born" when they are conceived.

Changes in technology threaten to undermine the Rule's assumptions that women cannot have children after they die and that men only have another nine months (or so). The possibilities of sperm and ova banks and frozen embryos challenge lawyers to rethink the rules. *See* W. Barton Leach, *Perpetuities in the Atomic Age: The Sperm Bank and the Fertile Decedent,* 48 A.B.A. J. 942 (1962); Daniel M. Schuyler, *The New Biology and the Rule Against Perpetuities,* 15 UCLA L. Rev. 420 (1968). For one attempt, see 765 Ill. Comp. Stat. 305/4(c)(3). The UPC solves the problem by disregarding post-death procreation for purposes of the Rule. *See* UPC § 2-901(d).

[20] *See* ALP § 24.54.

unborn sibling to be the oldest one to survive Ira. The second remainder for life fails. Samuel's remainder is vested, not subject to the Rule.[21]

These examples prompt some generalizations. Like all generalizations, these must be used with care, because they will not always apply. They can, however, help identify probable trouble spots. First, imagine a typical estate plan, with a life estate, a remainder for life, and an ultimate remainder. (See Chart 12-1.) The life estate is presently vested, not subject to the rule.

Chart 12-1

A Typical Perpetuities Scenario

Life Estate ⟶ Remainder for Life ⟶ Ultimate Remainder

The remainder for life is likely to be valid, because often the contingencies surrounding it will be resolved at the end of the first life estate. If that is the case, the first life tenant will be someone alive when the interests were created and can serve as validating life. The ultimate remainder, however, is more likely to be in trouble. The problem will arise because the lives relevant to that interest often will be those who hold the intermediate remainder for life. Those people may not qualify as validating lives because they might not have been alive at the beginning of the perpetuities period. While their own interest may be good, they may not be able to validate the ultimate remainder.

By paying careful attention to the language in question and taking things one step at a time, you can solve perpetuities problems. With a basic framework in mind, we now turn to some of the intricacies of the Rule.

§ 49 Craziness: If *Anything* Can Go Wrong

One troublesome aspect of the Rule is its requirement that the mere chance, however unlikely, of something going wrong is enough to invalidate an interest. The Rule will snare a drafter making reasonable assumptions about the way life works, rather than considering remote possibilities.[1]

---

[21] If this grant had been in trust, the UPC would change the result. Under Section 2-707(b), Samuel's interest would be contingent upon his survivorship until the time he could enjoy the property. Because the UPC's new survivorship rules significantly increase the number of contingent interests, they should be considered part of a package which includes perpetuities reform as well. *See* UPC § 2-707 comment. This text discusses the survivorship rules in § 45[B][2][c][iii], *supra*, and perpetuities reform in § 53, *infra*.

[1] For the view that the Rule's complex arbitrariness has advantages, in part because it lets the Rule sneak up on people, see Jeffrey E. Stake, *Darwin, Donations, and the Illusion of Dead Hand Control*, 64 Tul. L. Rev. 705 (1990).

Scholars have categorized these kinds of mistakes into three types, to which we now turn.[2]

[A] Fertile Octogenarians

The Rule assumes that anyone may have children, no matter what their age. This assumption poses problems because it can limit drastically the number of people who can qualify as validating lives. *Jee v. Audley*,[3] perhaps the most infamous of perpetuities cases, illustrates that point, among others.

Edward Audley's will directed that £ 1,000 be "placed out at interest" for his wife during her life, and at her death the money should go "unto my niece Mary Hall and the issue of her body lawfully begotten, and to be begotten, and in default of such issue I give the said £ 1,000 to be equally divided between the daughters then living of my kinsman John Jee and his wife Elizabeth Jee." Edward's wife predeceased him, so the initial gift went to Mary, who was unmarried and in her 40s. John and Elizabeth were in their 70s. Although the "issue of her body" language would have created a fee tail in real property,[4] such an estate could not be created in personal property. Therefore, Mary got an equivalent to a fee simple subject to an executory limitation, with executory interests in John and Elizabeth's daughters.[5] The question was whether the executory interests were valid. The court said no.

Much of the difficulty in the case surrounds the court's construction of the grant itself. The grant said that John and Elizabeth's then-living daughters took "in default of [Mary's] issue." The court applied an *indefinite failure of issue* construction, which means that the event of default would happen only when Mary's line runs out. To take, John and Elizabeth's daughters would have to be alive then.[6] To understand the case, it helps to try out the various relevant lives. First consider Mary. Because we cannot be sure that her line will run out at her death, she fails as a validating life.[7] Next consider John and Elizabeth. Again, because Mary's line might run out well beyond their deaths, they do not qualify.

---

[2] For the classic treatment, see W. Barton Leach, *Perpetuities in a Nutshell*, 51 Harv. L. Rev. 638, 642-646 (1938). For more variations and suggested solutions, see Robert J. Lynn, The Modern Rule Against Perpetuities ch. 5 (1966).

[3] 1 Cox 324, 29 Eng. Rep. 1186 (Ch., 1787). *See* W. Barton Leach, *The Rule Against Perpetuities and Gifts to Classes*, 51 Harv. L. Rev. 1331, 1338-1341 (1938).

[4] For a quick review of the fee tail, see § 34[D], *supra*.

[5] You might want to review defeasible fees in section 34[B], *supra*. *See especially* Figure 9-5. To modernize the language only slightly, you might consider the gift to read "to Mary, but if she dies without issue, to John and Elizabeth's daughters then living."

[6] While such a construction might make sense for a testator trying to keep land in the family by using a fee tail, it makes little sense with respect to a sum of money like the one involved here. A better approach would have been to adopt a *definite failure of issue* construction, meaning the default would happen, if at all, at Mary's death. For more on definite and indefinite failure of issue, see § 44[B], *supra*.

[7] If the court had applied a definite failure of issue construction, Mary would have been a validating life. See *supra* note 6.

The best candidates would seem to be John and Elizabeth's daughters. To take, they must survive until Mary's line runs out. Surely we will know at their deaths whether they lived long enough to qualify. While that statement is correct, the daughters cannot qualify as validating lives because validating lives cannot come from an open class. The court is unwilling to say that John and Elizabeth, in their 70s, will not have another daughter. This afterborn daughter could then survive all people now living and take the property. Because of the presumed possibility that John and Elizabeth could have more children, the gift to their daughters was void.[8] Because the daughter's gift was void, Mary was left with an unrestricted gift.[9]

Jee v. Audley is an example of a court applying rules without reference to their consequences. It shows the Rule at its most arbitrary. This court could have saved the gift to the daughters by construing the grant to mean the daughters took only if Mary died without issue surviving at her death,[10] by accepting evidence that John and Elizabeth could not have children,[11] or by waiting to see whether they had any more daughters.[12]

However much we might criticize the court's harsh approach, the presumption of fertility makes some sense in a modern context. It covers the possibility that someone might adopt a child. Now that adopted children increasingly qualify as class members,[13] a state which follows the traditional requirement of certainty should also recognize the risk of an "after-adopted" child.

The presumption of fertility (or possible adoption) is fairly easy to remember as an abstract rule. It is dangerous, however, because it is so easy to forget in particular circumstances. When clients describe elderly aunts, uncles, and grandparents, we must fight to remember that, theoretically, they could have or adopt more children, when we know in fact that they will not.

---

[8] This aspect of the case applied the "all or nothing" rule of class gifts. Unless all possible gifts to a class satisfy the Rule, gifts to all class members are void. *See* § 50[A], *infra*.

[9] For more discussion about how a fee simple subject to an executory limitation can become a fee simple absolute, see § 34[B], *supra*.

[10] Then Mary would have been a validating life.

[11] Then the daughters would have been validating lives.

This approach has some judicial support. *See In re* Lattouf's Will, 208 A.2d 411 (N.J. Super. Ct. App. Div. 1965) (court recognized that a woman who had had a complete hysterectomy could not bear children). For commentary, see Samuel M. Fetters, *The Perpetuities Period in Gross and the Child En Ventre Sa Mere in Relation to the Determination of Common-Law and Wait-and-See Measuring Lives: A Minor Heresy Stated and Defended*, 62 Iowa L. Rev. 309 (1976); Lawrence W. Waggoner, *In re Lattouf's Will and the Presumption of Lifetime Fertility in Perpetuity Law*, 20 San Diego L. Rev. 763 (1983).

[12] Rather than judging the validity of an interest at the time of its creation, jurisdictions embracing reform often "wait and see" how things turn out. *See* § 53[A], *infra*.

[13] *See* § 44[E][2], *supra*.

[B] Unborn Spouses

Jee v. Audley showed how the Rule can surprise drafters by not allowing people to serve as validating lives because there is a chance that someone as yet unborn could fill their role. The prototypical example of this rule is a testamentary grant in the following form: "To my son for life, then to his widow for her life, and at her death to his children then surviving." In *Pound v. Shorter*[14] Elizabeth Shorter's will created a trust for her then-unmarried son for life and, if he had no surviving children, then to "the wife of my said son" for her life, and finally, to "the children and descendants of children" of Elizabeth's brothers and sisters. The remainder to the "wife" was contingent upon being identified and was valid because the son could serve as the validating life. We would know at his death who his wife was. The court invalidated the final gift and gave a fee simple to the son's wife. Because the son might marry someone not alive when Elizabeth died, the "wife" could not serve as the validating life.[15]

Although its most common application is to spouses, the principle applies to anyone identified by description, rather than by name. Recall Example 12-6, in which Beth gave property to "Ira for life, then for life to Ira's oldest child who survives him, then for life to the first child of that child, then to Samuel."[16] Because Ira's oldest child who survived him might not be someone alive at the time of the grant, the following gift to that child's first child was void. You cannot use someone identified by description as a

---

[14] 377 S.E.2d 854 (Ga. 1989).

[15] Rather than recognizing a reversion in Elizabeth's estate, the court applied a statute giving a fee simple to the "last taker." *See* Ga. Code Ann. § 44-6-1 (repealed 1990). The court was unwilling to consider actual facts, to see if the son married someone who was unborn at his mother's death. The possibility that he might was enough. Georgia's legislature responded to this case by adopting the Uniform Statutory Rule Against Perpetuities Act. *See* Ga. Code Ann. 44-6-200 to 44-6-206. Section 53, *infra*, discusses the reform doctrine.

For a similar case, consider Perkins v. Iglehart, 39 A.2d 672 (Md. 1944). Lucy Dun left a trust with a life estate to her son, William, followed by another life estate to "his widow," with ultimate gifts to others. The court declined to consider the fact that when the will was made, William was engaged to be married in three weeks, that he did marry, and that his wife was alive at his mother's death. The ultimate gifts failed because the court said Lucy's intention was to benefit whomever became William's widow, not just his fiancee. Someone unborn at Lucy's death just might end up as William's widow.

Some courts have avoided the problem by interpreting general language as referring to specific people. *See, e.g., In re* Friend's Will, 28 N.E.2d 377 (N.Y. 1940) (interpreting will which said to "the widow of my said son Sol" as referring to Sol's wife when the testator died).

Courts sometimes *cause* a perpetuities problem by interpreting ambiguous grants as ones requiring survivorship. Consider Dickerson v. Union Nat'l Bank of Little Rock, 595 S.W.2d 677 (Ark. 1980). There the testator gave a life estate to her son's widow and a remainder "to the bodily heirs of my son." Although traditional rules would have us determine the son's heirs as of his death, the court interpreted the language as requiring the heirs to be identified at the widow's death. For more on when heirs are determined, see § 44[D][1], *supra*.

[16] The example is near the end of § 48, *supra*.

measuring life unless the description precludes the possibility that an afterborn might fit it.[17]

These examples illustrate how the second gift in a series (usually a remainder for life) can cause trouble for interests that follow.[18] If whoever holds that interest is certain to be someone who was alive when the interests were created, that person will often serve as a validating life to uphold the interest of the next in line. On the other hand, if someone not yet alive could later qualify to hold that second gift, then the holder of the second gift cannot be a validating life for the third gift.

[C] Administrative Contingencies

The third category of problems created by the Rule's willingness to consider all possibilities involves references to events which people expect will be completed within the perpetuities period, but which might not be. *In re Campbell's Estate*[19] involved Wesley Campbell's will giving the residue of his estate to the "four chair officers [of an Elks lodge] in office at the time of distribution of my estate." Because the estate might not be distributed within the lives of people alive at the testator's death, the court invalidated the gift to the officers.[20] Other suspect gifts are ones determined "when the mortgage is paid"[21] or "when the gravel pits are exhausted."[22]

Beware of finding administrative contingency problems which are not present. A testamentary gift "to my children living when my estate is distributed" is valid. The children are necessarily lives in being at the death of their parent, and the contingency surrounding their gift — being alive when the estate is distributed — will necessarily be resolved within their lifetimes. The children are their own validating lives.

To protect against the Rule's propensity for considering possibilities, use your imagination. Ask: "Could anything go wrong here?" If it could, you have identified a problem. Keep two points in mind in particular. First, remember that people can always have children. Second, watch the second gift in a line, to see whether holders of that gift can serve as validating lives for the third gift.

---

[17] A valid testamentary gift would be "to my son for life, then to his widow, *if she was alive at my death*, for her life, remainder to my son's then surviving children." Of course, that approach does limit the gift. Another technique is to leave the widow reference alone, but add a savings clause. Section 52, *infra*, discusses these clauses.

[18] See Chart 12-1 at the end of Section 48, *supra*.

[19] 82 P.2d 22 (Cal. App. 1938).

[20] The gift might have been saved, if the court had reasoned that the duty of personal representatives to secure the distribution of the estate would assure that the money would be distributed within the period. The court in Belfield v. Booth, 27 A. 585 (Conn. 1893), took such an approach.

[21] *See In re* Bewick, [1911] 1 Ch. 116.

[22] *See In re* Wood, [1894] 3 Ch. 381.

§ 50   Class Gifts

Class gifts pose special problems under the Rule, because all of the individual interests hang together.[1] In order for *any* class member's gift to be valid, the uncertainties surrounding *all* class members must be resolved in time. If a condition precedent for one class member might not be resolved in time, the whole class loses out. Moreover, for purposes of the Rule, one of the "uncertainties" which must be resolved is whether the class will remain open. Solving perpetuities problems thus requires mastery of the class closing rules.[2] Vested remainders subject to open are, despite their "vested" label, subject to the Rule.[3]

This section will first discuss problems posed by the "all or nothing" approach to class gifts, and then will turn to some doctrines which mitigate that approach in particular circumstances.

[A]   All or Nothing

The rule that all uncertainties, including class closing, be resolved for all class members means that class gift problems require a multiple-step analysis. First, ask whether the class will close in time. Because classes may close either physiologically or under the rule of convenience, you must consider both possibilities in your search for a validating life. Ask whether there is some validating life (or set of lives) you can look to and be sure that within 21 years after that life (or set), there will be no more "feeders" for the class. Ask also whether there is someone whose claim on the gift will be certain to close the class under the rule of convenience. If neither search uncovers a validating life, the gift is void. *If you do find someone to close the class in time, be sure not to stop there, but to ask the second question.*

Second, ask whether all conditions precedent for every class member will be resolved in time. This inquiry may yield different validating lives than the ones used to close the class. If you can find validating lives both to close the class and to resolve all of the conditions precedent, then the interests of all class members will be valid. If not, they will all be void.

A series of examples illustrates how these rules operate. First, consider a typical family. Clarence and Ruth have two children, Mike and Ellen. (See Chart 12-2.)

---

[1] The English case of Leake v. Robinson, 2 Mer. 363, 35 Eng. Rep. 979 (Ch. 1817), solidified what is now known as the "all-or-nothing" rule. In invalidating the gift to the daughters of John and Elizabeth, the court in Jee v. Audley, 1 Coc 324, 29 Eng. Rep. 1186 (Ch. 1787), assumed this approach. Section 50[A], *infra*, discusses *Jee*. For criticism of the all-or-nothing rule and discussion of other issues regarding class gifts, see W. Barton Leach, *The Rule Against Perpetuities and Gifts to Classes*, 51 Harv. L. Rev. 1329 (1938).

[2] This might be a good time to review § 43[B], *supra*.

[3] This rule is an exception to the general rule that the Rule Against Perpetuities does not apply to vested interests. For a review of vested remainders subject to open, see § 35[B][2][a][iii], *supra*.

Chart 12-2

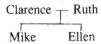

Recall that the Rule does not apply in the abstract, but to specific fact situations.

Example 12-7

John's will gives property "to Clarence for life, then to his children for their joint lives, remainder to their children."

Example 12-7(a). Assume all four family members survive John. Clarence's life estate is presently vested, not subject to the rule. Mike and Ellen have vested remainders for their joint lives, subject to open. Their remainder is good because the uncertainty about their class closing will be resolved physiologically at Clarence's death. Clarence is the validating life. Clarence's grandchildren have contingent remainders (on being born), subject to open. Their interest is void. Their class cannot close until the death of the last survivor among Clarence's children. Because Clarence is alive, he could have another child, Sue, who could survive Clarence, Mike and Ellen. Sue could have a child who could take more than 21 years after the deaths of all people now alive. It is scenarios like these which prevent members of open classes from serving as validating lives.[4] John's estate would keep a reversion.

Example 12-7(b). Suppose instead that Clarence died before John. Then the gift to Clarence's grandchildren would be good. Mike and Ellen would have presently vested life estates, not subject to the Rule. Their unborn children would have contingent remainders, subject to open. Mike and Ellen would serve as validating lives for both contingencies. The class of their children will close at the death of Mike and Ellen's survivor, and their deaths will also resolve the contingency about whether they have children.[5]

---

[4] Compare the unborn spouse problem discussed in § 49[B], *supra*. In each case, the problem is that someone not now living could meet the description of the person you would like to use as the validating life.

[5] This example illustrates another helpful rule. *In general*, gifts to grandchildren of living people will fail, but gifts to grandchildren of people who have already died will be valid.

Example 12-8

John's will gives property "to Ellen for life, remainder to her nieces and nephews."

Example 12-8(a). Now consider the same family, but a different gift. Ellen's life estate is presently vested, not subject to the Rule. Whether the remainder is good will depend upon who survives John. First suppose that Clarence and Ruth are alive, and that Mike has a daughter, Katie. Katie has a vested remainder, subject to open. It is valid, because the class of nieces and nephews will close under the rule of convenience at Ellen's death. At that time, Katie will be able to demand distribution.[6] Ellen is the validating life.[7]

Example 12-8(b). Suppose instead that Clarence and Ruth have died and Mike has no children. Mike's unborn children have contingent remainders, subject to open. Their interests are good because Mike's death will resolve both contingencies.[8] Although not named in the gift, Mike can serve as a validating life.[9]

Example 12-8(c). Now suppose that Mike has no children, but that Clarence and Ruth are still alive. Under these facts, the remainder is void. Unlike Example 12-8(a), Ellen cannot be a validating life, because there is no one now living who will be certain to close the class under the rule of convenience. Unlike Example 12-8(b), Mike cannot close the class physiologically. Because Clarence and Ruth are still alive, Mike is not the only possible "feeder" of the class of nieces and nephews. Clarence and Ruth could have another child (Remember Sue?). Mike, Clarence, Ruth, and Helen could all die. More than 21 years later, Sue could have a child who would qualify as a class member.[10]

---

[6] Even if Katie dies before Ellen, the successors to Katie's remainder will be able to demand distribution.

If this were a gift in trust and the local jurisdiction had adopted the UPC's rule keeping future interests in trust contingent upon survivorship until distribution, the gift would be void. For an explanation of why the contingent remainder would yield a void gift, see Example 12-9(c), below. For discussion of the UPC proposal, see § 45[B][2][c][iii], *supra*.

[7] For a case in which remainders like these would have been good, but for a later change, see Ward v. Van der Loeff, [1924] A.C. 653. The testator gave a life estate and a power of appointment to his wife. In default of the power's exercise, the property was to go to his brothers' and sisters' children. Because some of those children were alive at his death, they could close the class at the death of his wife, allowing her to be the validating life for their interests. Unfortunately, the testator changed his will and created contingent remainders, which were void. Note 12, *infra*, discusses this aspect of the case.

[8] They must be born and their class must close.

[9] Validating lives can be any that can affect the contingency. *See* § 48, *supra*.

[10] This analysis assumes, as is probable, that the rule of destructibility of contingent remainders does not apply, either because it has been abolished, or because the gift is in trust. Section 35[B][2][b], *supra*, discusses the destructibility rule. If the rule did apply, Ellen could serve as the validating life because any remainders contingent at Ellen's death would be destroyed.

The examples above concentrate upon the uncertainty about when a class will close. Resolving that problem becomes more complex when the remainder is contingent. The next series of examples considers the same family, but a slightly different grant.

Example 12-9

John's will gives property "to Ellen for life, remainder to her nieces and nephews who reach 21."

Example 12-9(a). Suppose Clarence and Ruth are alive, and that Mike has one child, Katie, who is 22. Katie has a vested remainder subject to open, which is valid under the Rule. Because she has met the condition precedent of reaching 21, Katie will be able to demand distribution at Ellen's death.[11] That event will close the class. Ellen serves as the validating life, because the class will close at her death and the age contingency will be resolved within 21 years of her death.

Example 12-9(b). Suppose instead that Clarence and Ruth have died, and that Mike's daughter, Katie, is 15. Katie's remainder is now contingent, subject to open. Mike can serve as the validating life. His death will close the class physiologically, and the age contingency will be resolved within 21 years thereafter.

Example 12-9(c). Now suppose that Clarence and Ruth are alive, and that Katie is 15. The remainder is void. Unlike Example 12-9(a), Ellen cannot serve as the validating life. Because Katie is not yet 21, we cannot count on her to close the class under the rule of convenience. Unlike Example 12-9(b), we cannot count on Mike to close the class physiologically. Clarence and Ruth could have another child, Sue. Everyone now living could die. More than 21 years later, Sue's child could reach 21 and take the remainder.[12]

Mastery of the principles behind examples like those above can lull you into a false sense of security. It gets easy to think that once we establish that the class will close in time, we have a valid interest. The next example illustrates that we must also consider the second half of the analysis: whether all conditions precedent for every class member will be resolved in time.

---

[11] Even if Katie does not survive Helen, Katie's successors will be able to demand distribution. This analysis assumes the traditional rule that Katie need not survive until the time of distribution. For discussion of the impact of the UPC's proposed reform on this point, see footnote 6, *supra*.

[12] For a case with similar facts, see *Ward v. Van der Loeff*, [1924] A.C. 653 (House of Lords). There the testator's will and codicil combined to leave a contingent remainder to the children of his brother and sister. Because the testator's parents were still alive, his siblings could not serve as validating lives for the gift to their children. Note 7, *supra*, discusses the validity of gifts under the original will.

Example 12-10

John's will gives property "to Ellen for life, remainder to Mike's children who reach age 30."

Clarence and Ruth have died, but Ellen, Mike and Mike's 32-year-old daughter, Katie, survive John. The remainder is void. The class will close physiologically at Mike's death and, because Katie is 32, we know that she will close the class under the rule of convenience at Ellen's death. Even though the class will close in time, we cannot be sure that all class members will reach 30 in time. Neither Ellen nor Mike qualify as validating lives because Mike could have another child who is younger than nine when Mike and Ellen die. Although a member of the class, that child could still reach 30 more than 21 years after their deaths.

When working on class gift problems, keep your eyes open for reasons a class might stay open, either because feeders are still alive or because you cannot count on the rule of convenience. Secondly, notice carefully the terms of any conditions precedent attached to the gift. Be especially wary of age conditions over 21.[13]

[B] Subclasses

A partial exception to the all or nothing approach is the rule that gifts to different subclasses stand or fall separately. Donors create subclasses when they divide a class gift among class members.[14] Subclasses are important to perpetuities analysis because within a single class, a gift to one subclass may be valid while a gift to a different subclass will be void.

American Security & Trust Co. v. Cramer[15] illustrates the subclass rule. Abraham Hazen's will created a trust for his wife for life, then for life to Hannah Duffey (whom Abraham called his "adopted daughter"), then for life to Hannah's children living at her death (or the issue of children who predeceased Hannah) and, finally, "upon the death of each the share of the one so dying shall go"[16] to that person's heirs. The family tree looked like this:

---

[13] When drafting, you might want to combine an older age limit and a savings clause. *See* § 52, *infra.*

[14] For example, you could create subclasses by directing a trustee to "pay income to my children for each of their respective lives, and upon the death of each, distribute the share from which that child has been receiving income to his or her children then surviving."

[15] 175 F. Supp. 367 (D.C. 1959).

[16] This is the key language creating the subclasses. Contrast "then to Hannah's grandchildren."

Chart 12-3

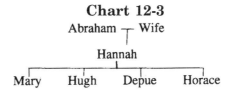

Mary and Hugh were alive when Abraham died. Depue and Horace were born later. When Depue died, the trustees sought instructions as to how to distribute the principal.

The court applied the subclass rule and treated separately the contingent remainders to Mary's, Hugh's, Depue's, and Horace's heirs.[17] Because Mary and Hugh were alive when Abraham died, they qualified as validating lives for the gifts to their heirs. On the other hand, because Depue and Horace were born later, the gifts to their heirs failed.[18]

The subclass rule can save some future interests in some contexts, but beware of the temptation to apply it when it does not fit. The rule works only when the document creates separate interests for the members of each subclass and when there are no possible late additions to the shares of those subclasses.[19]

[C] Per Capita Gifts

Another example of a donor expressly dividing a class gift into various parts is will language giving "$5,000 to each of my grandchildren, whether born before or after my death, who reach age 30." The "each" language means than rather than being grouped together, every grandchild is treated separately. Those grandchildren alive at the testator's death take valid gifts.[20] They can be their own validating lives. Those grandchildren born later lose out,[21] but their loss does not taint the other gifts.

---

[17] The remainders for life to Hannah's children were valid because Hannah could serve as the validating life.

[18] For a case which applied the subclass rule (also known as "vertical separability") to save all gifts, see Estate of Coates, 652 A.2d 331 (Pa. Super. 1994) (Because all grandchildren were alive at the testator's death, they could be validating lives for gifts to the great-grandchildren.).

[19] For example, if Mary's heirs' share could grow by receiving a gift over from Depue's heirs, the whole gift to Mary's heirs would fail. It might get larger after the expiration of the perpetuities period.

Another risk is that a court might apply the doctrine of "infectious invalidity" to invalidate all of the heirs' gifts. The question is whether the donor's intent would be better served by invalidating all of the interests or some of them. The doctrine can apply in a variety of contexts. *See* Simes & Smith § 1262.

[20] If the testator had not included the language "whether born before or after my death," standard class closing rules would have closed the class at the testator's death and left the then-living grandchildren as their own validating lives, without need for using the per capita perpetuities rule. For more on this class closing rule, see § 43[B], *supra*.

[21] Their gifts would have been valid if the age restriction had been 21. Then their parents, necessarily lives in being at their grandparent's death, could serve as validating lives.

In general, then, interests created in the form of class gifts live or die as a group. Where donors expressly have separated class members from each other, however, the Rule will apply to each subcategory individually.

§ 51 Powers of Appointment

Powers of appointment pose prickly perpetuities problems. To solve them, ask a series of questions: (1) What kind of a power do we have? (2) Is the power itself valid? and (3) Are *each* of the appointed interests valid?

The Rule distinguishes between two categories of powers, but divides them differently than the law does for other purposes.[1] In one category are general *presently exercisable* powers. These powers give their owners something very much akin to absolute ownership of the property. If they want it, they can reach out and take it. The Rule takes that reality into account. In the other category are general *testamentary* powers and special powers.[2] Because donees holding these powers cannot benefit themselves directly, general testamentary and special powers are subject to different rules. This section examines each of those categories in turn.

[A] General Presently Exercisable Powers

A power which allows the donee to benefit himself or his creditors is substantially the same as complete ownership. The Rule therefore treats general presently exercisable powers as it treats other interests. The power itself is *valid if it can be exercised within* the period. Apply standard perpetuities analysis, treating the question of when the power will become exercisable as you would any other contingency. Usually the question will be whether the donee will be identified (or whether the power will fail for want of a donee) within the period.[3] Similarly, each appointed interest created by the power's exercise is valid if contingencies surrounding it will be resolved within lives in being (+21) at the power's exercise.[4] Exercising the power is just like creating other interests.

[B] General Testamentary and Special Powers

Because general testamentary and special powers do not allow a donee to take the property for herself, they begin limiting the donee's freedom

---

[1] *See* Lawrence Burger, *The Rule Against Perpetuities as It Relates to Powers of Appointment*, 41 Neb. L. Rev. 583 (1962). You might want to review § 37[C], *supra*, on the various types of powers.

[2] Recall that this text frequently uses the term "special powers" to include what are sometimes called "non-general powers." *See* § 37[C]][1], *supra*. Because they do not give the donee the right to benefit from the property, non-general powers are subject to the same perpetuities rules as powers available to a limited class. *See* Restatement (Second) of Prop. § 1.2 cmt. d.

[3] Absent particular restraints, the power becomes exercisable for purposes of the Rule at the time the donee acquires it, even if the donee is a minor.

[4] This feature can be called a "fresh start," to distinguish it from the "second look" given to interests created by general testamentary or special powers. *See* § 51[B][2], *infra*.

at the time the donor creates the power. Thus, the policies of the Rule require ending those limitations within lives in being plus 21 years of the power's creation. This approach poses problems both for creating these powers and for validly exercising them.

[1] Validity of the Power

A general testamentary or special power is *void if it can be exercised beyond* the period. Now the question is not just getting the power into the hands of the donee in time, but assuring that the power will be exercised (or not) within the period. Consider the following will provision: "to my son for life, then to his widow for her life, remainder to whomever his widow appoints by will." Because we cannot be sure that the widow will be someone who was alive at the testator's death,[5] her power is void. It might be exercised more than 21 years after the deaths of all people living at the testator's death. The lesson: unless you take special precautions, do not create a general testamentary or a special power for someone not yet alive.[6]

A sleeper under this rule is a trustee's power to invade trust principal or allocate income. These powers, common devices to preserve flexibility,[7] are special powers of appointment, subject to the Rule. Because a trust can itself stretch beyond the perpetuities period, it is easy to forget that the trustee's discretionary powers must be time-limited. Suppose Dominic's will gave property in trust "to Vincent for life, then to his children for their lives, and after the death of his last surviving child, to San Francesco Church." Suppose also that Dominic gave the trustee the power to allocate trust income among Vincent's children. All of the beneficiaries' interests are valid under the Rule.[8] The power to allocate the income is void, however. More than 21 years after the death of everyone living when Dominic created the power, it might be exercised to allocate income among Vincent's children born after Dominic's death.[9]

[2] Validity of the Appointed Interests

The validity of interests created by the exercise of a general testamentary or a special power is measured from the time of the power's *creation*. Here

---

[5] For discussion of this point, see § 49[B], *supra*.

[6] You might give a power to an as-yet-unborn person (say, a grandchild), if you limited the time for the power's exercise to within lives in being (plus 21 years) at the time the document creating the power became irrevocable.

[7] For discussion of the powers themselves, see § 13[A], *supra*.

[8] Vincent's life estate is presently vested. The children's vested remainders for life, subject to open, will close at Vincent's death. The church's remainder is vested.

[9] *See* Arrowsmith v. Mercantile-Safe Deposit & Trust Co., 545 A.2d 674 (Md. 1988). George exercised a testamentary power created by his mother by creating life estates for his children, who were born after his mother created the power. Their income, however, was solely dependent upon the trustee's discretion. Because their income interests were not vested, they failed under the Rule.

Careful drafting can save discretionary powers by limiting their exercise to the maximum the Rule allows. This technique parallels the device of using savings clauses. *See* § 52, *infra*.

the Rule is following the notion that the donee of a special power is the agent of the donor.[10] The donee merely fills in words in the donor's document to identify who takes the property. We read the words as if the donor had written them, but we *do* consider facts we know at the time the donee actually exercises the power. This ability to consider facts at the time of exercise is called the "second look" doctrine. Sometimes a second look saves the gift, sometimes not.

Second National Bank of New Haven v. Harris Trust & Savings Bank,[11] illustrates how this two-step process works. In 1922, Caroline Trowbridge established a living trust for her daughter Margaret for life and gave Margaret a general testamentary power over the principal.[12] In default of the power's exercise, the property went to Margaret's surviving children or to other relatives. Caroline maintained the right to modify the trust terms regarding income, but as to the principal, the trust was irrevocable. In 1929, Margaret had a daughter, Mary. Margaret died in 1969, leaving a will purporting to exercise the power by creating a new trust, giving income to Mary for 30 years.[13] The remainder also went to Mary, but if she did not survive, then to her issue. The question was whether the interests Margaret tried to create were valid under the Rule.

Work through the appointed interests in order, measuring each from the time of the power's creation.[14] Because Caroline's trust was irrevocable as to principal, we read Margaret's appointed interests back into Caroline's trust as of the time it was executed (1922). We imagine that it read "to Margaret for life, then to Mary for 30 years, then to Mary, but if she does not survive, to Mary's issue." We consider facts we know at the time of the exercise, in part because we must in order to identify who takes the property. Once we do that, it makes sense to see if any newly identified people can serve as validating lives.

Mary's 30-year term is valid, because it vests at Margaret's death, and Margaret was alive when Caroline created the trust.[15] The court interpreted Mary's remainder following the term as a vested remainder, subject to divestment. It, too, must be measured from the time Caroline created the power in 1922.[16] Because it also vested at Margaret's death, Mary's

---

[10] For other examples of this idea, see § 37[E], *supra.*

[11] 283 A.2d 226 (Conn. Super. 1971).

[12] The power itself is good because Margaret is the validating life. The power cannot be exercised more than 21 years after her death.

[13] One wonders what prompted Margaret to design a plan which would keep the property in trust until Mary would be 70. Sometimes restrictive estate plans hurt family relationships. Part of a lawyer's job is to counsel the client about the personal costs of various plans.

[14] For the distinct minority view that the validity of interests appointed under a general testamentary power should be judged from the time of the power's *exercise,* see Industrial Nat'l Bank of Rhode Island v. Barrett, 220 A.2d 517 (R.I. 1966). *See generally* Laurence M. Jones, *The Rule Against Perpetuities and Powers of Appointment: An Old Controversy Revived,* 54 Iowa L. Rev. 456 (1968).

[15] It is not proper to say that Mary's term is valid because it is presently vested. It was not vested at the time Caroline created Margaret's power.

[16] For discussion of the problem of construing remainders as vested or contingent, see § 35[B][2][c], *supra.*

remainder was valid. The executory interest[17] in Mary's issue is void. Mary was not yet alive when Caroline created the power, so Mary cannot serve as a validating life. The court considered facts known at the time of the power's exercise, but those facts did not save the interest.[18] Because the executory interest was void, Mary's remainder was indefeasibly vested.[19]

The second look doctrine could have saved the gift to Mary's issue if the facts had been different. If Mary's gift of income had been for 21 years, the executory interests would have been valid. Margaret would work as the validating life. If Caroline had reserved a power to revoke the trust principal, we would measure the perpetuities period from the time that power expired, Caroline's death. Mary had been born by then and could serve as the validating life.

A different way to save appointed interests is to apply the doctrine of marshalling of assets, sometimes called allocation.[20] It applies to those cases in which a donee has blended assets subject to the power and assets from elsewhere. This blending often happens in a will which disposes of "all of my property, including property over which I hold a power of appointment."[21] Suppose Kristin used such a clause and also made two gifts: gift "One" would be invalid if made under the power, but gift "Two" would be a valid exercise.[22] A court might satisfy gift "One" with the other estate assets, and use assets subject to the power for gift "Two." That way both gifts would be valid.

[C] Takers in Default

Well-drafted documents creating powers of appointment will also identify people to take if the donee fails to exercise the power, or if the power fails for some other reason.[23] These gifts in default may raise perpetuities issues. Conceptually, gifts in default are remainders subject to divestment by the exercise of the power.[24] There is no perpetuities problem unless the

---

[17] The court called this interest a contingent remainder. Traditional analysis would call it an executory interest. *See* § 35[B], *supra*.

[18] For a case which applied the second look doctrine to validate the appointed interests, see Marx v. Rice, 67 A.2d 918 (N.J. Ch. Div. 1949). There Bernard Strauss left a will creating a general testamentary power for his wife, Florence. Florence executed the power at her death several years later by creating gifts for various relatives. Considering facts available at Florence's death, the court learned that the appointed interests went either to people alive when Bernard died or to children of those people. The people living when Bernard died served as validating lives. *See also In re* Bird's Estate, 37 Cal. Rptr. 288 (Cal. App. 1964) (same result).

[19] For another discussion of how the failure of an executory interest can yield an indefeasible estate, see § 34[B], *supra*.

[20] *See* Simes & Smith § 975; Restatement (Second) of Prop. §§ 22.1, 22.2.

[21] For discussion of the advisability of using such a clause, see § 39[A], *supra*.

[22] The disposition might violate the Rule or might be invalid as beyond the scope of a special power. For discussion of scope problems, see § 39[B], *supra*.

[23] On drafting powers, see § 40, *supra*.

[24] *See* Note, *Remainders Over in Default of Exercise of Powers of Appointment and Revocation*, 106 U. Pa. L. Rev. 420 (1958).

default gift is to an open class or subject to a condition precedent.[25] Many gifts in default, however, add these uncertainties. The question then becomes whether the second look doctrine applies to gifts in default. Case law is slim, and the commentators disagree.[26]

Sears v. Coolidge[27] is the principal American case on the question. Thomas Coolidge created a living trust in 1913. The trust divided the income among various beneficiaries, and then distributed the principal to Thomas' issue living at the trust's termination. The trust was to end at the first to happen of two events: (1) the death of the last survivor of Thomas' children, grandchildren and great-grandchildren living at his death, or (2) the time his youngest grandchild living at his death reached age 50. The restriction that everyone be living at Thomas' death would have created a large class of validating lives if the trust had been testamentary. Because he created the trust during his lifetime, however, Thomas left open the possibility that relatives born after the trust was created, but before he died, would postpone too long the time for identifying those issue who took the remainder.

Thomas had not reserved a power to revoke the trust, but he could change the beneficiaries, except to benefit himself. The court treated this reservation as a special power of appointment. Thus, the remainder to issue surviving at the trust's termination was a gift in default. The court considered facts available at the *non-exercise* of that power (Thomas' death) to determine the validity of the remainder. By then it was clear that no afterborns had sneaked in between the time of the trust execution and Thomas' death. The court upheld the gift.

The argument for applying the second look doctrine to gifts in default is not as strong as the argument for applying it to appointed interests. In the case of appointed interests, we must wait until the time of the appointment to know what interests to judge. At that point, it seems silly to ignore that we know who, in fact, was alive when. With gifts in default, we need not wait. The document creating the power also names the takers in default. We could apply a traditional "possibilities" analysis. Applying the second look doctrine to gifts in default is one small step toward an overall "wait and see" approach to perpetuities.[28]

The usual rule to take perpetuities problems one step at a time applies with particular vengeance when powers are involved. When identifying the type of power, watch for sleepers.[29] On questions of whether the power or

---

[25] The uncertainty about whether the remainder will be divested by the exercise of the power is not a factor. The remainder is just like any other vested interest, subject to being lost.

[26] *Compare* ALP § 24.36 (advocating taking a second look) *with* Simes & Smith § 1276 (opposing that view).

[27] 108 N.E.2d 563 (Mass. 1952).

[28] For discussion of this reform doctrine, see § 53[A], *infra*.

[29] A father giving his daughter a power "to appoint among my descendants" is creating a general power. A power in a trustee to allocate income among specified beneficiaries is a special power.

the appointed interests are valid, recall all of the traditional traps.[30] When judging the validity of interests created under a general testamentary or a special power, be sure to measure the time period from the power's creation.

§ 52 Savings Clauses

Because the Rule is so technical and so easily violated, drafters have developed fail-safe devices called "savings clauses."[1] These clauses have two functions. First, they protect the plan from the possibility that the Rule will strike some gifts, sending property back through the grantor's estate. Second, properly drafted savings clauses can extend a trust so that a grantor can make gifts which the Rule would prohibit.[2]

As *In re Lee's Estate*[3] illustrates, a poorly drafted savings clause can squander the opportunity to preserve most or all of a grantor's plan. Anna Lee created a testamentary trust for her son, Fairman, and her grandchildren. After Fairman's death, the trustee was to use the fund to support the grandchildren until each completed his education or turned 25. After each grandchild reached that point, the trust would provide $25.00 monthly "until the youngest of my said grandchildren shall have attained the age of forty (40) years."[4] Then the trust would terminate, with the principal going to the grandchildren then living. The gifts to the grandchildren were void.[5] The questions were whether and how a perpetuities savings clause affected the trust.

Savings clauses have two basic parts: one terminates the trust at the right time, and the other identifies the alternate takers. This one said that if any provisions were void on account of the Rule, the trusts "shall continue in force for the full period permitted by law and on the day prior to the expiration of such full period, [the] trustee shall make distribution of any remainder of the trust estate to the persons herein named who would be entitled to take distribution thereon upon termination of the trust."[6] Both parts of the clause posed problems.

---

[30] *See* §§ 49 (craziness) and 50 (class gifts), *supra.*

[1] *See* William M. McGovern, Jr., *Perpetuities Pitfalls and How Best to Avoid Them*, 6 Real Prop. Prob. & Tr. J. 155 (1971).

[2] Rather than relying upon a general savings clause to "cure" perpetuities problems, Professor Becker prefers more precise tailor-made provisions and offers numerous recommendations for how to draft them. *See* David M. Becker, Perpetuities and Estate Planning 133-184, 399-563 (1993).

[3] 299 P.2d 1066 (Wash. 1956).

[4] In some circumstances, the term "youngest grandchild" can pose some difficult construction problems. *See* § 44[C], *supra.*

[5] Because the son survived, the class of grandchildren was still open at Lee's death. Therefore, the grandchildren could not be their own validating lives. The age limitations established conditions which might be resolved more than 21 years after the son's death. For more discussion of the Rule as applied to class gifts, see § 50, *supra.*

[6] *In re* Lee's Estate, 299 P.2d at 1067-68.

First, the trust was to terminate one day prior to the expiration of the "full period permitted by law."[7] The trial court ordered the trust to end at the first of the following events: when the youngest grandchild reached 40, when the last surviving grandchild under 40 died, or 21 years less one day after the son's death. The Washington Supreme Court saw no justification for creating these alternative dates, however. It treated Fairman as the validating life and held that the "full period" was simply 21 years after his death.[8]

A more creative clause might have *extended* the time beyond the son's life plus 21. Suppose the clause had said, "unless terminated earlier according to its provisions, this trust shall end 21 years after the death of the last survivor of my descendants living at my death."[9] More than likely, that clause would extend the trust close to the time the testator contemplated. If there were no afterborn grandchildren, the trust could continue until the youngest grandchild reached 40. Even if another grandchild came along, he or she probably would reach 40 within 21 years after the other grandchildren died.

The second part of a savings clause identifies who is to take the property when the trust terminates. The clause said the property went "to the persons herein named who would be entitled to take distribution thereon upon termination of the trust." Fairman argued that this designation is too uncertain to be enforceable, because the identified takers are the very people whose interests violate the Rule. The court took the sensible approach of reading the clause as giving the property to Anna's grandchildren living when the trust terminates 21 years after Fairman's death. A better way to designate alternative takers usually will be to give the principal to those people entitled to the income right before the trust terminates.

Savings clauses are important tools. They protect against malpractice traps.[10] More importantly, they allow clients to structure a document so that actual, as opposed to hypothetical, events will control the estate plan. Savings clauses build in a "wait and see" feature similar to modern

---

[7] On this point the clause conflicts with itself, by saying continue as long as possible, but distribute one day before that time. The court read the clause as requiring termination one day before the expiration of the full period.

[8] *But see* Klugh v. United States, 588 F.2d 45, 48 (4th Cir. 1978) (interpreting "as far as the law will allow" and holding that the testator's descendants living at his death could be the validating lives); First Alabama Bank v. Adams, 382 So. 2d 1104, 1109 (Ala. 1980) (same interpretation where clause read that the trust could not "continue for a period of time longer than the time allowed by law for the vesting of the share of any beneficiary").

[9] For sample clauses, see Dukeminier & Johanson at 829-830; McGovern & Kurtz at 429-430; Waggoner, Alexander, Fellows & Gallanis at 1223. For an early version, with commentary, see W. Barton Leach & James K. Logan, *Perpetuities: A Standard Savings Clause to Avoid Violations of the Rule*, 74 Harv. L. Rev. 1141 (1961).

If a trust is an irrevocable living trust, so the perpetuities period runs from the date of the trust's execution, the reference should be to descendants (or others, as appropriate) "*now living.*"

[10] Their sloppy use, of course, presents different malpractice risks.

perpetuities reforms.[11] Their availability is not, however, a good excuse for not understanding the Rule's fundamentals. Like the reforms discussed in the next section, savings clauses build upon, rather than replace, the Rule.[12]

§ 53 Reform

As noted above,[1] the Rule's arbitrariness has prompted a series of reforms.[2]

One proposal is that the Rule ought not to consider mere, even fanciful, possibilities,[3] but rather ought to judge the validity of interests based on actual events. This approach is known as "wait and see." Another technique is to reform documents to make them conform to the Rule.[4] The reformation might take place at the testator's death or after a wait-and-see period has not solved the problem. Neither wait and see nor reformation is without problems of its own. This section discusses these two main reform doctrines,[5] and then examines the ongoing movement to abolish the Rule entirely.

[A] Wait and See

Few topics in property law have generated as much heated commentary as wait and see. At first the question was whether it is a good idea.[6] More

---

[11] *See* § 53[A], *infra*.

[12] *See* David M. Becker, *Estate Planning and the Reality of Perpetuities Problems Today: Reliance upon Statutory Reform and Saving Clauses Is Not Enough*, 64 Wash. U. L.Q. 287 (1986); Robert J. Lynn, *Perpetuities Literacy for the 21st Century*, 50 Ohio St. L.J. 219 (1989).

[1] *See* § 47, *supra*.

[2] One way to view these reforms is as a subset of the larger effort to prevent unjust enrichment when there has been a mistake. *See* Lawrence W. Waggoner, *Perpetuity Reform*, 81 Mich. L. Rev. 1718, 1719 (1983). For discussion of remedies for mistake, see §§ 7[B][4] (mistake in execution) and 41[B] (mistake and extrinsic evidence), *supra*.

[3] For some examples, see § 49, *supra*.

[4] This doctrine sometimes goes by the label *"cy pres,"* which means "as near as." Its origins are in the law of charitable trusts, where courts reform trusts which have become outmoded, so they can meet modern charitable needs. *See* § 53[B], *infra*.

[5] A few states have, or recently have had, statutes aimed at particular perpetuities problems. *See* Lawrence W. Waggoner, *Perpetuities Reform*, 81 Mich. L. Rev. 1718, 1726-1750 (1983).

Illinois, for example, has a set of provisions aimed at administrative contingencies, unborn widows, age contingencies over 21, and fertile octogenarians (really, those over 65). 765 Ill. Comp. Stat. 305/4(c). *See also* N.Y. Est. Powers & Trusts Law §§ 9-1.2 to 9-1.3 Rule entirely.

For analysis of the Illinois statute, see Daniel M. Schuyler, *The Statute Concerning Perpetuities*, 65 Nw. U. L. Rev. 3 (1970). For discussion of many of the problems this statute seeks to solve, see § 50, *supra*.

[6] *See, e.g.,* W. Barton Leach, *Perpetuities in Perspective: Ending the Rule's Reign of Terror*, 65 Harv. L. Rev. 721 (1952) (endorsing the reform); Lewis M. Simes, *Is the Rule Against Perpetuities Doomed? The "Wait and See" Doctrine*, 52 Mich. L. Rev. 179 (1953) (opposing). For more citations, see Simes & Smith § 1230.

recently, the debate has shifted to how it ought to work.[7] The basic idea is to wait after a testator's death to see if the horrible things the Rule imagines actually take place. The basic problem is: How long should we wait?

Three major approaches have emerged for determining how long to wait.[8] One is to identify people who are causally connected to the resolution of the contingency,[9] and then wait to see whether the problem is resolved within their lives plus 21 years.[10] The Restatement recommends a related approach, but creates a series of categories for identifying the lives.[11] The third technique, adopted by most states through the Uniform Statutory Rule Against Perpetuities (USRAP), avoids the difficulty of identifying lives and sets a 90-year waiting period.[12] With each of these approaches, the wait may still leave contingencies unresolved. In that situation, many places would reform the document to conform to the Rule.[13]

In re Estate of Anderson[14] shows a court willing to adopt wait and see

---

[7] The leading figures in this debate have been Professors Dukeminier and Waggoner. Dukeminier believes we should identify those lives causally related to vesting and wait to see how things turn out 21 years after their deaths. Waggoner favors waiting for a fixed period of years. Although each has expressed his views in other places, a good place to compare their approaches is a series of exchanges in the Columbia Law Review. The principal articles there are: Jesse Dukeminier, *Perpetuities: The Measuring Lives*, 85 Colum. L. Rev. 1648 (1985); Lawrence W. Waggoner, *Perpetuities: A Perspective on Wait-and-See*, 85 Colum. L. Rev. 1714 (1985).

For other perspectives, see Ira M. Bloom, *Perpetuities Refinement: There Is an Alternative*, 62 Wash. L. Rev. 23 (1987); Robert L. Fletcher, *Perpetuities: Basic Clarity, Muddled Reform*, 63 Wash. L. Rev. 791 (1988); Paul G. Haskell, *A Proposal for a Simple and Socially Effective Rule Against Perpetuities*, 66 N.C. L. Rev. 545 (1988).

[8] Some statutes have adopted wait and see but not made clear how it should work. *See, e.g.*, Ohio Rev. Code Ann. § 2131.08(c).

[9] These are the same people whom you would identify as relevant lives when solving problems under the traditional Rule. *See* § 48, *supra*. Although they would not qualify as *validating* lives under the Rule [If they did, there would be no need to wait and see.], they can work as *measuring* lives, defining how long to wait.

[10] *See, e.g.*, Ky. Rev. Stat. Ann. § 381.216.

[11] Restatement (Second) of Prop. § 1.4. Iowa took this approach. Iowa Code § 558.68. *See* Sheldon F. Kurtz, *The Iowa Rule Against Perpetuities — Reform at Last, Restatement Style: Wait-and-See and Cy Pres*, 69 Iowa L. Rev. 705 (1984).

[12] Originally a free-standing act, USRAP is now also part of the UPC. *See* UPC §§ 2-901 to 2-906. As of this writing, 28 states have adopted USRAP. *See* Uniform Statutory Rule Against Perpetuities (U.L.A.) § 1 (Supp. 1998). For a helpful short summary of USRAP, see Lawrence H. Averill, Jr., Uniform Probate Code in a Nutshell ch. 13 (5th ed. 2001).

For positive commentary on the statute, see Mary L. Fellows, *Testing Perpetuity Reforms: A Study of Perpetuity Cases 1984-89*, 25 Real Prop. Prob. & Tr. J. 579 (1990); Lawrence W. Waggoner, *The Uniform Statutory Rule Against Perpetuities: The Rationale of the 90-Year Vesting Period*, 73 Cornell L. Rev. 157 (1988). For criticism, see Ira M. Bloom, *Perpetuities Refinement: There is an Alternative*, 62 Wash. L. Rev. 23 (1987); James S. Chase, *Perpetuity Reform: How Much Do We Need?*, 11 Probate L.J. 1 (1992); Jesse Dukeminier, *The Uniform Statutory Rule Against Perpetuities: Ninety Years in Limbo*, 34 UCLA L. Rev. 1023 (1987).

[13] Reformation of this sort is discussed in § 53[B], *infra*.

[14] 541 So. 2d 423 (Miss. 1989).

without statutory authorization.[15] When Charles Anderson, a bachelor, died, he left much of his estate to his favorite nephew, Howard. Charles also created a trust to help pay education expenses for descendants of his father[16] for a 25-year period from the probate of the will. The remaining funds were payable to Howard, but if Howard died before then, to the heirs of his body. Howard challenged the trust as violative of the Rule.[17]

The gifts to the descendants violate the Rule because after Charles' death another descendant could be born, and everyone living at Charles' death could die, so the afterborn could take more than 21 years after Charles' death.[18] Rather than invalidating the trust because of that possibility, the court took into account facts known at the time of the decision. In particular, by then the date of the trust's termination was less than 21 years away, and people alive when Charles died were still alive. Therefore, by "waiting and seeing" until the time of the appellate decision, the court was able to be sure that the uncertainty about who would take from the education fund would be resolved within 21 years of the deaths of people alive when Charles died.

Another question was whether the gift to the heirs of Howard's body was valid. If the heirs are identified as of Howard's death,[19] Howard could serve as the validating life. If the heirs are identified as of the termination of the trust, the gift would be void. As in the situation above, an afterborn could sneak in, those living could die, and the afterborn could take more than 21 years after their deaths. The court validated the heirs' interest on the same reasoning it had used regarding the 25-year trust. Even if the heirs are not identified until the end of the trust, that will happen in fewer than 21 years from the time of the decision.

The facts in *Anderson* made it a good case for wait and see. Combining the 25-year period and the slow pace of litigation, the court was able to validate the scheme by using facts available as of the decision. The court expressly declined to say how much longer it would be willing to wait in different circumstances.[20] This case-by-case approach could lead to successive litigation.

---

[15] *Contra* Pound v. Shorter, 377 S.E.2d 854 (Ga. 1989). When the Georgia court declined the invitation to adopt wait and see, the legislature responded by adopting USRAP. *See* Ga. Code Ann. §§ 44-6-200 to -206. The case is discussed in § 49[B], *supra*.

[16] As a practical matter, the beneficiaries would be the children of Charles' nieces and nephews.

[17] Howard's lack of concern for the other nieces and nephews was not lost upon the court, which commented, "We are told that the bequest in trust violates the Rule against Perpetuities, and by this we are told that the testator has misjudged the nephew much more than the measure of the Rule." *Anderson*, 541 So. 2d at 424.

[18] Another possible challenge is based on the notion that Charles' will be probated well after everyone living at Charles' death had died. For discussion of this aspect of the Rule, see § 49[C], *supra*.

[19] For discussion of various approaches about when to identify heirs, see § 44[D][1], *supra*.

[20] *Anderson*, 541 So. 2d at 433 n.20.

Consider a testamentary gift from Bill to Ruth for life, then to her children who reach age 30. At Bill's death, Ruth has two children, Curtis and Mike. Applying wait and see, we do not invalidate the remainder immediately. Suppose Ruth has another child and later dies, leaving Mary Jane, Curtis, and Mike. Do we invalidate the remainder now, because Mary Jane could take more than 21 years after the validating lives? Or do we wait longer, hoping either Curtis or Mike will live until Mary Jane reaches 9? Like the *Anderson* case, many jurisdictions do not answer these questions.

Rather than using individual lives to set the time limit, the Uniform Statutory Rule Against Perpetuities (USRAP) simply says if we must, we will wait 90 years. The idea is to approximate the "lives-plus-21" period without the need for tracking lives.[21] If, from the beginning, we know the contingency will be resolved within lives-plus-21, the interest is valid.[22] If not, we wait and see for up to 90 years.[23]

The 90-year period also allows the reformed Rule to meet problems posed by modern science. Under UPC § 2-901(d), "the possibility that a child will be born to an individual after the individual's death is disregarded." The common law Rule includes actual periods of gestation, both to determine who can be a validating life and to identify who would be a beneficiary. With the advent of sperm banks, frozen embryos and like changes to come, a broader rule was needed. Now the possibility that Albert may have children long after death will not prevent him from being a validating life. Notice that the reform, however, also cuts off actual periods of gestation, which the common law Rule would have considered.[24]

One fear about the 90-year period was that it would prompt lawyers to draft documents setting 90 years as a *minimum* period.[25] They might, for example, create savings clauses which resolved ambiguities on the "later of" 21 years after lives in being at the trust's creation or 90 years from the trust's creation. USRAP's drafters in 1990 added a subsection designed to minimize the problem. Section 2-901(e) makes such "later of" clauses "inoperative to the extent that [they] produce a period of time that exceeds 21 years after the death of the survivor of the specified lives."[26]

---

[21] *See* UPC, Part 9, general comment.

[22] UPC §§ 2-901(a)(1) [nonvested property interests], (b)(1) [general power subject to a condition precedent], (c)(1) [nongeneral or testamentary power].

[23] UPC §§ 2-901(a)(2) [nonvested property interests], (b)(2) [general power subject to a condition precedent], (c)(2) [nongeneral or testamentary power].

[24] The change only affects the perpetuities analysis. It says nothing about whether people conceived after their parent's death will qualify for membership in a class, for example. *See* UPC § 2-901 comment.

[25] *See* Jesse Dukeminier, *The Uniform Statutory Rule Against Perpetuities: Ninety Years in Limbo*, 34 UCLA L. Rev. 1023, 1027 (1987).

[26] The statute poses significant problems for drafters seeking to take advantage of an exemption from the federal generation-skipping transfer tax. *See* Ira M. Bloom & Jesse Dukeminier, *Perpetuities Reformers Beware: The USRAP Tax Trap*, 25 Real Prop. Prob. & Tr. J. 203 (1990); Dukeminier & Johanson, at 846-849. A sketch of the generation-skipping tax appears in § 63, *infra*.

Despite the controversy surrounding wait and see, it is the reform of choice. The one problem wait and see does not solve is what to do when we have waited . . . and waited . . . and waited, but the contingency remains unresolved. At that point, many jurisdictions reform the document to conform to the Rule.

[B] Reformation[27]

Another method for easing the Rule's harshness is for courts to carry out simultaneous reforms. They reform the Rule by reforming offending documents to bring them into compliance with the Rule.[28] Courts either might reform the document immediately upon discovering the perpetuities violation, or they might first wait and see how things turn out, and then reform if they must. In either case, the basic problem is: How do we reform?

The goal of reformation is to follow the donor's intention as nearly as possible while still meeting Rule's limits.[29] Some courts have not been as aggressive as they might be in pursuing that goal. Consider *Estate of Chun Quan Yee Hop.*[30] Chun Quan Yee Hop left property in trust for his family, with directions that the trust terminate at his wife's death, or 30 years after his own death, whichever was later. At that point, the principal would be divided among his issue.[31] Under the Rule, the possible 30-year period invalidated the gift of principal. Rather than allowing the gift to fail, the court reformed the 30-year period to 21.[32]

While the reduction from 30 to 21 is an easy way to meet the Rule, it is not the best way to both meet the Rule and preserve the plan as much as possible. Interestingly, the court noted that Quan Yee's lawyer could have met Quan Yee's wishes by including a savings clause.[33] A clause might

---

[27] This doctrine is also known as *"cy pres."*

[28] Reformation of documents was one of the planks in Professor Leach's general reform platform. *See* W. Barton Leach, *Perpetuities in Perspective: Ending the Rule's Reign of Terror*, 65 Harv. L. Rev. 721, 734-735 (1952). The idea has been around for a long time. *See* James Quarles, *The Cy Pres Doctrine with Reference to the Rule Against Perpetuities—An Advocation of Its Adoption in All Jurisdictions*, 38 Am. L. Rev. 683 (1904). For short descriptions of the doctrine, see Bergin & Haskell at 218-221; McGovern & Kurtz at 434-436.

Reformation to cure a perpetuities violation is an exception to the traditional rule that courts will not reform wills to correct mistakes. For discussion of this question generally, see §§ 7[B][4] and 41[B][2], *supra.*

[29] *See* Restatement (Second) of Prop. § 1.5.

[30] 469 P.2d 183 (Haw. 1970). In 1992, Hawaii adopted USRAP. *See* Haw. Rev. Stat. §§ 525-1 to 525-6.

[31] His scheme reflected traditional Chinese favoritism of males. His four sons and their issue shared 3/4, while his 12 daughters and their issue shared the other 1/4.

[32] *See also* Berry v. Union Nat'l Bank, 262 S.E.2d 766 (W. Va. 1980). There Clara Post created a trust to pay education expenses for her husband's nieces and nephews for 25 years after her death. The court reduced the period to 21. In 1992, West Virginia enacted USRAP. *See* W. Va. Code §§ 36-1A-1 to -8.

[33] Chun Quan Yee Hop, 469 P.2d at 186-187 (1970). The clause the court proposed, however, would not have met Quan Yee's intention. It would have terminated the trust after 30 years even if his wife were alive.

have terminated the trust, if not already terminated, 21 years after the death of the last survivor of Quan Yee's wife and issue alive at his death.[34] By reforming the will to include such a clause, the court almost certainly would have preserved the plan, including the 30-year period.[35]

Like many wait-and-see statutes, USRAP gives courts the authority to reform documents if, at the end of the wait-and-see period, the offending contingency is still unresolved.[36] Perhaps more importantly in the short term, the statute also authorizes reformation of any document not covered by the wait-and-see provisions because those only apply prospectively.[37] The comments encourage courts to reform documents by inserting savings clauses.[38] If courts do that, of course, they effectively will be adopting a wait-and-see approach.[39] The Rule, as modernized by wait and see and reformation, seems likely to be with us for a while. When it comes to interests in trusts, however, the Rule has been effectively abolished in several states and is under siege in many others. We now turn to the repeal movement.

[C] Abolition

Spurred by wealthy individuals who would like to create perpetual trusts (and by the banks who would administer those trusts), a substantial block of states have effectively repealed the Rule as it applies to trusts in which the trustee has the power to transfer trust property.[40] The principal motivation of these donors is to take advantage of the exemptions created by the generation-skipping transfer tax (GST).[41] Properly-crafted, a $1 million trust could pass on vast amounts of wealth from one generation to another forever.[42]

---

[34] For discussion of savings clauses, see § 52, *supra*.

[35] *See* Olin L. Browder, Jr., *Construction, Reformation, and the Rule Against Perpetuities*, 62 Mich. L. Rev. 1 (1963). The court in *In re* Estate of Anderson, 541 So. 2d 423, 430 n.13 (Miss. 1989) endorsed such an approach. *Anderson* is discussed in § 53[A], *supra*. *But see* Trust under the Will of Shehan, 597 N.Y.S.2d 1017 (N.Y. Sur. 1993)(rejecting the suggestion of using rules of construction to (in effect) read a savings clause into the will).

[36] UPC § 2-903(1). The statute allows earlier reformation in some cases involving class gifts, in order to allow distribution to a class member. UPC § 2-903(2). Because drafters commonly create subclasses, this circumstance should not arise often. For more on subclasses, see § 50[B], *supra*.

[37] UPC § 2-905(b).

[38] UPC § 2-905 comment.

[39] For discussion of how savings clauses work, see § 52, *supra*.

[40] Though the methods differ, as of this writing the list includes Alaska, Arizona, Delaware, Idaho, Illinois, Maine, Maryland, Missouri, New Jersey, Ohio, Rhode Island, South Dakota, Virginia and Wisconsin. Other states are likely to jump on the bandwagon.

[41] *See* Ira Mark Bloom, *How Federal Transfer Taxes Affect the Development of Property Law*, 48 Cleve. St. L. Rev. 661 (2000); Ira Mark Bloom, *The GST Tax Tail is Killing the Rule Against Perpetuities*, 87 Tax Notes 569 (2000). The GST is highlighted in § 63, *infra*.

[42] An after-tax 6% return on an initial $1 million would produce a trust of $369 million in 100 years and $136.43 billion in 200 years.

States allowing perpetual dynasty trusts may be creating serious problems that will haunt society in the future.[43] Such trusts can concentrate enormous wealth—and the power wealth brings—in the hands of a relative few. Similarly, the influence of financial institutions that manage those trusts will grow. Administrative nightmares could arise as over time a trust for "my descendants" includes thousands of beneficiaries. Sources of venture capital could become scare as trustees—traditionally bound by more conservative investment rules[44] — hold a greater percentage of the nation's wealth. Whether other legal doctrines will arise or expand in order to meet whatever problems arise, only time will tell.[45]

---

[43] *See generally* Verner F. Chaffin, *Georgia's Proposed Dynasty Trust: Giving the Dead Hand Too Much Control*, 35 Ga. L. Rev. 1 (2000); Joel C. Dobris, *The Death of the Rule Against Perpetuities, or the RAP Has No Friends -An Essay*, 35 Real Prop., Prob. & Tr. J. 601 (2000).

[44] *See* § 56[A], *infra.*

[45] In particular, a rule against unreasonable accumulation of trust income may get more attention. *See* Restatement (Second) of Prop. § 2.2; Karen J. Sneddon, *The Sleeper Has Awakened: The Rule Against Accumulations and Perpetual Trusts*, 76 Tul. L. Rev. 189 (2001).

Chapter 13

PROBLEMS OF ADMINISTRATION

§ 54 Introduction

This chapter examines the major problems fiduciaries face when they administer estates or trusts. By their nature, those different jobs involve different considerations. Personal representatives of estates face a shorter time span, with limited goals. They must collect assets, pay off creditors, and distribute the funds to the appropriate beneficiaries.[1] Estate administration has the feel of holding things together.[2] Trust administration, on the other hand, usually has a longer time horizon. Trustees must be attuned to the changing personal needs of the beneficiaries and the changing markets which affect the management of the trust assets. Trust administration has a pro-active feel. Despite these differences, there often is no bright line dividing estate from trust administration.[3] Fiduciaries engaged in either type of administration face very similar problems, and the legal principles governing them tend to cut across the particulars of individual situations.[4]

---

[1] Section 2[A][1], *supra*, presents an overview of the probate process. Sometimes personal representatives get involved in will contests based on the doctrines discussed in Chapter 3, *supra*.

[2] *See* Estate of Beach, 542 P.2d 994 (Cal. 1975). During the period of estate administration, the value of a significant holding of stock dropped from $16 per share to $6. The executor was held not liable for having retained the stock. *See also* Estate of Knipp, 414 A.2d 1007 (Pa. 1980) (no surcharge although executor did not diversify stock holdings); *but see In re* Estate of Janes, 681 N.E.2d 332 (N.Y. 1997) (executor surcharged for not diversifying estate's portfolio).

[3] The line may be especially blurry towards the end of an estate administration when the personal representative is getting ready to hand over estate assets to itself as trustee. For many courts, the powers and duties change at the discharge of the personal representative after a final accounting. Others view the process as one which flows from one function into another. *See, e.g.*, Springfield Nat'l Bank v. Couse, 192 N.E. 529 (Mass. 1934) (no surcharge when bank/executor invested in securities not appropriate for executors to purchase, when decedent also had named bank as trustee). *See generally* Jay C. Baker, *The Executor-Trustee*, 13 Okla. L. Rev. 408 (1960).

[4] *See, e.g.*, UPC §§ 7-302 ("[T]he trustee shall observe the standards . . . that would be observed by a prudent man dealing with the property of another . . . ."); 3-703(a) (personal representative subject to standard of care for trustees); UTC § 804 ("A trustee shall administer the trust as a prudent person would . . . .").

This text focuses upon estate and trust administration, but much of this law applies to guardians as well. With the increased popularity of powers of attorney, related rules defining those powers will be developing further over the next several years. *See generally* William M. McGovern, Jr., *Trusts, Custodianships, and Durable Powers of Attorney*, 27 Real Prop. Prob. & Tr. J. 1 (1992). For discussion of powers of attorney, see § 22[A], *supra*.

Guard against the temptation to view this material as something only for paralegals, accountants, and trust administrators.[5] You could encounter these rules in a variety of contexts. You might become a fiduciary or represent one. You might represent a beneficiary in a dispute with a fiduciary. You might draft documents designed to avoid many of the problems identified here. In each of these contexts, your advice may significantly affect the people the donor wanted to benefit.[6]

This chapter seeks to give content to the general requirement that a fiduciary be prudent.[7] Because the problems of fiduciary administration of both trusts and estates flow together, any particular division is somewhat artificial. For example, a single investment decision may involve the duty of loyalty, a question of adequate care, and the interpretation of a will clause seeking to exonerate a trustee from liability.[8]

Despite the integrated nature of the topic, you are more likely to understand the basic concepts if you can group them into a few categories. It helps to consider together a set of problems involving a fiduciary's relationship with the beneficiaries. Somewhat different are issues revolving around the fiduciary's asset management. Some problems, including the scope of a fiduciary's powers, are best considered from the perspective of one drafting a document. Drafts can also alter fiduciary duties. Finally, remedies for breaches of fiduciary duty cut across the entire area. This chapter addresses each of those topics in turn.

§ 55 Relationships with Beneficiaries

This section discusses how the law regulates the relationships between fiduciaries and beneficiaries.[1] The primary topic is the duty of loyalty, but the section also covers the duty of fiduciaries to communicate with beneficiaries. Permeating these rules is the notion that both conduct and attitude matter.

---

[5] Indeed, banks and trust companies often hire lawyers as trust administrators.

[6] You may also face numerous ethical dilemmas. *See* Ronald C. Link, *Developments Regarding the Professional Responsibility of the Estate Administration Lawyer: The Effect of the Model Rules of Professional Conduct*, 26 Real Prop. Prob. & Tr. J. 1 (1991).

[7] Fiduciaries who have special skills, or represent that they have them, probably are bound to use them. *See* UPC § 7-302; UTC § 806.

For a striking application of this principle, see *In re* Estate of Lychos. 470 A.2d 136 (Pa. Super. 1983). A bank and a family member served as co-trustees. Among other mistakes, the bank deposited $15,000 in a non-interest-bearing account at the bank for a year. The court held the corporate trustee liable, but exonerated the individual trustee. Not all courts would be so kind to an individual trustee who did not object. *See also* § 55[A][1][b], *infra*.

[8] For just such a case, see In re Estate of Collins, 139 Cal. Rptr. 644 (Cal. App. 1977). There Ralph Collins named his business partner and his lawyer as trustees. Without adequate investigation of the facts or diversification of the trust fund, they loaned money to another client of the lawyer. A clause authorizing them to invest in "every kind of property . . . irrespective of whether said investments are in accordance with [California laws] pertaining to the investment of trust funds by corporate trustees" did not shield the trustees from liability.

[1] In this discussion, "fiduciaries" refers to persons who administer estates and trusts.

[A] The Duty of Loyalty

The duty of loyalty distinguishes fiduciary duties from other obligations the law imposes. Fiduciaries must place the beneficiaries' interests above their own. Loyalty has both a practical and an emotional component. Not only must fiduciaries follow certain rules, but they must also be above reproach. Trustees, in particular, carry a burden to be "squeaky clean."[2]

Two types of problems stem from a fiduciary's duty to place a beneficiary's interest first. Sometimes conflicts arise between a fiduciary and a beneficiary. For example, someone may have died owning bank stock and naming the bank as her testamentary trustee, thus placing the bank in the position of investing in itself.[3] Or a trustee may have other clients who would be interested in purchasing trust property.[4] Or a bank serving as guardian may want to hold a ward's funds in savings accounts or certificates of deposit at the bank.[5] Although courts and commentators discuss such conflicts as being between a fiduciary and a beneficiary, it may help to think of the conflicts as being between the fiduciary and the entity of the trust or the estate. The harm comes first to the asset, and secondarily to the beneficiary.

Another set of conflicts arises when different beneficiaries have different interests. A life tenant may seek high income, but the holder of the remainder may be more interested in preserving the underlying asset.[6] An executor may have the choice of allocating expenses in ways which help or hurt various beneficiaries.[7] The fiduciary's duty to each individual beneficiary is to treat that person impartially. This subsection first examines fiduciary-beneficiary conflicts, and then turns to the problem of impartiality.

---

[2] "The duty of loyalty owed by a trustee to a beneficiary in a trust relationship is more intense than in any other fiduciary relationship." Prueter v. Bork, 435 N.E.2d 109, 111 (Ill. App. 1982). *See generally* Karen E. Boxx, *Of Punctillios and Paybacks: The Duty of Loyalty Under the Uniform Trust Code*, 67 Mo. L. Rev. 279 (2002).

[3] *See In re* Will of Heidenreich, 378 N.Y.S.2d 982 (N.Y. Surr. 1976). *Heidenreich* is discussed in § 57[B], *infra*. A related issue is whether a corporate fiduciary which owns its own shares can vote those shares in elections to the corporate board of directors. *See* Cleveland Trust Co. v. Eaton, 256 N.E.2d 198 (Ohio 1970) (approving the practice).

[4] *See In re* Green Charitable Trust, 431 N.W.2d 492 (Mich. App. 1988) (surcharging the trustees $1.9 million, in part because they did not handle the sale with adequate investigation).

[5] *See In re* Estate of Swiecicki, 460 N.E.2d 91 (Ill. App. 1984). Although Illinois is one of several states with statutes allowing bank *trustees* to place deposits in their own institutions, the court held the bank *guardian* liable under the strict common law standard against self-dealing.

[6] *See* Dennis v. Rhode Island Hosp. Trust Nat'l Bank, 744 F.2d 893 (1st Cir. 1984) (trustee surcharged in part for maximizing income at the expense of failing to maintain rental property).

[7] *See* Joel C. Dobris, *Equitable Adjustments in Postmortem Income Tax Planning: An Unremitting Diet of Warms*, 65 Iowa L. Rev. 103 (1979).

[1] Fiduciary-Beneficiary Conflicts

Because some kinds of conflicts are virtually inevitable, the law recognizes degrees of conflict of interest between fiduciaries and beneficiaries. Self-dealing, in which the fiduciary transfers property with itself in its individual capacity, receives special treatment. Other conflict situations are subject to careful scrutiny. In either case, the settlor or the beneficiaries can consent to the conflict.[8]

[a] Self-Dealing

A fiduciary's self-dealing is particularly hazardous to a beneficiary's interest. Suppose Martin, as executor, owns land that Martin, as real estate developer, would love to purchase. Because of the temptation for the executor to give the developer a really good price, the law follows a "no-further-inquiry" rule in self-dealing situations.[9] Any beneficiary can undo the deal, regardless of its underlying fairness.

Self-dealing often arises when family members are fiduciaries. Consider *In re Estate of Allison.*[10] Hazel Allison died owning farmland she had leased to a company owned by her son, John. Hazel's will named John as her executor and gave her residuary estate, which included the farm, to her other children. John, as executor/landlord, signed up for a government subsidy program and then split the proceeds with himself, as tenant. When the residuary beneficiaries objected, the court viewed John's decision of signing up for the program as being good for the estate. The court said the payment to himself as tenant would have been valid if handled by a disinterested executor or approved by a court or the beneficiaries. Because of the self-dealing, however, the fairness of the arrangement was not relevant. Applying the rule that it should not inquire into the deal's fairness, the court held John liable for the amount he gained as tenant.

Settlors can approve transactions which would otherwise fall to the no-further-inquiry rule. Consider *City Bank Farmers Trust Co. v. Cannon.*[11] Mary Cannon named a bank as trustee of a revocable trust in which she placed National City Bank stock. Later, National City Bank merged with her trustee, so the trustee ended up owning its own stock. Then the stock market crashed. When a guardian ad litem for minor beneficiaries sought to surcharge the trustee for the loss resulting from holding its own stock, the court said it would not inquire into the trustee's good faith. Without

---

[8] *See* UPC § 3-713; Restatement (Second) of Trusts § 216.

[9] For shorter discussions, see Bogert § 95; Haskell at 276-280. For more extensive coverage, see Scott on Trusts § 170.

[10] 488 N.E.2d 1035 (Ill. App. 1986). *See also In re* Estate of Hines, 715 A.2d 116 (D.C. 1998) (personal representative of estate sold real property to herself as an individual and to her brother).

UTC § 802(c) presumes a conflict of interest is present in a variety of situations (like transfers to close relatives or corporations in which the trustee has an interest that might affect the trustee's best judgment).

[11] 51 N.E.2d 674 (N.Y. 1943).

more, the court would have set aside the transaction. Here, however, Mary had approved the investments with full knowledge of the conflict and had left unexercised her power to revoke the trust in light of the situation. Mary's approval of its conduct saved the bank.[12]

The no-further-inquiry rule is intentionally harsh. By making transactions voidable at a beneficiary's option, the rule hopes to prevent self-dealing in the first place.

[b] Other Conflicts of Interest

The duty of loyalty extends well beyond self-dealing, to any situation in which the interests of a fiduciary and those of the beneficiaries are in conflict. When such conflicts arise, courts will examine the underlying fairness of the situation.

In re Estate of Rothko[13] is among the best-known cases involving fiduciary conflicts of interest. Mark Rothko was an abstract expressionist painter whose works are now worth millions. His will named three co-executors. Bernard Reis was a friend and advisor who was also an officer of Marlborough Gallery, an art gallery which held several paintings owned by Bernard and his family. Theodoros Stamos was another artist. Morton Levine was a Fordham University anthropology professor.

At the time of his death, Mark had a contract with Marlborough Gallery to sell his paintings for a 10% commission. He then owned 798 paintings. Within three weeks after Mark's death, the executors arranged for the disposition of the paintings. One hundred were sold to Marlborough, A.G., another corporation associated with the gallery. The rest were consigned to the Marlborough Gallery, with a stipulation that the gallery receive a 50% commission. Mark's daughter, Kate, sued the executors for breach of fiduciary duty.[14]

Bernard and Theodoros were held liable for breach of the duty of loyalty in arranging the transfers. According to the court, both stood to gain

---

[12] *See also* Tracy v. Central Trust Co., 192 A. 869 (Pa. 1937). There a bank was one of three trustees who purchased as trust investments mortgages owned by the bank. Even though the other trustees participated in the purchase, they were able to invalidate it later because they were acting to protect the trust estate against the bank's breach.

[13] 372 N.E.2d 291 (N.Y. 1977). For more information about the circumstances of this case, see Lee Seldes, The Legacy of Mark Rothko (1979); Gustave Harrow, *Reflections on Estate of Rothko: The Role of the Legal Advisor in Relation to the Artist*, 26 Clev. St. L. Rev. 573 (1977).

[14] The bulk of the estate went to the Mark Rothko Foundation. Although not a beneficiary of the will, Kate had standing because New York's since-repealed mortmain statute limited gifts to charity. Standing is discussed in § 7[A][5][a][v], *supra*, and mortmain statutes are covered in § 30, *supra*.

Without Kate's involvement, the whole scheme might have remained hidden. The state attorney general, as supervisor of charities, would have had little reason to inquire closely about what happened. For more on supervision of charitable trusts, see Bogert § 156; Scott § 391-392. *See generally* § 15, *supra* (charitable trusts).

For another example of a charitable trust caught in a rush of conflicts, see Symposium, *The Bishop Estate Controversy*, 21 U. Haw. L. Rev. 2 (1999).

personally, although indirectly, from sales to or through the two Marlborough entities. Bernard was an officer in one of the corporations. More importantly, he and his family could expect favorable treatment in the future from the gallery for the sale of their own collections. Theodoros, a budding artist, might also appreciate a helping hand from a major gallery. Perhaps not coincidentally, less than a year after the sale of Mark Rothko's paintings, Marlborough Gallery agreed to be Theodoros Stamos' exclusive agent. Because of the conflicts, the court examined the fairness of the contracts, determined that they were inadequate, and assessed massive damages.[15]

Morton Levine, although not in a position of conflict, was also liable. His failure was that he watched in silence. By not stopping or reporting the deals,[16] he breached his duty to care for the estate's assets.[17]

Rothko raises a difficult question which affects all sorts of fiduciaries: when does mutual back-scratching become a breach of fiduciary duty? For example, does the bank trust department always use the same realtor because she offers the best service for the price, or because she refers her clients to the bank?[18] Because such conflicts do not rise to the level of self-dealing, the no-further-inquiry rule does not apply. The fiduciary must show, however, that the transactions are fair and reasonable. Nonetheless, sometimes close relationships cloud our judgment about what is in the best interest of the beneficiary. Beware of getting too cozy with other professionals.

Fiduciaries must constantly be alert to possible conflicts of interest.[19] They can arise both from innocent self-dealing and from sometimes-subtle benefits that flow from a particular course of action. As a guard against these dangers, ask: How would this look to an impartial observer?[20] Then follow the rule: "When in doubt, don't."

---

[15] For discussion of the damages question, see § 58, *infra*.

[16] Court approval of self-dealing transactions can be one way to protect a fiduciary such as Morton Levine. *See* UPC § 3-713; UTC § 802(b)(2).

[17] Morton Levine's plight serves as a warning to family members and friends tempted to take on fiduciary duties as a favor or to save money, with the expectation that a professional trustee or lawyer will handle the details. Indeed, the court rejected Morton's attempt to defend himself because he had acted upon advice of counsel.

[18] Consider a related question: Does the lawyer recommend a particular bank as trustee because it is the most competent, or because the bank's policy is to hire the lawyer who drafted a document to handle any legal problems involving that trust? *See generally* Gerald P. Johnston, *An Ethical Analysis of Common Estate Planning Practices — Is Good Business Bad Ethics?*, 45 Ohio St. L.J. 57, 115-124, 133-140 (1984).

Even if a will names a lawyer for the executor, courts routinely allow the executor to choose someone else. *See In re* Estate of Deardoff, 461 N.E.2d 1292 (Ohio 1984).

[19] For a case involving a lawyer/trustee who suffered a $1.9 million damage award, in part because he was not sensitive to the problem of wearing too many hats, see *In re* Green Charitable Trust. 431 N.W.2d 492 (Mich. App. 1988). *See also* State v. Wallace, 961 P.2d 818 (Okla. 1998) (lawyer/trustee suspended from law practice).

[20] Indeed, you might ask an *impartial* observer.

[2] Impartiality

In addition to not pursuing its own interests when they conflict with a beneficiary's, a fiduciary must treat each individual beneficiary impartially.[21] Sometimes these duties merge. Suppose Jonathan, as the executor for his mother's estate, has the power to allocate tangible personal property between himself and his sister, Kim. He cannot use that power simply to claim the hall clock for himself if Kim also wants it. Instead, Jonathan would have to use some neutral system for dividing the items.[22] Beneficiaries can be fiduciaries, but they must be careful because they will likely find conflicts at every turn.

Even an independent trustee, however, faces the competing needs of various beneficiaries. Conflicts are particularly common among income beneficiaries, and between them and those who expect to take the remainder.[23] The rest of this subsection focuses upon some common sources of conflict.

[a] Investment Strategy

Depending upon their individual situations, beneficiaries may disagree about what a trustee's investment strategy should be.[24] Income beneficiaries may want high income to live on, or they may prefer low current income and capital growth. Persons who hope to take the remainder will be concerned primarily with being sure the value of their interest has not eroded over time because of inflation.

Two somewhat similar cases illustrate the problem. *Commercial Trust Co. of New Jersey v. Barnard*[25] involved a trust established by Isaac Guggenheim for his daughters. In part because of the high tax brackets of the three income beneficiaries, the trustee invested fully in tax-exempt government bonds. The court approved this approach, even though the bonds produced low returns which were dissatisfying to one of the life tenants who was out of the country for a time and had fallen to a much lower tax bracket. Primary in the court's mind was the importance of preserving the principal.

Principal preservation also motivated the court in *In re Dwight's Trust*,[26] with opposite results for the accommodating trustee. The court surcharged the trustee for selling U.S. Savings Bonds at a loss in order to purchase tax-exempt securities for a high-tax-bracket life tenant. In general, trustees

---

[21] *See* UTC § 803.

[22] The siblings might, for example, flip a coin to decide who goes first, and then alternate choices. They might instead allocate 100 points to each beneficiary and hold an auction, with each beneficiary bidding points for the items he or she wanted most. An auction for real money would favor the wealthier beneficiary.

[23] For detailed coverage, see Scott on Trusts §§ 233-241A.

[24] For discussion of proper investing in general, see § 56[A], *infra*.

[25] 142 A.2d 865 (N.J. 1958).

[26] 128 N.Y.S.2d 23 (N.Y. Sup. Ct. 1952).

have been safe if they tuned into the needs of the life tenants without affirmatively diminishing the principal. This approach may change in light of the increased attention the law is giving to protecting the value of trust principal from the ravages of inflation. [27]

[b] Taxes

Tax rules also pose a conflict when they allow the fiduciary to allocate tax benefits or burdens among beneficiaries. For example, the tax code gives the executor the choice of claiming the expenses of estate administration against the income taxes due from the estate or against estate taxes. [28] The executor in *In re Estate of Bixby* [29] saved money overall, but incurred the wrath of the remainder beneficiaries. By taking administrative expenses against the income, he saved over $100,000 in *income* taxes, at the cost of an *estate* tax bill almost $60,000 higher than would have been the case had he taken the deduction there. While he was right to achieve the net savings, he should have allocated funds from the income beneficiaries to make up for the loss suffered by the remainder. [30]

[c] Principal-Income Allocation

Fiduciaries regularly receive and disburse money and other assets. A common question is whether particular receipts and disbursements should be credited or charged to the income beneficiaries or to the trust principal. [31] In identifying answers, the law faces a classic dilemma. The rules should be simple and inexpensive to apply. They should also be fair to all beneficiaries.

---

[27] *See In re* Estate of Cooper, 913 P.2d 393 (Wash. App. 1996) (trustee who was also income beneficiary breached fiduciary duty by weighting investments to income-producing assets); *see also* § 56[A][2], *infra.*

[28] I.R.C. § 642(g). *See* Joel C. Dobris, *Equitable Adjustments in Postmortem Income Tax Planning: An Unremitting Diet of Warms*, 65 Iowa L. Rev. 103 (1979).

[29] 295 P.2d 68 (Cal. App. 1956).

[30] Because the situs of the trust in *Bixby* was Illinois, but the decedent's domicile was Arizona, there was a question about which state's law should control. The court applied the law of the decedent's domicile because that approach would yield a consistent rule in different disputes involving the same estate. If the law of the trust situs controlled, and a decedent had established different trusts in several states, different apportionment rules might apply to the same levy of estate taxes. Also, the domiciliary state has an interest in protecting surviving family members who otherwise might not be able to recoup taxes paid. *See* Eugene F. Scoles, *Apportionment of Federal Estate Taxes and Conflict of Laws*, 55 Colum. L. Rev. 261 (1955). *See generally* William M. Richman & William L. Reynolds, Understanding Conflict of Laws ch. 4 (2d ed. 1993).

Another question is whether estate taxes should be apportioned among the estate beneficiaries. *See* Doetsch v. Doetsch, 312 F.2d 323 (7th Cir. 1963) (allowing widow who had paid taxes on entire estate to recover from beneficiaries of a living trust); Restatement (Third) of Prop. § 1.1, cmt. g (unless will provides otherwise, taxes should be equitably apportioned among probate and nonprobate assets); Carolyn B. Featheringill, *Estate Tax Apportionment and Nonprobate Assets: Picking the Right Pocket*, 21 Cumb. L. Rev. 1 (1990).

[31] *See* Bogert at ch. 13; Haskell at 298-304; McGovern & Kurtz at 329-338.

The basic vehicle for balancing those goals is the Uniform Principal and Income Act and its progeny. The Uniform Principal and Income Act was promulgated in 1931[32] and revised in 1962.[33] In 1997, a new version appeared,[34] primarily to account for the popularity of revocable living trusts[35] and the shift to new rules regulating trust investments.[36]

Among the most important innovations of the 1997 version is in Section 104, which gives the trustee the authority to adjust between principal and income instead of applying traditional rules that would be inappropriate for the trust in question. This power builds flexibility into the Act, and should help trustees reach sensible decisions in situations we cannot now anticipate. Because there are three versions and many adopting states have made changes of their own, the title "Uniform" is a bit overstated. More uniformity may arrive if states embrace the most recent version. Detailed examination of the various acts would not serve the purpose here, but remember that in specific cases, your local statute may answer a large number of questions about how to handle principal-income allocation. This subsection will highlight a few of the more notorious trouble spots.

First Wyoming Bank v. First National Bank & Trust Co. of Wyoming[37] illustrates a variety of problems. Charles Burdick placed 12,000 shares of Standard Oil of Indiana (SOInd) stock in a living trust, reserving the income to himself during his lifetime, and pouring the remainder into a trust he established with his will.[38] He named his daughter, Margaret, as trustee of the living trust. He appointed Margaret and her husband, George, to be trustees of the testamentary trust, which gave Margaret a life estate. The probate court also named them as Charles' executors. After Margaret's death some 50 years later, various trust beneficiaries challenged several of Margaret's and George's decisions.

After Charles' death, but before the estate was closed, SOInd declared a 50% stock dividend and issued shares in Margaret's name as trustee of the living trust. The final accounting for the estate, however, showed the original 12,000 shares as estate assets and the 6,000 shares from the stock dividend as having been distributed to Margaret as income beneficiary of the *estate*. A guardian ad litem was appointed for minor or nonresident estate beneficiaries, but no one challenged the accounting.

---

[32] *See* 7B Unif. Law. Ann. 242 (2000).

[33] *See* 7B Unif. Law. Ann. 131 (2000).

[34] *See* 7B Unif. Law Ann. 1 (2000). For background on this version, see a series of articles by Professor Joel C. Dobris: *Why Trustee Investors Often Prefer Dividends to Capital Gain and Debt Investments to Equity A Daunting Principal and Income Problem*, 32 Real Prop. Prob. & Tr. J. 255 (1997); *New Forms of Private Trusts for the Twenty-First Century Principal and Income,* 31 Real Prop. Prob. & Tr. J. 1 (1996); *The Probate World at the End of the Century: Is a New Principal and Income Act in Your Future?* 28 Real Prop. Prob. & Tr. J. 393 (1993).

[35] *See* § 12[E], *supra.*

[36] *See* § 56[A], *infra.*

[37] 628 P.2d 1355 (Wyo. 1981).

[38] Pouring over usually runs the other way, from a will to a preexisting trust. *See* § 16, *supra.*

Margaret and George made two mistakes regarding the stock dividend. First, they should have treated both the original stock share and the dividend shares as trust (not estate) assets. Charles did not own that stock when he died. The trust did. Second, they probably should have treated the dividend shares as principal, so that the trust's percentage of ownership in the corporation remained the same.[39] The remaindermen's challenge failed, however, because the court held that the original probate decree approving the final accounting was binding on the issue.[40] Because the SOInd stock should not have been subject to the probate court's jurisdiction, this holding is suspect. It does have the advantage, however, of avoiding the need to untangle everything after such a long time.

Another challenge went to how Margaret and George handled dividends which came in during the administration of the testamentary trust. SOInd owned stock in Standard Oil of New Jersey (SONJ). On different occasions, SOInd declared dividends out of its earned surplus, but paid those dividends by distributing SONJ stock. Margaret's estate claimed the SONJ shares as her income from the trust as the life tenant. The court agreed, applying the "Massachusetts rule," which is now widely accepted.[41] Under this rule, cash dividends and dividends payable in the form of stock of *another* corporation are income, while dividends payable in the stock of the *issuing* corporation are principal.[42] Thus, Margaret and George properly credited Margaret's account with the SONJ stock.[43]

A third challenge centered upon oil royalties paid to the trust. As you might have guessed, Margaret and George credited all of the royalties to Margaret's income account, with no allocation to those who held the remainder. The court approved this approach, relying by analogy on the "open mines" doctrine. This doctrine applies to legal life estates (i.e., those not in trust).[44] If a mine is already open when a grantor creates a life estate,

---

[39] At least this would be the result under the "Massachusetts rule" that the court adopts in a later part of the opinion, discussed just below. For discussion of the related issue of how to treat stock dividends earned between the time of a will's drafting and the date of death, see § 46[B], *supra*.

[40] For a concise discussion of issue and claim preclusion, see William M. Richman & William L. Reynolds, Understanding Conflict of Laws, 2d ed. 311-315 (1993).

[41] *See* Bogert §§ 115, 116. An earlier, more complicated approach is sometimes called the "Pennsylvania rule."

Section 401(c) of the 1997 Uniform Act allocates all stock dividends to principal.

[42] *See also* United States Trust Co. v. Cowin, 237 N.W. 284 (Neb. 1931) (adopting the "Massachusetts rule" for stock dividends paid by the issuing corporation).

There is some dispute about whether to apply new allocation rules to existing trusts, but most states have done so. *See, e.g., In re* Catherwood's Trust, 173 A.2d 86 (Pa. 1961) (applying Pennsylvania's version of the Uniform Act to pending and future distributions, regardless of when the underlying document was executed).

[43] A related question is whether mutual fund distributions, which generally include earnings from both dividends and capital gains, should be income or principal. *See* Tait v. Peck, 194 N.E.2d 707 (Mass. 1963) (allocating the capital gains portion to principal).

[44] *See* Scott § 239.3.

the life tenant gets all the proceeds of the mine. If no mine is open, neither the life tenant nor any remaindermen may open it without the others' consent. When a legal life estate is involved, the rule of not setting up a depletion fund makes sense because of the difficulty of monitoring and managing the fund. When there is a trust, however, creating a separate fund would be easy, and more fair to the holders of future interests.

In contrast to wasting assets (such as the oil fields in *First Wyoming Bank*), which hurt the principal beneficiaries by undermining the value of the principal, underproductive assets hurt the income beneficiaries.[45] Imagine, for example, farmland which produces low rentals, but then is sold for a subdivision development.[46] According to the Second Restatement, when under-productive assets are sold at a gain, the income beneficiaries should get some of that gain, to make up for the period of low income.[47] The 1997 Uniform Act allocates all the proceeds to principal[48] and relies upon the trustee's new adjustment power to fix any unfairness.[49]

The list of possible areas of principal-income disputes is as long as the list of possible sources of income or expense. Beneficiaries have litigated about what to do with income earned before a life tenant's death, but not paid until later,[50] and how to handle income earned on proceeds of property sold to meet probate administration expenses.[51] They have disputed whether income beneficiaries should be charged for depreciation.[52] They

---

[45] Often these assets come into a trust from an estate. The settlor may have given directions to hold the property, or to sell it, or may have said nothing. In most cases, a trustee will have the duty to sell such property. For a detailed discussion of these issues, see Scott on Trusts §§ 241.1-241.3A.

[46] These facts are adapted from In re Kuehn, 308 N.W.2d 398 (S.D. 1981) (allocating the gain according to the Restatement formula). *See also In re* Page's Estate, 18 Cal. Rptr. 886 (Cal. App. 1962) (same, for unproductive desert land sold for a gain).

Given the right facts, you might convince a court to allocate proceeds in less-obvious situations, like when a fiduciary finally recovers on a long-pending tort claim.

[47] The Restatement would give the principal an amount which can be expressed in the following formula:

$$\text{principal} = \frac{\text{net proceeds}}{1 + (\text{number of years})(\text{interest rate})}$$

Restatement (Second) of Trusts § 241.

[48] 1997 UPIA § 413(b).

[49] 1997 UPIA § 104.

[50] *See, e.g., In re* Appeal of New Britain Bank & Trust Co., 472 A.2d 1305 (Conn. Super. 1983) (allocating accrued income to life tenant's estate).

[51] *See, e.g.,* Proctor v. American Sec. & Trust Co., 98 F.2d 599 (D.C. Cir. 1938) (allocating to trust principal, income earned on property sold to pay probate expenses).

[52] The income beneficiary must pay maintenance costs to prevent waste, but the general approach is not to charge the income account with depreciation. *See, e.g.,* Chapin v. Collard, 189 P.2d 642 (Wash. 1948). If the trust is holding an ongoing business, a court may apply business accounting rules (which call for depreciation deductions) to the business itself. The net income of the *business* would then contribute to the income of the *trust* (determined under trust accounting rules). *See In re* Bailey's Trust, 62 N.W.2d 829 (Minn. 1954) (the trust owned an unincorporated nursery business). *See generally* Jan Z. Krasnowiecki, *Existing Rules of*

have fought over whether, and how, fiduciaries should allocate expenses of maintaining a residence and of converting it to other uses.[53] They have argued about who pays the fiduciary and its lawyers.[54] When resolving questions like these, start with the document in question;[55] then go to the local statute, then to local cases, and finally, to secondary authorities.

A relatively new way of conceptualizing trusts makes principal/income arguments irrelevant. A "unitrust" — sometimes called a "total return trust" — views the trust assets as a whole.[56] Instead of paying out "income," a unitrust typically distributes to the current beneficiary a pre-determined percentage of the trust's total market value.[57] This way both the current and the future beneficiaries share in the increases and decreases of the trust's value over time.

Balancing the needs of various beneficiaries can be difficult. Using good judgment and treating all beneficiaries with respect can solve many problems. One way to both serve beneficiaries and avoid litigation is to build good relationships through regular communication.

[B] The Duty to Communicate

Good lawyers and fiduciaries know that regular communication with clients and beneficiaries is good business. Communication is also an obligation. Ethics rules require lawyers to keep their clients informed.[58] Probate rules and trust documents regularly require that fiduciaries account to the beneficiaries.[59] The UPC requires trustees to answer beneficiaries'

Trust Administration: A Stranglehold on the Trustee-Controlled Business Enterprise, Part I: The Unincorporated Business, 110 U. Pa. L. Rev. 506 (1962), *Part II: The Incorporated Business,* 110 U. Pa. L. Rev. 816 (1962).

[53] For an interesting case which gets down to specifics like $6.00 plumbing bills and sharing the cost of a refrigerator, see *In re* Cronise's Estate, 6 N.Y.S.2d 392 (N.Y. Sur. Ct. 1937) (applying the general principle that income bears ordinary maintenance expenses and principal bears the expenses that go to increasing the value of the principal). *See* Scott §§ 233.2, 233.3.

[54] *See, e.g., In re* Lopez's Estate, 179 P.2d 621 (Cal. App. 1947) (charging the principal with costs of setting up the trust's operation); Davidson's Estate, 135 A. 130 (Pa. 1926) (dividing attorney's fees incurred when collecting on a promissory note).

[55] *See, e.g.,* Englund v. First Nat'l Bank of Birmingham, 381 So. 2d 8 (Ala. 1980) (General power to determine whether receipts should be income or principal did not empower trustee to violate local rules on specific topics.). For discussion of how document drafting can affect a variety of administration problems, see § 57[B], *infra.*

[56] Compare the modern portfolio theory of trust investing discussed in § 56[A][2], *infra.*

[57] *See generally,* Robert B. Wolf, *Estate Planning with Total Return Trusts: Meeting Human Needs and Investment Goals Through Modern Trust Design,* 36 Real Prop. & Prob. Tr. J. 169 (2001).

[58] Model Rules of Professional Conduct, Rule 1.4 (2002).

[59] Procedurally, a great many fiduciary duty cases arise as beneficiaries challenge accounts.

One reason for choosing a lifetime trust, instead of a testamentary one, is to avoid the need for regular accounting to the probate court. *See* § 11, *supra.* All trust documents, whether testamentary or lifetime, should require accounting directly to the beneficiaries. General trust principles require not only an accounting, but that the accounting be adequate. *See* Jacob v. Davis, 738 A.2d 904 (Md. Ct. Spec. App. 1999) (brokerage statements not enough). *See generally* McGovern & Kurtz at 552.

reasonable requests for information.[60] The UTC requires trustees to keep beneficiaries "reasonably informed about the administration of the trust and of the material facts necessary for them to protect their interests."[61]

Sometimes the duty may go beyond telling what has happened. Before making a major decision, a fiduciary should check with the beneficiaries to get their input.[62] *Allard v. Pacific National Bank*[63] illustrates the danger of acting alone. Freeman Allard and Evelyn Orkney were life income beneficiaries of testamentary trusts established by their parents to hold a quarter-block of commercial property in downtown Seattle. Under the trust documents, the trustee had "full power" to administer the assets without getting consent of the beneficiaries. Relying upon this authority, the trustees sold the property without telling Freeman and Evelyn.[64]

The court held that the trustee breached its duty to inform the beneficiaries, before the transaction, about all material facts of a "nonroutine transaction which significantly affects the trust estate and the interests of the beneficiaries."[65] On remand, the trial court assessed damages of about $1.2 million and an additional $1 million in attorney's fees.[66] Courts are beginning to demand that before fiduciaries finalize significant decisions about how to proceed with the trust, fiduciaries solicit the beneficiaries' involvement.[67] One way lawyers can help trustees avoid these sorts of problems is by drafting documents which require communication before the trustee decides how to handle important assets. With the duty expressed, trustees should be more likely to make communication a part of their routines.

Much of the law surrounding fiduciary-beneficiary relationships can be captured in one word: respect. Fiduciaries who think of their beneficiaries first will tend to avoid self-dealing and other conflicts of interest. Such fiduciaries will keep everyone informed, because if they were in the beneficiaries' position, they would like to be informed. Building relationships with those you serve not only avoids liability, it greatly lowers the chance that someone will complain if things do go wrong.

---

[60] UPC § 7-303(b).

[61] UTC § 813(a).

[62] A related obligation is for a fiduciary to keep itself informed about the status of the beneficiaries. *See* National Academy of Sciences v. Cambridge Trust Co., 346 N.E.2d 879 (Mass. 1976) (trustee surcharged when it continued to make payments to the testator's widow after she had remarried and her rights to income had ended).

[63] 663 P.2d 104 (Wash. 1983).

[64] The trustee also failed to get an independent appraisal or to test the market to identify an appropriate price.

[65] *Allard*, 663 P.2d at 110.

[66] *See* Allard v. First Interstate Bank, 768 P.2d 998 (Wash. 1989) (upholding the awards).

[67] For a case with many similarities to *Allard*, resulting in a $1.9 million surcharge, see *In re* Green Charitable Trust, 431 N.W.2d 492 (Mich. App. 1988) (when selling land, trustees breached many duties, including a duty to communicate imposed by statute).

§ 56　Managerial Issues

Another aspect of respecting beneficiaries is handling their assets carefully. This section addresses fiduciaries' management duties. Perhaps the most commonly quoted overall standard comes from Professor Scott, who would require trustees to exercise "such care and skill as a man of ordinary prudence would exercise in dealing with his own property."[1] As we shall see, that standard has taken some twists and turns with respect to investments, but in general it has dominated trust law.

Perhaps the most important point about fiduciary management is that good intentions are not enough. Consider the plight of Jane Ann Blair.[2] Her uncle Henry's will named her as trustee of a relatively modest fund to provide education for his daughter's children. Jane accepted the post, but treated the trust informally. Although the only beneficiary was nine years old at the beginning of the trust, Jane divided the assets among a checking account, a savings account, and certificates of deposit. Because she kept too much in the non-interest-bearing checking account over a period of 10 years, Jane was assessed almost $3,000 in damages. Unknowingly, she had breached her duty to invest the funds.[3]

This section will first discuss a trustee's investment obligations, and then highlight other management duties.

[A]　Investments

Determining the propriety of any trust investment requires asking two questions. The first is general: what *types* of investments can the trustee make? Statutes, case law, or the trust document may preclude investment in common stocks or real estate, for example. The second question is specific: assuming the type of investment is appropriate, is the *particular* investment proper? Although a document may authorize a trustee to buy common stocks, obtaining shares in Widgets, Inc., a company on the verge of bankruptcy, may be imprudent. The law on each of these points has been changing.

Over the space of about 160 years, the law is approaching coming full circle in terms of the way it judges trust investments. In 1830, *Harvard College v. Amory* gave us the "Prudent Man" rule: "[a trustee should] observe how men of prudence, discretion and intelligence manage their own affairs, not in regard to speculation, but in regard to the permanent disposition of their funds, considering the probable income, as well as the probable

---

[1] Scott on Trusts § 174; Restatement (Second) of Trusts § 174. For an insightful example, which draws upon Ann Landers to show what prudence means in the real world, see Shaffer, Mooney & Boettcher at 116-117. *See also* UTC § 804 ("reasonable care, skill and caution").

[2] *See* Witmer v. Blair, 588 S.W.2d 222 (Mo. App. 1979).

[3] For another case involving casual treatment by a family member trustee, see Jimenez v. Lee, 547 P.2d 126 (Or. 1976), discussed in § 12[A], *supra*. Cases like these suggest clients should use great caution when selecting a trustee. *See* § 12[D], *supra*.

safety of the capital to be invested."[4] Here was a flexible statement which could adapt to different circumstances, but such flexibility fell into disfavor.

The boom and bust economic cycles of the 19th century led many legislatures to provide "legal lists" of appropriate trust investments.[5] Some lists were mandatory, meaning that a trustee could not go beyond them. Others were permissive, allowing a trustee to buy something not on the list, but effectively placing the burden on the trustee to show that such a move was prudent. The lists tended to favor "safe" investments like government bonds and first mortgages on realty. Common stocks usually were omitted as too risky.

In the aftermath of the Great Depression of the 1930s, stocks recovered their value much better than bonds or mortgages.[6] By the 1940s, the move was on to broaden the scope of appropriate trust investments. With a push from Professor Scott and the Restatement of Trusts,[7] states dropped their legal lists and moved back to a more flexible "prudent man" approach.[8]

As fleshed out by Professor Scott in various sections of his treatise, this prudent man was more conservative than his earlier counterpart. In an influential article, Professor Gordon noted three ways that Scott narrowed the *Harvard College* approach.[9] First, Scott emphasized "preservation" instead of "permanent disposition" of the estate.[10] Second, when referring to investments, Scott shifted the prudent man standard, from one based on how people would manage their own property, to a standard based on those concerned about safeguarding the property of others.[11] Third, Scott drew a hard line between "prudence," which was mandated, and "speculation," which was prohibited.[12] The cumulative impact of these changes was

---

[4] 26 Mass. (9 Pick) 446, 461 (1830).

[5] *See* Bogert § 103.

[6] *See* Austin Fleming, *Prudent Investments: The Varying Standards of Prudence*, 12 Real Prop. Prob. & Tr. J. 243, 244-245 (1977).

[7] *See* Scott on Trusts § 227; Restatement (Second) of Trusts § 227. Scott was the Reporter for the First and Second Restatements.

[8] *See* Bogert at 386.

To eliminate the sexism of the old phrase, many statutes and commentators refer to this as a "prudent investor" rule. Because the Second Restatement retained the old term, but the Third Restatement and a new Uniform Act have adopted the modern one, this text hopes to avoid confusion by limiting the "prudent investor" usage to descriptions of the new rule. The prudent investor rule is discussed in § 56[A][2], *infra*.

[9] *See* Jeffrey N. Gordon, *The Puzzling Persistence of the Constrained Prudent Man Rule*, 62 N.Y.U. L. Rev. 52, 59-61 (1987).

[10] In an inflationary economy, nominal preservation of capital can hurt those who hold for long periods.

[11] Scott distinguished between the general obligation to handle trust affairs as one would handle one's own property, and a specific duty regarding investments. "A trustee must use the caution in making investments which is used by prudent men who have primarily in view the preservation of their property, of men who are *safeguarding property for others*." Scott on Trusts § 227 (3d ed. 1967) (emphasis added). With respect to investments, the "prudent man" became the "prudent trustee."

[12] Thus, new companies, companies which do not pay dividends, and new financial devices were out of bounds.

to give the hypothetical prudent man less flexibility when choosing investments.

More recently, economists and others have developed new views about how financial markets work. Collectively known as "modern portfolio theory," these ideas emphasize the risk and return of an entire portfolio, rather than an individual investment in isolation.[13] Modern portfolio theory is changing the law of trust investments.[14] In particular, the American Law Institute issued a new Restatement of Trusts devoted to creating a "prudent investor" rule shaped by modern portfolio theory,[15] and a Uniform Prudent Investor Act has been adopted in almost 40 states.[16]

This subsection will first discuss traditional trust investment rules and then will highlight the changes prompted by modern portfolio theory.

[1] The Traditional "Prudent Man"

Although the prudent man rule applies an objective standard, a personalized image may aid your understanding.[17] Visualize Stewart, the prudent man. He is, most of all, cautious. He dresses in blues and greys. He drives a four-door sedan with front and side airbags. He shuns football pools and has given up smoking. He plays not to lose.

As trustee of a family trust, Stewart is concerned most about safety. His primary goal is preservation of capital, without much regard for the corrosive effects of inflation.[18] He does not "speculate," but instead relies on investments with guaranteed returns, like government bonds or, at least, stocks with established records of paying dividends.[19] If he makes loans, he gets plenty of security.[20] Diversification is perhaps his most important device for achieving safety.[21] Because diversification is hard to achieve

[13] For an accessible introduction to the theory, see Burton G. Malkiel, A Random Walk Down Wall Street ch. 9 (Rev. ed. 1999).

[14] The writing is extensive. See, e.g., Bevis Longstreet, Modern Investment Strategy and the Prudent Man Rule (1986); Jeffrey N. Gordon, The Puzzling Persistence of the Constrained Prudent Man Rule, 62 N.Y.U. L. Rev. 52 (1987); Paul G. Haskell, The Prudent Person Rule for Trustee Investment and Modern Portfolio Theory, 69 N.C. L. Rev. 87 (1990).

[15] See Restatement (Third) of Trusts §§ 227-229; Edward C. Halbach, Jr., Trust Investment Law in the Third Restatement, 77 Iowa L. Rev. 1151 (1992).

[16] 7B Unif. Law. Ann. 56 (1998 Supp.). See generally John H. Langbein, The Uniform Prudent Investor Act and the Future of Trust Investing, 81 Iowa L. Rev. 641 (1996).

[17] See Bogert at 385-394; Scott at 434-458.

[18] "He has no duty to make investments for the purpose of increasing the value of the trust assets." Bogert at 387.

[19] For a case which endorsed a more extensive, and very detailed, set of criteria for judging safety, see First Alabama Bank v. Martin, 425 S.2d 415, 419-420 (Ala. 1982), discussed infra, this subsection.

[20] There should be an adequate margin of safety between the loan amount and the secured asset. Second mortgages are particularly dangerous, both because they may allow a smaller margin of safety and because they give up control to the senior creditor, who might force a sale at a bad time for the second mortgagee. See In re Estate of Collins, 139 Cal. Rptr. 644 (Cal. App. 1977) (trustees surcharged, among other things, for taking a second mortgage).

[21] See In re Estate of Janes, 681 N.E.2d 332 (N.Y. 1997) (executor surcharged over $4 million

without plenty of assets, Stewart may invest in nonspeculative mutual funds.[22]

As a traditional prudent man, Stewart also cares about his rate of return. He tends to think about the rate of return in absolute terms: is he generating enough income to meet the needs of the income beneficiaries? He tends not to focus on the total return of the whole portfolio over time. Avoiding individual losses is more important than achieving overall gains.

Depending upon the situation, our prudent man will face other problems.[23] One common concern is liquidity. Not only does he want to avoid being locked in to a bad investment, he also needs to anticipate the cash needs of the trust.[24] Another question is what to do if a beneficiary requests him to invest only in "socially responsible" companies. May a trustee consider factors other than obtaining the highest return for a given level of risk?[25] Trustees must watch the federal rules for handling pension investments, because those may impact private trusts.[26] Managing assets for someone else is no picnic.

One of the dominant features of the traditional prudent man rule is its one-investment-at-a-time approach. Consider what happened to the trustee

---

for decline of Kodak stock, which represented 71% of estate's value). *But see* Estate of Knipp, 414 A.2d 1007 (Pa. 1980) (executor escaped surcharge for decline in the value of Sears stock, which represented over 70% of the estate's value).

[22] There is some concern that investing in mutual funds is a breach of the duty not to delegate decisions (in this case, investment decisions about individual securities) to someone else. Because mutual funds allow smaller investors to diversify, many states allow the practice. *See* McGovern & Kurtz at 518.

Corporate trustees diversify small accounts by investing them in common trust funds. These essentially are mutual funds run by the trustee, pooling assets from a variety of trust accounts. They operate under specific authority to waive the rule against trustees commingling the assets of different trust accounts. *See, e.g.*, Uniform Common Trust Fund Act 7 (Part II), Unif. Law. Ann. 401. For a helpful discussion of common trust funds, see Mechanicks Nat'l Bank v. D'Amours, 129 A.2d 859 (N.H. 1957).

[23] For a list of additional criteria for the prudent man to consider, see Scott on Trusts § 227.12.

[24] If the trust is to care for his ailing mother, he would need to hold sizeable amounts in cash. If the trust is to provide college funds for his young grandchildren, he would not now need cash, but he would need to plan his investments so they are convertible to cash when tuition payments come due. If the trust provides both for his mother and his grandchildren, Stewart must balance their competing needs. *See* § 55[A][2][a], *supra*.

[25] The question of socially responsible investing became particularly important in the context of international efforts to isolate South Africa before it began to dismantle its system of apartheid, but the issues are broader. For a sampling of views regarding both charitable and private trusts, see Ronald A. Brand, *Investment Duties of Trustees of Charitable Trusts and Directors of Nonprofit Corporations: Applying the Law to Investments That Acknowledge Social and Moral Concerns*, 1986 Ariz. St. L.J. 631; Joel C. Dobris, *Arguments in Favor of Fiduciary Divestment of South African Securities*, 65 Neb. L. Rev. 209 (1986); John H. Langbein & Richard A. Posner, *Social Investing and the Law of Trusts*, 79 Mich. L. Rev. 72 (1980); Charles E. Rounds, Jr., *Social Investing, IOLTA and the Law of Trusts: The Settlor's Case Against the Political Use of Charitable and Client Funds*, 22 Loy. U. Chi. L.J. 163 (1990).

[26] *See* Symposium: *ERISA Fiduciary Responsibility*, 23 Real Prop. Prob. & Tr. J. 561 (1988). For a brief introduction into the federal statute, see § 21, *supra*.

in *First Alabama Bank of Montgomery v. Martin.*[27] The bank operated two common trust funds, one for equities and one for bonds.[28] When, in a down market, the bank sold some of the stocks and bonds for losses, beneficiaries of the individual trusts brought a class action against the bank. The trial court examined each individual security, found many of them imprudent, and surcharged the bank more than $2.5 million. The Alabama Supreme Court affirmed, ignoring the bear market conditions and, more importantly, ignoring the makeup of each portfolio as a whole. The court effectively made the trustee into an insurer against loss. Cases like this one, which are out of touch with modern portfolio theory, helped prompt the new prudent investor rule.[29]

[2]   The Prudent Portfolio Investor

In an effort to modernize the fiduciary investment law, the American Law Institute in 1990 approved new "prudent investor" rules.[30] The Uniform Prudent Investor Act (UPIA) followed in 1994.[31] In general, the new approach seeks to return to the flexibility of *Harvard College,*[32] but in a modern setting. Because other sources examine the new rules in detail,[33] this subsection need only highlight the major differences between the traditional and the new approaches.

Let us begin by imagining Jessica, a "prudent investor." She shares many traits with her conservative cousin, the prudent man.[34] She is careful, sensible. She has her share of dark suits, but occasionally wears pinks or reds for variety. She drives a two-door sporty car, but paid extra for airbags. She does not smoke, but buys a lottery ticket occasionally. She adjusts well to new situations.

---

[27] 425 So. 2d 415 (Ala. 1982).

[28] Common trust funds are rather like mutual funds run by the bank for its own trust accounts. *See* n.22, *supra*.

[29] For a case which seemed to take a one-stock-at-a-time approach, but did not apply the narrow standards of the *First Alabama* case, see In re Bank of New York, 323 N.E.2d 700 (N.Y. 1974). There the court said individual imprudent investments could not be offset by gain to the portfolio as a whole, but found no liability, because the individual losses were not caused by imprudent investing.

[30] Restatement (Third) of Trusts §§ 227-229.

[31] 7B Unif. Law. Ann. 56 (1998 Supp.)

[32] The new rule requires a trustee "to invest and manage the funds of the trust as a prudent investor would, in light of the purposes, terms, distribution requirements and other circumstances of the trust." Restatement (Third) of Trusts § 227; UPIA § 2(a). Compare the language of the *Harvard College* case quoted in § 56[A], *supra*.

[33] For a comprehensive discussion from the Restatement's Reporter, see Edward C. Halbach, Jr., *Trust Investment Law in the Third Restatement*, 77 Iowa L. Rev. 1151 (1992). *See also* John H. Langbein, *the Uniform Prudent Investor Act and the Future of Trust Investing*, 81 Iowa L. Rev. 641 (1996); Martin D. Begleiter, *Does the Prudent Investor Need the Uniform Prudent Investor Act—An Empirical Study of Trust Investment Practices*, 51 Maine L. Rev. 28 (1999).

[34] *See* § 56[A][1], *supra*.

Like her older counterpart, Jessica cares about risk and return, but she views a larger picture, based upon her understanding of modern portfolio theory and related concepts.[35] The prudent investor recognizes that the market values assets according to their potential returns and the risk of not achieving those returns. She views "return" to include both income and capital appreciation. Moreover, she sees two kinds of risk. Market risk, the chance that the whole market will go down, is reflected in prices generally. Specific risks, like the chance that new clean air rules will hurt electric utility stocks, are not part of the pricing system, because the market assumes these are covered by a diversified portfolio. The prudent investor reduces these specific risks through *diversification*.

Diversification is now both a more important and a more complex concept.[36] Diversification can occur at different levels. At its simplest, the level the traditional rules emphasize, "diversification" means merely increasing the numbers of different investments, to guard against individual losses. Many traditional investors also recognize that "diversification" should include holding different types of investments, some stocks, some bonds, some cash equivalents.

Now the focus is more precise. There is more attention to balancing the portfolio among investments that are unlikely to move in the same direction in the face of particular events.[37] For example, to offset stock of utilities using coal-fired power plants, Jessica might buy stock in a company manufacturing solar collection panels. Viewed in isolation, the solar stock might seem more risky than that of established utilities. Viewed in terms of the whole portfolio, however, the solar stock might lower the risk of loss caused by strict environmental rules. The insight that purchase of a "risky" stock actually can *lower* the overall risk to the portfolio means that the traditional, one-investment-at-a-time approach is counterproductive. Because the prudent investor must judge each investment decision in light of the overall portfolio and the needs of the trust, no investment is imprudent per se.[38]

The "big picture" approach affects other rules as well. Allocation decisions regarding principal and income should be less traumatic in some situations.[39] The focus on the trust portfolio's overall return, combined with

---

[35] *See* Edward C. Halbach, Jr., *Trust Investment Law in the Third Restatement*, 77 Iowa L. Rev. 1151, 1159-1166 (1992).

[36] Despite the increased emphasis on diversification, the new rule recognizes that in some situations, like when a trust holds stock in a family corporation, a duty to diversify may give way to more specific settlor goals, like maintaining control of the company. *See* Restatement (Third) of Trusts § 227, cmt. q; UPIA § 3, cmt.

[37] *See* James S. McDonald, *Considerations of Asset Allocation in Trust*, 130 Tr. & Est. Apr. 1991 at 51, 55.

[38] *See* Edward C. Halbach, Jr., *Trust Investment Law in the Third Restatement*, 77 Iowa L. Rev. 1151, 1184 (1992). International investments, once taboo, are now part of the mix trustees should consider. *See* Frederic J. Bendremer, *Modern Portfolio Theory and International Investments Under the Uniform Prudent Investor's Act*, 35 Real Prop. Prob. & Tr. J. 791 (2001).

[39] Indeed, the new investment rules prompted revisions in the Uniform Principal and Income Act. *See* § 55[A][2][c], *supra*.

overall flexibility, should make it easier for trustees to meet different needs in different circumstances. Remaindermen now have the benefit of rules attentive to inflation's corrosive effect on purchasing power.[40] By liberalizing non-delegation rules,[41] but admonishing trustees to avoid unwarranted expenses,[42] the new rule encourages those who need advice to seek it, but also suggests that purchasing broad-based market funds might be appropriate.[43]

Although the prudent investor rules affect a variety of doctrines regarding fiduciary responsibility,[44] their most significant impact is likely to be furthering the movement toward judging investments as part of a whole, rather than on a one-at-a-time basis. While understanding that trust investment law seems increasingly likely to recognize elements of modern portfolio theory, lawyers should also be cautious. In several jurisdictions, the traditional rule is still the law.

[B] Other Managerial Duties

Fiduciaries have a variety of other managerial duties designed to safeguard the beneficiaries' assets. One which seems obvious enough is the duty to take control of the assets.[45] For executors, this is usually the first step in probate administration.[46] Trustees normally take some or all of the assets from the executor, so trustees need to watch what the executor has done. In one interesting case,[47] a bank served as both executor and trustee. As executor, it mistakenly overpaid inheritance taxes and then turned the estate assets over to itself as trustee. Trust beneficiaries recovered from the bank, as trustee, for failure to object to the bank/executor's tax overpayment.

Other duties protect the integrity of the process. Unless otherwise authorized, trustees cannot mingle funds from one trust account with those of another.[48] The idea is to be sure that gains and losses stay with the right accounts. A related obligation is the duty to identify trust assets as such. This act is called "earmarking," and avoids confusion about whether assets are the trustee's property personally or belong to the trust. Earmarking

---

[40] Restatement (Third) of Prop. § 227 cmt. i, § 232 cmt. c.

[41] Non-delegation rules are discussed in § 56[B], *infra*.

[42] Restatement (Third) of Prop. § 227(c)(3).

[43] For the view that trustees should be investing in unmanaged funds which seek to reproduce the market, see John H. Langbein & Richard A. Posner, *Market Funds and Trust Investment Law*, 1976 Am. B. Found. Res. J. 1.

[44] *See* § 57 (drafting), *infra*.

[45] *See* UTC §§ 809 & 812.

[46] *See* § 2[A][1], *supra*.

[47] *In re* First Nat'l Bank, 307 N.E.2d 23 (Ohio 1974).

[48] These rules have been relaxed to allow corporate fiduciaries to combine trust money in common trust funds. *See* § 56[A][1], *supra*. UTC § 810(d) covers individual trustees as well: "If the trustee maintains records clearly indicating the respective interests, a trustee may invest as a whole the property of two or more separate trusts."

protects the trust assets from the risk that the trustee's personal creditors will claim those assets and the risk that the trustee will sell them to a bona fide purchaser.[49] Because holding securities in the name of individual trusts burdens easy transferability,[50] many states eliminate or soften the earmarking rule for securities.[51]

Trustees also have a duty not to delegate to others obligations they ought to perform themselves.[52] To decide what acts a trustee may delegate, courts apply the familiar rule of prudence under the circumstances, with particular attention to how much discretion the act involves.[53] With respect to delegation of investment decisions, the modern portfolio theory views delegation more positively than do traditional rules, which tend to allow delegation of investment decisions only in very narrow circumstances.[54]

[C] Liability for Contracts and Torts

Under traditional rules, fiduciaries may be personally liable for contracts even if the contract is within the fiduciary's authority,[55] and they may be personally liable for torts[56] even when they have personally done no wrong.[57] When fiduciaries have acted properly, they usually will have a right of indemnification against the estate or trust. If that entity has plenty of assets, the liability should pose no problem; if the claim exceeds the assets, however, the fiduciary is stuck. Of course, if the contract were beyond the scope of the trustee's power or if the tort resulted from the trustee's

---

[49] An older rule held trustees liable for any loss which occurred while assets were not earmarked, even if the loss was the result of general economic conditions. The modern rule holds trustees liable only if the failure to earmark caused the loss. *See* Miller v. Pender, 34 A.2d 663 (N.H. 1943) (adopting the modern rule); Bogert § 100.

[50] Transfer agents, quite rightly, want to be sure that the trustee has the power to sell, so they may ask for lots of documentation. The widely adopted Uniform Act for Simplification of Fiduciary Security Transfers is designed to ease the paperwork burden. 7B Unif. Law. Ann. 689.

[51] Probably the most common solution is for a corporate trustee to have the securities issued in the name of a "nominee," often a partnership established just for the purpose of nominally owning the shares. The trustee credits the securities to various trust accounts, but can easily transfer them on the open market.

[52] *See* Scott on Trusts § 171.

[53] *See* UTC § 807, which moves from a "one size fits all" standard to one which recognizes different skill levels. Trustees with lower skill levels can delegate more. The emphasis is on exercising care, skill and caution in selecting the agent to do the delegated work.

[54] *Compare* Restatement (Second) of Trusts § 171 *with* Restatement (Third) of Trusts § 227 and UPIA § 9. *See* John H. Langbein, *Reversing the Nondelegation Rule of Trust-Investment Law,* 59 Mo. L. Rev. 105 (1994).

[55] *See* Atkinson § 119 (personal representative); Bogert § 125 (trustees).

[56] *See* Atkinson § 118 (personal representative); Bogert § 129. The basis for liability would be the *respondeat superior* doctrine. This rule does not usually apply to trustees of charitable trusts.

[57] The traditional rules on personal liability of trustees for contracts and torts contrast with the usual rules for agents of disclosed principals. *See* Restatement (Second) of Agency §§ 320 (in general, agent acting for a disclosed principal not a party to a contract), 358(1) (unless at fault, agent of a disclosed principal not liable for the conduct of other agents).

negligence, then personal liability would attach without a right of indemnification.

Traditionally, fiduciaries could be sure of avoiding contract liability only if the contract explicitly excludes personal liability.[58] Even signing in a representative capacity, like "Warren Magnuson, Executor of the Estate of Ruth Magnuson," is not enough to avoid liability under the traditional rule. In contrast, the UTC absolves the trustee of personal liability on a contract "properly entered into in the trustee's fiduciary capacity . . . if the trustee in the contract disclosed the fiduciary capacity."[59]

A solution for tort liability is insurance that runs personally to the fiduciary. *Johnston v. Long*[60] illustrates why insurance is important. Ralph Long was the executor of C. A. Gray's estate. Gray had owned an automobile agency. As directed by Gray's will, Long hired John Berger to manage the business after Gray's death. When Harold Johnston stopped to deliver gasoline, an overhead door fell and cut off the end of his nose. The court noted that when a fiduciary is not at fault, the estate should bear the ultimate cost, but applied the respondeat superior doctrine and held Long personally liable for the loss. The court did not view a trust or estate as a separate entity, like a corporation, so the negligent employee was *Long's* employee. Moreover, the court saw procedural advantages to allowing suit against the fiduciary personally.

In response to the harshness of these traditional rules, many states have reversed them. Under the UPC and the UTC a trustee is personally liable for torts only if personally at fault.[61]

Managing a trust or an estate requires both a grasp of the big picture and attention to detail. It is not a duty which should be accepted lightly. Fortunately, good drafting can make life a bit easier for fiduciaries.

§ 57 Drafting: Powers and Duties

Testators and settlors can alter virtually all of the rules described in this chapter. They can approve of self-dealing, devise their own principal-income allocation formulae, set their own investment policies, authorize commingling of assets, and even exonerate fiduciaries for negligent acts. For the overwhelming percentage of estates and trusts, clauses describing fiduciary power or liability never reach litigation. Rather, fiduciaries simply rely upon such clauses in the day-to-day course of business. Case law is helpful, however, for determining the outer boundaries of fiduciary behavior.

Depending upon the nature of a fiduciary's situation, well-drafted documents grant a wide range of powers.[1] A "simple" will covering modest assets

---

[58] *See* Scott § 263. If the *trust* document excludes personal liability and the other party has notice of that provision, the trustee may avoid personal liability. Haskell at 313.

[59] UTC § 1010(a).

[60] 181 P.2d 645 (Cal. 1947).

[61] UPC § 7-306(b); UTC § 1010(b).

[1] The law treats different kinds of fiduciaries differently. Personal representatives are likely

should provide basic authority to act, usually without the need for court approval.[2] If a business is involved, more detailed provisions will be needed. Because of the ongoing nature of a trust, trustee powers provisions often are very long and detailed.

Because all of these individualized grants operate against a background of legislation, this section first identifies the various approaches different states take. It then turns to common problems regarding drafting provisions about fiduciary powers and duties.

[A] Legislation

Legislation regarding fiduciary powers takes a variety of forms.[3] Some states give particular powers, like the power to sell on credit.[4] Still others give fiduciaries a long list of powers.[5] Sometimes drafters will incorporate a list of powers by reference to other documents or to statutes.[6] Incorporating a list by reference can be risky, because you must be sure you really want all those powers in a particular circumstance, or know how future amendments to the incorporated document will affect your document. On the other hand, statutes which give powers to fiduciaries put the burden on the drafter to negate unwanted powers. Check your local statute before drafting a document which reads "in addition to all other powers granted by law . . . ."

[B] Language in the Document

Documents can both help and hurt fiduciaries trying to perform their jobs. Testators and settlors can grant helpful authority and give guidance. On the other hand, directions can become so restrictive that they hurt the will or trust beneficiaries. This subsection offers some examples of common problems, ranging from grants of power to exculpatory clauses. To some extent these issues overlap, because a fiduciary's liability may depend upon whether a document has given the fiduciary the power to do something.

Among the most vexing of administrative questions is how to allocate receipts and disbursements between income and principal.[7] Sometimes

---

to have some inherent powers to handle the estate. *See, e.g.,* Atkinson at 645 (power to sue). Although trustees are without inherent powers, courts may imply powers for them in particular circumstances. *See* Smith v. Mooney, 139 A. 513 (N.J. Ch. 1927) (court found an implied power to sell real estate when otherwise distribution to beneficiaries would be in very small fractions of ownership); Scott § 186.

[2] In particular, allowing for the private sale of real estate without court approval of the appraisal or the ultimate sale can save time and money. Of course, the client needs to trust the executor before adopting such a course.

[3] *See* Shaffer, Mooney & Boettcher 111-115.

[4] R.I. Gen. Laws § 18-4-2.

[5] This is the approach of the UTC. *See* UTC § 816. *See also* UPC § 3-715.

[6] For a discussion of the incorporation by reference doctrine as it applies to wills, see § 8[B], *supra.*

[7] *See* § 55[A][2][c], *supra.*

drafters attempt to ease this burden by giving fiduciaries broad discretion to allocate items as they wish. Courts often read these clauses narrowly. *American Security & Trust Co. v. Frost*[8] involved Mary Lincoln's will, which gave her trustees the power "to decide finally any question that may arise as to what constitutes income and what principal,—it being my wish however, that whenever feasible their decision be in favor of the life beneficiaries named herein."[9] When two individual trustees, who favored the income beneficiaries, disagreed with the corporate trustee over how to allocate various receipts, litigation followed. The court ruled that under settled rules the receipts should go to the principal account, and that the discretionary clause only operated when there was reasonable doubt about what to do. The broad clause did not override the settled rule.

Hildegard Clarenbach used even stronger language in her will, saying that a fiduciary's decision on principal-income allocation "shall be final and not subject to question by any court or any beneficiary hereof."[10] Her children were trustees and life income beneficiaries. When stock they sold produced almost $20,000 in capital gains, the trustees allocated $10,000 to their own income accounts. The court saw their action as more in the nature of invading the principal (which they had no independent authority to do) than as one involving principal-income allocation. In the court's view, their discretion did not extend this far.[11] If the trustees had possessed an invasion power, the result might have been different.[12]

Different problems center around a fiduciary's power to sell.[13] Even if a document has given the fiduciary a power to sell, related obligations may still restrict the power. For example, *Durkin v. Connelly*[14] involved an executor who had the power to sell real estate and invest the proceeds. She agreed to sell some land, taking some cash and a second mortgage from the purchaser. When the executor changed her mind, the court refused to specifically enforce the contract. Although she had the power to sell, her taking a second mortgage for some of the balance meant that she was, in effect, investing estate funds imprudently.[15] Similarly, the trustee in *Allard v. Pacific National Bank*[16] had full power to administer the trust

---

[8] 117 F.2d 283 (D.C. Cir. 1940).

[9] 117 F.2d at 284.

[10] *In re* Clarenbach's Will, 126 N.W.2d 614 (Wis. 1964).

[11] The court also noted that, at the time the will was drafted, Wisconsin followed the complicated Pennsylvania rule for allocating stock dividends. The broad clause could have been intended to avoid disputes under that rule. For discussion of the changing rules regarding stock dividends, see § 55[A][2][c], *supra*.

The trustees' conflict of interest may also have influenced the court.

[12] Perhaps the best solution is to establish benefits without regard to either principal-income allocation rules or need. For example, a "unitrust" approach allocates everything to principal and gives current beneficiaries a set percentage of that. *See* § 55[A][2][c], *supra*.

[13] *See* McGovern & Kurtz at 504–510. For discussion of self-dealing, see § 55[A][1][a], *supra*.

[14] 92 A. 906 (N.J. Ch. 1915).

[15] Second mortgages are generally prohibited under traditional prudent investor rules. *See* § 56[A][1], *supra*.

[16] 663 P.2d 104 (Wash. 1983).

whose principal asset was commercial property. That power, however, did not relieve the trustee from its duty to consult with the beneficiaries before selling the parcel.[17]

Similar problems surround efforts to continue a decedent's business. Consider Don, a pilot who owns an airplane which tests for air pollution. While working under a contract with the National Park Service to measure particulates in the air around North Cascades National Park, Don dies. Anticipating this possibility, Don's will names his wife, Joan, as executor and gives her "full power to continue the Testem business."[18] Even though she has the power, Joan must be able to exercise it competently.[19] Her level of expertise will be critical in deciding whether she should simply hire a pilot to complete the contract or to continue the business throughout the estate administration to preserve it for the beneficiaries. Suppose she continues the North Cascades project, but a key instrument breaks. Can she borrow money or spend other estate assets to get it fixed? Without more specific language, a court would probably say "no" to either option.[20]

Just as drafters should be sensitive to the family situation when designing powers to invade a trust,[21] so should they know the family's assets when designing management powers. If a particular asset, or kind of asset, dominates the holdings, then draft with that situation specifically in mind. General directions to "do all things necessary" can be helpful, but are not as useful as specific directions tailored to the client's particular situation.

Another way in which clients can personalize their documents is by telling a trustee what investment strategy to follow. When particular assets are important to a client, the document should identify them. Donors may want to absolve the trustee from liability for holding onto close corporation stock in the face of declining value or the lack of diversification.[22] Others might identify favored investments.[23] Some donors go further, however,

---

[17] Section 55[B], *supra*, discusses this aspect of the case.

[18] If the document did not give her power to continue, Joan would need the consent of interested parties (including creditors) or a court order. *See In re* Estate of Kurkowski, 409 A.2d 357 (Pa. 1979) (surcharging widow for continuing, without authorization, to run decedent's business for 20 months); Atkinson § 121.

[19] *See* Estate of Baldwin, 442 A.2d 529 (Me. 1982). Stephen and Tracy Baldwin ran a general store. When Stephen died, a bank accepted the job of executor and was surcharged for letting Tracy continue to run the store unsupervised.

Both *Baldwin* and *Kurkowski*, cited in the previous note, involved widows sued by children of a prior marriage. When dealing with combined families, have a heightened sense of danger. For discussion of this issue in the context of planning to avoid will contests, see § 7[A][5], *supra*.

[20] *Compare In re* Estate of Muller, 248 N.E.2d 164 (N.Y. 1969) (without specific authorization, general assets are not available to continue the business), *with* Willis v. Sharp, 21 N.E. 705 (N.Y. 1889) (language authorizing the executor to "sell or make such other disposition of my real and personal estate as the safe conduct of such business shall seem to require" was enough to allow executor to buy business goods on credit, with the general estate assets liable for the debt).

[21] *See* § 13[A], *supra*.

[22] *See* McGovern & Kurtz at 516.

[23] *See In re* Kettle, 423 N.Y.S.2d 701 (N.Y. App. 1979), *appeal after remand*, 434 N.Y.S.2d 833 (N.Y. App. 1980) (enforcing a desire to retain TRW, Inc., securities).

and authorize only some kinds of investments. This approach can hurt the beneficiaries if conditions change. The question then becomes whether a court should allow a trustee to deviate from those instructions.[24]

Consider *In re Trusteeship Agreement with Mayo.*[25] In 1917 and 1919, Charles Mayo established two trusts and directed the trustees not to invest in real estate nor corporate stock. Because the period of inflation following World War II substantially eroded the value of the principal,[26] the trust beneficiaries sought, and got, court permission for the trustee to invest in corporate stocks. On very similar facts, other courts have held fast to the documents' expressed intentions.[27] The lesson for drafters is to be sure the client fully understands the risk that what looks wise today may look foolish in the future.

Sometimes courts read grants of authority very broadly as a device for relieving trustees of liability. *In re Heidenreich*[28] involved a trust established by Alice Heidenreich. She named two individual trustees, with a corporate trustee to serve as successor. Alice and her husband had been principal shareholders of Citizens Bank of Brooklyn, which by the time of the litigation had become part of Franklin National Bank. As a consequence, the trust held Franklin National stock. Franklin National also took over as successor trustee when one of the individual trustees died. After Franklin National Bank collapsed and its stock became worthless,[29] a guardian ad litem for the minor beneficiaries objected to the bank's account.[30] The guardian's theory was that the bank's retention of its own stock was a breach of the duty of loyalty.[31]

What saved the trustee was the court's willingness to read trust language which authorized the fiduciary "to retain any property . . . however acquired" as a waiver of the duty of loyalty regarding the bank stock. We should ask whether Alice really intended[32] such a clause to have the broad

---

[24] For discussions which raise related themes, see §§ 14 (modification of trusts) and 53[A] (reformation of documents to bring them into compliance with the Rule Against Perpetuities), *supra*.

[25] 105 N.W.2d 900 (Minn. 1960).

[26] For discussion of how this period of inflation influenced investment rules generally, see § 56[A][1], *supra*.

[27] *See, e.g.*, Stanton v. Wells Fargo Bank & Union Trust Co., 310 P.2d 1010 (Cal. App. 1957); Toledo Trust Co. v. Toledo Hospital, 187 N.E.2d 36 (Ohio 1962).

[28] 378 N.Y.S.2d 982 (N.Y. Sur. 1976).

[29] As the end neared, Franklin National was in a difficult position. If the trust department had sold the stock on the basis of inside information that a collapse was imminent, the bank could have violated federal securities law. *See generally* Daniel M. Schuyler, *From Sulphur to Surcharge? — Corporate Trustee Exposure Under SEC Rule 10b-5*, 67 Nw. U. L. Rev. 42 (1972).

[30] The adult beneficiary did not object. One possible explanation for this position is that the remaining individual trustee may have been a relative. Any liability attached to the bank would also affect the individual trustee.

[31] On the duty of loyalty generally, see § 53[A], *supra*.

[32] Because the clause was part of a long list of trustee powers that Alice probably never read carefully, perhaps we should say "should be deemed to have intended." For more on the problem of attributing intention to donors, see § 41[A], *supra*.

meaning the court gave it. Courts probably should interpret clauses like this as intending to soften the rules about appropriate trustee investments.[33] Because individuals often own assets which are too speculative or undiversified, such clauses make sense as a way of easing a portfolio towards trust investment quality.[34] Courts should not read an "any property, however acquired" clause as a waiver of a breach of loyalty. Because the duty of loyalty goes to the heart of the trustee-beneficiary relationship, the donor would have some chance of seeing the issue. Courts should at least require that the clause specifically refer to the conflict.[35] A stricter approach would hold the trustee liable unless the settlor made a knowing waiver.[36]

Rather than waiving objections to particular trustee activities, donors sometimes insert very broad exculpatory clauses in their documents. In general, courts honor these clauses except in situations of gross negligence or willful default,[37] but states range from being very restrictive to very liberal when enforcing exculpatory clauses.[38] Many professional trustees avoid such clauses as bad for public relations.

The UTC bars enforcement of exculpatory clauses to the extent they (1) protect the trustee against breaches "committed in bad faith or with reckless indifference to the purpose of the trust or the interests of the beneficiaries" or (2) are "inserted as a result of" the trustee's abuse of a fiduciary or confidential relationship to the settlor.[39] The second element has real power because exculpatory language "drafted or caused to be

---

It is hard to know what Alice's intention on the loyalty question would have been. She and her husband had close ties to the Brooklyn bank and presumably would have trusted it. Whether she would have had similar faith in Franklin National's ability to act in the trust's interests is a more difficult question.

[33] For discussion of trustee investment duties, see § 56[A], *supra*.

[34] Recall that under the prudent investor rule no investment is per se imprudent. *See* § 56[A][2], *supra*. On the other hand, trustees will be acting at their peril if they rely upon such clauses as an excuse to hold onto inappropriate investments, without examining those investments in light of the trust's needs. *See* Edward C. Halbach, Jr., *Trust Investment Law in the Third Restatement*, 77 Iowa L. Rev. 1151, 1177-1180 (1992).

[35] The document might say that the trustee "may retain any assets, including securities of any corporate fiduciary serving as trustee, ..." Even if a document waives the loyalty duty, the trustee might be liable for breach of the duty of care. *See* Robertson v. Central N. J. Bank & Tr. Co., 47 F.3d 1268 (3d Cir. 1995) (holding the trustee liable for keeping 95% of the principal in the bank's own stock).

[36] For a case which applied estoppel, see City Bank Farmers Trust Co. v. Cannon, 51 N.E.2d 674 (N.Y. 1943). Mary Cannon put National City Bank stock in a trust held by Farmers Loan & Trust Company. After the two merged, the new bank held its own stock. By the time Mary died in 1938, the stock market crash and Great Depression had left the stock worth only a fraction of its earlier value. Because Mary had retained powers to revoke the trust or remove the trustee and had consented to the bank's retaining the stock, the court held that her relatives were estopped from objecting.

[37] *See* Bogert § 94; Scott at 429-431.

[38] *See* Robert Whitman, *Exoneration Clauses in Wills and Trust Instruments*, 4 Hofstra Prop. L.J. 123 (1992).

[39] UTC § 1008(a).

drafted by the trustee" is invalid as an abuse *unless the trustee proves* the term is fair *and* its contents were adequately communicated to the settlor.[40] To be safe, trustees will need to build a record showing adequate communication.

The law surrounding fiduciaries' powers and duties is more flexible than it first appears. Because courts allow wills and trusts to modify most of the basic rules, you should be careful not to relegate these issues to boilerplate language. Rather, view draft provisions covering powers and duties as additional opportunities to help your clients meet their individual objectives.

§ 58 Remedies

Beneficiaries who have suffered from breaches of duty have available a wide range of remedies against their fiduciaries.[1] They can invalidate deals, get specific performance, impose constructive trusts, deny fiduciary fees, remove fiduciaries, and recover damages (surcharges).[2] This section highlights some of the questions surrounding damages. First it takes up the problem of when appreciation damages are appropriate, and then it turns to damages involving investment decisions.

One of the more controversial damage awards came in *In re Estate of Rothko*.[3] The case involved executors who breached their duty of loyalty when they sold a famous artist's paintings.[4] Rather than basing damages on the difference between the prices paid and the paintings' value at the time of the sales, the court assessed "appreciation damages" of the difference between the sale price and the value of the paintings at the time of the trial. Appreciation damages are proper when a trustee is under a duty to retain specific property, but sells it instead.[5] In such cases, the trustee is doing more than merely selling for too low of a price — it is also violating a separate duty. The *Rothko* court thought that a breach involving a "serious conflict of interest"[6] called for the same measure of damages.

Professor Wellman has criticized *Rothko's* damage award as one which imposed punitive damages under the guise of compensating the trust.[7] He is particularly sensitive to the problem faced by fiduciaries when the relevant assets are rare. Experts who can appraise or purchase such assets will often be members of a relatively small group, inclined to have the same

---

[40] UTC § 1008(b).

[1] In appropriate cases, beneficiaries can also recover trust property (or its proceeds) from third parties, subject to the doctrine protecting bona fide purchasers. *See* Bogert ch. 19.

[2] *See. e.g.,* UTC § 1001. *See generally* Bogert ch. 18 and Scott on Trusts §§ 197-215.

[3] 372 N.E.2d 291 (N.Y. 1977).

[4] For discussion of the loyalty issue, see § 55[A][1][b], *supra*.

[5] *See* Scott on Trusts § 208.

[6] *Rothko*, 372 N.E.2d at 297.

[7] *See* Richard V. Wellman, *Punitive Surcharges Against Disloyal Fiduciaries—Is Rothko Right?*, 77 Mich. L. Rev. 95 (1978).

sorts of conflicts as those present in the art world of Mark Rothko. To avoid liability, fiduciaries might not consult the best people, or might be forced to get court approval for what should be routine transactions.

On the other hand, appreciation damages might be appropriate in situations like Rothko's, where a market has not had time to form. Artists' works often appreciate after their deaths, as people realize that no more works will be completed. An approach which measures damages as of the date of sale could encourage quick sales to interested parties who stand to gain handsomely over time.

Trust investments pose some different problems for setting damages. One traditional doctrine is the "anti-netting" rule. It says that a trustee who breaches trust duties may not offset gains against losses if the breaches were separate and distinct.[8] Suppose a trust document prohibits Carol, as trustee, from buying stocks, but she buys IBM and General Motors stock anyway. The IBM goes down; the GM goes up. Carol is liable for the full loss on the IBM. The trust gets the full benefit of the gain on the GM. On the other hand, if Carol first bought IBM, then sold it at a loss and used the proceeds to buy the GM, she would be liable only for any net loss.[9]

At first blush, the anti-netting rule would seem to cause problems for those endorsing modern portfolio theory, which focuses on total gains or losses.[10] The two rules are not at odds, however, because modern portfolio theory applies to determine *whether* there is a breach. The anti-netting rule applies only *after* there has been a breach.[11]

Modern portfolio theory does suggest that courts measure damages differently, however. No longer should they look to each investment but, rather, to the portfolio as a whole. Trustees who fail to diversify or who invest too conservatively for the situation ought not to be insulated by a rising market.[12] Courts should compare a trustee's performance to the returns of market indexes and comparable trust funds.[13]

This chapter has discussed a wide range of topics involving fiduciary administration. Perhaps its most important lesson is that careful attention to detail and concern for your clients' interests are important in all aspects of practice.

---

[8] *See* Bogert at 563; Scott on Trusts § 213. The rule is not restricted to damages from investment decisions, but it arises frequently in that context.

[9] Sometimes deciding whether two breaches are separate and distinct can be difficult. The Restatement provides a list of factors to help. Restatement (Second) of Trusts § 213.

[10] For discussion of modern portfolio theory and the prudent investor rule, see § 56[A][2], *supra*.

[11] *See* Jeffrey N. Gordon, *The Puzzling Persistence of the Constrained Prudent Man Rule*, 62 N.Y.U. L. Rev. 52, 96-97 (1987); Edward C. Halbach, Jr., *Trust Investment Law in the Third Restatement*, 77 Iowa L. Rev. 1151, 1181 (1992).

[12] *See* Edward C. Halbach, Jr. *Trust Investment Law in the Third Restatement*, 77 Iowa L. Rev. 1151, 1181-1183 (1992).

[13] In a down market, this approach has the advantage of protecting trustees from beneficiaries who would like to be insured against loss. For discussion of this problem, see § 56[A][1], *supra*.

Chapter 14

A SKETCH OF FEDERAL WEALTH TRANSFER TAXES

§ 59   Introduction

This chapter pursues a modest, but important, goal: to introduce you to the federal system for taxing wealth transfers. With a basic understanding of the system, you will better appreciate cases involving estate plans constructed for tax reasons. Research and advanced course work should be easier. Perhaps most importantly, you should be able to identify situations which call for more expertise than you have acquired. Then you will know it is time to learn more or send your client elsewhere.[1]

Not surprisingly, the current system developed over time. Although Congress had imposed various inheritance-related taxes for short periods in the 18th and 19th centuries, it turned to an estate tax in 1916, and we have had one ever since.[2] The gift tax followed, with some fits and starts, as a backup to the estate tax[3] and the income tax.[4] The estate and gift taxes operated separately from 1932 until 1976, when they were unified into one system which taxes cumulative lifetime transfers and the estate at death. Major reforms in 1981 shifted the tax burden off of the middle class, by raising effective exemption levels and allowing an unlimited marital deduction. Those reforms, however, left intact provisions which benefited very rich people who set up dynastic trusts. In 1986, Congress added a separate generation-skipping tax (GST), which seeks to impose a wealth transfer tax upon each generation of our wealthiest families.[5]

---

[1] Remember, of course, that a great many clients need estate planning even if they do not have tax problems. *See* McKen V. Carrington, *Estate Planning for the Non-Taxable Estate*, 21 St. Mary's L.J. 367 (1989); Thomas L. Shaffer, *Nonestate Planning*, 42 Notre Dame Law. 153 (1966); William D. Zabel, *Time Out for the Human Side of Estate Planning*, Tr. & Est., May 1988, at 8.

A related problem is that clients who face tax liability also need advice on non-tax issues. Avoid the tendency to treat tax saving as the exclusive goal of an estate plan.

[2] An *inheritance* tax imposes taxes on recipients, often with different rates or exemptions depending on how closely related the recipient was to the decedent. An *estate* tax falls on the decedent's estate.

[3] At first, people could avoid estate taxes by emptying their estates with lifetime gifts. The gift tax eliminated some, but not all, of the advantages of lifetime giving. *See* § 61, *infra*.

[4] Lifetime gifts can divide among family members the income which will be earned on those assets. Because of progressive tax rates, the total tax bill may be lower.

[5] Congress created one round of generation-skipping rules in 1976, but retroactively repealed and replaced them in 1986. *See* Tax Reform Act of 1986, Pub. L. No. 99-514, 100 Stat. 2085 § 1433(c)(1) (1986).

Inflation-indexed protections and higher effective exemptions came in 1997. We now have a three-part system which taxes gifts, estates and generation-skipping transfers in the hope of limiting the power which great wealth can bring.[6]

Shifting directions in 2001, Congress started phasing out the system until there will be no estate and GST taxes for decedents dying in 2010. The gift tax will remain, but at lower rates. In an interesting political game with future Congresses, much of the system is scheduled to be reinstituted in 2011 (at levels that would have been reached before the 2001 amendments).[7]

As you consider the topics in this chapter, note in particular how the unified system works, what sorts of assets are included in the gross estate, and how married couples maximize use of the unified credit. Understanding these elements will not make you a competent estate planner, but will move you closer to that goal.

§ 60   A Unified System

The unified gift and estate tax system works rather like a large beaker, with a scale printed on the side. Each time we make a lifetime taxable transfer, we pour a little water into the beaker. Later additions are assessed at a higher rate, but we do not actually pay any tax until we fill past the threshold Congress has set. Until then we use bits and pieces of our "unified credit" to offset tax we would otherwise owe.[1]

Our transfers are technically taxable transfers, but because we use the credit, we actually pay no tax until the total of our transfers rises above the threshold. The amount which goes tax-free is usually known as an "exclusion" or an "exemption equivalent."

To phase out the estate tax, Congress increased exemption levels in stages. Table 14-1 shows the exemption amounts established for each year until 2009.

---

[6] For a sampling of commentary and proposals for reform, see Mark L. Ascher, *Curtailing Inherited Wealth*, 89 Mich. L. Rev. 69 (1990); Christopher E. Erblich, *To Bury Federal Transfer Taxes Without Further Adieu*, 24 Seton Hall L. Rev. 1931 (1994); John E. Donaldson, *The Future of Transfer Taxation: Repeal, Restructuring and Refinement, or Replacement*, 50 Wash. & Lee L. Rev. 539 (1993); Edward J. McCaffery, *The Uneasy Case for Wealth Transfer Taxation*, Yale L.J. 283 (1994); J.D. Trout & Shahid Buttar, *Resurrecting "Death Taxes": Inheritance, Redistribution and the Science of Happiness*, 16 J. L. & Politics 765 (Fall 2002).

[7] 26 U.S.C.A. §§ 2210 and 2664 (2002).

[1] *See* IRC §§ 2010, 2505.

Table 14-1

Year	Exemption Amount
2003	$ 1,000,000
2004	$ 1,500,000
2005	$ 1,500,000
2006	$ 2,000,000
2007	$ 2,000,000
2008	$ 2,000,000
2009	$ 3,500,000

To see how the unified credit works, imagine Marc, who has incurred no prior transfer tax liability. Because his son, Ben, needs a down payment for his first house, Marc gives Ben $31,000 in 2003. Eleven thousand dollars of that amount is exempt under the gift tax annual exclusion, explained below.[2] The other $20,000 is subject to a tentative tax.[3] Rather than actually paying any tax, however, Marc uses up a small piece of his unified credit. Figure 14-1 illustrates Marc's situation after making the gift.

Figure 14-1

Marc's First Gift

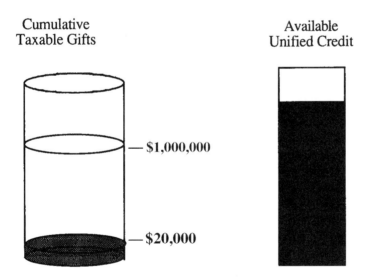

Suppose further that in 2004, Ben's roof collapses, so Marc gives him another $31,000 to repair the damage. Again, the annual exclusion shelters

---

[2] See § 61[B], infra.

[3] See IRC § 2001(c).

$11,000[4] and the other $20,000 is subject to tax. This second gift is taxed at a higher rate, however, because it comes on top of Marc's earlier gift. (See Figure 14-2.[5])

Figure 14-2

Marc's Second Gift

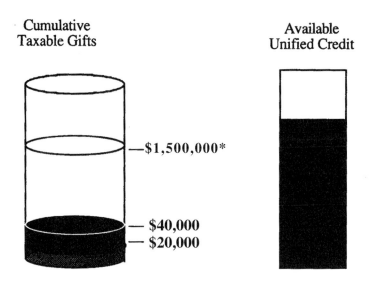

Cumulative
Taxable Gifts

Available
Unified Credit

—$1,500,000*

— $40,000
— $20,000

To achieve that result as an accounting matter, we add in the prior gift and figure the tax on the cumulative total.[6] Marc is not taxed twice on the 2004 gift, however, because we later credit him with the amount of the tentative tax he was assessed in 2003. The earlier gift only serves to push the second gift into a higher bracket. Marc still uses his unified credit and pays no tax.

If Marc makes other taxable gifts, they will be treated the same way. Suppose that Marc dies in 2008 after having given away $750,000 in taxable gifts. Figure 14-3 illustrates the situation just before his death. Now that he has died, the value of his taxable estate will be added in, just like the series of lifetime gifts. If the taxable estate is $1,250,000 or less, the rest of his unified credit can cover the tax. If the taxable estate pushes his lifetime-plus-death total over $2,000,000, his estate will be able to use the rest of his available credit to offset some of the tax, but will be liable for the rest.

---

[4] Because the exclusion is indexed for inflation, the amount may be higher in 2004.

[5] Note that the exemption amount has increased as part of the phase-out.

[6] You might say that we account for the water already in the beaker.

Figure 14-3

Marc's Lifetime Gifts

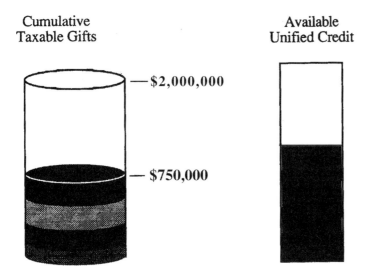

Cumulative
Taxable Gifts

Available
Unified Credit

—$2,000,000

—$750,000

With the basic framework in mind, we now turn to identifying taxable gifts and estates.

§ 61   The Gift Tax

The Internal Revenue Code imposes a tax on any "transfer of property by gift,"[1] while also excluding many gifts of $11,000 or less.[2] This section first addresses what constitutes a gift, and then turns to the annual exclusion.

[A]   What Is a Gift?

Deciding whether something is a "gift" for gift tax purposes[3] often involves questions of valuation and of whether a transfer is complete. Some gifts are obvious. If Monica hands $50 to her son, Mark, and tells him "happy birthday," she has made a gift. Some are more subtle. Suppose Monica sells Mark her car for $2,000. The Code says when "property is

---

[1] IRC § 2501(a)(1).

[2] The amount will increase with inflation in $1,000 steps. IRC § 2503(b)(2). As a practical matter, deductions for qualifying gifts to a charity or to a spouse mean that those gifts escape tax. *See* IRC §§ 2522 (charity) & 2523 (spouse). For discussion of the parallel estate tax deduction for spousal gifts, see § 62[B], *infra*.

[3] Familiarity with the law of gifts for purposes of transferring title is helpful for understanding the law of gift taxation, but always remember that it is the tax definitions which control tax cases. For a review of the property rules, see § 17, *supra*.

transferred for less than an adequate and full consideration in money or money's worth . . . the amount by which the value of the property exceeded the value of the consideration shall be deemed a gift . . . ."[4] If the car is worth $5,000, Monica has made a $3,000 gift.[5] Thus valuation determines both *whether* there is a gift and the *size* of that gift.[6]

Sometimes donors will give away property, but hold onto some strings. Then the question is whether the strings are strong enough to mean there was no completed gift.[7] Only if the donor has parted with all "dominion and control," is there a gift.[8] For example, there is no gift if Monica created a trust for Mark, but retained a power to revoke.[9] Similarly, there may be no gift because the trustee has the power to invade the principal for Monica's benefit.[10] If there is not a gift, the property probably will be included in the donor's gross estate at death.[11] The converse is not true, however. It is possible that a gift will be complete for gift tax purposes, but still in the donor's gross estate.[12]

Just as retaining powers can prevent a gift from being complete, so can giving up powers make a gift complete. In particular, releasing a general power of appointment[13] over the remainder of a trust would create a gift

---

[4] IRC § 2512(b). There is no gift if the transfer was made in the ordinary course of business, free from donative intent. Thus, you can buy shoes on sale without receiving a gift. *See* Treas. Reg. § 25.2512-8. On the other hand, there is a gift if the transferor does not receive "money or money's worth" in return. *See* Commissioner v. Wemyss, 324 U.S. 303, 65 S. Ct. 652, 89 L. Ed. 958 (1945) (William Wemyss's transfer of stock to induce Ellen More to marry him was a gift because his estate was depleted and he received only a promise in return.). Free services, like a lawyer preparing a tax return for a family member, are not gifts. Also, some property settlements reached in the context of divorce are not "gifts." IRC § 2516.

[5] On the other hand, if the car is worth $1,000, Mark made a $1,000 gift to Monica.

[6] Valuation problems arise under both the gift and estate tax schemes. For example, life expectancy tables help to value present and future interests and annuities. Special rules apply to valuing real property used in farming or closely-held businesses. *See* McGovern & Kurtz at 622-623.

[7] *See* McGovern & Kurtz at 614-617.

[8] *See* Treas. Reg. § 25.2511-2.

[9] Recall that for the purpose of judging the validity of a living trust, a beneficiary has something, even if the settlor reserves a power to revoke. For the purpose of taxing the transfer, however, the beneficiary does not have enough to mean there is a completed gift. *See* § 12[E], *supra* (the problem of revocability in trust law).

[10] The result will turn on the scope of the trustee's discretion. If the discretion is limited by a standard which would allow the donor to force distributions, there is no gift because the donor has retained some control. *See* Estate of Holtz v. Commissioner, 38 T.C. 37 (1962) (no gift when Leon Holtz created a living trust giving the trustee the power to invade the principal "for the welfare, comfort and support of Settlor, or for his hospitalization or other emergency needs"). For discussion of the property law aspects of invasion powers, see § 13[A], *supra*.

[11] For discussion of the elements in the gross estate, see § 62[A], *infra*.

[12] Suppose Susan gives property to Peter to hold in trust with income to Susan for life, remainder to Sarah. The remainder is a completed gift to Sarah, but the entire value of the trust is in Susan's gross estate because of her retained life estate. IRC § 2036(a)(1). Under the unified system, Susan would be credited for any taxes attributable to the gift to Sarah. *See* § 60, *supra*.

[13] For discussion of powers, see Chapter 10, *supra*.

of the remainder. Similarly, if the general power is time-limited and the person holding the power allows it to lapse, there is a gift.[14] An important exception, however, limits the impact of the lapse-creates-gift rule. The lapse of a power of appointment is a release only to the extent that the property which could have been appointed in a calendar year exceeds $5,000 or 5% of the assets subject to the power.[15] Because of this rule, donors who create general powers to invade trust principal frequently limit them to $5,000 or 5% of the assets. That way, there is no gift if the powers are not exercised. These "five and five" powers figure prominently in plans which utilize the annual exclusion, to which we now turn.

[B] The Annual Exclusion

To avoid the recordkeeping which would follow if all gifts, including birthday presents, were taxable, Congress created the annual exclusion.[16] Because it allows each donor to give $11,000[17] annually to *each* donee, however, the exclusion encourages wealthy taxpayers to reduce their estates by making lifetime gifts.

To see how the exclusion might work, imagine Jan and Mike, who have accumulated substantial assets. Their daughter, Danielle, is married and has two children. Their son, Michael, is married with one child. Together, Jan and Mike could transfer $154,000 annually to their family without even filing a gift tax return. Jan could give $11,000 to each of seven people: Danielle, her husband, their two children, Michael, his wife, and their child. Mike could do the same.[18] In just four years, they could transfer over $600,000 tax free, without touching a dime of their unified credits.

The annual exclusion applies only to unrestricted rights to the use, possession, or enjoyment of property or its income.[19] Thus, a donor cannot apply the exclusion to income interests given in trusts if the trustee has discretion to allocate income among various beneficiaries.[20] Similarly, the exclusion does not cover future interests.[21] Many taxpayers, however, want to use the annual exclusion, but restrict gifts to minors until they reach

---

[14] Be especially careful with the language you use in this context. The donee of the power is also the donor of the gift made when the power lapses.

[15] IRC § 2041(b)(2).

[16] IRC § 2503(b).

[17] This amount will rise in $1,000 increments to keep pace with inflation. IRC § 2503(b)(2).

[18] If Mike could not afford to make such large gifts, they could still use the annual exclusion in either of two ways. First, Jan could give Mike the necessary funds, shielding them from tax by the unlimited marital deduction. *See* IRC § 2523. Then Mike could make his own gifts. Second, they could elect to "split" each $22,000 gift Jan makes, with $11,000 attributable to Mike. *See* IRC § 2513. Most couples will prefer the first approach, because gift splitting requires filing a tax return and meeting some additional requirements.

[19] Treas. Reg. § 25.2503-3(b).

[20] For discussion of these trusts, see § 13[A], *supra*.

[21] *See* Jeffrey G. Sherman, *'Tis a Gift to be Simple: The Need for a New Definition of "Future Interest" for Gift Tax Purposes*, 55 U. Cin. L. Rev. 585 (1987).

majority. In response, the Code allows the annual exclusion for future gifts to minors in some circumstances.[22]

Finding these rules restrictive, lawyers have invented alternative approaches. One common way to get the annual exclusion for a gift in trust with a delayed distribution to a minor is to create a *"Crummey* power." The name comes from the case of *Crummey v. Commissioner*,[23] and the principal device is a general power of appointment, limited in time and amount.

D. Clifford Crummey and his wife created an irrevocable living trust to hold gifts for their children, one of whom was an adult. The trust gave each child (or the guardian of a minor child) the right to withdraw from the trust the amount their parents added to the trust in any given year. If, as was planned, the child did not exercise the withdrawal right during the year, the right lapsed, and the property stayed in the trust. The question was whether the minor children's powers to withdraw principal meant that the gifts they received in a particular year were present interests which would qualify for the annual exclusion. Because each child had a right to get the money, even though needing a guardian, the court held that the annual gifts qualified for the exclusion. The key for the court was the power's existence, not the unlikelihood of its being exercised.[24]

A variation on the original *Crummey* power can help in other contexts. Careful use will yield the annual exclusion, even though the income beneficiary has only a discretionary right to income. Suppose Jan put $5,000 in trust, with the income payable to Danielle in amounts the trustee sets and with a remainder to Danielle's children. Suppose also that Danielle has a non-cumulative power to withdraw up to $5,000 or 5% of the principal in any given year. Under *Crummey*, Danielle's withdrawal power lets Jan use the annual exclusion. The "five and five" limit means Danielle has not made a gift to her own children if she lets the withdrawal power lapse.[25] Moreover, the trust corpus is not in Danielle's gross estate, except to the extent that it includes property she could still withdraw in the year of her death.[26] Such a plan is most useful, of course, if Jan makes regular contributions to the trust.[27]

---

[22] IRC § 2503(c).

[23] Crummey v. Commissioner, 397 F.2d 82 (9th Cir. 1968). *See* Willard H. Pedrick, *Crummey is Really Crummy*, 20 Ariz. St. L.J. 943 (1988).

[24] For the gift to qualify for the annual exclusion, the holder of the power must have notice of the annual contribution and a reasonable time to exercise the power. *See* Rev. Rul. 81-7, 1981-1 C.B. 474; Priv. Ltr. Rul. 90-04-172 (30-day period is enough).

[25] For discussion of the "five and five" power, see the end of § 61[A], *supra*.

[26] Neither IRC §§ 2036 (retained life estate), nor 2041 (powers of appointment) applies. The "five and five" limit means Danielle has not made a gift to her children with a retained life estate, nor does she have a power of appointment over more than the unexercised power pending in the year of her death.

[27] When the trust principal breaks $100,000, 5% will be greater than $5,000. Jan then can begin increasing her contributions to the lesser of 5% of the principal or the annual exclusion amount. If she goes over 5%, she will create gift tax problems for Danielle on the lapse of the power. If she goes over the annual exclusion amount, she no longer will have the annual exclusion's complete shelter.

Because the annual exclusion proved too restrictive in some situations, Congress added separate gift tax exclusions for taxpayers who pay college tuition or medical expenses for someone.[28]

§ 62　The Estate Tax

The federal estate tax resembles a fishing net. It snares a large number of different assets, but its holes allow escapes in some situations. The basic approach is to include assets in a "gross estate," allow some deductions to produce a "taxable estate," and then assess taxes on that amount, taking into account gifts made during the decedent's lifetime. This section first introduces the gross estate, then discusses the marital deduction, and closes with a look at how couples can use the marital deduction and unified credit together to shelter estates of up to $1.2 million.

[A]　The Gross Estate

The gross estate is an accounting concept which attributes to a decedent property in the decedent's probate estate and nonprobate property which benefited the decedent.[1] Knowing the basic elements in the gross estate is important so you can judge whether your clients face estate tax problems.[2] This subsection introduces the most common of those elements, first by considering a typical, middle-class family, and then by noting some complications. It closes with a comment on stepped-up basis.

[1]　Basic Provisions

With the phase-in of larger exclusions so that in 2003, the unified credit shields $1,000,000, Congress has shifted the transfer tax burden to wealthier taxpayers. Nonetheless, many families who do not consider themselves "rich" may need tax planning advice because their total assets exceed the amount the unified credit shelters.[3] One of the most important points to get across to clients is that avoiding probate does not, of itself, mean avoiding federal estate taxes. Moreover, married couples need to think in terms of their total wealth. Their tax problems are most likely to arise at the death of their survivor.[4]

---

[28] IRC § 2503(e). The payments must go directly to the school or the caregiver, not to the student or patient. Also, only *tuition*, not living expenses, is excluded. Of course, the annual exclusion might cover contributions toward living expenses.

[1] When we say some asset is "in the gross estate," we do not mean that the asset itself becomes subject to the jurisdiction of a court. Rather, we are including its *value* in a computation to determine tax liability. The UPC's original version of the "augmented estate" for spousal election adopted the same concept, while changing some of the details. *See* § 28[C][3][a], *supra*. "Hotchpot" calculations for handling advancements take a similar approach. *See* § 24, *supra*.

[2] *See* McGovern & Kurtz § 15.3.

[3] For discussion of the unified credit, see § 60, *supra*.

[4] The unlimited marital deduction can shield assets passing to the surviving spouse, but if the survivor dies unmarried, no such deduction will be available. *See* IRC § 2056, discussed in § 62[B], *infra*.

A few basic provisions bring in most of the assets of typical families: the estate at death,[5] joint property,[6] life insurance,[7] and retirement benefits.[8] Consider Arlan and Jane, a couple in their 50s. Right now, their potential probate estates are relatively small: each one owns a car, some jewelry, and their clothes (total: $35,000).[9] Everything else is nonprobate assets. Some of it is joint property: a suburban house ($150,000); furniture and appliances ($15,000); various bank accounts and certificates of deposit ($15,000); and shares in a mutual fund ($20,000). Much of it is life insurance: Arlan's $75,000 life insurance policy, payable to Jane; Arlan's $100,000 group policy through his employer; Jane's $75,000 policy, payable to Arlan; and Jane's $120,000 policy through her employer. The catch may be their retirement benefits, which total $200,000. Their total: $805,000.

Notice how they might well have over $1,000,000. In many parts of the country, a "typical suburban house" would be worth much more than the $150,000 estimate above. The couple might also own a vacation cabin or a timeshare condo. Their furniture might include a few antiques, or their cars might be more valuable. They might own more life insurance, or have better group policies. Their retirement funds might be larger if their employers have been contributing, or if they had started saving sooner. Moreover, the value of their assets may well increase with time. The point is that many families who know nothing of trusts with retained life estates and general powers of appointment may face estate tax problems.[10]

---

[5] IRC § 2033.

[6] When joint property is held by a married couple, half of the value of the property will be in the estate of the first to die. *See* IRC § 2040(b). This is another example of policy-makers' treating marriage as a partnership. For discussion of this theory in the context of spousal election, see § 28, *supra*.

If the decedent and the other joint tenant(s) are unmarried and purchased the property, the Code values the decedent's share, based on the percentage the decedent contributed to the purchase. The Code presumes the decedent furnished all of the consideration, and therefore puts the burden on the estate to show that others contributed. If the joint tenants were given the property by someone not a joint tenant, the decedent's estate gets a fractional share equaling the decedent's share of the joint property (as if they were all tenants in common). *See* IRC § 2040(a).

At the death of the last surviving joint tenant, all of the property will be in that person's estate. IRC § 2033.

[7] The value of life insurance will be in the gross estate of someone who retained an "incident of ownership," like changing the beneficiary, over the policy. *See* IRC § 2042(2). Once the benefits are paid to the survivor, they will be in the probate estate of that person and thus in the survivor's gross estate under Section 2033.

[8] Annuities and other forms of retirement saving are included in the gross estate under section 2039.

[9] The value of these items may be higher than most clients realize. They might forget, for example, the antique pin inherited from Aunt Lucy or the original painting bought from a then-unknown artist 25 years ago.

[10] On the other hand, they may live a long time and spend almost all of it. As lawyers, we must advise them about both prospects.

[2]   Some Complications

The estate tax, of course, is designed to cover persons wealthier than Arlan and Jane. This subsection highlights provisions more likely to affect those taxpayers. In particular, it discusses transfers within three years of death, transfers in which the decedent retained some interests, and powers of appointment.

A successor to provisions which captured lifetime gifts made "in contemplation of death," Section 2035 brings into the gross estate the value of certain gifts made within three years of the decedent's death, and it brings in the value of *taxes paid* on all gifts made during that period. The three-year rule is easier to enforce than the "contemplation" standard, but it aims at the same problem: reducing the advantage of lifetime giving.[11] Consider two examples.

Michelle, dying of cancer, has a life insurance policy with a face amount of $500,000 and a cash value of $200,000. Lucy is the beneficiary. If Michelle gives Lucy the policy, Michelle will incur tax liability on $189,000.[12] If Michelle dies having control over the insurance, the whole $500,000 will be in her gross estate.[13] To negate Michelle's incentive to make that gift, the Code includes in her estate the face value of the policy if Michelle dies within three years of the gift.[14]

Suppose instead that Michelle simply gave Lucy $500,000, paid $100,000 as taxes due on the gift, and died within three years. The $100,000 is included in Michelle's gross estate.[15] The reason for this rule is to negate— during the three-year period—the tax advantage of making taxable gifts instead of leaving the property to be part of one's estate.

The advantage comes from an important difference between the gift and the estate taxes. The gift tax is *exclusive*; the taxes paid come on top of the gift. The $100,000 Michelle paid in taxes is gone. It will not be in her estate, subject to tax there. In contrast, the estate tax is *inclusive*. The taxable estate includes the funds which eventually will be used to pay the tax. That approach means the money used to pay the tax is itself subject to tax. If Michelle had given Lucy a $500,000 testamentary gift, that amount, and the $100,000 needed to pay the tax, would both be in Michelle's taxable estate. While the Code allows an advantage to lifetime giving in general,[16] the Code eliminates that advantage in the last three years by taxing the gift tax paid earlier.

---

[11] The advantages were greater before Congress established the unified system. At first there was no gift tax, and later the gift tax rates were lower than estate tax rates.

[12] $200,000 minus the $11,000 (for now) annual exclusion. *See* § 61[B], *supra.*

[13] *See* IRC § 2042.

[14] *See* IRC §§ 2035(a)(2), 2042.

[15] *See* IRC § 2035(c).

[16] Another advantage of lifetime giving is the ability to shield transfers with the annual exclusion, which has no parallel in the estate tax. *See* § 61[B], *supra.*

The Code also captures for the gross estate the value of lifetime transfers in which taxpayers retain beneficial interests. In particular, the gross estate will include the value of property in which the decedent kept a life estate,[17] or kept a reversionary interest worth more than 5% of the value of the property which can only be enjoyed by surviving the decedent,[18] or retained various powers to control the property.[19] These provisions have generated a great deal of litigation, as taxpayers seek to retain benefits without suffering tax consequences.[20] In general, the courts have looked at the substance, rather than the form, of the arrangements in question.[21]

Finally, the gross estate includes property subject to a general power of appointment.[22] Property subject to a special power, however, generally will not suffer the same fate.[23] Because of this distinction, donors create different sorts of powers in different situations. For example, planners often recommend that clients create special powers in order to give a donee considerable authority but still not incur taxes on the property subject to the power.[24] On the other hand, a client may decide to give a surviving

---

[17] IRC § 2036(a)(1). Sometimes disputes arise about whether someone retained a life estate. *See* Estate of Rapelje v. Commissioner, 73 T.C. 82 (1979) (retained life estate where decedent transferred residence to daughters, but stayed on the property); Estate of Linderme v. Commissioner, 52 T.C. 305 (1969) (same, involving sons).

Similar disputes appear when courts determine, for property law purposes, whether there has been a gift. *See* § 17, *supra*.

[18] IRC § 2037.

[19] IRC §§ 2036(a)(2) (the right to designate who shall enjoy the property), 2036(b)(2) (voting rights in controlled corporations), 2038 (the right to amend or revoke). *See generally* Joseph Isenbergh, *Simplifying Retained Life Interests, Revocable Transfers, and the Marital Deduction*, 51 U. Chi. L. Rev. 1 (1984); C. Douglas Miller & R. Alan Rainey, *Dying with the "Living" (or "Revocable") Trust: Federal Tax Consequences of Testamentary Dispositions Compared*, 37 Vand. L. Rev. 811 (1984).

The fact that the donor is acting as a trustee will not necessarily keep the assets out of his estate. *See, e.g.*, Old Colony Trust Co. v. United States, 423 F.2d 601 (1970) (Where the settlor also served as co-trustee, administrative powers over the trust were not enough to include it in the gross estate, but the trustees' powers to increase the size of a beneficiary's interest did bring the value of the trust into the settlor's gross estate.).

Powers which otherwise would bring property into the gross estate will not do so if they are limited by an "ascertainable standard" enforceable in the courts. For discussion of what constitutes an ascertainable standard, see § 37[D], *supra*.

[20] *See* McGovern & Kurtz at 625-634.

[21] *See, e.g.*, United States v. Estate of Grace, 395 U.S. 316 (1969). There Joseph created a living trust for his wife, Janet, giving her a life estate. Janet obligingly created a trust with a life estate for Joseph. Noting the reciprocity of the arrangement, the court included in Joseph's gross estate value of the life estate Janet created.

[22] This discussion expands upon the overview in § 37[D], *supra*. Recall that a general power is one exercisable in favor of the donee, the donee's creditors, the donee's estate, or creditors of the donee's estate. IRC § 2041(a). If the owner is properly restricted by an ascertainable standard, it is not a general power. IRC § 2041(b)(1)(A).

[23] For a discussion of the gift, estate, generation-skipping and income tax aspects of non-general powers, see Amy M. Hess, *The Federal Taxation of Nongeneral Powers of Appointment*, 52 Tenn. L. Rev. 395 (1985).

[24] These powers often fit nicely with the credit shelter trust described in § 62[C], *infra*.

spouse a general power as a way of equalizing the estate tax burden between each spouse.[25]

A donor can give the donee of a power a great deal of benefit without adverse estate tax consequences to the donee by giving the donee a power to invade a trust's principal to benefit the donee, but limiting the power's exercise by an "ascertainable standard relating to the [donee's] health, education, support or maintenance . . . ."[26] The limit keeps the power out of the definition of a general power. Creating such a power requires careful attention to detail, because courts will subject to taxation property subject to a power which is not limited properly.[27]

In terms of taxing property a decedent has earned or received outright, the Code casts a broad net. On the other hand, it is much more generous toward property people receive with strings attached. Donees can receive a good deal of power over property, short of absolute ownership, without that property being taxed in their own estates. For example, suppose Jennie creates a trust naming Sheila as trustee and giving her typical management powers. Jennie can also give Sheila (as beneficiary) a right to the trust's income, a non-general power of appointment over the remainder, a power (limited by an ascertainable standard) to invade the principal to benefit herself, and an annual "five and five" power to invade the principal. Sheila has something very close to complete ownership, yet the trust will not be in her gross estate, except to the extent the "five and five" power lapses in the year she dies. The ability to shield donees' estates from tax makes estate planning popular.

[3] Stepped-Up Basis

The tax system offers a particularly valuable benefit to families who own property which has appreciated in value during their ownership. For income tax purposes, property which transfers at death takes on a new, "stepped-up" basis,[28] its value in the decedent's gross estate.[29] Suppose Hans bought

---

[25] Property subject to that power would both qualify for the marital deduction in the donor's estate and put the property in the donee-spouse's gross estate. See § 62[B], infra.

[26] IRC § 2041(b)(1)(A).

[27] See, e.g., Miller v. United States, 387 F.2d 866 (3d Cir. 1968). Because a power to invade the principal for "proper maintenance, support, medical care, hospitalization, or other expenses incidental to [the donee's] comfort and well-being" was too broad, the property was taxed in the donee's estate. Miller, 387 F.2d at 867, 870.

[28] "Stepped-up" is a common, but misleading, term. Basis can also be "stepped-down" if an asset declines in value. See generally, Karen C. Burke & Grayson M.P. McConch, Death Without Taxes, 20 Va. Tax Rev. 499, 510-518 (2001).

[29] IRC § 1014. In contrast, the donee of a lifetime gift takes on the donor's basis, adjusted upward for gift taxes paid. IRC § 1015.

Other possible benefits of waiting until death include favorable valuation of farmland or land used in a closely-held business (IRC § 2032A), favorable income taxation of redemption of stock in a closely-held corporation (IRC § 303), and deferral of estate taxes attributable to a closely-held business (IRC § 6166).

The step-up is particularly valuable in community property jurisdictions because it applies to the entire community property, not just the decedent spouse's half. See IRC §§ 1014(a), (b)(6). For more on community property, see § 28[A], supra.

stock in 1980 for $1,000, but that it is now worth $10,000. If Hans sold the stock, he would realize a $9,000 capital gain. Suppose that the stock does not change in value, but that Hans leaves it to Dietrich at Hans' death. Dietrich's basis will be $10,000.[30] Dietrich could sell it immediately without realizing a taxable gain. If he later sells the stock for $15,000, Dietrich will only realize a $5,000 gain. Either way, the $9,000 gain Hans experienced escapes income tax. As part of the phase-out of the estate tax, the stepped-up basis approach is scheduled to end in 2010.[31]

[B] The Marital Deduction

Once the value of the gross estate is established, various deductions apply, reducing the gross estate to the "taxable estate." For our purposes, the most important deduction is the one for transfers to surviving spouses.[32] Although the details can get quite complex, the basic principle of the marital deduction is straightforward: the law treats married couples as units, not individuals. It allows each spouse to give unlimited amounts of property to the other without incurring transfer taxes, so long as the property will be exposed to tax once it leaves the marital unit.[33] This subsection identifies the four types of transfers which will qualify for the marital deduction.

The easiest way to be sure a transfer qualifies for the marital deduction is to **give the property outright** to the surviving spouse. In many situations, however, such an approach may be undesirable. The surviving spouse may need the management a trust provides, or the decedent spouse may want to be sure children from an earlier marriage get a share after the survivor's death. By carefully following the Code's rules, drafters can create trusts which will qualify for the marital deduction. In each case, the tradeoff is that the property then will be in the survivor's gross estate.

One trust which will qualify for the marital deduction is a trust giving the surviving spouse a **life estate plus a general power of appointment**.[34] Various rules protect the trust from being a shell with little value

---

[30] Dietrich will not get the benefit of the step-up if Dietrich had given the stock to Hans within a year of Hans' death. *See* § IRS 1014(e). This provision discourages people from avoiding capital gains by giving property to donees near death and then expecting to get it back with a higher basis at the donee's death.

[31] IRC § 1014(f).

[32] The marital deduction comes from IRC § 2056. The other available deductions are: administration expenses, debts, and funeral expenses (§ 2053); casualty losses (§ 2054); and charitable transfers (§ 2055).

[33] For simplicity, the text speaks in terms of the estate tax. The gift tax marital deduction works along the same lines. *Compare* IRC § 2056 (estate tax) *with* IRC § 2523 (gift tax). *See* McGovern & Kurtz at 620 & 644-648.

[34] *See* IRC § 2056(b)(5). The language describing this material can get confusing because of the common use of a double negative: to qualify for the deduction, the interest passing to the survivor must not be a nondeductible terminable interest. In this case, the life estate itself is a terminable interest and would not qualify, but the other elements of the trust make it deductible.

to the spouse. The spouse must have the right to receive all, or a specified portion,[35] of the trust income, at least annually. Moreover, the trust assets must be property which will produce income.[36] No person, including the trustee, can have the power to give the property to anyone other than the spouse.[37] The general power may be testamentary, but otherwise cannot be limited by time, events, purposes, or permissible donees.[38]

Once Congress adopted an unlimited marital deduction, it faced a dilemma. Some taxpayers might well want to care for their surviving spouses (and not-so-coincidentally qualify their estates for the marital deduction), but at the same time not want the spouse to have a general power of appointment over the remainder. Perhaps the most telling case for restricting the survivor's power is when a decedent has left children from a prior marriage. The surviving spouse might cut out the children. With that problem in mind, Congress developed the **QTIP trust** alternative for getting a marital deduction.[39] "QTIP" stands for "qualified terminable interest property."

A QTIP trust is a lot like the life-estate-plus-general-power trust, without the need for the general power. The spouse still has the right to income from productive property, but the decedent can identify who gets the remainder. The QTIP trust, however, adds a restriction that no person, including the surviving spouse, may give the property to anyone except the surviving spouse during the survivor's lifetime. Also, property in a QTIP trust does not qualify for the deduction unless the executor elects that it should. The election feature is attractive to some taxpayers because it allows last minute adjustments to minimize taxes by deciding which estate (the decedent's or the survivor's) should get the property.[40]

A final, seldom-used way to qualify for the marital deduction is to create an **estate trust**, with income for life to the surviving spouse and a remainder to the *surviving spouse's* estate. Here, the trustee can have discretion regarding payments of income, and the property need not even produce income, but because the remainder goes to the survivor's estate, it will be subject to tax there. The extra administrative costs of passing the property through probate make this an unattractive alternative, except

---

[35] If the income right is limited, so will be the value of the marital deduction.

[36] If the property is not income-producing, the spouse must have the power to force the trustee to change non-income-producing property for property which will produce income, or to otherwise compensate the spouse for the income loss. *See* Treas. Reg. § 20.2056(b)-5(f)(5).

[37] For example, a trustee power to invade the principal to pay for the children's educations would disqualify the trust.

[38] Restrictions which go to the procedure for exercising the power are permissible. *See* Treas. Reg. § 20.2056(b)-5(g)(4). For discussion of why such restrictions might be desirable, see § 39[A], *supra*.

[39] *See* IRC § 2056(b)(7).

[40] Decisions about whether and how much to elect can get very complicated. *See* Mark L. Ascher, *The Quandary of Executors Who Are Asked to Plan the Estates of the Dead: The Qualified Terminable Interest Property Election*, 63 N.C. L. Rev. 1 (1984).

in situations when the decedent owns non-income-producing property which ought not to be sold, like stock in a family corporation.[41]

Deciding how best to structure an estate plan utilizing the marital deduction requires lawyers and clients to consider a wide range of variables. In addition, marital deduction planning often places the lawyer in a difficult position, because the spouses' interests, or desires, may be different. In particular, spouses who expect to survive their mates may object to plans which leave themselves with less than complete ownership. In some cases, each spouse may need a separate lawyer. At the very least, they must give their informed consent to a dual representation, and they probably should waive their confidentiality rights as well.[42]

[C] Using the Unified Credit

Because the unified credit is personal to each taxpayer, its value can be lost in large estates if it is not fully utilized. By making lifetime transfers between each other, or by structuring the estate plan in various ways, married clients can maximize the use of both of their unified credits, in 2006 effectively shielding $2 million from estate tax. The options are numerous and complicated.[43] Perhaps the most important technique is to balance the sizes of both estates during the lifetimes of both spouses, so that each has at least the amount sheltered by the unified credit.[44] This subsection illustrates why planning is important. For simplicity, the examples which follow take place when the exclusion amount for each taxpayer is $1 million.[45]

Example 14-1. Consider Judy and Paul, a married couple who have made no taxable gifts. They have assets of $2,400,000, all in Paul's name. If Judy dies first, her estate owes no tax, and her unified credit is wasted. When Paul dies later, his estate will have the full $2.4 million[46] and pay taxes on the $1.4 million by which the estate exceeds the $1 million exemption equivalent created by the unified credit. If Paul dies first, leaving everything to Judy, his estate pays no tax because of the marital deduction.

---

[41] Recall that both the life-estate-plus-general-power trust and the QTIP trust require that the spouse have authority to demand that the trust produces income.

[42] For discussion of the similar problem of representing both spouses when they may be waiving marital rights, see the end of § 28, *supra. See also* §§ 6 (couples seeking wills) & 10 (couples making contracts regarding wills), *supra.*

[43] *See* Carolyn B. Featheringill, *The Unified Credit: Tax Plans and Family Ties*, 16 Cumb. L. Rev. 517 (1986); Thomas M. Featherston, Jr., *The Funding of Formula Marital Deductions Gifts After the Economic Recover Tax Act of 1981*, 27 S. Tex. L. Rev. 99 (1985); Sheldon F. Kurtz, *Marital Deduction Estate Planning Under the Economic Recovery Tax Act of 1981: Opportunities Exist, But Watch the Pitfalls*, 34 Rutgers L. Rev. 591 (1982).

[44] A less attractive option is for surviving spouses to achieve some balance by using disclaimers or spousal election claims. *See* §§ 27 (disclaimers), 28[C] (spousal election), *supra.*

[45] For a review of the unified credit, see § 60, *supra.*

[46] For simplicity, the example assumes no expenses or other deductions and no change in the value of the estate over time. In real planning situations, these variables could be very important.

Again, the unified credit is wasted. Judy later dies owning $2.4 million, and her estate suffers tax on $1.4 million. Whatever the order of death, the total amount subject to tax in both estates is $1.4 million.

Example 14-2. One starting place would be to equalize the estates, in this case by having Paul give Judy $1.2 million. If that is the only change, however, the result is the same. Suppose Paul dies first,[47] leaving everything to Judy. The marital deduction still covers his estate, and Judy is left with the same $2.4 million, of which she can shelter only $1 million.[48]

The problem is that the plans in both examples overutilize the marital deduction and waste the unified credit in the estate of the first to die. The solution, from a tax perspective, is to give less to the surviving spouse and more to a separate trust which will be able to use the unified credit in the first estate. A "credit shelter trust" can work differently in a variety of situations, but the basic idea is to create an entity which does not use the marital deduction. This approach leaves enough money in the taxable estate of the first to die to use up that person's unified credit.

Example 14-3. Return to Example 14-1, where Paul owned the entire $2.4 million, but with a difference. Suppose Paul dies first, but instead of giving everything to Judy, he creates a trust, and funds that trust with the amount necessary to make maximum use of his unified credit. In this example, the credit shelter trust would be for $1 million.[49] Everything else could still go directly to Judy.[50] At Paul's death, his estate still pays no tax. The unified credit covers the $1 million in trust, and the marital deduction covers the rest. The payoff comes at Judy's death. Now her gross estate is only $1.4 million, and her unified credit shelters $1 million of that. Her estate pays tax only on $400,000.[51]

The cost of this arrangement is that Judy no longer gets everything at Paul's death. The credit shelter trust could give Judy income for life, powers to invade, special powers to appoint and the like, while still keeping its value out of her gross estate.[52] Make no mistake, however; Judy would have something less than complete ownership. The clients need to decide whether the tax savings is worth the loss of control.

---

[47] Since their estates are equal, the order of death is irrelevant.

[48] The same result follows if all of the property is joint. Whoever dies first, the marital deduction will cover the half which goes to the survivor. Again, the survivor will hold the whole $2.4 million at death.

[49] If Paul had made lifetime gifts using part of the unified credit, the trust would be smaller. Also, if Paul held other property which would not qualify for the marital deduction (for example, joint property with a child), then some of the unified credit would be needed to shelter that property, and the credit shelter trust would again be smaller.

[50] Common alternatives to the outright gift are a life-estate-and-general-power trust and a QTIP trust. *See* § 62[B], *supra*. While they may meet other planning objectives, neither of these devices is necessary in order to make optimal use of the unified credit and marital deduction.

[51] Recall that when Paul left everything to Judy outright, she paid tax on $1.4 million. The difference is the $1 million in the credit shelter trust, using up Paul's unified credit.

[52] For a list of powers Judy could have without subjecting the trust to taxation in her estate, see the end of § 62[A][2], *supra*.

There is one major flaw in our revised plan. Suppose Judy dies first. The inability to use Judy's unified credit would again leave Paul with $1.4 million subject to tax.[53] Unless Paul and Judy equalize their estates, at least to the extent of giving each enough to use up the unified credit, those credits could be lost.[54]

Example 14-4. Let us finally consider Paul and Judy with equalized estates ($1.2 million each) and plans which utilize the credit shelter trust. Whoever dies first leaves $1 million in trust and $200,000 outright to the survivor. As usual, no tax. The unified credit covers the $1 million, and the marital deduction takes care of the rest. The survivor's estate will be $1.4 million (their own $1.2 million plus the $200,000 from the first to die). The survivor's unified credit covers $1 million, leaving $400,000 exposed to tax.

This discussion of the estate tax is no substitute for a course on that topic. It should, however, alert you to the elements of the gross estate, so that you can recognize clients who need more sophisticated estate plans. The discussion of the unified credit should illustrate why married couples who together have more than the exemption-equivalent amount should consider establishing credit shelter trusts.

§ 63   The Generation-Skipping Transfer Tax

To plug some holes which the gift and estate tax system had left open, Congress enacted the generation-skipping transfer tax (GST) in 1986.[1] The GST applies in addition to gift and estate taxes, but was designed with those taxes in mind. The rules surrounding the tax, and lawyer's strategies for coping with those rules, are very complex. The purpose of this section is not to summarize those rules,[2] but rather, to help you understand why they developed. As part of the phasing-out of the estate tax, the GST is scheduled for abolition in 2010 (and re-introduction in 2011).

The previous section noted that clients might want to establish credit shelter trusts which confer substantial benefits on income beneficiaries without subjecting the value of those trusts to taxation in the life tenant's estate. Credit shelter trusts are just one variety of a common species: a life estate in trust with considerable benefits, but not so many as to subject the trust to tax. When trusts line up such life estates in succession until the Rule Against Perpetuities calls a halt,[3] property can escape estate tax for several generations. These trusts are the primary targets of the generation-skipping tax.

---

[53] If you need to check the figures, see Example 14-1, *supra*.

[54] Decisions about whether and how much to equalize estates can be difficult, because the spouses' life expectancies are also relevant.

[1] IRC ch. 13. For commentary, see Howard E. Abrams, *Rethinking Generation-Skipping Transfers*, 40 Sw. L.J. 1145 (1987); Ira M. Bloom, *Federal Generation-Skipping Transfer Taxation: How Should the States Respond?*, 51 Alb. L. Rev. 817 (1987).

[2] *See* McGovern & Kurtz at 650-660.

[3] For discussion of the Rule, see Chapter 12, *supra*.

The overall goal is to tax wealth once in each generation. To accomplish this, the GST taxes transfers to a "skip person," someone two or more generations below the transferor's generation.[4] To help visualize these transfers, consider gifts from Genevieve, to her daughter Peggy, and to Peggy's son, Troy. From Genevieve's perspective, Troy is a skip person.

Taxable transfers to a skip person might happen any of three ways. There could be a "taxable termination," like a trust from Genevieve which ends at Peggy's death, with distribution to Troy.[5] There could be a "taxable distribution," like Peggy's exercise of a special power of appointment to invade for Troy's benefit the principal of a trust Genevieve established.[6] Finally, to prevent direct avoidance of the rules aimed at trusts, there could be a "direct skip," like a gift straight from Genevieve to Troy.[7]

The GST is a wealthy person's tax. Each transferor has a $1 million exemption, which the transferor can allocate among GST transfers.[8] For example, if Genevieve put $2 million in trust for Peggy for life, remainder to Troy, she could allocate all of her exemption to the trust. When the tax became due at Peggy's death, half of the trust would be exempt.[9] Moreover, spouses can combine their exemptions, for an overall shelter of $2 million.[10] Taxable transfers which exceed these limits generate tax liability at the federal estate tax's highest rate.[11]

With much of the system scheduled to expire within the decade, estate planners need to stay on top of the continuing changes — and assess the political climate.

---

[4] IRC § 2613(a).

[5] *See* IRC § 2612(a).

[6] *See* IRC § 2612(b).

[7] *See* IRC § 2612(c). Gifts from grandparents to the children of their predeceased children do not count as skips. The descendants of the predeceased child "roll up" a generation. IRC § 2612(c)(2). Thus, if Peggy were not alive when Genevieve made the gift to Troy, it would not be taxable. A gift from Genevieve to Troy's son (her great-grandson) would be taxable as a direct skip.

The gift tax annual, tuition and medical exclusions also shelter transfers from the GST. IRC §§ 2611(b)(1), 2642(c). For discussion of these exclusions, see § 61[B], *supra*.

[8] The exemption is indexed to increase over time with inflation. IRC § 2631(c). An "inclusion ratio" determines the proportion of GST assets which the exclusion shelters. IRC § 2642(a). Default rules apply if the transferor makes no allocation. IRC § 2632(c).

For discussion of how the exemption is driving the move to abolish the Rule Against Perpetuities, see § 53[C], *supra*.

[9] The $1 million exemption effectively can shelter larger amounts. If the trust has grown to $6 million before Peggy's death, $3 million is still exempt.

[10] The system is similar to the one available for splitting gifts under the gift tax. *See* IRC § 2513, discussed in § 61[B] n.18, *supra*.

[11] IRC § 2602.

Chapter 15
LOOKING AHEAD

One of the few things that can be said with confidence about the future is that it will be different from the present. Change makes our lives interesting, but throws us off our bearings from time to time. Part of preparing for a career is developing a set of personal and professional values to help you through those challenges.

We have seen how the staid old law of wills and trusts is changing. Walls between probate and nonprobate doctrines are collapsing. Formality is in decline. Changes in the structure of our families, from the pattern of dual-career marriages to the spread of step-families to more non-marital couples, are forcing the law to adapt.

Moreover, in response, wills and trusts law practice increasingly involves planning for life, with at-death plans taking a secondary role. For example, younger clients may need advice on how best to save for their children's college costs. Your middle-aged clients may need trusts to care for aging parents. Older clients may want to anticipate their potential loss of capacity. Durable powers of attorney to handle property and health care decisions are becoming standard fare. You will have the chance to develop new devices to handle as-yet-unknown problems. Because these lifetime decisions affect the clients themselves, not just their survivors, the clients are even more interested in tailoring their plans to meet their specific situations.

At the same time as pressure increases to individualize planning, technological change promises the opportunity to meet those needs. Word processing allows lawyers to reformulate standard documents quickly. Increasingly, more sophisticated planning programs are using facts about clients to produce plans and documents. Properly used, computer programs can be excellent tools for helping to identify quickly the choices a client needs to make.

Computerization also carries a risk. Poorly designed programs may not ask enough questions, or may present too few choices. Perhaps a greater risk is that, like the form books of old, the programs may become seductive. When in a hurry, you may be tempted to make choices for the client, instead of checking first. Seeing the program's three choices, you may be lured away from considering—or inventing—a fourth. It will take constant attention to be sure that you are using the technology to your clients' benefit, not just your own.

Whatever changes occur during your career, one thing will remain: you will have the power to affect people's lives. Every day, you will be influencing how families function. With that power comes the responsibility to structure plans with a sensitivity to the different needs of different clients. As you develop your own set of values to guide your professional growth, aim to be the kind of lawyer you would like to have.

Finally, as you strive to balance the needs of your private and professional lives, consider some advice from Charles Schultz. Linus wonders, "If you work real hard, and you get everything you've always wanted, is it worth it?" Snoopy responds, "Not if your dog doesn't like you."[1]

---

[1] For a copy of the cartoon, see Andersen & Bloom, Fundamentals of Trusts and Estates 589 (2d ed. 2002).

TABLE OF CASES

[References are to pages.]

[References are to pages.]

[References are to pages.]

[References are to pages.]

[References are to pages.]

[References are to pages.]

[References are to pages.]

TABLE OF UNIFORM PROBATE CODE

[References are to pages.]

[References are to pages.]

TABLE OF UNIFORM TRUST CODE

[References are to pages.]

INDEX

[References are to pages.]

[References are to pages.]

[References are to pages.]

[References are to pages.]

[References are to pages.]

[References are to pages.]

[References are to pages.]

[References are to pages.]

[References are to pages.]

[References are to pages.]

[References are to pages.]